ECONOMIC HISTORY OF HYDERABAD STATE

(Warangal Suba : 1911-1950)

V. RAMAKRISHNA REDDY

GIAN PUBLISHING HOUSE
DELHI

GIAN PUBLISHING HOUSE
29/6 Shakti Nagar, Delhi-110007

ISBN 81-212-0099-7

The publication of this book was financially supported by the Indian Council of Historical Research, and the responsibility for the facts stated, opinions expressed or conclusions reached, is entirely that of the author and the Indian Council of Historical Research accepts no responsibility for them.

PRINTED IN INDIA

Published by Gian Publishing House,
Printed at Godwall Printers, Delhi.

FOREWORD

There are not many studies available on the economic history of South India. This book "Economic History of Hyderabad State (Warangal Suba), 1911-1950" written by Dr. V. Ramakrishna Reddy is a welcome addition in the field of economic history. It throws vivid light on the economic conditions in the Nizam's dominions in general and of the districts of Warangal, Karimnagar and Adilabad in particular.

Dr. V. Ramakrishna Reddy who, at present is an Assistant Professor in History at the Andhra Pradesh Open University, has taken great pains in consulting several original files in Urdu and English at the Board of Revenue and Andhra Pradesh State Archives which is no mean task as the files at these centres are yet to be properly indexed.

He also consulted the relevant files in the Statistics Department and the several Commission reports on tenancy, banking and agricultural conditions in the erstwhile Hyderabad State besides referring to several contemporary Newspapers in Telugu, Urdu and English.

The scholar has dealt in detail about the village administration and has brought out the subtle differences in the then existing land tenure systems in the Hyderabad State like the *Ijara*, *Kowl*, *Banjar* and *Agrahara* apart from delineating on the different set ups in *sarf-i-khas*, *paigah*, *Inam*, *Jagir*, *Samsthan* and the difference between the *Shikmidars* and *Pattedars*. The then existing agricultural conditions, production and prices in the Hyderabad State have been dealt with.

On the whole, the material drawn by the scholar from primary and secondary sources is rich in variety and magnitude. It adds to the value of the book as an original source material. Dr. Ramakrishna Reddy is to be congratulated for having brought out such a valuable book in the realm of economic history. This being his doctoral thesis, one hopes that he wo ld come out with similar scholarly works in future.

15th June 1987
Dean,
Faculty of Social Sciences
Osmania University
Hyderabad *SAROJINI REGANI*

PREFACE

Beneath the pomp and splendour of the Nizam's rule in Hyderabad State, lay hidden the depressed and exploited lives of the common people. If Warangal Suba is taken as a unit for study in this regard, it could be seen clearly that whereas the region abounded in natural, forest, agricultural, industrial, labour and trade resources, the actual economic development that has been experienced was not at all commensurate, ultimately resulting in a far lower standard of living than that was witnessed in adjacent states. The intricate reasons that lay behind this situation and the effects that emanated from it, had been examined, basing primarily on the rich wealth of information that was contained in voluminous Warangal Subedari Records and State Departmental Files, the former of which are all in Urdu language, and have been for the first time brought to use.

My grateful thanks, in this connection are due to Prof. Sarojini Regani, Dean, Faculty of Social Sciences, Osmania University, for guiding me at each and every stage in my endeavour. I owe a deep sense of gratitude to her for having spared her valuable and precious time in going through the work and writing a 'Foreword'. I am also obliged to the authorities and the concerned staff of State Archives, the Andhra Pradesh Board of Revenue, State Library, Salar Jung Museum Library, Osmania University Library and Bureau of Economics, Hyderabad, the National

Archives, Nehru Memorial Museum Library and Jawaharlal Nehru University Library, New Delhi, and the Collectorate of Warangal, for rendering me valuable cooperation in the collection of relevant data that is available at their respective centres. I am very much grateful to Md. Asadullah, S. Zia-ul-Haq and M.A. Alavi for assisting me in the examination of Urdu records.

My special thanks are due to U.G.C., New Delhi for granting me the Teacher Fellowship, Director of Higher Education, Andhra Pradesh, for sponsoring my candidature for the Fellowship and the Director, Indian Council of Historical Research, New Delhi and the Registrar, Telugu University, Hyderabad for extending me grant for printing this work. Last, but not the least, I am obliged to Gian Publishing House, Delhi, for having successfully brought out the work within a short time.

V. Ramakrishna Reddy

ABBREVIATIONS

Dn	=	Deccan
NMML	=	Nehru Memorial Museum Library
W.S.	=	Warangal *Subedari*
I.G.I.	=	Imperial Gazetteer of India
R.A.R.	=	Revenue Administration Report
A.P.D.G.	=	Andhra Pradesh District Gazetteers
A.R.	=	Administrative Report
E.L.O.H.	=	Economic Life of Hyderabad
O.S.	=	Osmania *Sicca*
REE	=	Rural Economic Enquiries
R.No.	=	Record Number
I.S.	=	Industrial Statistics
D.G.R.	=	Director-General of Revenue
F.R.	=	Fortnightly Report
T.C.R.	=	Tenancy Committee Report
RARC	=	Report of the Agrarian Reforms Committee
HSSM	=	Hyderabad Survey and Settlement Manual
SYB	=	Statistical Year Book
A.S.	=	Agricultural Statistics
H.C.C.C.	=	Hyderabad Co-operative Commercial Corporation.
TRAIC	=	Triennial Report on the Administration of the Department of Industries and Commerce
H.E.H.	=	His Exalted Highness
A.S.I.T.	=	A Survey of Industries in Telangana
A.I.T.U.C.	=	All India Trade Union Congress
Acc.No.	=	Accession Number
A.I.S.P.C.	=	All India State People's Conference.

CONTENTS

CHAPTER ONE

INTRODUCTION

THE PRESENT study intends to portray the economic history of Warangal *Suba*[1] or the Eastern Division of H.E.H. the Nizam's Dominions from 1911 to 1950. It consisted of the three Districts of Warangal, Karimnagar and Adilabad. Though Nizamabad District also formed part of this *Suba* from 1929 to 1937,[2] it is not taken into this study as it was there only for a temporary period.[3] The *Suba* was bounded on the north by Berar and the Central Provinces, on the East by the Pranhita and Godavari rivers and by the Godavari District of Madras Presidency, on the South by the Krishna river and the Krishna District of Madras Presidency and on the West by the districts of Nizmabad, Medak, Atraf-i-balda and Mahbubnagar of the Nizam's Dominions.[4] The headquarters of the Commissioner was at Hanamkonda, located between Kazipet and Warangal stations on the Nizam's State Railway, it being a town of much commerical and historical importance, at a distance of 84 miles north-east of Hyderabad city. The region comprised of 11 Divisions,[5] 25 Taluqs and 4842 villages out of which 4036 were *Diwani*,[6] 29 *Sarf-e-khas*[7] and 777 *Jagir*[8] areas.[9] It is proposed in this work to examine the economic aspects of crown and *Jagir* lands also, so that a totality of the picture might be arrived at. The period of the topic fully covers the reign of the last and the VII *Nizam*, Mir Osman Ali Khan (1911-1948) and hence the depiction of the economic conditions in the *Suba* would, at the same time throw much light on the conditions existing in the State as a whole.

Warangal after which the *Suba* was named had a glorious history extending from the last quarter of the 12th Century. Its rulers, the Kakatiyas, established their hegemony over the eastern and central Deccan which continued for more than two centuries ending in 1323 A.D. The region witnessed all-round prosperity, especially in the domains of foreign trade, irrigation and art. The famous tanks of Ramappa, Pakhal, Laknavaram, and Ghanpur, the Thousand-Pillared Temple at Hanamkonda, the temples at Palampet and the fort at Warangal are the standing monuments to their economic and artistic zeal. Similarly, Karimnagar could revel in the historical glory of Vemulawada Chalukyas (731 A.D. to 966 A.D.)[10] and Adilabad in that of the Gond Rajas (A.D. 1240 to A.D. 1750).[11] Besides royal eminence, the region was renowned for the products of its cottage industries. The cotton, silk and woollen carpets, rugs, *shatranjis*[12] and durries of Warangal, the brass articles and silver filigree work of Karimnagar and the wooden toys and handicraft works of Nirmal, had even before the advent of the modern period, become well-known in the markets of India and abroad. Warangal rugs and silk carpets had won acclaim in the great London Exhibition of 1851, rugs priced at £ 100 per square yard and were the only example in which silk was used in carpets with a perfectly satisfactory effect.[13] Regarding the fine cotton stuffs produced in the Kingdom of Warangal, Marco Polo, the Venetian traveller observed in the 13th century that :

"In this Kingdom are made the best and most delicate buckrams and those of highest price ; in sooth they look like tissue of spider's web. There is no king nor queen in the world but might be glad to wear them". In a note to this passage Colonel Yule remarks : "Here buckram is clearly applied to fine cotton stuffs......."[14]

During the heyday of the Kakatiyas, the region had enjoyed extensive foreign trade with Burma, China, East Indies and Ceylon in the East and Persia and Egypt on the West. Sandalwood, camphor, pearls, ivory, metals, handwoven clothes, carpets, perfumes, pepper and diamonds used to be exported and silkgoods, lead, china, camphor, sugar and horses used to be imported.[15] Thus, in every phase of life and activity, the Kakatiya age formed an age of transition between the ancient and the modern times.[16]

During the period under review also, the *Suba* made significant contribution in political and economic fields. All the three Districts abounded in rich forests, water and mineral resources, Warangal and Karimnagar led in the production of rice, being the staple food next to jawar, in the entire Dominions. Coal mining, one of the few large-scale industries in the State and employing the largest number of workers than any other industry in the Dominions, was exclusively confined to the *Suba* Districts. Not only the coal requirements of the State Railways were met but exports of coke and coal were made, fetching as much as Rs. 103.28 lakhs in the year 1945-46.[17] Ajamjahi Spinning & Weaving Mills, Carpet Factory in Warangal and Sirpur Paper Mills and Sirsilk Factory in Sirpur, Adilabad District, were some of the other notable large-scale industries of the *Suba* that contributed immensely to the cloth, Paper and Rayon Production of the State. The area did not lag behind in political activity. Both the Congress and the Communist parties which dominated the political scene of the period had considerable following in the Division.[18]

But, all the same, the economic development of the area during the period under study, was not in commensuration with its plentiful resources. A fair number of people in the rural areas seldom got two square meals a day.[19] *Economic enquiries held in 1949-51* revealed that the monthly per capita income worked at Rs. 15-11-0, whereas per capita expenditure was Rs. 14-7-0, thus giving a bare margin of Rs. 1-4-0. Compared to adjacent States, the standard of life in Hyderabad was decidedly lower.[20] The reasons that lay behind this paradox have not been critically analysed by the extant works on the subject.[21] Whereas Qureshi and B.K. Narayan have dealt with the economic development of Hyderabad State in a general and descriptive manner. Bedfords and Pavier have concentrated and confined their study to the single aspect of the Telangana Movement. Even Mr. I. Thirumali (of the J.N.U.) in his recent M. Phil work on 'Agrarian Relations in Telangana 1928-48' has only tried to trace the developments on the agrarian front, that led to the Telangana Struggle and its course upto 1948. Critical tracing of the economic development in its various aspects, vis-a-vis the resources and the potential, basing primarily on the huge and voluminous records that are available in Urdu and Persian, has not been so far done. Hence, the present effort is an attempt made in that direction with reference to Warangal *Suba*.

The sources that are available for study on the subject may be broadly divided into four categories, i.e., (1) Manuscript Records, (2) Official Reports, Surveys, and Census, (3) News papers and journals, and (4) individual writings. Among the Manuscript Records, first and foremost are the Warangal *Subedari* records which are in Urdu and all in the form of files. Majority consist of appeal cases preferred on the decisions of lower Revenue Officers to *Subedar*. Here and there '*Jamabandi*'[22] and Administrative Reports of the *Suba* are to be found. But, they are not evenly spaced chronologically to give a continuous data. There are as many as 150 bundles, each on an average containing 80 files. Index lists exist only for 109 bundles. Even these do not give correct inkling of the subject matter contained in the files. But, the most unfortunate thing is that papers that are there in several files dealing with important matters of economic interest such as 'Inspection Notes of Director-General of Revenue',[23] cases of land transfers and evictions and even *Jamabandi* Reports in some bundles were destroyed and only fly-leaves are kept. On the other hand, files dealing with 'succession' to property and 'adoption' cases which are also good many in number, are fully preserved in their entirety. Yet, the revenue appeal cases and reports that are available are of immense use in studying about the character of revenue system, its practical functioning, the various difficulties experienced and represented by the ryots and the extent and the manner in which they were attended to by the revenue authorities. The innumerable and valuable records have been for the first time put to use.

In Manuscript Records, next come the Secretariat Records of H.E.H. the Nizam's Government, preserved in State Archives and Secretariat, Government of Andhra Pradesh, Hyderabad. They are kept Department-wise but the indexes are prepared in a defective manner, so much so that considerable time is taken in picking out the files from the Stack. Files of the Departments of Agriculture, Finance, Revenue, Supply, Industries, Rural Reconstruction and Social Welfare are available, majority in Urdu and a few in English. These mainly dealt with the conditions pertaining to the entire Dominions and only here and there files relating to Warangal *Suba* or matters relating to it are to be found. But yet, the information that is found therein is of a substantial nature and very much helped in supplementing the data collected from *Subedari* Records.

Reports submitted by the committees or commissions appointed by Government provide basic information on the matters investigated. *Report on Agricultural Indebtedness* (*1937*) *Tenancy Committee Report* (*1940*), *Report of the Royal Commission on Jagir Administration and Reforms* (*1947*), *The Banking Enquiry Committee Report* (*1930*) and the *Agrarian Reforms Committee Report* (*1949*) give useful data on the different aspects that are enquired into. But, no such reports are found in the fields of industry, commerce, trade, transport and communications, even though they do have considerable bearing on the economic situation. These committee Reports are supplemented by *General Administrative Reports and Administratrative Reports* of different Departments of the Government such as Agriculture, Revenue, Excise, Forest, Industries & Commerce, Trade, Co-operative Societies etc. But, these Reports are not available for continuous period nor were they issued so. Further, they were published long after the period for which they were intended. *The Report on the Administration of the State pertaining to the period October 1941 to October 1942* was published in 1945. Thereafter no consolidated Report on the Administration of the State has been published until the *Report for the period from the middle of September 1948 to 31st March 1950* was published (n.d.). Even the data that is given in them is also very much restricted to the period of the Report which was generally one year and hence not much useful to form a comparative or background idea on the related aspect. But still, they proved of much value in corroborating and supplementing the facts gathered from Manuscript Records.

Economic investigations or surveys were held in the State first in 1929-30 and later in 1949-50, under the supervision of S. Kesava Iyengar who served the Government first in the capacity of special Officer for Economic Investigations and later as Economic Adviser. Whereas only Warangal District of the *Suba* was covered in the 1929-30 survey, all the three Districts of the *Suba* and as a matter of fact, of the entire State were covered in the 1949-50 enquiry. Landholdings, assessment, land transfers, *begari*,[24] debt, co-operative societies, agricultural labourers and wages, etc,. have been examined. They being rural economic enquiries, the aspects of industry, trade, markets, local bodies and urban life were not covered. Further, it was a sample survey confined to a few select villages in a Taluq, having its own limitations, consequent on local variations in soil, land holdings, natural resources, transport facilities etc., from one quarter of a Taluq to another. In spite of these limitations, the surveys are of immense value in the study of rural economic scene and they being physical enquiries, the data that is furnished enables in forming a comparative idea of the economic conditons existing during the twenty years active period that was there between the two surveys held.

Census Reports, both demographical and others, form an important source of information. Whereas the Decennial Reports on population deal with the growth or decline of population, its movement, the occupation of the people, vital statistics etc. Census is also collected, though belated and not regularly spaced, on the aspects of labour, livestock and agriculture. Agricultural Census in the Dominions was started as late as 1943-44 and until that time, the crop acreage and yield statistics were simply based on the figures of a few villages or figures sent in the past years by village officers supplemented by personal guesses by the *Tahsil* Staff both in the cases of area and yield. Hence, they remained far from being accurate.[25] Further, *Jagir* areas never used to submit even these imperfect particulars.[26] With the introduction of agricultural census, acreage and yield particulars of each crop of every village whether *Diwani* or non-*Diwani*, was arranged with checking of figures at different levels which has definitely ensured greater accuracy of the statistics. The Labour and Livestock Census were held quinquennially. The former were held in 1920, 1928[27], 1930, 1935 and 1940. They mainly dealt with the number of labour employing concerns, strength employed, both agricultural and industrial, wages, working conditions and general conditions of labour. But, it is important to note that in the case of the fisrt three census, though some data is collected, neither they were analysed nor published at all.[28] The work gained due sincerity, thoroughness and publication only with the Fourth Quinquennial Report of 1935. Hence, though they are of limited use, yet they are helpful in getting a glimpse of the labour scene in its fullness. The cattle or Livestock census were held rather systematically once in every five years starting in 1919 and ending in 1945. Types of cattle, their breeding, distribution, diseases, unserviceable cattle, and exports and imports of cattle and cattle products, are the items and are drawn upon in them. But these Reports, except those of 1935 and 1940 are not available for study. Measures for the scientific breeding of cattle and effective prevention of cattle diseases, seem not to have been given much attention in these census. Yet, they help informing a basic idea of the cattle life in the State.

Information of much value on agriculture, land revenue, rationing, labour and Communist activities, can be gleaned from contemporary newspapers and journals. But, the newspaper issues are available for different periods. '*Golkonda Patrika*', a Telugu bi-weekly and in the later forties a daily, is available from 1934 to 1950, with some gaps in between. It has been the largest circulated Telugu Newspaper, very much representing the cause of Telangana[29] ryots. Next comes '*Meezan*', another popular daily that was in good circulation in the *Nizam's* Dominions and is available now only from 1944 to 1948, with again, a few gaps. It is the only newspaper that was simultaneously published in three languages of English, Telugu and

Urdu. Another newspaper of much local coverge and importance which continues in the present times, is *The Deccan Chronicle*' in English, which is available only from 1947 'These newspaper issues are very much in a brittle condition and the way they are preserved, especially at State Central Library, Hyderabad, leaves much to be desired. But, in whatever form and sequence they are available, they being contemporary sources, are of considerable value in studying the developments from 1934 onwards.

Among the contemporary journals that are available, the prominent one is '*Hyderabad Government's Bulletin on Economic Affairs*', a monthly in English, published under the editorship of S. Kesava Iyengar.[30] The issues are available from 1947. They deal with different aspects of the economic scene indicating the nature and character of the Governmental measures introduced from time to time. Another notable journal of the period whose issues are now available is '*Hyderabad Information*' published by the Information Bureau, as a Monthly in Urdu, English, Telugu, Marathi and Kannada. It is available from 1941 to 1944 with many missing numbers in between. The journal very much tried to highlight the importance and scope of the various measures introduced by the Government from time to time. In both these journals, they being Government-sponsored, critical and objective analysis of the measures taken is very much lacking. Other magazines entitled '*Hyderabad Farmer*' a quarterly issued by the Hyderabad Farming Association in English, Telugu and Urdu and '*Hyderabad Bulletin*'[31] Published in English, are there in the references, but are not available now for study.

Besides the works by individual writers already referred to[32], there are others that are useful for background study on the subject. They can be broadly divided into two categories. The first one comprises of writings by leaders of *Andhra Maha Sabha*,[33] and Communist party who were actively associated with the literary, social and economic awakening that characterised the period.[34] Objectivity in these writings is marred to a considerable extent by inter and inner party recriminations and slander. If this is left aside, they would help in having a deep insight into the problems that afflicted the State and the course that the events have taken. The second category covers those works which are free from any bias, either party or otherwise and are devoted to dispassionate study. A.M. Khusro's '*Economic and Social effects of Jagirdari abolition and land reforms*', '*Andhra Pradesh District Gazetteers*', S.C. Dube's '*The Indian Village*', Zaheer Ahmed's '*Dusk and Dawn in Village India*', N.G. Ranga's '*Economic Organisation of Indian Villages*' ; 2 vols, etc., are some such writings that help in forming a fairly comprehensive idea of the village life in Telangana, economic structure and the changes it underwent. '*Tribal Hyderabad*' by Christoph-Von-Furer-Haimendorf is also a valuable work, depicting the history and the economic condition of tribals and aboringinals in Hyderabad State, in a critical and analysing manner.

The sources thus enumerated above, are numerous and varied but none of them gives us a complete and comprehensive account of the economic condition of Warangal *Suba* during the period under review. Further, except the Warangal *Subedari* Records, all other sources mainly dealt with development in the State as a whole. Consequently, information relating to the *Suba* was carefully sifted out of them and given a shape. Using all the available sources to the best advantage, an effort has been made to present the economic history of the *Suba* during the period under review in a full and comprehensive manner.

For the convenient treatment of the matter, it is divided into different chapters. Scope, importance and sources for the subject are examined in first chapter. As the physical features, natural and mineral resources of the area had a decisive influence on the economic life of the people, their impact has been assessed in second chapter. Political and administrative conditions had their bearing on the economic changes of the region. Hence, a brief survey has been made of them in Chapter III. The general economic policy of the State and its relation with the cultivators were mainly determined by the different systems of land tenure that prevailed in it. Consequently, the various systems of land tenure, their impact on the Government, landlords and ryots, the system of Survey and Settlement, the rates of assessment and their effect on the economic condition of the cultivators at large, and land revenue remissions and their impact, have all been traced in IV Chapter.

The nature and the volume of agricultural production are influenced by landholdings, pattern of land distribution, irrigational facilities, character of agriculture, agricultural research and experimentation, improved seeds, manures, implements, pesticides and the extent of their application, supply of working cattle and cattle manure, agricultural credit requirements and the pattern of their fulfilment, agricultural indebtedness and debt control measures and rainfall or crop conditions. These agricultural conditions of manifold nature have been portrayed in Chapter V. Pattern of land utilization, crop acreages, and price trends, have got an immediate bearing on agricultural production. These, along with the actual crop out-turns and the systems of procurement and rationing that had considerable bearing on the economic condition of ryots and others, have been vividly dealt with in Chapter VI.

Industrial production, labour, marketing and trade and transport and communications, form other significant facets of economic arena. Their condition, extent of growth and its impact on the economic condition of the *Suba*, have been extensively treated in VII Chapter. Education, health, urban development and tribal welfare, have also exercised considerable influence on the economic condition and development of the *Suba* people. Telangana Struggle came as a climax to the events of the period. making an unmistakable impression on the minds of the people and the authorities. These different aspects have been analysed in Chapter VIII. Conclusive assessment of the economic condition of the *Suba* during the period formed the IX Chapter.

REFERENCES

1. It refers to a 'Province' or 'Division' consisting of 3 or 4 Districts headed by a '*Subedar*' or 'Commissioner'. This unit of administration was derived from Maughal system.
2. *Administrative Report for 1338 Fasli (6-10-1928 to 5-10-1929)* Government Central Press : Hyderabad-Dn, 1932), p. 2 ; *The Economic Life of Hyderabad* (Government Central Press : Hyderabad-Dn, 1937), pp. 33-34.

3. *Golkonda Patrika* (Bi-weekly), 10-8-1936.
4. *Imperial Gazetteer of India, Provincial Series, Hyderabad State,* (Superintendent of Government Printing : Calcutta, 1909), p. 161.
5. It was an administrative Unit consisting of two or three Taluqs headed by a Division Officer or Second *Taluqdar.*
6. It was derived from '*Diwan*' or 'Prime Minister, referring to areas directly administered by the State.
7. Refers to lands meant for personal expenses of the crown or in other words crown lands.
8. *Jagir* was a tenure in which the Public revenues of a given tract of land were made over to a servant of the state, together with the powers requisite to enable him to collect and appropriate such revenue and administer the general Government of the area. The assignment was either conditional or unconditional. In the former case, some public service such as performance of prayer duties in religious institutions, or the levy and maintenance of troops etc,. was prescribed. The latter was left to the entire disposal of the State.
9. Warangal Subedari *File* No. 38 of 1356 Fasli (1947) & Record No. 2469 of 1357 Fasli (1948) ; *Report of the Royal Commission on Jagir Administration and Reforms* (H.E.H. the Nizam's Government, Bangalore Press : Bangalore City, 1947), p. 37.
10. Prof. K.A. Nilakantha Shastry & Dr. N. Venkataramanayya, 'The Chalukyas of Vemulawada' in G. Yazdani (edited) *Early History of the Deccan,* Vol. II, pp. 504-505.
11. M.V. Rajagopal (edited) *Andhra Pradesh District Gazetteers. Adilabad,* (Government Central Press : A.P. Hyderabad, 1976), p. 23.
12. Used for spreading on floor and also on beds.
13. S.H. Bilgrami & C. Willmott : *Historical and Descriptive Sketch of His Highness the Nizam's Dominions,* (Bombay : 1883) pp. 397 & 416.
14. *Ibid.,* p. 395.
15. Maremanda Rama Rao (edited) '*Kakatiyu Sanchika*' (Andhra Historical Research Society, Rajahmundry : 1935), p. 175.
16. P. Sreenivasachar, 'Political social and religious conditions of the Deccan under the Kakatiyas' in *the Proceedings of the Hyderabad Archaeological & Historical Society, January to August 1941,* (Government Central Press, Hyderabad-Dn : 1942), p. 19.
17. H.E.H. the Nizam's Government : *Trade Statistics for 1356 Fasli (1946-47),* p. 80.
18. Here-in after whenever 'Division' is referred to, 'Division' with

Capital 'D' refers to *Suba* and 'division' with small 'd' refers to unit consisting of 2 or 3 Taluqs.

19. A.I. Qureshi : *The Economic Development of Hyderabad*, Vol. I, (The Orient Longman's Ltd., Madras : 1941), p. 34.
20. S. Kesava Iyengar : *Rural Economic Enquiries in Hyderabad State, 1949-51*, pp. 382 & 588.
21. A.I. Qureshi, *Op. Cit* ; B.K. Narayan : *Agricultural Development in Hyderabad State, 1900-56*, Secunderabad, 1960 : B.K. Narayan : *A Survey of Industries in Telangana*, Secunderabad, 1962 ; Ian Bedford, *Telangana Insurrection : A Study in the cause and development of Communist Insurrection in Rural India* (Unpublished Ph. D. thesis, Microfilm available in Nehru Memorial Museum Library, Delhi) & Barry Pavier, *Telangana Government, 1944-51* (Ph.D. Thesis, available in JNU, Delhi).
22. Annual meet of Revenue Officers and staff at divisional level in which the revenue collections made during the year were reviewed, revenue demand for the ensuing year was fixed and land *Pattas* or ownership rights were granted.
23. He also held simultaneously the post of Revenue Secretary and decided appeal cases preferred by the *Subedaries* and also supervised their functioning.
24. It is a kind of forced labour extracted mostly without payment from village menials and even from smaller ryots and tenants by Government Officials and big landlords.
25. Office of the Financial Secretary and Financial Adviser (Supply Finance) *File* No. 53 of 1353 Fasli (1944) and serial No. 480.
26. *Ibid.*
27. Exceeded the quinquennial limit. It was due to late starting, reason being not much importance seems to have been attached to this work.
28. H.E.H. the Nizam's Government : *Report on Labour Census, 1935* (Government Central Press, Hyderabad-Dn : 1937), p. 1.
29. Refers to eight Telugu-speaking Districts which included the three Districts of Warangal *Suba*.
30. See the earlier para regarding 'Surveys' in this Chapter.
31. Type and duration of its publication are not known.
32. In the critique of the existing literature on the subject, in this chapter.
33. Though in its genesis as *Andhra Jana Sangham* in 1922 started as a literary movement, it after 1930, very much highlighted and worked for the redressal of social and economic grievances of the people in the State.
34. Madapati Hanumantha Rao : *Addhrodyamam*, 2 vols ; Mandumula Narsinga Rao : *Fifty years Hyderabad* : P. Sundarayya : *Telangana*

Armed Struggle and its Lessons : Ravi Narayana Reddy : *Heroic Telangana* : *Reminiscences and Experiences* : D. Venkateshwar Rao : *Telangana Armed Struggle and the path of Indian Revolution* : M. Bosava Punnaiah : *Telangana Armed Struggle-Realities* ; Swamy Ramananda Tirtha : *Memoirs of Hyderabad Freedom Struggle*, etc.

CHAPTER TWO

PHYSICAL FEATURES AND NATURAL RESOURCES

Location and Natural Divisions

WARANGAL *Suba* lay Lat. 16° 50′ to 19° 55′ N and Long. 77°57′ to 81°35 E. It is situated in the east of an extensive plateau with an average elevation of about 1,250 feet above the level of the sea, but with summits here and there rising to 2,500 and even 3,500 feet. The State was divided into two natural divisions, geologically and ethnically distinct, separated from each other by the Manjira and Godavari rivers. The portion to the north and west formed the trappean region, that to the south and east remained granitic and calcareous.[1] Ethnically the trappean region was inhabited by speakers of Marathi and the Kannada languages and the granitic region by those of Telugu. The difference between these two tracts in respect of soils, vegetation and hill features had its direct and profound influence on crop pattern, type of cultivation, habits and the economic well-being of the people inhabiting them. Whereas rich crops of wheat and cotton were cultivated in the black soils of the trap region, rice, maize and groundnut were mainly grown in the *Chalka*[2] soils of Telangana. The Marathwada region was covered with luxuriant vegetation, with cliffs, crags and undulating hills. In the granatic and calcareous region, on the other hand, the hills were denuded of vegetation, but the plains were covered with scattered brushwood of every description ; domeshaped hills and wild fantastic boulders abounded in many parts, giving the region a gloomy aspect. Black soils, being more retentive of moisture encouraged dry cultivation in the north and west, whereas red loamy soils, being less retentive of moisture forced the ryots in the south and east to predominantly resort to cultivation under tanks. Similarly, the sandy soils of Telangana resulted in the stunted growth of men and cattle and they remaining rather idle and backward in working for the development of agriculture[3], whereas the black soils in the north and west naturally helped in the vigorous growth and swift movements of the beings which, in the natural course of things, were accompanied by better economic conditions.

Area and Population

Warangal Division in 1911, as shown in Table 1, measured an area of 20,970 sq. miles. The average area of a district in the State was 5,166 sq. miles, while the average population was 8,04,628.[3a] Warangal with an area of 7,943 sq. miles became the largest District in the State as well as the *Suba.* Adilabad District with an area of 7,294 sq. miles and Karimnagar District with an area of 5,733 sq. miles occupied respectively second and third places in the Division. Population of the *Suba* in the same year numbered 26,57,477, out of which urban population was 1,51,928 and rural population 25,05,549, which unmistakably pointed to the predominant concentration of people in villages. As a matter of fact, towns[4] numbered only 15 in the Division in contrast to as many as 4,002 villages. The mean density of the *Suba* which was 132 per sq. mile was far less than that of the State, which stood at 162.[4a] This was mainly because of the low densities of the Districts of Warangal and Adilabad compared to their hugeness in area. In fact, they occupied in this respect the last two places respectively among the sixteen districts[5] of the State. Density in Telangana was very much dependant on the proportion of cultivated area under rice and also that which was irrigated. Accordingly, Adilabad which had the lowest percentage of its cultivated area under rice as also under irrigation in the whole of Telan-

TABLE I
Area, Population and Density in the year 1911

Division/ District	Area in Sq. Miles	Towns	Villages	Persons			Mean density per Sq. Mile	Percentage of total area		Percentage of cultivated area which is irrigated	Percentage of cultivated area under rice
				Urban	Rural	Total		Cultivable	Cultivated		
1	2	3	4	5	6	7	8	9	10	11	12
Warangal Division	20,970	15	4,002	1,51,928	25,05,549	26,57,477	132	41.3	32.7	10.7	9.2
Warangal District	7,943	5	1,244	73,373	8,32,041	9,05,414	114	38.3	32.8	12.9	10.2
Karimnagar District	5,733	7	1,135	54,418	10,77,219	11,31 637	197	52.5	43.2	16.5	12.3
Adilabad District	7,294	3	1,623	24,137	5,96,289	6,20,426	85	33.4	22.1	2.7	5.1

These figures are not given in the Census Report, but are calculated by averaging the District figures.

Source : *Census of India*, 1911, Volume XIX, *Hyderabad State*, pp. 2-3, 6-7 & 16.

gana, combined with the presence of huge forests accounting for as much as 44 percent[6] of the total area of the District, ranked lowest in the State. On the other hand, Warangal, as indicated in the Table, had better percentages both in respect of the rice cultivated and irrigated areas. It occupied the proud positions of number two in rice area and number one in gross irrigated area in the entire State.[7] But, curiously, it stood last but one in respect of density of population, the reason being that it had one of the largest forest areas in the State, spread in the Central and northern parts of the District. These areas were highly infested with malaria and consequently discouraged settlement of the people on the land. Some of the forest area Taluqs in the Division were so sparsely populated that their densities per square mile had been so low such as 25 (Mulug), 48 (Paloncha), 75 (Yellandlapad), 81 (Pakhal), all in the Warangal District ; 70 (Mahadeopur) in Karimnagar District ; 70 (Adilabad), 48 (Rajpura), 72 (Asifabad), 77 (Kinwat and Yelgadap), 85 (Chinnur), and 89 (Sirpur), all in the Adilabad District.[8]

But, if the area cultivated is only taken into consideration, then the density per square mile shoots up to 384.6 in the case of Adilabad and 347.5 in respect of Warangal.[9] Further, it deserves to be noted that in view of the vast scope for land development and the exploitation of mineral resources, especially coal, the densities in respect of both these Districts kept on rising.[10] In contrast to these two Districts, Karimnagar which had the highest percentage of rice-cultivated as well as irrigated area, recorded highest density, exceeding both the *Suba* and State averages. Its density kept on increasing steadily and by 1951, it had become the most densely populated District in the State,[11] if the figures of the Capital City were removed from those of Hyderabad District. It had 80.70 per cent of its area and 93.2 per cent of its population distributed in the densities between 150-300 per square mile.[12]

Hill Features

There are numerous clusters of hills of minor importance. They are generally 50 miles or less in length, and their only importance lies in the fact that they are in many cases the sources of petty local streams which go to feed the larger rivers of the region.[13] In Warangal District, a range of low hills runs from Pakhal and Singareni to Aswaraopet in the south-east, bounding the lower Godavari Valley. The Kandikal Gutta range extends from the south-east to Chinnur in Adilabad District. Ten miles north-west of Warangal are the Chandragiri hills and 14 miles west of it the famous iron hills of Hasanparthi. The country around the town of Hanamkonda is about 1,700 feet above sea level, but the average elevation of the District is only about 870 feet.[14] The whole area is dotted with isolated hills.

In the District of Karimnagar, a range of hills commencing at Gurrapalli, runs in a north-easterly direction as far as Jagtial, from where it proceeds to Vemalkurthi near the Godavari. A second range, known as Sanigaram range,[15] proceeds from Sanigaram and Mallangur Parallel to the above range, at a distance of 32 miles. The villages of Kuncherla, Minola and Marmulagutta on this range are between 2,200 and 2,300 feet above the sea. A third range starts in the south-west corner of the District from the valley of the Maner river, and runs in a north-easterly direction. Intersecting the Sanigaram range, it passes beyond Ramgir, where it is about 1,600 feet above the level of the sea. The range ends near the Godavari.

In Adilabad District, the Sahyadriparvat of Satmala range runs from the north-west to the south-east for about 175 miles. In this range, the Mahbubghat is the highest peak. Hills of minor importance lie in the east.[16] The centre of the District is characterised by a plateau containing hill ranges which reach a height of 2,000 feet in some places. These uplands cover nearly half the area of the District and are the home of the well-known tribe Raj Gonds and the lesser known sub-tribes of Kolams, Thollis, Naikpods and Pradhans.[17]

Rivers

As the Deccan Plateau slopes down eastwards to the Madras seaboard from the long flanking wall of the Western Ghats, all the flow of the rivers is from the West to the East. The two main lines of drainage are represented by the two great river systems of Godavari with its tributaries and the Krishna with its confluents.[18]

Godavari which is the most important river in peninsular India, forms as southern, northern and north-eastern and eastern boundary to the Districts of Adilabad, Karimnagar and Warangal respectively. At the same time, it separates the former two Districts from Central Provinces and the latter one from Madras Presidency. This river which flows in the northern half of the region, has the important tributaries of Penganga, Wardha, Wainganga, Pranhita[19] and Kadam on the left and Manjira, Sabari, Kinnerasani and Maner on the right. The river when it enters the Dominions does not exceed a quarter of a mile in breadth with steep banks. But, on entering into Karimnagar District, it attains a width of half a mile to a mile. Lower down, the stream becomes still more imposing and the surrounding landscape highly attractive. It is on account of this beautiful scenery that the Godavari has received the name of the 'Indian Rhine.'[20] Though the river has bounded all the three Districts of the *Suba*, no effort has been made during the period under review, in utilising its waters either for irrigation or for generation of power.[21] But however, construction of dams over its two tributaries Kadam[22] in Adilabad District and Maner[23] in Karimnagar District has been taken up with an irrigation potential of 26,325[24] hectares and 17,680[25] acres respectively. Their completion went beyond the period under study.

River Krishna, the second largest river flowing in the Dominions, passes along the southern boundary of Khammamet Taluq of Warangal District for a short distance only. It thus acts as the southern boundary of the Division separating it from the Krishna District of the Madras Presidency. Important among its confluents are the Maner, Paler and Wyra. The Maner river takes its birth in Pakhal Taluq of Warangal District, flows southwards and after draining the Taluqs of Yellandu and Khammam,[26] falls into the river Krishna after a course of 154 kilometres. River Paler flows almost parallel to the Muner, and also falls into the Krishna, 7 miles south of Jaggayyapeta in Krishna District of Madras Presidency. A reservoir was constructed over it in 1930 in

Khammam Taluq at a cost of Rs. 24,65 lakhs.[27] It was expected to irrigate 19,650 acres, but rarely did it even reach one thousand mark in actual area irrigated.[28] The Wyra is a tributary of the Muner and joins it near Jalpalli in Khammam Taluq before falling into the Krishna. A masonry dam with earth backing was constructed over it in Khammam Taluq in 1933 with an anticipated *ayacut* of 17,390 acres.[29] Here, in this case also, the full *ayacut* has never been irrigated,[30] and the reasons that led to this development would be examined separately.

River Valleys in the region had their influence in the formation of different and distinct social, cultural and ethnical units in the area, besides, of course acting as convenient boundaries for delimiting States and Districts. As far as Adilabad District is concerned, two distinct units are noticeable. While the Nirmal side of the North Godavari Valley consisting of the Taluqs of Nirmal, Yelgadap,[31] Asifabad, Luxettipet, and Chinnur is Telangana and has the closest affinities with the Nizamabad and Karimnagar side of the river, the upper strip of the District along the Penganga consisting of the Taluqs of Kinwat, Boath, Utnur, Adilabad, Rajura and Sirpur is distinctly Marathwada and has the closest affinities with the Central Provinces just across the river.[32] From this northern area people sent their children to Yeotmal in Marathwada region for education and had property, including *Jagirs* in the Central Provinces. This movement or exchange was very much reciprocal in the sense that rich persons from beyond the river came to Adilabad, Rajura and Sirpur and set up cotton pressing and ginning units. Further, all the cotton produced in the area moved northwards. Regarding Karimnagar and Warangal Districts, the Taluqs bounded by river Godavari on the north-east and east, such as Sultanabad and Mahadeopur in Karimnagar and Mulug, Pakhal and Paloncha in Warangal, remained deep forest and malaria-ridden, very much cut-off from the rest of the country due to poor means of communication and transport[33] and consequently very much backward, socially, economically and culturally. In contrast to this, the people inhabiting the two southern Taluqs of Khammamet and Madhira of Warangal

District bounded by river Krishna, developed intimate social, economic and cultural contacts with the people of the Krishna District on the other side of the river and as a result, they looked more Andhra[34] rather than Telangana and markedly different from the people of inner Taluqs of the District in their accent, dress, manners, customs, agricultural methods and way of living.

Lakes and Tanks

In parts of the Deccan which includes the *Suba* area, the rainfall, though normally sufficient to ripen the crop, is yet so precarious that without irrigation, there can be no assurance to the cultivator that his crops will mature.[35] The heavy sand content in the soils of the region also prompted the ryot to depend on sources of irrigation.[36] There are no natural lakes, but from the earliest times dating as far back as 700 years, advantage has been taken of the undulating character of the country to dam up some low ground or gorge between two hills, above which the drainage of a large area s collected. The Pakhal lake in the Pakhal Taluq of Warangal District, originally constructed in 1213 A.D. by Yagala-Ummidi, a General of Ganapati Raja of Kakatiya dynasty[37] and restored in 1922 at a cost of Rs. 450 lakhs to irrigate 8,910 acres with an annual revenue of Rs. 77,460, is by far the most important of such tanks in the *Nizam's* Dominions and has been formed by throwing a bund across the Pakhal river between two low head-lands. The dam is 2,000 yards long and the lake formed is 8,000 yards long, 6,000 broad and when full, covers an area of 13 square miles.[38]

Next to Pakhal, the tanks that ranked in importance from the point of view of their contribution to irrigation are Ramappa, Laknavaram, Ghanpur, Waddepalli, Dharmasagar[39] and Singabhupalem tanks in Warangal District ; Baithpalli, Sanigaram, Chegaon, Parkal and Kothapally tanks in Karimnagar District and Thorri Cheroo[40] in Adilabad District. Tank irrigation in the State as a whole was led by the two former Districts.[41] Though wells and river projects were there as other sources of irrigation; tanks, both small and large, far outsurpassed them in the extent of their contribution to land irrigation. The number of tanks and their state of repair, afford a fair criterion of the prosperity of the country.[42] But, the restoration and maintenance of these tanks left much to be desired, as a result of which the *ayacuts*[43] under them got greatly diminished and it is not surprising that the State very often found itself in the grip of a formidable food crisis, spelling disaster for the people.[44]

Soils

Reddish sandy to sandy loams known as *Chalkas* and darkish grey to dark loams, to clay loams were the types of soils that occurred in the region.[45] Warangal and Karimnagar Districts contained greater proportion of sandy loams, whereas black soils predominated in Adilabad District. This was probably due to the reason that the latter District was partly situated in trap and partly in granitic region, whereas the former two were completely in the granitic tract.[46] Reddish sandy or loamy sands occurred mostly along the banks of the streams, at the foot of the hillocks and at the lower end of steep slopes. They were suitable for rain-fed crops during *Kharif*[47] season and for raising paddy under intensive irrigation. They were also good for growing crops under protective irrigation during *Rabi*[48] season. In order to get good yields in these soils, it was found that quick acting and readily soluble fertilisers in smaller doses at frequent intervals were to be used.

Sandy loams which covered the largest area in the *Suba* as a whole, were generally non-saline, non-alkaline and well-drained. They were very poor in fertility but responded well to irrigated crops with proper application of manures. If the lands were dry, neither they were cultivated every year, nor was the same crop repeated owing to the poor quality of the soil. These lands were intented chiefly for *Kharif* Crops of *til*[49] and jawar and were cultivated only for two successive years, after which they remained fallow for three or more years.[50] With proper and sufficient supply of water, they were very much suitable for cultivation of paddy, sugarcane, groundnut, vegetables and pulses. These soils were usually deficient in nitrogen and phosphoric acid contents. The application of green leaf, superphosphate and nitrogen were recommended as good manures for these soils.[51]

Black soils or *requr* occurred mostly in the Taluqs of Mahboobabad, Khammamet, Madhira, Yellandu, Paloncha and Pakhal, all in Warangal District; Sultanabad, Mahadeopur, Jagtial and Huzurabad Taluqs in Karimnagar District, and Kinwat, Adilabad, Rajura, Nirmal, Luxettipet, and Chinnur Taluqs in Adilabad District. *Requr* is a highly agillaceous, very finely grained, dark or black soil containing a high proportion of calcium and magnesium carbonates. It is very tenacious of moisture and extremely sticky when wet. The dark colour appeared to be due in reality to the large proportion or iron contained in the finest soil particles.[52] These soils, being generally more fertile, were found highly suitable for the cultivation of *Rabi*, jawar and cotton in the black type, whereas paddy, maize, chillies and tobacco were grown in clay loam variety.[53] The black soils, being calcareous, required the application of superphosphate. The alluvial soils in the river valleys and borders, were highly fertile, and were used for growing paddy, sugarcane, wheat and cotton. But, they were found in small pockets and patches and formed a negligible percentage of the total area cultivated.

Forest Resources

The total forest area of the State, being 11.7 percent of the total area, was inadequate for meeting the requirements of the country, in view of the fact that 15 per cent was generally accepted as the minimum required for an agricultural population.[54] In contrast to this, the *Suba* Districts occupied the premier position in the State in being endowed with rich and extensive forests along the river Godavari.

In the protected forests, trees were under the control of the Forest Department; but in the open forests, only sixteen species[56] were reserved for protection.[57] The entire forests in the State were divided into Eastern and Western Circles, each consisting of seven divisions. The divisions of Warangal, Khammamet and Karimnagar formed part of the former, while those of Asifabad and Nirmal, of the latter.[58] Each division was under an Assistant Conservator and the department was headed by

TABLE II

Distribution of Forests in 1324 Fasli (1914-15)

Name of the District/ Region	Total area	Forest area: Protected	Forest area: Open	Forest area: Total	Percentage of forest area to total area	Remarks
1	2	3	4	5	6	7
	Sq. Miles	Sq. Miles	Sq. Miles	Sq. Miles		
Total Maharathwada	41,378	617.50	801.19	1,418.69	3.42	Note :—In this Table, figures of total area as well as forest area of Telangana and the State do not include those pertaining to the Sarf-i-Khas District of Atraf-i-Balda, as the same are not available.
Warangal District	7,943	2,124.38	926.00	3,050.38	38.40	
Adilabad District	7,294	1,831.50	982.66	2,814.16	38.58	
Karimnagar District	5,733	1,038.68	280.55	1,319.24	23.01	
Total Telangana	38,709	6,573.23	2,770.49	9,343.72	24.13	
Grand total for the State	80,087	7,190.73	3,571.68	10,762.41	13.43	

Compiled from : *Revenue Administration Report, 1324 Fasli (1914-15)*, p. 128

the Conservator who was empowered to exercise full control over protected forests and 'reserved' species of trees in open forests. Taken as a whole, the open forests formed less than half of the area covered by Protective forests and the opportunities for free and unrestricted exploitation of forest products by the ryots, had thus been very much narrowed down. The forest demarcation line was in many places contiguous with cultivated land. The ryot had to secure his fuel and timber at non-competitive rates from contractors who bought blocks marked out by the Forest Department.[58a] The economic life of our peasantry was affected as they could not secure their requirements of forest products cheaply and easily.[58b]

Regarding the percentage of forest area to total area,[59] the *Suba* Districts of Adilabad, Warangal and Karimnagar occupied the first three places respectively in the State. Their percentages, especially of the two former Districts were far higher than those of the State, the Marathwada and Telangana regions. The distribution of the forests in the State was uneven. The forests were not equally distributed in all parts, the two Districts of Osmanabad and Bhir having no forests at all, while the forests in Karimnagar (Elgandal), Warangal, and Adilabad (Sirpur-Tandur) occupied half the area of the State lands. The Maratha Districts were far less wooded than the Telangana Country.[59a] The eastern half of the State comprising of Telangana Districts has 29.1 per cent of forest land and the Western half consisting of Marathwada and Karnataka is poor in forest land, with hardly 3.4 percent.[60]

Forests capable of yieding good timber were confined to the eastern parts of Adilabad, Karimnagar and Warangal Districts along the river Godavari. The notable species that occurred in them were teak (*Tectonagrandis*), ebony (*Diospyros melanoxylon*), *shisham* (*Dalbergia Sisoo*), satin-wood (*Chloronylon swietenea*), sandal-wood (*Santalum Album*), *bhandara* (*Adina Cardifolia*), *tirman* (*Anogeissus latifolia*), *eppa* (*Hardwickia binata*), *Chinnangi* (*Lagerstroemia Parviflora*), *Kodsha* (*Cleistanthus Collinus*), *bijasal* (*Pterocarpus Marsupium*), *mokab* (*Schrebera Swietenioides*), *somi* (*Soymida fabrifuga*), *nallamaddi* (*Terminalia Tomentosa*) *sandra* (*Acacia catechu*), bamboo and *jittigi* (*Dalbergia*

Latifolia).[61] With the exemption of a few *coupes*[62] that were worked departmentally for the supply of agricultural requirements to the local ryots and timber to the saw mills, forest produce was generally sold to be exploited by the contractors, wherever demand existed and labour was available. *Tectona Grandis* (Teak) was the principal marketable species and this found its way to the Chief and distant markets of consumption such as Hyderabad and Secunderabad. The other species, such as *Terminalia Tomartosa* (*Nallamadi*), *Acacia Catechu* (*Sandra*), *Pterocarpus Marsupium* (*Bijasal*), etc., were locally consumed and were not exported to the above mentioned markets either because of heavy railway freights or for want of popularity.[63] Sleepers for State Railways, soft-wood species for use in the Match Factory started at Mahboobabad in the year 1928, and beedi-leaves for the widespread cottage industry, were all supplied from the eastern forests. Timber requirements (Pit-props) for the Singareni Coal mines at Bellampalli, Mandamarri and Ramakrishnapur in Adilabad District and Ramagundam in Karimnagar District, had been largely met from the forests of Adilabad.[63a] The Singareni Collieries Company Limited, at Kothagudem needs about 24,000 pit props for its mines at Kothagudem. All these are obtained from the local forests. Some of the forest *coupes* within a radius of about 32 kilometres from Kothagudem are taken by the Singareni Collieries Company Limited at the rates fixed by the Government.[63b]

The sources of income to the Division from the District forests were different and diverse. An idea could be had of them and their extent of contribution, from Table III, for the period 1922-36 of which period only, item-wise District figures[64] are available. Timber and fuel formed the major source of revenue and it generally approximated to 50 per cent of the total revenue of the Dapartment. There was big increase amounting to nearly 100 per cent in this item during the period 1922-26 in the case of Warangal and Karimnagar Districts whereas there was a decrease in the case of Adilabad. This pointed to the better utilisation of the resources in the case of former two Districts in view of the better means of transport they had, and on the other hand, poor facilities in this respect in the latter District had its adverse impact, even though it had

TABLE III

Value of the out-turn of Forest Products, Revenue and Expenditure of Forest Department—1331-1345 Fasli (1922-36)

WARANGAL DISTRICT

Value of the out-turn of products in O. S.* Rs.

Sl. No.	Fasli/ Year	Timber and fuel	Bamboo	Grass and Grazing	Fruits	Bark and leaves	Other minor Products	Miscellaneous receipts including revenue collected by Revenue Dept.	Total Revenue	Total expenditure
1	2	3	4	5	6	7	8	9	10	11
1.	1331F/1922	81,713	5,858	46,057	177	3,048	288	21,365	1,52,506	1,11,306
2.	1335F/1926	1,65,935	26,065	1,50,908	1,078	9,513	377	20,492	3,74,369	96,829
3.	1340F/1931	1,63,392	9,533	..	..	31,217	1,445	12,837	2,18,424**	1,06,649
4.	1345F/1936	1,41,094	9,529	66,221	..	35,110	1,623	14,676	2,68,253	1,26,800

(Contd.)

KARIMNAGAR DISTRICT

Sl. No.	Fasli/ Year	Value of the out-turn of products in O.S. Rs.								
		Timber and fuel	Bamboo	Grass and Grazing	Fruits	Bark and leaves	Other minor Products	Miscellaneous receipts including revenue collected by Revenue Dept.	Total Revenue	Total expenditure
		12	13	14	15	16	17	18	19	20
1.	1331F/1922	24,902	275	36,798	18	1,072	352	4,698	68,015	44,156
2.	1335F/1926	93,356	1,216	1,36,013	258	5,064	180	12,960	2,51,097	52,188
3.	1340F/1931	80,087	568	90,000	..	7,116	2,519	5,454	1,85,744	44,755
4.	1345F/1936	63,974	2,214	38,388	..	7,906	1,442	16,504	1,30,428	49,829

(*Contd.*)

ADILABAD DISTRICT

Value of the out-turn of products in O.S. Rs.

Sl. No.	Fasli/ Year	Timber and fuel	Bamboo	Grass and Grazing	Fruits	Bark and leaves	Other minor Product	Miscellaneous receipts including revenue collected by Revenue Dept.	Total Revenue	Total Expenditure.
		21	22	23	24	25	26	27	28	29
1.	1331F/1922	75,996	5,474	31,604	796	3,943	8,783	3,708	1.30,304	1,33,267
2.	1335F/1926	52,569	12.561	1,17,112	1,145	4,726	1,729	52,545	2,42,387	1,34,123
3.	1340F/1931	1,26,529	11,195	..	..	27,536	4,193	43,919	3,49,232	1,11,207
4.	1345F/1936	1,14,525	18,532	1,33,586	..	24,530	2,160	39,198	3,27,631	1,53,107

* Osmania *Sicca*, meaning the currency (*Sicca*) that was in vogue during the time of MIR OSMAN ALI KHAN, the VII Nizam.

** In the statement it is given as Rs. 33,38,636 which does not tally with the total of columns 3 to 9.

Compiled from : *Hyderabad District Gazetteers*, Tables Volume, *1340 & 1345 Fasli (1931 & 1936 A.D.)*, *Warangal*, pp. 94-95, *Karimnagar*, pp. 94-95 & *Adilabad*, pp. 94-95.

equally good timber and fuel resources. On the other hand, there was a slide down from 1926 to 1936 in respect of Warangal and Karimnagar but increase in respect of Adilabad. The pre-and post-Depression period had its diminishing effects in respect of the former two and the low wages and easy availability of labour in latter District has resulted in increasing exploitation of the material by timber contractors. Leaving aside this contingent factor, the effective prevention of smuggling of teak[65] into British territory and providing easy and better means of transport to the timber areas, would have greatly helped in augmenting the revenue from this item. But, little progress was recorded in this direction, especially in the latter aspect.

Next to timber and fuel, grass and grazing charges formed a significant source of income from the forests. The types of grasses found in the area were *Heteropogon contortus* (*Eddigaddi*),[66] *Aristida Adscencionis* (*Pillipesaragaddi*), *Cynodon dactylon* (*Gerichagaddi*), *Cymbopogon Martini* (*Kachigaddi*), *Andopagon Pumilus* (*Semalagaddi*), *Andropogon contortus* (*Yadagaddi*), *Aristida Setacea* (*Chipuru gaddi*), *Themeda Quadrival vis* (*Molvagaddi*) *Saccharum* species (*Koprigaddi*) besides the local varieties of *Yelaka Chevulagaddi*, *Kakkelagaddi*, *Kolinigaddi* and *Echinochloa* species.[67] Grazing in the 'reserved' and 'Protected' forests was regulated by the Forest Department, and the fees was collected either Departmentally or through contract agency. Grazing rights in the 'Open' forests were auctioned annually by the Revenue Department.[68] Thus, the ryot was made to pay grazing tax[69] both to Forest and Revenue Departments. But, the Forest Department was found paying particular attention only to timber producing areas and neglecting grazing grounds and grass lands which were generally left to themselves.[70] The Government *Bancherai* was situated in many villages at a distance and there was no controlling authority to enforce steps to ensure proper growth of grass by preventing indiscriminate grazing. As such, it served to useful purpose.[71] Further, at many places, the area fixed for *Banchcrai*, being 10 per cent of the total land of the village, was not given to the full. In some villages of Warangal District, it was only 4 to 14 per cent, in Karimnagar, it was 10 to 15 per cent and in

Adilabad, no figure could be given as the Settlement[72] was not over.[73] The growing of grass and fodder crops in the cultivators' own lands which was in vogue already both in Telangana and Marathwada offered the only hope for making good the shortage of common grounds.[74]

Income from fruit trees was not much, they being very much grown in private gardens. Bamboo, which was available in huge quantities especially in the Adilabad District,[75] had become the basic raw material for the paper industry at Sirpur which started production in March 1942 and had gradually become the largest paper mill in the whole of the Southern Zone.[76] Another good revenue yielding produce was *Gulmohwa* which was collected in the forest areas by the Excise Department in large quantities for making country liquor.[77] For the year 1323 Fasli (1913-14 AD) the revenue demand for *Gulmohwa*[78] from the Districts of Warangal, Karimnagar and Adilabad was Rs.15,720, Rs. 52,867 and 2,76,163 respectively.[79] The tribesmen such as Gonds, Koyas and Lambada, residing in the neighbourhood of the forest regions of Godavari, used the flowers of the *Mohua* (*Bassia Latifolia*) both as a part of their staple food as well as drank liquor prepared out of them.[80] They resented its auction by the Government as the contractors demanded payments from them even though they were entitled to free use of the flowers for their domestic consumption.[81] Lac, a forest product of much economic importance, was collected in the forests of Nirmal, Hanamkonda and Karimnagar and the quantity gathered in Nirmal alone in 1328 *Fasli* (1918-1919 A.D.) fetched a profit of Rs. 5,500 to the Government.[82]

Leaving aside stray cases just as in 1922 as shown in the table above, forest expenditure usually formed not more than 50 per cent of forest revenue. If the figures available for the period 1913 to 1945[83] are examined, they would indicate that whereas the increase in Revenue during this 32 year period, ranged from 3 to 20 times,[84] that in expenditure ranged only from 2 to 6 times,[85] in the 5 Forest Division of the *Suba*. Surplus had accrued thus, from year to year. But, on the other hand, schemes of re-afforestation, prevention of soil erosion and promotion of the means of transport required increasing funds to be spent.[86]

Forests yielding good timber had been so drastically over-exploited that unless immediate steps are taken to re-stock them with valuable hard-woods and industrial soft-woods, the future supply of timber from them would suffer great shortages.[87] The hilly and reverine areas of Mulug, Khammam, Madhira, Yellendu, Paloncha, Mahadeopur, Chinnur, Utnur and Nirmal were prone to the danger of erosion whenever heavy rains occurred, due to the slopy and undulating topography of the land. Remedial measures like regulated forestry, controlled grazing, revegetation, etc., needed the attention of the Department.[88] Poor communications that existed in the eastern area which was capable of yielding good timber had very much hindered the exploitation of forest resources in this area. As a matter of fact, except teak, other varieties such as *Satin*, *Nalla Tumma*, *Sandra*, *Bandaru*, *Chiriman*, *Jitiqi*, *Yeqi*, *Neredu*, *Eppa*, *Chinnangi*, *Vepa*, *Somi* and *Maddi*, which were equally good to serve as beams, rafters, poles, door-frames and scatlings[89] had not been very much exploited, mainly due to the transport and marketing bottlenecks.

Rainfall

Crops in the area being very much monsoon-dependant, the amount, time and distribution of rainfall had a direct and proportional bearing on the agricultural production.[89a] Even the tanks and wells in which the *Suba* abounded did not also serve the purpose, if the rains were deficient. The figures given in table attached pertaining to 1925-26 and 1926-27 illustrate this dependence. Rice, being the main irrigated crop in both Warangal and Karimnagar, the decrease in acreage and out-turn was very much marked and corresponded with the decline in rainfall. Jawar, not being so much an irrigated crop, the impact of the decline in rainfall was rather not so much except in the District of Adilabad where it covered considerable acreage. The effect on cotton crop was mixed. This might be due to differing conditions regarding soil adaptability and time of rainfall. But, all the same, the fact was clearly established that the crops in the region were fully dependant and thrived on rainfall.

TABLE IV

Effect of Rainfall on Acreage

Sl. No.	Year	Rainfall in inches	WARANGAL DISTRICT Rice Acreage	Rice Out-turn in tons	Jawar Acreage	Jawar Out-turn in tons	Cotton Acreage	Cotton Out-turn in tons
1	2	3	4	5	6	7	8	9
1.	1925-26	46.09	1,52,995	75,101	4,30,422	72,865	27,398	7,034
2.	1926-27	26.35	97,714	44,314	4,05,349	72,763	12,751	3,188
Decrease		19.74	55,281	30,787	25,073	102	14,647	3,846
Increase		—	—	—	—	—	—	—
Percentage (Decrease)		40.65	36.13	40.99	5.77	0.13	53.09	54.67
Percentage (Increase)		—	—	—	—	—	—	—

KARIMNAGAR DISTRICT

Sl. No.	Year	Rainfall in inches	Rice		Jawar		Cotton	
			Acreage	Out-turn in tons	Acreage	Out-turn in tons	Acreage	Out-turn in tons
		10	11	12	13	14	15	16
1.	1925-26	46.29	2,04,883	1,29,493	4,50,424	76,725	64,804	6,661
2.	1926-27	23.50	73,838	25,946	3,73,472	66,690	72,604	12,973
Decrease		22.79	1,31,045	1,03,547	76,952	10,035	—	—
Inerease		—	—	—	—	—	7,800	6,312
Percentage (Decrease)		49.23	63.96	72.24	17.08	13.07	—	—
Percentage (Increase)		—	—	—	—	—	10.74	48.65

ADILABAD DISTRICT

Sl. No. Year	Rainfall in inches	Rice		Jawar		Cotton	
		Acreage	Out-turn in tons	Acreage	Out-turn in tons	Acreage	Out-turn in tons
	17	18	19	20	21	22	23
1. 1925-26	43,69	29,876	10,780	6,47,117	89,736	2,30,030	80,870
2. 1926-27	31,50	25,020	6,702	3,44,944	58,251	2,05,849	72,047
Decrease	12.19	4,856	4,078	3,02,173	31,485	24,181	8,723
Increase	—	—	—	—	—	—	—
Percentage (Decrease)	27.90	16,25	37.82	46.69	35.08	10.51	10.78
Parcentage (Increase)	—	—	—	—	—	—	—

Compiled from : *Statistical Abstract, 1922-31*, pp. 272-73.
Agricultural Statistics, 1925-26 to 1934-35, (Government Central Press, Hyderabad-Dn : 1938), pp. 18, 20, 26, 28, 72, & 74.

TABLE V **Normal, good and bad Rainfall**

(Figures in inches)

Sl. No.	District/division	Normal Rainfall (50 years) in 1944-45	Exceptionally good Rainfall	Year	Exceptionally bad Rainfall	Year
1	2	3	4	5	6	7
1.	Marathwada Acreage	28.53	—	—	—	—
2.	Warangal District	36.01	54.31	1918	19.93	1920-21
3.	Karimnagar ,,	33.31	51.26	1935-36	14.23	1920-21
4.	Adilabad ,,	39.97	52.67	1933-34	20.38	1920-21
5.	Telangana Acreage	32.92	—	—	—	—
6.	Dominions ,,	33.73	44.53	1917	15.13	1920-21

Compiled from : *Decennial Report on Administration, 1912-22 A.D.* p. 16 ;
S.M. Bharucha, *Agricultural Indebtedness in H.E.H. the Nizam's Dominions, 1937*, p. 24.
and
Statistical Year Book, 1935 & 1942-45, pp. 294 & 881 ; *1941*, p. 529.

It is clear from Table V that the normal rainfall of the *Suba* Districts was above that of all the three averages--Marathwada, Telangana and the State. In other words, the heaviest amount of rainfall was experienced in the Eastern Division for the reason that the amount of rainfall in the State increased from the South-west to North-east. The South-west monsoon most copiously precipitated on the forest area of Asifabad and Eastern Warangal District. The precipitation was especially prominent along the forested hills which surrounded the Pranhita and Godavari Valleys.[90] About three-fourths of the yearly rainfall in the Telangana Districts was caused by the South-west Monsoon,[91] the remainder falling in the early part of the North-west monsoon, i.e., in October and November.[92] The South-west monsoon occurs between June and September, rainiest month being July.[93] The rainfall in the State was highest in Adilabad District and lowest in Raichur District[94] which lay in the South-west. Variations in the quantity, time or season and distribution of rainfall were considerable and not infrequent. From a maximum of above 50 inches, the rainfall as shown in the Table V had fallen, in respect of all the Districts to a minimum of even less than 20 inches in a period of 50 years, amounting to a decrease of more than 40 per cent. During the ten years period 1910-11 to 1919-20 that commenced the reign of the VII *Nizam*, as many as seven years witnessed insufficient or damagingly heavy rainfall, coupled with variation in distribution and this had its disastrous and unfavourable effect on crop condition.[95] Hail-storms, which fall in the pre-monsoon period,[96] also caused damage to *Rabi* crop.[97] In 1946, as many as 54 villages out of 180 in Warangal Taluq of Warangal District, suffered damage to *Rabi* crop, due to hailstorms that fell in the month of April.[98]

Climate

The climate of the Division is hot and damp from March to the end of September and temperate for the rest of the year.[99] The year is divided into four seasons. The winter season from December to February, is followed by the Summer season from March to May. The period from June to September is the south-west monsoon season and October and November constitute the post-monsoon or retreating monsoon season.[100] Climate in the areas which were hilly and nearer to Godavari and Pranhita was unhealthy as they were malarious. On the other hand, the climate prevailing in the central and plain areas was non-malarious and healthy.

Humidity

Corresponding with the arrival of the south-west monsoon, the relative humidity of the atmosphere rises suddenly in June. It continues high during the rainy season with humidities between 65 and 80 per cent,[100a] and gradually decreases with the advent of the cold, dry weather. The humidity is lowest, even coming down to 25 per cent, during the hot months from March to May. However, it is to be noted that the atmosphere in the hot weather in the Telangana is not so dry as in the Marathwada. The Telangana was studded with a large number of water tanks and reservoirs for irrigation purposes ; these and the large forest areas in the region make the air somewhat humid in the hot season.[101]

Temperature

Rise in the temperature starts from about the end of February. May is the hottest month in which, on some days, the temperature at places like Hanamkonda, Khammam, Bhadrachalam and Ramagundam, reaches 47° C (116.6° F). Afternoon thunder showers which occur on some days bring welcome relief. With the arrival of the south-west monsoon by about the second week of June, there is significant drop in temperature. By about the first week of October, the monsoon withdraws and there is a slight decrease in the day temperature. After October, both day and night temperatures decrease rapidly. December is the coldest month in which the night temperatures sometimes drop down to about 9°C (48.2°F). After February, temperatures begin to increase.[102]

Cloudiness

During the period of the south-west monsoon, the skies are heavily overcast with clouds. There is rapid decrease in cloudiness during the post-monsoon season. The skies are generally clear or lightly clouded in the remaining part of the year.

Winds

The winds are generally westerly in June, July, August and September ; during October, November, December, January and February, the blow from the east ; and in March, April and May, the north-westerly breezes are frequent.[103] The winds are light to moderate with some increase in force in the later part of summer and the early part of the south-west monsoon season.

Special Weather Phenomena

Storms and depressions which originate in the Bay of Bengal during the monsoon and post-monsoon seasons and move west-wards and north-westwards, affect the weather in the area causing widespread heavy rain and strong gusty winds. Thunderstorms occur mainly during summer and south-west monsoon seasons. Dusty winds are common in summer afternoons.[104]

Flora

Flora that existed in the rich forests of the area has already been examined. Villages and cultivated fields were also associated with trees of much economic value. Mango, custard-apple, *tarvar* (*Cassia Auriculata*), *babul* (*Acacia Arabica*), Tamarind (*Tamarindus Indica*), *Mushti* (*Strychnos Nuxvomica*), *Velaga* (*Feronia Elephantum*), *Amla* (*Phyllanthus emblica*), Margo (*Azadirachta indica*), Peepal (*Ficus religiosa*) and Banyan (*Ficus Vengalensis*) are commonly grown. *Topes* of toddy palms and large size *sendhi* (*Phoenin sylvestris*) are a common sight in the rural landscape and their ownership is well preserved as they yielded *sendhi*,[105] drunk by most of the rural folk.[106] But, however, the *pattadar* having toddy and *sendhi* trees within the limits of his *patta* land, was entitled only to the use of their leaves, fruits and wood, but not juice, the trees being deemed to be the property of Government.[107] This restriction however, had no effect on the increasing and widespread consumption of this drink by the people in the region that Warangal ranked first in 1945 among all the Districts in contributing as much as Rs. 39,53,543 towards revenue from toddy and *sendhi*.[108] As a matter of fact, next to Land Revenue, Excise Revenue became the main source of income to the State[109] and the efforts made to promote temperance were minimal with negligible effect.[110]

Fauna

The region being dominated by vast and thick forests, a greater variety of wild animals and feathered game is not to be met with in any other part of India excepting perhaps Mysore State.[111] Tigers and leopards are found everywhere, while bison and occasionally elephants are met with in the immense jungle about the Pakhal lake. The highlands are resorted to by spotted deer (*Cervus arus*), *nilgai* (*Boselaphus tragocamelus*), sambar (*Cervus Unicolor*), four-horned antelope, hog deer, and ravine deer or gazelle.[112] Wild hog are found in the jungles and numerous kinds of antelope in the plains. Hyenas, wolves, tiger-cats, bears, hares, jackals etc., are in great abundance. In the vicinity of tanks and rivers, water-fowl, duck, teal etc., are abundant. Wild duck, patridges, jungle-fowl and pea-fowl are to be found everywhere. Florican and flamingo are occasionally seen on the banks of the Godavari and the Krishna.

Principal shooting grounds were situated in the Madhira, Yellandu and Pakhal Taluqs of Warangal District. Game rules that came into force as early as 1st July, 1917, declared them to be Government preserves and no shooting licence was given except to nobles, *Jagirdars* and high Government Officials.[113] The forest preserve or '*Shikargah*' at Pakhal, covering vast expanse of cultivable land,[114] was kept exclusively for the sport of H.E.H. the *Nizam* and his family members. But human life, besides that of cattle, did not remain completely free from the danger of man-eaters. As late as 1949, a man eating tiger played havoc by killing four human beings in the Luxettipet Taluq of Adilabad District.[115] Only nominal allotments were made in the Budget for the killing of such wild animals to be given as *Inam* or gift for the shooters.[116]

There were as many as 2,308 tanks and 6,056 *Kuntas*,[117] in the *Suba*.[118] They contained good and rich wealth of fish. Large and small rivers passing through the territory, also formed convenient sources for fish exploitation. The Fisheries Department which came into existence as late as 1941, conducted practical survey in the *Suba* Districts as a result of which 99 species were identified, out of which a large variety of them were found to be quite good for propagation. Some larvicidal fishes suitable for the control of malaria and guienea-worm diseases were also found out.[119] Fishes of commercial importance like *Boche* (*Catla Catla*), *Murrel* (*Ophiocephalus strtatus*), *Waluga* (*Wallago Attu*), *Arzu* (*Wirrhina reba*), *Chitra Gande* (*Labeo Fimbriatus*), *Nallaganda* (*Labeo Calbasu*) etc., are found in abundance in the lakes of Pakhal, Ramappa, Laknavaram and Ghanpur, all in Warangal District.[120] These lakes are thus ideal for fishing. But, as the tree stumps have been removed at the formation of these reservoirs, only experienced fishermen could fish in them with nets. It is really regrettable that the Department due to lack of proper facilities and encouragement from the above,[121] could not do much in increasing the production of fish, even though there were abundant and inexhaustible sources.

Natural and Mineral Resources

Warangal Division, true to its physical geography, forms the richest region of the State in respect of mineral resources, Coal, iron ore, graphite, mica, garnets, talc, soap-stone, limestone, marble and granite stones, are in short, some of the minerals[122] that have been identified in the *Suba* Districts, but exploited only partially. Only coal out of the above has been put to large scale exploitation. The geological formations that are existent in the region such as Gondwana, Archean, Laterite etc., have a close bearing on the type and extent of the mineral wealth that is contained in it.

Coal

Coal as mineral is found in the Gondwana[123] series of geological strata towards the eastern portions of the Hyderabad State in the Districts of Adilabad, Karimnagar and Warangal in the Pranhita and Godavari river valleys.[124] The series form as a continuous strip from the Wardha valley through the State into the Madras Presidency and occupy about 3,800 sq. miles, but the actual coal seams are located only in particular areas.[125] The first coal field to be opened was the Singareni field in Yellandu Taluq of Warangal District. Where production started in 1887, and to the time of its closing down in 1941 after working the "Kingseam",[126] nearly 30 million tons of coal were extracted from a number of mines situated within an area of 10 miles long and two to three miles broad.[127] This coal field has been reopened towards the close of the period under review, to work the thick seam which is expected to contain considerable reserves of Coal. With the exhaustion of the king seem at Yellandu, the exploitation of the mines at Kothagudem in the same Taluq and also connected by rail, was started as late as 1938 and rapidly developed into the most important coal field in the State, its output rising to the record figure of over 8,44,000 tons in 1942. The area has great potentialities and has an estimated reserve of 80 million tons.[128]

The Tandur collieries in the Asifabad Taluq of Adilabad District have been developed since 1927. Here, two mines are being worked, each equipped for an output of 750 tons per day. Further in the same District, there are three coal mines near Sasti and Paoni in Rajura Taluq which are being worked since 1916 on the Wardha river opposite Balharshah, with an annual output of 73,000 tons reached in 1939.[129] The coal mining is carried on by the Singareni Collieries Co. Ltd. in the Coal fields of Singareni, Kothagudem and Tandur by Sir Maneckji Dadabhoy and Sir Bishweswardas Daga in Sasti and Paoni Collieries.[130] Besides these, another important field was discovered by prospecting conducted by Sir Fazalbhoy Currimbhoy to the South of the Godavari which included the Sultanabad Taluq of Karimnagar District in which about 38 million tons of coal has been estimated.[131] The yearly output of coal from all the mines that are being exploited is just over a million tons which worked out just four percent of All India output.[132] Considering the estimated resources of 1,000 million tons kept at the disposal of the Singareni Collieries Co. Ltd. for exploitation, the quantity extracted during 45 years was only about 33 million tons and this was very inadequate.[133] Hence, H.E.H. the *Nizam's* Government took on its own shoulders the responsibility for developing coal mining in the State by acquiring 88 per cent shares of the Company on the 14th November, 1944.[134]

Coal in the *Suba*, right until 1950 has been used mainly for steam raising purposes in railways, mills and power houses. As it is non-cooking, it is unsuitable for mettalurgical purposes.[135] But, from coal it is possible to develop coal distillation and dye-stuffs industry with the recovery of such by-products as tar, synthetic petrol and synthetic fertilizers. Coal-tar vaporization at different temperatures condenses in some 300 by-products. About 75 per cent of the 1,500 materials manufactured from these are dye-stuffs, 25 per cent drugs, perfumes and explosives.[136] As it provides cheap power,[137] coal conservation has become imperative in view of it being wasted by allowing raw coal to be exported to the neighbouring provinces.[138]

Iron Ore

Workable iron ore is found concentrated in the upper beds of the Gondwana series and intensive deposits are noted in the portions of Adilabad and Warangal Districts.[139] The Department of Geology,[140] in the course of its surveys, has noted extensive occurrences of iron ores in Nirmal, Yelgadap, Utnoor, Luxettipet, Chinnur and Sirpur Taluqs of Adilabad District ; Parkal, Jagitiyal and Sirsilla Taluqs of Karimnagar Districts.[141] In Warangal District, the Taluqs of Warangal and Yellandu are noted for this mineral.[142] They exist in the form of haematite, magnetite and ferruginous schists.[143] The quality of iron found in the ore varied from 47 per cent in Thimmapur lateritic (Karimnagar Taluq) to 93 per cent in Parkal (Parkal Taluq) and 97 per cent in Sankaram (Chinnur Taluq).[144]

Iron smelting has been known from time immemorial since the neolithic times as evidenced by the neolithic implements with iron slags. Swords famous for their strength and peculiar damascening lustre,[145] manufactured from Konasamudram[146] steel by the local iron industry of Nirmal attained world-wide fame and formed an important source of commerce between Hyderabad and other countries.[147] Nirmal steel was also used in the manufacture of surgical instruments in the Roman empire.[148] Steel weapons of different sorts, such as swords, daggers and knives with massive ivory handles are manufactured at Hanamkonda from Konasamudram steel.[149] But, with the introduction of modern methods of iron smelting,[150] and the competition of imported metal, the ancient industry got a severe blow from which it could never regain its original importance. The indigenous smelting by primitive methods, though still persisting in certain of the iron ore localities such as in Sirpur Taluq of Adilabad District, does not satisfy even a small fraction of the local needs. Hence, most of the finished and unfinished products of iron and steel are imported and this cottage industry is fast dying.[151]

Graphite

Graphite is reported from Paloncha in Warangal District in schistose garnetiferous gneiss in beds varying from a few inches upto 2 ft. in width. It is much impregnated with earthy material. Good quality graphite has also been reported from the area and an improvement both in quality and quantity in depth is indicated. A small deposit of graphite is reported from near Hasnabad in Karimnagar District.[152]

Being one of the natural forms of Carbon, graphite has a wide industrial application for the manufacture of crucibles used for melting metals. It is extensively used in the manufacture of 'lead' pencils, in the preparation of paints, for the prevention of scale formation in boilers, for stone polishing and in electrodes and batteries.[153] In spite of these varied uses, the mining leases granted to different persons for different periods between 1918 to 1949 did result in the extraction of only a small quantity.[154]

Mica

Mica occurs in flakes and looks about 1½ to 2 sq. inch indicating economic possibilities in depth. Mica of commercial sizes has been reported from the villages of Kallur in Madhira Taluq ; Tailpalli ; Nelakondapalli and Wandanum of Khammam Taluq of Warangal District.[155] Small size mica and flakes are in demand for making miconite and for dry lubrication along with the graphite. For its heat resistance, transparency and frictionlessness, the ground mica is used for patent roofing, wall-paper packing, in axle and pipes, boiler coverings, fire proof and fancy paints.[156] Prospecting licenses for mica were granted to Messrs. Vazir Sultan & Sons, Hyderabad[157] in 1944 for exploiting the mines at Kallur and Gokawaram in Madhira Taluq. The mines were worked upto 1950,[158] but the details of the quantity of the mineral extracted are not available after 1945.[158a] But, however, the fact that the mining operations were confined only to two villages and that too, for a short period of six years, indicate the least importance given to the matter.

Garnets

Translucent and transparent varieties of red almandine garnets in the Garibpet area in Madhira Taluq have long been known to yield material for the lapidary industry.[159] The crystals have a diameter of 0.3 to 0.5 cm ; the maximum being 2 cms. A rough estimate of about 32 million tons was made for this mineral.[160] But, no extraction of the mineral seems to have taken place during the period. Long platy-crystals of Kyanite are also found associated with garnets in this area.[161]

Talc and Soapstone

Powdered talc is an important mineral 'filler' used in industry. The best grade is used in the manufacture of toilet powder and certain types of soaps. It is also used in the leather and rubber industries and in the manufacture of foundry facings and for metal polishing.[162] Talcose rocks have been noted round about the Singareni coal mines in the Yellandu Taluq of Warangal District. They are used by school boys locally as slate pencils and also for making inkstands, geometrical models, etc.[163]

Varieties of soapstone and potstones occur commonly as alteration product of the amphibolites and periodtites, potstones are reported from Metpalli[164] in Karimnagar District and Dammapalli in Warangal District.[165] Soapstone is quarried near

Tukal Muddikunta in Karimnagar District. It is used by the Sirpur Paper Mills as a 'filler' to improve the surface and increase the capacity of the paper.[166]

Marble

Marble occurs in an extensive area in Yellandu Taluq of Warangal District. It is in three alternate layers from 15″ to 18″ in thickness of white and gray colour. The white Predominates.[167] The villages are Munditog, Jastapally and Raghunathapalem, for which the Deccan Marble and Mining Company have been granted mining lease for 30 years commencing from 1931.[168] It was estimated that between 25,000 and 30,000 tons of marble can be quarried from the mines at Yellandu, 15 miles from Jastapally, out of which about 5,000 tons as per the estimate of the expert, compare favourably with good Italian marble.[169] In 1933, the company wound up its operations at Jastapally and shifted its machinery and workshops to the Yellandu quarries.[170] After cutting out blocks from the quarries for making flooring tiles, table tops and other decorative articles, the waste chips are used for making marble lime which is claimed to have better properties of setting strength and finish than the ordinary lime prepared from *Kunkar*.[171]

The Company produced 2,597 tons during the eleven years ending in 1942 and the quarrying operation was stopped till 1950 when the work was resumed.[172] The stoppage was due to the fact that marble products being non-essential for war, railway wagons for transport and steel for cutting marble were not supplied ; further, as building material prices had abnormally increased, construction of buildings had been very much suspended which affected the demand for marble and its products.[173] The output figures that are available for the period 1940-42 show that on an average, the marble extracted from Munditog quarries did come to only 253 tons per year and marble lime from Jastapally quarries to only 64 tons.[174] The mineral whose slabs are exported to Bombay besides commanding local markets,[175] appears not to have been exploited in commensuration with the potentialities that are available.

Limestone

Lime stones in the *Suba* occur fringing the Gondwana formations in the Adilabad, Karimnagar and Warangal Districts. About 242 million tons of limestones suitable for cement manufacture are available from Putnur (Peddapalli Taluq, 89 million tons) and Nerella (Jagtial Taluq, 153 million tons) forests of Karimnagar District. These limestones are high in calcium carbonate and low in magnesium carbonate. In Ramagundam area of the District, there are dolomitic limestones containing about 40 per cent magnesium carbonate. These can be used for the production of magnesia used in the preparation of refractory linings in metallurgical furnaces.[176]

In Adilabad District also, there are fairly extensive deposits of Cement grade limestone in the Ryali Reserve Forest area in Luxettipet Taluq and to the north of Asifabad and Adilabad. The former has a reserve of 600 million tons of cement grade lime stone which are exploited by the cement factory set up at Mancherial later in 1958. 50 million tons of flux grade limestone are indicated to have been there in the Asifabad area by the Geological Survey of India and this is being exploited by the Sirpur Paper Mill. Local people in the District used the limestones for lime.[177] The potentialities of deposits of limestone and dolomite occurring over considerable areas in Warangal District, are still to be worked out.[178] The limestones of Sirpur Taluq near Kolihal and of the hills north of Luxettipet in Adilabad District occur extensively, but are not worked on any commercial scale for want of transport facilities.[179] Figures of output extracted out of the vast reserves are not available.

Building Stone

The granites and dyke rocks of the Archaeans and the sandstones of the sullavais provide excellent building stone. The reserves of these are enormous.[180] The iron-free Barakar and Kamthi sandstones are used for building purposes in Rajura, Chinnur and other Taluqs in Adilabad District.[181]

Diamonds

This precious stone is found along the banks of the river

Krishna, the southern boundary of the State. The famous parital group of diamond mines lie on the north bank of the Krishna in Madhira Taluq of Warangal District.[182] But, it has not proved profitable to work the small diamond layers found round about parital as the diamonds imbedded there under black cotton soil have proved to small to be of much value.[183]

Water Power Resources

The main rivers Godavari and Krishna and their many tributaries including Manjira and Kadam[184] have rapids and also falls which could be utilised for generating hydro-power.[185] At the end of the period under review, the following are the important Hydro-electric schemes under investigation pertaining to the *Suba* area.[186]

Sl. No.	River	Plant capacity in K.W.
1	Manair	1,200
2	Kadam	1,75,000
3	Penganga	40,000
4	Pranhita	50,000
	Total	2,66,200

The cost of these installations along with seven more in the other areas of the State was estimated at approximately Rs. 28 crores with a total installed capacity of about 5,00,000 K.W. of hydro-power.[187] But, none of the schemes investigated in the region has been put into effect until the end of the period, even though the prosperity of the country very much depended on the supply of power to irrigation and industry. Whatever industries existed were mostly dependent on fuel. Thus, the possibilities in the way of natural water power in the area remained unexploited[188] during the period under review.

REFERENCES

1. *Administrative Report of His Highness the Nizam's Dominions for the year 1322 Fasli (6th October, 1912 to 5th October, 1913)*, (Hyderabad-Dn : 1915), p. 1.
2. Finely pulverized reddish soil with sand and traces of lime, being well suited for rainy season crops.
3. S.H. Bilgrami and C. Willmott, *op. cit.*, pp. 299-331.

3(a). *Census of India, 1911*, Vol. XIX *Hyderabad State*, Part I, (Bombay : 1913), p. 1.

4. As per the *Census of India, 1911*, these places which were inhabited by 5,000 persons and above and possessing urban characteristics were classified as towns.

4(a). *Census of India*, 1921, Vol. XXI. *Hyderabad State*, Part I, (Hyderabad: Government Central Press, 1923), p. V.

5. Eight districts were in Telangana and eight in Marathwada region.
6. W.S. *File* No. 36/86 of 1343 Fasli (1934) Record No. (n.g.).
7. *Census of India, 1941*, Vol. XXI, *H.E.H. the Nizam's Dominions (Hyderabad State)*, part I, *Report* (Hyderabad-Dn : 1945), p. 51.
8. *Census of India, 1911*, Vol. XIX, *Hyderabad State., op. cit.*, p. 9.
9. *Ibid.*, p. 6.
10. From 114 and 85 in 1911 the densities per sq. mile of Warangal and Adilabad rose to 116 and 90 in 1921; 141 and 104 in 1931; 167 and 113 in 1941 and 194 and 123 in 1951 respectively—*Census of India, Hyderabad State, Reports, 1921* (p. 33), *1931* (p. 37), *1941* (p. 3) and *1951* (p. 10).
11. *Census of India, 1951*, Vol. IX, *Hyderabad State*, part I.A. *Report* (Hyderabad-Dn : 1955). p. 22.
12. *Census of India*, 1911, *op. cit.*, p. 9.
13. H.H. the Nizam's Government : *Revenue Administration Report 1324 Fasli (1914-15 A.D.)*, (n.p), (n.d)., p. 4.
14. I.G.I., *op. cit.*, p. 161.
15. Named after a village of the same name in the District.
16. M.V. Rajgopal, *Andhra Pradesh District Gazetteers, Adilabad*, (Government Central Press, Hyderabad-Dn : 1976), p. 3.
17. *History and Legend in Hyderabad* (Department of Information and Public Relations, Osmania University Press, Hyderabad : 1953), p. 3.
18. H. Raychaudhuri, 'Geography of the Deccan' in the *Early History of the Deccan*, Parts I-VI, edited by G. Yazdani (London : 1960), p. 9.
19. Wardha, after it is being joined by Penganga on the right side and then Wainganga on the left bank, flows as a united stream, known as Pranhita Dr. W.W. Hunter, 'Imperial Gazetteer of India', Vol. III, in *Hyderabad Affairs*, Vol. I by Moulvi Syed Mahdi Ali, (Bombay : 1883), p. 349.

20 R.A.R., *op. cit.*, p. 6.
21. A dam was subsequently constructed over Godavari at Poehampad, irrigating vast areas in Karimnagar District.
22. Started in 1949 and completed in 1955.
23. Commenced in 1945 and finished in 1952.
24. A.P.D.G.. Adilabad, *op cit.*, p. 53.
25. Abdul Qayyum Khan, 'Irrigation in Hyderabad State' in *Hyderabad Government Bulletin on Economic Affairs.* Vol. I, No. 9, (December 1948), p. 1071.
26. It is the short name for Khammampet.
27. *A.R. for 1349 Fasli* (*6-10-1939 to 6-10-1940*), (Hyderabad-Dn : 1942), p. 96.
28. The reasons for this short fall are discussed in Chapter V.
29. *The E.L.O.H.* (Government Central Press, Hyderabad-Dn : 1937; p. 119.
30. W.S. *File* No. 1 of 1357 Fasli (1948) & Record No. 2064 of 1357 Fasli.
31. It was administered as a *paigah* area. In other words. a *Jagit* bestowed for the maintenance of troops for the protection of the *Nizam*—see the sub-section i. *Paigah* in Chapter IV.
32. Tour Notes of Director—General of Revenue (R.M, Crofton) in Western Adilabad, dated 6-12-1934 in W.S. *File* No. 36/86 of 1343 Fasli (1934) and Record No. (n.g.).
33. This is discussed in Chapter VII.
34. It refers to the Circar and Ceded Districts of Madras Presidency.
35. *Report of the Royal Commission on Agriculture in India* (Bombay : 1928), p. 324.
36. See the first para in the chapter.
37. Abdul Qayyum Khan, *op. cit.*, p. 1068
38. I.G.I., Hyderabad State, *op. cit.*, p. 161.
39. This centuries old tank being nearer to Warangal, the head quarters town, its waters have been diverted for town water supply in 1946—W.S. *File* No. 12 of 1347 Fasli (1938) and Record No. 1104 of 1356 Fasli (1947).
40. Cheruo in Telugu refers to tank.
41. *A.R. for 1303 Fasli* (*8th October, 1893 to 7th October, 1894*), p. 6 ; The E.L.O.H., *op. cit.*, p. 117.
42. Moulvi Syed Mahdi Ali, Vol. I, *op. cit.*, p. 918.
43. Area proposed for irrigation.
44. *Immediate Agrarian Problems, Hyderabad State*, (Hyderabad-Dn : Agriculturists' Association, 1949), p. 12
45. Rural Reconstruction Secretariat, Hyderabad-Dn, *File* No. 139 & Ser ial No. 2 of 1358 Fasli (1949).
46. I.G.I., Hyderabad State, *op. cit.*, p. 187.
47. The first or the monsoon season in which the sowings are made in the month of June.

48. It follows the *Kharif* season and the sowings are made in September or October.
49. Oil is extracted out of it, which is considered to be very good, tasty and healthy for cooking. As it is, *til* is used in preparation of sweets.
50. *Settlement Report of Warangal Taluka of Warangal District 1302 Fasli (1893)*, (Central Jail Press, Hyderabad) : (n.d,), p. 31.
51. *A.P.D.G., Karimnagar*, (Hyderabad : 1974), p. 85.
52. Royal Commission on Agriculture in India, Report, *op. cit.*, p. 72.
53. *A.P.D.G. Warangal*, (Hyderabad : 1976), p. 72.
54. E.L.O.H. *op. cit.*, p. 8.
55. It is for this reason that the total area of the State in the *Table* appears less than the usual figure of 82,698 sq. miles, whereas the percentage of forest area to total area is more than the accepted figure of 11.7 stated as above.
56. Sandal, teak, *shisham*, ebony, satin-wood, *eppa*, *nallamaddi*, *bijasal*, *batta*, gunam, *somi*, *dhaura* or *tirmani*, *Kodsha*, *sandra*, *bhandara*, *mokab*, and *chinnanyi*.
57. The I.G.I., Hyderabad State, *op. cit.*, p. 36.
58. *Statistical Abstract of H.E.H. the Nizam's Dominions from 1321 Fasli to 1330 Fasli (1912-1921)*, (Gevernment Central Press, Hyderabad-Dn : 1925), pp. 96-97.

58(*a*) S. Desava Iyengar, *Economic Investigations in the Hyderabad State*, 1929-30, *Vol. III*, *Warangal District*, (Government Central Press, Hyderabad-Dn : 1932), p. 7.

58(b) Extract from a broadcast talk by Shri Daulat Rai, Chief Conservator of Forests from A.I.R. Hyderabad station, on July 3, 1950 in S. Kesava Iyengar, *Rural Economic Enquiries* in Hyderabad State, 1949-51, (Goverment Press, Hyderabad -Dn : 1951), p. 137.

59. The calculation of these percentages differed from one source to another. For example, regarding Adilabad, whereas the *Revenue Administration Report for 1914-15* gives it as 38.58, W.S. *File* No. 36/86 of 1343 Fasli (1934) states the same as much as 46 per cent. This might be probably due to the differing criterion adopted in computing the forest area.

59(*a*) I.G.I., Hyderbad State, *op. cit.*, p. 38.

60. B.K. Narayan, *Agricultural Development in Hyderabad State, 1900-1956*, (Secunderabad : 1960), p. 8.
61. The I.G.I., Hyderabad State, *op. cit.*, pp. 166 & 187.
62. Forest areas demarcated for Departmental exploitation.
63. The E.L.O.H., *op. cit.*, p. 9.

63(*a*) A.P.D.G. Adilabad, *.op cit.*, p. 67.

63(*b*) *A.P.D.G. Khammam*, (Government Central Press, Hyderabad-Dn : 1977), pp. 15-16.

64. Annual figures of just Revenue and Expenditure, forest division-wise are available from *Statistical Year Books* and *Statistical Abstract for the period 1322 Fasli to 1350 Fasli* (*1913-1941 A.D.*), but they only indicate fluctuations in net income and expenditure.
65. *The Deccan Chronicle*, 4-3-1949.
66. Gaddi means grass in Telugu language.
67. A.P.D.G. *op. cit.*, Khammam (p. 13), Karimangar (pp. 18-19) and Warangal (p.12).
68. The I.G.I., Hyderabad State, *op. cit.*, p. 37.
69. It also used to be known as *Bancherai* (Public grazing land) Cess.
70. M.M. Ali Baig, 'Cattle improvement in Hyderabad' in *The Hyderabad Forest Magazine* (Quarterly) No. II, (July 1942), No. 1, p. 5.
71. Immediate Agrarian Problems, *op. cit.*, p. 56.
72. The process by which survey, measurement and fixation of Category and assessment of land is made by the Settlement Departmemt.
73. W.S. *File* No. 103 of 1338 Fasli (1929 A.D.) Record No. 3100 of 1339 Fasli (1930 A.D.).
74. R.A.R. *op. cit.*, p. 189.
75. It was spread within a radius of 1,012 miles to Sirpur Paper Factory and spread over an area of 36,000 acres, with an average of 4.5 tons per acre-*Golkonda Patrika* (Bi-weekly), 23-2-1939.
76. L.S. Habib Ahmed : *An Economic Survey of the Sirpur Paper Mills Limited*, unpublished M.A. (Economics) dissertation, (Osmania University, 1960), p. 19.
77. Kind of leaves or flowers that caused intoxication when used in the preparation of liquor.
78. The E.L.O.H., *op. cit.*, p. 11.
79. R.A.R. *op. cit.*, p. 213.
80. Syed Khaja Abdul Gafoor, *Tribes and Tribal Welfare in Hyderabad*, (Government Press, Hyderabad-Dn : 1953), p. 16.
81. Christoph-von-Furer-Haimendorf, *Tribal Hyderabad*, (Hyderabad : 1945) p. 105.
82. *A.R. for 1328 Fasli 6 10-1918 to 6-10-1919*), (Hyderabad-Dn : 1920), p. 6.
83. *Statistical Abstract-1912-21 A.D. 1922-31.A.D.* and *Statistical Year Books, 1935-1945 A.D.*
84. 20 times increase in Asifabad Division.
85. 6 times increase in expenditure in Nirmal Division.
86. R.V. Rao, *A Review of Hyderabad Finance* (Hyderabad : 1951), p. 134.
87. Rural Reconstruction Department, Serial No. 27, *File* no. 261/50 Misc. of 1950 A.D.
88. A P.D.G., *op. cit.*, Warangal, p. 72, Khammam, p. 54, Karimnagar, p. 84 and Adilabad, p. 55.

89. A.P.D.G. Warangal, *Ibid.*, p. 87.
89(*a*). Refer to the section 'M. Crop conditions' in Chapter V.
90. Abdul Qayyum Khan, *op. cit.*, p. 1067.
91. In the Suba Districts, it was 81 to 85 per cent.
92. Department of Agriculture, H.E.H. the Nizam's Government, *File* No. 42, Serial No. 97 of 1357 Fasli (1948).
93. W.S. *File* No. 58 of 1350 Fasli (1941) and Record No. 2506 of 1351 Fasli (1942).
94. R.E.E. *op. cit.*, p. 18.
95. Census of India, 1921, Vol. XXI., Hyderabad State, Part I. *op. cit.*, pp. 5-6. Also see the first para in the Section 'M, Crops conditions' and Table XXXIII in Chapter V.
96. January to May,
97. It is the hot-season rice crop sown from December to February, the other and the earlier one, also for rice, known as *Abi,* is sown in July to August.
98. W.S. *File* No. 16 of 1355 Fasli (1946) and Record No. 69 of 1356 Fasli (1947).
99. I.G.I. Hyderabad State, *op. cit.*, p. 27.
100. A.P.D.G. Warangal. *op. cit.*, p. 21.
101(*a*). *Ibid.*, p. 22.
101. Department of Agriculture, H.E.H. the Nizam's Government, *File* No. 35, Serial No. 97 of 1357 Fasli (1948).
102. A.P.D.G., *op. cit.*, Warangal, p. 22, Khammam, p. 19 and Karimnagar, pp. 29-30.
103. Edward Thornton, Imperial Gazetteer of India, Vol. III, in Moulvie Syed Mehdi Ali, *Hyderabad Affairs*, Vol. I, (Bombay: 1883), p. 349.
104. A.P.D.G., Adilabad, *op. cit.*, p. 19.
105. It is the fermented juice extracted from toddy and *Ita* trees.
106. A.P.D.G., Warangal, *op. cit.*, p. 14.
107. Government of Hyderabad, Revenue Department, *Selected Laws and Rules of the Revenue Department*. (Hyderabad-Dn : 1950), p. 15.
108. The contributions of Karimnagar and Adilabad Districts were comparatively, less they being Rs. 17,31,650 and Rs. 10,26,758 respectively, *Statistical Year Book*, *1942-45*, p. 676.
109. Decennial Report on the Administration of the H.E.H. Nizam's Dominions, *op. cit.*, p. 210.
110. R.V. Rao, *op. cit.*, p. 143.
111. I.G.I. Hyderabad State, *op. cit.*, p. 8.
112. *Ibid.*
113. First *Taluqdar*, Warangal, *File* No. *Munshikhana* 191 of 1320 Fasli (1911) and R. No. 2874 of 1311 Fasli (1912).
114. W.S. *File* No. 76 of 1343 Fasli (1934) and R. No. 2474 of 1344 Fasli (1935).

115. *The Deccan Chronicle*, 14-7-1949.
116. W.S. *File* No. 1 of 1355 Fasli (1946) and R.No. 1286 of 1355 Fasli-only Rs. 25 for the State and Rs. 7 for Warangal *Suba* were allotted for the year.
117. Smaller tanks. Refer to the sub-section '*Kuntas*' in the Chapter V.
118. W.S. *File* No. 71 of 1319 Fasli (1910) and R. No. 3757 of 1321 Fasli (1912).
119. Rural Reconstruction Department, S. No. 27, *File* No. 261/50, Misc of 1950.
120. A.P.D.G., Warangal, *op. cit.*, pp. 20-21.
121. Agriculture Department, S.No. 17, *File* No. 51 of 1354 Fasli (1945).
122. Mr. Syed Kazim Ali, Director of Mines, Hyderabad Government, States that the term 'mineral' applies to not only products or metals below the earth's surface, but also those on earth's surface like clay, sand and build ing stones which have a market value-*The Deccan Chronicle*. 27-5-1950.
123. Named after Gonds inhabiting the tracts, *Ibid.*
124. H.E.H. the Nizam's Government, *Industrial Statistics, 1935-36 to 1944-45* (Government Central Press, Hyderabad-Dn : 1948), p. 308.
125. Khurshid Mirza, *A Brief outline of the Geological History of Hyderabad with a reference to its Mineral Resources*, (Hyderabad- Dn : 1937), p. 31.
126. Named after W. King of the Geological Survey of India who discovered it in 1871.
127. Syed Kazim Ali, 'Mineral Resources of Hyderabad' in *The Deccan Chronicle*.
128. *Ibid.*
129. B.K. Narayan, *A Survey of Industries in Telangana*, (Secunderabad : 1962), p. 21.
130. I.S., *op. cit.*, p. 310.
131. *Hyderabad Information*, Vol. IV., No. 10, July 1944, p. 17.
132. *The Deccan Chronicle*, 26-3-1949.
133. H.E.H. The Nizam's Government : *Statistical Year Book, 1941-42 to 1944-45*, p. 1125.
134. *Ibid.*
135. Syed Kazim, *op. cit.*
136. I.S. *op. cit.*, p. 313.
137. Realising the importance of thermal power and the immensity of coal resources, the construction of a Thermal power plant at Ramagundam in Karimnagar District, was taken up towards the close of the period.
138. Nawab Ahsan Yar Jung Bahadur, *Conservation of Coal and Manufacture of Gasoline* (Hyderabad-Dn : 1904), P. 1.
139. Khurshid Mirza, *op. cit.*, p. 26.

140. Established in 1922.
141. I.S., *op. cit.*, p. 320.
142. *Ibid.*, p. 323.
143. *Ibid.*, pp. 323-324.
144. *Ibid.*, p. 322.
145. Hence called 'Damascus Swords'.
146. A place in Nirmal Taluq of Adilabad District.
147. I.S. *op. cit.*, p. 319.
148. *Ibid.*
149. Settlement Report of Warangal Taluka, *op. cit.*, p. 19.
150. In modern times, cooking coal is used instead of Charcoal as in earlier times, for smelting.
151. I.S. *op. cit.*, p. 322.
152. Khurshid Mirza, *op. cit.*, p. 40.
153. *Hyderabad Information*, Vol. IV. No. 10. (July 1944), p. 34.
154. Available figures show that it never averaged more than 50 tons per year-*A. Rs. for 1328 Fasli* (*1918-1919*), p. 27 ; *1330 Fasli* (*1920-21*), p. 28 ; *1347 Fasli* (*1937-38*), p. 108 ; *1349 Fasli* (*1939-40*), p. 109 and 1350 Fasli (1940-41), p. 115.
155. I.S. *op. cit.*, p. 324.
156. *Ibid*., pp. 324 & 327.
157. They are the proprietors of 'Charminar Cigarette Factory' of Hyderabad.
158. B.K. Narayan, A survey of Industries in Telangana, *op. cit.*, p. 40.

158(*a*) During the first 2 years prospecting, there was an output of 16,618 Ibs-*Statistical Year Book*, *1941-42 to 1944-45*, p. 1126.

159. *Hyderabad Information*, Vol. IV. No. 9, (June, 1944), p. 7.
160. A.P.D.G., Khammam, *op. cit.*, p. 10.
161. *Hyderabad Information*, Vol. IV. No. 9, p. 7.
162. *Hyderabad Information*, Vol. IV. No. 10, p. 34.
163. *Ibid.*
164. A *Jagir* Area.
165. Khurshid Mirza, *op. cit.*, p. 49.
166. *Hyderabad Information*, Vol. IV No. 10, p. 34.
167. I.S. *op. cit.*, p. 329.
168. *A.R. for 1345 Fasli* (*7-10-1935 to 5-10-1936*), (Hyderabad-Dn : 1838), p. 93.
169. E.L.O.H. *op. cit.*, p. 69.
170. *Ibid.*
171. Pieces of gravel stone, Khurshid Mirza, *op. cit.*, p. 57.
172. B.K. Narayan, A survey of Industries in Telangana, *op. cit.*, p. 40.
173. *A.R. for 1350 Fasli* (1941), p. 103.

174. *A.R. for 1349 Fasli (6-10-39 to 6-10-1940)*, p. 109 ; *1350 Fasli (6-10-1940 to 6-10-1941)*, p. 116 and 1351 Fasli (6-10-1941 to 5-10-1942), p. 102.
175. Statistical Year Book, *op. cit.*, p. 1126.
176. A.P.D.G. Karimnagar, *op. cit.*, p. 8.
177. A.P.D.G. Adilabad, *op. cit.*, pp. 10-11.
178. A.P.D G. Warangal, *op. cit.*, p. 9.
179. Khurshid Mirza, *op. cit.*, pp. 56-57.
180. A.P.D.G. Warangal, *op. cit.*, p. 9.
181. Khurshid Mirza, *op. cit* , p. 58.
182. I.S., *op. cit.*, p. 316.
183. Information Bureau, *Some Aspects of Hyderabad*, (Hyderabad -Dn : 1941), p. 8.
184. Has a vertical drop of about 120 ft. in Yelgadap Taluq, Adilabad District and forms an ideal site for hydro-electric scheme to supply power to the District, Khurshid Mirza, *op. cit.*, p. 55.
185. Abdul Qayyum Khan, *op. cit.*, p. 1075.
186. R.V. Rao, *op. cit.*, p. 316.
187. *Ibid.*
188. The E.L.O.H., *op. cit.*, p. 18.

CHAPTER THREE

ADMINISTRATIVE AND POLITICAL CONDITIONS

Administrative System, Subedari

The State having once[1] formed a Mughal provinces or *Suba*, it adopted the Mughal system of civil divisions.[2] It was divided for convenience of administration, during the period under review into four Divisions, out of which Warangal formed the eastern one. *Subedar* or Commissioner who was appointed by the Revenue Department with the sanction of the *Nizam* to head a Division, acted as the chief controlling authority in all matters connected with the land revenue, besides exercising civil and criminal authority and powers of supervision over all the districts in his Divisions.[3] He was, however, subject to the control of the Director-General of Revenue-cum-Revenue Secretary who, in turn, functioned under the direct orders of the Minister.[4] Separation of judicial powers from the Revenue officers, though introduced by Sir Ali Imam, the prime Minister in the later part of the 1920s, this was resented by higher Revenue officers and consequently withdrawn.[5] But, however, in dealing matters of a technical nature pertaining to land and land revenue, the Revenue courts could better be regarded as Administrative courts, rather better equipped to deliver the goods than ordinary judges.[6] Besides hearing appeals from lower courts and calling for reports on different matters of administration from District heads, the *Subedar* also undertook frequent tours of inspection in the *Suba* area to keep himself in touch with local conditions, and instruct the local officials as and when necessary and pass on the information that was necessary and called for, to the higher ups in the Government. He, in fact, served as the connecting link between the Government and the District adminstration.

Districts

The *Suba* consisted of three Districts, each under a First *Taluqdar* who was subordinate to the *Subedar* and acted as the executive chief in revenue, civil and criminal matters. The responsibility for maintaining peace and order in the District was put more on his shoulders than that of District police officials and the District police *Mohatmim* or Superintendent had to obey his orders.[7] First *Taluqdar* also supervised the work of Second or Third *Taluqdars* appointed over a division into which a District was divided and *Tahsildars* appointed over a Taluq into which the division was divided in turn. Two or three divisions constituted a District and similarly, a division consisted of two or three Taluqs.

It is seen from Table VI that the divisions containing both the maximum as well as the minimum number of Taluqs and villages were located in Adilabad District. On an average, each division comprised 2.5 Taluqs and each Taluq 206 villages, whereas in the State as a whole it was only 160.[8] Utnoor was given the unique distinction of being formed into a single Taluq division, for the purpose of bringing out its development, it being the most backward area in the District, by stationing a special officer, Development, at Utnoor who also functioned in the capacity of a division officer.[8a] Not less than three divisions were there in each District of the *Suba*. Number of villages recorded for administrative units differed[9] from one report to another, either due to deserting of villages or due to the merger of hamlets or smaller villages into neighbouring bigger villages for purposes of computation. Tahsildar who was kept under the immediate supervision of division officer, was assisted in Taluq administration by a

Deputy or *Naib* Tahsildar. This arrangement was mainly done in order to keep one of the two at the head quarters while the other was on tour, they being mainly touring officers.[10] Each Taluq was divided into three or four circles called "*Halkas*" over each of which was placed a Revenue Inspector called "*Girdawar*.[11] He took a prominent part in the collection of land revenue, measurement and demarcation of land and collection of foodgrain levy[12] from cultivators. A *Halka* consisted of a number of villages.

Villages

The absolute unit for administrative purposes was the "Village" which had definite boundaries fixed by Settlement and might contain one or more hamlets.[13] Each village had its regular complement of officers who were usually *Watandars* or hereditary village officers.[14] They mainly consisted of the *Mali Patel* for revenue collection and *Police Patel* for maintaining law and order ; the *Patwari* for keeping and maintaining accounts of land holdings and land revenue ; the *Talari* who was the village peon for collection purposes ; a *Setsindhi* for every 50 houses in the village as a watchman ; *Neri* or *Neredu* who looked after irrigational works and water supply to fields ; and a *Dheir*, a man of low caste employed as a watchman, messenger and *Begari*[15] in the village establishment.[16] These village officers were paid by the Government as well as the village community. The cash remuneration, allowed to the *patels* and *patwaris* was calculated according to a progressively decreasing scale fixed by Government, i.e., the larger the collection, the smaller the rate at which remuneration was calculated.[17] Besides this fixed scale, they were also paid at the rate of 2 pies each out of one *anna*[18] from the village service fund.[19] Their salaries were increased by 50 per cent in the closing forties.[20] Each *Talari* and *Setsindhi* got Rs. 24 and a Neri Rs. 36 per annum from the Government.[21] The *Talari* also shared 3 pies per *anna* of the village service fund. The *Dheir* got 4 pies out of the one *anna* cess of the service fund.[22] In addition to this cash remuneration, some of the village staff such as the *Neri*, the *Setsindhi*, received, along with artisans such as the Potter, blacksmith, the goldsmith, the

TABLE VI

Administrative Units of the Suba For 1353 Fasli (1944)

Sl. No.	Name of the District	Name of the Division	Details of Taluqs (No. of villages in brackets)	Number of Taluqs	Number of Villages
1	2	3	4	5	6
1.	Warangal	Warangal	Warangal (206) ; Pakhal (207) ; Mulug (195)	3	608
		Khammam	Khammam (156) ; Madhira (211)	2	367
		Yellandu	Yellandu (65) ; Mahbubabad (307) ; Palvancha (180)	3	452
			Total Warangal :	8	1427
2.	Karimnagar	Karimnagar	Karimnagar (160) ; Sultanabad (176)	2	336
		Jagtiyal	Jagtiyal (241) ; Sircilla (171)	2	412
		Huzurabad	Huzurabad (132) ; Parkal (116); Manthani (238)	3	486
			Total Karimnagar :	7	1234

3.	Adilabad	Adilabad	Adilabad (214) ; Kīnwat (175) ; Boath (239)	3	628
		Asifabad	Asifabad (286) ; Sirpur (448) ; Rajura (323) ; Chinnur (211)	4	1268
		Nirmal	Nirmal (192) ; Luxettipet (161)	2	353
		Utnoor	Utnoor (259)	1	259
			Total Adilabad	10	2508
			Grand total	25	5169

Source : W.S. *File* No. 38 of 1354 Fasli (1945) and R.No. 706 of 1354 Fasli.

carpenter, the barber, the washerman, etc., *Balota Inams*[23] or lands with only $\frac{1}{4}$th of the original assessment.[23a] These were given in consideration of the service they rendered to the village community and Government officials. These *Balotadars* had also received fixed quantity of grain per plough from the cultivators at the time of harvest.

The *Patels* and *Patwaris*, though their salaries are nominal and rather meagre, had, due to their landed property and local background, commanded considerable influence in rural administration.[24] Every villager, right from a middle farmer down to an artisan was made to feel their impact either in the payment of land revenue, recording of land rights, claiming of *talaf-mal*[25] and *taccavi*,[26] or in the collection of food grain levy. Besides these officials, there were *Deshmukhs*, *Deshpandyas*, *Sirdeshmukhs* and *Sirdeshpandayas*,[27] all hereditary landlords who before 1860 functioned as tax-farmers[28] but afterwards were allowed to retain their huge landed estates, besides being given an annual pension known as *Rusum*. They had the opportunity of seizing these lands by way of compensation for being deprived of their right of tax-collection.[29] Further, they indulged in the most lucrative trades of money and grain-lending and also liquor and toddy contracts which not only made them exceedingly rich but more important than that, completely kept the different sections of rural population under their strong and unrelenting thumb, Added to this, very often the *Watans* of *Patelgi*, *Patwarigiri* and *Deshmukhi* or *Deshpandyagiri* were all concentrated in one person and in some other cases, *Watan* rights of several villages were confined to the members of a single family.[30] These factors naturally encouraged them to perpetrate different types of excesses including *Vetti*[31] and the punishments inflicted on them by the *Suba* authorities were not only rare but seldom effective and deterrent.[32] Even though *Asaldars*[33] appointed *Gumasthas*[34] on their behalf to discharge their duties in different villages, this made no difference to the enjoyment and exercise of vast and varied powers and authority by these big *Watandars*,[35] for the reason that the *Gumasthas* being dependant on the will and pleasure of *Asaldars* had, in short, become their tools and mouthpieces. Not infrequently they even exceeded their masters in subjecting the ignorant and illiterate masses to various atrocities.[36]

Central System

Adminstrative machinery at the State level consisted, besides the *Nizam*, an Executive Council and a Legislative Council. The former, headed by His Excellency, the President consisted of seven members, each heading a ministerial department. It rendered advice to the head of the State on all important and policy matters of the State but it was not, however, binding on him to go by it. It was fully a nominated body continuing in office at the will and pleasure of the Ruler and was not responsible to the Legislative Council either for the advice that it rendered or the administrative measures that were undertaken.[37] Further, it is significant to note that the three important and key branches of Finance, Revenue and Police were kept under the control of English Civil servants[38] which, naturally pointed to strong British influence over the Dominions' administration.[39] The Legislative Council established in 1894 for the purpose of enacting laws for the State was composed of a President, a Vice-president and 23 members out of whom three were ex-officio.[40] The remaining twenty members were appointed by the Prime Minister or the President for a period of two years at a time and out of them nine were Government officials and eleven non-officials. Again, only one member was taken from the general public out of the non-official seats,[41] which clearly and unmistakably reflected the preponderant official character of the Legislature. Its powers remained purely deliberative and nominal. The Council had no power to criticise or discuss the budget or put any questions as to the maladministration of government officials.[42] His Highness, further, had the right to order the repeal or amendment of any enactment.[43] Though promise had been made by the *Nizam* as early as 1920 and schemes submitted in the year 1939 and the following years for the enlargement of membership as well as the introduction of elective element in the Legislative Council, they had not come into effect, mainly due to the fact that the two leading political parties in the State were at loggerheads with each other over this issue.[44] In fact, Hyderabad and Gwalior were the only two Indian States out of 12 States where no Elected Members were there in the Legislature, whereas from Revenue and population point of view, Hyderabad stood first and Gwalior sixth among them.[45]

Local Government

Lack of elective element and domination of officials characterised the organisation and composition of local bodies, too. They consisted of District Boards, Taluq Boards and Panchayats in the rural areas, Town and Municipal Committees in the urban areas. Actually the beginning of Local Government in the Hyderabad State outside the city municipality may be seen in the levy in 1297 *Fasli* (1888 A.D.) of a local cess in all *Khalsa*[46] districts at the rate of one *anna* on every rupees of land revenue.[47] This was to be spent on conservancy, sanitation and works of public utility in the ratio of 3 pies for Education, 2 pies for Medical, 2 pies for Roads, and 5 pies for works of public utility.[48] Besides this, in towns other taxes like house tax, lighting tax, toll-tax. vehicle tax and market fees were also levied by local bodies.[49] The official and non-official members in these bodies were appointed in equal number, presided over by the respective official heads[50] that were there at the headquarters. Over-all control and supervision was exercised by the Local Fund Department. All the non-official members were nominated by the ex-officio chairman and even the members of the village *Panchayats* which were formed only in a meagre fraction of the total number of villages,[51] were also selected in an open meeting of the adult householders of the village and one of the *panchas* was again nominated as *Surpanch** by the *Taluqdar* of the district.[52] They were taken from amongst the *zamindars*, lawyers, traders, and merchants and were appointed every three years.[53] The existence of only one budget for the whole district, towns, and villages alike, resulted in the negligence of developmental work in the villages and complete concentration in headquarter towns.[54] This was rectified after 1928-29 by the separation of district and town funds but even after the performance of these local bodies remained far behind the expectations. This was examined in Chapter VIII.

Administrative Changes

From 1911 to 1914 only transfer of a few outlying villages from one Taluq to another as dictated by experience and change of the names of a few Taluqs as a matter of sentiment had taken place. Thus, Rajura was called Ahmedapur, Jammikunta was transformed into Huzurabad and Jangaon into Asifabad.[55] In the year 1914, two important changes were made in the Adilabad District; first one was the transfer of headquarters of the District from Adilabad to Asifabad. But, this was done on the incorrect presumption that it would be on the projected railway route to Balharshah and at a time when Adilabad, with the Godavari at Soan unbridged was very difficult for access.[56] The bridge was later built, but the railways line did not touch Asifabad. Further, it had other disadvantages of being on lower altitude and malaria-infested, compared to Adilabad. On the other hand, the latter was located in the open with ample room for planned expansion, with a dry and healthy climate and above all gained importance as a centre of Marathwada culture in the northern half of the District.[57] Consequently, the District headquarters was again shifted in December 1940 from Asifabad to Adilabad.[58] The second measure was that two new Taluqs of Boath and Utnoor were created by detaching sufficient number of villages from the Taluqs of Adilabad, Kinwat, Asifabad, Nirmal and Luxettipet. This was done as the existing Taluqs were found to be too large in view of the lack of roads and communication with ryots.[59]

Significant change in the set-up of the administrative Divisions was effected in the year 1922 when Sir Ali Imam, the Prime Minister, after undertaking a tour of India in the middle of the year, got the four *Subas* into which the State had been divided, abolished and *Taluqdars* were kept in charge of district administration directly under the Revenue Secretariat.[60] It was felt that there would be no need of an intermediary between *Taluqdar* and the Government and hoped that people would not experience difficulties under the new system.[61] But, even under the new arrangement, the role of supervisory head had not been completely dispensed with. Two Inspecting Officers, one for each natural division were appointed. As they had no executive powers, the arrangement could not work and was done away with.[62] Then, the two natural divisions, Marathwada and Telangana, under two Directors-General of Revenue, came to be regarded as convenient units in 1925. Each unit was termed as a 'Range' and the Telangana Range consisted of as many as 7 Districts, 48 Taluqs and 9,639 villages.[63] These, however, were subsequently found to be unwieldy and not conducive to efficient administration. In this system, many difficulties were experienced in the collection of land revenue arrears. Consequently, the four *Subas* were reconstituted in 1929.[64] These administrative experiments had thus proved firmly that the *Subedari* system of administrative divisions was the best and most suited under the local conditions obtaining. In the reconstituted arrangement, Nizamabad District which georaphically lay to the west of Karimnagar District and formerly in Medak *Suba*,[65] was now joined in Warangal *Suba* for the purpose of facilitating the execution of irrigation works under Nizamsagar Project and accordingly, when these arrangements were over around 1936-37, the said District was rejoined in its original Division.[66] This temporary development had no bearing on the study of the economic history of the Eastern Division, for the District of Nizamabad did not very much share the physical, social and economic conditions that obtained in the *Suba* Districts.[67]

Minor changes to suit administrative convenience are to be noted during the decade that followed. On representation from *Taluqdar* of Karimnagar and *Subedar* of Warangal, the name of Mahadeopur Taluq whose headquarters was Manthani had, now in 1941, been changed as Manthani Taluq to avoid postal delay and confusion.[68] 15 villages including the major ones of Bhimghanpur, Eturnagaram, Buddharam and Kamlapur, were taken out from Manthani Taluq and attached to Parkal Taluq of the same District of Karimangar. This was done on the basis of Revenue Member, W.I. Grigson's finding that the area covered by those villages was far off from Manthani and communication became difficult.[69] But, changes highly significant and momentous from administrative as well as economic points of view, took place in 1949. Consequent on the abolition of princely rule in September, 1948,[70] the administration of *Sharf-e-Khas*[71] villages which had previously been under the personal management of the ruler of the State and constituted virtually a State within a State,[72] had now been taken over by the State on 5th February, 1949. This definitely helped in striving for uniformity of the administration and also the amelioration of the condition of the people in the former crown lands. The take over of these villages made the task of *Jagir*[73] assumption by Government easier. *The Abolition of Jagirs Regulation* came into force on the 15th August, 1949 and they were placed under a *Jagir* Administrator[74] for the settlement of immediate problems like compensation to *Jagirdars*, survey of Jagir lands, etc. The removal of these *Jagirs* which got spread all over the region in varying proportions,[75] not only helped in bringing the cultivators in these areas into direct contact with the Government by removing the intermediaries, but also immensely contributed for administrative uniformity and efficiency.

Another significant change in the field of administration that took place in the year and more so for present study was the abolition of *Subedaries* once for all and their replacement by a Board of Revenue. With the abolition of the post of Director-General of Revenue in 1947, the executive functions of the Director-General disappeared and the Land Revenue Department remained the only Department in the State without a single head. There was no Central Executive authority to which the Government could look for the execution of the measures and Policies initiated by them.[76] Further, it was found that due to change in the form of Government, development of communications and formation of numerous Departments at the headquarters, the Commissioners were not able to exercise effective control over the activities of Government in their Divisions.[77] Hence, a Board of Revenue was formed in their place to function from 1st August, 1949 as the highest executive and appellate authority for all revenue-earning and allied Departments of the State. It consisted of four Members out of whom one was designated as Senior Member and presided over its meetings. The distribution of work was functional and not territorial.[78] This Board was established on the analogy of the Madras system.[79]

With the inauguaration of rule by Military Governor, Civil Administrators mostly drawn from outside the State and holding the same status as that of First *Taluqdars* were appointed one for each district to deal with the immediate problems that were confronted in the transitional period. Consequent on *Sarf-e-Khas* and *Jagir* abolition and exchange of village[80] with neighbouring States, a reorganisation was brought about in the composition of administrative units. The Taluqs of Khanapur, Metpalli, both formerly *Jagir* areas and Boorgampad, newly created from Palvancha Taluq, were freshly added to the Districts of Adilabad, Karimnagar and Warangal respectively.[81] Regarding Revenue Sub-Divisions, the number remained the same in respect of Karimnagar, whereas Warangal gained one in that of Kothagudem,[82] Adilabad lost one. Compared to the number of villages that obtained in 1944,[83] there was an increase of 27 in respect of Warangal District, whereas decrease of 6 and as many as 460 villages was there in respect of Karimnagar and Adilabad Districts respectively.[84] This was largely due to the reconstitution and re-arrangement of the *Tahsils* that had taken place consequent on the attendant changes. When the Military Government was carried on approximately for a period of two years, it was replaced by a popularly elected ministry headed by Shri M.K. Vellodi, an I.C.S. man in June, 1950.[85] This Ministry was there in office until March 1952 when Indian General Election was held. It was creditably associated with the enactment of *the Tenancy and Agricultural Lands Act* on 10th June, 1950 which, for the first time, brought into being protected tenants, as well as minimum and maximum holdings. In accordance with the practice prevailing in other Indian Provinces, the designation of the revenue officials in the districts had been suitably modified[86] with effect from 1st November, 1950.

Administrative Conditions

The procedure most commonly adopted by the people of the *Suba* for the redressal of their grievances and difficulties such as grant of remission of land revenue, land *pattas*, agricultural loans, excesses inflicted by village officials and tenure-holders,[87] etc., was by filling preliminary cases and appeals. Preliminary case was filed with the immediate Revenue Officer having powers to decide in a particular matter, who normally happened to be Tahsildar and if the applicant was dissatisfied with the decision given, he was given the facility of going on appeal to the next higher court. It is really a point to be appreciated that a citizen if need be and resources permitted, could on appeal, approach even the Prime Minister. But this method resulted in considerable delay, sometimes even extending for more than a decade[88] in having a final say in an appeal case. Not infrequently the persons who filed the case at the lower court or the officer who gave the judgement therein had not the fortune of surviving until the final decision in the matter was given.[89] This inordinate delay was mainly due to conflicting and contradictory decisions given by the Presiding Revenue Officers, one above the other.[90] The variance was again due to the exceeding of powers in giving judgements even by First *Taluqdars*[91] and also the fact that harsh or lenient attitude was adopted by the deciding officers being influenced by extraneous considerations other than legal.[92] Instance was recorded where even *Subedar* was strongly reprimanded for giving decision in a case ignoring an earlier order of the Government.[93] Number of preliminary and appeal cases decided by the district heads and also the *Subedar* generally formed not more than 50 percent of the total number that remained to be disposed off in a year.[94] It was also complained by applicants that they had been subjected to much expense and inconvenience due to shifting of dates of hearing in cases without prior intimation by Presiding Officers.[95]

The element of corruption that loomed large in different branches of the Government including the Police[96] affected administrative efficiency and resulted in much inconvenience and suffering to the people. As early as 1923 the, *Firman*[97] of the *Nizam* had stated that :

"Corruption and dishonesty are spreading in different branches of the Government. Its bad effects have reached upto districts. I want this evil to be removed in every office (whether it is judicial or administrative departments). Why because due to this evil, bad complaints are being made about Government job."[98]

Records show that matters had not improved since then. Taking of *mamul*[99] had become common in different transactions that the people made with Revenue, Forest, Police and Customs Departments. Non-payment of this not only resulted in deliberate delay and deadlock in the transactions,[100] but, not less often, brought physical beating to the economically ill-affording rural poor.[101] Collection of illegal and extra cesses other than land revenue,[102] swallowing of *taccavi*,[103] *talafmal* and levy grain amounts[104] by *Patels*, *Patwaris* and *Girdavars* entailed considerable hardship to peasants. The ignorance of the illiterate farmers in understanding the complex revenue regulations that applied to them was fully exploited by village-officials and Revenue Inspectors to their advantage.[105] Opportunities for illegal gratification encouraged employees to seek transfer from *Subedari* to Hyderabad Commercial Corporation.[106] Next to land revenue and excise, customs formed the major source of income to the Government. But large-scale smuggling was done from the border areas of the *Suba* with the conniving of Customs officials.[107] It was felt that if this large-scale corruption was rooted out, the income of the State from the source would get trebled.[108] Dishonesty of the officers was also not on the wane. Village Officers, Revenue Inspectors and Clerks of Revenue Department were found resorting to malpractice and impersonation in appearing for village Officers' Test and Telugu Test.[109]

Conditions of law and order had an important bearing on the economic condition of the people. Though crime was not on the decrease,[110] yet no major disturbances affecting peace in the area had taken place until the advent of parties with strong and narrow religious affiliations,[111] towards the close of thirties. The next decade saw the birth of *Andhra Maha Sabha* and Hyderabad State Congress which further complicated the political scene.[112] Divergence in political aims came to widen the gulf, rather unfortunately from a religious and communal angle. Whereas the latter had the ideal of striving for the establishment of a responsible Government under the headship of the *Nizam*, the *Ittehad* on the other hand, became firmly determined to maintain status quo. In 1940, however, there was the rising of Gonds, an aboriginal tribe at Babijheri, 11 miles west of

Asifabad in Adilabad District. This, in which 10 were killed including their leader Bhimu and 13 were injured, was due to the long friction between the Forest and Police subordinates on the one side and the aboriginals on the other.[113] But, more than this, the strong attachment of Gonds to Babijheri which they were forced to vacate, might have moved them to rebel. Though it was crushed, it had the beneficial effect of including the Government to take up tribal welfare measures in a bigger way. The entry of Communism from the border district of Krishna of Madras Presidency into Warangal District after 1940[114] and to a smaller measure into the other two Districts, had added a new dimension to the political and economic scene. Economically, the high prices of essential commodities and also their scarcity consequent on the Second World War coupled with black market and rigours of levy inflicted untold misery on the population. Politically, the events had taken a swift and worst turn after 1956 consequent on the eventual declaration of Indian Independence and the people, especially, in the Taluq of Mahboobabad, Khammam, Madhira, Palvancha, Mulug, Sirsilla, Manthani and Jagtiyal, had been subjected to the three-pronged attack of the Police, the Communists and the *Razakars*.[115] There was utter insecurity to life and property and consequently huge exodus of population into the border districts of Madras Presidency. During this period, the Arab and Irani irregulars carrying arms with them had their heyday in different towns and villages of the area and caused complete panic and terror among the local populace.[116] Even the formation of Military Government did not give respite to the people from the excesses indulged in by the Communists and the Indian Army. Only after the struggle was given up by the Communists in October 1951 after the installation of a People's ministry, there was complete peace and tranquility in the entire area again.

Administrative condition of the area has been very much influenced by the pattern of the growth of education and the development of transport and communications. In the field of education,[117] the facilities for instruction were not provided in proportion to the number of villages. In Mahboobabad Taluq, for instance, there were 181 villages for which there existed in

1949 only 2 or 3 Middle Schools and 80 or 90 primary schools.[118] Facilities for higher education were thus completely deficient in the Taluq. The discouraging of the establishment of private schools and the teaching of Telugu which was spoken by the majority of the population but at the same time neither medium of instruction nor taught beyond primary stage, had been very much responsible for the prevalence of these meagre facilities for instruction.[119] The number of Libraries and Reading Rooms which could very much help in promoting the enlightenment of the local population, was highly insignificant. They numbered in 1939, 5 in Warangal District, 1 in Karimnagar District and none in that of Adilabad.[120] To add to this, restrictions imposed on the freedom of the Press, speech and assembly by the widely hated Gashti[121] No. 53 had very much deprived the administration of making use of the representative opinion of the people on different matters affecting it. About a dozen urdu dailies functioned under the patronage of the *Nizam*. But, on the other hand, cabinet approval became necessary not only for bringing out any Telugu newspaper, but also for its contents.[122]

Transport and Communication facilities[123] act as main props for administrative machinery. But, these were inadequate not only for several villages but even some of the Taluqs of the *Suba*. Kinwat in Adilabad District and Borgampahad in Warangal District, both Taluq headquarters remained completely land-locked, unconnected either by road or rail transport.[124] This seriously affected not only grain movement, but even carrying of mail, to and from the District headquarters.[125] Road mileage worked out in 1949-50 at one mile for every 15 sq. miles and vast areas with Gonds in Adilabad, Karimnagar and Warangal still continued as if in the days of the Ramayana[126] without any contact with modern life.[127] Only the Taluqs of Madhira, Khammam, Yellandu, Mahboobabad, Warangal, Huzurabad, Sultanabad, Luxettipet, Asifabad, Sirpur and Adilabad were traversed by rail line. The remaining 14 Taluqs were completely untouched by this modern transport. Though the State had the distinction of running its own post-offices, they were only few and far between.[128] Each Post Office covered an average area of 59 sq. miles.[129] For some villages, for miles together, there were no post offices and even two weeks' time was taken for letters to reach.[130] Even letters were not received in time in those places which had Postal facilities.[131] Telephone and tele-communication services had been extended only to Warangal District and the other two Districts had not received this facility during the period under study.[132] The administrative and the business-wings had, to that extent, lost the quick means of communication provided by these services.

Political Condition

The Commencement of the reign of VII *Nizam* witnessed the emergence of the library movement in the region. The 'Raja Raja Narendra *Bhasha Nilayam*' established at Hanamkonda in 1904 and the 'Mahabubia *Grandhalayam*' opened at Errupalam in Khammam Taluq, were the notable ones among the libraries opened at this time in this area. This intellectual movement which had for its object the noble ideal of promoting literary and cultural consciousness among the Telugu people,had gained momentum with the starting of the publication of a Telugu weekly, entitled *'Telugu Patrika'* on 27-8-1922 from Inugurthi, a village in Mahboobabad Taluq under the editorship of Dr. Baddiraju Seetaramachandra Rao, a *Deshmukh.*[133] Though this paper did not continue after five years, it worked tremendously during this period to promote the intellectural awareness among its readers. In order to bring together men and women from different places who were associated with the running of libraries and promote mutual sympathy and co-operation between them, the First Telugu Library Conference was held on 22-2-1925 at Madhira, Taluq Headquarters in Warangal District. Good number of delegates from the Capital City as well as the villages, attended this Conference Presided over by Sri Pingali Venkatrama Reddy, a wealthy *Deshmukh* and honorary justice from Warangal District.[134] The library movement under the auspices of *Andhra Jana Sangham*, an organisation formed on 12th November, 1921 to bring about literary and cultural re-awakening among Telugu people,[135] had taken up as part of its work, publication of cheaply placed but valuable books and pamphlets highlighting historical background, social and economic problems that beset the people. Some of them were "*Nizam Andhra Rashtra Prashamsa*", "*Nizam Rashtra Andhra-ways of improvement*", both of historical nature, "*Vartaka Swatantriyamu*" (Freedom of the Merchants) enjoining the merchant community to resist official pressure in demanding provisions either freely or at nominal rates and "*Vettichakiri*" which resented the extraction of forced labour by officials from village service staff, even though it was prohibited by a *Firman* in 1923.[136]

Even problems of still greater economic importance like the reduction of taxes on dry lands, introduction of the system of *Bandobast*[137] in Jagir lands, early enactment of a statute specifying the rights and responsibilities of the *Jagirdars* and *Jagir* ryots and protest against the imposition of an illegal tax on handlooms in *Jagir* lands, known as "*Mohtarfa*", were taken up with the Government by *Andhra Jana Sangham* and the people were educated about them by issuing booklets.[138] The movement, under the spirited leadership of Sri Madapati Hanumantha Rao,[139] marched forward even though district and village officials tried to obstruct it by denying permission for the opening or continuance of libraries. As a matter of fact, the then Home Secretary, Sir Akbar Hydari, was kind enough to state that such a permission was not necessary.[140] The library movement thus not only helped the growth of Telugu language and literature but contributed much to the development of political consciousness and created a sense of self-confidence among the Telugu-speaking people.[141] It also created the necessary leadership among them. Almost all the political leaders of Telangana who dominated the scene up to 1950 and even after, had something or the other to do with the library movement of the earlier days.[142]

Even though the *Nizam* very much remained as the true and faithful ally of the British[143] and espoused their policies both within and outside India, the people of the *Suba* along with those of the other areas of the State, had expressed their support for the *Khilafat* agitation of 1920 as well as for the Gandhian programme of '*Charkha* Spinning' and 'Prohibition'. *Khilafat* Day was observed in the months of March and April, 1920 at places like Karimnagar, where both Hindus and

Muslims joined together to pass resolutions urging the redressal of the injustice done to Turkey. In the meeting at Karimnagar held in *Idgah*,[144] the First *Taluqdar* Syed Mohiuddin Ali Khan and the Joint Magistrate Rai Ratanchand were present, even though police-report states that permission was not obtained for it.[145] The strong influence of the agitation on the local people including the highest officials had thus become clear.

Regarding *charkha*-spinning, reports show that Nirla Narasimaha Sahu of the Forest Department prepared several *Charkhas* in his own factory at Warangal and sent them to Vijayawada of Madras presidency for sale.[146] A person by name Gandham Lakshminarasimha Rao of Vimanur Taluq, Krishna District, had come to Karimnagar under Gandhiji's inspiration. He collected subscription for the Tilak *Swarajya* Fund and left the place. The people of the Adilabad District started leaning towards prohibition, rather influenced by the highhandedness of Pestonjee, the excise contractor. Such influences spread from Chanda and other border districts. Villagers of Poolpad in Warangal District had taken oath to give up drinking.[147]

The wide-ranging activities of the *Andhra Jana Sangh*, coupled with the desire of the people to closely follow the developments that were taking place in British India, made the Government so much apprehensive that it clamped the famous restrictive order known as *Ghasti* No. 53, on 21st November, 1929 which regulated that any person holding a public meeting should not only give ten days' prior notice to the Police Commissioner or the First *Taluqdar*, but also send in advance the agenda of the meeting so that the Government would decide whether the meeting was of a political nature or not and then give the permission.[148] But, this did not deter *Andhra Jana Sangham* to get expanded into a large body, that came to be known as *Andhra Maha Sabha* in 1930. During the sixteen year period upto 1946, as many as thirteen conferences of this *Sabha* were held, out of which three in Warangal District[149] and one in that of Karimnagar,[150] had taken place. As the *Maha, Sabha* activity in Adilabad District had started only in 1942[151] no meeting had taken place in it. This late starting might be due to the difficulty of communication as well as the Marathwada character of the northern half of the District. The demands made by the *Maha Sabha* in these sessions were all-embracing and very much served as a mirror reflecting the social, economic and political problems that affected the people. Financial assistance to libraries, removal of difficulties of *Balotadars*, formation of village panchayats and introduction of elective element in Municipalities, prohibition, toning up of the administration of *Jagirs*, reduction in land revenue rates, improvement of the condition of backward classes, formation of legislature by democratic election and appointment of the Ministry from it, etc., formed some of the main items on which the attention and consideration of the Government was requested.[152] The democratic and the political nature of the demands was clearly manifest.

Around 1940, an extremist section under younger elements in the *Sabha* had developed which came to advocate stronger measures like abolition of *vetti*, reducion of high *Kowls*,[153] non-eviction of tenants, grant of *pattas* to actual cultivators of land, abolition of *Jagirdari* system, complete responsible Government and compulsory Survey and Settlement of lands.[154] They emerged as the Communist group under the energetic leadership of Ravi Narayana Reddy and Baddam Yella Reddy[155] and had come to dominate the sessions of *Andhra Maha Sabha* from 1941. As a result, the older and moderate elements among whom were Madiraju Ramakotiswara Rao and Jamlapuram Kesava Rao who presided over the 9th and 13th sessions of the *Sabha* respectively and were formed Warangal District, got separated and themselves into the Nationalist *Andhra Maha Sabha*. Their separate conferences were held in 1945 and 1946 which lacked the earlier lustre and appeal and finally in the latter year got themselves merged into the State Congress whose membership extended over both the natural divisions of the State.[156] The Communist group, on the other hand, continued to play a crucial role in the State and *Suba* politics under the old banner.

The year 1938 was memorable in the history of Hyderabad for the smouldering embers of agitation in the minds of the people burst out in a flame. Associations like the Civil Liberties union[157] the *Arya Samaj* and the State Congress began to offer peaceful resistance to the laws of the Government considered as oppressive. The entire atmosphere was surcharged with a mood of agitation, very much inspired by the Gandhian Non-violent and Non-co-operation Movement set in motion in British India. A provisional committee to work out the formation of State Congress was formed in the middle of July, 1938 and within a month about twelve hundred primary members were enrolled in the capital city and the districts[158] and it was decided to hold a general body meeting on the 9th September, 1938 for the election of office bearers and adoption of the Constitution. But, the meeting was prohibited by an Extra-ordinary Gazette notification of the Government issued on September 8, 1938 which declared the proposed Congress to be a communal organisation and hence an unlawful association under the public safety Regulation.[159] This took the Congress leaders by surprise, who after failing in all their attempts to convince the Government regarding the removal of the force, started *Satyagraha*[160] on the 24th October, 1938. As many as thirteen batches took part in it by turns in which Pelbaraja Ranga Rao, Kallur Narasimham, and Kanaka Prasada Gupta from Warangal District, B Yella Reddy and K.V. Muralidhar Rao, D. Narasaiah, G. Rama Reddy, Raja Reddy, Ratna Reddy and Konda Reddy from Karimnagar District had taken part.[161] The *Satyagraha* was suspended on the 24th December, 1938 mainly on the advice of Mahatma Gandhi, hoping that the Government would generally respond to this gesture. But, no such thing had happened and inspite of efforts by Gandhi as well as State Congress leaders, the ban on the State Congress was not lifted untily April, 1946.

The year 1938 also witnessed the strike of Osmania University students in December, when the authorities refused to give them permission for singing *Vandemataram*[162] song in the hostel prayer halls. It was really unfortunate that feelings of suspicion lurking in the minds of the authorities induced them to conclude that this song was political and controversial. As many as 3,000 students had boycotted their respective schools and colleges in the city as well as the districts, out of whom 600 had been rusticated.[163] Nookala Ramachandra Reddy and Achyuta Reddy, P.V. Narasimha Rao, Hayagrivachari and D. Venkateswara Rao, who hailed from Warangal and Karimnagar Districts took an active part in this *Vandemataram* Movement.[164] *Satyagraha* was further resorted to in September and October, 1942, when as part of and in aid to the British Indian agitation, Quit India Movement was undertaken in Hyderabad against the British.[165] M.S. Rajalingam, Kaloji Narayana Rao and Krishna Dube[166] were among those who participated from Warangal District.[167]

Tension in the districts mounted up when in June, 1947 the Central office of the Hyderabad State Congress had issued circular to its branch organisations in the districts to hold public meetings and adopt resolutions stating that Hyderabad should join the Indian union in the new constitutional set-up that would emerge on the handing over of power by the British on 15th August.[168] Government did not agree with this stand and very much decided to maintain a separate existence. Consequently, permisssion was not given for the Congress meetings to be held[169] and further Home Department in July, 1947 declared the whole of Warangal District as a 'Disturbed Area', thereby banning all meetings and processions.[170] Inspite of such restrictions being imposed, the State Congress had called upon the people to observe 7th August, 1947 as "Join Indian Union" day. Workers in the factories were asked to stop work and students to abstain from schools and colleges. Quite in response, processions were taken out, even though there was police *lathi charge*.[171] Feelings ran high when the *Satyagrahis*, in accordance with the directive from State Congress leaders, and very much against the ban clamped by the State Government, began to hoist the Indian union flag on 15th August, the Day of Indian Independence. People in villages, students and Congress workers took part in these flag hoisting ceremonics which continued in September also,[172] in large numbers[173] and as a result, mass-arrests had taken place. Kaloji Narayan Rao, Krishna Dube. M.S. Rajalingam, Keshav Reddy and Smt. Rajeshwari from Warangal District, Kacha Raghunatha Rao, Ramapati Rao, Hanumantha Rao and

Lakshminarayana from Karimnagar District were among those who courted arrest during this period.[174] Among student-leaders, Mr. Goutama Rao from Karimnagar was sentenced to two and half years' rigorous imprisonment.[175] Besides flag-hoisting at defiance of Government orders, people at this time resorted to civil disobedience aimed at making the administrative control over them inoperative. Customs regulations were flouted,[176] excise trees were cut[177] and officers of the Government were not allowed even to enter villages and meddle with the situation.[178]

This confrontation between the Government and the people did not get lessened even after the conclusion of the Standstill-Agreement on 29th November, 1947 between Hyderabad and the Dominion Government of India, according to which Defence and External Affairs came under the control of India. The political situation in the *Suba* and also the State, from now onwards until the end of 1950 had become highly delicate and explosive. Hyderabad, at this time became a battlefield of four struggling powers : His Exalted Highness, the *Majlis-i-Ittehad-ul-Muslimeen*, the Hyderabad State Congress and the Communist party of India.[179] The Ruler of the State had very much become prisoner in the hands of the *Majlis* organisation which asserted that he and his "crown" were the embodiment of the political and cultural sovereignty of the Muslims of the Deccan.[180] Bahadur Yarjung, the president of this party which was declared by the *Nizam's* Government to be a communal organisation and whose membership was prohibited for State servants,[181] went a step further to openly announce that the king owed his existence to them.[182] The Ruler was never allowed by this organisation to use his discretion and wise-counsel in considering the proposal consistently put forward by the State Congress of joining the State in Indian union. On the other hand, he was kept under the false impression that with the support of the *Razakar* force[183] and the strength of the Hyderabad Army, he could successfully resist even the contingency of armed intervention by India. As a result, the *Stand-still Agreement* was observed more to gain time than to strive for the peaceful solution of the constitutional problem that had arisen.

The efforts of the Communists[184] to fish in troubled waters had made the situation all the more graver. The huge concentration of *Jagirs* in the Districts of Nalgonda and Warangal and the great amount of exploitation to which the rural population was subjected at the hands of the feudal elements provided the fertile ground for them to operate[185] their strategy of establishing a Red Raj in this part of the Deccan.[186] The deep political crisis that over took the State since the second half of 1946 was chosen by them as the right moment to start their depredations. Life and property of the people had become so much insecure due to raids day in and day out, either by *Razakars*, Police, or the Communists, or sometimes by all,[187] that the Indian Government took the inevitable step of armed intervention, resulting in the installation of Military Governor's rule on 18th September, 1948. But, even after police Action, 147 were killed in Warangal District only upto 9th July, 1949 by the Communists and out of these, 96 were from Mahboobabad Taluq alone.[188] Large-scale looting of property had also been reported.[189] By December, 1949, when the Military Government was replaced by a civilian Ministry, the trouble besides not being fully suppressed in Warangal District, had now spread to other Districts of Karimnagar and Adilabad.[190] Duplicate administration in each district, manned by the Hyderabad and Indian union officials hampered the Government and it was reasonably believed by the Government that the Communist raiders acquired their weapons at a low price from the State police.[191] Raids continued throughout 1950 also and for the first time in March, 1950, they were extended to town areas also when the godown at Illendu Collieries containing explosive material was looted and rail-route between Dornakal and Kothagudem was subjected to destruction.[192] Even after long experience, Government machinery had not come to full grips with the situation. Normalcy came to prevail only after the Communists had called off their struggle in October, 1951. Subsequently, General Elections were held in March, 1952 in which the Communists also took part.

REFERENCES

1. 1687-1724 A.D.
2. Decennial Report on the Administration, *op. cit.*, p. 49.
3. Selected Laws and Rules of the Revenue Department, *op. cit.*, p. 4.
4. R.A.R., *op. cit.*, p. 42.
5. W.S. *File* No. 103 of 1338 Fasli (1929) & R. No. 3100 of 1339 Fasli (1930).
6. M.A. Muttalib, *The Administration of Justice under the Nizams* (*1724-1947*), Unpublished Ph.D. Thesis, (Osmania University, Hyderabad : 1957), p. 257.
7. *Golkonda Patrika* (Bi-weekly), 15-9-1938.
8. Hyderabad Government, *Memoranda submitted to the Taxation Enquiry Commission, 1953*, (Government Central Press, Hyderabad-Dn : 1953), p. 54.
   (a) W.S. *File* No. 38 of 1354 Fasli (1945) & R. No. 706 of 1353 Fasli.
9. See Page 1.
10. W.S. *File* No. 88 of 1354 Fasli (1945) & R. No. 19 of 1356 Fasli (1947).
11. Revenue Administration Report, *op. cit.*, p. 25.
12. Introduced in 1944.
13. R.A.R. *op. cit.*, p. 25.
14. Moulvi Cheragh Ali, *Hyderabad* (*Dn*) *Under Sir Salar Jung*, Vol. I, (Bombay : 1884), p. 124.
15. One from whom forced labour, mostly unpaid, was extracted by Government officials and village landlords.
16. Moulvi Cherag Ali, *op. cit.*. p. 124.
17. R.A.R., *op. cit.*, p. 58.
18. 12 pies made one *anna* and 16 *annas* a rupee.
19. Collected @ one *anna* per rupee on land revenue for village development.
20. *Golkonda Patrika*, 13-9-1949.
21. Moulvi Cheragh Ali, *op. cit.*, p. 124.
22. *Ibid.*, p. 125.
23. Land grants given for the maintenance of the village artisans and service staff.
   (a) Settlement Report of Warangal Taluka, *op. cit.*, p. 67.
24. Syed Abid Ali Hassan, *Whither Hyderabad*, (The B.N. Press, Madras; 1935), p. 79.
25. Claiming land revenue remission for crop-damage, either due to excess or less rainfall or any other natural factors.
26. Government loans advanced to farmers either for cultivation purposes or for digging wells.
27. *Deshmukh* refers to village-headman and *Deshpandya* to District Accountant; *Sirdeshmukh* and *Sirdeshpandya* refer to headship in the respective categories.
28. The right of tax-collection was auctioned and tax-farmers enjoyed the authority and advantage of collecting from the ryots much over and

above the fixed amount that they paid to Government.

29. Barry Pavier, 'The Telangana Armed Struggle' in *the Economic & Political weekly*, special number (August 1974), Vol. IX, p. 1413.
30. The family of Mr. Ramchandra Rao, *Deshpandey* had *Mali* (*Mali Patel*), *Kotwali* (*Police patel*) and *Patwarigiri* rights over 105 villages in the Manickgadh area of Rajura Taluq in Adilabad District—W.S. *File* No. 27 of 1345 Fasli (1936) & R. No. 830 of 1348 Fasli (1939).
31. Forced labour which was mostly unpaid or very meagrely paid.
32. Several such instances are recorded in Warangal *Subedari* Records. To quote two : W.S. *File* No. 60 of 1322 Fasli (1913) & R. No. 2202 of 1324 Fasli (1916); W.S. *File* No. 93 of 1341 Fasli (1932) & R. No. 830 of 1348 Fasli (1939).
33. Village officials enjoying original *Watan* rights by means of *Sanad* or grant from the Ruler.
34. Persons appointed by *Asaldars* with the permission of the Government, to carry on duties on their behalf.
35. *Deshmukhs*, *Deshpandyas*, *Patels*, *Patwaris*, *Sirdeshmukhs* & *Sirdeshpandyas* were regarded as such on account of their power and position.
36. Several such instances are there in *Suba* history. To quote two : W.S. *File* No. 24 of 1354 Fasli (1945) R. No. 907 of 1354 Fasli : W.S. *File* No. 98 of 1341 Fasli (1932) & R. No. 456 of 1342 Fasli. (1933).
37. All India State People's Conference, *File* No. 65 (Available in Nehru Memorial Museum Library (NMML) Delhi), Part I, p. 237.
38. Mandumuia Narasinga Rao, *Fifty years Hyderabad* (Hyderabad : 1977), p. 90.
39. It was so all-pervasive and complete that even on matters concerning the roy al family such as the wedding of Princes, their education and succession to the throne, the opinion and advice of the British Resident carried all weight and approval.
40. Chief Justice of the Hyderabad High Court, The Judicial Secretary and the Legal Adviser to the Government.
41. *Administrative Report for 1322 Fasli* (*6 10 1912* to *5-10-1913*), (Hyderabad-Dn : 1915), p. 9.
42. A.I.S.P.C. File No. 65, Part I., *op. cit.*, p. 237.
43. M. Fathulla Khan, *A History of Administrative Reforms in Hyderabad State* (Secunderabad-Dn : 1955), p. 116.
44. Whereas the 'State Congress' strongly supported and strived for the measure, the *Ittehad-ul-Muslimeen*, backed by the sympathy and support of the Ruler, vehemently opposed it, for the fear that the reform would affect the Muslim rule and domination over the State.
45. *Report of the Reforms Committee*, *1938* (Government Central Press, Hyderabad-Dn), p. 96.
46. Under the direct administration of the Government
47. H.E.H. the Nizam's Government, *Local Government*, (n.y.), p. 1.

48. *Report of the Departments Working under the Secretary and Director-General of Revenue, 1336 Fasli (1926-27)*. p. 91. The ratio fixed in the beginning was 4 pies for the remuneration of village police, 2 pies for education, 2 pies for road cess and 4 pies for general improvements which was changed to the above cited in 1917-18 when Government decided to pay the village police from general revenues, R.V. Rao., *op. cit.* p. 334.
49. *Ibid.*, p. 92.
50. First *Taluqdar* in the case of District Board and Tahsildar or Second *Taluqdar* in the case of Taluq Board.
51. As against total number 19,909 villages in the State (*1951 Census Report*, Part II, P. 4), *Panchayats* were formed only in 378 villages until the end of March 1950—*Report on the Administration of Hyderabad State, September 1948 to March 1950* (Government Press, Hyderabad-Dn), p. 89.
52. *Ibid.*
53. R.A.R. *op. cit.*, p. 229.
54. Madiraju Ramakoteswara Rao, *Sweeyacharitra*, (Warangal : Sarvari Telugu calendar); Local Government, *op. cit.*, p. 3.
55. R A.R., *op. cit.*, p. 20.
56. 'Notes' by T.J. Tasker, Revenue Member, dated 17-2-1938, in W.S. *File* No. 36 of 1343 Fasli (1934) & R. No. 1450 of 1352 Fasli (1943).
57. *Ibid.*
58. W.S. *File* No. 36/86 of 1343 Fasli (1934) & R. No. (n.g.).
59. R.A.R., *op. cit.*, p. 20.
60. W.S. *File* No. 103 of 1338 Fasli (1929) & R. No. 3100 of 1339 Fasli (1930); *Census of India, 1931*, Volume XXIII, Hyderabad State, Part I, 1933, (Hyderabad-Dn), p. 1.
61. W.S. *File* No. 103 of 1338 Fasli (1929), *op. cit.*
62. *Census of India, 1931*, Hyderabad State, *op. cit.* p. 1.
63. W.S. File No. 103 of 1338 Fasli (1929), *op. cit.*
64. *Census of India, 1931*, Hyderabad State, *op. cit.*, p. 1.
65. The second Division in Telangana besides that of Warangal, consisting of the Districts of Medak, Talgonda, Mahboobnagar and Nizamabad.
66. *Golkonda Patrika* (Bi-weekly), 10-8-1936; *Census of India, 1941*, Vol. XXI, *Hyderabad State*, Part I, (Hyderabad-Dn : 1945), p. 2.
67. Physically, hill and forest features were not so prominent in Nizamabad as they were in Adilabad, Warangal and Karimnagar; Socially, aboriginal and backward tribal population was very much predominant in the latter Districts compared to the former; and economically, the former District was very much better off due to rich black soils, getting the benefit of Nizamsagar Project, whereas the Eastern Districts enjoyed these benefits to a lesser degree.

68. W.S. *File* No. 8 of 1349 Fasli (1940) & R. No. 371 of 1351 Fasli (1942).
69. Revenue Secretary's Letter No. 2384 dated 9-5-1358 Fasli (1949) in W.S. *File* No (n.g.).
70. On 18th September, 1948, the *Nizam* surrendered his authority to General J.N. Chaudhary of Indian Army who then took over as Military Governor.
71. See p. 1.
72. *Census of India, 1951, Hyderabad State*, Volume IX, Part I, (1955, Hyderabad-Dn), p. 6.
73. See pages 1 & 2.
74. *The Report of the Agrarian Reforms Committee, 1949*, (Hyderabad-Dn), p. 2.
75. This question is examined in detail in Chapter IV.
76. Report on the Administration of Hyderabad State, September 1948 to March 1950, *op. cit.*, pp. 9-10.
77. Memoranda submitted to the Taxation Enquiry Commission, *op. cit.*, p. 54.
78. *Ibid.*
79. *The Deccan Chronicle*, 18-7-1949.
80. Whereas 10 villages of Warangal District were transferred to Krishna District of Madras, 3 villages from the latter were transferred to the former—*Census of India, 1951*, Hyderabad State, Part I, *op. cit.*, p. 8.
81. *Golkonda Patrika* (Daily), 26-4-1950.
82. The Taluqs of Palvancha and Boorgampad were put under this Division—*Golkonda Patrika*, 11-5-1950.
83. See Table VI.
84. *Census of India, 1951*, Hyderabad State, Part I, *op. cit.*, p. 7.
85. Mandumula Narasinga Rao, *op. cit.*, p. 390.
86. Civil Administrator or First *Taluqdar* was now called as 'Collector'; Second *Taluqdar* as 'Deputy Collector'—*Golkonda Patrika* (Daily), 22-11-1950.
87. *Jagirdars, Ijaradars, Maqtadars*, etc. For detailed explanation, see Chapter IV.
88. W.S. *File* No. 7 of 1340 Fasli (1931) & R. No. 862 of 1348 Fasli (1939).
89. *Ibid.*
90. W.S. *File* No. 67 of 1338 Fasli (1929) & R. No. 3160 of 1339 Fasli (1930).
91. Office of the Director-General of Revenue, Telangana Range, *File* No. 3 of 1336 Fasli (1927) & R. No. 10574 of 1338 Fasli (1929); W.S. *File* No. 21 of 1334 Fasli (1925) & R. No. 13329 of 1338 Fasli (1929); W.S. *File* No. 18 of 1334 Fasli (1935) & R. No. 856 of 1334 Fasli.
92. W.S. *File* No 79 of 1339 Fasli (1930) & R. No. 1263 of 1340 Fasli (1931); Director-General Revenue, Telangana Range, *File* No. 16 of 1338 Fasli (1929) & R. No. 2908 of 1339 Fasli (1930).

93. W.S. File No. 3 of 1343 Fasli (1934) & R. No. 636 of 1344 Fasli (1935).
94. W.S. *File* No. 132 of 1320 Fasli (1911) & R. No. 3793 of 1321 Fasli (1912); W.S. *File* No. 38 of 1354 Fasli (1945) & R. No. 706 of 1354 Fasli.
95. W.S. *File* No. 60 of 1356 Fasli (1947) & R. No. 96 of 1356 Fasli.
96. Meezan, 17-1-1947; W.S. *File* No. 167 of 1355 Fasli (1946) & R. No. 57 of 1356 Fasli. (1947).
97. Royal Order.
98. *Golkonda Patrika*, (Bi-weekly), 14-12-1939.
99. Dignified name given for the bribes that were commonly collected.
100. W.S. *File* No. 3 of 1950 Fasli (1941) & R. No. 1365 of 1352 Fasli (1943).
101. *Golkonda Patrika*, 3-9-1949.
102. D.G.R. Telangana Range, *File* No. 89 of 1334 Fasli (1925) & R. No. 10007 of 1338 Fasli (1929).
103. W.S. *File* No. 3 of 1352 Fasli (1943) & R. No. 1991 of 1352 Fasli.
104. *The Deccan Chronicle*, 13-5-1950.
105. *The Golkonda Patrika*, 25-8-1938.
106. It was entrusted with the monopoly of grain purchase from ryots, W.S. *File* No. 30 of 1354 Fasli (1945) & R. No. 1639 of 1355 Fasli (1946).
107. W.S. *File* No. 31 of 1352 Fasli (1943) & R. No. 5 of 1357 Fasli (1948).
108 *The Golkonda Patrika*, 25-8-1938.
109. W.S. *File* No. 70 of 13 Fasli (1947) & R. No. 1511 of 1357 Fasli (1948); W.S. *File* No. 117 of 1351 Fasli (1942) & R. No. 2216 of 1352 Fasli (1943).
110. *The Golkonda Patrika*, 5-9-1939.
111. *Ittehad-ul-Muslimeen* was founded in 1927 and already *Arya Samaj* was functioning.
112. *Andhra Maha Sabha* was started in 1930 and Hyderabad State Congress in 1938. Their Political role is discussed in the next section.
113. Christoph-von-Fuhrer-Haimendorf, *op. cit.*, p. 122.
114. *The Golkonda Patrika* (Daily), 13-1-1949.
115. Irregular troops working under the direction of *Ittehad* Organisation.
116. W.S. *File* No. 30 of 1354 Fasli (1945) & R. No. 61 of 1357 Fasli (1948); W.S. *File* No. 43 of 1355 Fasli (1946) & R. No. 68 of 1356 Fasli (1948); *Meezan*, 16-8-1946; *Golkonda Patrika* (Daily), 17-1-1948.
117. It is discussed in detail in Chapter VIII.
118. *The Golkonda Patrika* (Daily), 17-6-1949.
119. *Meezan*, 12-8-1944.
120. A.K. Waghmare, 'Education in Hyderabad', in A.I.S.P.C. *File* No. 70 (Part I), 1947-48, p. 17.

121. Government circular.
122. Ravi Narayana Reddy, *Heroic Telangana, Reminiscences and Experiences* (Published by the Communist Party of India, Delhi : 1973), p. 1.
123. Discussed at a greater length in Chapter VIII.
124. W.S. *File* No. 43 of 1355 Fasli (1946) & R. No. 68 of 1356 Fasli (1947); W.S. *File* No. 16 of 1355 Fasli (1946) & R. No. 69 of 1356 Fasli.
125. *Ibid.*
126. Refers to 2000 B.C.
127. R.E.E., *op. cit.*, p. 332.
128. R.V. Rao, *op. cit.*, p. 364.
129. *Statistical Year Book*, 1941-42 to 1944-45, (Nizam's Government, Hyderabad-Dn), p. 394.
130. *The Golkonda Patrika* (Daily), 5-8-1950.
131. *Ibid.*
132. R.E.E., *op. cit.*, pp. 343-344.
133. Madapati Hanumantha Rao, *Telangana Andhrodyamam*, Part I, (Hyderabad-Dn : 1949), p. 128.
134. *Ibid.*, p. 60.
135. *Ibid.*, p. 148.
136. Sarojini Regani, "The Social Background, for the rise of the *Andhra Maha Sabha* Movement in Telangana" in *Itihas,* Journal of Andhra Pradesh Archives, Vol. 1, No. 1, (January to July, 1973), p. 188.
137. Measurement and survey of land and then fixing the assessment.
138. Madapati Hanumantha Rao, *op. cit.*, Part II, 1950, pp. 274-76.
139. A lawyer from Hyderabad who took active interest in carrying on the activities of *Andhra Jana Sangham* and later from 1930 of *Andhra Maha Sabha.*
140. N. Ramesan (ed), *The Freedom Struggle in Hyderabad*, Vol. IV, (Published by the Andhra Pradesh State Committee appointed for the compilation of a history of the Freedom Struggle in Andhra Pradesh : 1966), p. 44.
141. K. Subhas Chandra Reddy, *Telangana : A Study in Regionalism,* unpublished Ph. D. Thesis (Osmania University, 1978), p. 34.
142. Sarojini Regani, *op. cit.*, p. 189.
143. He bore a title to that effect.
144. Place where Muslim festival prayers are held.
145. The Freedom Struggle in Hyderabad, Vol. IV, *op. cit.*, pp. 88-89.
146. Sarojini Regani, *Highlights of the Freedom Movement in Andhra Pradesh*, (Hyderabad : 1972), p. 175.
147. The Freedom Struggle in Hyderabad, Vol. IV, *op. cit.*, p. 25.
148. Highlights of the Freedom Movement in Andhra Pradesh, *op. cit.*, p. 180.
149. Third at Khammamet in 1934, 9th at Dharmavaram in 1942 and 12th at Madikonda in 1945.

150. Fourth at Sirsilla in 1935.
151. *Meezan*, 4-1-1945.
152. Madapati Hanumantha Rao, *op. cit.*, Vol. II, pp. 258-280, 342-354.
153. Rates of land lease.
154. P. Sundarayya, *Veera Telangana Viplava Poratam-Gunapatalu*, (Vijayawada, 1973), p. 26.
155. Hailed from a village official family in the village of Galipalli in Sirsilla Taluq of Karimnagar District. Entering political arena in 1930 by undergoing imprisonment at Rajahmundry in Madras Presidency because of participation in Civil Disobedience Movement, began to take interest in the politics of *Andhra Maha Sabha* since 1934 and finally became its General Secretary in 1946. He remained as the foremost Communist leader in the *Suba* area—*Meezan*, 21-9-1944.
156. Highlights of the Freedom Movement in Andhra Pradesh, *op. cit.*, p. 182.
157. A Hindu Organisation which fought for the grant of Civil rights in the Dominions.
158. The Primary membership in 1949 was as following : Warangal District : 1,55,944, Karimnagar District : 71,698, Adilabad District : 60,482 : Total Telangana : 7,18,886. Warangal stood first, Karimnagar fourth (Second Nalgonda, Third Mahboobnagar), and Adilabad last in the 8 districts, *Golkonda Patrika* (Daily), 6-9-1949.
159. The Freedom Struggle in Hyderabad, *op. cit.*, pp. 135-36.
160. Peaceful Resistance.
161. The Freedom Struggle in Hyderabad, *op. cit.*, p. 57.
162. It was a patriotic song written in reverence of Motherland by Bankim Chandra Chatterjee.
163. Jawaharlal Nehru Subject *File* No. 102, Part II, 1938-42, p. 28 (Preserved in the Nehru Museum Library, Delhi).
164. Highlights of the Freedom Movement in Andhra Pradesh, *op. cit.*, pp. 186-187.
165. The Freedom Struggle in Hyderabad, *op. cit.*, p. 246.
166. Trade Union leader of Singareni Collieries at Kothagudem in Khammam Taluq of Warangal District.
167. Highlights of the Freedom Movement in Andhra Pradesh, *op. cit.*, p. 195.
168. *The Deccan Chronicle*, 25-6-1947.
169. W.S. *File* No. 140 of 1356 Fasli (1947) & R. No. 58 of 1357 Fasli (1948).
170. W.S. *File* No. 169 of 1356 Fasli (1947) & R. No. 73 of 1357 Fasli (1948).
171. Highlights of the Freedom Movement in Andhra Pradesh, *op. cit.*, p. 202.
172. *Meezan*, 9-9-1947; *The Deccan Chronicle*, 11-9-1947.
173. As many as 21,000 people participated in this *Satyagraha*—Highlights

of the Freedom Movement in Andhra Pradesh, *op. cit.*, p. 202.

174. *Ibid.*, pp. 202-203.
175. A.I.S.P.C. *File* No. 70 (Part I), 1947-48, p. 363.
176. *Meezan*, 12-9-1947.
177. *Ibid.*, 16-9 1947.
178. *Ibid.*
179. K.M. Munshi, *The End of an Era*, (Bombay, 1957), p. 19.
180. Fortnightly Report of the Hyderabad Resident to the Viceroy for the period ending 31st March, 1944, in *Reel 2, Accession No. 45, Crown Representative Reports* (Micro Films available in National Archives, Delhi).
181. F.R. for the first half of September 1938, *Reel 2, Accession No. 45*, File No. 28P (s)/38, *Crown Representative Reports.*
182. F.R. for the first half of January 1941, *Reel S., Acc. No. 52*, File No. 5(2)P (Secret), *Crown Representative Reports.*
183. A para-military organisation functioning from 1940 under *Ittehad's* direction. It numbered 50,000 on 3rd November, 1947 and got enormously increased as the days rolled by. It was supplied with uniforms, firearms and regular military training, very much at State's expense, Highlights of the Freedom Movement in Andhra Pradesh, *op. cit.*, p. 206.
184. A detailed examination of the Communist activities and their effects on the economic condition of the *Suba* is made in Chapter VIII.
185. *The Deccan Chronicle*, 12-2-1949.
186. *Ibid.*, 17-7-1949.
187. *The Hindu*, 21-1-1948, Hyderabad Residency *Files* No. F. 141 (14)P/48, dated 24-3-1948; No. 434-F./141/(1)/P. 148, dated 15-3-1948. There are many such *Files* preserved in National Archives, Delhi; *The Golkonda Patrika* (Daily), 28-1-1948.
188. *The Golkonda Patrika* (Daily), 9-7-1949.
189. *Ibid.*, 14-1-1949; *The Deccan Chronicle*, 20-5-1949.
190. *The Golkonda Patrika*, (Daily) 8-7-1950, & 19-11-1950.
191. *The Deccan Chronicle*, (Editorial), 19-6-1949.
192. *The Golkonda Patrika* (Daily), 7-3-1950, & 31-10-1950.

CHAPTER FOUR

LAND TENURES AND LAND REVENUE ADMINISTRATION

THE REGION being primarily agricultural, the pride of place in economic relations is occupied by its land system. Conditions of agricultural production are, to a great extent, determined by the relation that existed between the owners and cultivators of land and the rights and status of the actual cultivators.[1] The assessment and collection of such a widely levied impost as that of land revenue, demanded an intimate knowledge of land customs and the social features of country life.[2]

A. Land Classification

For purposes of land revenue administration, the lands were broadly divided into Government and Non-Government lands. The former, also known as *Diwani* or *Khalsa* lands, were under the direct management of the Government and revenue from them went to the Government exchequer. They formed as much as 83 per cent of the total number of villages in the *Suba*.[3] Non-Government lands were those whose revenue had been wholly or partially assigned for some special purpose. These extended over all the three Districts, but in varying proportion and Warangal ranked high in this respect. Land of the second category were further sub-divided into (a) *Sarf-i-khas* lands, which were the property of the *Nizam* and the revenue from which went to his privy purse and (b) lands which had been the result of State grants and the revenue from which had been assigned wholly or partially as *Jagir* or *Inam* in favour of some person or persons.[4]

(*a*) *Land Rights* : Different types of land tenures, as indicated in Table VII were in vogue both in *Khalsa* and Non-*Khalsa* areas. In *Diwani* villages *Ryotwari* tenure based on Bombay system was widely prevalent. *Ryotwari* villages formed 75 per cent of the total number of villages in the *Suba*.[5] Under *Pattedari* tenure, the owner or *Pattedar* was himself the cultivator of the land and as long as the assessment that was determined and fixed from time to time was paid, no interference was made with his land rights. In *pot-pattedari*, on the other hand, two or more cultivators worked together on joint-stock principle and the rights of all the partners remained equal. The *pattedar* could neither evict the *pot-pattedar* nor enhance the assessment payable by him. Meagreness or insufficieny of agricultural inputs had generally induced the cultivators to resort to this type of cultivating tenure, but anyhow, it did not appear to be much in vogue in the area.[6]

(*b*) *Tenants* : The Ryotwari tenure never intended to recognise any middleman between the landholder and the State and the owner becoming an absentee. But, factors like old age, sickness, lack of heirs, indebtedness, staying away from the place of land, large holdings and the owner adopting a non-agricultural profession, etc., had all resulted in inducing many a land holder to lease his land. Further, as land became a commodity of value owing to the security it offered and the prestige and status it conferred on its owner, many non-cultivators began to acquire lands which they leased out to others for cultivation.[7] *Shikmidars* and *Asami-Shikmis* were otherwise known as protected tenants and tenants-at-will respectively. Whereas the former enjoyed the right of remaining on the land as long as he fulfilled the terms of the agreement with the owner, the latter, on the other hand, enjoyed a temporary or annual

TABLE VII

Types of Land Tenures

Diwani or *Khalsa lands*	Other tenures of *Khalsa land*	*Non-Khalsa lands*
Ryotwari tenure	1. Pan-maqta	1. Sarf-e-Khas
Cultivating tenures	2. Pahud or Sarbasta	2. Samasthan or Peshkash
1. Pattadari	3. Ijara	3. Jagir
2. Pot-Pattadari	4. Agrahar	(a) Paigah or Jamiat Jagirs
3. Shikmidari		(b) Al-Tamgha Jagirs
4. Asami-Shikmi		(c) Zat-Jagirs
		(d) Tankha-Jagirs
		(e) Mashrooti Jagirs
		(f) Madad-maash Jagirs
		4. Inam

tenancy. An *Asami-Shikmi* could become a *Shikmidar*, if he had been a partner in the cultivation of the holding from the time it was first cleared or had been in uninterrupted occupation for twelve consecutive years.[8] But, rarely was the same tenant allowed to cultivate the same land for more than two to five years.[9] *Pattedars* very much resorted to changing their *Kowldars* frequently so that the latter might not claim a prescriptive right on the strength of long possession.[10] This had also given them the benefit of claiming higher rents, as there was keen competition among landless tenants to take land on lease. As a matter of fact, the percentage of landless to occupancy tenants had increased rather alarmingly from 24 to 71 in Warangal District between 1929-30 to 1949-50.[11] It was with the same intention to deprive the *Kowldars* of occupancy rights over the lands which they cultivated that the *pattedars* showed aversion to enter into written agreements with them. That was the reason why leases were mostly oral[12] and as many as 75 per cent of them remained tenancies-at-will that got terminated after one year.[13] If at all a written agreement was executed, its terms and conditions had only put the tenant completely at the mercy of the landlord. A typical specimen of such an agreement executed in Warangal District is enclosed in *Appendix I*.

It can be seen from Table VIII that whereas Warangal and Adilabad Districts fell short of State percentage both in respect of occupant cultivators and occupant-cum-tenant cultivators, they had exceeded it in respect of landless tenants. Karimnagar District, on the other hand, very much recorded an opposite trend to this. The huge presence of landless tenants in Warangal District which in this respect ranked highest in the State,[14] had immensely served as a contributory factor for the eruption of peasant discontent and struggle under Communist leadership. The appointment of a Committee in 1940 to enquire into the Tenancy problem and the passing of the *Asami-Shikmis* Act in 1945 based on its recommendations, though well-intentioned, had failed to bring any perceptible change in the condition of the tenantry. Though the Act which came into operation in 1947 had regulated that those *Asami-Shikmis* who were in continuous occupation of land for six years between 1933-43 were to be recognized as permanent or protected

TABLE VIII

Cultivating Occupants and Tenants (in Surveyed Villages) in 1949-50

Sl. No.	District	Occupant Cultivators	Occupant-cum-tenant Cultivators	Landless tenants	Mortgages (with possession only)	Total
1	2	3	4	5	6	7
1.	Adilabad	1280 (67.5)	274 (14.4)	340 (17.9)	4 (0.2)	1898 (100.0)
2.	Karimnagar	1161 (79.9)	173 (11.9)	119 (8.2)	...	1453 (100.0)
3.	Warangal	1711 (66.4)	251 (9.8)	613 (23.8)	...	2575 (100.0)
	State	17162 (69.4)	3960 (16.0)	3554 (14.4)	60 (0.2)	24736 (100.0)

Figures in brackets denote the percentages to total number of cultivators given in col. 7,

Source : S. Kesava Iyengar, *Rural Economic Enquiries*, 1949-51, p. 78.

tenants and the period of lease in case of tenants-at-will was to be for not less than ten years, these were not implemented due to Governmental indifference, the intransigence of the landlords and the ignorance of the tenants.[15] Government at that time very much got pre-occupied with problems of political nature that arose consequent on the declaration of Indian Independence.[16] The tenants, besides being generally ignorant of the beneficial provisions of the Act, were not allowed to take advantage of them if at all they willed, by the strong-arm tactics adopted by wealthy *Pattedars*. Sample survey conducted by a Special Officer in Warangal District in April, 1949 and also the gathering of opinion by the Agrarian Reforms Committee in the same year, revealed that insecurity of tenure created by short and yearly leases, frequent evictions and rack-renting, had characterised the situation in different parts of the area.[17] More and more lands were resumed under the guise of bringing them under personal cultivation.[18]

The condition of *Kowldars* in the other tenures of *Jagir*, *Magta*, *Ijara*, *Agrahar* and *Inam* was no better. It was even graver in the sense that even cultivators of long standing extending to even a period of 90 years had come to be regarded as tenants-at-will with no independent rights of sale, mortgageability and transfer[19] and were also evicted freely as and when they refused to pay higher *Kowls*.[20] Even in Jagirs which were Surveyed and Settled, *pattedars* were regarded as *Shikmidars* who, in turn, let their lands on rent to *Asami-Shikmis*.[21] In other words, unlike in *Ryotwari*, these tenure-holders or assignees came to regard themselves as the sole *Pattedars* of all villages that were under their charge. If at all permission was ever accorded by *Jagirdars* for sale, transfer, heirship or according of *pattedari* rights, *nazars* or *nazarana*,[22] amounting to one or two years' assessments were demanded from cultivators.[22a] These evils were more pronounced in unsurveyed and unsettled *Jagirs* which numbered in 1949 as many as 1,137 villages out of 5,800 *Non-Diwani* villages in the State.[23] Whenever Government decided to undertake Survey and Settlement of a *Jagir* village rather compulsorily, then the alienator took all care to get the village records prepared in such a way that the actual land holders were showed as tenants.[24] There was no supervision or scrutiny by Government officers of the village papers of alienated villages, nor did the Survey Officers hold a detailed enquiry into the rights of occupants of land in Non-*Khalsa* villages.[25] As a matter of fact, Government rules regarding grant of *pattedari* rights in Non-*Khalsa* villages were only issued in *Jarida* No. 32 of 19th *Thir* (May) 1356 *Fasli* (1947)[26] and even these legal provisions had remained mostly on paper.[27] Further, it is significant to note that chapter 7 of section 169 of the Hyderabad Land Revenue Act which referred to Survey and Settlement was made not applicable to Non-*Khalsa* villages, except on the written application of the holder of any such village,[28] which under the circumstances stated above, would never the forthcoming. The rights of the tenants in both *Khalsa* and Non-*Khalsa* villages and their relationship with *Pattedars* and landlords was put on proper footing ensuring occupancy rights, security of tenure and reasonable lease rates, only with the passing on 10th June, 1950, of the Hyderabad Tenancy and Agricultural Lands Act. Its implementation, however, was witnessed only after the close of 1950.

c. Maqtas: In *Diwani* lands there were, besides *pattedari* and cultivating tenures, *Maqtas*, *Sarbastas* or *Watans*, *Ijaras* and *Agrahars*. The holders of these Non-*Ryotwari* tenures being invariably landlords or officials of considerable wealth and power,[29] the economic condition of the cultivators, tenants and other sections of rural population, had come to be immensely influenced by the way of their functioning. The fact that tenurial rights over a number of villages was vested in one person[30] had led to vast concentration of landed power which, in turn, promoted them to indulge in different kinds of excesses, causing misery to the local population.

Pan-Maqta or *Maqta* was a *kowl* or tenure by contract granted by former Governments under which lands extending from small isolated fields to whole villages and even groups of villages, were given to the holders on a fixed quit-rent without liability to enhancement.[31] These were granted either permanently or for a life or lives. There were also some *Maqtas* on which no quit-rent was levied and thus, they very much resembled *Iname* or revenue-free grants.[31a]

The quit-rent or the *pan* was always less than the full assessment of the lands assigned and this concession was intended to benefit the tenure holders. For a land of 1,009 acres and 26 *quntas* given on *Maqta* and whose land revenue was Rs. 1,160-8-0, the *Pan* fixed per year was only Rs. 32.[32] Consequently, the *Maqtedars* and *Agraharuiks* of Warangal *Suba* in 1929 had a net revenue surplus of Rs. 4,89,695-11-03, after paying *pan* as well as meeting the administrative expenditure involved in the management of these villages.[33] Even this small proportion of land revenue was not paid in time by some of the *Maqtedars* and they fell into huge arrears. Ajam Gavri, *Maqtedar* of three villages in Parkal Taluq covering an area of 2,712 acres and 33 *quntas*, was found in arrears of land revenue for the period 1933 to 1944 to the extent of Rs. 27,966-3-3.[34] He being an influential person and also the only *Pattedar* in all those villages, became confident that none would come forward to purchase his lands if at all they were auctioned for the realisation of revenue arrears.[35]

Besides being benefited in the meagre payment of *pan*, the *Maqtedars* further got consolidated in their power by indulging in huge occupation of uncultivated Government lands which, by using their influence in official circles, they succeeded in getting allotted on *patta* at the payment of usual revenue.[36] It was reported in the *Settlement Report of Warangal Taluka for 1893* that such surreptitious increase of *Maqta* lands had increased by 406 percent.[37] But, more dangerous and significant to note from the view point of land rights was the fact that these *Maqtedars* who had only been assigned a portion of land revenue of the villages under their charge, began to regard themselves as the sole owners and *pattedars* of the lands. They frequently resorted to changing the names of old and real cultivating *pattedars* as tenants[38] and if at all they ever accorded *pattedari* rights to old cultivators, or permitted sale, mortgageability or even recognized heirship, *nazrana* or *peshkash* in the shape of one or two years' assessment was extracted from them.[39] Just like *Jagirdars*, they even collected, besides land revenue, '*patties*' or subscription on certain occasions like marriage in a *Maqtedar's* family,[40] which were absolutely illegal and unjust. The distinction in question of land rights between *Khalsa* and Non-*Khalsa* land had only become blurred and bleak in respect of this tenure.

As indicated in Table IX, there were 271 *Maqtas* in the *Suba* and next to *Ryotwari* villages, they formed the largest group in *Diwani* lands. It is significant to note that these were concentrated in the Taluqs of Warangal, Yellendu, Madhira, Mahaboobabad, Manthani, Sirsilla, Adilabad, Asifabad, Rajura and Sirpur which consisted of fertile soils with facilities for irrigation. Though the creation of new *Maqtas* was not resorted to during the time of the last *Nizam* in view of the increasing demand for land,[41] yet the continuance of those that were earlier granted, was itself sufficient enough to give rise to peasant disaffection and discontent in the area.

d. Kowldars and Banjardars : Though statistics regarding their exact number in different Taluqs of the *Suba* are not available in the records, yet sufficient information was there to show that these *Diwani* tenures prevailed in the area and were quite significant to note as they were concerned with land development. In some of the areas, they were quite extensive. In Warangal Taluq itself there were as many as 820 *Kowldars*.[42] *Kowli* tenures were granted either to convert dry lands into wet at the prevailing dry rates, or to cultivate waste lands overgrown with trees called *banjar* lands. The duration of lease for the former was thirty years and for the latter from five to forty years[43]. *Banjardars* were no other than those holders who took *banjar* land on *Kowl*. Even high Government officials of the rank of Chief Secretary[44] and First *Taluqdar*[45] vied for *banjar* tenures. This naturally became a contributory factor for the growth of absentee landlordism which, in turn, had a baneful effect on agricultural development of the region. Even in the case of allotment of *banjar* lands to non-officials, there were cases of absentee landlordism.[45a]

These tenure holders, on the expiry of the *kowl* period and the fulfilment of lease conditions, were granted these newly developed lands on *patta* and in the case of *banjar* lands where new villages and sprung up, the *Banjardars* were also conferred *patelgi* rights in those villages.[46] The main condition to get these land and *watan* rights in the case of *banjar* lands only to see that 40 huts or houses were laid in the area allotted, besides of course, bringing greater part of the lands under cultivation.[47]

TABLE IX

Taluq-wise Picture of Diwani and Non-Diwani Villages of Warangal Suba as in 1941

Sl. No.	Name of the Taluq	Area-wise number of villages									Total No. of villages	Deserted villages in Diwani
		Diwani	Sarf-i-Khas	Jagirs			Paigah	Samas-than	Maqtas	Agra-hars		
				Exem-pted	Non-Exem-pted	Total						
1	2	3	4	5	6	7	8	9	10	11	12	13
1.	Warangal	175	4	4	16	20	—	—	14	2	215	1
2.	Pakhal	195	—	—	2	2	—	—	9	2	208	45
3.	Mulug	193	—	—	1	1	—	—	—	1	195	52
4.	Paloncha	56	—	—	40	40	—	116	3	12	227	18
5.	Yellandu	45	—	—	3	3	—	—	13	4	65	9
6.	Khammam	144	—	—	4	4	—	—	—	8	156	3
7.	Madhira	153	—	7	5	12	—	—	22	17	204	—
8.	Mahabcobabad	146	—	—	21	21	—	—	25	15	207	4
	Warangal District Total	1,107	4	11	92	103	—	116	86	61	1,477	132

9.	Karimnagar	134	20	—	15	15	—	—	6	5	180	2
10.	Sultanabad	122	4	46	8	54	—	—	6	2	188	5**
11.	Jagtiyal	187	—	9	1	10	—	—	9	8	214	2
(a)	Metpalli (Jagir-Taluq)	—	—	27	—	27	—	—	—	—	27	—
12.	Manthani	149	—	—	5	5	—	—	31	—	185	82
13.	Parkal	101	—	—	6	6	—	—	9	—	116	—
14.	Huzurabad	121	—	—	6	6	—	—	2	2	131	—
15.	Sircilla	150	—	1	4	5	—	—	13	2	170	6
	Karimnagar District Total	964	24	83	45	128	—	—	76	19	1,211	97
16.	Adilabad	190	—	3	5	8	—	—	12	—	210	27
17.	Chinnur	172	—	—	2	2	—	—	1	—	175	21
18.	Luxettipet	138	—	—	4	4	—	—	8	1	151	13
19.	Asifabad	259	—	—	9	9	—	—	18	—	286	—
20.	Rajura	245	—	—	6	6	—	—	26	—	277	—
21.	Kinwat	158	—	—	11	11	—	—	2	—	171	11
22.	Sirpur	164	—	—	3	3	—	—	27	—	194	18
23.	Utnur	176	—	—	—	—	—	—	4	—	180	45

24.	Nirmal	184	—	1	5	6	—		2	—	192	22
(a)	Yelgadap (Paigah Taluq)	—	—	—	2	2	65	—	—	—	67	14
25.	Boath	219	—	—	4	4	—	—	9	—	232	68
	Adilabad District Total	1,905	—	4	51	55	65	—	109	1	2,135	239
	Warangal Suba Total	3,976	28	98	188	286	65	116	271	81	4,823	468

*It refers to 'Ryotwari'

**Includes one in 'Maqta'

Source : Compiled from : *Village Lists of Warangal, Karimnagar and Adilabad Districts* (prepared by the Department of Statistics & Census ; Hyderabad, 1950), pp. 30-291.

Further, remission of land revenue permanently for 1/4th area was also granted in those cases where wet lands were developed and waste lands were populated.[48] But, this concession was withdrawn in respect of the latter category where dry lands were developed since 1346 *Fasli* (1937).[49]

Not satisfied with these huge accretions of land power and revenue concessions, these *Banjardars*, and *Kowldars* just like *Maqtedars*[50] resorted to huge unauthorised and illegal occupation of forest and uncultivated land, which, with the help of their influence in Governmental circles, they could succeed in getting on *Patta*.[51] An increase of 53.11 per cent in *Kowli* lands of Warangal Taluq was due to the area not being demarcated and the *Kowldars* thus were left free to encroach upon the adjoining jungle tracts and show their limits accordingly.[52] True to their concentrated land power, these holders, just like *Maqtedars*, indulged in unjustifiable seizure of lands from tenants and increase in taxes from them.[53] It was a case of single *pattedar* invariably an absentee, served by a number of *Asami-Shikmis*, and consequently the attendant evils of exploitation of hunger for land were manifest.

(*e*) *Tahud/Sarbasta/Watandari* : *Tahud* or *Sarbasta* tenure was prevalent before 1866, when tax-farming was there. Under this system, wealthy and influential persons from the Districts, otherwise known as *Deshmukhs* and *Deshpandyas*[54] like Pingali Venkatrama Reddy, *Deshmukh* of Waddepalli in Warangal Taluq and Tungaturthi Narasimha Rao, resident of Hanamkonda but absentee landlord at Medarmula in Mulug Taluq, both of Warangal District,[54a] served as tax-farmers or contractors. They remitted a fixed amount to the treasury but extracted the last pie from the ryots and thus retained considerably more for themselves than what they despatched to the Government treasury.[55] Besides land revenue, the collection of certain other cesses such as excise, (*abkari*) tax on professions (*mohtarfa*), garden produce (*baghat*) tax on trees (*sardarkhti*), mango fruit (*amrai*) etc., which formed considerable sources of revenue to the State, was also farmed out to *Tahuddars*.[56] *Deshmukhs* and *Deshpandyas* further got strengthened very much in their economic and land power by the grants of revenue-free lands known as *Seri* and *Sawaram* respectively, made by former *Nizams* in remuneration for their services and in consideration of their official position.[57] This accretion of vast land power combined with huge tax surplus enjoyed under *Tahud* system went a long way in establishing these landlords as supreme rulers in their villages. So much so, that the period before 1853 had very much come to be regarded as a golden time for them.[58]

But it was a bad time for the State and its treasury. Scared by the extravagant demands made by *Tahuddars* or *Sarbastadars*,[59] many of the cultivators had given up their lands and as a result, the income of the Government tended to diminish.[60] Further, accounts were not kept regularly.[61] The cumulative effect was that the revenue of the State fell far below the expenditure.[62] In order to reverse this trend, Sir Salar Jung I, who became Prime Minister in 1853, had put an end to the system of revenue-farming in 1854 and introduced in its place, the method of assessing each individual cultivator.[63] This change, however, did not affect much the strength and position of *Deshmukhs* and *Deshpandyas*. On the other hand, it was further strengthened. In consequence of the abolition of tax-farming, the former revenue-farmers were given land in compensation and most of them availed of the opportunity to seize as much of the best land as they could.[64] Further, they were also allowed an annual pension on hereditary basis known as *Rusum-i-zamindari*, calculated at 7½ per cent on the revenue collections out of which 5 per cent was the share of *Deshmukhs* and 2½ per cent that of the *Deshpandyas*.[65] This cash grant which amounted to Rs. 1,10,671 for Warangal *Suba* for 1321 *Fasli* (1912),[66] was paid to them during the present century, without requiring them of any service.[67]

Thus, even after the introduction of beneficient reforms during the second half of the last century, the *Deshmukh* and *Deshpandyas* continued to enjoy their dominant position in the rural economy which they proceeded resolutely to further strengthen and consolidate during the succeeding decades by resorting to grain and money-lending and also liquor and toddy contracts.[68] The distribution and the concentration pattern of these *Watandars*[69] who played a significant and crucial role in the economic development of the region during

TABLE X

Taluq-wise Particulars of Rusum allotment for 1338 Fasli (1929) in respect of Deshmukhs and Deshpandyas

Sl. No.	Amount sanctioned for the District/ State	With-held during the year	Balance	Name of the Taluq	Amount allotted	Remarks
1	2	3	4	5	6	7
1.	Warangal District ; Rs. 29,642	—	Rs. 29,642	Warangal	Rs. 4,600/-	
2.	" "	—	"	Pakhal	Rs. 3,029/-	
3.	" "	—	"	Mulug	Rs. 931/-	
4.	" "	—	"	Mahboobabad	Rs. 6,000/-	
5.	" "	—	"	Yellandu	Rs. 202/-	
6.	" "	—	"	Palvancha	Rs. 5,702/-	
7.	" "	—	"	Khammam	Rs. 6,500/-	
8.	" "	—	"	Madhira	Rs. 2,600/-	
9.	Karimnagar District Rs. 43,021	Rs. 9,425-2-0	Rs. 33,595-14-0	Karimnagar	Not mentioned	
10.	" "	--	"	Sircilla	Rs. 7,500/-	
11.	" "	—	"	Huzurabad	Rs. 8,500/-	
12.	" "	—	"	Jagtiyal	Rs. 8,700/:	
13.	" "	—	"	Parkal	Rs. 4,400/-	
14.	" "	—	"	Mahadeopur	Rs. 1,495-14-0	The with-held amount was of this Taluq

15.	,, ,,	—	,,	Sultanabad	Rs. 3,000/-
16.	Adilabad District ; Rs. 12,000/-	—	Rs. 12,000/-	Adilabad	Rs. 4,016-6-7
17.	,, ,,	—	,,	Sirpur	Rs. 2052-10-8
18.	,, ,,	—	,,	Rajura	Rs. 1,548-4-3
19.	,, ,,	—	,,	Nirmal	Rs. 909-14-6
20.	,, ,,	—	,,	Kinwat	Rs. 342-15-9
21.	,, ,,	—	,,	Chinnur	Rs. 1,530-7-3
22.	,, ,,	—	,,	Luxettipet	Rs. 1,462-9-0
23.	,, ,,	—	,,	Asifabad	Nil
24.	,, ,,	—	,,	Boath	Rs. 112-8-0
25.	,, ,,	—	,,	Utnoor	Rs. 24-4-0
	Total Warangal Suba : Rs. 84,663/-, Rs. 9,425-2-0, Rs. 75,237-14-0				
	Total for the State : Rs 6,18,000/-	—	Rs. 6,18,000/-		

Source : Subedari Warangal *File* No. 23 of 1337 Fasli (1928) & R. No. 687 of 1339 Fasli (1930).

TABLE X(a)

Rusumdars of Suba Warangal for the Year 1343 Fasli (1934)

Sl. No.	Name of the Taluq	Deshmukhs	Categories of Rusumdars: Desh-pandyas	Sir-Muqaddams	Rusum-Patwari-giri	Rusum-Qanungoi	Sir-Desh-mukhs	Sir-Desh-pandyas	Total	Remarks
1	2	3	4	5	6	7	8	9	10	11
1.	Adilabad	2	2	2	—	—	—	—	6	
2.	Sirpur	1	—	—	—	—	—	—	1	
3.	Rajura	5	1	2	—	—	—	—	8	
4.	Nirmal	3	1	—	—	1	—	—	5	
5.	Boath	—	2	—	—	—	—	—	2	
6.	Utnoor	—	—	—	1	—	—	—	1	
7.	Luxettipet	2	—	—	—	—	—	—	2	
8.	Chinnur	2	—	—	—	—	—	—	2	
9.	Kinwat	6	4	—	—	—	—	—	10	
10.	Asifabad	—	—	—	—	—	—	—	Nil	
	Total Adilabad District	21	10	4	1	1	—	—	37	
11.	Khammam	25	—	—	—	—	—	—	25	The number
12.	Warangal	27	,,	—	—	—	—	—	27	referred to
13.	Mahboobabad	26	,,	—	—	—	—	—	26	both Desh -

14. Madhira	20	,,	—	—	—	—	—	20	mukhs &
15. Pakhal	13	,,	—	—	—	—	—	13	Deshpandyas.
16. Paloncha	6	,,	—	—	—	—	—	6	"(out of these 2 belonged to Raja of Paloncha)"
17. Yellendu	5	,,	—	—	—	—	—	5	,,
18. Mulug	3	,,	—	—	—	—	—	3	,,
Total of Warangal District	125	,,	—	—	—	—	—	125	
19. Sultanabad	13	13	—	—	—	7	2	35	
20. Mahadeopur	--	—	—	—	—	3	—	3	
21. Parkal	44	11	—	—	—	—	—	55	
22. Jagtiyal	17	31	—	—	—	—	1	49	
23. Sircilla	18	14	—	—	—	—	26	58	
24. Huzurabad	36	21	—	—	—	1	6	64	
25. Karimnagar	21	15	—	—	—	=	2	38	
Total of Karimnagar District	149	105	—	—	—	11	37	302	
Suba Total :	295	115	4	1	1	11	37	464	

Compiled from : Warangal Subedari *File* No. 5 of 1340 Fasli (1931) & R. No. 1596 of 1343 Fasli (1934) the period of the present study, could well be gleaned, rather in an indirect manner, from Table X in which the *Rusum* allotments Taluq-wise for 1929, were indicated and also rather directly from Table X (a). They were spread over all the Taluqs except that of Asifabad in Adilabad District. But the concentration, however, was there in the Taluqs of Khammam, Mahboobabad, Madhira, Palvancha and Warangal in Warangal District ; Mahadeopur, Jagtiyal, Huzurabad and Sirsilla in Karimnagar District ; and Adilabad, Sirpur, Rajura, Chinnur and Luxettipet in Adilabad District. Among the three Districts, Karimnagar and Warangal were more pronounced in this respect than Adilabad. But, if the 15 Districts of the State were taken as a whole, then the three *Suba* Districts of Karimnagar, Warangal and Adilabad, ranked only 7th, 11th and 14th respectively, in the order.[70] As against this picture, the fact that Warangal and Karimnagar Districts, next to that of Nalgonda, were in the forefront of the peasant Revolt against landlord domination that commenced in Telangana in 1946, has got to be understood and explained by the interplay of other factors like the easy infiltration of Communists from the border District of Krishna in Madras Presidency, the hilly and forest-infested nature of the region, huge tribal population, poor economic condition of ryots and most important of all, greater intensity of peasant exploitation at the hands of *Watandars* and *Jagirdars*. But, all the same, it can't be lost sight of the fact that all those Taluqs in the *Suba* where there was significant concentration of *Deshmukhs* and *Deshpandyas* as could be noted from Table X (a), witnessed in greater or lesser degree, depending on the intensity and magnitude of the compelling forces, events and developments characteristic of the peasant uprising.

These *Watandars* including *Patels* and *Patwaris*,[71] who had entire villages or thousands of acres of land[72] under their ownership, got it cultivated mostly either by *Kowldars* or by employing *bhagelas*.[73] One-fourth of the large wet area in Warangal District was managed by tenants and almost the whole of the rest by *bhagelas*.[74] The tendency of big landlords belonging to cultivating classes giving up cultivation work and taking up grain and money-lending, liquor and toddy contracts and establishment of mills, had become more pronounced, especially in Warangal District.[75] But, the condition of tenants, agricultural serfs and even of independent *pattedars* was far from happy under these non-cultivating and absentee landlords. Eviction of tenants, rack-renting, subjecting of *bhagelas* to bonded labour, unjust and forcible occupation of lands of *pattedars* and above all, collection of various illegal cesses and extraction of *vetti* from all sections of the rural population, had very much characterised agrarian relations under this *watandari* tenure.[76] To add to these evils, *patels* and *patwaris* using their official position besides their land power, indulged in different excesses like collection of excess amounts of land revenue, demanding of gratis for entry of cultivation and land revenue payment details in *pavni patrak*,[77] improper and corrupt dealings in the conduct of land auctions and allotment of *laoni* land[78] etc., which caused much heart-burning and misery to the cultivating farmers and tenants.[79] The mild reaction and reprimand from the administration, or sometimes even conniving, in these misdeeds had only emboldened these big *Watandars* to further intensify their atrocities on the rural helpless.[80]

(*f*) *Ijaras* : Just like *Kowl* and *Banjar* tenures that were traced earlier, *Ijara* tenure was also primarily concerned with land development. This tenure was introduced in the Dominions in 1878 A.D., in order to get numerous deserted villages repopulated and bring under cultivation large tracts of cultivable lands lying waste, which had arisen and rather increased owing to the mal-administration of Governments that were there previous to Salar Jung I.[81] As a special inducement to attract people to take up the development of these lands, the *Ijara* system was introduced, under which land was given on lease, assessed at light rates subject to progressive increase till the full assessment was reached, the period of concession varying from 5 to 30 and in some cases to 40 years.[82] On the expiry of the *Kowl* period, the village was surveyed and settled and was given permanently on *Bil-Maqta* or a fixed annual quit-rent equal to half the settlement assessment, provided that the *Ijaradar* during the period of the lease had brought 1/3rd of the land allotted to him under cultivation and he was also given the rights of *Patelgi* of the village if there were 40 houses or huts in it.[83] But, instances were there persons of influence got this allotment in spite of the non-fulfilment of the conditions stipulated.[84] A factor which significantly contributed towards concentration of land was the provision that the *Ijaradar*, on the expiry of the *Kowl*, was given land on *Bil-Maqta* double to the land that he got cultivated during the lease tenure[85]. In making for this arrangement, even the usual allotments of land that were to be made in respect of village *gairan*, pasture land and *Inam* for *Sethsindhi* were ignored or else made from Government *poramboke* or forest land, if the land in the village was just sufficient to meet the requirement of the *Ijaradar*.[86] As the system of leasing out land was found to cause unnecessary loss to Government and as the demand for land and consequently its value having considerably increased, it was felt that no special inducements were any longer necessary to attract people to the land and hence, it was abolished in 1318 *Fasli* (1909). A special officer, called the *Ijara* Settlement Officer was appointed in 1322 *Fasli* (1913) to go into each case on the spot and submit a report to Government for final decision.[86a] But the *Ijara* leases that were granted earlier which were, for the most part, subject to the fulfilment of lease conditions, converted into permanent *Bil-Maqtas*, were sufficient and numerous enough to continue as a separate tenure, having its own impact on the economic development of the region.

These *Ijaras* were there only in the Telangana part of the State, for the reason that it only consisted or vast number of deserted, waste and forest lands. Again, in this Region, 89 per cent of the *Ijaras* were granted in Warangal *Suba* itself. Out of the total number of 356 *Ijara* villages in the State, as many as 317 were there in the Eastern Division in the order of Adilabad 172 ; Warangal 96 and Karimnagar 49 and these formed the highest numbers respectively among all the Districts in the Sate.[87] As a matter of fact, the forest and deserted lands in the State were prevalent among the Districts in the same order. But, the revenue from these villages for 1320 *Fasli* (1912) was estimated to be only Rs. 22,000, Rs. 20,000 and Rs. 9,292 respectively for the *Suba* Districts.[88] Whereas the area occupied by leased and *Bil-Maqta* lands formed more than

50 per cent of the total area of the villages concerned, the assessment paid to the Government for both the categories amounted to only 40 per cent of the total assessment of those villages.[89] The concessions thus enjoyed by *Ijaradars* in land allotment, revenue-payment and the grant of *Watan* rights were so liberal and extensive that they had more or less acted as if they were the *Jagirdars* for all purposes.[90]

The *Ijaradars* who were usually absentee landlords came to regard the actual cultivators as only tenants-at-will, even though they had been on the land since it was first brought under cultivation and had, in fact, put in almost all the labour for reclaiming the land or populating the villages for which the *Ijaradars* received rich rewards from the Government.[91] Permission was not given even to old tenants to sell the right of tenancy.[92] Lands of the royts were forcibly taken away and given to others after taking *nazarana*.[93] Tax demands were increased as and when the *Ijaradars* liked and they very much exceeded the rates fixed by the Settlement.[94] In fact, they generally strived to get the implementation of the Settlement wherever done, rather delayed inordinately.[95] They often took as rent double the assessment, but, in practice, extra amount twice this accepted figure was collected from tenants without of course any receipts being given and hence no proof of it.[96] It was also found that *Ijaradars* were generally in the habit of unlawfully encroaching on lands of neighbouring villages with a view to take benefit from the valuable forests and also cultivable lands, thereby causing considerable loss to Government and needy ryots.[97] But, the *Ijaradars* instead of being evicted from such unjust encroachments, were, on the other hand, granted *patta* of huge lands at the concessional rate of two annas per rupee for 15 years and then full assessment.[98] This only helped in the further concentration of land power and forest wealth in the hands of these *Ijaradars*. It being a *Diwani* tenure, tenants in *Ijara* villages were provided with assured hopes to attain *Shikmidari* status and even purchase lands from their *pattedars* only when the Hyderabad Land Revenue Act was suitably amended in 1952.[99]

(g) *Agraharas* : *Agrahar* tenure like that of *Maqtas*, was also based on the arrangement that the assignee has to pay a fixed quit-rent permanently.[100] These were granted for the support of Hindu or Muslim places of worship. Most of these were made in favour of Brahmans who served as *pujaris* or performers of worship at Hindu temples[101] and only a few to Muslim performers of worship.[102] It can be seen from Table IX that 81 *Agrahar* villages were there in the *Suba*, out of which Warangal District contained as many as 61, whereas Adilabad District had only one. This is mainly due to the fact that the former, being the centre of the kingdom of medieval Hindu dynasties such as that of the Kakatiyas, naturally abounded in temples, whereas the latter did not possess such a background and hence places of worship.

Absentee landlordism had been there even in respect of *Agraharik*s. Shankaracharya of Pushpagiri *peetham*[103] was granted rights of *Agraharik* over Dharmavaram village in Sirsilla Taluq of Karimnagar District, who in turn, appointed one Mr. Sivakumara Pantulu, resident of Secunderabad, as his attorney or *Muqtar-e-am* to carry on the administration on his behalf. This *Muqtar-e-am* who also stayed far away from the said *Agrahar*, in turn, fixed one Mr. Raji Reddy, resident of Timmayapalli, a village in Medak District, again of a place away from the *Agrahar* and of a different District of a different *Suba*, to look after land-tax collection and other affairs of the village.[104] As no *bandobast* of the lands was done, the agent kept on the scene levied high rates and those ryots who refused to pay were evicted. If *talaf-mal* was done by *Diwani* administration, no exemptions were given by him. The *Agraharik* being independent in revenue administration, the cultivators could neither represent their sufferings to *Ryotwari* officials nor the *Agraharik* bothered at all about them, even when the ryots took all the trouble of going all the way to represent to him in person.[105]

Added to absenteeism, concentration of more than one *Agrahara* tenurial right in one person was also there. Shankarachary was given these rights over four villages in Sirsilla Taluq of Karimnagar District and Jamal Baig over 3 villages in Huzurabad Taluq also of the same District.[106] The latter besides being the *Agrahardar* of these 3 villages, was also *Maqtedar* of 7 villages in the same Taluq.[107] In the unsurveyed village of Polepalli in Khammam Taluq of Warangal District, the *Agraharik* was found collecting as high a rate as Rs. 100 for a piece of land from the ryots and evicted those who could not pay it.[108] Though on the spot official enquiries on representation from the local people led to recommendations for the conduct of Survey such as in the village cited above, its actual conduct and the necessary follow-up measures were not taken up with due promptitude and interest,[109] which, in turn, was very much due to the care that these assignees had taken to see that these operations were delayed as long as possible, so that they could have a free field for exploitation. Just like *Ijaradars*, the *Agrahardars* also indulged in illegal occupation of lands of neighbouring villages and sometimes in the same village over and above the extent that they were granted.[110] These included Government lands also.[111] Even when the lease-holder had confessed about the excess occupation of land, no action was taken.[112] The *Agrahardars* thus, though they were supposed to carry on the noble task of religious worship, proved in practice, that they were no less than other tenure-holders such as *Maqtedars*, *Ijaradars*, *Watandars* and *Banjardars* in exploiting the peasantry for their self-aggrandizement. Only forms varied but basic methods remained the same.

(*h*) *Sarf-i-Khas* : These crown lands which covered an area of one-tenth of the[113] dominions and spread over eighteen Taluqs,[114] did not form any sizeable portion in Warangal *Suba*. These included 20 villages in Karimnagar, 3 in Sultanabad[115] and 4 in Warangal Taluq and Adilabad District had none.[116] The area being very much hilly and forest-infested, it did not attract the *Nizam* to bring many villages under his personal occupation. These villages, though belonged to the Ruler, were kept under the administration of *Diwani* officials, who, of course, managed them on behalf of the *Serf-i-Khas* Department. Revenue from these villages, after deducting management charges, was credited to *Sarf-i-Khas* treasury.[117] The *Diwani* officials, though they were put in charge of the administration of these *Sarf-i-Khas* villages, never used their independent discretion in deciding cases relating to revenue matters for fear of incurring the displeasure of the Ruler and all such matters were simply forwarded to be decided by *Sarf-i-Khas* Chief Secretary.[118] Further, it also became the practice that on personal approach to the *Nizam*, persons of influence who were involved in offences of serious nature such as the illegal occupation of forest land, could get themselves not only absolved of the charges but even get rewarded by huge allotment of land.[119]

Revenue demand from the *Sarf-i-Khas* villages of Karimnagar District amounted to Rs. 2,89,482-3-0 and from those of Warangal Taluq to Rs. 55,730-10-0.[120] The amounts were not inconsiderable in view of the fact that dry lands formed 70 per cent of the total area.[121] To add to this, the taxes were collected in such a rigorous manner that even in the Depression years of 1933 and 1934, 100 per cent collections were recorded.[122] But, on the other hand, the *Sarf-i-Khas* administration was so stringy and regardless of the welfare of the agriculturists in its spending that when, due to scarcity of water, one-fourth remission of land revenue was granted in all *Diwani* lands for 1933 and when the same was recommended for *Sarf-i-Khas* areas by the First *Taluqdars* of Karimnagar and Warangal, it was flatly denied by the Secretary, *Sarf-i-Khas* and repeated representations in this regard were made even by *Subedar* of Warangal but to no effect.[123] Even in respect of maintaining sources of irrigation also on which the development of agriculture has fully depended, the amounts spent were so negligible or nil that during the fifteen year period between 1933 to 1948, whereas the total number of sources remained the same, the number of sources to be repaired or unserviceable ones, had increased considerably.[124] The miserliness of the *Sarf-i-Khas* administration failed to attract men of efficiency to serve it, on account of the d.pressingly low salaries offered. A clerk in *Diwani* area was paid Rs. 30/- per month, whereas he was paid only Rs. 15/- under *Sarf-i-Khas.*[125]

Details of the cultivators in these *Sarf-i-Khas* areas of the *Suba* for the fifteen year period of 1933-48 are given in Table XI. They go to show that the number of *Shikmidars* and *Hissedars*[126] or joint-holders during this period had nearly increased three times and six times respectively to that of *pattedars*. As a matter of fact, the number of *pattedars* in Sultanabad Taluq showed a decrease. In other words, whereas

TABLE XI

Details of Cultivators in Sarf-i-Khas Areas, 1933-1948

Sl. No.	Year	Name of the Taluq	No. of Villages	Details of Cultivators				Total
				Patt-dars	Shikmi-dars	Hisse-dars		
1	2	3	4	5	6	7	8	9
1.	1342 Fasli (1933)	Warangal	4	566	70	155	791	1357 Fasli (1948)
2.	–do–	Karimnagar	20	1,250	600	680	2,530	-do-
3.	–do–	Sultanabad	3	354	132	236	722	-do-
		Total	27	2,170	802	1,071	4,043	

Sl. No.	Year	Name of the Taluq	Year Details of Cultivators Patte-dars	Shikmi-dars	Hisse-dars	Total	Difference— Increase (+) or Decrease(−) Patte-dars	Shikmi-dars	Hisse-dars	Total
			10	11	12	13	14	15	16	17
1.	1342 Fasli (1933)	Warangal	598	253	1,146	1,997	+32	+183	+1,091	+1,206
2.	—do—	Karimnagar	1,572	1,056	1,146	3,774	+322	+456	+466	+1,244
3.	—do—	Sultanabad	340	530	382	1,252	−14	+398	+146	+530
		Total	2,510	1,839	2,674	7,023	+330	+1037	+1,703	+2,980

Source : Warangal Subedari *Files* No. 1 of 1342 Fasli (1933) and R. No. 486 of 1343 Fasli (1934) and No. 1 of 1357 Fasli (1948) and R. No. 25 of 1357 Fasli.

the percentage of increase in respect of *pattedars* of all the three Taluqs was only 15 per cent during this period, it was stupendously so high as 129 per cent and 159 per cent in the case of *Shikmidars* and *Hissedars* respectively. Comparatively, this increase was for less pronounced in *Diwani* area.[127] *Pattedars* giving up cultivation of the land by themselves was very much evident. Even in joint cultivation also, the tenants appeared to be more alive to its advantages than landholders.[128] Though, as seen above, only a fraction of the revenue was utilised in *Sarf-i-Khas* villages for the benefit of the cultivators,[129] yet they enjoyed the benefit of Survey and Settlement and the non-presence of the overlord of their villages on the spot.[130] Consequently, compared to alienated villages like *Jagirs*, these were relatively free from those exploitations which arose either due to the presence of the assignees on the spot or frequent visits to receive various kinds of payments in money, kind and labour.[131]

(*i*) *Samasthan or Peshkash* : *Samasthans* were former Hindu States which after losing their independence during medieval times to Muslim conquerors, continued their existence in modern period by paying annual tribute to the reigning Muslim sovereigns. In other words, they came to function as vassal territories. The annual tribute that used to be paid since the Mughal times by these *Samasthandars* had come to be called *peshkash* or *pan*, both terms being used synonymously.[132] Out of fourteen *Samasthans* in the State,[132a] Palvancha lying in the eastern part of Warangal District, was one. In area which consisted of 3,090 sq. miles, it remained the biggest of them all.[133] It was rural in its composition that it comprised 69 villages[134] and only 2 towns.[135] To its eastern border lay the East Godavari District and to its south Krishna District, both of Madras Presidency. River Godavari formed its natural boundary on the east and in the ridges and valleys of the Eastern Ghats inhabited predominantly the aboriginal tribes who went by the name of the Konda or Hill Reddis and the Koyas.[136] Out of a total population of 64,973 in the *Samasthan* as per the 1931 census, tribal population numbered as much as 26,251[137] or, in other words, formed 40 per cent.

Like *Pan-Maqtadars* and *Agraharikss*, the Raja[138] of Palvancha was put in an advantageous position that he enjoyed a huge revenue surplus over and above what was paid by means of *peshkash.* His annual income was Rs. 6,78,382[139] and as against this, he remitted only Rs. 45,875 towards *peshkash* into the Government treasury.[140] As long as this fixed amount was paid, he was left free to administer the area without interference from the Imperial Government.[141] Even more, the *Samasthan* had its own District and Taluq judicial courts.[142] The administration, however, did not remain free from making improper and illegal demands on ryots[143] and even on inferior tenure-holders like *Agraharikss*[144] and *Banjardars*[145] In some instances, it was so adamant to accept the decisions given by First *Taluqdar* and even *Subedar* of Warangal that the affected persons were compelled to approach the Prime Minister for getting the wrongs redressed.[146] But, more than this, the absenteeism of the Raja,[147] the long and frequent periods of takeover of the *Samasthan* administration by the Court of Wards for the settlement of disputes that arose over succession to the *gaddi*[148], and the administrative apathy and indifference exhibited by the *Samasthandars*[149] had contributed in a large measure for creating administrative vacuum and anarchy which were fully exploited by *Watandars,* big and immigrant merchants and forest officials in inflicting different types of excesses on the local population, and especially the tribal farmers and labourers.[150]

The *Patels* and *Patwaris* collected the revenue at their own discretion, very much out of proportion to the size of the fields and receipts were given for smaller sums than they actually collected.[151] Besides land revenue, they collected from the *Koyas,* fire-tax, house-tax and *Ippa* flower-tax,[152] even though these were not authorised by Raja.[153] The result of this crushing burden of taxation was that much cultivable land suitable for rain-fed rice had changed hands during the generation before 1945 from Hill Reddis and Koyas into the hands of *Patwaris* and merchants who, in turn, got them cultivated by employing these same tribals as daily labourers, or hired it out against 50 per cent of the crop.[154] Even as labourers engaged in the exploitation of rich timber from the *Samasthan* forests and its export to the British side, which was taken up as a thriving business by merchants from the East Godavari District of the Madras Presidency, the Hill Reddis were paid only a fraction of the rates that were prevalent in the British as well as the *Samasthan* areas which rather remained the same. To all intents and purposes, these were regarded by the merchants as their personal property and an article of trade.[155] So much so, that these tribals came to feel strongly that their lot as cultivators was much better under Raja's administration than that under the Court of Wards.[156] Their large scale emigration to British territory under the latter regime, during later thirties and forties, proved a pointer to this.[157] To combat the spread of discontentment and sense of frustration among the aboriginals in the area, a Tribal Reclamation Scheme had been prepared but the Tribal Areas Regulation and necessary rules to bring about the rehabilitation work were framed and brought into force only in 1950[158]. In the half yearly budget of 1950-51, Rs. 10,308 was provided for Koya Welfare Scheme in Paloncha Taluq and Rs. 60,356 for Tribal Reclamation Scheme covering all the areas, but the success and extension of these measures was very much hampered by the lack of communications and accessibility to the far and wide scattered hamlets of the aboriginals.[159]

(*j*) *Jagirs*[160] : Among non-*Khalsa* tenures, *Jagirs* occupied premier place both in respect of number as well as impact on the economic system. The word '*Jagir*' is a contraction from the persian *Jai*=place, and *ir*=holding or taking possession.[161] The Mughal system of making land grants to noblemen was introduced in eastern Deccan with necessary modifications occasioned by place and time, by Nizam-ul-Mulk, the first *Nizam* who distinguished himself in Mughal administrative and military service, before he became the ruler in 1724.[162] So greatly did he come to depend on the support of the Muslim and Hindu noblemen that he brought with him to the Deccan for his strength and stability that one-third of his territory was distributed among them, the Muslims being engaged for military service and the Hindus in administrative work.[163] Of these land grants, the most important from the view point of wide and sovereign rights enjoyed by the fief-holders, were the *paigah*[164] or *Jamiat Jagirs*, which were bestowed by the second *Nizam*, Nizam Ali (1761-1803) to provide for the maintenance of

Household Troops which was aimed to serve as a counter-balancing military force between himself and his troops.[165]

(*i*) *Paigah* : Yelgadap, Taluq, lying between the Taluqs of Nirmal and Luxettipet in Adilabad District, was the only *paigah* in the *Suba*. It was held by *Nawab* Sultan-ul-Mulk Bahadur and consisted of 65 villages.[166] Their total population in 1941 was only 23,452 and 48 villages had only a population of 7,410 which unmistakably pointed to the sparseness of the population.[167] The Taluq formed a compact unit but got tucked in between *Diwani* Taluqs. As the condition of military service was not in force long before the turn of this century, the keeping of troops became only symbolic and ceremonious, serving no worth-while purposes. Though freed from this obligation, the *paigah* noblemen had full control of revenue and judicial administration and ran their own Departments of education, health, public works, Survey and Settlement, etc. But, the efficiency of these was often absurdly low.[168] It had proved almost impossible for Government to secure effective co-operation from *paigah* Departments in public health administration, food control and similar matters.[169] Further, there was excessive interference of the *Nizam* not only in the administration and succession of these estates, but even in family matters such as marriages, disposal of personal property, etc., for he came to treat these families as mere branches of the Asaf Jahi family.[170] Thinking that these *Paigahs*[171] were not serving any useful purpose, the Reilly Commission had recommended as early as 1927 to disband their armies and recover the *Jagirs* from them.[172] But, the *Nizam* in his *Firman* issued on 23rd April, 1929, did not favour these recommendations, stating that the Rulers were served hereditarily by these noblemen.[173] The result was that most of these *paigahs* continued to be happy hunting grounds for interested noblemen[174] and the land rights and condition of the cultivators was none the better than in other assigned lands.

ii. Other Jagirs : These could be better classified as 'exempted' or 'non-exempted' ; 'conditional' or 'unconditional', and 'rent-free' or 'rent-paying'. *Al-tamgha*[175] *Jagirs* were revenue free grants[175a] made permanent and hereditary and *Zat Jagirs* were unconditional in the sense that large areas of land were granted for the maintenance of the grantees without any stipulation of service. *Mashrooti Jagirs* were, on the other hand, granted for the performance of some definite service, religious, civil or military and were continued only so long as the conditions of the grant were fulfilled. Religious grants made for the support of religious or charitable institutions, mainly dominated this category. *Madad Mash Jagirs* were granted as a gratuity, either as the sole means of maintenance for the donee, who might be the holder of *Mashrooti* grants, or as a supplement to his other means of livelihood. Opportunity was thus provided for an individual to receive two types of *Jagirs*, and thereby get strengthened enormously in land and revenue power. *Tankha Jagirs*, were, of course, granted when the State was in financial difficulties before 1853, in lieu of the payment of salaries to military and civil establishments.[176] But, these were resumed or redeemed with the assumption of power by Salar Jung I in 1853,[177] as he was able to put the finance of the State in sound state by his wise and beneficient reforms. A significant factor which contributed for the growth of the feudal system was that the grants of *Jagirs* which were originally meant for definite periods not extending beyond the lives of the grantees and were resumable with the office, became in course of time permanent and hereditary either because it was thought below the dignity of the Ruler to assume, or by mere usurpation made possible by the weakness of the Central Government before 1853.[178]

Exempted *Jagirdars* could otherwise be considered as big *Jagirdars*. 98 such *Jagirs* were there in the *Suba*, (Table IX) with concentration in the Taluqs of Sultanabad and Metpalli, the latter being a *Jagir* Taluq by itself. Raja Dharam Karan Bahadur with as many as 40 villages under his control[178a] in the former and *Nawab* Gazi Jung Bahadur with all the 27 villages in the latter under his control, ranked highest in feudal monopolistic power of his category.[179] Excepting some minor control over their judiciary and police by the *Diwani* administration, these big *Jagirdars* functioned as independent princes with having the administration of their territories completely at their disposal and this feature was so horrible that one shuddered at the very sight of it.[180] They maintained a complete system of private Government with their own courts of justice, police, revenue staff and also Survey and Settlement Departments.[181] Non-exempted *Jagirs* in the *Suba*, were almost double the number of the exempted ones (Table IX). Concentration of these *Jagirs* was there in the Taluqs of Palvancha, Mahboobabad, Warangal, Karimnagar and Kinwat. It is significant to note that nearly 50 per cent of them were to be found in Warangal District only and the other two Districts have accounted for nearly 25 per cent each. *Jagirdari* oppression and the intensity of the peasant struggle that followed it, naturally corroborated with this distribution pattern.[182] State[183] Manmanga Ramanajavaram with 22 villages, State Rajput with 18 villages, both in Palvancha Taluq, *Nawab* Shaokat Jung Bahadur with 20 villages in Mahaboobabad Taluq and Raja Shivraj Dharmvanth Bahadur[184] with all the 9 villages of this category in Jagtiyal Taluq, ranked highest in *Jagirdari* concentration of landed power of the non-exempted type.[185] These tenure-holders, majority of whom held one *Jagir* village and hence be considered as small *Jagirdars*, had full revenue jurisdiction but their judicial and police powers varied considerably according to their status and the income of their *Jagirs*.[186] They were, however, not free from Government control and majority of them remitted *Haq-e-malikana* or royalty which ranged from 2 to 5 per cent in normal cases to 25 per cent in exceptional cases.[187]

In accordance with revenue laws, the proprietory rights over all *Jagir* lands vested with the Government and the *Jagirdars* were entitled only to revenues upon these lands and never to the rents from them. As the value of lands rose, the *Jagirdars* started claiming rents as well as *pattedari* rights on these lands.[188] Many of them began to treat their hereditary cultivators as if they were tenants-at-will.[189] This led to the enhancement of rent or assessment even in respect of old cultivators.[190] These absentee landlords collected 25 to 50 per cent more revenue than the *Khalsa* villages[191] and freely evicted even cultivators of long standing if they failed to pay these abnormal assessments.[192] To add to the burden, majority of the *Jagirdars* never granted their ryots remission and suspension of land revenue on the scale it was sanctioned by Government to the ryots in *Diwani* areas.[193] Due to this denial, the impact of the usually heavy assessment was felt with crushing weight by the cultivators whenever there was crop failure due to natural and unforeseen calamities which sometimes happened in seven years out of ten.[191] Even in Surveyed villages, *nazarana* in the shape of one or two years' assessment was extracted by *Jagirdars* before according *pattedari* rights even to old cultivators, to permit them to sell or mortgage their lands and also to recognise heirs.[195] These evils of high assessments, rack-renting, easy evictions and *nazars* were resorted to by *Jagirdars* in a more candid and pronounced manner in unsurveyed villages which formed 20 per cent of the total non-*Diwani* villages in the State in 1949.[196] The main reason for a large number of *Jagirs* to remain unsurveyed and unsettled was the absence of any legal provision for compulsory Settlement of these villages[197] and the *Jagirdars* had, on their part, always longed its non-conduct or at least postponement, in order that they could have a free field for exploitation.[198]

Besides the collection of land revenue assessments or rents whose burden itself was more than what the peasants with their meagre incomes could bear, the *Jagir* holders levied a motley of irregular cesses. The nature and the number of these extra payments differed from one *Jagir* to another, but in to these numbered as many as 35.[199] '*Shadi-patti*'[200] (Marriage cess), '*Gharpatti*' (House-tax), '*Mohtarfa*' (Tax on handlooms), 'grazing tax' and fine at a rate Rs. 12 to 50 for every cattle trespassing into *Jagirdar's* fields, collection of one anna per rupee extra on Local Fund, collection at a rate of 100 maize *Kankulu*[201] from every ryot for the food of *Jagirdar's* horses irrespective of the fact whether they were maintained by him or not, *mamul* at a rate one ram from each herd of sheep or goats per year and even tax for cremating dead bodies at a rate Rs. 0-6-6, etc., were among these sundry duties.[202] This long list makes the point clear that these tenure-holders in order to satisfy the too many demands of their city or town life filled with luxury and vaingloriousness[203], laid their huge tax net not only around the necks of the ryots but also all other sections of the rural population such as weavers, shepherds, etc. The ryots were made to shut their mouths and undergo hardships caused by these hated cesses, on account of *Gashti* No. 53.[203a] More than the collection of these illegal cesses, the one which earned utmost odium to *Jagirdars* and caused untold suffering to the populace was the extraction of *Vetti* or forced labour from different sections of the local population. Occupants, tenants, labourers, weavers, shepherds, washermen, etc., each being made to serve the needs of the *Jagirdar* in the sphere relating to his profession,[204] as and when demanded even relegating personal necessities to the background, failing which the defaulters were subjected to physical torture and deprivation of basic necessities of life like taking of water from village wells and provisions from shops.[205] Its prohibition by a *Firman* of the *Nizam* as early as 19,[206] made no impression on these hard-headed feudal lords. Compared to these vexatious exactions, the contributions made by the *Jagir* administration towards the development of agriculture, irrigation, education, health and water supply was dismal.[207] There did not seem to be a single *Jagir* which spent at least one rupee out of hundred rupees on education. 75 per cent of the villages did not seem to be having even primary schools.[208] Their huge incomes which in respect of some exceeded one lakh rupees per year[209] were rather spent unproductively far away from the concerned *Jagirs*, in leading a life of extravagance, pomp and ceremony, generally exceeding the limits of their purse and consequently throwing the *Jagirs* into deep indebtedness.[210] It is no wonder then, that popular opinion or the masses at large clamoured for the removal of these intermediaries and directed their vehement attack against then during the crisis period of 1946-48.

(*k*) *Inams* : '*Inam*' is an Arabic word which means favour or reward. An *Inam* holding was thus a grant of land in which the State had given up its right to the land revenue, or a portion of it, in favour of an individual or an institution, in return for the performance of certain duties or as a charitable endowment without the obligation of service, or as a reward to favourites.[211] These grants were usually hereditary and permanent and varied from small isolated fields to whole villages or several villages.[212] Besides the *Inams* which were usually granted for the staff associated with religious institutions,[213] the one which had been coming by way of convention or practice, were the *balota Inams*,[214] otherwise also known as *chowtai Inams*.[215] Probably, in view of the greater amount of service taken from *Dheds* by the village officers as well as the officers on tour and also their general non-possession of private land and poor economic condition, they were given preference, compared to other *balotadars*, both in respect of the extent of *Inam* land granted and also the percentage of land revenue remission enjoyed.[216] *Inam* tenures were granted in such a liberal manner that even public women were also bestowed with them.[217]

During the days of administrative confusion and disorder that prevailed before Salar Jung I, the grant of these lands had been greatly abused and the impoverished condition of the treasury prompted the Ministers to issue these grants as a means to meet the claims on it. But, they were often fraudulent and their number got so much multiplied that they threatened to eat up a large portion of the revenue of the State.[218] In order to set right this mal-administration, a Commission, known as the *Inam* Commission, was established in 1865 A.D. which carried on its work till 1912 when it was abolished in view of the major part of the work being over and the Revenue Department took up the completion of the remaining work.[219] As a result of this enquiry, *Inams* that were proved to be valid were granted fresh title deeds and others where sufficient evidence or continuity of possession were not forthcoming, were either resumed or charged with a portion of the full revenue at the direction of the Government.[220] Though it was stated that the total number of *Inamdars* in the State was 83,000 of which 57,000 were in *Diwani* and 26,000 in *Jagirs*,[221] area-wise figures are not available. Consequently, *Inam* Land area particulars to the extent available, are given in Tables XII and XIII which provide a gleaning about the distribution pattern of these tenures in the *Suba* area. Adilabad District had the largest area under these grants, mainly on account of vast uncultivated but cultivable lands that were available in it. These lands were more than the combined area of the other two Districts.[222] Warangal District which stood next to Adilabad District in respect of the extent of the uncultivated land available (*f.n. No. 222*), naturally occupied the same place in respect of *Inam* land area (Table XIII). Karimnagar District stood at the end in both the respects.

TABLE XII

Area of Inam Lands of Warangal District for the year 1320 Fasli (1911)

Sl. No.	Name of the Taluk	Area in Acres—Guntas
1	2	3
1.	Pakhal	759-01
2.	Mulug	338-02
3.	Khammam	18,899-20
4.	Mahboobabad	6,104-25
5.	Yellandu	2,762-17
6.	Warangal	6.897-22
7.	Madhira	8,057-11
	Total	43,818-18

Source : Office of the First Taluqdar, Warangal, *File* No. 35 of 1320 Fasli (1911) & R. No. 2312 of 1321 Fasli (1912).

TABLE XIII

Cultivated Area and Inam Area of Warangal Suba for the year 1356 Fasli (1947)

Sl. No.	Name of the District	Cultivated area occupied by ryots A — G	Inam area A — G
1	2	3	4
1.	Warangal	17,72,455-33	47,816-00
2.	Karimnagar	14,69,235-00	43,306-29
3.	Adilabad	15,24,964-29	72,040-39
	Suba Total :	47,66,655-22	1,63,163-28

Source : Jamabandi Report in Warangal Subedari *File* No. 36 of 1356 Fasli (1947) and R. No. 2469 of 1357 Fasli (1948)

Taluq-wari details of *Inam* land area in respect of Warangal District, furnished in Table XII[223] show that Khammam had the largest area forming 43 per cent of the total area, followed by Madhira, Warangal and Mahboobabad. Taluq-wise statistics of uncultivated land are not available but the line up indicated in the Table reveals the fact that *Inam* land areas were in high proportion in those Taluqs of the District where *Deshmukhs* and *Deshpandyas* were also in good number [See Table X(a)]. This had naturally resulted in intensification of pressure on the peasantry. *Inamdars* of minor holding and *Dhed balota Inamdars* were not allowed to enjoy water supply to their lands[224] and occupancy rights over them,[225] on account of the exercise of domination by *Deshmukhs*, *Patels* and *Patwaris*. Representation at the *Taluqdari* and *Subedari* level in this regard did not result in much change in this situation as the *Watandars* enjoyed considerable influence with higher Revenue Officials. Further, some of the *Inamdars* themselves like temple priests[226] and *Sethsindhis*,[227] showed little interest in cultivating the lands allotted. Even after grant periods running over decades, the lands remained uncultivated, the reasons being that they primarily remained non-agriculturists, not cultivating the land by themselves, and the lands, on the other hand, fetched poor rents or no rents at all, as they remained undeveloped. At the same time, *Inamdars* with necessary potential and interest in land development were permitted by Circular No. 4 of 1298 *Fasli* (1889) to bring excess lands under their occupation over and above the extent prescribed in the *sanad*, without any extra tax being levied, as long as they were within the broad demarcated limits.[228] This provision contributed towards concentration of land in the hands of big *Inamdars*. Though the *Inamdars* thus enjoyed concessions in land occupation and revenue payment yet, as they did not enjoy the right of revenue collection like *Jagirdars*, *Maqtedars*, *Ijaradars*, etc., much was not heard in the records of any excess perpetrated by them in the matter of enjoyment of land rights by *pattedars* and tenants. It was for the same reason that these lands did not come under the purview of the *Jagir* (Abolition) Regulation.[229] Yet, vesting of vast lands, even extending to several villages, with a marginal or no revenue payment, had by itself, led to land monopolization with necessary attendant evils.

B. Land Revenue Administration

Besides land tenures which formed the life layer of revenue administration, other aspects which had an important bearing on it and also very much on the condition of the ryots, were Survey and Settlement, assessments and their incidence, rents and remissions. The success and failure of land revenue system and to a greater extent, the prosperity of agriculture depended on how these items were administered. Hence, a close and an in-depth examination of them would enliven the study of economic history of this region as well as of the State.

(*a*) *Survey and Settlement* : For fixation of assessment on each individual holding, land survey and settlement became the first pre-requisite. The abolition of tax-farming[230] by Salar Jung I was accompanied by the establishment of a Survey and Settlement Department in 1875. The entire Dominions were divided into four circles, Warangal, being one of them, each under a Superintendent and after the initial survey of all the *Diwani* districts was over, only two circles, Marathwada and Telangana, were retained under two Superintendents with headquarters at Hyderabad and Warangal respectively.[231] The chief functions of the Department had been to carry out the surveys of *Khalsa* and Non-*Khalsa* villages and attend to the Revisions at the termination of the sanctioned periods of Settlement.[232] As conditions in Hyderabad resembled those of Bombay, the Bombay system which was already worked successfully for 30 years was adopted.[233] In the case of *regar*[234] soils, the relative value was determined according to their depth and in the case of *chalka*[235] soil and wet garden lands according to the relative proportions of clay and sand in them. In the case of wet and garden lands, in addition to the soil value of the land, the water class of source of irrigation was fixed with the help of an *annawari*[236] table and this was taken into account in fixing the assessment of wet lands.[237]

As there were considerable wet lands in the *Suba* area as well as in Telangana producing rice, the system adopted for assessment was different from that of the Bombay system, which was fully introduced in Marathwada.[238] In Bombay, the assessment on rice lands was fixed at a low rate, but collected whether the crop was raised or not, while in Telangana the practice adopted by the Government was to take a high assessment when a wet crop was raised and to give remissions in whole or part, when there was no crop, or it had partially failed due to natural or unforeseen conditions. In other words, the main principle was that the assessment fluctuated according to the state and the nature of the crop.[239] But, the conditions of the ryots in Telangana were such that even if the Government were to reduce the rates on rice crop, it was found that the cultivators would get all the advantages of the rules in years of good crop, while in bad years they would even be unable to pay their rents.[240] In Hyderabad, every valuable acre was included in the *ayacut*[241] of a source and consolidated wet rates were charged.[242] This provision gave scope for the corruption of village officials at the expense of the ryots, for they included even land not actually irrigated under the category of wet land.[243] This troublesome clause was removed only in September, 1949 when the Revenue Department had issued orders stating that only land under cultivation from waters of the *ayacut* at least for four years in the last ten years would be classed as wet land for assessment.[244] The maximum rates proposed by the Settlement Department were submitted to the Government for sanction and after they had been sanctioned, assessments for individual fields were calculated according to the classification values[245] and they were then announced to the cultivators.[246]

The progress of Survey and Settlement in the *Suba* Districts was very much slow and unsatisfactory which, in turn, had seriously impaired the growth of agriculture by subjecting the ryots to high and long-drawn assessments. The introduction of First Settlement itself extended from 1895 in Warangal Taluq to 1937 in Asifabad and Sirpur Taluqs.[247] Mulug Taluq, even until 1952, remained without this.[248] When such was the neglect of a Taluq in which 193 out of 195 villages were under *Ryotwari* or *Diwani* administration directly,[249] the situation in respect of villages under *Jagirdars* on whom there was no legal compulsion to undertake this work right until 1946,[250] was definitely worse.[251] In Karimnagar District also, four villages remained yet to be surveyed as on 20-9-1950.[252] Though originally the period of Settlement was stated to be for 30 years, it was reduced to 15 years when the operations were extended to Telangana.[253] After the expiry of the original Settlement, a Revision Settlement was to be made and though re-survey and re-classification were provided for by the rules, in practice, they were not undertaken.[254] But, rates were revised which, on all occasions, except during the Depression,[255] resulted in increased assessment. The percentage of net increase in dry rates ranged from 14 to 14½ and in the case of wet rates from 12½ to 16⅔ in the Revisions carried in the year 1917 (Nirmal Taluq) and 1926 (Yellandu and Karimnagar Taluqs).[255a] To cite an instance for knowing its magnitude, revised rates announced for 442 villages belonging to the Warangal, Khammam and Parkal Taluqs led to an increased assessment of Rs. 4,07,435.[256] Further, Original Settlement of First Setllement periods of some of the *Tahsils* expired long back and were not accompanied since then, by Revision Settlements. First Settlements of both Pakhal and Palvancha Taluqs which ended in 1918 remained even until 1952, unaccompanied by either Second or Revision Settlements.[257] This affected those cultivators who brought new lands under cultivation after the introduction of the First Settlement, for they had to pay high rates of assessment under *Siva-i-Jamabandi*[258] and also those assessed wet cultivators whose lands got periodically subject to water scarcity as they had to run for remissions every time which involved considerable hardship to small and illiterate peasants,[259] etc.

Frequent complaints were heard of mistakes and lapses, sometimes deliberate with pecuniary motive, committed by Settlement and Survey staff in fixing village boundaries,[260] demarcating *Poramboke*[261] and *gairan* land[262] and Revision of Settlement. It was observed by First *Taluqdar* of Adilabad in a case that more often, the land of poor ryots was included in *Poramboke* and *gairan* by the Settlement people and it became a troublesome job for the peasants to get this corrected, for they were ignorant of the rules that were in operation in this regard.[263] Regarding the lapses in Revision Settlement, it so happened that when the Revision Settlement of Sirsilla Taluq was announced in 1936, the mistakes were so wide-ranging that as many as four to five hundred people gave their petitions to *Tahsildar* for their correction. Writing of one crop land as of two crops, declaring dry land as wet, joining plots that were being cultivated into *bancherai*[264] and giving it on *Patta*, fixing of wet rate for those lands where the agriculturist at his own expense dug a new well and took the water by *mote*, etc., were some of them.[265] Out of such a large number of petitioners, only those who went to Settlement Department headquarters got their requests accepted and the rest did not receive consideration even after two years had passed.[266]

Land Record Offices with District Officers as heads were started in 1918 in Warangal and Karimnagar, for the purpose of maintaining *Ryotwari* records in an up-to-date condition and attending to the change brought on the field from time to time.[267] These became part of the Settlement Department along with the Record of Rights Section which was introduced in 1936 to compile registers showing particulars of rights over the lands, in order to prevent litigation and simplify land transactions.[268] The Record of Rights Act which was promulgated in 1936 failed to serve the purpose of protecting the rights of actual holders of land for which it was intended, because it continued to recognise only *pattedars*.[269] The actual holders had been ignored in favour of the old *pattedars*. Consequently, a new Record of Rights Act had been enacted in 1949, giving a fair deal to the tillers of the soil and paving the way for the disappearance of nominal *pattedars* by recognising the actual holders of the land.[270]

b. Land Revenue Assessments and Their Incidence : Land Revenue assessments formed the main source of income to the *Suba* administration. *Ryotwari* income to the Division increased from Rs. 47,23,000[271] in 1911 to Rs. 83,34,000[272] in 1948, which amounted to 76 per cent growth in a span of 37 years. Prior to Salar Jung I, land Revenue assessments used to be received in kind, the system being known as '*battai*.'[273] On 'dry crops', the State received about one-fourth of the produce, and on 'wet' lands irrigated from tanks and wells, it received half and two-fifths respectively of the produce.[274] This *battai* not only proved heavy but the sufferings of the ryots were intensified under tax-farmers who did not allow the standing crops to be removed until the demand was met and further, the loss caused to Government demand by desertion of the lands by some ryots was made good from those who remained cultivating.[275] In order to give relief to farmers from these vexatious demands, *battai* was replaced by cash payment, along with the removal of tax-farming by the great benefactor of modern Hyderabad, Salar Jung I.[276] *Pattedar* in the case of *Khalsa* land and superior holder in the case of non-*Khalsa* land, were made primarily responsible for the payment of land revenue.[277] It was collected in four *kists* or instalments, the first in the month of November, the second in January, the third in April and fourth in June.[278] At the time of every instalment, review would be made at the District and the Division level and instructions would be issued for strict supervision and better collection.[279] The percentage of tax-collected to the total demand was extremely good going as high as 99.13.[280] The Administration was usually so eager about maintaining this, that when in Telangana Districts 1914-15 it fell to 95.46 from 96.11 of the previous year, the Telangana officers were warned that trouble would await them if the same thing continued.[281]

On the other hand, little interest was shown by revenue officers, including First *Taluqdars*[282] and Second *Taluqdars* in the collection of tax arrears and even threats were issued to the latter as well as Tahsildars that their increments would be stopped if improvement was not made in this respect.[283] These tax arrears which stood at Rs. 7,55,472-10-10 in 1910,[284] got accumulated to Rs. 21,53,513-7-4[285] at the end of 1946, in spite of the fact that an amount of Rs. 7,18,137-8-7, being the accumulated arrears of the *Suba* upto 1933, was granted as remission in 1938 to commemorate the Silver Jubilee of the accession to power of the VII *Nizam*.[286] The percentage of collection recorded in this respect was as low as 7.88 in 1944-45[287] in respect of the *Suba* as a whole and it even touched 0.02 in the case of Parkal Taluq for the year 1946-47.[288] It is significant to note that a huge portion of these arrears was due from those Taluqs which, comparatively, were better off economically such as Madhira, Warangal, Mahboobabad, Yellendu,

Khammam, Karimnagar, Jagtiyal, Huzurabad, Parkal, Nirmal, Adilabad, Chinnoor and Rajura[289] the reason being that rich landlords who were also tenure-holders,[290] indulged in delaying tactics of filing appeal cases regarding the payment of their huge arrears[291] and ultimately succeeded in getting them written off.[292] *Jagirdars* showed utmost indifference and non-co-operation in this respect. Out of twelve *Jagirdars* who figured in tax collections in Warangal District for the month of *Ardibehist* 1355 *Fasli* (March, 1946), only one *Jagirdar* had made full collection, three partial and the rest nothing, the most significant point to note in it was that *Nawab* Showkat Jung Bahadur, a *Jagirdar* of twenty villages in Mahaboobabad Taluq[293] failed to pay a tax demand of Rs. 2,173.[294] In contrast to this lenient and complacent attitude adopted by the Revenue administration towards the collection of tax arrears from wealthy landlords and tenure-holders, illegal and unjust collections in the name of these arrears were made by *Patwaris* in collaboration with Taluq officials forcing the ryots to sell their property including cattle, in spite of the fact that they had already paid their land revenue dues and receipts were produced to that effect.[295] A case of privileged and the unprivileged, reminiscent of the pre-Revolutionary days of France of 1789, was clearly manifest in this situation. In other words, history repeated itself.

It could be seen from Table XIV that the rates of assessment, both dry and wet during thirty-three year period of 1912-1945, were on the increase in both the regions of Telangana and Marathwada, excepting the slight decrease in dry rate of Telangana in 1945. The same increasing trend, though gradual, was there during the remaining period upto 1950.[296] Whereas assessment on dry lands was higher in the case of Marathwada, it was so in respect of wet lands in Telangana Districts, which was mainly based on the predominance of respective soils in the regions.[297] Table XV reveals the interesting fact that the *Subu* maximum averages both in respect of dry and wet lands were far higher than those given in respect of the two regions and the State for 1934 in Table XIV. This variation was mainly because of the different soil classifications and the predominant wet cultivation in

TABLE XIV

Rates of assessment (1912-1945) in Marathwada and Telangana (in Diwani Area)

Sl. No.	Name of the Division	Average Rates of assessment: Before 1912		1912-1922		1934		1945	
		Dry	Wet	Dry	Wet	Dry	Wet	Dry	Wet
		Rs. As. Ps.	Rs. As. Ps.	Rs. As. Ps.	Rs. As. Ps.	Rs. As. Ps.	Rs. As. Ps.	Rs. As. Ps.	Rs. As. Ps.
1.	Marathwada	0- 13- 10	5- 0- 9	1- 0- 1	5- 8- 4	1- 1- 11	5- 15- 5	1- 2- 2	9- 12- 3
2.	Telangana	0- 11- 11	11- 1- 3	0- 12- 5	11- 6- 7	0- 15- 6	12- 3- 6	0- 14- 2	12- 5- 3
3.	State Average	0- 12- 10	8- 1- 0	0- 14- 3	8- 7- 5	1- 0- 8	9- 1- 6	1- 0- 7	11- 2- 0

Compiled from : *Decennial Report on Administration 1912-22*, p. 90.
and
Agricultural Statistics, H.E.H. the Nizam's Dominions, *1936-40* and *1941-45* (Maps).

TABLE XV

Maximum and Minimum Rates of Assessment in Warangal Suba (1931-36)
and
Incidence of Land Revenue (1922-31 to 1944-45)

(*In Rupees, Annas & Paise*)

Sl. No.	Name of the District	Rates of Assessment in 1931-36 Highest Dry	Highest Wet & Baghat*	Lowest Dry	Lowest Wet & Baghat	Average Dry	Average Wet & Baghat
1	2	3	4	5	6	7	8
1.	Warangal	2-4-0 to 2-14-0 (Khammam)	8-0-0- to 14-0-0 (Yellandu)	1-4-0 to 2-0-0 (Mulug & Paloncha)	6-0-0 to 12-0-0 (Mulug & Paloncha)	1-4-0 to 2-14-0	6-0-0 to 18-0-0
2.	Karimnagar	2-0-0 to 3-0-0 (Jagtiyal, Karim-nagar, Sirsilla & Huzurabad	8-0-0 to 20-0-0 (Sirsilla)	1-2-0 to 1-10-0 (Mahadeo-pur	6-0-0 to 12-0-0 (Sultanabad)	1-2-0 to 3-1-0	5-0-0 to 20-0-0

3. Adilabad*	1-4-0 to 2-0-0 (Chinnur & Nirmal)	8-0-0 to 16-0-0 (Nirmal)	0-8-0 to 1-8-0 (Boath)	5-0-0 to 9-0-0 (Rajura)	0-8-0 to 2-0-0	5-0-0 to 16-0-0
4. Suba average	1-13-0 to 2-15-0	8-0-0 to 16-10-0	0-15-0 to 1-11-0	5-10-0 to 11-0-0	0-15-0 to 2-15-0	5-5-0 to 18-0-0

	Incidence of Land Revenue on fully assessed area per acre						Land revenue assessed per head of population of fully assessed area		
	1922-31		1939-40		1944-45		1922-31	1939-40	1944-45
	For Total area	For cultivated area	For Total area	For cultivated area	For Total area	For cultivated area			
	9	10	11	12	13	14	15	16	17
1. Warangal	1-4-2	1-8-3	1-2-10	1-4-9	0-14-11	1-0-5	...	2-8-10	2-2-8
2. Karimnagar	1-10-7	1-14-0	1-5-1	1-6-2	0-14-0	1-14-10	...	2-9-9	2-4-5

3. Adila-bad	0-10-11	0-13-6	0-13-0	0-14-6	1-0-8	0-15-9	...	1-15-6	1-12-8
4. Suba average	1-3-2	1-6-7	1-1 7	1-3-1	0-15-2	1-8-0	...	2-6-0	2-1-3

*Means garden lands.

**Settlement Rates were not yet announced for Asifabad, Sirpur and Utnoor Taluqs.

***Not given.

Compiled from : *Hyderabad District Gazetteers, 1931, & 1936, Warangal* (pp. 66-67) *Karimnagar* (pp. 66-67) & *Adilabad* (pp. 66-67)

and

Agricultural Statistics, 1922-31 (pp. 296-297), *1936-40* (pp. 200-201); *1941-45* (pp. 364-365).

Warangal and Karimnagar Districts. This could be verified by the fact that the averages of Adilabad District, both highest, lowest and also the mean, in respect of dry and wet lands, were far below than those of the other two *Suba* Districts, mainly because of the low grade soils and meagre wet cultivation that obtained there. But, all the same, the tax burden on the people of *Suba*, especially wet cultivators was far heavy. This can be gauged from the fact that in the neighbouring State of Madras, the average wet assessment per acre was only Rs. 7-1-6,[298] compared to Rs. 18 to Rs. 20 in Warangal Division. In other States, there was the practice which gave much relief to cultivators that wet rate was collected only when the lands were actually irrigated and on other occasions, only dry rate was collected.[299] The absence of this welcome feature in the area had only heightened the tax burden, for there were frequent occasions when the ryots could not carry on wet cultivation, such as failure of timely rains, non-repair of irrigation sources, non-availability of agricultural inputs, etc.[300] Another disability which affected wet cultivators was the rule that wells which were constructed before 1908 and were outside the *ayacut*, had been classed as Government wells, and a consolidated wet assessment was levied on lands under these wells, whereas lands under wells constructed after 1908[301] had been assessed at dry rate.[302] Even though a remission of 0-10-8 for a Rupee of land revenue was given for these lands since 1931,[303] it did not very much lessen the burden of these cultivators who consequently neglected the repair of such wells, once they went out of order.[304] This anamoly was corrected only in the year 1949, bringing much relief to these vexed cultivators.[305]

The figures of incidence of land revenue on fully assessed area per acre and population as given in Table XV are not much illustrative of the impact of assessments since they are only quantitative but not qualitative, in the sense that they do not give any inkling of the differing effects of these on different segments of agricultural and rural community. Though the increase in the assessments was not sudden and drastic, its non-elasticity compared to periodical and violent changes in the prices of agricultural commodities and other basic necessaries required by agriculturists, made all the difference to the different categories of cultivating population and others. Low prices during Depression and rising prices during the wars had both worst hit the small peasants and the landless labourers, the former by bringing far too low prices for agricultural commodities and the latter offsetting the rise in the prices of agricultural commodities by the rise in the wages of labour, cost of cattle, manure etc., so much so that they were hard put for the payment of land revenue and at least some of them sold their land at below the market price for the purpose.[306] On the other hand, the big land holders and agriculturist-cum-traders who formed not more than twenty per cent total agricultural population, with their huge surplus in agricultural production and bullock-capacity, had no depressing effect of low prices and their effects were more than neutralised by the huge profits enjoyed on account of war time rise in prices.[307] As a result, the rise in assessment had only insignificant effect on them.[308] In view of this strong influence of price cycle on agricultural economy, the system of assessment fixed by Government was regarded as irrational and unscientific and it was felt that a scientific basis should be imparted to the assessment by correlating it to the price of the agricultural produce.[309]

Land Revenues was highest as a percentage of net income as could be seen from Table XVI, in respect of 'C' grade lands. Warangal and Adilabad in respect of jawar, Karimnagar in respect of paddy and Adilabad in the case of cotton, marked the highest percentages in this category. As a matter of fact these Districts led in the out-turn of these crops noted against them. According to S.M. Bharucha, Additional Revenue Secretary, who conducted an enquiry into agricultural indebtedness in 1936-37, the land revenue on an average farm of 16 acres worked at 9.4 per cent.[310] As the grade of land had slided down, the percentage had increased. With the increased cost of production and the prices of the commodities that were witnessed with the advent of the Second War, demand was made by the people and the press that land revenue should also be proportionately reduced, so that the land revenue should be taken out of the production surplus alone and not

TABLE XVI

Land Revenue as a Percentage of Net Income

(before payment of land revenue)

Sl. No.	District	Crop	A Grade		B Grade		C Grade	
			Maximum Percentage	Minimum Percentage	Maximum Percentage	Minimum Percentage	Maximum Percentage	Minimum Percentage
1	2	3	4	5	6	7	8	9
1.	Adilabad	Jawar	4.6	1.0	12.0	1.0	33.3	1.6
2.	Karimnagar	-do-	5.7	2.2	6.6	2.6	16.6	2.7
3.	Warangal	-do-	8.0	2.3	12.9	3.3	44.4	5.3
4.	Adilabad	Paddy (Single crop)	5.3	3.2	9.4	4.0	28.6	5.6
2.	Karimnagar	-do-	5.9	2.7	11.4	1.2	54.5	11.4
1.	Warangal	Groundnut	2.2	0.8	3.6	0.7	28.6	0.8
1.	Adilabad	Cotton	6.3	1.5	8.3	2.2	42.9	9.1

Source : S. Kesava Iyengar, *Rural Economic Enquiries, 1949-51*, pp. 293-296.

out of the gross income of the cultivator.[311] As the incidence of assessment was heavier on dry as well as wet lands than in British India,[312] it was observed by no less a person than Mr. O. Connor, Director-General of Statistics that a reduction of land revenue by 25 to 30 per cent would very much help in the improvement of the Peasantry.[313] But, no such benefit was extended until the close of the period which only kept the farmers in a mood of resentment biding their time.

c. Rents : With the increase in the value of land and competition for land among the landless that were witnessed in the first decade of the present century,[314] landlords with big holdings found it rather profitable to give land on rent rather than cultivate themselves. In the northern and central parts of Warangal District, the entire cultivation work was done by tenants and *bhagelas*[315]. With risks of cultivation involved in owner-framing being now shifted to *Kowldars*, and with opportunities to extract maximum rents, tenancy, in fact, became a lucrative business for many a landlord than owner-framing.[316]

Table XVII shows that not only highest number of *Kowls* were given in Warangal District, but its number almost equalled that of the other two Districts combined. Adilabad and Karimnagar came next in the order. Among the different modes of lease payment, cash rents were extensively used. These cash rents were, in turn, mostly in vogue in respect of dry lands. They covered more than 60 per cent of these leased lands, whereas the State percentage in this respect was only 40. In this system, the entire risk involved in reaping good crop or not, was borne by the tenant and the landlord was assured of his fixed rent by only paying land revenue. Table XVIII indicates that cash rents in the surveyed villages compared to average rents of the Districts, got multiplied two to three times in respect of dry lands and also wet lands. Adilabad and then Warangal led in this respect and Karimnagar remained far behind. The dearness of these cash rents could be gauged from the fact that district average rents over which they recorded much increase were themselves two to three times higher than the assessment rates.[317] In other words, lease-holders under these cash rents paid four to six times of the assessment rates.

TABLE XVII

Rents—Modes of Payment

Sl. No.	District	No. of Contracts	½ share in produce			Specific Rents in cash		
			Dry A. G.	Wet A. G.	Garden A.G.	No. of Contracts	Dry A.G.	Wet. A.G.
1	2	3	4	5	6	7	8	9
1.	Adilabad	203	923-11 (19.8)	127-8 (26.1)	—	369	3,261-20 (70.2)	110-11 (22.7)
2.	Karimnagar	93	111-32 (11.5)	140-5 (47.0)	0-17 (17.5)	235	638-8 (65.6)	127-9 (41.7)
3.	Warangal	446	920-22 (25.5)	744-0 (63.9)	0-19 (24.7)	618	2,402-3 (66.6)	341-27 (29.3)
	All Districts (State)	4,595	41,935-24 (51.2)	2,407-33 (42.8)	543-33 (58.5)	3,619	33,334-4 (40.7)	1,773-31 (31.5)

	Garden A.G.	Specific Rents in Kind				Other Cases			
		No. of Contracts.	Dry A.G.	Wet A.G.	Garden A.G.	Total No. of Contracts	Dry A.G.	Wet A.G.	Garden A.G.
	10	11	12	13	14	15	16	17	18
1. Adilabad	16-4 (100.0)	116 (2.7)	124-22 (49.9)	243-3	—	47	338-29 (7.3)	6-15 (1.3)	—
2. Karimnagar	—	—	—	—	—	10	223-18 (22·9)	30-22 (10.3)	2-0 (82.5)
3. Warangal	13-27 (75.3)	71 (7.3)	263-12 (6.4)	73-38	—	5	19-25 (0.6)	5-12 (0.5)	—
All Districts (State)	345-27 (37.2)	543 (2.2)	1,768-13 (17.8)	1,002-5 (0.9)	8-12	567	4,867-33 (5.9)	443-31 (7.9)	31-12 (3.4)

Note :—Figures in brackets denote the percentage to the total land leased dry, wet or garden, as the case may be.
A=Acres. G=Guntas

Compiled from :—S. Kesava Iyengar, *Rural Economic Enquiries, 1949-51*, pp. 59-60.

It was on account of these heavy rents and at the same time risk-covering that the tenants usually preferred and also stood to gain under what was known as *battai* or division of produce system[318] or crop-sharing method. Gross produce was shared half each by *Kowldar* and the landlord ; land revenue was paid by the latter and regarding the sharing of other items like manure, seed, cultivation expenses, etc., practice differed from one District to another, as shown in Table XVIII. The main advantage of this system, in contrast to cash rents was that the cultivational risks were borne by both the leaseholders and the landlords. This mode of rent was mostly used in respect of wet lands. The percentage of Warangal and Karimnagar Districts in this respect, for outweighed the State average. '*Gallu Makhtha*' or taking of fixed grain as rent was prevalent mainly in respect of a few wet holdings in Adilabad and Warangal Districts. The rent varied from six maunds to twelve maunds depending upon the fertility and water sources[319]. But this, as well as certain other methods were not very much in usage as *battai* and cash rents.

The incidence of the rent payment on the incomes of the poor tenants, acted as a great drag. It formed 35-45 per cent of the gross produce in the case of the tank irrigated lands ; 25 to 30 per cent in the case of the lands irrigated by wells and for dry lands it was about 15 to 25 per cent for food crops and 25 to 40 per cent for cash crops.[320] After making this bulky payment and meeting his cultivation expenses, there would be very little margin to the actual cultivator to make his both ends meet. Furthermore, he suffered on the count that the rent demand had no relation to the frequent changes in the price of the agricultural produce and the periodical remissions of land revenue granted by the Government to the landlords were not accompanied by proportionate reductions in rents.[321] That the prevalence of high rents had brought about a deterioration in the economic condition of the tenants was brought to light by the Famine Commission as early as 1901 when they observed that :

"There is a universal agreement that the expropriated owner (the present tenant) has as a rule sunk to the condition of a mere serf tilling the very land he owned once and making over the produce to the owner. In good years he has nothing to hope for except a bare subsistence, in bad years he falls back on public charity".[322]

d. Remissions : Remissions which had been granted when there were unfavourable crop conditions on account of shortage or excess of rain, their late coming, breach of irrigation sources, pest attack on crops, etc., formed a significant item in the revenue budget of the land. Depending on the intensity of the conditions, they ranged from 25 to even 51 per cent[323] of the assessments made in respect of Telangana District. But, this benefit was normally and mostly extended to wet lands only, reasons being comparatively, heavy incidence of assessment,[324] less margin of profits or return over and above the investment and also limitations in the choice of crops for cultivation.[325] But, even among wet lands also, an invidious distinction was made in that only those lands which were cultivated under wells constructed before 1317 *Fasli* (1908)[326] and 1324 *Fasli* (1914)[327] had been made eligible to receive this revenue concession and the rest were deprived of it, the reasons being that the former lands were subjected to consolidated wet assessment[328] unlike the latter. Link with payment of wet rate had thus deprived until 1949, vast number of otherwise wet cultivators for all practical purposes, from enjoying this benefit, even though crop conditions in general remained the same for all.

On the other hand, only those dry lands which were in unsettled village or Taluq and were affected by bad seasonal conditions including excessive rain, were granted remission, due to the fact that these areas, compared to settled ones, were subjected to heavier assessment.[329] Dry crops of *kharif* and *rabi*[330], in other areas, were allowed remission only on those occasions when there prevailed extremely unfavourable crop conditions bordering famine.[331] Otherwise, remission granted to these crop lands were, as could be seen from Table XIX, minor and insignificant. Their percentage in the entire State was only 3.47 as against 43.86 in respect of wet crop lands. As Marathwada, compared to Telangana, contained vast number of black fields watered by walls, percentage of dry crop remissions was higher in it than that of Telangana. Similarly the

TABLE XVIII

Average cash rent per acre and details of other terms in respect of lands leased on crop sharing basis

(Rent figures are in Rupees, Annas and Paise)

Sl. No.	District	Dry Land			
		No. of Cases	Average Rent per acre in the District	Maximum average rent per acre among the surveyed villages	Minimum average rent per acre among the surveyed villages
1	2	3	4	5	6
1.	Adilabad	261	4-0-0	11-4-0	2-6-0
2.	Karimnagar	130	6-2-0	8-1-0	2-7-0
3.	Warangal	359	4-13-0	11-13-0	2-0-0
	All Districts (State)	2,355	5-5-0	21-10-0	1-5-0

		Wet Land				Garden Land			
		No. of Cases	Average rent per acre in the District	Maximum average rent per acre among the surveyed villages	Minimum average rent per acre among the surveyed villages	No. of cases	Average rent per acre in the District	Maximum average rent per acre among the surveyed villages	Minimum average rent per acre among the surveyed villages
		7	8	9	10	11	12	13	14
1.	Adilabad	36	36-8-0	110-0-0	12-10-0	13	8-0-0	8-0-0	8-0-0
2.	Karimnagar	17	20-5-0	20-5-0	20-5-0	—	—	—	—
3.	Warangal	49	17-13-0	33-13-0	8-4-0	3	11-8-0	11-8-0	11-8-0
	All Districts (State)	690	40-14-0	165-0-0	8-4-0	43	30-7-0	53-5-0	6-6-0

		Share of net yield or gross yield	Land Revenue by	Manure by	Seed by	Cultivation expenses, viz., ploughing, sowing, weeding and harvesting by	Appropriation of hay or stalks by
		15	16	17	18	19	20
1.	Adilabad	Gross Yield	Land Lord	Tenant	Shared equally	Shared by both according to the proportion	Tenant
2.	Karimnagar	Do	Do	Do	Tenant	Do	Shared according to the proportion
3.	Warangal All Districts (State)	Do	Do	Land lord	Do	Tenant	Tenant

Note :—The particulars given in this Table refer only to those villages of the *Suba* Districts in which Economic Surveys were held in 1949-51.

Compiled from :—S. Kesava Iyengar, *Rural Economic Enquiries, 1949-51*, pp. 62-63 & 65.

latter being a land of tanks and rice, it far exceeded the former in respect of wet crop remissions. Again, among wet crops, *tabi*[332] claimed maximum percentage of remissions, and this was mainly due to the fact that many of the water sources failed to supply required water to fairly good number of fields under their *ayacuts*, for the hot summer winds had their effect on water tables. Failure to remove the suit under tank beds as well as canals, and erect the broken bunds or close the breaches, had contributed not a little towards this end.[333]

In Warangal *Suba*, the Districts of Karimnagar and Warangal, true to their irrigational importance, received higher percentage of remissions and Adilabad, on account of its meagre facilities for irrigation, got not even one-third of what the former were granted.[334] But, all the same, the *Suba* had a higher percentage than that of the State which was primarily due to vast amount of wet cultivation in Karimnagar by means of wells and in Warangal by means of tanks. It would have exceeded even that of Telangana also, but for the poor ranking of Adilabad District in respect of wet cultivation.

But, it is necessary to realise that these remissions which were granted on such an enormous scale did not really benefit the cultivators. To get their applications for remissions approved, they were made to satisfy Taluq employees, *Girdavars* and village officials by offering suitable *mamuls*. These payments had so much neutralised the expected benefit that the ryots on many an occasions got prepared to the assessment rather than to go around these minions for a mere pittance.[335] The real beneficiaries turned out to be big *Deshmukhs* and landlords in whose hands the wet lands, especially in Warangal District, were concentrated. *1929 Economic Investigations* revealed that 2.5 per cent of occupants held more than 50 per cent of the total wet area and further, most of the land available for cultivation in the north and centre of the Warangal District was in the hands of big landlords or *Deshmukhs* who got it cultivated by serfs and tenants.[336] Their influence with high revenue officials enabled the concessions to flow freely as they desired. They got doubly benefitted by not allowing a proportionate reduction nor even a marginal one in the rents which they extracted from the land-hungry tenants.[337] In *Sarf-i-Khas* and

TABLE XIX

Nature and Extent of Grant of Remissions in 1336 Fasli (1927)

(In 0.5 Rupees)

Kind of Cultivation	Crop	Marathwada			Telangana		
		Assessment	Remission	Percentage	Assessment	Remission	Percentage
1	2	3	4	5	6	7	8
Dry	Kharif	65,63,777	6,03,735	9.18	33,08,101	14,400	0.44
	Rabi	65,53,743	42,082	0.64	32,21,880	22,835	0.68
	Total dry	1,31,17,520	6,45,817	4.92	65,29,981	36,235	0.55
Wet	Abi	5,39,871	1,89,081	35.02	69,27,087	30,94,317	44.57
	Tabi	1,92,309	63,784	33.16	43,35,324	24,86,877	57.36
	Garden	9,72,245	6,582	0.68	4,05,640	25,574	6.30
	Total wet	17,04,425	2,59,447	15.22	1,46,68,051	56,06,768	48.05
	Grand Total	1,48,21,945	9,05,264	6.11	1,81,98,032	56,43,003	31.09

(In O.S. Rupees)

		Total			Warangal Suba			
		Assessment	Remission	Percentage	Name of the District	Total assessment	Remission	Percentage
		9	10	11	12	13	14	15
Dry	Kharif	98,71,878	6,18,135	6.26				
	Rabi	97,75,623	63,917	0.65	Warangal	133,69,020	9,54,921	28.34
	Total dry	1,96,47,501	6,22 052	3.47	Karimnagar	36,11,605	22,39,672	34.32
Wet	Abi	74,66,958	32,83,398	43.97				
	Tabi	45,27,633	25,550,661	56.34	Adilabad	16,568	1,28,707	9.37
	Garden	13,77,885	32,156	2.33				
	Total wet	1,33,72,476	58,66,215	43.86	Suba Total	83,97,193	23,23,300	27.66
	Grand Total	3,30,19,977	65,48,267	19.83				

Compiled from :—H.E.H. The Nizam's Government : *Report on the Working of the Departments under the Secretary and Director-General of Revenue, 1336 Fasli (1926-27)*, pp. 18 & 20.

Jagir villages, these remissions were denied in toto, though Government's orders were given for their grant.[338] In short, basically, they acted as birds of the same feather. In fact, they were.

REFERENCES

1. Vera Anstey, *Economic Development of India*, (London 1929), p. 97.
2. Baden Powell, B.H., *Administration of Land Revenue and Tenure in British India*, (New Delhi, 1978), p. 2.
3. Royal Commission Report, *op. cit.*, p. 37.
4. Decennial Report on the Administration, *op. cit.*, p. 73.
5. W.S. *File* No. 103 of 1338 Fasli (1929) & R. No. 3100 of 1339 Fasli (1930).
6. Rural Economic Enquiries, *op. cit.*, pp. 79-80.
7. A.M. Khusro, *Economic and Social effects of Jagirdari Abolition and Land Reforms in Hyderabad*, (Hyderabad, 1958), p. 18.
8. Decennial Report on the Administration, *op. cit.*, p. 76.
9. *Report of the Tenancy Committee*, (Hyderabad, 1940), p. 3.
10. *Ibid.*, p. 4.
11. Economic Investigations and Rural Economic Enquiries, *op. cit.*, pp. 11 & 56.
12. R.A.R.C., *op. cit.*, p. 112.
13. Economic Investigations, *op. cit.*, p. 21.
14. R.E.E., *op. cit.*, p. 368.
15. R.A.R.C., *op. cit.*, p. 111.
16. See the last three paragraphs in the section 'Political Conditions' in Chapter III.
17. R.A.R.C., *op. cit.*, pp. 111 & 113.
18. *Ibid.*, p. 111.
19. *Meezan*, 19-10-1945.
20. *Meezan*, 4-12-1945.
21. T.C.R., *op. cit.* p. 15.
22. Means present or gift but compulsorily extracted.

22(a). T.C.R., *op. cit.*, p. 11.

23. *The Hyderabad Survey and Settlement Manual*, (Government Press : Hyderabad-Dn, 1952), p. 3.
24. Government of Hyderabad, Revenue Department, *File* No. 444-28-50 & R. No. 369 of 1950.
25. T.C.R., *op. cit.*, p. 10.
26. Selected Laws and Rules of the Revenue Department, *op. cit.*, p. 67.
27. Circular No. 2 of the Revenue Department, Dated 18-10-1949 in *File* No. 444-28-50, R. No. 369.
28. T.C.R., *op. cit.*, p. 11.
29. Moulvi Cheragh Ali, *op. cit.*, p. 24.

30. There were several instances in the Records to that effect. To quote two instances, Rani Lakshmi Bai was the *Maqtedar* of 13 villages in Jagtiyal Taluq of Karimnagar District (W.S. *File* No. 155 of 1325) Fasli (1916) & R. No. (n.g.) Murli Manohar Rao was the *Maqtedar* of 12 villages, six in Luxettipet Taluq and six in Chinnoor Taluq of Adilabad District, W.S. *File* No. 8 of 1351 Fasli (1942) & R. No. 141 of 1352 Fasli (1943).
31. R.A.R., *op. cit.*, p. 53.

31(a). *Ibid.*

32. W.S. *File* No. 9 of 1319 Fasli (1910) & R. No. 651 of 1322 Fasli (1913).
33. W.S. *File* No. 103 of 1338 Fasli (1929) & R. No. 3100 of 1339 Fasli (1930).
34. W.S. *File* No. 62 of 1355 Fasli (1946) & R. No. 1847 of 1355 Fasli.
35. *Ibid.* The lands were ordered for auction by the *Subedar* until the dues were realised. It is not known from the *File* whether the said arrears were realised or not.
36. W.S. *File* No. 10 of 1340 Fasli (1931) & R. No. 2982 of 1344 Fasli (1935).
37. Settlement Report of Warangal Taluka, *op. cit.*, p. 27.
38. W.S. *File* No. 2 of 1340 Fasli (1931) & R. No. 532 of 1342 Fasli (1933).
39. T.C.R., *op. cit.*, pp. 11-12.
40. *Ibid.*, p. 12.
41. R.A.R., *op. cit.*, p. 53.
42. Settlement Report of Warangal Taluka, *op. cit.*, p. 64. These were different from tenants who were also referred to as '*Kowldars*'. Though both held land on lease or *Kowl*, the conditions and terms of the *Kowls* and also their status and rights were completely dissimilar.
43. *Ibid.*
44. *Nawab* Ahmadullah Khan *Saheb*, *Banjardar* of Dornakal in Warangal District—*Meezan*, 14-6-1944.
45. Syed Nayeemuddin, First *Taluqdar* of Warangal as *Banjardar* of Habibnagar in Warangal Taluq—W.S. *File* No. 4 of 1339 Fasli (1930) & R. No. 532 of 1344 Fasli (1935).

45(a). W.S. *File Nos.* 174, 175 & 176 of 1325 Fasli (1916) & R. Nos. 4107, 4104 & 4105 respectively of 1325 Fasli (1916).

46. W.S. *File* No. 23 of 1349 Fasli (1940) & R. No. 36 of 1355 Fasli (1946).
47. W.S. *File* No. 4 of 1339 Fasli (1930) & R. No. 532 of 1344 Fasli (1935) and *File* No. 144 of 1334 Fasli (1925) & R. No. 5329 of 1344 Fasli.
48. W.S. *File* No. 3 of 1324 Fasli (1915) & R. No. 729 of 1331 Fasli (1922); W.S. *File Nos.* 174, 175 & 176 of 1325 Fasli (1916) and R. Nos. 4107, 4104 & 4105 respectively of 1325 Fasli.

49. W.S. *File* No. 1 of 1339 Fasli (1930) & R. No. 200 of 1346 Fasli (1937).
50. See the Section '*Maqtas*' in this chapter.
51. W.S. *File Nos*. 174, 175 and 176 of 1325 Fasli (1916) & R. Nos. 4107, 4104 and 4105 respectively of 1325 Fasli.
52. Settlement Report of Warangal Taluq, *op. cit*., p. 27.
53. *Meezan*, 14-6-1944.
54. See 'Village Administrative System' in Chapter III.

54(a). D.G.R. Telangana *File* No. 14 of 1334 Fasli (1925) & R. No. 3909 of 1338 Fasli (1929) and W.S. *File* No. 88 of 1329 Fasli (1920) & R. No. 795 of 1331 Fasli (1922).

55. Mehdi Ali, *Hyderabad Affairs*, p. 321.
56. Decennial Report on Administration, *op. cit*., p. 77.
57. R.A.R., *op. cit*., p. 59.
58. Mehdi Ali, *op. cit*., p. 321.
59. Zamindars serving as tax-farmers were known as *Sarbastadars*.
60. The Hyderabad Survey and Settlement Manual, *op. cit*., p. 2.
61. Mehdi Ali, *op. cit*., p. 321.
62. *Ibid*.
63. The Hyderabad Survey and Settlement Manual, *op. cit*., p. 7.
64. See Section on 'Village Administration' in Chapter III.
65. R.A.R., *op. cit*., p. 58.
66. W.S. *File* No. 99 of 1320 Fasli (1911) & R. No. 3771 of 1321 Fasli (1912).
67. R.A.R., *op. cit*., p. 58.
68. See Section 'Village Administration' in Chapter III.
69. Holders of revenue-free lands granted by former Governments. But, these lands during the reign of the last *Nizam* were assessed as *Ryotwari* lands, as *Rusum* or scale (remuneration for *Patels* and *Patwaris*) was allowed to *Watandars*—Revenue Administration Report, *op. cit*., p. 58.
70. W.S. *File* No. 23 of 1337 Fasli (1928) & R. No. 687 of 1339 Fasli (1930). This line-up was in respect of *Rusum* allotments. The same was not available in respect of direct number of these big *watandars*. This, in turn, was due to variation in the size and concentration of *watans* that obtained in the *Suba* Taluqs.
71. See the Section 'Villages' in Chapter III.
72. Kalluru *Deshmukh* in Madhira Taluq owned 100,000 acres and ranked second highest in the State itself, first being Jannareddy Pratap Reddy, owning 1,50,000 acres in Suryapet Taluq of Nalgonda District P. Sundarayya, *op. cit*., p. 19 (Telugu edn.); 77 holdings in Warangal District and 53 holdings in Karimnagar District were from 1,000 to 2,500 acres; 10 in Warangal and 6 in Karimnagar Districts were from 2,500 to 5,000 acres, Immediate Agrarian Problems, *op. cit*., p. 43.
73. Agricultural serfs (In Telugu '*Jeetagadu*') employed extensively in the Central and Northern parts of Warangal District by every big land-holder—Economic Investigations, *op. cit*., p. 12.

74. *Ibid.*, p. 20.
75. *Ibid.*, p. 15.
76. *White Paper on Hyderabad*, 1948, p. 20.
77. Official record in which details of land ownership, cultivation and revenue payment were entered.
78. Uncultivated land newly allotted for cultivation.
79. See the Section 'Villages' in Chapter III. More about these excesses and their effects are discussed in chapter VIII.
80. *The Deccan Chronicle*, 5-11-1949.
81. A.I. Qureshi, *op. cit.*, p. 109.
82. Decennial Report on Administration, *op. cit.*, p. 77.
83. W.S. *File* No. 2 of 1354 Fasli (1945) & R. No. 2468 of 1357 Fasli (1948).
84. W.S. *File* No. 59 of 1323 Fasli (1914) & R. No. 2531 of 1325 Fasli (1916).
85. W.S. *File* No. 3 of 1346 Fasli (1937) & R. No. 809 of 1347 Fasli (1938).
86. W.S. *File* No. 7 of 1342 Fasli (1933) & R. No. 2631 of 1343 Fasli (1934).

86(a). R.A.R., *op. cit.*, p. 122.

87. Revenue Department *File* No. A3/9/1/59 Fasli (1950) & R. No. 110.
88. W.S. *File* No. 111 of 1320 Fasli (1911) & R. No. 3777 of 1321 Fasli (1912).
89. Revenue Department *File* No. A3/9/1/1359 Fasli (1950) & R. No. 110.
90. *Ibid.*
91. F.R. for the first half of January, 1934 in Political Department *File* No. 34-P (Secret) of 1934, microfilmed in Hyderabad, New Delhi & Simla List, *Reel 8, Acc. No. 51* (Available at National Archives, Delhi).
92. T.C.R., *op. cit.*, p. 14.
93. W.S. *File* No. 23 of 1326 Fasli (1917) & R. No. 4094 of 1326 Fasli; W.S. *File* No. 51 of 1344 Fasli (1935) & R. No. 2054 of 1344 Fasli.
94. D.G.R. Telangana *File* No. 9 of 1337 Fasli (1928) & R. No. 1678 of 1338 Fasli (1929).
95. D.G.R. Telangana *File* No. 113 of 1338 Fasli (1929) & R. No. (n.g.).
96. T.C.R., *op. cit.*, p. 14.
97. W.S. *File* No. 2 of 1334 Fasli (1935) & R No. 1680 of 1334 Fasli; W.S. *File* No. 39 of 1340 Fasli (1931) & R. No. 3081 of 1340 Fasli.
98. W.S. *File* No. 26 of 1348 Fasli (1939) & R. No. 847 of 1343 Fasli.
99. Revenue Department, *File* No. A3/9/1/1359 Fasli (1950) & R. No. 110.
100. *Administrative Report for 1308 to 1312 Fasli* (*1899 to 1903*), (Hyderabad, 1907), p. 13.
101. *Ibid.*
102. Village Lists, *op. cit.*, pp. 30-291.

103. Outside State boundaries.
104. *Golkonda Patrika* (Bi-weekly), 4-8-1938.
105. *Ibid.*
106. W.S. *File* No. 155 of 1325 Fasli (1916) & R. No. (n.g.).
107. *Ibid.* The figures that were given in respect of *Maqtas* and *Agraharas* pertaining to Huzurabad Taluq, in this *File* and Village Lists cited for Table IX, do not tally. The difference might be due to the joining of some of them in *Ryotwari*, either because of non-payment of *pan*, or because of lack of heirs, or non-sanction of *virasat* or succession, etc.
108. W.S. *File* No. 22 of 1340 Fasli (1931) & R. No. 2059 of 1341 Fasli (1932).
109. *Ibid*. W.S. *File* No. 33 of 1353 Fasli (1944) & R. No. 1330 of 1356 Fasli (1947).
110. W.S. *File* No. 22 of 1340 Fasli (1931) & R. No. 2059 of 1341 Fasli (1932); W.S. *File* No. 133 of 1335 Fasli (1926) & R. No. 6041 of 1338 Fasli (1929).
111. W.S. File No. 22 of 1340 Fasli (1931) & R. No. 2059 of 1321 Fasli (1932).
112. W.S. *File* No. 133 of 1335 Fasli (1926) & R. No. 6041 of 1338 Fasli (1929).
113. *The Deccan Chronicle*, 8-2-1949.
114. The Decennial Report on Administration, *op. cit.*, p. 78.
115. Table IX gives it as 4. One more village might have been acquired or purchased by the Ruler. However, as the contemporary *Subedari File* quoted at *116* (*f.n.*) gives it as 3, that is taken as more authentic.
116. W.S. *File* No. 1 of 1357 Fasli (1948) & R. No. 25 of 1357 Fasli.
117. Decennial Report on Administration, *op. cit.*, p. 79.
118. W.S. *File* No. 1 of 1344 Fasli (1935) & R. No. 22 of 1344 Fasli.
119. W.S. *File* No. 2 of 1352 Fasli (1943) & R. No. 1140 of 1352 Fasli; W.S. *File* No. 40 of 1334 Fasli (1925) & R. No. 2264 of 1340 Fasli (1931).
120. W.S. *File* No. 1 of 1357 Fasli (1948) & R. No. 25 of 1357 Fasli.
121. *Ibid.*
122. W.S. *File* No. 3 of 1342 Fasli (1933) & R. No. 494 of 1343 Fasli (1934); *File* No. 4 of 1342 Fasli (1933) & R. No. 475 of 1343 Fasli; W.S. *File* No. 2 of 1343 Fasli & R. No. 476 of 1343 Fasli; W.S. *File* No. 2 of 1343 Fasli & R. No. 481 of 1343 Fasli.
123. W.S. *File* No. 4 of 1342 Fasli (1933) & R. No. 454 of 1343 Fasli (1934).
124. *Ibid*, W.S. *File* No. 1 of 1357 Fasli (1948) & R. No. 25 of 1357 Fasli.
125. W.S. *File* No. 1 of 1342 Fasli (1933) & R. No. 450 of 1343 Fasli (1934).
126. See '*Pot-pattedari*' discussed earlier in this chapter.

127. See Table VIII.
128. R.E.E., *op. cit.*, p. 81.
129. *The Deccan Chronicle*, 8-2-1949.
130. A.M. Khusro, *op. cit.*, p. 4.
131. *Ibid.*
132. K. Krishnaswamy Mudiraj, *Pictorial Hyderabad*, Vol. II, (Hyderabad, 1934), p. 619.
132(a) Royal Commission Report, *op. cit.*, p. 30.
133. A.M. Khusro, *op. cit.*, p. 7.
134. Table IX gives them as 116. This figure appears to be rather exaggerated in view of the fact that both *Hyderabad District Gazetteers, Warangal (1931-1936)* and A.M. Khusro, *cited above* gave them as only 69 and 70 respectively. Gazetteers' figure is adopted for the purpose.
135. *Hyderabad District Gazetteers, Warangal*, Tables Volume, *1340 & 1345 Fasli* (*1931 & 1936*), (Hyderabad, 1939), p. 3.
136. Christoph-Von-Fuhrer-Haimendorf, *op. cit.*, p. 1.
137. *Hyderabad District Gazetteers*, Warangal, *op. cit.*, pp. 10 & 11.
138. Title borne by former Hindu rulers.
139. A.M. Khusro, *op. cit.*, p. 7.
140. R.A.R., *op. cit.*, p. 57.
141. A.I. Qureshi, *op. cit.*, p. 112.
142. M.A. Muttalib, *op. cit.*, p. 245.
143. N.G. Ranga, *Economic Organisation of Indian Villages*, Vol. II, (Bombay, 1929), p. 21.
144. D.G.R. Telangana Range, *File* No. 31 of 1338 Fasli (1929) & R. No. 2900 of 1339 Fasli (1930).
145. W.S. *File* No. 41 of 1340 Fasli (1931) & R. No. 56 of 1341 Fasli (1932).
146. *Ibid.*
147. N.G. Ranga, *op. cit.*, p. 19.
148. From 1935, it was continuously under the management of Court of Wards, a body created to look after the taken over *Samasthans* and *Jagirs* either for want of determination of succession or non-payment of *Peshkash*, etc., W.S. File No. 30 of 1334 Fasli (1925) & R. No. 2456 of 1344 Fasli (1935); *Hyderabad Information*, Vol. III, No. 11, August, 1943; *Meezan*, 22-1-1946.
149. He was so indifferent that he slept for 22 years over the allotment of 100 acres of his *Poramboke* land by the Government to a *baggal* (*Bania*) on *patta* and nothing could be done later in that regard even though appeal went up to Revenue Secretary—W.S. *File* No. 97 of 1338 Fasli (1929) & R. No. 2236 of 1341 Fasli (1932).
150. Christoph-Von-Fuhrer-Haimendorf, *op. cit.*, p, 27.
151. *Ibid.*, pp. 6-7.
152. See Section 'Forests' in Chapter II.

153. N.G. Ranga, *op. cit.*, p. 21.
154. Christoph-Von-Fuhrer-Haimendorf, *op. cit.*, p. 8.
155. *Ibid.*, pp. 16 & 18.
156. *Ibid.*, p. 28.
157. *Ibid.*, p. 27.
158. Syed Khaja Abdul Gafoor, *op. cit.*, pp. 40-41.
159. *Ibid.*, pp. 41 & 47.
160. For definition see f.n. 8 in Chapter I.
161. Baden Powell, B.H., *op. cit.*, p. 54.
162. Bawa, V.K., *Hyderabad in Transition under Salar Jung I, 1853-1883, An Indian State Under British Influence*, unpublished Ph. D. Thesis (Available in Micro Film, NMML, New Delhi), (Tulane University, 1967), p. 35.
163. J.D.B. Gribble, *A History of the Deccan*, Vol. I, (London, 1896), p. 337.
164. *Paigah* means stables, indicating the maintenance of cavalry—Decennial Report on Administration, *op. cit.*, p. 79.
165. As there was the domination of the Minister, Rukhn-ud-Daula over the *Nizam*, Nizam Ali, he took this step after the death of the Minister in 1775, in order to have military support in case the regular troops acted under the orders of any future Minister—K. Krishnaswamy Mudiraj, *op. cit.*, p. 187.
166. Village Lists, Adilabad District, *op. cit.*, pp. 250-251.
167. *Ibid.*
168. A.M. Khusro, *op. cit.*, p. 5.
169. Political Department, *File* No. 242-P(S)/45, of 1945 in Hyderabad, New Delhi and Simla Lists, Micro Film *Reel 7, Acc. No. 50*, p. 23.
170. *Ibid.*
171. There were in total 1,194 *Paigah* villages in the State, spread over 23 Taluqs and 10 District, A.M. Khusro, *op. cit.*, p. 6; K. Krishnaswamy Mudiraj, *op. cit.*, p. 187.
172. A.I.S.P C. *File* No. 65, Part I, p. 292.
173. *Ibid.*
174. Political Department, File No. 242-P(S)/45 of 1945, in Hyderabad, New Delhi and Simla Lists, Micro Film, *Reel 7, Acc. No. 50*, p. 23.
175. It is a Turkish compound word made up of two words 'Al' and 'Tamgha' both of which signified the royal signet-A.I. Qureshi, *op. cit.*, p. 115.

175(a). But, a kind of royalty called *Haq-e-Malikana* was collected from almost all *Jagirs* which were originally absolutely rent-free-Royal Commission Report, *op. cit.*, p. 33.

On certain *Jagirs* this royalty was fixed at each succession and ranged nominally from 2 per cent to 5 per cent but, in certain exceptional cases rose to 25 per cent—*File* No. 334-P(S)/44, of 1944, in Hyderabad, New Delhi and Simla Lists, Micro Film, *Reel 3, Acc. No. 46*, p. 6.

176. The entire Rajura Taluq of Adilabad District remained as *Tankha Jagir* of Hasan Khan Hindojai and it became a *Khalsa* territory only in 1281 Fasli (1872)-W.S. *File* No. 1 of 1325 Fasli (1916) & R. No. 1886 of 1327 Fasli (1918).
177. Decennial Report on Administration, *op. cit.*, p. 80.
178. Revenue Administration Report, *op. cit.*, pp. 60-61.
178(a). He had such *Jagirs* in other areas of the State also, which altogether numbered as many as 186 villages with an annual income of Rs. 13,51,333. Besides scope for feudal oppression, the administrative complexity that arose due to the scattering of these *Jagirs* and their immensity, could well be imagined, A.M. Khusro, *op. cit.*, p. 7.
179. Village Lists of Karimnagar District, *op. cit.*, pp. 70-71 & 104-105.
180. "History of Paigahs", a printed booklet in A.I.S.P.C. *File* No. 65.
181. K. Krishnaswamy Mudiraj, *op. cit.*, p. 201.
182. This aspect was examined in detail in Chapter VIII that dealt with the Peasant Struggle.
183. Refers to estate.
184. Besides this landed estate, he, as *Qanungoi*, a hereditary *watan* office carrying no work received as *Rusum* Rs. 82,000, for the year 1321 Fasli (1912) from the four *Subas*, out of which the share of Warangal *Suba* was Rs. 13,000. This amount varied only marginally, as it was calculated on the revenue that was received—W.S. *File* No. 99 of 1320 Fasli (1911) & R. No. 3771 of 1321 Fasli (1912). His *Jagir* estate was spread over 11 other Districts of the State with a total number of 222 villages, with an annual income of Rs. 7,00,000, Definitely an example for large concentration of landed power, *The Golkonda Patrika* Bi-weekly), 13-8-1936.
185. Village Lists of Warangal and Karimnagar Districts, *op. cit.*, pp. 118-121, 288-289 and 62-63.
186. A.M. Khusro, *op. cit.*, p. 8 ; K. Krishnaswamy Mudiraj, *op. cit.*, pp. 201-202.
187. *File* no. 334-P(S)/44 of 1944 in Hyderabad, New Delhi and Simla Lists, Micro Film, *Reel 3*, *Acc. No. 46*, p. 6.
188. Government of Hyderabad, Revenue Department, *File* No. 444-28-50 and R. No. 369, p. 12.
189. *File* No. 334-P (S)/44 in Hyderabad, New Delhi and Simla Lists, Micro Film (National Archives, Delhi), *Reel 3*, *Acc. No.* 46, p. 3.
190. T.C.R., *op. cit.*, p. 10.
191. Ravi Narayana Reddy, *Heroic Telangana, Reminiscences and Experiences*, (Delhi, 1973), p. 3.
192. *The Golkonda Patrika* (Bi-weekly), 29-6-1939 ; W.S. *File* 15 of 1350 Fasli (1941) & R. No. 149 of 1357 Fasli (1948).
193. V. Venkataraman, *Land Reforms in India with Special Reference to Hyderabad*, unpublished Ph. D. thesis, (Osmania University, 1957), p. 38 ; Royal Commission Report, *op. cit.*, p. 71—There were *Jagirs*

where the benefit was completely denied—*Golkonda Patrika* (Bi-weekly), 5-4-1934.

194. See Section 'Rainfall' in chapter II.
195. T.C.R., *op. cit.*, p. 11.
196. The Hyderabad Survey and Settlement Manual, *op. cit.*, p. 3, Statistical data of vital importance and of a reliable nature relating to *Jagirs*, is not available for the reason that no records were maintained in *Jagir* areas. This was admitted by the Revenue Department. Even the information given by big estates and that regarding population census and statistics was of doubtful nature ; Royal Commission Report, *op. cit.*, pp. 10 & 21.
197. *Administrative Report for 1349 Fasli (6-10-1939 to 6-10-1940)*, (Hyderabad-Dn, 1942), p. 18.
198. For further elaboration on this point, see discussion '*Kowldars*' in the Section titled 'Land Rights' in this Chapter.
199. T.C.R., *op.cit.*, p, 15.
200. *Patti* refers to compulsory cess.
201. Maize tops containing grain.
202. *Golkonda Patrika* (Bi-weekly), 29-6-1939 & 3-7-1939 ; *Meezan*, 11-10-1945 ; W.S. *File* No. 11 of 1341 Fasli (1943) & R. No. 3341 of 1343 Fasli (1934).
203. K. Krishnaswamy Mudiraj, Vol. II, *op. cit.*, p. 202.

203(a) W.S. *File* No. 89 of 1352 Fasli (1943) & R. No. 119 of 1352 Fasli.

204. Economic Investigations, *op. cit.*, p. 13.
205. *Meezan*, 4-12-1945.
206. See the section 'Political conditions' in Chapter III.
207. Government of Hyderabad, *Jagir Administration*, Vol. I, 1952, pp. 15-16 ; *Golkonda Patrika* (Bi-weekly), 10-4-1939 ; Royal Commission Report, *op. cit.*, pp. 79-81.
208. *Golkonda Patrika*, (Bi-weekly), 29-6-1939.
209. Essay in '*Rayyat*' Paper, incorporated in *Golkonda Patrika* (Bi-weekly), 13-8-1936.
210. *Jagir Administration*, Vol. I, *op. cit.*, p. 16.
211. Decennial Report on the Administration, *op. cit.*, p. 80.
212. A.I. Qureshi, *op. cit.*, p. 117.
213. Land grants to Mosque staff at the rate of 150 acres to *Pesh Imam*, 50 acres to *Mauzan* and 25 acres to water carrier in Asifabad District Headquarters—W.S. *File* No. 38 of 1336 Fasli (1927) & R. No. 6572 of 1338 Fasli (1929) ; 1 Acre and 10 bombs of wet land was granted to a temple priest in Basavapur, Taluq Karimnagar W.S. *File No.* 7 of 1339 Fasli (1930) & R. No. 1806 of 1340 Fasli (1931).
214. See the Section "Villages" in Chapter III.
215. As the holders of those *Inama* had to pay ¼th or *chowta* (in Urdu) of the original assessment, they were called so.

216. Whereas even in a small village, *Dheds* were granted land upto 20 acres, others like *Dhobies* (washermen) were granted only 6 acres. Regarding remission, *Dheds* were eligible for full remission of Rs. 30 whereas the latter were given only upto Rs. 15 W.S *File* No. 28 of 1343 Fasli (2934) & R. No. 471 of 1344 Fasli (1935).
217. W.S. *File* No. 94 of 1325 Fasli (1916) & R. No. 4037 of 1326 Fasli (1917).
218. R.A.R., *op. cit.*, p. 125.
219. Decennial Report on Administration, *op. cit.*, p. 80.
220. Government of Hyderabad, *Memoranda Submitted to the Taxation Enquiry Commission*, 1953, p. 51.
221. R.A.R.C., *op, cit.*, p. 8.
222. In the year 1929, the area of these lands in the *Suba* Districts was (in acres and *guntas*) : Adilabad, 2,57,403-11¾ ; Warangal, 1,00,282-36 ; and Karimnagar, 58,516-14—*Suba* Administrative Report for 1339 Fasli (1929) in *File* No. 103 of Fasli (1929) & R. No. 3100 of 1339 Fasli (1930).
223. Particulars of Palvancha Taluq were not furnished in the Source cited. It is difficult to conclude that there were no *Inam* lands in it. The omission might probably be due to the fact that the Taluq particulars might not have reached the office of the First *Taluqdar*, by the time this statement was prepared and submitted to *Subedar*.
224. W.S. *File* No. 69 of 1340 Fasli (1931) & R. No. 2491 of 1340 Fasli.
225. W.S. *File* No. 72 of 1348 Fasli (1939) & R. No. 1253 of 1352 Fasli (1943).
226. W.S. *File* No. 17 of 1325 Fasli (1916) & R. No. 4003 of 1326 Fasli (1917).
227. W.S. *File* No. 15 of 1356 Fasli (1947) & R. No. 1096 of 1356 Fasli. For definition and functions of *Sethsindhi*, see section 'Villages' in Chapter III.
228. W.S. *File* No. 59 of 1319 Fasli (1910) & R. No. 2412 of 1325 Fasli (1916).
229. *Memoranda Submitted to Taxation Enquiry Committee, op. cit.*, p. 51.
230. See Section '*Tahuddars/Sarbastadars/Watandars*' in this Chapter.
231. *Statistical Year Book, 1941-42 to 1944-45*, p. 614.
232. *Ibid.*, p. 615.
233. The Hyderabad Survey and Settlement Manual, *op. cit.*, p. 8.
234. See Section 'soils' in Chapter II.
235. *Ibid.*
236. The water supply potential was divided into 16 groups, just as there were 16 *annas* in a rupee. Hence, it was known as *annawari.*
237. The Hyderabad Survey and Settlement Manual, *op. cit.*, p. 13.
238. Here, the wet lands formed only a small proportion of the available and cultivated lands.
239. The Hyderabad Survey and Settlement Manual, *op. cit.*, p. 14.

240. *Ibid.*
241. Irrigable area.
242. HSSM, *op. cit.*, p. 14.
243. *The Deccan Chronicle*, 13-9-1949.
244. *Ibid.*
245. See the first para in this section.
246. HSSM, *op. cit.*, p. 14.
247. *Ibid.*, pp. 20-23.
248. *Ibid.*, pp. 20-21.
249. See Table IX.
250. See the last para in the sub-section 'b-Tenants' in this Chapter.
251. *Ibid.*, See the section '*Jagirs*' in this Chapter.
252. Agriculture Department, Nizam's Government *File* No. 96/59F of 1359 Fasli (1950) & R. No. 83.
253. HSSM, *op, cit.*, p. 10.
254. *Ibid.*, p. 15.
255. *A.R. for 1347 Fasli* (*6-10-1937 to 5-10-1938*), (Hyderabad, 1940), p. 5.

255(a). *Memoranda Submitted to the Taxation Enquiry Committee*, *op. cit.* p. 58.

256. *Report on the working of the Departments under the Revenue Secretariat 1328 Fasli* (*1918-1919*), (Hyderabad-Dn), p. 25.
257. HSSM, *op. cit.*, pp. 20-21.
258. Land Revenue collected from such lands whose *Patta* was not granted.
259. See the Section 'Remissions' in this Chapter.
260. W.S. *File* No. 37 of 1323 Fasli (1914) & R. No. 2237 of 1325 Fasli (1916).
261. Government uncultivated land but cultivable.
262. Pasture land for grazing.
263. W.S. *File* No. 31 of 1349 Fasli (1940) & R. No. 1354 of 1350 Fasli (1941).
264. See the Section 'Forests' in Chapter II.
265. *Golkonda Patrika* (Bi-weekly), 27-3-1939.
266. *Ibid*.
267. SYB, 1941-42 to 1944-45, *op. cit.*, p. 615.
268. *Ibid.*
269. *The Deccan Chronicle*, 28-6-19-49.
270. *Ibid.*
271. W.S. *File* No. 111 of 1320 Fasli (1911) & R. No. 3777 of 1321 Fasli (1912).
272. W.S. *File* No. 599 of 1357 Fasli (1948) & R. No. 46 of 1358 Fasli (1949).
273. HSSM, *op. cit.*, p. 5.
274. IGI, *op. cit.*, p. 58.
275. HSSM, *op. cit.*, p. 3.

276. *Ibid.*, p. 5.
277. Selected Laws and Rules of the Revenue Department, *op. cit.*, p. 40.
278. K. Krishnaswamy Mudiraj, Vol. II, *op. cit.*, p. 520.
279. W.S. *File* No. 7 of 1347 Fasli (1938) & R. No. 687 of 1347 Fasli.
280. For the year 1927, the percentages that were recorded in respect of Warangal, Karimnagar and Adilabad Districts were respectively 90 48, 99.13 and 99.06. For the State and Telangana, they were 97.45 and 95.72 respectively=*Report on the working of the Departments under the Secretary and Director-General of Revenue, 1336 Fasli* (*1926-27*), p. 22 ; W.S. *File* No. 38 of 1354 Fasli (1945) & R. No. 707 of 1354 Fasli.
281. R.A.R., *op. cit.*, p. 104.
282. W.S. *File* No. 25 of 1355 Fasli (1946) & R. No. 71 of 1356 Fasli (1947).
283. W.S. *File* No. 16 of 1355 Fasli (1946) & R. No. 69 of 1356 Fasli (1947).
284. W.S. *File* No. 73 of 1320 Fasli (1911) & R. No. 3759 of 1321 Fasli (1912).
285. W.S. *File* No. 38 of 1355 Fasli (1946) & R. No. 875 of 1357 Fasli (1948).
286. W.S. *File* No. 35 of 1346 Fasli (1937) & R. No. 1839 of 1351 Fasli (1942).
287. W.S. *File* No. 38 of 1354 Fasli (1945) & R. No. 706 of 1354 Fasli.
288. W.S. *File* No. 78 of 1355 Fasli (1946) & R. No. 56 of 1356 Fasli (1947).
289. *Ibid.*
290. See the sub-section 'C. Maqtas' in this chapter.
291. W.S. *File* No. 25 of 1355 Fasli (1946) & R. No. 71 of 1356 Fasli (1947).
292. An amount of Rs. 24, 747-12-11, being the revenue arrears standing for 17 years in the name of Pingali Raghava Reddy, an influential landlord and also excise contractor in Warangal District, was ultimately written off, thereby confirming the vast Governmental influence that the family (Pingali Venkatrama Reddy) Kodanda Rama Reddy and Pratap Reddy, other known figures) had=W.S. *File* No. 30 of 1335 Fasli (1926) & R. No. 1681 of 1339 Fasli (1930).
293. See the second para in the sub-section 'ii. Other *Jagirs*' in this chapter.
294. W.S. *File* No. 16 of 1355 Fasli (1946) & R. No. 69 of 1356 Fasli (1947).
295. W.S. *File* No. 58 1339 Fasli (1930) & R. No. 85 of 1341 Fasli (1932).
296. The average dry assessment of the State in 1952 was Rs.1-1-0 per acre and Rs. 10-8-11 for an acre of single crop wet land. The slight reduction in wet rate compared to that of 1945 (See *TableXIV*) might have come after the change of Government in September, 1948-HSSM, *op. cit.*, p. 15.

97. See the section 'Natural divisions' in Chapter II.
98. HSSM., *op. cit.*, p. 15.
99. *Golkonda Patrika* (Daily), 12-4-1949.
00. See the section 'a Survey and Settlement' in this chapter.
01. The sanctity of this year was that the Hyderabad Land Revenue Act was passed in it.
02. RARC, *op. cit.*, p. 179.
03. *Golkonda Patrika*, (Daily), 7-4-1949.
04. RARC, *op. cit.*, p. 179.
05. *Golkonda Patrika*, (Daily), 7-4-1949.
06. W.S. *File* No. 17 of 1352 Fasli (1943) & R. No. 576 of 1353 Fasli (1944).
07. R.E.E., *op. cit.*, pp. 457 & 459.
08. R.V. Rao, *op. cit.*, p. 291.
309. Immediate Agrarian problems, *op. cit.*, p. 63.
10. REE, *op. cit.*, p. 298.
311. L.G. Ganu, 'Land Revenue and Rural Indebtedness' in (Finance Department, English Branch, File No. 1 of 1937) *The Hyderabad Bulletin*, 28-8-1937.
312. *Ibid.*, p. 3.
313. *Ibid.*, p. 14.
314. During the decade 1901-1911 A.D., rent receivers in the State showed an increase of 1, 748.8 per cent. This was a great indicator of the new trend-R.A.R., *op. cit.*, p. 28.
315. See f.n. 3 in this chapter.
316. V. Venkatraman, *op. cit.*, p. 51.
317. See Tables XIV & XV.
318. T.C.R , *op. cit.* p. 8.
319. Immediate Agrarian problems, *op. cit.*, p. 30.
320. These included in Telangana, groundnut, castor, tobacco, sugarcane, etc.,—Immediate Agrarian Problems, *op. cit.*, p. 37.
321. *Ibid.*, pp. 39-40.
322. *Indian Famine Commission Report 1901*, p 110.
323. *A.R. for 1328 Fasli (6th October 1918 to 6th October 1919)*, (Hyderabad, 1920), p. 2.
324. See Table XV.
325. *Proceedings of the conference of Subedars held at the Revenue Secretariat on 18th, Sharewar (July), 1342 Fasli (1933)*, Hyderabad, p. 2.
326. For this category of lands in 1356 Fasli (1947), Rs. 1,58,344-5-0 was granted as remission in the *Suba* area—W.S. *File* No. 36 of 1356 Fasli (1947) & R. No. 2469 of 1357 Fasli (1948).
327. W.S. *File* No. 13 of 1355 Fasli (1946) & R. No. 157 of 1357 Fasli (1948).
328. See the third para in the section 'b. Land Revenue Assessments and their incidence' in this chapter.
329. John Law, *Modern Hyderabad* (Deccan, Calcutta, 1914), p. 65.

330. See the Section 'Soils' in Chapter II.
331. A.I. Qureshi, *op. cit.*, p. 127.
332. It was a second crop of rice, sown in January-February and harvested in April-May. In other words, was a summer crop of rice.
333. Settlement Report of Warangal Taluka, *op. cit.*, p. 49.
334. See Table I.
335. *Golkonda Patrika* (Bi-weekly), 12-12-1938.
336. S. Kesava Iyengar, *op. cit.*, pp. 2 & 2.
337. See the last para of the section 'c. Rents' in this chapter.
338. W.S. *File* No. 3 of 1342 Fasli (1933) & R. No. 453 of 1343 Fasli (1934).

CHAPTER FIVE

AGRICULTURAL CONDITIONS

AGRICULTURAL production is very much determined by factors like the size of landholdings and the pattern of land distribution, irrigation facilities, type of cultivation and methods employed, the type and the extent of the use of seeds, manures and pesticides and also the extent and the manner in which agricultural credit is made available and debt relief is organised. The influence of these factors could, of course, be seen only when there was sufficient amount of rainfall and the land was not visited by any epidemic or internal catastrophe, either political or economic. The latter has a direct and an immediate bearing on the condition of crops.[1] An assessment is made in this chapter of how these natural and human agencies contributed for, or retarded the pace of agricultural production in the *Suba* area.

A. *LAND HOLDINGS* : On account of the increase in the value of land and also the lack of suitable and remunerative subsidiary occupations, more and more number of people began to depend, as years rolled by, on land for their living. In contrast to this, big landlord *Deshmukhs* who owned entire villages[2] found it profitable to let their vast lands on lease[3] and themselves take up non-cultivating occupations like excise contracts, money and grainlending and running of mills etc. Both these developments, combined with the exercise of the rights of inheritance, sale and transfer of land by *Pattedars* led to the holdings, both occupant and cultivating, becoming smaller in size from year to year. Though fluctuations were there in the figures recorded in *Table XX* for the middle period of thirties and forties which were mainly due to difference in the scope and method of computation adopted,[4] the fact was unmistakably clear that during the thirty seven year period between 1913 and 1950, landholdings, especially relating to dry lands, suffered a reduction in size amounting to not less than 30%. The position obtained in respect of Warangal District in 1929-30 after excluding the lands owned by seventeen big landlords, each of whom possessed more than 100 acres and ranging upto 1,500 acres and even more,[5] and that of Karimnagar District in 1949-50, was significant to be observed from the point of view of the economic condition of the farmers in these areas. For a peasant and his family to lead a reasonable life of comfort in Telangans, Kesava Iyengar after detailed enquiry in 24 villages in 1929-30 opined that 15 acres of dry land or 5 acres of wet land should be the minimum or economic holding[6] and the Agrarian Reforms Committee after detailed enquiry in 1949-50, came to the conclusion that 8 or 10 acres of wet land and 50 acres of dry land would constitute an economic holding.[7] Viewed in the light of these expert recommendations, holdings in all the three Districts throughout the period covered in *Table XX*, excepting some stray exceptions in respect of dry lands, were far below the minimum level required for the cultivators to lead a normal life. Even in 1929-30, as many as 75% of the total number of occupant ryots in Warangal District were found possessing insufficient land.[8]

The enormity of the extent of these small holdings could better be appreciated from *Table XXI* which shows that in 1945, the number of those *pattedars* who had the lowest holding of 5 acres formed as much as 43.78% of the total number of *pattedars* in Warangal District, 41.04% in Karimnagar District and 30.64% in Adilabad District. In the *Suba* taken as a whole, they formed as much as 38.42%. The holdings in the region, besides being small in size, were also characterised by excessive fragmentation which considerably affected scope for increased agricultural investment and production. In Thimma-

TABLE XX

Average sizes of Land Holdings, 1913-50

Sl. No.	Name of the District	Average sizes of land Holdings in acres						
		1322 Fasli (1913-14)		1331 Fasli (1922-23)		1929-30***		
		Dry	Wet	Dry	Wet	Dry	Wet	Garden
1	2	3	4	5	6	7	8	9
1.	Warangal	18.6	2.7	14.9	2.3	11.31	3.4	0.11
						18.5	11.22	10.10
2.	Karimnagar	13.2	2.5	13.1	2.5	—	—	—
3.	Adilabad	11.6	0.3	14.6	0.4	—	—	—
4.	Suba	14.4	1.38	14.2	1.37	—	—	—
5.	Telangana	14.1	1.8	14.8	1.9	—	—	—
6.	State	19.8	1.3	19.4	1.2	—	—	—

Average sizes of Land Holdings in acres

	1343 Fasli (1934-35)		1354 Fasli* (1945-46)		1949-50***		
	Dry	Wet	Dry	Wet	Dry	Wet	Garden
	10	11	12	13	14	15	16
1.	18.0	...	15.2	...	12.29**	2.34	0.4
2.	11.0	...	12.3	...	8.4	1.20	0.8
3.	12.0	...	14.1	..,	11.12	1.12	0.1
4.	13.66	...	13.86	...	10.28	1.35	0.4
5.	12.51	1.58	9.14	1.25	—	—	—
6.	17.23	1.04	12.14	0.83	13.17	1.1½	0.8

*Diwani Taluqs only

**In Acres and Guntas.

***Figures were of the survey, conducted in selected villages of each District.

...Figures were not given.

)(Excluding the area held by 17 big landholders.

Compiled from : 1. *Decennial Report on Administration, 1912-22*, p. 89.

2. S. Kesava Iyengar, *Economic Investigations in the Hyderabad State, 1929-30*. Vol. I, p. 11.

3. *Agricultural Statistics, 1936-40*,

4. *Agricultural Statistics, 1941-45*, p. 363.

&

5. S. Kesava Iyengar, *Rural Economic Enquiries, 1949-51*, p. 33.

TABLE XXI

Pattadars and classification of their holdings in 1945

Sl. No.	Classification of holding	Number of Pattadars in Warangal District	Karimnagar District	Adilabad District	Total in the Suba
1	2	3	4	5	6
1.	5 acres	24,103	34,825	20,346	79,274
2.	5 to 10 acres	9,049	14,332	10,528	33,909
3.	10 to 15 ,,	5,550	9,022	8,584	23,156
4.	15 to 20 ,,	4,281	6,616	7,850	18,747
5.	20 to 25 ,,	2,923	5,238	4,883	13,044
6.	25 to 50 ,,	5,021	6,773	8,195	19,989
7.	50 to 100 ,,	2,841	4,763	3,822	11,426
8.	100 to 150 acres	913	1,642	1,095	3,650
9.	150 to 200 ,,	512	710	730	1,952
10.	200 to 250 ,,	292	364	458	1,114
11.	250 to 500 ,,	341	893	421	1,655
12.	500 to 1,000 ,,	139	114	345	598
13.	1,000 to 2,500 ,,	77	53	127	257
14.	2,500 to 5,000 ,,	10	6	14	30
15.	Above 5,000 ,,	1	..	4	5
	Grand Total :	55,053	84,851	66,402	2,06,306

Compiled from : *Agricultural Statistics, 1940-41* to *1944-45*, pp. 392-393.

pur village of Jagtiyal Taluq, a dry land plot of 16 acres and 5 *quntas* was held by as many as twelve *hissedars*[8](a) among whom one had a share equivalent to ten paise in a rupee.[9] Wet lands were even more prone to fragmentation. As per the tests conducted by the Settlement Department, it was found that the proportion of holdings of wet lands under one acre, as compared to those above one acre was 1 to 7 in Warangal District and 1 to 5 in Karimnagar District.[10] *Rural Economic Enquiries held in 1949-50* revealed that on account of scattering of holdings, every occupancy consisted on an average 2.5 plots and the size of the average plot in a cultivation holding was smaller than that in an occupancy holding in all the three Districts of the *Suba*, which pointed to the large presence of tenants and greater pressure on land.[11] Break-up of the joint family system, irregular expansion of cultivation over waste lands, purchases and sales, and division of property amongst a large number of distant relatives in case of the absence of direct heirs of families, were all responsible for accentuating fragmentation of lands.[12]

Small and fragmented holdings had their definite impact on agricultural production and also the condition of their cultivating owners. The holdings being uneconomical, restricted the scope and the capacity of the cultivator to invest profitably on well construction, better seeds and fertilisers and commercial crops. The cost of production per acre was higher than in the case of larger farms. Even resources that existed in the shape of man-power, bullocks, carts, etc., could not be put to sufficient and full use, due to the meagre holdings. This compelled many such small farmers owning insufficient holdings to leave their fields during the off-season and serve themselves as agricultural labourers.[13] In fragmented plots, much cultivable land was wasted on hedges and paths. Besides, there was the wastage of considerable time and labour in going from plot making also difficult proper supervision and easy rotation of crops and cattle breeding on sound lines. But, the worst of all the effects of these unprofitable holdings was that they formed one of the basic causes of debt.[14] This hand-to-mouth existence with little surplus in crop yield put them in such a delicate and precarious condition that any slight adversity in the shape of rainfall, water supply or other crop conditions, threw them fully into the hands of village money-lender who invariably aimed at land grabbing and then reducing the hapless peasant to the status of a serf.

B. *PATTERN OF LAND DISTRIBUTION* : It can be seen from the classification of holdings as shown in the *Table XXI* that land in the three Districts got distributed in such a way that there were good many small or uneconomical holdings[15] on the one hand and excessive monopolization or concentration of greater percentage of land in fewer hands, on the other. Whereas big *Pattedars* owning more than 100 acres formed only 4.15%, 4.45% and 4.81% out of the total number of *pattedars* in the Districts of Warangal, Karimnagar and Adilabad respectively, on the other hand, those *pattedars* who held land from 5 acres to 10 acres formed 60.21%, 58.02% and 46.49% respectively. In terms of land, the pattern concerning Warangal District was clearly brought out by 1929-30 Survey in 12 villages which stated that 1.7% of the occupants held more than 35% of the total dry land and 2.5% of the occupants held more than 50% of the total wet area.[16] The position in respect of other Districts[17] and during the rest of the period differed only in degree but not in kind.[18]

This inequality in land distribution had its adverse effect on agricultural growth. On one hand, the holdings of small farmers were so meagre in size, frequently characterized by fragmentation also that they did not possess sufficient economic wherewithal to contribute their mite for the increase of agricultural production.[19] This was further affected by the various disabilities like the extraction of *vetti*, collection of illegal cesses etc., inflicted on these small ryots by big landlords, village officials and also revenue officials.[20] On the other, excessive monopolization of land led to absenteeism and diminishing returns in productivity. The big landlords got their huge lands cultivated either by *bhagelas* or by tenants. But, high rents coupled with insecurity of *kowls* incapacitated the latter from taking up cultivation on an intensive and profitable level.[21] Further, holdings which ranged from 500 to 5,000 acres and even above, became so unwieldy and difficult to supervise effectively that after a stage, with every increase in the size of the holding, the yield per acre tended to decrease.[22]

Though there was slight decrease in the percentage of absentee *pattedars* to that of total *pattedars* in the Warangal *Suba* from 7.83% in 1937[23] to 6.35% in 1949-50,[24] the effect on agricultural production was none the less effective in view of the enormity of these holdings which extended from particular pieces to several villages.

C. IRRIGATIONAL FACILITIES : *Chalka* soils with their non-retentiveness of the moisture and the precarious nature of the monsoons made irrigation vitally essential for the agricultural well-being of the people in *Suba*.[25] Its importance was realised as early as thirteenth century by Kakatiyas of Warangal but for whose beneficent care, Warangal District during the present century would not have occupied the first place in the State in respect of tank irrigation. From the point of view of income to the Government, it could be seen that whereas wet cultivated land in the Districts of Warangal and Karimnagar formed less than 15% of the total cultivated land, land revenue from wet lands accounted for more than 63% of the total land revenue demand from these two Districts. Even in respect of Adilabad District, though the wet lands formed only less than 3% of the total cultivated land, wet assessment formed more than 20% of the total assessment for the District.[26] Development of irrigational facilities became all the more important in view of the fact that rice, maize, jawar and wheat, being the main food items of the people in the region, were grown under irrigation in the respective order.[27]

(*ii*) *Sources of Irrigation, Their Construction and Maintenance* : These consisted in the main of tanks, *Kuntas*, wells and river projects, both Government and private. An idea could be had of the sources available, both good and damaged, in 1910 and 1926 from *Table XXII*. Wells, whose cost of construction varied according to local conditions from Rs. 39 in Karimnagar District, Rs. 47 in Warangal District to Rs. 116 in Adilabad District[28] and which were administered by the well-sinking Department that was started in April, 1928,[29] accounted for as much as 79.09% and 80.85% of the total number of sources in the *Suba* in 1910 and 1926 respectively. Karimnager District ranked highest in the State in respect of well cultivation, whereas Adilabad District suffered a decrease of 75.27% in the already meagre number between the

TABLE XXII

Sources of Irrigation for the years 1319 Fasli (1910) & 1335 Fasli (1926)

Name of the District	Tanks						Kuntas				Total	
	In good condition		Damaged		Total		In good condition		Damaged			
	1910	1926	1910	1926	1910	1926	1910	1926	1910	1926	1910	1926
1	2	3	4	5	6	7	8	9	10	11	12	13
Warangal	421	559	525	234	946	793	497	1,213	1,235	735	1,732	1,948
Karimnagar	671	840	219	157	890	997	2,885	3,097	625	590	3,510	3,687
Adilabad	236	307	186	162	472	469	310	450	504	286	814	736
Suba Total	1,378	1,706	930	553	2,308	2,259	3,962	4,760	2,364	1,611	6,056	6,371

	Wells						Other Sources							
	In good condition		Damaged		Total		In good condition		Damaged		Total		Serviceable	
	1910	1926	1910	1926	1910	1926*	1910	1926	1910	1926	1910	1926	1910	1926
	14	15	16	17	18	19	20	21	22	23	24	25	26	27
Warangal	12,053	14,093	2,012	1,783	14,065	15,876	205	63	21	46	226	109	13,176	15,928
Karimnagar	16,611	22,791	5,106	3,262	21,787	26,053	367	1,082	37	100	404	1,182	20,604	27,810
Adilabad	632	242	1,220	217	1,852	459	33	56	29	59	62	110	1,264	1,055
Suba Total	-7,366	37,126	8,338	5,262	3,70,704	42,388	605	1,201	87	205	692	1,401	35,044	44,793

	Total Unserviceable Last year		Total Unserviceable this year		Grand Total This year		Grand Total Total		Repairs undertaken during the year: Through Revenue Department: Emergent Repairs		Through Revenue Department: Kowli Dastaband Repairs		Through Irrigation Department		Total	
	1910	1926	1910	1926	1910	1926	1910	1926	1910	1926	1910	1926	1910	1926	1910	1926
	28	29	30	31	32	33	34	35	36	37	38	39	40	41	42	43
Warangal	6,779	2,533	14	265	3,793	2,798	16,969	16,726	13	68	2	—	—	43	15	111
Karimnagar	5,957	3,956	30	153	5,987	4,109	26,591	31,919	9	137	254	—	139	17	402	154
Adilabad	1,915	705	—	19	1,915	724	3,179	1,779	28	55	—	—	—	—	28	55
Suba Total	11,651	7,194	44	437	11,695	7,631	46,739	52,424	50	260	256	—	139	60	445	320

Source : Subedari Warangal *Files* No. 71 of 1319 Fasli (1910) & R. No. 3757 of 1321 Fasli (1912) & R. No. 103 of 1338 Fasli (1929) & R. No. 3100 of 1339 Fasli (1930).

years and one strong reason for this great divergence was the big margin that existed, in well cost. Though *taccavi* was advanced for well-sinking, only those ryots who promised to grow food crops for first five years could get the benefit[30] and besides this, they were made to do lot of *pairavi*[31] involving considerable expenditure before they got it.[32] Most of the wells remained private and their service in wet cultivation depended on the variation in the amount of rainfall for they were not dug to the ground-water level, the reason being the poor financial condition of the average farmer. On the other hand, this type of water source very much suited the Deccan Trap in which lay the *Suba* region[33] and further, it gave the facility to a ryot of changing crops according to his need and demand, which was very much restricted in the case of tank and canal irrigation. But, the discrimination that was rather obscurely and unjustly made in respect of rate of assessment between those wells which were constructed before and after 1908 had became not only a source of long-standing grievance to the farmers, but led to the farmers, but led to deliberate neglect in repairing the demand ones.[34] Though there was decrease in the number of damaged wells between the years and their number in 1926 formed 12.41% of the total number, yet the fact that as many as 5,262 wells remained unserviceable in the *Suba* in 1926 was to be reckoned with significance, especially in view of the growing scarcity of foodgrains that was experienced in the Dominions from time to time.

KUNTAS : After wells, *Kuntas* and tanks formed the largest source of irrigation. The former were smaller in command area and bounded with earth. Though they were 50% higher in number than larger tanks, yet, due to vagaries of the monsoon, water sufficient for wet cultivation could be collected only once in four or five years.[35] But, the cultivations were charged wet rate even during this lean period and if at all remission was to be sought in this respect, they were made to go round *Patwaris* and *Girdavars* for recommending *talaf-mal* on account of crop failure.[36] The bunds being earthen, got breached even in years of normal rainfall and the accumulation of alluvial deposits year by year raised the level of the river bed making it after some time completely unserviceable. Consequently, the number of damaged *Kuntas* as shown in *Table XXII* was far higher than that in respect of tanks and the percentages were as higher as 59.66% in 1910 and 33.84% in 1926. But, the repair work was usually undertaken by the P.W.D. at such a snail's pace that even Director-General of Revenue in his tour of Warangal District in 1944 expressed his unhappiness at delaying repairs to twenty major *Kuntas* in that District.[37] The result of such apathy was that the farmers in the *Suba* were deprived of taking the benefit of water s pply from as many as 1,611 *Kuntas* in 1926.

TANKS : Excepting the few river projects of Palair, Wyra, Manair and Kadam,[38] rest of the major irrigation in the area was done by means of tanks, both natural and artificial.[39] Intending and affording *pattedars* were allowed to construct tanks with the permission of the Government and they were also held responsible for their repair and unkeep.[40] *Netris* or *Neerudus* were appointed to look after the tank sluices and release of water to the fields pertaining to Government tanks for which purpose they were granted *Balota Inam* land and also tax remission amounting to Rs. 36/- per year.[41] For the construction and repair of private tanks, *Dastband*[42] *kowls* were granted by the Government. According to these *kowl* agreements, the *Dastbanddar* for maintaining the sluices, bunds and bed of the tank in good condition was allowed payment of one-tenth of land revenue that would accrue to the Government from the lands irrigated under the said tank. Failure to discharge his obligation resulted in the forfeiture of the *Dastband* and cancellation of *Kowl.* But, in practice, the *Kowl* amount proved so meagre compared to the rising costs of repair and tank maintenance and further its non-payment for years together extending to even 37 years[43] that the *Kowldars* or their successors voluntarily opted for termination of their *Kowls*. This disinterestedness of the *Dastbanddars* could be seen from *Table XXII* that *Kowli Dasband* repairs of damaged tank formed only 27.52% of the total damaged tanks in 1910 and zero per cent in 1926.

Taking both tanks and kuntas into consideration for which the repairs were undertaken by the different agencies, the number of sources repaired out of the damaged ones formed only

13. 50% in 1910 and 14.78% in 1926. The position was deplorable in the case of *Jagirs* and *Sarf-i-Khas.* When First *Taluqdar* of Adilabad reported to *Subedar* that many irrigation sources which were under the control of *Jagirdars* that were paying ¼th of their revenue to Government[44] were not repaired, the matter was passed over as of least importance.[45] A tank in Jafargadh, a *Sarf-i-Khas* village in Warangal District that got breached in 1901 was not repaired even upto 1933.[46] As against 44 repairable sources that were there in 1934 in *Sarf-i-Khas* area of Karimnagar Taluq, not even a single one was repaired.[47]

iii. Potential and Actual Irrigation : Though wells far outnumbered other sources mumerically.[48] Yet, in the actual area irrigated as shown in *Table XXIII*, tank irrigation formed as much as 78.32% of the total area irrigated and far exceeded other sources including well-irrigation which accounted for only 9.91% Canal irrigation managed by Government formed only 7.13% and others were still behind. In both tank and well-irrigation as well as in the total area irrigated, Karimnagar led the other Districts and also the State. On the other hand, Warangal District dominated in respect of canal irrigation mainly because of the concentration of river projects in its Taluqs. Adilabad lagged far behind in respect of each source and its area irrigated formed only 17.06% of the total area irrigated in the *Suba*. But, it is significant to note that the two Taluqs of Nirmal and Chinnoor together accounted for 50% of the total area irrigated in the District and as a matter of fact, these two always remained in the forefront of economic dominance in Adilabad. The Taluqs of Mahaboobabad, Pakhal and Khammam in Warangal District and Sirsilla, Karimnagar and Jagtiyal in Karimnagar District ranked high in area irrigated and these were the same which in the latter forties spearheaded the Peasant Struggle.

But, irrigated area treated as a proportion of cultivated area looked quite meagre and insignificant. It could be seen from *Table XXIV* that it was never more than 19%[49] and though there was some increase in it between 1911-21, it fell appreciably then onwards until 1941 (see *chart I*). Though there was element of variation in rainfall, yet, this unwholesome trend speaks of the fact that the actual *ayacuts*, as

TABLE XXIII

Area under Irrigation for 1345 Fasli (1936)

Sl. No.	Taluq	Total area sown (including area sown more than once)	By Canals		Area Irrigated			
			Government	Private	By Tanks	By Wells	Other Sources	Total***
1	2	3	4	5	6	7	8	9
1.	Warangal	3,33,192	4,019	955	12,330	4,581	155	16,961
2.	Khammam	3,13,005	3,910	349	29,812	3,243	1,905	33,957
3.	Mahboobabad	3,43,052	2,617	601	32,353	..	..	42,359
4.	Madhira	1,94,427	1,249	107	16,337	..	..	16,407
5.	Pakhal	67,362	950	500	27,646	1,438	..	38,084
6.	Paloncha	1,27,460	1,071	300	2,618	..	..	7,618
7.	Mulug	91,825	549	169	..	1,564	..	564
8.	Yellandu	86,620	744	201	16,514	..	..	16,514
9.	Paloncha (s)*	..	989	..	2,575	..	..	2,575
10.	Kanath	19,341	239	709	731	966	97	109
Total Warangal District		15,76,784	16,337	3,946	1,40,916	11,792	2,157	1,75,148

11. Jagtiyal	2,66,521	4,426	. .	20,215	4,635	1,321	42,987
12. Sultanabad	1,99,909	1,500	. .	20,398	1,800	4,369	17,619
13. Karimnagar	3,31,942	2,044	1,511	28,550	4,200	529	47,723
14. Sirsilla	2,17,606	2,355	550	25,150	5,120	910	47,199
15. Huzurabad	1,78,884	1,500	. .	16,714	7,277	1,454	19,891
16. Parkal	1,73,173	. .	. .	18,596	2,117	1,886	14,599
17. Mahadeopur	1,38,841	170	. .	20,664	325	. .	11,159
18. Metpalli (J)*	40,299	. .	. .	5,894	900	432	5,235
19. Peddapalli (J)*	94,403	. .	350	2,936	1,576	. .	4,662
20. Vemalwada (J)*	1,862	. .	. .	811	15	. .	126
21. Kamanpur	13,812	. .	47	1,443	3	. .	1,493
Total Karimnagar District	16,57,452	11,995	2,458	1,61,371	27,968	10,901	2,14,693
22. Adilabad	2,05,897	1,079	200	638	. .	251	3,889
23. Chinnur	1,00,000	. .	97	16,427	. .	. .	16,400
24. Asifabad	73,527	. .	113	1,176	. .	74	1,258
25. Luxettipet	1,23,180	975	. .	6,143	222	951	14,441
26. Kinwat	1,85,577	1,077	109	69	2,340	. .	369
27. Utnoor	55,040	. .	. .	285	2	. .	287
28. Boath	1,08,700	997	144	597	. .	12	669

29. Nirmal	1,68,615	. .	. .	25,703	3,696	110	26,703
30. Rajura	1,37,897	. .	. .	424	560	. .	484
31. Sirpur	1,06,780	1,080	249	8,168	. .	. .	9,168
32. Yelgadar (P)**	20,200	. .	. .	. .	. .	. .	. .
Total Adilabad District	12,85,413	5,208	912	65,909	6,842	1,498	80,269
Suba Total	45,19,649	33,540	7,406	3,68,196	46,602	14,456	4,70,110

*(S) *Samasthan*

**(P) *Paigah*

***This does not tally with the total of items 4 to 8.

*(J) *Jagir*

Source : *Hyderabad District Gazetteers, Tables Volumes 1931 & 1936., Warangal* (pp. 300-301), *Karimnagar* (p. 300) & *Adilabad* (p. 298).

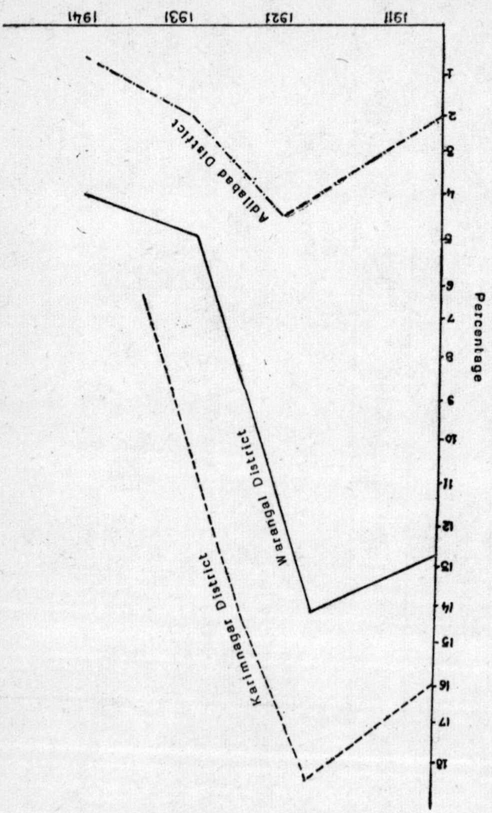

Chart I : Percentage of Cultivated area which was irrigated 1911-1941

TABLE XXIV

Percentage of Cultivated area which was irrigated, 1911-1949

Sl. No.	Name of the District/ region/State	Percentage of cultivated area which was irrigated 1911	1921	1931	1941	1949
1	2	3	4	5	6	
1.	Warangal District	12.9	14.4	5.1	4.2	
2.	Karimnagar ,,	16.5	18.6	12.4	6.6	
3.	Adilabad ,,	2.7	4.6	2.1	0.8	
4.	Telangana Region	. .	14.1	8.6	40,3	
5.	State	. .	8.2	5.3	2.8	7*

Compiled from : *Census Reports, Hyderabad State, 1911* (p. 16), *1921*, (p. 33), *1931* (p. 37) & *1941* (p.3)
&
**Report of the Agrarian Reforms Committee, 1949*, p. 177.

against the potential under bigger tanks and river projects got shrunk considerably. *Table XXV* indicates that neither in river projects like Palair and Wyra nor in the case of large tanks like Pakhal and Laknavaram, did the area irrigated ever reach the forecast figures fixed by P.W.D. or the Settlement Department. It in some years touched as low a figure as forming 12.22% and 13.51%[50]. On account of this declining trend in the area irrigated, the percentage of return on cost was also not much.[51] Government suffered considerable loss in revenue in the case of the historic Laknavaram project as the return worked out to only 2% on the restoration cost, even though there was sufficient water all the time in the tank.[52] Whereas the anticipated percentage of return in the case of Palair and Wyra projects was 6.56% and 4.16% respectively, the actual percentage of return was only 2.83% with concession[53] and 4.56% without concession in respect of Palair and 2.73% with concession and 3.82% without concession in respect of Wyra.[54] There was sufficient water in the reservoirs of the famous Pakhal and Ramappa projects to take up '*Do Fasla*' cultivation,[55] but the big and absentee landlords

TABLE XXV

Area Forecast and Irrigated under Some Important River Projects and Tanks

(In Acres & Guntas)

PALAIR Project				WYRA Project			PAKHAL Tank	
	Forecast Area by P.W.D	Area irrigated	Percentage of return on expenditure	Year	Forecast area	Area irrigated	Percentage of return on expenditure	Year
1	2	3	4	5	6	7	8	9
*1928	19,650	551	. .	1931*	17,390	2,280	. .	1938
1929	,,	2,564	. .	1932	,,	3,585	, .	1939
1930	,,	4,248	. .	1933	,,	7,912	. .	1940
1931	,,	3,565	. .	1934	,,	11,941	3.53	1941
1932	,,	5,860	. .	1935	,,	13,493	3.80	1942
1933	,,	3,449	. .	1936	,,	9,249	2.48	1943
1934	,,	9,714	4.25	1937	,,	13,593	3.80	1944
1935	,,	12,729	4.63	1938	,,	13,664	3.82	1945
1936	,,	12,889	4.56	1939	,,	13,751	. .	1946
1937	,,	6,607	1.88	1940	,,	9,906	. .	1947

1938	,,	12,860	4,56	1941	,,	13,281	..	..
1939	,,	7,341	1.22	1942	,,	870	..	..
1940	,,	6,632	..	1943	,,	12,560	..	..
1941	,,	11,921	..	1944	14,542**	7,637	..	..
1942	16,084-33**	6,800	..	1945	,,	3,212	..	..
1943	,,	7,564-14	..	1946	,,	11,151	..	..
1944	,,	4,806-8	..	..	..	..	..	..
1945	,,	11,419-12	..	..	..	..	..	..
1946	,,	9,355-13	..	..	..	..	..	..
1947	,,	10,631-31	..	..	..	..	..	..
1948	,,	12,703-12	..	..	..	..	..	..

			(in Acres & Guntas)					
			Laknavarem		Tank	Bhimghanpur		Tank
	Forecast area	Area irrigated	year	Forecast area	Area irrigated	Year	Forecast area	Area irrigated††
	10	11	12	13	14	15	16	17
1928†	8,910	2,400-39	1920	3,535-34	2,274-31	1943	2,000	3,590-28
1929	,,	5,547-17	1921	,,	1,248-39	1944	,,	2,681-29
1930	,,	3,682-18	1922	,,	3,031-17	1945	,,	4,162-18
1931	,,	5,848-01	1923	,,	1,972-37	1946	,,	2,742-35
1932	,,	2,962-12	1924	,,	2,823-09	1947	,,	1,916-12
1933	,,	6,168-21	1925	,,	2,829-04	..	..	..
1934	,,	5,985-25	1926	,,	2,432-17	—	—	—
1935	,,	3,836-23	1927	,,	2,402-20	—	—	—
1936	,,	4,705-33	1928	,,	2,793-25	—	—	—
1937	,,	4,201-35	1929	,,	2,522-02	—	—	—
1938	,,	—	1930	,,	2,044-00	—	—	—
1939	,,	—	1931	,,	2,780-00	—	—	—
1940	,,	—	1932	,,	2,514-00	—	—	|

1941	,,	—	1937	,,	†4,193-00	—	—	—
1942	,,	—	1938	,,	3,021-00	—	—	—
1943	,,	—	1941	,,	2,470-9	—	—	—
1944	,,	—	1942	,,	493-4	—	—	—
1945	,,	—	1943	,,	1,268-1	—	—	—
1946	,,	—	1944	,,	2,477-38	—	—	—
1947	,,	—	1945	,,	2,013-38	—	—	—
1948	,,	—	1946	,,	2,637-20	—	—	—
	,,	—	1947	,,	3,435-38	—	—	—
			1948	,,	432-14	—	—	—

*Year of commencement of the project.

**Fixed in Revision Settlement.

†This was due to expansion in the *ayacut*.

††The fact that it looked more than the forecast area in many of the years might be due to the fact that some nearby drylands or those outside the fixed *ayacut* might have utilised the waters on payment of *Sivai-Jamabandi*.

Compiled from :

1. W.S. *File* No. 10 of 1349 Fasli (1940) & R. No. 683 of 1357 Fasli (1948).
2. W.S. *File* No. 32 of 1355 Fasli (1946) & R. No. 685 of 1357 Fasli (1948).
3. W.S. *File* No. 19 of 1356 Fasli (1947) & R. No. 1740 of 1357 Fasli (1948).
4. W.S. *File* No. 1 of 1357 Fasli (1948) & R. No. 2064 of 1357 Fasli.
5. Agriculture Department, Government of Hyderabad, S. No. 21 & *File* No. 56 of 1354 Fasli (1945).

&

6. W.S. File No. 7 of 1346 Fasli (1937) & R. No. 1587 of 1352 Fasli (1943)

were not prepared for it and in the case of Pakhal, the largest natural lake in the Dominions, there was as much as 3,196 acres and *guntas* of fallow land in 1944.[56] Even the State taken as a whole, the position was all the same discouraging. Besides the river waters of Godavari and Krishna with their tributaries, it received annually from rainfall more than two million cubic feet of water out of which barely 10% was utilised for irrigation and the rest ran to waste.[57]

(*iv*) *Reasons for low utilisation of irrigational resources* : Under both Ramappa and Pakhal projects[57a] whose settled *ayacut* extended to 5,177 acres and 8,910 acres respectively,[58] low utilisation of the irrigation potential had mainly occurred because of the notable presence of big *pattedars* with vast estates of irrigable land under their absentee ownership. Pingal Partap Reddy had a holding of 2,113 acres out of the net ayacut of 3,001 acres and 39 *quntas* that remained after deducting *Inam* land under Ghanpur project in Warangal Taluq and 1,899 acres and 37 *quntas* out of a net *ayacut* of 4,927-32 *quntas* that remained after deducting *Inam* land under Ramappa project.[59] The respective percentage worked out to 70.38% and 38.53%. Under Pakhal project, Mr. Mahboob Reddy, another big *pattedar* alone possessed about 10,000 acres, which amounted to total monopolization of the *ayacut*.[60] These landlords who never stayed on these lands took no interest in cultivation. They got their land cultivated in *tabi* only by giving them on *battai*[61] to the ryots of Huzurabad, Pakhal, Karimnagar and also of surrounding villages where there were no water sources for *tabi*.[62] Even though water in the reservoirs was there for *tabi* cultivation, they never took it up for the reason that none came from the other tracts during this crop season to cultivate these absentee lands on exorbitant rents as they could get profitable *kowls* in their own areas.[63] When other cultivators with small or no holdings came forward from local villages to cultivate these lands on double crop basis[64] and consequently First *Taluqdar* and also *Subedar* of Warangal proposed to the Government for compulsory introduction of '*do-fasla*' under these *ayacuts* and most important of all, redistribution of these absentee lands among small and needy cultivators. Such attempts time and again, were foiled by absentee landlords like Pingal Partap Reddy whose influence and leverage at higher Governmental circles was so complete that even *Subedar* could do nothing but express his anguish.[65] Thus, available water resources could not be utilised to the possible extent, due to the vested interests of the dominant feudal section of the area.

Shrinkage in the area irrigated was mainly due to the insufficiency of water in the tanks brought about by the lowering of F.T.L. (Full Tank Level) at the time of the restoration of tanks inordinate delay in the construction of field channels and the neglect and indifference with which the tanks and canals were maintained.[66] *Table XXV* indicates that the forecast area, as a result of Revision, had been reduced in respect of Palair project from 19,650 acres to 16,084-33 acres and in respect of Wyra project from 17,390 acres to 14,542 acres in the years 1942 and 1944 respectively. The construction of field channels to supply water for an *ayacut* of 3,300 acres under Baithpally project in Madhira Taluq was not done even upto 1948 when the tank was restored in 1938[67] with a forecast area of 4,800 acres. But for the indifference of the Revenue and Irrigation Departments, the matter should not have been delayed for a decade and above in view of the prevailing practice that the cost of excavation of field channels was advanced by Revenue Department to ryots under the *ayacut* by way of *taccavi* and was collected back in instalments along with interest also.[68] In view of the fertile soils in the *ayacut* and the keenness of the cultivators towards wet cultivation,[69] the loss to agricultural production on account of this Departmental lapse was definitely of huge dimensions.[69a] Serviceability of tanks and *kuntas* very much depended on the removal of alluvial deposits that got accumulated in tank beds, cleaning or removal of slit in feeders and field channels and instant repair of sluices and bunds that went out of order. These matters, if attended to promptly would, in fact, increase the scope for greater utilisation of irrigational sources.[70] But, these were given the least care even though separate Department of Irrigation was there right from 1896 A.D. and cognizance was taken in this respect only when a source had completely gone out of service.[71] Failure to clean the field channels, though not the tank beds, resulted in immediate suffering of the cultivators that the tailend ryots got deprived cf water supply to their fields.[72] The spending by the State on this nation-building service through the period did not speak much for its keenness in this regard. It rose from 23.27 lakhs in 1911-12 to 30.17 lakhs in 1948-49, an increase of 6.90 lakhs over a period of 37 years, with of course, wider falls in between amounting to 9.36 lakhs in 1934-35 and 8.01 lakhs in 1935-36.[73] The financial stringency of the Government in this respect could well be gauged from the fact that the Manair river project, the only one of its kind in Karimnagar District proposed to irrigate 23,000 acres in 18 villages of Sirsilla Taluq[74] and produce 1,076 k.w. of electricity,[75] at an estimated expenditure of Rs. 35,80,000/-[76] though earnestly submitted by First *Taluqdar* for the sanction of the Government in 1928,[77] was approved by the P.W.D. only in 1939[78] and the actual work commenced only in 1945 to be completed towards the end of 1949.[79]

Late release of water, non-provision of water for sowing of seedlings for transplantation, unpredictability regarding the release of water, corruption in the release of water, faulty fixing of forecast areas and also height of sluices of flank channels, delay in conducting *phodi*[80] of *ayacut* lands and grant of their *pattas*, forest and *shikargah*[81] areas intervening cultivated lands, prevalence of malarial climate and poor communication facilities to majority of the villages, were several other factors that accounted for poor utilisation of the irrigational facilities in the area. Water used to be released in the month of *Meher*[82] or August by which time *abi* sowing was generally completed by ryots.[83] Further, farmers in the area adopted the practice of growing paddy seedlings for transplantation. As water was released late from tanks and as all the cultivators did not possess wells whose water supply also very much varied with the timing and the amount of rainfall, *abi* cultivation of rice was considerably affected. Very much appreciating this situation, First *Taluqdar* of Warangal while submitting Progress Report on irrigation under Palair project for the year 1948 expressed the opinion that if the P.W.D. arranged to supply water in time for growing seedlings, a large area could be brought under wet cultivation, which was then cultivated under crops or allowed to lie fallow.[84] But, neither this was given effect nor the construction of wells which was suggested as an alternative was feasible due to differing physical features and construction costs nor was it encouraged as a special and emergent Governmental measure. Not only the release of water was late, but the very supply became uncertain for ryots. They, in the hope of getting water to their fields, grow seedlings under their private arrangement and just before '*Magha Karthi*',[85] the Irrigation Department announces its inability to supply water and the ryots in utter disappointment, were made to go for dry crops, suffering their seedlings wasted.[85] The embarassment and loss to ryots would have been avoided if the average area irrigated actually under a sources during the last four or five years was fixed as the *ayacut limit*.[87] But, contrary to this, the Officers of the Department satisfied themselves by keeping ambitious forecast acerage that was never and could be reached. The result would be that the more of '*tahbandi*'[88] the less was the crop and more applications for *talaf-mal*.[89]

Irrigation in the area did not remain free from the hand of official corruption. Even though there was 12' water in Palair reservoir, some of the ryots of Nelakondapalli village of Khammam Taluq were not released water for their paddy fields as they did not satisfy the P.W.D. officers and the result was that the crops got dried up.[90] Similarly, the ryots of Kalakota village of Khammam Taluq getting their lands irrigated under Wyra project, were forced to pay bribe to Mohammad Ismail Khan, *Mojinidar*[91] @ Rs. 14-8-0 per acre in 1938 at the time of doing *Phodi* of their lands.[92] These collections acted as a drag on the limited finances of the cultivators and consequently affected their capacity for investment on agricultural imputs, wrong fixing of channel sluices on a higher level than water level in the reservoir could normally reach it, had also affected in no small measure the irrigational development. The head sluice of the Right Flank channel of Palair project was constructed in such a way that it remained eight feet higher than left Flank channel and consequently, only when there was 13' level of water in the reservior, the Right channel could catch the water.[93] This became such a rare possibility that during the 13 year period preceding 1941, the 1,200 acre *ayacut* under the Right channel received water in *abi* season only twice.[94] As this phenomenon proved to be a source of loss both to Government and the ryots, these lands were finally in 1946, on the wise initiative of Revenue Member who paid a visit to the area in 1941, removed from the *ayacut* and classed as dry.[95]

The undue delay that took place in the Survey and Settlement of *ayacut* lands of some of the projects like those of Bhimghanpur and Baithpalli had definite impact on irrigation under these sources. The former in Mahadeopur Taluq of Karimnagar District was restored in 1917 A.D. at a cost of Rs. 50,326/- to irrigate an *ayacut* of 2,000 acres.[96] Matters went on in such a slow and haphazard pace that by 1948, only 1,160 acres out of the estimated area, forming 58% was cleared of forest whose demarcation was done in 1940 after a gap of 23 years since tank restoration and even these few surveyed lands were not brought under *Jamabandi* and granted *attas*, but on the other hand, the unfortunate ryots were allowed to cultivate these lands only on *Sivai-Jamabandi*.[97] The result of non-grant of *pattas* was that the farmers resorted to shifting cultivation from one plot to another and evinced no interest in land development. Consequently, the maximum area cultivated at any time until 1946 was only 567 acres-16 *quntas*.[98] The remaining 840 acres of proposed *ayacut* was allowed to remain as a forest area right throughout.[99] In the case of Baithpalli,[100] even though irrigation started in 1943, *Phodi* work of the *ayacut* lands was not done until 1948 and Settlement Commissioner was only asked to take it up.[101] This slackness on the part of the official machinery was in great variance with the eagerness of the cultivators in this *ayacut* for wet cultivation.

Prevalence of thick forests and *shikargah*[102] interspersed between cultivated lands and their non-demarcation and clearance had not only restricted the irrigable area, but, on the other hand, immensely contributed for the prevalence of acute malarial conditions which, in turn, resulted in sparseness of population and scarcity of agricultural labour. These conditions existed in varying degrees, in the *ayacut* areas of Ramappa, Pakhal, Laknavaram and Bhimghanpur. Under Laknavaram project, one *Pattedar* alone by name Venkat

Krishna Shastry possessed about 2,561 acres and 23 *guntas* located in thick forest and he began to make huge profit by cutting and selling the trees rather than to bring these vast lands under the plough.[103] In Pakhal area, the Royal Hunting Preserve consisted of 1,000 acres out of the total *ayacut* of 9,000 acres[104] and section. 2669 Vol. IV of Revenue code strictly prohibited ryots to cultivate within 300 yards of the *shikar-gah.*[105] The First *Taluqdar* of Warangal expressed that if the limits of Government land and Hunting Preserve were settled and demarcated, hundreds of acres could be brought under cultivation.[106] Under Bhimghanpur, 840 acres of *ayacut* land consisting of dense jungle was left uncleared throughout the period.[107] Thousands of acres of irrigable land thus left uncleared and unutilised in dense jungles had adversely affected the scope for increased agricultural production.

The incidence of malaria was so acute in these forest-ridden *ayacuts* that cultivators and labourers came from the adjoining tracts to take up cultivation work in these areas only during *tabi* season and that too, when they failed to get work in their own and other villages for want of water supply for irrigation. They left these villages immediately after the harvest was over and *abi* crop could not be raised in these areas even though there was sufficient water in the reservoirs fortaking it up.[108] Population, on account of this frightening disease, became so much sparse that under Laknavaram project, out of 17 villages only three were really populated and the rest 14 were deserted.[109] Under Bhimghanpur and Pakhal also, the malaria was so rampant that people got afraid to settle in these *ayacut* areas, whatever might be the scope for possession of land and irrigational facilities.[110] On the other hand, the efforts made by the Government to contain and combat this widespread and dreadful disease, had never been in commensuration with the magnitude of the task and hence, the areas continued to remain backward and sparsely populated. The benefits of its eradication to agriculture were so much that when the Government in 1950 decided to spend Rs. 1,00,000 on its removal in the areas of Laknavaram and Ramappa projects, it was estimated that these efforts would lead to the increase of land cultivated under these tanks additionally by 6,000 acres.[111]

Lack of proper roads[112] in the *ayacut* areas of Pakhal, Laknavaram, Bhimghanpur, Singabhupalem, Baithpalli and Chegaon[113] projects acted as a hindrance for the development of irrigation and also the all-round prosperity of the village covered by them. In fact, they being not only endowed with irrigation but also rich timber yielding forests.[114] they deserved special attention and development roads should have been undertaken[115]. But, unfortunately, the very fact that they contained thick forests, had thrown them into utter neglect in this respect. Irrigation in the case of these projects commenced respectively in 1920, 1919, 1917, 1941 and 1942.[116] On the other hand, Irrigation Progress Reports in respect of these tanks, submitted for the year 1948 recorded dismal picture in respect of road development.[117] In other words, such a long period of 31 to 28 years in present century witnessed the neglect of this vital sector of rural development. The unwillingness of cultivators to settle in these areas in spite of sufficient water in reservoirs and fertile or suitable lands for wet crops, the non-seriousness of Health Officials in working for the eradication of malaria in these areas,[118] short supply of manures to ryots, non-exploitation of forest resources in an effective manner, etc., were all linked with road development. Even the few roads that were taken up were executed in portions and the whole length never got completed for years.[119] The feeder road from Chegaon project to the main Karimnagar-Luxettipet road which was started as a famine measure in 1939 could not yet be completed in 1948.[120] Further, the existing roads were badly maintained.[121] Thus, diverse factors more administrative than natural, had contributed for poor utilisation of irrigational potential in the region.

D. *CHARACTER OF AGRICULTURE* : Agriculture formed the predominant occupation of the people. For every 1,000 of population in 1911, people pursuing cultivation numbered 536, 466 and 673 in the Districts of Warangal, Karimnagar and Adilabad respectively.[122] As dry holdings formed more than 80% of the total cultivated area,[123] agriculture in the area remained primarily dependent on monsoons and its att ndant fluctuations.[124] Further, none of the irrigational sources was perennial in nature and consequently, they too served only when there was adequate rainfall. The methods of agriculture that were adopted remained rather crude, primitive and unscientific.[125] The average cultivator was generally illiterate, unprogressive and was of a very suspicious nature. ever opposed to new methods and experiments, he was stubbornly unwilling to depart from his old traditional methods, however unsuitable and unprofitable they proved to be.[126] Ploughing was done by the traditional bullock-drawn wooden ploughs which was definitely slow and laborious[127]. Except in irrigated tracts where pressure of population was great and holdings were relatively small, the preparation of soil was hurried and unsatisfactory, manuring inadequate, and interculture not what it should be. The seed used was a mixture of types, and on the whole, low yielding. The improved seed developed by the Agriculture Department covered only about 5% of the total cultivated area.[128] Insect pests and plant diseases caused a huge loss annually both in the fields and store houses. To add to these handicaps, the financial resources of an ordinary cultivator remained very much limited, not leaving margin for investment on agricultural inputs.[129] The net result of all these factors was that the average yield per acre of most of the crops was decidedly low and compared unfavourably with the yields that obtained in adjacent British Indian Provinces.[130]

E. AGRICULTURAL RESEARCH AND EXPERIMENTATION : For a long time in the past, agriculture as a State subject was so much neglected that there used to be no separate grant for the improvement of agriculture in the State Budget till as late as 1911.[131] The reign of Mir Osman Alikhan was credited with the constitution of the Department of Agriculture in 1913 with Mr. Kenny as Director.[132] Till 1928, it mainly had the object of saving Gaorani[133] Cotton from deterioration. In 1928-29, the Department was reorganised and it started systematic efforts with Research, Experiments, Demonstration and propaganda wings, for the general improvement of the agriculture of the country.[134] For conducting crop experimentation of rice, groundnut, tobacco, cotton, maize, etc., and demonstrating the cultivators in improved methods of cultivation, Main Farm with a total area of 105 acres was opened at Warangal in 1933 to serve the cultivators of East Telangana Division which comprised the Districts of Karimnagar, Nalgonda, Warangal and Adilabad.[135] It also comprised in an area of 10 acres, a Horticultural Section, designed for fruit plantation and also of flowering and ornamental plants.[136] Supplementary efforts of directing Hyderabad Farming Association[137] and publishing '*Rahbar*', a magazine in Urdu[138] and distribution free of cost, among ryots of six printed leaflets in Urdu and Telgu languages, for the purpose of propagating the improved varieties of seeds, manures, implements and methods of cultivation, were also undertaken by the Department.[139] The success of these educative efforts of the Department was greatly limited by the poor percentage of literacy among the people of the *Suba*, which during the period 1911-50 remained only below 9% whereas the State's figure touched 25.2%.[140]

The basis of all agricultural progress is experiment. The strength of demonstration and propoganda wings depended on research.[141] The production of improved varieties of crops suited to different soil and climatic conditions was the most important activity of the Agricultural Department. The demonstration of Kharif jawar P.B. 4-K in Adilabad District giving an average yield of 538 lbs. as against 462 lbs per acre of the local variety, Gaorani Cotton 12 F.2 in Adilabad District yielding 220 lbs. of *kapas*[142] per acre as against 185 lbs. of the local variety, the early maturing paddy varieties of H.S. 12 and H.S. 19 in the Districts of Warangal and Karimnagar yielding 791 lbs. and 1,479 lbs. of paddy respectively as compared with 536 lbs. and 1,233 lbs. of the local varieties and the late maturing variety of H.S. 35 in Warangal District yielding an average of 2,260 lbs. per acre as against 1,766 lbs. of the local variety, marked some such activity of the Department.[143] But, the results of these experiments reached only an insignificant proportion of the cultivating population. Only one Government Farm at Warangal was meant to serve the farming needs of the three *Suba* Districts besides Nalgonda. The field staff or the *Kamgars* who came in personal contract with the ryots and on whom very much depended the success of improved varieties and methods, were so few and inadequate in number that even among these four Districts, the demonstration and propaganda activities were not extended to Karimnagar District until 1936 and to Adilabad District excepting Sirpur Taluq even beyond that.[144] In 1948-49 the staff who got engaged in Extension work in the entire State consisted of only 35 Agricultural Assistants and 165 *Kamgars* which was not able to contact more than one-third of the number of villages in the State.[145] Very few of these men stayed beyond the Taluq headquarters.[146] Further, most of the village level workers had no knowledge of the local languages and were not even able to talk to the agriculturists in their own language.[147] Having experienced these inadequacies, the agriculturists' Association rightly expressed in 1949 that, besides an experimental farm in a *Suba* of four Districts, there should be a 'demonstration farm' in each Taluq in order to translate into practical agriculture the results of research achieved in the experimental stations[148]. Besides being thus inadequate in personnel and equipment, the experimental farms were also felt to be of not much help by agriculturists, for the models and methods that were evolved were not in conformity with their purse and means.[149] The insufficiency of the field staff and demonstration farm was, in turn, very much due to the meagre funds that had been allotted to the Department right throughout. Their percentage to total expenditure of the State ranged from 0.94 in 1934-35 to 1.57 in 1950-51.[150]

F. SEEDS, THEIR SUPPLY AND UTILISATION: One of the quickest methods of increasing production is by the use of improved seeds. Selected improved seeds gave 10 to 30% increased production.[151] Use of better seeds was expected, in terms of quantity, to increase food production in Hyderabad State by at least one lakh tons per year, which would have significantly lessened the food imports.[152] But, the usual practice adopted by majority of ryots in the area was that they made their own seed arrangements, some preserved out of the previous crop, some borrowed from his neighbours and the rest taken on loan or '*Nag-Pech*'[153] from the money-lender-cum-grain-lender who extracted repayment in extra ranging from 25 to 50% for the season.[154] The supplies of the Agricultural Department were extended only to particular areas and for particular crops.[155] In fact, improved seed, fertilizers and implements such as tractors, were put to use only by a few large-scale farmers.[156] Until the year 1929-30, the farmers in Telangana Districts received no help at all, either of seed or manure from the Agricultural Department which only supplied cotton seeds to Marathwada Districts.[157] The very existence of the Department was not known to ryots in this earlier period.[158]

Table XXVI in which the acerage figures of East Telangana Division[159] under improved varieties of crops were given for the period 1933-34 to 1938-39, clearly reveals the fact that the seed supplied by the Department compared to the one produced and procured by cultivators locally, covered an insignificant proportion of the total acerage in an year. In fact, this percentage during the six year period suffered a steep decline from 13.42 in 1933-34 to 1.16 in 1938-39. Groundnut, bajra[160] and Paddy varieties occupied highest acerages, the former far outstripping the latter two combined, which only pointed to the onset of commercialization in agricultural production. When the stoppage of imports of rice and wheat from other Indian provinces during the Second Great War focussed the importance and necessity for increased food production, the Department intensified its efforts for the supply of varieties of food crops.[161] But, even then also, the extent of cultivators covered was not much. To cite an instance, among the ryots of Khammam and Madhira Taluqs under Wyra project with an *ayacut* area of 17,390 acres and an actually irrigated area of 870 acres in 1942, only 337 cultivators spread over 60 villages were supplied for *abi* crop with *taccavi* seed[162] of 2,543 bags.[163] The average worked roughly at 6 cultivators per village and 8 bags of seed per cultivator. For *abi* 1356 *Fasli* (1947), Paddy seeds covering only one cultivator in one village, consisting of 30 bags, covering 90 acres under Palair Project and none from Wyra Project, were supplied by the Department.[163a] Further, the confidence of ryots in Departmental seed was shaken by reported cases where it failed to sprout under wet cultivation.[164] The Department with its meagre resources and inadequate staff[165] found it so difficult to cope up with the work of seed multiplication consistent with even the limited demand, that seed purchased

TABLE XXVI

Area in acres under new and Improved varieties of crops in East Telangana Division, 1933-34 to 1938-39

Name of the crop	1933-34			1934-35			1935-36		
	Departmental seed	Natural seed	Total	Departmental seed	Natural seed	Total	Departmental seed	Natural seed	Total
1	2	3	4	5	6	7	8	9	10
Sugar cane varieties	40	243	283	77	235	312	393	194	587
Groundnut varieties	1,757	12,951	14,703	715	7,620	8,335	886	7,508	8,394
Cotton varieties	—	—	—	—	—	—	—	—	—
Wheat varieties	—	—	—	—	—	—	1	—	1
Paddy varieties	22	13	35	215	527	742	168	242	410
Bajra varieties	97	1 061	1,158	448	1,352	1,800	413	1,122	1,535
Jowar varieties	—	—	—	—	—	—	1	—	1
Castor varieties	—	—	—	—	—	—	35	—	35
Potatoes	—	—	—	—	—	—	1	—	—
Guinea grass	—	—	—	—	—	—	3	—	3
Total	1,916	14,268	16,184	1,455	9,734	11,189	1,901	9,066	10,967

Name of the crop	1936-37			1937-38			1938-39		
	Departmental seed	Natural seed	Total	Departmental seed	Natural seed	Total	Departmental seed	Natural seed	Total
	11	12	13	14	15	16	17	18	19
Sugar cane varieties	11	224	235	7	287	294	13	237	250
Groundnut varieties	611	92,800	934,11	2,318	1,26,059	1,28,377	1,225	1,42,051	1,43,276
Cotton varieties	—	—	—	75	—	75	12	80	92
Wheat varieties	—	—	—	5	—	5	—	—	—
Paddy varieties	86	302	388	340	907	1,247	438	4,128	4,566
Bajra varieties	104	675	779	290	1,187	1,477	44	2,500	2,544
Jowar varieties	—	—	—	29	—	29	—	—	—
Castor varieties	107	40	147	42	42	84	36	110	146
Potatoes	1	—	—	—	—	—	—	—	—
Guinea grass	—	—	—	—	—	—	—	—	—
Total	919	94,041	94,960	3,107	1,28,482	1,31,589	1,768	1,49,106	1,50,874

Compiled from :—*Annual Administration Reports of the Department of Agriculture, H.E.H. the Nizam's Government, for the years 1933-34* (p. 41), *1934-35* (p. 41), *1935-36* (p. 42), *1936-37* (p. 43), *1937-38* (pp. 38-39), & *1938-39* (pp. 40-41).

in the open market was also on occasions, distributed as improved seed,[166] which gave much room for suspicion in the minds of the farmers about the quality of the Departmental seed. Thus, the question of production and distribution of improved seed varieties, though fraught with immense possibilities of increased agricultural production, failed to receive the required strength and attention at the hands of the Government which had its consequential effect on the decline in the volume of production as well as yield per acre.

G. MANURES AND THEIR EXTENT OF USAGE : Lack of proper and sufficient manuring contributed not a little for low yields in the area. Dry crop land was ever hardly manured, for it became very expensive costing about three times the land revenue per acre.[167] Even with regard to wet and garden crops, the peasant depended mostly on that which was collected from his backyard or farmyard.[168] The practice of herding goats and sheep at night time on cultivated fields, especially paddy fields, was very much adopted by ryots in Telangana Districts, to provide fertility to the soils.[169] This did not cost the peasant much, for he paid only Re. 1/- for folding 500 goats for a single day and three such sittings proved enough for $\frac{3}{4}$th acre of wet land.[170] But, it proved really unfortunate that when by proper manuring, the yields of crops could be increased easily by 50%, the ryots due to shortage of fuel, burnt a large quantity of cowdung as fuel after getting it dried up.[171]

It can be seen from *Table XXVII* that though different types of manure were supplied by the Agricultural Department, the acreage covered appeared to be a meagre fraction of the total area cultivated. As there were four Districts in East Telangana Division, the supply of Departmental manures during the period 1931-32 to 1938-39, did not cover even 100 acres in each District. Though manures like castor cake, Ammonium Sulphate and Nicifos proved much useful in the cultivation of paddy, sugarcane groundnut, etc., the high cost of these fertilisers together with non-education of the cultivators by the Extension Staff of the Department about their benefits in cultivation yields, had led, in the main, to this poor utilisation. For *abi* 1336 *Fasli* (1947), among the manures of groundnut

TABLE XXVII

List of Manures Distributed (Through Department) East Telangana Division, 1931-32 to 1938-39

Name of the Manure	1931-32 Amount of manure	1931-32 Corres-ponding area	1932-33 Amount of manure	1932-33 Corres-ponding area	1933-34 Amount of manure	1933-34 Corres-ponding area	1934-35 Amount of manure	1934-35 Corres-ponding area
1	2	3	4	5	6	7	8	9
	Lbs	Acres	Lbs	Acres	Lbs	Acres	Lbs	Acres
Ammophos	..	..	..	..	..	..	..	..
Ammonium Sulphate	1,840	23	1,300	13	2,000	25	..	..
Super Phosphate	224	2	400	4	..	..	..	..
Castor Cake	32,000	10	39,040	..	33,440	10	1,61,120	51
Ground-nut Cake	..	..	..	..	..	..	..	..
Nicifos	..	..	19,152	171	18,550	186	12,230	122
Total	34,064	35	59,892	200	53,990	221	1,73,350	173

Name of the manure	1935-36 Amount of manure	1935-36 Corres-ponding area	1936-37 Amount of manure	1936-37 Corres-ponding area	1937-38 Amount of manure	1937-38 Corres-ponding area	1938-39 Amount of manure	1938-39 Corres-ponding area
	10	11	12	13	14	15	16	17
	Lbs	Acres	Lbs	Acres	Lbs	Acres	Lbs	Acres
Ammophos	..	.	..	..	..	..	..	..
Ammonium Sulphate	2,960	37	1,440	18	1 0,800	135	1,040	13
Super Pho-sphate	..	..	..	..	..	..	..	..
Castor Cake	3,51,330	139	11,200	24	22,240	11	7,680	10
Groundnut Cake	.. 3,650	.. 108	.. 11,680	.. 146	.. 12,084	.. 151	.. 3,840	.. 48
Total	3,62,940	284,	24,320	188	45,124	297	12,560	71

Compiled from : *The Annual Administration Reports of the Department of Agriculture, H.E.H. The Nizam's Government, for the years 1931-32* (p. 50), *1932-33* (p. 47), *1933-34* (p. 46) *1934-35* (p. 46), *1935-36* (p.54), *1936-37* (p. 52), *1937-38*, (pp, 50-51) & *1938-39* (p. 51).

cake, bonemeal, superphosphate, only 194 cultivators spread over 15 villages under Palair project and 313 cultivators of 17 villages under Wyra project were supplied with only 4,137 bags of groundnutcake (Area 1,400 acres) and 7,901 bags of the same (Area 2,935 acres) respectively[171a]. Oil cakes of castor and groundnut,[172] being obtained locally and found of immense use in paddy and sugarcane growing, were put to greater use than other varieties. But, higher prices prevailing for these items in British India amounting to a difference of even Rs. 100/- per ton, encouraged exports from the State and the Government, at times, taking the local demands into consideration, was compelled to ban the export of these manures.[173] Green manures, though of much utility in paddy growing, were not very much resorted to. Only big farmers who had '*Kanchas*'[174] could go for them.[175] Manurial crops which required only one or two waterings, could be grown if water was there in the tanks after the *abi* season and was supplied free of assessment.[176] Such conditions did not obtain in the area during the period of study. Preparation of compost manure out of town refuse had just begun only in the year 1950 and this could not meet to some extent the manurial requirements of the farmers of the near-by villages.[177] The net result that obtained in the overall situation was that though the manure distribution programme of the State aimed at supplying manure for three to four lakh acres every year, the off-take of manure from the godowns had been considerably below the expectation.[178] This naturally led to low production.

H. CROP DISEASES AND CONTROL MEASURES : Insect pests and crop diseases took a heavy toll every year in the State. This was particularly the case in Telangana Districts where, on account of irrigation and double cropping, the attack of insect pests became a regular feature of rice cultivation. Hispa (*nalla purugu*), grass hopper (*midatha*), swarming caterpillar (*prakudu purugu*), and gall-fly (*dumparogam*) did lot of damage to rice crop every year.[179] Other important crops of jawar, groundnut and castor were also not free from insect damages. It was estimated that on an average about 1,00,000 tons of jawar grain was destroyed every year on account of smut disease (*kani*) alone in the State.[180] The enormity of the damage could be realised from the fact that for the year 1931-32, the Department received from the Districts as many as 190 reports of insect damage to various crops including extensive damage to paddy crop in Warangal and Karimnagar Districts due to *Schoenobius incertellus* (Paddy stem-borer) attack.[181]

When such was the magnitude and seriousness of the nature and effect of crop diseases, it was unfortunate and of great loss from the view point of agricultural production that until the end of 1949, no regular research work had been carried on by the Agricultural Department on either the extent of loss caused by the weeds or on the method of their eradication[182] Only general and salient measures like 15" deep tractor ploughing,[183] setting up of light traps[184] and rat poison-baits[185] etc., were advocated for the removal of weeds and insects. But, these processes naturally involved much expense as tractor ploughing was to be done on hire by majority of the cultivators and also much cumbursomeness in arranging traps as climatic conditions did influence their set-up. Though the invention of B.H.C and its various preparations since 1950 has helped very much in counteracting most of the crop diseases that were experienced,[186] yet, the entire reign of the last *Nizam* remained without any systematic or scientific crop control measures and as a result, the cultivators of the region were made to suffer heavy crop losses from time to time.

I. AGRICULTURAL IMPLEMENTS : These remained mostly of traditional pattern only. Bullock drawn wooden ploughs and carts continued to be the prime possession of the cultivators.[187]. Improved implements such as iron ploughs, 'Persian wheel water lift', 'power-pumping plants', 'oil engine', 'tractors', etc., were supplied by the Department of Agriculture. Though the cultivators came to appreciate the advantage of some of the new implements like iron ploughs and 'power-pumping plants' in the sense that the former helped in the ploughing of more acerage at greater depth than the wooden one and the later helped in quick extraction of water from wells, avoiding at the same time great amount of exertion for weak-bodied bullocks in drawing the *mhote*[188] of the country type, yet their cost was beyond the reach of most of them.[189] Besides the cost, the operational mechanism of some of these improved implements like 'oil engines' and 'water pumping sets' proved beyond the grasp of the ordinary ryo.[190] The lack of repair and replacement facilities that existed in the case of traditional implements, was also a strong factor that turned the ryots against these new appliances.[191] Love and strong attachment to the traditional implements, born out of inbred conservatism, also very much prompted the ryots not to opt for the improved implements.

The net result of these cumulative factors was that only an insignificant percentage of the total number of cultivators in East Telangana Division came forward to purchase the new appliances from the Department. To cite the trend in the case of iron ploughs between the years 1931-32 to 1938-39, the number distributed ranged from 2 to 45 and it was 1 to 4 in the case of 'power-pumping plants'.[192] These few also might have been taken by rich farmers. Though tractor owing was beyond the reach of ordinary cultivators, these were supplied by the Department since 1947 on hire @ Rs. 20/-per acre.[193] As these were alloted at such a wide margin of five for one district[194] and as one tractor ploughed four acres per day.[195] the intending cultivators would be made to wait rather too long for their time and under such circumstances, frequent tractor ploughing would neither be possible nor advantageous to soil from the view point of retention of fertility.[196] It was however, most suited for the cultivation of '*banjar*' lands[196a].

If both the old and new types of ploughs and carts were taken together into consideration, then the *Suba* Districts, excelled in the number possessed. In 1919, in respect of ploughs, Karimnagar District with 1,23,097 and Warangal with 1,10,255, occupied the second and third positions in the State and regarding carts in the same year, Karimnagar with 56,068 and Adilabad with 41,910 stood second and third in the State.[197] These numbers got further increased to the extent of 50% by 1935[198]. But, it is interesting to note that these imposing figures look small if they were considered as an average per 100 of population. If considered so, the averages in

1935, in respect of ploughs for the three Districts of Warangal, Karimnagar and Adilabad were 15.7, 12.4 and in respect of carts, they averaged 4.1, 5.7 and 8.3 respectively.[199] Even the cultivating population of these Districts did not fall below 50% of the total population.[200] Not only thus there was deficiency in these prime requisites of cultivators, but that with the introduction of controls in 1944 which included iron also, iron components that were required in the manufacture of agricultural implements began to be sold at exorbitant rates in black market. This situation of undue suffering to ryots was traceable even in 1950.[201] Thus, in the matter of agricultural implements, tradition and deficiency prevailed, with natural tendency for decrease in production.

J. ANIMAL HUSBANDRY AS AN AGRICULTURAL ADJUNCT : The fact that agricultural operations in the *Suba* were mainly carried by means of bullock power[202] and cattle refuse was chiefly used as manure to the fields[203], made it clear that the growth of agricultural production was dependent on adequate growth of livestock. The success of the ryot, the intensity and the extent of his operations was determined not only by the availability of sufficient number of draught animals, but more by their strength and working capacity. It can be seen from *Table XXVIII* that on an average, a *pattedar* possessed only one pair of working animals. If both *diwani* and non-*diwani pattedars* and draught animals were taken into consideration as it was done in the case of 1930 Livestock Census, Karimnagar *Pattedar* had an average of two pairs and Adilabad's not even one animal. Of all the *Suba* Districts, Karimnagar had the highest number of working animals and more so in bullocks. On the other hand, Adilabad had the least number of this working cattle, even though the area occupied was the highest.[204] This was due to the fact that the distribution of agricultural cattle depended on the extent of the land cultivated, the extent of land irrigated, the strength of the rural population and the size of the holdings.[205] Though bullock-power formed the main motive force for cultivation in the Eastern Division, he-buffaloes were also used in wet cultivation as they could bear the strain involved in it well. Not only their purchase and upkeep cost the ryots comparatively less,

TABLE XXVIII

Number of working animals per Pattedar, in 1930 & 1935

Name of the District	Number of: Bullocks		Number of: He-Buffaloes		Number of: Total		Number of Pattedars		Average Number of Working animals per Pattedar	
	1930	1935	1930	1935	1930	1935	1930	1935	1930	1935
1	2	3	4	5	6	7	8	9	10	11
Warangal District	2,05,788	. .	83,971	. .	2,89,759	3,76,815	1,04,518	98,973	2.77	3.8
Karimnagar District	2,77,360	. .	75,099	. .	3,52,459	3,72,607	83,210	1,51,011	4.24	2.4
Adilabad District	2,37,496	. .	19,797	. .	2,57,293	2,42,372	2,92,514	1,17,011	0.88	2.0
Telangana	. .	. .	. .	. .	. .	23,39,535	. .	6,47,196	. .	3.6
Marathwada	. .	. .	. .	. .	. .	21,54,451	. .	5,67,925	. .	3.7
State	34,07,443	. .	5,80,637	. .	39,88,080	44,93,986	13,81,175	12,15,121	2.88	3.6

. . Figures not given in the census.

Note : The Livestock Census figures of 1930 were given for both *Diwani* and non-*Diwani* areas of the Districts, and on the other hand, those of 1935 were given only for *Diwani* areas of the Districts. It is because of this, significant fluctuations are noticeable in the number of *Pattedars* and even in the average. Hence, for a totality of the situation, figures of 1930 are considered.

Source : H.E.H. the Nizam's Government's, *Report on the Administration of the Department of Statistics for the year 1339 Fasli (6th October 1929 to 5th October 1930 A.D.—Third Quinquennial Livestock Census*) Part II, *1932*, p. 98

&

Fourth Quinquennial Livestock Census, 1935, p. 18.

further they were also used for carrying loads such as sand, toddy and other articles of utility.[206] But, it was a point of concern from the view point of agriculture that Telangana between 1930 and 1935 suffered loss in male oxen and buffaloes amounting to 8 and 6% respectively.[207] Even between 1935 and 1940, there was a decrease of 2.9% in the total number of cattle.[208] Further, as per the cattle census of 1945, the working animals enumerated showed a decline of 2% over 1940. Average number of working animals (cattle) per cultivator (in the Government sown area) was 2.4, 1.8 and 1.7 respectively in the years 1935, 1940 and 1945. It is heartening to note that the total number of buffaloes during the quinquennium of 1940-45 decreased by 9% and those in milk by 11%.[208a]

The strength and sustenance of the working cattle depended on the type of breed, facilities available for fodder and grazing and the extent of medical care that was provided in the event of the outbreak of a cattle disease and preventive measures in this regard. Deccani, Mahadeopuri or Manthani and Ongole or Nellore breeds of bullocks were prevalent in the area, out of whom the first one and commonly prevalent was a shorter and lighter variety and the other two belong to good-sized and well-built ones. Among buffaloes, the Mahori, Marathwari and Deccani breeds were there among which the first one, largely prevalent in the Nirmal, Boath and Kinwat Taluqs of Adilabad District, proved the well-built and heavy type[209]. For having oxen or he-buffaloes of choice and good breed, the farmers or cattle owners have got to arrange for the coverage of their female cattle by a stud or pedigree bull or he buffalo. But, the agriculturists, except those who kept cattle herds, usually were not in the habit of devoting much attention to this aspect and the result was a weak and degenerating progeny.[210] This situation was further aggravated by the fact that the stud bulls were so scarcely and sparsely supplied by the Veterinary Department that during the quinquennium of 1930-35, for the three districts only one was supplied for Warangal for 1930-31 only and for the remaining four year period all remained blank[211].

As the demand for allotment of fresh lands began to increase with the growth that was witnessed in rural population since the second decade of the present century, the extent of grazing lands that were earmarked for each village got shrunk from time to time since these came to be allotted for cultivation. The percentage of grazing lands to total area of a village that was formerly fixed at 25% was brought down to 10% and even 5% in some cases[212]. Warangal, Karimnagar and Adilabad Districts, in spite of their considerable forest lands, had only percentages of 9.4, 8.0 and 4.3 respectively in 1935[213]. If the forest area was excluded, the percentage of grazing area worked out only to 7.3% for the State as a whole[214]. Even these much reduced areas were also sacrificed whenever lands fell short in making land grants on *patta* to *Maqtedars*, *Ijaradars* and *Kowldars*[215]. Consequently, the ryots were compelled to raise fodder crops among which *Kadbi* or jawar stalks, was the most important[216]. In view of the land holdings being small in respect of majority of the cultivators[217] and the inadequacy of grazing facilities provided by Government, it would have very much benefited the ryots and the cattle if Government provided free irrigation facilities or reduction in land taxes for growing fodder crops which were not of commercial value to the farmer[218]. Such an incentive had never come forth and the end result was weak and emaciated cattle prone to succumb easily to any disease or exertion[219].

The predominant wet cultivation in the Eastern Districts gave rise not only to malarial conditions[220], but also to frequent cattle diseases that took a heavy toll. Their ravage coincided with the rainy and cold season[221]. The incidence in particular years was so telling that in the year 1932-33, agricultural cattle numbering 2,45,934 in Warangal District, 3,69,944 in Karimnagar District and 2,10,900 in Adilabad District suffered mortality[222]. The most deadly of cattle diseases that caused plague-like havoc was rinderpest[223]. The serum-simultaneous method of inoculation was adopted for its treatment[224]. But, though the diseases were of a recurring nature spreading over almost all the Taluqs at some time or other, no preventive measures were undertaken by the Department which would have saved much recurring loss to the farmer whose finances were already limited. On the other hand, even the diseased cattle failed to receive timely treatment, in spite of representations from the cultivators[225]. One Veterinery Hospital at District headquarters and a few itinerary dispensaries spread over all Taluqs[226], were hardly enough for the *Suba* Districts among whom Warangal with 20,78,204 total livestock and Karimnagar with 20,20,497 occupied third and fourth places in the State as a whole[227]. Construction of the hospital at Warangal was over only in 1930[228] and in the other two, none was there until 1936[229]. Even the existing dispensaries were poorly equipped and under-staffed with inadequately trained personnel[230].

Supply of manure from the cattle, of which statistics are not available, must also had suffered, what with poor grazing and fodder facilities and heavy incidence of morality. Export-import statistics of the livestock for the period 1921-1935 showed that the former outstripped the latter, three to four times which had its debilitating effect on the manurial resources and other agrarian aspects[231]. This pointed towards the depressing condition of the agrarian economy. Further, the prevalence of unserviceable cattle numbering 76,171 ; 63,722 and 45,925 of oxen (both male and female) and 24,542 ; 18,161 and 7,204 buffaloes (both male and female) in the Districts of Warangal, Karimnagar and Adilabad respectively[232], acted as a considerable drag on the limited maintenance opportunities of the cultivators and even restricted scope for better feeding of the serviceable cattle. Animal husbandry conditions, as analysed above, would go to show that the ryots, at large, were neither assured of adequate and well-built working cattle, nor of sufficient manurial supply from the cattle. These tendencies were definitely inimical to agricultural growth.

K. AGRICULTURAL CREDIT REQUIREMENTS AND THEIR PATTERNS OF FULFILMENT : In Warangal *Suba* when majority of the holdings were below the optium level[233] and vagaries of monsoon determined the fate of the crops[234], the agriculturists who had little surplus incomes left over after meeting their domestic requirements, for the sake of investments and their extent and nature of fulfilment had significant effects on the character of agricultural production. Statistics of the credit requirements of the *Suba* in any particular year or period are not available as no attempts had been made neither by the State nor by the voluntary organisations to collect information in this regard. However, particulars of a survey of 27 villages spread over all the three Districts at the rate of one for each Taluq[235] conducted in 1949-50 as part of an intensive rural economic survey of the State, are available that provide a glimpse of the capital requirements. It would be only a partial indication of the situation that obtained earlier, because changes such as rise in the prices of agricultural commodities, hike in the value of land, improvement in irrigational, marketing and transport facilities, had contributed to some extent, for strengthening the capital position of the *pattedars*.

Table XXIX shows that 24.2 to 55.2% of the resident families in the surveyed villages were in need of additional capital. Both in the number of families requiring credit and the extent required, Warangal District stood highest among all the 16 Districts in the State.[236] This was due to the fact that small and at the same time rich farmers, were in heavy numbers here.[237] It can be seen from *Table XXX* that the number of those farmers whose incomes ranged from Rs. 500 and below Rs. 1,000 and those of Rs. 1,000 and above that were in need of further credit in Warangal District was again highest not only in the *Suba* but in the entire State.[238] These ryots with such higher incomes desired additional capital mainly for the purpose of purchasing land. 57.18% of this amount was sought in the case of Warangal District for land purchase as against 33.5% in the case of all the Districts taken as a whole.[239] Other purposes for which the amounts were sought in order, for the State were : cattle (27.5), wells (10.2), farm buildings (7.6), agricultural machinery (6.6), embankments (4.0), land improvement (3.3), agricultural implements (2.1) etc[240]. Compared to 1929-30 period of investigations when the ryots took greater proportion of loans to meet household expenses rather than cultivation expenses[241], the ryots in 1949-50 appeared to have developed longing for a productive type of investment that would pay them dividends in return.

L. CREDIT AGENCIES AND EXTENT OF CREDIT SUPPLIED : Credit needs of the people in the rural areas had been met broadly by the money-lenders, Co-operative Credit

TABLE XXIX

Additional Capital requirements : Amounts (of Surveyed villages) 1949-51

Sl. No.	Districts	Total No. of resident families	Total No. of families requiring additional capital	Percentage of Col. 4 to Col. 3	Amount required in Rs.	No. of villages surveyed
1	2	3	4	5	6	7
1.	Warangal	3,624	2,002	55.2	24,83,918	9
2.	Karimnagar	2,175	677	31.1	1,53,479	7
3.	Adilabad	3,203	774	24.2	2,08,505	11
	All Districts in the State	36,013	13,066	36.3	87,48,318	118

Source : S. Kesava Iyengar, *Rural Economic Enquiries in the Hyderabad State, 1949-51*, p. 461.

TABLE XXX

Additional Capital Requirements : Size Groups, 1949-51 (of surveyed villages)

Sl. No.	District	Below Rs. 100		Rs. 100 and below Rs. 300		Rs. 300 and below Rs. 500	
		No. of families	Amount Rs.	No. of families	Amount Rs.	No. of families	Amount Rs.
1	2	3	4	5	6	7	8
1.	Warangal	93	4,750	138	26,235	142	54,600
2.	Karimnagar	292	14,282	78	16,140	277	85,167
3.	Adilabad	101	5,025	422	63,480	156	52,600
	All Districts in the State	895	43,700	4,094	6,88,363	3,146	10,95,679
	State percentage	6.9	0.5	31.3	7.9	24.1	12.5

Sl. No.	District	Rs. 500 and below 1,000		Rs. 1,000 and above		Total		No. of villages surveyed
		No. of families	Amount Rs.	No. of families	Amount Rs.	No. of families	Amount Rs.	
		9	10	11	12	13	14	15
1.	Warangal	479	3,52,511	1,150	20,45,822	2,002	24,83,918	9
2.	Karimnagar	24	30,980	6	7,000	249	1,52,760	7
3.	Adilabad	71	38,700	24	48,700	774	2,08,505	11
	All Districts in the State	2,262	14,39,509	2,669	54,81,067	13,066	87,48,318	118
	State percentage	17.3	16.5	20.4	62.6	100	100	

Source :—S. Kesava Iyengar, *Rural Economic Enquiries in Hyderabad State, 1949-51.*, p. 463.

Societies, Banks and Government Departments. Joint-stock Banks like the Imperial Bank and the Central Bank began to function as commercial banks, very much catering for their profit. They concentrated chiefly on deposit receiving and exchange, rather than on loan advancing.[242] Even Co-operative Banks like the Dominion Co-operative Bank and the Prudential Bank also indulged in profit making[243]. In other words, the banks and the bankers became more the agencies for the encashment of *hundis*[244] Demand Drafts, than agencies for credit[245]. The fact that Central Banks at Warangal, Khammam, Karimnagar, Jagtiyal, Chinnoor and Manthani had, during the five year period of 1929-33 advanced loans to the extent of Rs. 1,93,000/-, 1,52,000/-, 76,000/-, 59,000/-, 50,000/- and 33,000/-[246] indicated that the rural credit sector was only given meagre allotment. The advances made in respect of the first two areas looked comparatively bigger, mainly due to huge allotments that might have been made to the vast business community that flourished at these two headquarter towns. Besides, the non-establishment of Land Mortgage Banks to provide for the long-term credit needs of the farmers such as purchase of land, had considerably affected the credit opportunities to farmers in the entire State. Though proposal was made in this regard as early as 1939[247] and representations to that effect were made by Agriculturists Association[248] and such Banks had been functioning in the neighbouring States of Madras and Mysore since 1930 and lent out 7 crores and 71 lakhs of rupees respectively to needy ryots until 1949, the Hyderabad Government right until October, 1950,[249] did not come forward to fulfil this long cherished desire of the cultivators. To climax it, right until almost the close of the period under study, it became difficult for Indian Banks to start branches in the Dominions and more difficult for local capitalists to start new Banks.[250] Private investment efforts were treated with doubt and misgiving, thereby closing normal channels of economic development.

M. CO-OPERATIVE INSTITUTIONS AND THEIR CONTRIBUTION TO CREDIT STRUCTURE: The object of the Co-operative Movement that was started in Hyderabad in 1913 was to establish Rural Credit Societies for financing the cultivators for constrictive purposes and liquidating their private debts borrowed on high rates of interest.[251] But, even after 37 years had elapsed since its ambitious beginning, the Societies failed to make any significant contribution in either of these objectives.[252] Regarding the spread of these Societies in the *Suba* Districts, it ranged only from 8.49 to 30.71% of the total number of villages of a District in 1944 (See *Table XXXII*). Even for the State also, it remained only 21.40%. The fact that even on an average three-fourth of the *Suba* villages and even of the State were not brought under the impact of Co-operation after an existence of 31 years had testified not only to the ineffective functioning of the Propoganda wing of the Department,[253] but also to the utter neglect of the Government in allotting staff and apportioning expenditure and subsidies to the Department. As per Government of India Co-operative Planning Committee's recommendations, it was reported that there was a shortage of 561 Supervisors, 269 Auditors, 80 Inspectors, 3 Assistant Registrars and 3 Deputy Registrars in the State.[254] Average cost per Society being Rs. 73/- and subsidy at Rs. 45,000/- put Hyderabad at the lowest rung of the Co-operative ladder, in comparison with other provinces or States.[255] Complete disregard of this movement in *Jagirs*, *Paigahs*, and *Samasthans*, was also responsible for its meagre coverage in the area.[256] Average membership per society was also not at all encouraging. It could be seen from *Table XXXII* that it having never exceeded 25, had, in fact, slid down except in respect of Adilabad. The general illiteracy of the cultivators, the corruption that was involved in the grant of advances and the distance of the Credit Societies from the villages, had, in the main, led to this poor membership of the agriculturists in these societies.[257] For a peasant to receive a loan of Rs. 100/-, he was made to spend Rs. 50/- in whetting those officials who helped him in securing it and if he wanted any extensions of the date or instalments of repayment, he was made to satisfy the officers again.[258]

Table XXXI indicates that Co-operative institutions in the Surveyed villages of Warangal and Adilabad Districts, had contributed credit only for 2.99% and 0.45% of the debts that were recorded in respect of the said Districts. In the case of

TABLE XXXI

Debts & Credit agencies in 1949-51

(In Rupees) (In surveyed Villages)

Sl. No.	District	Professional-Money-lenders	Cultivating families	Non-Cultivating-non-Professional Money-lenders	Co-Operative Institutions	Government Departments	Total
1	2	3	4	5	6	7	8
1.	Warangal	1,18,893	3,09,550	1,34,415	32,562	18,352	6,13,772
2.	Karimnagar	1,21,705	54,323	4,812	—	—	1,80,840
3.	Adilabad	1,68,741	1,67,327	70,786	1,878	230	4,08,962
	Total (16 Districts)	17,11,628	20,88,392	11,63,423	3,58,985	1,30,235	54,52,663
	Percentage (To col. 8)	31.39	38.30	21.34	6.58	2.39	100.0

Source : S.K. Iyengar, *Rural Economic Enquiries, 1949-51*, p. 412

the seven Surveyed villages of Karimnagar District, the contribution was nil (See *Chart II*). The percentages fell far below that of the State which stood at 6.58%, thereby pointing to the still weaker role played by these institutions in the *Suba* area. The amounts of loan advanced year-wise, as indicated in *Table XXXII*, show that they formed only around 25% of the total working capital of the Societies in a District. For the year 1945, the percentages that would come in respect of Warangal, Karimnagar, Adilabad and the State are 23.43, 23.57, 65.88 and 25.11 respectively. Only Adilabad showed a departure which might be due to comparatively smaller number of Societies that were there compared to its total number of villages and hence better concentration by the Departmental officials on the credit objective. The charging of 9% rate of interest and the inordinate delay that was experienced in securing the loans,[259] the domination of these Societies by official element due to the ignorance and illiteracy of the cultivators[260] and above all, the non-democratic character of the Government until the middle of 1950,[261] had been several other important factors that accounted for the poor performance of these bodies. The net result was low and negligible amount of co-operative credit got available to agriculturists in the area.

ii. Governmental Credit and the Extent of its Contribution to Agricultural Credit Structure : Advances were made by the Government in the shape of *taccavi* to agriculturists for specific purposes of land improvement such as construction of embankments, wells[262] or irrigational channels and secondly for short-term agricultural needs of purchase of bullocks, seeds, manures and agricultural implements.[263] They carried an interest rate of 6%[264]. But, these loans, as could be seen from *Table XXXIII*, appeared to have been granted not as a regular policy of the Government, but very much as relief measures undertaken in times of distress.[265] Allotment columns for the three *Suba* Districts right from 1922 to 1928, look blank except one or two here and there, for the reason that this period was not visited by any calamity. For the period of the Economic Depression of 1929-33, advances were made in comparatively good proportion and there was general slackness again during the post-Depression period[266] right until 1942 when the Grow

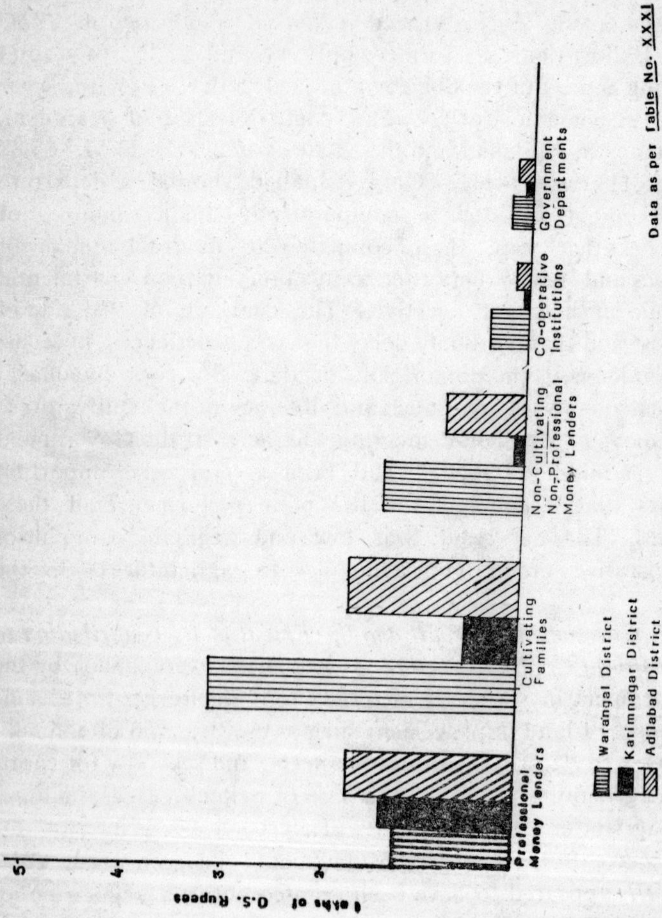

Chart II : Debts-Creditor Agencies in 1949-51

TABLE XXXII

Number, Membership and Financial Position of Co-operative Agricultural Societies, 1351-1354 Fasli (1942-45)

Sl. No.	District	No. of villages	No. of Societies at the end of the year	Percentage of of Col. 4 to Col. 3	No. of Members	Average** membership per society
1	2	3	4	5	6	7
1.	Warangal 1942	—	293	—	7,303	25
	,, 1943	—	336	—	8,288	—
	,, 1944	1,427	353	24.73%	9,925	—
	,, 1945	—	373	—	5,789	15
2.	Karim-nagar 1942	—	303	—	6,451	21
	,, 1943	—	351	—	7,506	—
	,, 1944	1,234	379	30.71%	8,436	—
	,, 1945	—	390	—	7,855	20
3.	Adilabad 1942	—	169	—	3,996	23
	,, 1943	—	188	—	4,585	—
	,, 1944	2,508	213	8.49%	5,231	—
	,, 1945	—	219	—	5,520	25

1	2	3	4	5	6	7
State	1942	—	3,565	—	89,068	25
,,	1943	—	4,516	—	1,10,299	—
,,	1944	22,360*	4,787	21.40%	1,19,160	—
,,	1945	—	5,549	—	1,41,964	20

*See Table VI in chapter III.

*As given in *1941 Census Report, Hyderabad State*, part II., p. 2.

**All fractional figures are avoided in calculating the average.

Sl. No.	District	Year	Working capital at the close of the year							
			Loans and deposits from		Share Capital	Deposits from individuals and other sources (members and non-members)	Loans and deposits held by Government	Reserve and other funds	Total working capital	Loans issued to members and other societies
			Banks	Societies						
			8	9	10	11	12	13	14	15
1.	Warangal	1942	3,46,693	4,134	1,74,319	16,929	100	8,58,358	8,00,358	1,31,699
		1943	3,03,266	4,126	1,82,892	18,385	100	2,58,522	7,67,291	1,56,833
		1944	2,35,433	—	1,91,183	24,502	100	2,71,365	7,22,583	1,10,112
		1945	2,00,996	4,078	1,96,451	21,398	100	2,89,829	7,12,852	1,67,025
2.	Karimnagar	1942	2,23,221	222	77,782	2,575	—	24,270	3,28,070	80,118
		1943	2,12,536	7	86,770	2,855	—	29,714	3,31,882	82,716
		1944	1,77,436	—	96,784	3,141	—	38,233	3,15,594	77,926
		1945	1,78,503	142	1,03,117	5,237	—	43,557	3,30,556	77,939

			8	9	10	11	12	13	14	15
3.	Adilabad	1942	85,605	—	40,999	278	—	6,711	1,34,593	50,757
		1943	87,197	—	49,999	386	—	9,449	1,47,031	85,436
		1944	93,730	—	38,366	770	—	13,598	1,66,472	1,23,457
		1945	95,115	—	66,429	1,326	—	19,660	1,82,530	1,20,254
	State	1942	38,00,441	13,903	20,42,009	2,45,101	32,826	20,59,162	79,93,442	14,07,499
		1943	42,41,796	23,495	22,00,645	3,76,357	14,149	24,26,989	92,33,411	21,26,144
		1944	38,18,515	—	23,47,904	3,89,653	13,439	26,56,724	92,25,225	23,13,172
		1945	36,53,016	20,788	25,06,956	3,91,139	12,924	46,99,952	1,12,84,775	28,42,768

Compiled from : *Statistical Year Book, H.E.H. the Nizam's Government, 1351—54 Fasli (1942-45)*, pp. 842-845.

TABLE XXXIII

Land Improvement and Agriculturists' Loans (Taccavi) Issued During 1922-1945

(In urpees)

Sl. No.	District	1922	1923	1924	1925	1926	1927	1928	1929	1930	1931	Total including outstanding balance at the beginning of the year 1931	Total recovered
1	2	3	4	5	6	7	8	9	10	11	12	13	14
1.	Warangal	—	—	—	10,000	800	—	—	500	10,100	6,320	69,344	1,93,885
2.	Adilabad	—	—	—	—	—	—	—	2,400	500	9,865	7,057	3,843
3.	Karimnagar	—	—	—	—	—	—	400	200	—	—	6,595	2,601
	All Districts (State)	7,425	9,705	1,82,674	38,111	10,859	1,20,088	13,515	23,545	1,91,485	1,08,570	8,50,034	8,90,810

(In rupees)

Sl. No.	District	1932	1933	1934	1935	Total including outstanding balance at the beginning of 1935	Total recovered
		15	16	17	18	19	20
1.	Warangal	20,284	2,28,786	42,811	33,199	3,00,426	31,915
2.	Adilabad	46,990	46,660	29,425	8,125	1,22,071	17,926
3.	Karimnagar	14,666	2,525	12,078	1,78,000	60,366	9,821
	All Districts (State)	4,80,673	5,82,715	2,93,681	5,95,899	16,49,244	2,19,070

(In rupees)

Sl. No.	District	1936	1937	1938	1939	1940	1941	Total including outstanding balance at the opening of 1941	Total recovered
		21	22	23	24	25	26	27	28
1.	Warangal	20,550	5,090	12,814	6,000	7,800	3,563	75,301	25,280
2.	Adilabad	—	—	2,115	31,280	—	—	1,58,843	47,418
3.	Karimnagar	15,000	13,000	8,000	1,12,000	1,86,000	23,000	1,94,369	33,006
	All Districts (State)	1,50,152	2,50,452	1,34,155	4,61,581	9,41,221	9,81,160	31,25.984	7,54,864

Sl. No.	District	(In rupees) 1942	1943	1944	1945	Grand Total including outstanding balance at the beginning of 1945	Total recovered
		29	30	31	32	33	34
1.	Warangal	32,000	39,21,945	550	5,700	3,77,146	40,136
2.	Adilabad	—	—	—	—	2,37,730	65,642
3.	Karimnagar	22,960	56,000	29,460	565	2,83,378	30,296
	All Districts (State)	13,52,323	54,83,212	12,65,357	15,53,154	53,13,575	7,32,417

Source : H.E.H. the Nizam's Government, *Statistical Abstracts, 1922-31* (pp. 156-57); *Statistical Year Books, 1935* (p. 90), *1941* (pp. 128-29) & *1942-45* (pp. 602-603).

More Food Campaign was launched by the Government, as a result of which *taccavi* advances in the shape of improved seeds, manures and implements were granted in an all time higher proportion. Leaving aside the special allotments made under the influence of crisis conditions, the usual allotment of Rs. 13,000/- for Warangal *Suba*,[267] consisting of more than three lakh *pattedars*[268] spread over more than five thousand villages[269], was like a drop in the ocean for the credit-thirsty cultivators. It is unfortunate that the District Revenue authorities had been so indifferent and disinterested in this laudable activity that they failed to spend the meagre and insignificant allocations of Rs. 6,000/- for Warangal, Rs. 3,000/- each for the other two and showed savings to the Government to the extent of Rs. 2,090/-.[270]

This was so because, on the one hand, the Revenue officers were generally reluctant to grant loans because of the trouble involved in investigating applications and in recovering the instalments of the loans as they fell due.[271] Their slackness in collection could very well be guaged from *Table XXXIII* that the outstanding balances between 1931-1945 had increased by approximately more than five times in the case of Warangal, thirty times in the case of Karimnagar and forty times in that of Adilabad. It is no wonder then that the amounts got dragged on for such an inordinate period that interest which accrued on the loans far exceeded the principal in the case of the Taluqs of Madhira, Pakhal as well as the entire District of Warangal as in the year 1941.[272] On the other hand, ryots applied for *taccavi* only when they were in extreme need and failed to get credit through other sources for it involved lot of delay, effort and expense to get through.[273] Another significant point that emerged in this connection was that the lists of loan distribution showed that real, needy and poor ryots were not benefited out of this, but instead, influential big landlords, *patels*, *patwaris* and *Deshmukhs* received the gains that resulted.[274] Very often, the latter even misused them in the sense that *taccavi* wheat and paddy taken for the purpose of sowing, were used instead, for domestic purposes.[275]

The cummulative result of the situation that obtained was that, the credit supplied by Government Departments in the surveyed villages of 1949-50, as could be seen from *Table XXXI*, formed only 2.99%, nil and 0.05% of the total debts that stood in respect of Warangal, Karimnagar and Adilabad Districts. The percentage of the State which remained at 2.39 looked far better than that of the two latter Districts. With both Co-operative and Governmental Credit together not forming even 5% of the total debt amount in respect of any of these Districts, the emphasis and importance in rural credit structure naturally shifted to money lenders.

iii. The Money Lenders and Their Contribution to Agricultural Credit : *Table XXXI* indicates that the three classes of money lenders-professional, cultivating and non-professional and non-cultivating-together provided credit for as much as 91% of the total debts in the Districts as a whole and the same was 95% and even above in the *Suba* Districts. Among them, the cultivating families who took to money lending as a subsidiary occupation, led the others in the volume of credit supplied. The difference in the volume of credit supplied by them and other categories of indigenous bankers, was the highest in Warangal District among all the other Districts in the State.[276] Whereas 50.43% of the total debts in that District were due to cultivating families, the respective percentages for the categories of professional—money lenders and non-professional—non-cultivating money lenders were only 19.37% and 21.89%. Marwaris, Reddy and Telanga raiyats and Komties[277] were the significant communities who carried on the trade in the three categories respectively.[278] As early as the year 1937 itself, this became so thriving a business that it attracted as many as 22,343 persons in the State, of whom 10% were there in the City of Hyderabad.[279] The point of importance was that these money lenders were in preponderance in the rural areas where grain lending got clubbed with cash lending.[280]

The fact that credit supply in these areas was made by those persons who held vast landed estates and also the *watans* of *Deshmukh*, *patel* and *patwari*, had added new dimensions to the situation.[281] They found it profitable to indulge in grain-cum-money lending as well as rents-receiving rather than cultivate the lands by themselves.[282] The rates of interest mostly ranged from 12% to 18% in cash and 25% to 125% in kind.[283] Whether the loan was given in cash or kind, the *sowcars*[284] preferred always to get it back in kind only for by this, they not only received the usual rate of interest but also had the added advantage of receiving the grain at the rate of Rs. 5/- per *khandy*[285] less than the then prevailing market price which was in turn either sold if high prices prevailed in the market or else was given on loan again that fetched him higher interest than advanced. If the ryots returned cash loans in cash only with 12% interest, then the money lender not to get deprived of his additional benefit, demanded payment of extra interest at the rate of Rs. 5/- per *khandy*, the number of *khandies* calculated being the equivalent of the amount of the cash loan taken at the prevalent market rates of the produce.[286] These transactions worked in such a grind-like manner that a ryot who once got involved in them which became rather inevitable in view of the fact that other sources of credit were extremely limited, it became extremely difficult, with his small holding and frequent failure of crops to get out of them without losing his only piece of land.[287] In case of alienation, he was not even allowed to remain at least as a tenant on his land.[288]

Money lending proved, under the circumstances, such a profitable calling that whenever ryots joined as members of Co-operative Societies, it came to be strongly resented by concerned village *Patels* and *Patwaris* who tried to dissuade the members by suing them in the Civil Court for the payment of their dues, which became more than enough for the ignorant and poor peasants to get back from the influence of the Societies.[289] Though Money Lenders' Act was passed in 1940 requiring them to obtain licenses, maintain correct accounts, not to molest the debtors for default and even reduce the rates of interest to 6% and 9% in respect of secured and unsecured debts, its implementation rather became inadequate and ineffective.[290] Even in 1949-50, one-third of their number carried on unlicensed.[291] Further, necessity made the ryots to tolerate any amount of breach of the provisions of the Act. Thus, the irony that lay in the credit situation for agriculturists was that agencies which provided cheap credit could supply only a fraction of what was required and those that gave at mere asking, put a great premium on the independence and enterprise of the farmers. It had an unsettling and weakening effect on the growth of agriculture.

l. Agricultural Indebtedness and Relief Measures : The seriousness or the importance of the problem of agricultural indebtedness in the Dominions could be judged from the fact that, by 1940, about one-third of the agricultural land had gone out of the possession of the owners into the hands of *sowcars* and money lenders in the *Diwani* area and the former were, thenceforth made to cultivate their lands as tenants-at-will.[292] It has gained added dimension in view of the development that greater percentage of debts, amounting to as much as 50.43 of the total debts in Warangal District as against 38.30 in respect of the State, was provided by members of the cultivating families such as *Reddys* and *Kapus*,[293] whose primary interest remained to grab the lands of the debtors at the earliest opportunity and then get their huge landed estates cultivated, as absentee or mostly non-cultivating landlords, either by tenants or by *bhagelas*.[294] Besides land transfer or dispossession, indebtedness of agriculturists led to poorness of agriculture, for the debt burden little enabled them to spend on inputs.[295] The practice that the indebted ryots were bound to sell their produce at 20% less than the prevailing market prices to their creditors and thereby get their debt Commitments fulfilled at least partially though not fully in a crop year, left little income remaining over and above their needs of subsistence.[296] The occurence of only one good crop year in a cycle of five years on the average,[297] had rarely allowed the cultivator to extricate himself entirely from his debt burden and consequently, it kept on recurring and rather increasing, in view of the frequent adverse crop conditions and violent fluctuations in commodity prices and demand, occasioned by wars and trade cycles.[298] This rising debt burden during the period in the *Suba* Districts and also the State could be gleaned from *Table XXXIII-(a)* and *Chart II-(a)*.[299]

i. Causes of Indebtedness : Small and fragmented holdings, accumulation of high rates of compound interest, crop insecurity, cattle deficiency, improvident expenditure on marriages and other ceremonies, the fixed and

TABLE XXXIII-(a)
Debts in 1931, 1939 and 1950*

Sl. No.	District	1931	1939	1950
1	2	3	4	5
		Rs.	Rs.	Rs.
1.	Warangal	2,50,845	3,06,270	6,13,772
2.	Karimnagar	1,04,589	1,32,996	1,80,840
3.	Adilabad	85,095	2,52,137	4,0,9862
4.	All (16) Districts Total	18,26,593	29,80,620	54,52,663

*Refers to surveyed villages only.

Source : S. Kesava Iyengar, *Rural Economic Enquiries in the Hyderabad State, 1949-51*, p. 436.

burdensome character of land tax and unproductive expenditure on liquor and litigation, had all contributed in varying degrees for indebtedness among the peasantry. Accumulation of a good number of debts for ten to twenty years[300] mainly because of the exorbitant rates of interest ranging from 12% in cash to 125% in kind[301] and the amounts being compounded for every two or three years, proved the major source of drag on the incomes of the ryots. Consequently, the the highest percentage of Co-operative loan amount, amounting to as 43.1 in 1917, was utilised for the discharge of these old debts.[302] But, the dangerous feature was that non-land mortgage debt which dragged on for several years tended to get consolidated into land-mortgage debt.[303] Crop insecurity caused by frequent unfavourable rainfall conditions at times bordering on famine[304] and deficiency of cattle, working as well as of other types, occasioned by different factors like defective breeding, poor grazing and veterinary facilities coupled with rates of cattle mortality and greater prevalence of unserviceable numbers,[305] had the effect of adding to the debt burden of the cultivating community. The fact that the average number of working cattle per cultivator in the Government sown area stood at 2.4, 1.8 and 1.7 in 1935, 1940 and 1945 respectively,[306] did certainly not look ominous in a region which had 75% of its population engaged in agriculture.[307]

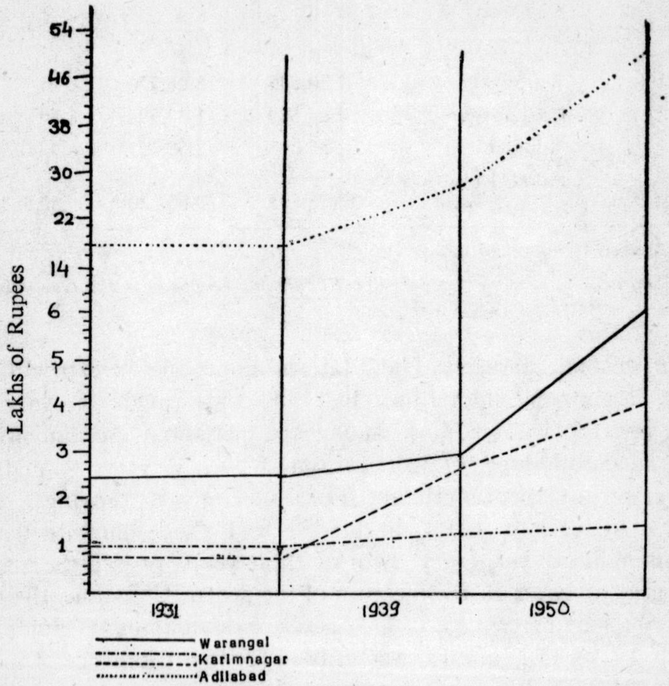

Chart II (a) : Volume of Debt, 1931-50.

Small and fragmented holdings that very much characterised the land organisation in the *Suba* Districts[308], formed strong bases for money lending and hence, became one of the basic causes of debt[309]. Excepting some stray exceptions in respect of dry lands, these, throughout the period, remained in size far below the minimum level required for the cultivators to lead a normal life and fragmentation went to such a level that 33 *quntas* or slightly more than ¾th of an acre formed a cultivating unit[310]. Their hand-to-mouth existence hardly enabled them to strive for the improvement in agriculture and on the other hand, forced them to contract debts even to meet slightest contingency, either agricultural or otherwise. To add to these uneconomical holdings, the incidence of land revenue which was always on the rise and which was more by as much as 157 to 185% than the rates prevalent in the neighbouring State of Madras, was felt with crushing weight by the ryots that they, whenever crop yields were not good, were forced to go for loans in order to meet the demand.[311] The Government demand, which rather remained inelastic and very much unaffected by the significant and at times, such as during the Depression and the Inflationary periods, violent changes in the prices of the agricultural produce, came to be regarded not only as irrational and unscientific[312], but expert opinion in the State felt that a reduction of 25 to 30% was essential for the improvement of the peasantry, which of course, was never considered by the Government right until the close of the period.[313]

Expenditure on marriages, funerals and other ceremonies of a social and unproductive nature, formed an important cause for debts both among the peasants and also the labourers, ranking in value next only to accumulated or ancestral debts.[314] Economic Investigations carried out in 1990-30 and 1949-51 in the Dominions revealed that debts on account of marriages were so numerous that in the latter year, among the Surveyed villages land-mortgage and non-land-mortgage debts contracted for marriages accounted for 25.6 and 18.1% respectively of the total loan amount which marked the highest among those of all other items.[315] The cultivators and workers in Telangana being improvident, conservative and tradition-minded, attached utmost importance to celebrating these social ceremonies going beyond their means incurring huge debts which, with high rates of compound interest and also because of their unproductive nature proved in the succeeding period, a drag around their necks. Many of this order became *Bhagelas* in Warangal District, under such compelling circumstances, finding no other way to clear off such debts.[316]

Huge unproductive expenditure resulting in indebtedness was also incurred in drinking and litigation in rural as well as urban areas.[317] Though climatic factors such as that the peasants and workers who worked in wet lands all through the day felt the need of hot drinks, or *sendhi*[318] was considered as having the effect of keeping the body cool in hot summer days are involved yet, neither the beverages were taken in moderate quantity, nor were they of unadulterated or non-fermented type.[319] The consequence was that both the monetary and health resources of the people were sqandered. Warangal District with as many as 932 country liquor shops and 3,725 today *sendhi* shops, ranked first and second in the State respectively.[320] Karimnagar District with 1,011 toddy *sendhi* shops occupied third place, first being Nalgonda District with 3,779 shops[321], thereby indicating that the drink incidence was more in Telangana region than in Marathwada which, in turn, was due to the preponderance of wet cultivation and prevalence of toddy trees in the former than in the latter. Allowing a margin for the periodic rise in excise duties, the tremendous increase in the consumption of intoxicants during the period could be well noticed from the fact that the excise income of Warangal *Suba* rose from Rs. 12,99,600/- in 1911[322] to Rs. 1,05,95,946/- in 1945[323], the growth amounting to as high as 715.32% in a period of 34 years.

The very facilities that the citizens were provided to represent their different grievances ranging from land revenue remission to official excesses by means of filing preliminary cases and appeals, the ladder extending from the court of Tahsildar up to that of the Prime Minister, gave vast scope for litigation and consequent expenditure that made the lowest strata of the rural society to contract debts. The inordinate delay, some times even extending for more than a decade, in giving the final decision in a matter and the conflicting and contradictory verdicts given by the presiding Revenue Officers one against the other, had further accelerated the litigationary difficulties of the people. Only 50% of the cases on hand in an year were disposed off. Shifting of the dates of hearing in cases without prior intimation, had further cost the poor purse of the people, proning them to run into further indebtedness.[324]

ii. Extent and Effects of Debts : The debt figures given in *Table XXXIII-(a)*, though they pertained to only 11,9 and 7 Surveyed villages in Adilabad, Warangal and Karimnagar Districts respectively, yet, they being the only data available could be considered as representative of the extent of debt during the period. Compared to 1931, debts in 1939 increased by 22.09, 27.16 and 196.30% in Warangal, Karimnagar and Adilabad Districts respectively[325] as against 63% in the State.[326] The respective District percentages in 1949-50 compared to 1939, rose by 100.40, 35.97 and 62.19[327] as against 83% in respect of the State[328]. It could thus be seen that though there was increase in debts throughout this period, the rate or the proportion of growth was, excepting in Adilabad District, considerably higher in the latter year than in 1939. The distinct upwardness in debt curve could easily be noticed from *Chart II (a)* in respect of all excepting Karimnagar District for the year 1949-50. In the latter District, the percentage rise amounted to only 8.81 as against, on the other hand, 78.31, being the highest, in respect of Warangal District. It is, on the other hand, significant to notice that unlike in other units, the proportionate percentage rise in debts in the case of Adilabad District, fell by 134.11 in 1949-50 as against increase by 196.30 in 1939. This differential situation in respect of the *Suba* Districts was due to the fact that in the former year, the percentage of families requiring additional capital out of the total number of resident families in the Surveyed villages, was 55.2 in Warangal as against 31.1 in Karimnagar and only 24.2 in Adilabad. Even for the State as a whole also, it being only 36.3, was well below that of Warangal District. It is important to note that 57.18% of this additional capital was sought for land purchase in the latter as against 33.5%

in the case of the former.[329]. Further, 82.36% of this capital required was sought in Warangal District by only 31.73% of the resident families who were in need in Rs. 1,000/-and above, which again, formed the highest among all the Districts in the State and the respective State percentages stood at 62.6 and 20.4.[330]

It also deserves observation that excepting in the case of Adilabad in 1939 and Warangal in 1949-50, the State percentages of growth in debts remained considerably above those of the *Suba* Districts. In other words, either in volume of debt or the average debt per resident family, the latter figured only in the lower order, next to those of Medak *Suba.* On the other hand, the Districts of the Marathwada region ranked far higher in this respect. The average debt per resident family in 1929-30 in the surveyed villages of Warangal, Mahaboobnagar[331] and Aurangabad[332] Districts stood at Rs. 103-4-7, Rs. 85-11-2 and Rs. 150-2-7 respectively.[333] Indebtedness calculated in terms of land revenue assessment in 1937 amounted to the highest figure of 118 times in Hingoli Taluq of Parbhani District[334] to the lowest figure of 10 times in Devarkonda Taluq of Nalgonda District.[335] In *Suba* Districts, this ranged from 60 times in Rajura Taluq to 10 times in Luxettipet Taluq, both of Adilabad District.[336] This situation in the debt position seemed to have got topsyturvy during the period that followed 1939 for, average debt per resident family in 1949-50 stood at Rs. 169-6-0, Rs. 219-7-0 and Rs. 62-0-0 in the respective Districts of Warangal, Mahboobnagar and Aurangabad.[337] In fact, the latter formed the lowest in the State, in contrast to the average of the same District in 1929 30 ranking the highest in the State among the Surveyed Districts.[338] The respective averages in Karimnagar and Adilabad Districts in 1949-50 stood at Rs. 83-2-0 and Rs. 127-11-0, both ranking respectively first and second in the lowest order among Telangana Districts.[339] The change in the situation in the latter year was due to the vigorous practising of credit supply by the affluent members of the cultivating classes in Telangana on one hand[340] and greater spread of debt-relief and control agencies in Marathwada,[341] on the other. If the rise in the debts between 1931 and 1949-50 was compared, the percentage increase was of the order of 144.67, 72.95 and 389.59 in Warangal, Karimnagar and Adilabad Districts respectively,[342] as against 199 in the ease of the State as a whole.[343] The rise in the volume in the case of the two former Districts was not insignificant, though it was below that of the State. However, Karimnagar's formed only half of that of Warangal's and only slightly more than one-third of that of the State. On the other hand, the growth in respect of Adilabad District which was double of even that of the State, was due to the backwardness of agricultural production even during the inflationary period and increasing credit needs of the ryots. But, though the volume of debt over the period had increased considerably, it was an encouraging development that the *Economic Enquiries held in 1949-50*, revealed that excluding the Co-operative and Government dues, 56.7% of the debt in the Districts was productive, 40.2% was unproductive and 3.1% was utilised for the repayment of prior debt.[344]

(*a*) *Land Transfer* : Among the effects of indebtedness, the most significant one was, of course, large-scale land transfers The wave of land transfers alternated between rise and fall during Depression, post-Depression and Inflationary periods. In 1929-30, in the Surveyed villages of Warangal District, the lands that were transferred due to debts and mortgage amounted to 36% of the total land transfers that had been effected during the preceding twenty five years.[345] The corresponding percentages in Aurangabad and Raichur.[346] Districts had been more than 50% and 33% respectively.[347] Considerable extents of lands in Warangal and also Nanded[348] Districts that belonged to cultivating and non-cultivating classes had passed into the hands of non-cultivating persons belonging to cultivating classes.[349] This applied very much in the cases of wet lands that 848-5 acres out of a total of 912-2 acres got transferred to persons not actually cultivating in the former District.[350] Hereditary village officers or *Watandars*[351] in this District who also carried on money and grain-lending exerted considerable pressure or force in getting these transfers effected.[352] Not only these wet land transfers became pronounced as years advanced, but unlike in Aurangabad and Raichur where 20% and 10% respectively of the transferred area was cultivated by the ex-occupants as tenants, none were continued, except rarely in Warangal.[353]

During the post-Depression period when the *Debt Investigations were held in 1937*[354], it was found that the total area of land that was transferred during 1922-35 in Warangal *Suba*[355] into the hands of money-lenders and village officials formed only 17.80% of such land in the State. Other *Subas* of Aurangabad, Gulbarga and Medak accounted for 46.87, 23.75 and 11.57% respectively of similar transactions in the State[356]. As there was trade and economic recovery during the post-Depression period,[357] decline was experienced in land alienations on account of debts, compared to huge rise during the Depression period[358]. The percentage of fall was far more in the case of Warangal *Suba* than those of Aurangabad and Gulbarga. In this respect, it was, as in the case of volume of debt,[359] second only to Medak *Suba* in the State. Even in the State as a whole also, if viewed in terms of total occupied land, the land that had passed during the fifteen years preceding the Survey, from the possession of cultivators into the hands of money-lenders and village officials, had amounted to only 10.35%[360].

But, the situation regarding land transfers due to adjustment of prior debt, had gone for the worse during the post-war period when the Enquiries were held in 1949-50. The number of such cases in the Surveyed villages had been of the order of 112, 63 and 43 in the respective Districts of Adilabad, Warangal and Karimnagar, which ranked respectively, first, second and fourth, third being Gulbarga, among all Districts in the State. As much as 787-32 acres and 670-16 acres of dry land had been transferred from Adilabad and Warangal Districts respectively that had put them again, in first and second places in the State. Similarly, in respect of wet lands also, Warangal and Adilabad Districts which recorded transfer of 65-9 acres and 53-16 acres respectively, came to occupy first and second places among the Districts in the State[361]. It is, on the other hand, significant to note that the acerage transferred in the case of Karimnagar District, as in respect of volume of debt [362], which amounted to 108-8 acres of dry, wet and garden land put together[363], was far less than that of Adilabad and Warangal Districts forming only one-eighth of the former and one-seventh of the latter respectively. This naturally reflected on the comparatively better economic soundness of the ryots in this District and their lesser requirements of additional capital[364]. But, however, the *Suba* taken as a whole, contributed for as much as 50% of the dry land, 81.25% of wet land and 20% of garden land that was transferred towards adjustment of prior debt in the Surveyed villages of all the Districts in the State. This, in fact, proved the highest among all the *Subas* in the State[365].

Majority of the peasants and labourers could not take advantage of the prevailing rising commodity prices for they had been more than offset by the increasing costs of cultivation and further the scarcity of foodstuffs and articles of daily use experienced during most of the period, affected their condition further[366]. This inequitous situation coupled with not infrequent crop failures[367], forced the indebted farmers to dispose off their few land bits for meagre amounts in order to get freed from the debt burden, however, small or big it was[368]. Conditions were so pressing that 30 acres for Rs. 840/-[369], 29 acres for Rs. 1,450/- and 10 acres for Rs. 2,150/-[370] were sold to clear the debts by some land owners in Mahaboobabad and Khammam Taluqs of Warangal District in 1944 and 1945. The price for acre, in these cases of dry land, ranged from Rs. 28/- to Rs. 215/-. Wet land sale which was resorted to only scarcely in view of their limited availability and greater usefulness, fetched in Hanamkonda of Warangal Taluq, a far better price of Rs. 500/- for 29 *guntas* or nearly ¾th acre in 1945[371]. Sale price also varied according to the location and type of soil. But, all the same, it was found as late as 1955 in an *Enquiry held in a typical Telangana village* that even according to a rough estimate, 55 to 60% of the families were indebted[372].

(*b*) *Effect on Agriculture and Industry* : The effect on agriculture was diversified. Where as the indebted peasants found themselves incapable of investing on agricultural inputs that contributed for efficient production[373], the landlord and *Sowcar* creditors, on the other hand, emerged as the controllers of the levers of production and distribution in the countryside. The latter, in fact, always tried to ensure that the debtors, though alientated their land, had not fully cleared their debt for, this became the instrument through which they exercised their domination over the peasantry and extracted maximum service obligations from them in their agricultural operations, mostly free and even if paid, only very nominally[374]. They utilised their huge resources in land, cattle and capital to augment production which had more than offset the rising costs of production or the declining prices and this, coupled with their profits from excise contracts and investment in agro-based industries, had put enough surplus resources in cash and kind in their hands, a part of which flowed into the trade of grain and money-lending that acted as an important leverage to retain their hold over the masses. Things worked up in such a manner that the latter rarely got freed from their stranglehold[375].

In the case of industrial labourers, amounts were offered on daily or weekly basis, but at very high rates of interest ranging from 75 to 380% per annum. Consequently, the amounts of loan remained smaller, but generally these were contracted for unproductive purposes like spending on marriages, funeral rites and festivals and hence, turned into a drag on their limited purse[376]. The effect of drink evil on worker indebtedness was also significant[377]. But, the most dangerous practice that affected them was that, due to their ignorance and illiteracy, no debt and repayment accounts were kept and hence, the debts continued to remain unpaid life-long, irrespective of the repayments that the workers used to make from time to time[378]. In the case of artisans who manufactured goods on home or cottage basis, on borrowed capital either from bigger *Sowcars* or master-craftsmen, the former by paying interest of not less than 12% was obliged to sell products to the capitalists or the creditors who paid them far less than market rates prevailing[379]. Whenever the demand for their products suffered either due to war, Depression, external competition etc. their debt burden increased further. As a result, these base industries continued in a famished condition for most of the time during the period.[380]

(c) *Debt Control Measures and Their Impact* : The Enquiry into Agricultural Indebtedness held in 1936-37 in the Dominions recommended among other things, steps to regulate money-lending, conciliation of the accumulated debt by agreement and arbitration, prevention of land alienation, establishment of Land Mortgage Banks and widespread use of Co-operative Societies, greater promotion of cottage industries and village panchayats, etc., all of which were intended as debt remedial measures for the relief and prosperity of the agriculturists.[381] The Government, which even before this investigation started measures in this direction, now took up the task in earnestness.[382] The three salient Debt Relief Regulations viz., the Money-Lenders' Regulation, the Debt Conciliation Regulation and the Land Alienation Regulation, which were brought into being on the basis of the findings of the *Inquiry*, had been converted into full fledged Acts in the year 1940 when they had been passed by the State Legislature and then received the assent of the Ruler.[383]

(a) *The Money-Lenders' Act* : It became clear that the *sahukar* or the local money-lender was serving as the chief pillar of agricultural credit in the State and the arrears of debt accrued mainly because of the exorbitant rates of compound interest that had been extracted an both short and long term loans.[384] The fact that these indigenous banks provided for uneconomic borrowing that was denied by the Co-operative Societies and the easy and quick access that the peasants and the workers had to the former as against delaying procedure of the latter and also Banks and Government Departments made the former the most popular credit agency than any other.[385] As a result, the Government by means of this Act, tried to regulate money-lending rather than replace it, which well-neigh looked neither feasible nor wise.

Under this Act, all money-lenders were required to obtain license, maintain accounts of principal and interest and give a copy of it to the debtor, and the rates of interest which were originally fixed at a maximum of 9% in the case of secured loans and 12% in the case of unsecured loans, had been later reduced to 6% and 9% respectively. Charging of compound interest was forbidden. Another significant feature of the Act was that molestation of a debtor for the recovery of debt was made a cognizable offence and further no agriculturist owing land and paying a land revenue of Rs. 50/- or less, could be arrested for detention in prison.[386] So far so good. But, the effort made by the Government to implement the provisions of the Act remained inadequate right from the beginning. This could be seen in the fact that out of 23,343 thriving money-lenders in the State, only 14,667 obtained license during the initial years of 1939 and 1940 and in the subsequent years, as the Agricultural Reforms Committee gathered the opinion, little attention was paid by the administrative machinery to the fact whether all the money-lenders registered themselves or not.[387] Further, the fact that the scope of this Measure did not extend to non-*Diwani* areas had affected its implementation and provided opportunity for money-lenders from the *Diwani* areas to evade the provisions of the Act by carrying on their activities from the former.[388]

But, the more harmful and immediate effect, from the view point of cultivators, that emerged from the Act was that the *Sahukars* who had developed antagonism towards it, not only completely stopped giving any credit at all to the former, but, on the other hand, began to collect previous loans by some means or the other open to them.[389] As a result, the ryots got extremely starved of credit and some of the worst sufferers even took their lives out of desperation.[390] Though the Government tried to meet their contingency by granting *taccavi* to ryots, it could hardly meet the requirement. As a matter of fact, between 1940 and 1945, the amounts of these grants in Warangal and Karimnagar Districts showed a decline of the order of 25% and 99% respectively excepting in 1943 and Adilabad District to be worse still, drew simply blank in this respect.[391] Neither the revenue officials were anxious to advance these loans nor the ryots, though needy, showed eagerness to receive them, because each of them came to regard the transaction and troublesome and cumbersome one.[392] Credit supply from Banks and Co-operative Societies during the period remained even more inadequate and trifling. The fact that the Co-operative loans advanced in the *Suba* Districts between 1942 and 1945 only, formed around 25% of the share capital amount of the societies in them and further, the percentage of the Co-operative debts in the surveyed villages in 1949-50 formed only 2.99, nil and 0.45 of the total debts in the respective Districts of Warangal, Karimnagar and Adilabad, spoke about the meagre and declining nature of co-operative credit in the area during the period.[393] The difficulties of the local population could very well be imagined under these circumstances that the usual local credit source got tightened and others became mostly unavailable.[394] Compelling necessities of the ryots naturally prompted the underhand dealings of the money-lenders that ran counter to the provisions of the Act.

(b) *Debt Conciliation* : For the settlement of long and outstanding debts, conciliation by agreement or arbitration was tried.[395] Taluq Boards, each consisting of two representatives of the agriculturists and two of the *sowcars* with a revenue or judicial officer as chairman, were for the first time, formed in the middle of 1938 in as many as nine Taluqs comprised in four Districts of which, Warangal was the only one from Telangana.[396] These Boards which had been established for one year originally, but were renewed finding their usefulness, got increased in number to twenty-six in 1940, but, subsequently, got abolished to the extent of eleven by 1944, five in 1946 and one later, so that by 1949, only nine were functioning of whom one each was there at Warangal and Khammam in the *Suba* area.[397] The other *Suba* Districts seem not to have been covered by these.[398] Needy persons were made to apply to a Board and get their cases registered. An idea of the work turned out by these bodies could be had from the fact that during the ten years period of 1938-48, the amount in respect of which conciliation was attempted stood at 57.5 lakhs, out of which debts aggregating 34.35 lakhs were scaled down to 21.5 lakhs, the reduction secured thereby working out to 32.43%.[399] This remission, however, as in the first year of 1938-39 varied from Board to Board, to the effect that the percentage ran from 6.67 in Tuljapur[400] to 90.75 in Khammamet.[401]

But, these Boards proved so slow in their work that it was ever unlikely that they would complete it within any reasonable period of time. Thus, during the year 1938-39, out of 2,743 cases that had been registered, only 893 cases had been dealt with, of which, again only 277 were settled by agreement and the remaining were either closed or rejected,[402] Similarly, at the end of 1940-41, as many as 1,813 cases amounting to Rs. 21,42,392 were left pending.[403] The reasons for this slow performance of the Debt Conciliation Boards are not far to seek.

There was the extreme hostility of the money-lenders to debt conciliation, even though they stood to gain in view of the Act which prevented the alienation of agricultural lands for clearing the debts.[404] They probably, were unwilling to forego not only the difference in the interest amount over and above what the Money Lenders' Act had permitted, but more important was the factor that they never wanted the entire clearance of debts due to them, for thereby, they felt, their hold or domination over the community would be lost.[405] It is rather more unfortunate that even the indebted ryots also did not very much come forward to take up proceedings under the Act against the village *sahukar* for the fear that the only available source of credit would get closed to them thereby.[406]

Besides this genuine fear in the minds of the cultivators, their necessity to seek conciliation under the Act had got somewhat lessened in the forties in view of the inflationary conditions and a consequent rise in their agricultural incomes.[407] Further, in view of the voluntary nature of the awards, the scope of the Act became very much limited and the relief that a Board could give to a debtor became not only slender but also dependent on the consent of the creditors. The latter would not always readily agree to any settlement, which often resulted in merely declaring the amount of debts due to them without enabling the debtors to discharge their debts except by the disposal of their properties. The Agricultural Reforms Committee rightly felt in this connection that arbitration should be made obligatory on the creditors and the Board should be given powers to reduce the debt to a level that would be within the paying capacity of a debtor, if at all the Act was to be of any real benefit to the latter.[408] But, neither these beneficial recommendations took shape, nor at least the Land Mortgage Banks had been there in the State to provide required credit to ryots to meet the debt awards made under conciliation.[409] As a result, the Act proved of no tangible benefit to the peasants that suffered from serious indebtedness in the area.[410]

(c) *The Prevention of Agricultural land Alienation Act* : The passing of agricultural lands from cultivating classes into the hands of non-cultivating classes became so marked during the

Depression and the post-Depression period that the Government felt impelled to bring out a measure for preventing this.[411] The important features of this Act had been that alienation could take place only in such cases where, even after alienation, land with an annual assessment of Rs/- 50 at least would remain in the proprietory possession of the alienor and the alienee was to be a member of an agricultural class having lands of the land revenue of not more than Rs. 500/- annually, or belonged to the same class to which the former belonged. Conditional sale under mortgage of land was forbidden and twenty years was fixed as the period of limit for leasing of land by a member of an agricultural class.[412] The importance that the Government attached to this measure could be judged from the fact that the jurisdiction of the civil courts was excluded in the matters that were disposed under this Act or powers exercised by it under this Act.[413] Excepting in the cases stated above, permanent alienation of land of the member of a cultivating class required the sanction of the First *Taluqdar*.[414]

This Act was also not free from certain shortcomings that affected its enforcement. The division of communities into wholly agricultural and wholly non-agricultural ones, was regarded as arbitrary, discriminatory and indefensible, for each had both the classes in its fold, though the proportion of the categories varied from one caste to another.[415] As a result of this unwarranted classification, the benefits under this Act were totally denied to certain castes and communities, while others enjoyed them with no better claim to be regarded as hereditary agriculturists. To prevent entire communities from acquiring land amounted to perpetually restricting them to urban life and non-agricultural pursuits.[416] There was also another clause in the Act that provided scope for land alienations with official connivance. It provided that if the First *Taluqdar* and *Subedar* had agreed, then member of an agricultural class could alienate his land, even when his holding, after alienation, fell below the annual assessment limit of Rs. 50/- which was prescribed as the normal requisite for carrying on land transfers under this Act.[417] Influencing of officials by fair or foul means in land transactions was not an uncommon thing during the period in the *Suba* area.[418]

Even otherwise also, the number of agricultural land transfers in the *Suba* Districts and especially in those of Warangal and Adilabad, had increased rather heavily during the forties, whereas considerable fall was noticed in this respect during the post-Depression period. In fact, they proved the highest, compared to other *Subas* in the State.[419] In spite of the safeguarding provisions of the Act, the rising costs of production, the increasing value of land, the scarcity of essential commodities and inputs and not infrequent crop failures, had the cummulative effect of prompting and rather forcing the peasants to effect agricultural land alienations.[420] Besides debt, absenteeism of the owners, staying mostly in Hyderabad and Secunderabad as Government employees or Military Solidiers and in some cases, in British Indian provinces as far as Punjab, old age and heirs not available or not staying on the land, daughter's marriage and movement between villages in different Taluqs of a District or even of the same Taluq due to difference in the value of land, had, in the main, contributed for increasing number of land transfers in the *Suba*, the first one accounting for around 33% and the latter three for 13% each of the total transfers that had been effected during the years 1944-46.[421]

It is significant to note that, excepting in Warangal District, though more than 80% of the total transferred area was from cultivating classes, they, on the other hand, received even far greater percentage of the area, in return.[422] This had very much come to serve the purpose for which the Act was intended. Karimnagar District in the State had the double distinction of recording the highest percentage of area both transferred from and received by the cultivating classes and on the other hand, the least percentage of area transferred from and received by the non-cultivating classes.[423] Further, this District had witnessed the second least amount of total land that was transferred among all Districts in the State, first being Osmanabad.[424] In the *Suba*, of course, it remained the least in this respect. These facts very much stood as the indicators of the agricultural soundness of this *Suba* District which was also reflected in its volume of debt being the least in the *Suba*.[425] In contrast, Warangal and Adilabad Districts had

TABLE XXXIII (b)

Land Transfers in Surveyed villages-1948-50, Pattern of Distribution

(Area in acres and Guntas)

Sl. No.	District	Area transferred from cultivating classes	Area transferred from non-cultivating Classes	Total	Area received by persons actually cultivating at present	Area received by persons not actually cultivating at present	Total
1	2	3	4	5	6	7	8
1.	Adilabad	1,928-14 (81.8)	428.38 (18.2)	2,357-12 (100.0)	2,039-5 (86.5)	318-7 (13.5)	2,357-12 (100.0)
2.	Karimnagar	440-17 (91.4)	41-22 (8.6)	481.39 (100.0)	476-1 (98.8)	5-38 (1.2)	481-39 (100.0)
3.	Warangal	2,908-5 (53.0)	2,581-8 (47.0)	5,489-13 (100.0)	3,746-38 (68.3)	1,742-15 (31.7)	5,489-13 (100.0)
4.	All Districts (State)	16,006-1 (63.8)	9,064-6 (36.2)	25,070-7 (100.0)	20,103-2 (80.2)	4,967-5 (19.8)	25,070-7 (100.0)

Figures in brackets denote percentage to the total area transferred.

Source : S. Kesava Iyengar : *Rural Economic Enquiries in the Hyderabad State, 1949-51*, p. 116.

recorded the first and second highest areas of total land that was transferred respectively in the State.[426] In fact, as noted earlier, even in respect of land transfers due to prior debt, the latter and the former stood in the same places in the State.[427] On the other hand, in respect of the distribution of transferred area, Warangal District had its own markedness in the *Suba* as well as the State. In the case of percentage of the area transferred from and also received by the cultivating classes, it stood only far above the other Districts of the *Suba,* but in the area received, it stood second in the State, next only to Parbhani.[428] But, it is significant for the study to realise that in the actual area both transferred as well as received and again, by both the classes, this *Suba* District excelled among all others in the State.[429] Naturally, the poverty and the suffering of the peasants and other weaker sections of the population touched the peak points in this and Adilabad Districts.

(d) *Other Contributory Measures* : (*i*) *Land Mortgage Banks and Co-operative Credit Societies* : When Governmental and Co-operative credit supply to ryots became not only meagre and scarce, but also could not meet the long-term credit needs of which, clearance of prior debt proved the foremost, the establishment of Land Mortgage Banks was regarded as the right step to meet the deficiency. As a matter of fact, these had been functioning in the neighbouring States of Madras, and Mysore since 1930 and lent out until 1949 as much as 7 crores and 71 lakhs of rupees respectively to needy ryots.[430] But, on the other hand, in Hyderabad State, even though proposal was made in this regard as early as 1939, and even though the Hyderabad Land Mortgage Bank Act providing for their establishment was enacted as early as around 1941[431] and further even though the Hyderabad Agriculturists' Association made representations for the opening of these Banks in the countryside, the Government, very much unfortunate to credit-thirsty peasants, did not come forward right until October, 1950, the fag end of the period to fulfil this long-felt need of the farming community.[432] To add to this costly developmental lapse, the Co-operative credit societies also, at least to compensate by looking after the immediate and short-term needs of the local population in full, did register no satisfactory growth either in their number, or in their membership, or in the amount of loan advanced. During an existence of 31 years ending in 1945, the movement could spread, on the agricultural side, to only around 25% of the villages in the *Suba*, with an average membership of 25 and loans advanced never exceeding 2 lakhs in an entire District and also 25% of the share capital of its total societies[433], which certainly did not augur well either for relieving the debt burden of the ryots or for promoting the development of the agriculture as a whole.

(*ii*) *Village Panchayats* : For the settlement of disputes, even of a minor nature, relating to land division, boundaries, property sharing, protection of crops, personal rivalries, debt cases, etc., the villages where panchayats did not exist, were made to trek long distances to headquarter towns where revenue and Judicial courts had been usually located. This involved considerable expenditure which, in turn, proved a substantial source of rural indebtedness, besides taking their energy and time.[434] The establishment of *Gram Panchayats* whose members were selected in an open meeting of the villagers[435] and who had thorough knowledge of village affairs, would have come very much in handy for the poverty-stricken farmers. But, the State lagged far behind in this respect. The panchayat *A'in*[436] was itself promulgated as late as 1941-42[437] and the process of formation thereafter went so slow that even by March, 1950, only 378 Panchayats had been formed in the entire State[438] that comprised as many as 22,498 towns and villages alike, working out to a dismal percentage of 1.67.[439] The complete absence of these self-governing bodies in non-*Diwani* villages had, besides the Governmental disinterestedness towards the functioning of these units on democratic basis, in the main, led to its poor show. Even in these few bodies that came to function, the principle of selection of *panch* members from the assemblage of the adult householders of the village and the nomination of *sarpanch* from among the former by the First *Taluqdar*, had been observed in place of their election by the villagers.[440] Thus, a useful arm that had great potentialities in debt control and rural upliftment, had been, for known reasons,[441] laid to waste.

(*iii*) *Cottage Industries*: Cottage industries such as hand-loom-weaving and spinning, cotton ginning and pressing, tailoring, carpentry, pottery, poultry, dairying, etc., had, as agricultural ancillaries, vast potentialities for bringing about debt relief in the countryside, by substantially adding to the agricultural incomes. The potentialities for the development of these industries remained immense in the *Suba* Districts, especially in Karimnagar and Warangal, even to the extent of ranking pre-eminent in the State. But, due to reasons stated elsewhere, these home and ancient industries lost their former prosperity and experienced considerable decline during the period. The severe fall in handloom-weaving which, next to agriculture, formed the major occupation of the people in the *Suba* as well as the State, due mainly to lack of sufficient patronage by the Regime, the middle and the upper classes and great amount of competition from external and mill products, had brought much deterioration in the economic condition of the lower strata of the society.[442] Due to unfavourable setting, the weaving craftsmen also did not remain free from debt burden. As a matter of fact, because of lack of financial independence, these were made to function as mere piece-wage earners under *Sahukars* or master weavers.[443] Until 1946, the Commerce and Industries Department's attention was mainly confined to Hyderabad only and there was no permanent District organisation for a systematic development of small and cottage industries[444]. Thus, cottage industries in the area, as a debt control organ, failed to receive growth during the period.

M. *CROP CONDITIONS*: In the first year of the reign, there had been sufficient rains and consequently rice and oil seeds crops which required good rainfall, came exceptionally good.[445] But, cotton crop suffered due to the late coming of rains.[446] With the decline in the amount of rain-fall in the next year ranging from 8" to 9" in respect of Karimnagar and Warangal Districts as could be seen from *Table XXXIII-*(*c*), crop out-turn was much below the average.[447] Added to crop deficiency, the ryots suffered on account of the outbreak of plague epidemic which continued throughout the decade until 1919-20, claiming as many as 1,94,325 lives in the

TABLE XXXIII (c)

Actual Rainfall

AVERAGE CUM ACTUAL RAINFALL (in inches)

Sl. No.	District	1911-12*	1912-13	1913-14	1914-15	1915-16	1916-17
1	2	3	4	5	6	7	8
1.	Warangal	38.5	29.00	32.97	38.54	42.87	40.55
2.	Karimnagar	33.7	25.82	29.20	44.68	38.92	36.70
3.	Adilabad	37.2	38.42	38.13	50.04	39.54	47.19
	State Average	30.0	25.90	26.45	37.82	35.21	44.53

AVERAGE CUM ACTUAL RAINFALL (in inches)

Sl. No.	District	1917-18	1918-19	1919-20**	1920-21	1921-22	1922-23	1923-24	1924-25
		9	10	11	12	13	14	15	16
1.	Warangal	54.31	***38.33	30.56	**28.73	**39.10	32.35	34.80	39.63
2.	Karimnagar	41.99	***31.66	28.61	**18.62	**36.36	26.57	24.30	39.41
3.	Adilabad	52.22	31.76	28.81	20.90	**48.43	36.40	36.10	44.97
	State Average	42.11	27.43	26.80	17.00	31.63	26.24	25.81	30.90

AVERAGE CUM ACTUAL RAINFALL (in inches)

Sl. No.	District	1925-26	1926-27	1927-28	1928-29	1929-30	1930-31	1931-32	1932-33
		17	18	19	20	21	22	23	24
1.	Warangal	46.09	26.35	39.20	39.99	32.17	35.90	46.74	42.13
2.	Karimnagar	46.29	23.50	35.09	38.62	23.63	35.04	44 58	41.04
3.	Adilabad	43.69	31.50	42.22	44.11	32.58	37.83	51.96	50.30
	State Average	32.54	23.37	32.60	36.93	23.88	29.05	39.16	36.52

AVERAGE CUM ACTUAL RAINFALL (in inches)

Sl. No.	District	1933-34	1934-35	1935-36	1936-37	1937-38	1938-39	1939-40	1940-41
		25	26	27	28	29	30	31	32
1.	Warangal	44.39	41.23	44.72	45.39	31.31	35.40	39.29	42.66
			**					***	***
2.	Karimnagar	43.83	38.97	40.70	51.26	31.87	43.73	28.13	34.22
								**	**
3.	Adilabad	52.67	43.54	47.50	56.53	43.06	56.67	33.16	48.91
	State Average	38.23	32.86	36.74	34.12	29.00	37.34	27.36	32.46

AVERAGE CUM ACTUAL RAINFALL (in inches)

Sl. No.	District	1941-42	1942-43	1943-44	1944-45	1945-46	1946-47	1947-48
		33	34	35	36	37	38	39
1.	Warangal	27.64***	38.53	36.96	33.54	26.68	24.68	44.36
2.	Karimnagar	22.55	37.89	40.94	37.31	21.45	21.89	38.66
3.	Adilabad	28.43	44.64	41.93	41.07	43.44	35.89	38.92
	State Average	21.96	33.95	35.44	29.44	28.85		35.22

*Normal rainfall.
**Famine in the entire District,
***Famine in part of the District.

Compiled from : *Census Report of India, 1911, Hyderabad State*, Part I, p. 16.
Decennial Report on Administration, 1912-22, p. 16.
Statistical Abstract, 1922-31, pp. 272-73.
Statistical Year Book, 1935, p. 294.
Statistical Year Book, 1941, p. 529.
Statistical Year Book, 1942-45, p. 881.
W.S. *File* No. 38 of 1355 Fasli (1946) & R. No. 875 of 1357 Fasli (1948).
W.S. *File* No. 36 of 1356 Fasli (1947) & R. No. 2469 of 1357 Fasli (1948) and
Hyderabad Government Bulletin on Economic Affairs, vol. I, No. 5, April 1948, p. 554.

State.[448] This, combined with two other virulent diseases of cholera and influcnza which also ravaged the Dominions during this decade, led to shortage of agricultural labour and consequent rise in wages.[449] The next three years of 1913-14 to 1915-16 had excellent and well-distributed rains corresponded by good crop yields but, the two that followed immediately had heavy but unseasonable rains falling in September and November that damaged both *kharif* and *rabi* crops and also rice.[450] Food grain prices rose to record height which made the Government to open cheap grain shops and undertake relief measures.[451] The four year period, 1918-19 to 1921-22, proved the worst in the economic history of the region and of the State. Failure of monsoons, insufficiency or unseasonable heavy rains coupled with heavy attack of epidemic diseases, brought in famine conditions either totally or partially. (see the *Table XXXIII*). There was huge loss of human and cattle life due to shortage in food and fodder, and, infact, the mean density of population per sq. mile in respect of Karimnagar District which suffered heavier losses due to lesser rainfall than the other two, came down from 197 persons in 1911 to 191 persons in 1921.[452] Agricultural depression characterised by rising prices of food grains and bullocks stalked the land during this period[453] and relief measures organised by the Government could only lessen but hardly mitigate the suffering of the rural population.[454]

The decade 1921-31, excepting the initial year of famine declared in parts of all the *Suba* Districts (see *Table XXXIII* (*c*)) which was due to reasons other than less rainfall, the remaining years, though alternated between good and moderate crop conditions, were nevertheless free from any extreme conditions bordering on famine. The crop years of 1924-25, 1925-26 and 1928-29 proved good, while the rest ranked moderate to less.[455] Economic Depression during the year 1929-34 had only worsened the economic condition of the ryots in all the Taluqs of the *Suba* in the sense that the crop out put that turned out good and satisfactory only once in three or four years at an average due to precariousness of the monsoons received, constantly declining prices, thus depriving them of their little benefit.[456] The grant of remission and *taccavi* by the Government to alleviate the distress had only marginal effect.[457]

The next decade of 1931-41 had equal number of satisfactory and unsatisfactory crop years. Whereas 1931-32, 1932-33, 1933-34, 1935-36 and 1940-41[458] had witnessed favourable seasons, those of 1934-35, 1936-37, 1937-38 & 1939-40 had-unfavourable crop conditions.[459] In 1934-35, both *kharif* and *abi* suffered due to indifferent weather conditions and there was even scarcity of water and fodder for some months in certain Districts.[460] Prevalence of such unsatisfactory crop conditions in parts of Karimnagar District brought them under famine-affected areas.[461] While record rainfall in south-west monsoon period and nil rainfall in north-east monsoon season was responsible in 1938-39 for below average yields of both *kharif* and *rabi* crops it was below normal and required quantity of rainfall from south-west monsoon and its late arrival that led to poor out-turn of crops in the years 1936-37, 1937-38, 1939-40 & 1940-41.[462] In the latter two years, scarcity conditions existed in all the Taluqs of Karimnagar District and parts[462](a) of Addilabad District.[463] Whereas the normal amount of rainfall prescribed for crop conditions in the State was 34.32"[464], the figure recorded in respect of both the Districts in 1939-40 and that of Karimnagar in 1940-41 also was, as could be seen from *Table XXXIII-(c)* below this minimum.

Rainfall and seasonal conditions proved unsatisfactory in 1941-42 also. There was below the normal yield of rainfall from south-west monsoon which was fixed at 24.81."[465] Whereas 35" of rainfall was found, after several years of experience, as necessary for growing a successful paddy crop in Warangal Taluq[466], the total amount of rainfall that was received in respect of all the *Suba* Districts as well as the State in the year, as could be seen from *Table XXXIII-(c)*, fell far below the required minimum. As a result, scarcity conditions prevailed in all the Taluqs of Warangal District[467] and huge loss was suffered in respect of total area cultivated and the out-turn received, including important crops of rice and groundnut.[468] Remission and relief work was hardly able to compensate the loss. The next two years of 1942-43 and

1943-44 had been years of sufficient rainfall and accordingly of good crop yields.[469] In the following year, the rainfall was inadequate in the case of Warangal District as well as of the State as a whole and consequently, there was decrease in acreage and outturn of crops.[470] On the other hand, Karimnagar had good *kharif* and *abi* crop conditions, as the rainfall was adequate in that District.[471] Crop conditions got considerably deteriorated in 1945-46 and 1946-47 in the two Districts of Warangal and Karimnagar as well as of the State as a whole, due to rainfall that was far below the required minimum the shortage ranging from 7.64″ to 12.43″. This had its inevitable effects on crop average and out-turn, though the value of principal crops started showing increasing trend right from 1939 or the out-break of the Second Great War, due to the phenomenal increase in prices, particularly of oil seeds.[472] 1947-48 had been a favourable crop year but, this and the succeeding two years had experienced political and economic convulsions that had an unsettling and damaging effect on crop conditions in the area.[473] It is, however, significant to note that though rainfall variations and timing had been responsible for producing alternating years of favourable and unfavourable crop conditions during the last decade of 1941-51, yet, the conditions never deteriorated to such an extent that they approximated to the horrifying years of famine before 1922-23.[474]

Small and fragmented holdings, large-scale absentee landlordism and excessive monopolization of land, poor utilisation of irrigational facilities, centuries-old type of agriculture, insignificant and ineffective efforts of propaganda and research, meagre application of improved seeds, manures, pesticides and implements, inadequate supply of well-built agricultural cattle and cattle manure, ryots forced to get more than 90 per cent of their credit needs met by the exacting money-lenders who aimed at expropriating the small holdings of the debtors, increasing debt burden and ineffective remedial measures, frequent failure of the precarious monsoons and prevalence of famine conditions coupled with out-break of virulent epidemics during the first decade, these developments, in short, characterised the agricultural situation of the period. These certainly created an atmosphere which was not conducive for agricultural growth. It would be significnat to note that in the various facets of agricultural arena that had been analysed, events sailed more in the direction of stabilising the economic power of big landlords rather than enabling the small farmers to march forward. Besides land concentration, the various facilities provided by the Government such as improved seeds, manures, pesticides and implement, irrigational facilities under tanks and rivers, *taccavi* and agricultural loans, etc., were more utilised by the former than the latter.[475] The letter's ignorance, weak financial resources and standing at the Governmental leval as against the former's position of strength and influence, worked out towards this situation.[476] But, the unfortunate factor from the point of view of agriculture was that these big landlords who commanded vast landed, irrigational and credit resources, allowed them to be frittered away with, as they remained invariably absentee landlords, more interested in enjoying high rents rather than maximising production.[477] The *Kowldars* were neither allowed nor capable to invest and work for augmenting the land yields.[478] The whole thing that transpired finally was that those agricultural classes who were capable of investing and augmenting production had no interest in agriculture and on the contrary, the sections who had abiding interest in own cultivation, had neither the capacity nor the wherewithal for increased production. The definite indicator was low agricultural production.

REFERENCES

1. For the influence of rainfall on crop condition, see section 'Rainfall' in Chapter II. For an idea of the impact of political convulsions, see section 'Political conditions' in Chapter III.
2. W.S. *File* No. 24 of 1357 Fasli (1948) & R. No. 1676 of 1357 Fasli.
3. See the section c. 'Rents' in Chapter IV.
4. The figures of 1945-46 were meant for *Diwani* area only and similarly those of 1929-30 and 1949-50 were based on the survey conducted in selected villages. Another important reason for major fluctuations

in respect of Warangal and Adilabad was that vast new uncultivated areas were brought newly under cultivation which contributed for the rise in the size of holdings.

5. Economic Investigations, 1929-30, Vol. III, Warangal District, *op. cit.*, p. 5.
6. Economic Investigations, Vol. I, 1929-30, *op. cit.*, p. 15.
7. RARC, *op. cit.*, p. 154.
8. Economic Investigations, Vol. I, 1929-30, *op. cit.*, p. 15.

8(a). See the section '*Sarf-i-khas*' in chapter IV.

9. It amounted to 1/19th share, as a rupee during the period under study consisted of 192 paise and in terms of land 33 *quntas* or slightly more than ⅘th of an acre—W.S. *File* No. 31 of 1358 Fasli (1949) & R. No. 735 of 1358 Fasli.
10. A.I. Qureshi, *op. cit.*, Vol. I, p. 159.
11. R.E.E., *op. cit.*, p. 94.
12. *Report of the Royal Commission on Agriculture in India* (Bombay 1928), p. 134.
13. H.E.H. the Nizam's Government, *Report on Labour Census, 1935*, (Hyderabad, 1937), p. 17.
14. M.L. Darling, 'Punjab Peasant in prosperity and debt,' p. 29, quoted in V. Venkataraman, *op. cit.*, pp. 84-85; RARC, *op. cit.*, p. 75.
15. See the section 'Land holdings' in this chapter.
16. Economic Investigations, Vol. III, *op. cit.*, p. 4.
17. They were not covered by 1929-30 Survey, but were surveyed in 1949-50.
18. REE, *op. cit.*, pp. 40-41.
19. See the section 'Land Holdings' in this chapter.
20. See Chapter IV and section 'Land Rights' in it.
21. See the sections 'Tenants' and 'Rents' in Chapter IV.
22. V. Venkatraman, *op. cit.*, p. 72.
23. S.M. Bharucha, *Agricultural Indebtedness* (Hyderabad, 1937), p. 56 (Computed out of the figures given for all the *Suba* villages).
24. REE, *op. cit.*, p. 30 (Computed out of the figures given for selected villages only).
25. See the sections 'Soils' and 'Rainfall' in Chapter II.
26. Hyderabad District Gazetteers, Tables volumes, *op. cit.*, Warangal (pp. 68-99), Karimnagar (pp. 66-67) & Adilabad (pp. 66-67).
27. There was slight variation in respect of Adilabad that unlike the other two Districts, jawar and maize occupied second and third places among crops irrigated-Hyderabad District Gazetteers, Tables volumes, *op. cit.*, Warangal (pp. 304-305), Karimnagar (pp. 302-303) & Adilabad (pp. 302-303).
28. Report on the working of the Departments under the Secretary & Director-General of Revenue, *op. cit.*, p. 29.
29. D. V. Rao, *Manual on groundwater and well-sinking*, (Hyderabad, 1947), p. 2.

30. *Golkonda Patrika* (Daily), 20-4-1950.
31. In Telangana parlance, it referred to efforts made by customers with staff in Government offices to get things done.
32. *Golkonda Patrika* (Daily), 23-4-1950.
33. D.R. Gadgil, *The Industrial Evolution of India,* Oxford University Press, 1942, p. 132.
34. See the section 'Rates of assessment and their incidence' in Chapter IV.
35. Immedaite Agrarian Problems, *op. cit.*, p. 65.
36. *Ibid.*
37. W.S. *File* No. 27 of 1353 Fasli (1944) & R. No. 1944 of 1355 Fasli (1946).
38. For construction particulars, irrigation potential and its realisation of these river projects, see the section 'Rivers' in Chapter II.
39. See the section 'Lakes and Tanks' in Chapter II.
40. Selected Laws and Rules of the Revenue Department, *op. cit.*, p. 25 6.
41. D.G.R. (T) *File* No. 4 of 1337 Fasli (1928) & R. No. 3795 of 1338 Fasli (1929).
42. Means in Urdu 1/10th.
43. W.S. *File* No. 2 of 1344 Fasli (1935) & R.No. 602 of 1344 Fasli.
44. Smaller or non-exempted *Jagirdars* paid this.
45. W.S.*File* No. 250 of 1338 Fasli (1929) & R. No. 2165 of 1340 Fasli (1931).
46. W. S. *File* No. 4 of 1342 Fasli (1933) & R. No. 454 of 1343 Fasli (1934).
47. See the section 'Sources of Irrigation' in this Chapter.
48. The percentage shown in respect of Telangana for 1941 appears to have been given by mistake or oversight, as the same was not in line with the percentage recorded in respect of other administrative units.
49. They were recorded in respect of Laknavaram in 1918 and Palair in 1929 respectively.
50. See Table XXV in respect of Palair and Wyra Projects.
51. This was recorded for the years 1930-32-W.S.*File* No. 7 of 1346 Fasli (1937) & R. No. 1587 of 1352 Fasli (1943).
52. Remission of land revenue.
53. W.S. *File* No. 52 of 1350 Fasli (1941) & R. No. 540 of 1354 Fasli (1945).
54. Double wet crop or two wet crops.
55. Agriculture Department, Hyderabad Government, S. No. 21 & *File* No. 56 of 1354 Fasli (1945), p. 3.
56. Statistical Year Book. 1941-42 to 1944-45, *op. cit.*, p. 288.
57. (a) Also under Laknavaram and Singabhupalem projects-W.S. *File* No. 1 of 1357 Fasli (1948) & R. No. 2064 of 1357 Fasli.
58. Much surplus water would be there even after these *ayacuts* were

fully irrigated- W.S.*File* No. 1 of 1357 Fasli (1948) & R.No. 2064 of 1357 Fasli.

59. W.S. *File* No. 5 of 1340 Fasli (1931) & R. No. 2458 of 1344 Fasli (1935).
60. Agriculture Department, Hyderabad Government, S.No. 21 & *File* No. 56 of 1354 Fasli (1945), p. 4 (As the settled *ayacut* was only 8,910 acres, his possession might have included considerable unsurveyed or forest lands).
61. See the section' c. Rents' in Chapter IV.
62. Agriculture Department, Government of Hyderabad, S. No. 21 & *File* No. 56 of 1354 Fasli (1945) pp. 1 & 4.
63. W.S. *File* No. 5 of 1340 Fasli (1931) & R. No. 2458 of 1344 Fasli (1935).
64. As many as 235 people came forward to cultivate '*do-fasla*' lands under Ramappa, under which 7,000 acres(might be including both settled and unsettled *ayacut* lands) were under big *pattedars* that were reluctant to take up '*do-Fasla*' cultivation.
65. W.S *File* No. 5 of 1340 Fasli (1931) & R. No. 2458 of 1344 Fasli (1935).
66. Immediate Agrarian Problems, *op. cit.*, p. 65.
67. W. S. *File* No. 1 of 1351 Fasli (1948) & R.No. 2064 of 1354 Fasli.
68. W.S. *File* No. 120 of 1354 Fasli (1945) & R.No. 1259 of 1354 Fasli.
69. Agriculture Department, Government of Hyderabad, S. No. 21 & *File* No. 56 of 1354 Fasli (1945), p. 16.

69. (a) Such delay in the completion of the excavation of field channels between 1927 to 1948 and beyond was experienced in the case of Bhimghanpur project also—W.S. *File* No. 1 of 1357 Fasli (1948) & R. No. 2064 of 1357 Fasli.

70. W.S. *File* No 1 of 1357 Fasli (1948) & R.No. 2064 of 1357 Fasli.
71. Settlement Report of Warangal Taluka, *op.cit.*, p. 50
72. W.S. *File* No. 1 of 1357 Fasli (1948) & R. No. 2064 of 1367 Fasli.
73. R.V. Rao, *op. cit.*, p. 251.
74. D.G.R. (T) *File* No. 86 of 1335 Fasli (1926) & R. No. 10721 of 1338 Fasli (1929).
75. W.S. *File* No. 1 of 1352 Fasli (1943) & R. No. 1225 of 1355 Fasli (1946).
76. D.G.R. (T) *File* No. 86 of 1335 Fasli (1926) & R. No. 10721 of 1338 Fasli (1929).
77. *Ibid.*
78. W.S. *File* No. 1 of 1352 Fasli (1943) & R. No. 1225 of 1355 Fasli (1946).
79. *The Deccan Chronicle*, 15-8-1949.
80. See the section 'Survey & Settlement' in Chapter IV.
81. See the section 'Fauna' in Chapter II.
82. Arabic calender.
83. W.S. *File* No. 1 of 1357 Fasli (1948) & R.No. 2064 of 1357 Fasli,

84. *Ibid.*
85. '*Karthis*' form the seasonal calender of Telangana ryots. There are altogether 27 *Karthis* in an agricultural year each extending roughly for 15 days. *Magha Karthi* corresponds to the period of August 15th to 28 th-S.H. Bilgrami, Vol. I, *op.cit.*, p. 284.
86. W.S. *File* No. 1 of 1357 Fasli (1948) & R.No. 2064 of 1357 Fasli.
87. W.S. *File* No. 10 of 1349 Fasli (1940) & R.No. 483 of 1357 Fasli (1948).
88. Area fixed for wet crop.
89. W.S. *File* No. 6 of 1355 Fasli (1946) & R.No. 2285 of 1355 Fasli.
90. *Meezan*, 24-10-1946.
91. Settlement Inspector.
92. *Golkonda Patrika* (Bi-weekly), 25-7-1938.
93. W.S. *File* No 54 of 1355 Fasli (1946) & R.No. 1880 of 1355 Fasli.
94. *Ibid.*
95. W.S. *File* No. 1 of 1357 Fasli (1948) & R No. 2064 of 1357 Fasli.
96. W.S. *File* No. 4 of 1355 Fasli (1946) & R. No. 923 of 1356 Fasli (1947).
97. W.S. *File* No. 2 of 1353 Fasli (1944) & R. No. 794 of 1358 Fasli (1949); W.S. *File* No. 1 of 1357 Fasli (1948) & R. No. 2064 of 1357 Fasli.
98. W.S. *File* No. 4 of 1355 Fasli (1946) & R.No. 923 of 1356 Fasli (1947).
99. W.S. *File* No. 1 of 1357 Fasli (1948) & R.No. 2064 of 1357 Fasli
100. See the second para in this section.
101. W.S. *File* No. 1 of 1357 Fasli (1948) & R.No. 2064 of 1357 Fasli.
102. *Shikargah* was there only in the case of Pakhal.
103. W.S. *File* No. 1 of 1357 Fasli (1948) and R. No. 2064 of 1357 Fasli.
104. *Ibid.*
105. Agriculture Department, Government of Hyderabad, S.No. 2 & *File* No 56 of 1354 Fasli (1945).
106. *Ibid.*, p. 4.
107. See the previous para in this section.
108. Agriculture Department, Government of Hyderabad S.No. 21& *File* No. 56 of 1354 Fasli (1945), p. 4.
109. W.S. *File* No. 19 of 1356 Fasli (1947) & R. No. 1740 of 1357 Fasli (1948).
110. W.S. *File* No. 4 of 1355 Fasli (1946) & R.No.923 of 1356 Fasli (1947).
111. *Golkonda Patrika* (Daily), 26-5-1950.
112. See last para in the section 'Administrative conditions' in Chapter III.
113. See section 'Lakes and Tanks' in chapter II.
114. The latter three were not forest-ridden.
115. E.L.O.H., *op. cit.*, p. 110.
116. The last one was not yet completed by 1948—Agriculture Depart-

ment, Government, of Hyderabad, S. No. 21 & *File* No. 56 of 1354 Fasli (1945).

117. W.S *File* No. 1 of 1357 Fasli (1948) & R.No. 2064 of 1357 Fasli.
118. The last three were not malaria-infested.
119. *A.R. for 1322 Fasli* (*6th October, 1912 to 5th October, 1913*), Hyderabad-Dn 1915) p. vii.
120. W.S. *File* No. 1 of 1357 Fasli (1948) & R. No. 2064 of 1357 Fasli.
121. *A.R.* for 1322 Fasli (1912-13), *op. cit.*, p. vii.
122. Census of India, 1911, Hyderabad State, Part I *op. cit.* p. 157.
123. Decennial Report on Administration, *op.cit.*, p. 85.
124. See the section 'Rainfall' in Chapter II.
125. M. Gopalan 'Scheme for the Agricultural Development under the Irrigation Projects in Hyderabad' in *Hyderabad Government Bulletin on Economic Affairs*, Vol. I, No. 9, December, 1948, p. 1086.
126. *Ibid.*
127. S.C. Dube, *The Indian Village* (London, 1955), p. 82; Immediate Agrarian Problems, *op. cit.*, p. 9.
128. Director of Agriculture, Hyderabad State, 'A Note on Agricultural Conditions in Hyderabad State in the year 1947-48' 'in Agriculture Department, S. No. 103, *File* No. 40/8 of 1357 Fasli (1948).
129. *Ibid.*
130. M. Gopalan, *op.cit.*, p. 1086.
131. A. I. Qureshi, *op.cit.*, p. 57.
132. H.E.H. the Nizam's Government, *Annual Administration Report of the Department of Agriculture for the year ending 1325 Fasli* (*7th October 1915 to 5th October, 1916*), (Hyderabad-Dn, 1918), p. 1.
133. Indigenous species of cotton.
134. ELOH, *op. cit.*, pp. 34-35.
135. Excepting Nirmal Taluq which was included in Western Telangana Division for the sake of administrative convenience. The entire State was divided into four Division, East Telangana Division, Gulbarga Division and Karnataka Division, each under a Deputy Director of Agriculture and each provided with one or more Government Farms-H.E.H. the Nizam's Government, *Annual Administration Report of the Director of Agriculture for the year 1346 Fasli* (*6th Juue, 1936 to 5th June, 1937*), (Hyderabad-Dn, 1938), p. 11.
136. *Annual Report of Research and Experimental work of the Department of Agriculture for the year 1345—46 Fasli* (*1936-37*), (Hyderbad-Dn, 1937), p. 476.
137. It received annual grant of Rs. 2,500/- for publishing a useful quarterly magazine, "*The Hyderabad Farmer*" and also helped needy farmers to get grants-in-aid from the Government-H.E.H. the Nizam's Government, *Annual Administration Report of the Department of Agriculture for the year 1341 Fasli* (*9th June, 1931 to 5th June 1932*), (Hyderabad-Dn, 1933), p. 43.

138. H.E.H. the Nizam's Government, *Annual Administration Report of the Department of Agriculture for 1328 Fasli* (*1918-1919*), p. 45.
139. H.E.H. the Nizam's Government, *Annual Administration Report of the Department of Agriculture for 1342 Fasli* (*6th June, 1932 to 5th June, 1933*), (Hyderabad, 1935), p. 29.
140. Census of India, 1951, Hyderabad State Part I-A Report, *op. cit.*, p. 473.
141. Royal Commission on Agriculture in India, Report, *op. cit.*, p. 38.
142. Local name for raw cotton.
143. Rural Reconstruction Secretariat, Hyderabad-Dn, *File* No. 9/1 & S. No. 48 of 1358 Fasli (1949).
144. H.E.H. the Nizam's Government, *Annual Administration Reports of the Department of Agriculture for the year 1344 Fasli* (*6th June, 1934 to 5th June, 1935*), (Hyderabad-Dn, 1936), p. 20 and *for the year 1345*), *Fasli* (*6th June,1935 to 5th June 1936*), (1938), p. 22.
145. The Department of Agriculture, Government of Hyderabad, *Towards Self-sufficiency in Hyderabad, 1950-51 to 1951-52* (1952) p. 3.
146. *Ibid.*
147. *Ibid.*
148. Immediate Agrarian Problems, *op.cit.*, p. 67.
149. W.S. *File* No. 11 of 1342 Fasli (1933) & R.No. 26 of 1342 Fasli (1933).
150. Memoranda submitted to the Taxation Enquiry Committee, *op.cit.*, p. 189.
151. Towards self-sfficiency in Hyderabad, *op. cit.*, p. 9. See the second para in the section 'Research and Experimentation' in this chapter only.
152. *The Deccan Chronicle*, 4-5-1950. The State had normally a deficit of 70,000 to 80,000 tons of rice and 10,000 tons of wheat-*The Deccan Chronicle* 23-12-1948.
153. The system of grain loans transacted in Telangana went by the name '*Nag Pech*'.
154. Economic Investigations, Vol. III, *op. cit.*, p. 20; REE, *op. cit.*, p. 202.
155. REE, *op. cit.*, p. 202.
156. Immediate Agrarian problems *op.cit.*, p. 68.
157. Economic Investigations in Hyderabad State, Vol. I, *op. cit.*, p. 35.
158. Economic Investigations, Vol. III,*op. cit.* p. 20.
159. See the section 'Research and Experimentation' in this chapter.
160. A food crop, grown in *Kharif* season, black in colour and much used by the ordinary village folk both for meal and bread purposes.
161. Agriculture Department, H.E.H. the Nizam's Goverment *File* No. 40/8 & S.No. 103 of 1357 Fasli(1948).
162. W.S. *File* No. 22. of 1351 Fasli (1942) & R. No. 1170 of 1352 Fasli (1943).

163(a) W.S.*File* No. 1 of 1357 Fasli (1948) & R.No. 2064 of 1357 Fasli.

164. Such case was reported by Madhria Tahsildar regarding the Paddy seed supplied for Baithpalli-Gangaram Project in Madhira Taluq for the year 1945-W.S. *File* No. 30 of 1354 Fasli (1945) & R.No. 6 of 1357 Fasli (1948).
165. See the section 'Research and Experimentation' in this chapter.
166. RARC, *op. cit.*, p. 181.
167. TCR *op. cit.*, p. 5.
168. REE *op. cit.*, p. 203:
169. Settlement Report of Warangal Taluka, *op. cit.*, p. 29.
170. *Ibid.*
171. RARC, *op. cit.*, p. 182.
171(a) W.S. *File* No. 1 of 1357 Fasli (1948) & R. No. 2064 of 1357 Fasli.
172. In forties, it came to be used greatly in paddy cultivation—Rural Reconstruction Department, H.E.H. the Nizam's Government, *File* No. 261/50 Msc. of 1950 & S. No. 27.
173. *The Deccan Chronicle*, 8-7-1949.
174. Pastures owned as *Patta* land by individual rich farmers.
175. Immediate Agrarian Problems *op. cit.*, p. 56.
176. RARC, *op. cit.*, p. 182.
177. Rural Reconstruction Secretariat, H.E.H. the Nizam's Government S. No. 27 *File* No. 261/50 of Msc. of 1950.
178. Towards Self-sufficiency in Hyderabad, *op. cit.*, p. 13.
179. *Ibid.* p. 14.
180. *Ibid.* p. 15.
181. *Annual Report of Research and Experimental work of the Department of Agriculture for the year 1341 Fasli (7th June, 1931 to 5th June, 1932)*, H.E.H the Nizam's Government, 1933), p. 59.
182. Rural Reconstruction Secretariat, H.E.H. the Nizam's Government *File* No. 139/6 & S.No. 2 of 1358 Fasli (1949).
183. Rural Reconstruction Secretariat, H.E.H. the Nizam's Government *File* No. 139/6 & S.No. 2 of 1358 Fasli (1949).
184. Annual Administration Report of Research and Experimental work of the Department of Agriculture for 1341 Fasli, *op. cit*, p. 63.
185. Field rates also caused crop damage, especially in the case of root crops like groundnut, potato, etc., and for killing them poison-baits were put-Annual Report of Research and Experimental work of the Department of Agriculture for the year 1341 Fasli *op. cit.*, p. 65.
186. Towards self-sufficiency in Hyderabad, *op. cit.*, p. 15.
187. See the section 'character of Agriculture' in this chapter.
188. Water lift of the country type, in which the bullocks would be made to move forwards and backwards to lift the bucket of water from out of the well. The repetition of this process as a regular feature affected the bullock strength very much.
189. *Annual Administration Report of the Department of Agriculture, H.E.H. the Nizam's Government for 1341 Fasli (1932)*, p. 41.
190. R.E.E., *op. cit.*, p. 203,

191. H.E.H. the Nizam's Government, *Live stock Census of H.E.H. the Nizam's Dominions, 1935*, p. 31.
192. *Annual Administration Report of the Director of Agriculture, H.E.H. the Nizam's Government for the year 1932-33*, (p. 48); *1933-34*, (p. 47) *1934-35*, (p. 47) & *1938-39*, (p. 52).
193. *Golkonda Patrika* (Daily),8-3-1949.
194. *Golkonda Patrika* (Daily), 2-7-1950.
195. *Golkonda Patrika* (Daily), 8-3-1949.
196. Expert opinion is deeply divided on the fact that soil loses fertilty due to frequent deep ploughing-REE, *op. cit.*, p. 209.
196(a) *Golkonda Patrika* (Daily) 2-7-1950.
197. Adilabad in respect of ploughs and Warangal in that of carts, numbered in the same year 81,437 and 29,058 respectively-Livestock Census Report, 1935, *op. cit.*, p. 12.
198. *Ibid.*
199. *Ibid*
200. See the section 'Character of Agriculture' in this Chapter.
201. *Golkonda Patrika* (Daily), 12-4-1949 & 17-3-1950.
202. See the section 'Character of Agriculture' in this chapter.
203. See the section 'Manures and their Utilisation' in this chapter.
204. See Table I.
205. Livestock Census, 1935, *op.cit.*, p. 12.
206. *Ibid.*, p. 23.
207. *Ibid.*, p. 12.
208. A. I. Qureshi, *op. cit.*, p. 75.
208(a) RARC, *op. cit.*, pp. 89 & 93.
209. Livestock Census, 1935, *op. cit.*, pp. 35-38.
210. A. I. Qureshi, *op. cit.*, p. 77.
211. Livestock Census, 1935, *op. cit.*, p. 40.
212. A. I. Qureshi, *op. cit.*, p. 78.
213. Livestock Census, 1935, *op. cit.*, p. 46.
214. RARC, *op. cit.*,p. 90.
215. See the section '*Ijaras*' in Chapter IV.
216. Imperial Gazetteer of India Hyderabad State, *op. cit.*, p. 32.
217. See the section 'Land holdings' in this chapter.
218. Agriculture Department, H.E.H. the Nizam's Government, *File* No. 45 of 1359 Fasli (1950) & S. No. 92, p. 42.
219. See the section 'Forests' in Chapter II.
220. See the sub-section iv. in section 'Irrigational Facilities' in this chapter.
221. A. I. Qureshi, *op. cit.*, p. 84.
222. Livestock Census, *op. cit.*, p. 78.
223. Caused by a minute organism which gains entrance to the body in food which has been contaminated by the discharges of an infected animal-Royal Commission on Agriculture in India, Report, *op. cit.*, p. 282.

224. *Ibid.* p. 319.
225. *Golkonda Patrika* (weekly), 7-9-1933.
226. Rural Reconstruction, Department, H.E.H. the Nizam's Government, *File* No. 261/50 Msc. of 1950 and S. No. 27.
227. *Hyderabad Information*, Vol. I, No. 2, Dai 1350 Fasli (November, p. 27-Nalgonda with 26,09,916 and Mahaboobnagar with 20,78,710, occupied first and second places respectively.
228. *Administrative Report of H.E.H. the Nizam's Dominion far 1339 Fasli (6-10-1929 to 5-10-1930)*, (Hyderabad-Dn 1933), p. 60.
229. Hyderabad District Gazetteers, Tables Volumes, Karimnagar and Adilabad, *op. cit.*
230. A. I. Qureshi, *op. cit.*, p. 107.
231. Livestock Census, 1935, *op. cit.*, pp. 57-58; *Golkonda Patrika* (Bi-weekly),19-10-1936.
232. *Ibid.*, p. 21.
233. See the section 'Land Holdings' in this chapter.
234. See the section 'Rainfall' in Chapter II.
235. Besides the previous 25 Taluqs of the *Suba* (See *Table VI* in chapter III), the two Taluqs of Yelgadap (*Paigah*) in Adilabad District and Boorgampahad in Warangal District, (newly constituted) were added. Hence, the number of Taluqs became 27 in this Survey-See the section 'Administrative changes' in Chapter III.
236. REE, *op. cit.*, p. 461.
237. See the section 'Land Holdings' and 'Pattern of Land Distribution' in this chapter.
238. REE, *op. cit.*, p. 463.
239. *Ibid.* p. 465.
240. *Ibid.*, pp. 465-66.
241. Economic Investigations, Vol. III, *op. cit.*, p. 20-In Warangal District, whereas household expenses led to debts in 447 cases, cultivation expenses led to in 268 cases only.
242. H.E.H. the Nizam's Government, *The Banking Enquiry Committee Report*, (*1930*), p.22.
243. B.V. Ramnarsu, 'Banking Structure in Hyderabad',--in *Hyderabad Government Bulletin on Economic Affairs*, Vol. I, 1947—48, p. 1059.
244. These were drawn on the name of Bombay creditors by the purchasers of produce in the Dominions in O.S. Rupees and were purchased in turn by the importers of piece goods, local banks and bankers for they gained profit in this transaction by exchanging their surplus O.S. cash for B.G. (British Government) Rupees- The Banking Committee Report, *op. cit.*, p. 58.
245. *Ibid.*, p. 63.
246. Agriculture Department, H.E.H the Nizam's Government, *File* No. 62/43 of 1343 Fasli (1934) & S.No. 10.
247. *The Deccan Chronicle*, 23-6-1949.
248, Immediate Agrarian Problems, *op. cit.*, p. 61,

249. *Golkonda Patrika* (Daily), 31-10-1950.
250. R.V. Rao, *op. cit.*, p. 364.
251. Madhava Rao, Anvari, 'The Co-operative Movement in Hyderabad' in *Hyderabad Government Bulletin on Economic Affairs*, Vol. I, 1947-48, p. 1063.
252. REE, *op. cit.*, pp. 439-440.
253. Agriculture Department, H.E.H. the Nizam's Goverument, *File* No. 106/58 Fasli (1949) of 1358 Fasli (1949) & S. No. 131.
254. Rural Reconstruction Secretariat, H.E.H. the Nizam's Government, *File* No. 41/58 Fasli (1949) of 1358 Fasli (1949) & S No. 35.
255. *Ibid.*, pp.3-4.
256. Rural Reconstruction Secretariat, H.E.H. the Nizam's Government *File* No. 36/58 & S. No. 36 of 1358 Fasli (1949).
257. Immediate Agrarian Problems, *op.*, *cit.*, p. 60.
258. S. Abid Ali Hussain, *Whither Hyderabad*, (Madras, 1935). p. 82.
259. Immediate Agrarian Problems, *op. cit.*, p. 60.
260. Madhava Rao, Anvari, 'Are Existing Co-op. Societies being squeezed out ?', in *the Deccan Chronicle*, 19-6-1949.
261. Madhava Rao, Anvari, 'The Co-operative Movement in Hyderabad' in the *Hyderabad Government Bulletin on Economic Affairs*, Vol. I, 1947-48, p. 1064 ; See the section 'Administrative changes' in Chapter III.
262. See the Sub-section 'ii. Sources of irrigation, their construction and maintenance' in this chapter.
263. S.C. Ray, *Agricultural Indebtedness in India and its remedies*, (Calcutta, 1915), p. 67.
264. W.S. *File* No. 55 of 1341 Fasli (1932) & R. No. 2012 of 1343 Fasli (1934).
265. *Golkonda Patrika* (Daily), 13-10-1949 ; RARC, *op. cit.*, p. 167.
266. There were some exceptions here and there, as for example in the case of Karimnagar District in the years of 1939 and 1940. These generally consisted of *taccavi* financing for the purpose of digging irrigation channels @ Rs. 3/- per acre - W.S. *File* No. 47 of 1345 Fasli (1936) & R. R. No. 1820 of 1354 Fasli (1945).
267. W.S. *File* No. 22 of 1348 Fasli (1939) & R. No. 1475 of 1348 Fasli ; W.S. *File* No. 12 of 1350 Fasli (1941) & R. No. 2979 of 1350 Fasli.
268. See Table No. XXVIII in this chapter.
269. See Table No. VI in Chapter III.
270. W.S. *File* No. 12 of 1350 Fasli (1941) & R. No. 2979 of 1350 Fasli.
271. RARC, *op. cit.*, p. 168.
272. W.S. *File* No. 40 of 1349 Fasli (1940) & R. No. 91 of 1351 Fasli (1942).
273. *Golkonda Patrika* (Daily). 23-4-1950.
274. *Golkonda Patrika* (Daily), 13-10-1949.
275. *Golkonda Patrika* (Daily), 23-4-1950.
276. REE, *op. cit.*, p. 412.

277. Essentially a business community.
278. Economic Investigations, Vol. III, *op. cit.*, pp. 16 & 19.
279. Department of Statistics, H.E.H. the Nizam's Government, *Some Economic Facts and Figures of H.E.H. the Nizam's Dominions*, (Hyderabad-Dn, 1937), p. 18.
280. *Ibid.*
281. See the sections on 'Villages' in Chapter III and '*Tahud/Sarbasta/Watandari*' in Chapter IV.
282. See the sections on 'Watandari' and 'Rents' in Chapter IV.
283. S.M. Bharucha, *op. cit.*, p. 84 ; REE, *op. cit.*, p. 432.
284. Big money lenders were locally and popularly referred by this appellation.
285. Measure of 20 maunds grain.
286. S.M. Bharucha, *op. cit.*, p. 84.
287. *Ibid.*
288. Barry Pavier, *op. cit.*, p. 1417.
289. *Fifth Annual Report on the Working of the Co-operative Societies of H.E.H. the Nizam's Government for the year 1328 Fasli (1919)*, (Hyderabad-Dn, 1919), p. 15.
290. RARC, *op. cit.*, p. 166.
291. *Ibid.*
292. TCR, *op. cit.*, p. 1.
293. See the sub-section' iii. Money-lenders and their contribution to agricultural credit', in this chapter.
294. See the second para in section 'B. Patterns of Land Distribution', in this chapter.
295. Government of Madras : *Report of the Economist for enquiry into rural indebtedness*, (Madras, 1946), p. 57.
296. Settlement Report of Warangal Taluka, *op. cit.*, p. 37 ; see para II in the sub-section 'iii. Money-Lenders and their contribution to agricultural credit' in this chapter.
297. RARC., *op. cit.*, pp. 75-76 ; Also refer to the section 'M. Crop conditions' in this chapter.
298. See the section 'D. Price variations and their effects' in Chapter VI and sub-section 'Trade Development, 1911-1950' in Chapter VIII.
299. Attached to this section.
300 Economic Investigations, Vol. III, 1929-30, *op. cit.*, p. 17.
301. S.M. Bharucha, *op. cit.*, p. 84.
302. *Third Annual Report on the working of the Co-operative Societies of H.E.H. the Nizam's Government for the year 1326 Fasli* (1917), (Hyderabad-Dn, 1917), p. 4.
303. Economic Investigations, Vol. I, *op. cit.*, p. 27.
304. See Table XXXIII-(c) and section 'M. Crop conditions', in this chapter.
305. See the section 'J. Animal Husbandry as an agricultural adjunct', in this chapter.

306. RARC, *op. cit.*, p. 89.
307. *The Hyderabad Government Bulletin on Economic Affairs*, Vol. I, No. 9, p. 106.
308. See the section 'A. Land holdings', in this chapter.
309. M.L. Darling '*Punjab Peasant in prosperity and debt*', p. 29.
310. See the section 'A. Land holdings', in this chapter.
311. See third para in sub-section 'b. Land Revenue assessments and their incidence', in Chapter IV. (Percentage is calculated).
312. *Ibid.*, (fifth para).
313. *Ibid.*, (Sixth para),
314. Labour Census, 1935. *op. cit.*, p. 64 ; A.S. Raju : *Economic Conditions in the Madras Presidency, 1800-1850*, Published Ph. D thesis, (University of Madras, 1941), p. 137 ; RARC, *op. cit.*, p. 75, N.G. Ranga, *op. cit.*, p. 71.
315. Economic Investigations, Vol. II, *op. cit.*, p. 20 ; REE, *op. cit.*, pp. 417 & 479.
316. See the sub-section '*Bhagelas*', in Chapter VII.
317. RARC, *op. cii.*, p. 75.
318. Juice of toddy or palmyra trees taken as an intoxicant but considered of having cooling effect, especially in summer season if taken unfermented.
319. Settlement Report of Warangal Taluka, *op. cit.*, p. 38.
320. The number of country liquor shops in Karimnagar and Adilabad Districts was only 131 and 378 respectively—*Statistical Year Book, H.E.H. the Nizam's Government, 1945 Fasli (1945)*, p. 118.
321. The number of toddy *sendhi* shops was only 253 in Adilabad District being the lowest in Telangana, which was due to the less number of trees, on account of forests in the District—*Ibid.*
322 W.S. *File* No. 112 of 1320 Fasli (1911) & R. No. 3778 of 1321 Fasli (1912).
323. Statistical Year Book, 1351-54 Fasli (1942-45), *op. cit.*, pp. 676-77.
324. See the first para in section 'Administrative Conditions', in Chapter III.
325. Percentages are calculated.
326. REE, *op. cit.*, p. 435.
327. These are calculated.
328. REE, *op. cit.*, p. 435.
329. See Table XXIX and para two in the section 'K. Agricultural Credit requirements and their pattern of fulfilment', in this chapter.
330. The percentages of the District are calculated on the basis of the figures given in Table XXIX attached in this chapter—For data on district on other *Subas*, See REE, *op cit.*, p. 463.
331. A District in Medak *Suba*.
332. A Marathwada District in the *Suba* of the same name.
333. Economic Investigations in Hyderabad State, Vol. I, 1929-30 *op cit.*, p. 29.

334. In Marathwada.
335. In Medak *Suba*.
336. RARC *op. cit.*, pp. 74-75. (Based on the data collected by S.M. Bharucha in 1937).
337. REE, *op. cit.*, p. 437.
338. *Ibid* : Economic Investigations, 1929-30, Vol. I, *op. cit.*, p. 29.
339. REE. *op. cit.*, pp 410-11.
340. See the sub-section 'iii. Money lenders and their contribution to agricultural credit', in this chapter.
341. For example, the first nine Taluq Debt Conciliation Boards established in 1938-39 convered the Marathwada Districts of Aurangabad, Osmanabad and Gulbarga and only one District from Telangana, i.e., Warangal—*Hyderabad Information*, Vol. I, No. 2 June, 1941, p. 26. Even in December, 1949, out of 9 Debt Conciliation Boards existing in the State, 6 remained from the former and only 3 from the latter—*The Deccan Chronicle*, 3-12-1949.
342. Percentages are calculated on the basis of the figures given in Table XXXIII-(a) attached in this section.
343. REE, *op. cit.*, p. 435.
344. *Ibid.*
345. Percentage calculated on the basis of the relevant figures given in Table VII in Economic Investigations, 1929-30, Vol III, *op. cit.*, p. 9.
346. In Gulbarga *Suba*.
347. Economic Investigations, 1929-30, Vol. I, *op cit.*, p. 18.
348. In Aurangabad *Suba* and it was surveyed in 1929-30.
349. Economic Investigations, 1929-30, Vol. I *op. cit.*, p. 18.
350. *Ibid.*, Vol. III. p. 9.
351. See the sub-section 'E. *Tahnd/Sarbasta/Watandari*', in Chapter IV.
352. Economic Investigations, 1929-30, Vol. III, *op. cit.*, p. 8.
353. *Ibid.*, Vol. I, pp. 1819. (Among the 12 Surveyed villages of Warangal District, Ammapalem village in Mahaboobabad Taluq was mentioned as the only exception to this practice).
354. By S M. Bharucha, Additional Revenue Secretary H.E.H. the Nizam's Government.
355. It, of course, at this time comprised Nizamabad District also, besides the usual three Eastern Districts.
356. The percentages are calculated from the figures given in Appendix I contained in S.M. Bharucha, *op. cit.*, pp. 50-51.
357. See last para in the sub-section 'ii. Depression and Recovery 1929-38', in Chapter VI.
358. 1929-30 figures cited in the earlier para may be considered as representing the Depression period.
359. See the second para in this sub-section.

360. In terms of actual acerage the figures were : occupied area= 10,27,675 ; Transferred land=1,06,454 acres—S.M. Bharucha, *op cit.*, p. 6.
361. REE *op. cit.*, p. 125.
362. See the first two paras in this sub-section.
363. 89-10 acres of dry land, 15-4½ acres of wet land and 3-34 acres of garden land-REE, *op. cit.*, p. 125.
364. For an observation on the additional capital requirements of this District, see the first para in this sub-section.
365. REE *op. cit.*, p. 125.
366. See the second para in the sub-section 'iii. Period of Inflation 1939-1950', in Chapter VI.
367. See the section 'M.Crop conditions', in Chapter V.
368. 100 *Files* of 1350-1358 Fasli (1941-1949) of Warangal *Subedari*, dealt with such cases of land sale, spread over the three Districts of Warangal, Karimnagar and Adilabad, but majority in the first one.
369. W.S. *File* No 67 of 1353 Fasli (1944) & R. No. 1411 of 1353 Fasli, S. No. 37.
370. W.S. *Files* Bundle containing 33 files with Nos. (123 of 1354 Fasli (1945) & R. No. 619 of 1355 Fasli (1946); (S. No. 1) to 49 of 1355 Fasli & R. No. 654 of 1355 Fasli (S. No. 33). These two particular cases are with S. Nos. 15 & 30 respectively.
371. W.S. *File* (Bundle same as above) S. No. 23.
372. S.C. Dube : *The Indian village*, (London, 1955), p. 78. (The enquiry was held in Shamirpet a suburban village to Hyderabad, very much included in Telangana during the period).
373. See the starting para of this section.
374. Pradhan, H. Prasad : 'Reactionary Role of usurer's capital in rural India', in *Economic and Political weekly*, special number, August, 1974, Vol. IX, pp. 1305-1307.
375. S.M. Bharucha, *op. cit.*, p. 84.
376. Report on Labour census 1935, *op cit.*, p. 64.
377. Refer to the last but one para in the sub-section 'ii. Causes of Indebtedness', in this section.
378. Report on Labour census, 1935, *op. cit.*, p. 64
379. See the sub-section 'Private Finance', in Chapter VII ; Royal Commission Report on Agriculture in India, *op. cit.*, p. 435.
380. See the Section 'Small, Medium and Cottage Industries', in Chapter VII.
381. S.M. Bharucha, *op. cit.*, p. 30.
382. The Government promulgated in 1932 a Regulation for the Relief of Indebted Agriculturists and the prevention of usury and in 1934 the Land Alienation Regulation. The latter was enforced at first only in the two Districts of Aurangabad. Others also remained essentially

experimental measures—*Hyderabad Information*, Vol. I, No. 1, Thir, 1350 Fasli (May, 1941), p. 19.

383. *Hyderabad Information*, Vol. I, No. 1 Thir, 1350 Fasli (May, 1941), p. 20.
384. R.V. Rao, *op. cit.*, p. 308 ; RARC, *op. cit.*, p. 75.
385. A.1. Qureshi., *op. cit.*, pp. 176-177.
386. RARC, *op. cit.*, pp. 76-77 ; also see the sub-section 'iii. The money lenders and their contribution to agricultural credit, in this chapter.
387. See the first and third paras in the sub-section iii. the money-lenders and their contribution to agricultural credit', in this chapter.
388. *Golkonda Patrika* (Bi-weekly), 10-9-1936 & 5-9-1938.
389. *Administrative Report for 1348 Fasli* (*1938-39*), (H.E.H. the Nizam's Government : Hyderabad-Dn, 1941), p. 18.
390. *Golkonda Patrika* (Bi-weekly), 25-7-1938.
391. See Table XXXIII in this chapter. (percentages are calculated).
392. See the second para in sub-section 'ii. Government credit and the extent of its contribution to agricultural credit structure', in this chapter.
393. See para two in sub-section 'i. Co-operative institutions and their contribution to credit structure', in this chapter.
394. The frequent failure of crop conditions further intensified their suffering—see the section 'M. crop conditions', in this chapter.
395. 1941 Census Report, Part I, *op. cit.*, p. 19.
396. *Hyderabad Information*, Vol. I, No. 2 June, 1941, pp. 26-27.
397. RARC, *op. cit.*, p. 77.
398. No mention about these Districts in the data available was made.
399. RARC, *op. cit.*, p. 78.
400. In Marathwada Region.
401. *Hyderabad Information*, Vol. I, No. 2, June 1941, p. 26.
402. *Ibid.*
403. *Ibid.*, p. 27.
404. *Ibid.*
405. Pradhan H. Prasad : 'Reactionary Role of usurer's capital in Rural India', in the *Economic and Political Weekly*, August 1974, Vol. IX, pp. 1305-1309.
406. RARC, *op. cit.*, p. 165.
407. *Ibid.*
408. *Ibid.*
409. See the sub-section 'i. Credit Agencies and extent of credit supplied', in this chapter.
410. RARC., *op. cit.*, p. 165.
411. See the sub-section 'a. Land Transfers', in this section.
412. Selected Laws and Rules of the Revenue Department., *op. cit.*, pp. 133 & 139.

413. *Ibid.*, p. 142.
414. *Ibid.*, p. 133.
415. RARC. *op. cit.* p. 166 ; Immediate Agrarian Problems, *op. cit.*, p. 43.
416. RARC., *op. cit.*, p. 166.
417. Selected Laws and Rules of the Revenue Department *op. cit.*, p. 133.
418. See the first three paras in the section 'Administrative Conditions', in Chapter III.
419. See the sub-section 'a. Land Transfers', in this section.
420. *Ibid.*
421. W.S. *File Nos.* 4 of 1350 Fasli (1941), S. No. 42 & R. No. 465 of 1350 Fasli to No. 6 of 1350 Fasli (S.No. 46) & R. No. 468 of 1350 Fasli : No. 3 of 1350 Fasli (S. No. 25) & R No. 1190 of 1350 Fasli to No. 27 of 1350 Fasli (S. No. 35) & R.No. 1204 of 1350 Fasli ; No. 13 of 1350 Fasli (S. No. 50 to No. 18 of 1350 Fasli (S. No. 51) & R. No. 1261 of 1350 Fasli ; No. 85 of 1350 Fasli (S. No. 1) & R. No. 1603 of 1353 Fasli to No. 109 of 1353 Fasli (S. No. 10) & R. No. 1612 of 1353 Fasli ; No 83 of 1353 Fasli (S. No. 14) & R. No. 1660 of 1353 Fasil to No. 93 of 1353 Fasli (S. No. 19) & R. No. 1665 of 1353 Fasli ; No. 16 of 1357 Fasli (1948) (S. No. 49) & R. No. 706 of 1357 Fasli ; No. 67 of 1353 Fasli (S. No. 27) & R. No. 1411 of 1353 Fasli to No. 99 of 1353 Fasli (S. No. 30) & R. No. 1414 of 1353 Fasli ; No. 59 of 1353 Fasli (S. No. 32) & R. No. 1428 of 1353 Fasli to No. 87 of 1353 Fasli. (S. N. 42) & R. No. 1441 of 1353 Fasli ; No. 15 of 1354 Fasli (1945) (S. No. 19) & R. No. 1 of 1354 Fasli to No. 35 of 1354 Fasli & R. No. 37 of 1354 Fasli ; No. 3 of 1354 Fasli (S. No. 48) & R. No. 51 of 1354 Fasli to No. 7 of 1354 Fasli (S. No. 52) & R. No. 55 of 1354 Fasli ; No. 90 of 1355 Fasli (S. No. 30) & R. No. 1955 of 1355 Fasli ; No. 96 of 1355 Fasli (S. No. 43) & R. No. 1958 of 1355 Fasli to No. 113 of 1355 Fasli (1946) S. No. 47) & R. No. 1963 of 1355 Fasli ; No. 27 of 1357 Fasli (1948) (S. No. 75) & R. No. 1101 of 1357 Fasli ; No. 167 of 1356 Fasli (1947) (S. No. 86) & R. No. 1117 of 1357 Fasli No. 75 of 1355 Fasli (S. No. 1) & R. No. 1955 of 1355 Fasli to No. 114 of 1355 Fasli (S. No. 22) & R. No. 1936 of 1355 Fasli.
422. See Table XXXIII (b).
423. REE, *op. cit.*, p. 116
424. In Gulbarga *Suba*, *Ibid.*
425. See the Table XXXIII (a) and first two paras of sub-section 'i. Extent and effects of debts', in this section.
426. REE, *op. cit.*, p. 116.
427. See the sub-section 'a. Land Transfers', in this section.

428. Percentages are in terms of total transferred area in the District. Parbhani was in Aurangabad *Suba*-REE, *op. cit.*, p. 116.
429. REE., *op. cit.*, p. 116.
430. See the sub-section 'i. Credit Agencies and extent of credit supplied', in this chapter.
431. *Hyderabad Information*, Vol. I, No. 1, May 1941. p. 18.
432. See the sub-Section 'i. Credit agencies and extent of credit supplied', in this chapter.
433. See Table XXXII and sub-section 'i. Co-operative Institutions and their contribution to credit structure', in this chapter.
434. K. Venkataranga Rao, 'Causes of debt', in *Golkonda Patrika* (Bi-weekly), 19-5-1938.
435. Report on the Administration of the Hyderabad State, September, 1948 to March 1950, *op. cit.*, p. 89.
436. It means Governmental Regulation or Act.
437. R.V. Rao, *op cit.*, p. 337.
438. Report on the Administration of Hyderabad State, September, 1948 to March, 1950, *op. cit.*, p. 89.
439. 1941 Census Report Part I, *op. cit.*, p. 67. (percentage is calculated on the total numbers of villages. The number of villages with population ranging from 2,500 to 5,000 (Panchayats were formed in such villages) is not available, but even then however the percentage would be between 5 and 10 only).
440. See the section 'Local Government' in Chapter III,
441. The minority character of the rural community and friction that developed in political arena during the forties are prominent in this respect—Also see RARC, *op. cit.*, p. 200.
442. See the section 'Small, Medium and Cottage Industries', in Chapter VII.
443. See the sub-section 'Private Finance', in Chapter VII.
444. See the section 'Small, Medium and Cottage Industries', in Chapter VII.
445. *Census of India, Hyderabad State, 1921,* Volume XXI, Part I, (Hyderabad-Dn, 1921).
446. *Administrative Report for 1320 and 1321 Fasli* (*6th October, 1910 to 5th October, 1912*), p. 37.
447. *Ibid.*
448. Census Report, 1921, *op. cit.*, p. 5.
449 *Ibid.*, p. 6.
450. *Ibid.*, pp. 5-6.
451. *Ibid.*
452. Census Reports, *op cit.*, 1911, (p. 16) & 1921, (p. 33).
453. *Administrative Report for 1329 Fasli* (*7th October, 1919* to *5th October, 1920* Hyderabad-Dn, 1921) ; *Annual Average Retail Prices of principal commodities in H.E.H. The Nizam's Dominions, 1319-50 Fasli* (*1921-41*), pp. 6-93.

454. *Administrative Report for 1330 Fasli (6-10-1920 to 5-10-1921)*, (Hyderabad, 1922), p. 1.
455. *Agricultural Statistics, H.E.H. the Nizam's Government, 1925-26 to 1934-35*, (Hyderabad, 1938), p. 20 ; Census Report, 1931, *op. cit.*, pp. 20-21.
456. This aspect was discussed in greater detail in chapter VI—*Administrative Report for 1343 Fasli (6-10-33 to 5-10-34)*, Hyderabad, 1937), p. 15 ; W.S. *File* No. 125 of 1343 Fasli (1943) & R. No. 54 of 1343 Fasli, ; W.S. *File* No. 48 of 1343 Fasli (1934) & R. No. (n. g) and W.S. *File* No. 14 of 1343 Fasli (1934) & R. No. 8 of 1343 Fasli.
457. *Administrative Report for 1343 Fasli (6-10-1933 to 5-10-1934)* (Hyderabad, 1937), pp. 15-16.
458. Excepting Karimnagar District where in all its Taluqs drought conditions prevailed which made the Government to declare it a famine-striken area and undertake relief measures. Such condition was also there in the Taluqs of Chinnoor and Luxettipet of Adilabad District—W.S. *File* No. 58 of 1350 Fasli (1941) & R. No. 2506 of 1351 Fasli (1942) ; *File* No. 11 (2)—P (S), 40, political Department Hyderabad, New Delhi & Simla Lists, *Micro film, Reel 8, Acc. No. 51.* (At National Archives, Delhi).
459. *Census Report, Hyderabad State*, 1941, part I pp. 7-9 , *Trade Statistics, H.E.H. the Nizam's Government, 1935-36*, (p. 2) *1936-37*, (pp. 3-4), *1937-38* (pp. 2-3), *1939-49*, (pp. 11-12) & *1940-41*, (pp. 11-12) ; W.S. *File* No. 58 of 1350 Fasli (1941) & R. No. 2505 of 1351 Fasli (1942).
460. Census Report, 1941, *op. cit.*, p. 7.
461. *Statistical Year Book, H.E.H. the Nizam's Government*, 1941-42 to 1944-45, p. 1059.
462. Census Report, 1941, *op. cit.*, pp. 7-9 ; Trade Statistics, *op. cit.*, 1936-37, (p. 2), 1937-38, (pp. 2-3) 1939-40, (pp. 11-12) & 1940-41 (pp. 11-12) ; W.S. *File* No. 58 of 1350 Fasli (1941) & R. No. 2,506 of 1351 Fasli (1942).
462.(a) Adilabad, Chinnur and Asifabad Taluqs.
463. Statistical Year Book, 1941-42 to 1944-45, *op. cit.*, pp. 1059 and 1061,
464. *Trade Statistics, H.E.H. the Nizam's Government, 1351 Fasli (1941-42)*, p. 13.
465. *Ibid.*
466. Settlement Report of Warangal Taluka, *op. cit.*, p. 23
467. Sandy loans proportion was more in the soils of Warangal compared to those of other *Suba* Districts As these required greater amount of water at regular intervals compared to other types (See Section 'Soils', in Chapter II), famine conditions stalked the land on the failure of the south-west monsoon—Statistical Year Book, 1941-42 to 1944-45. *op. cit* , p. 1061.
468. Trade Statistics 1351 Fasli (1941-42) *op. cit.*, p. 13.

469. Trade Statistics for 1352 Fasli (1942-43), *op. cit.*, pp. 15-16 ; Political Department Hyderabad, New Delhi & Simla Lists, *Micro Film, Reel 2, Acc. No. 45* (Available at National Archives, Delhi).
470. Statistical Year Book, 1941-1945, *op. cit.*, p. 994.
471. *Meezan*, 5-1-1945.
472. *Trade Statistics for 1356 Fasli (1946-47)*, pp. 22-25.
473. See the section 'Political Conditions', in Chapter III.
474. *Census of India, 1951 Hyderabad State*, Part I, p. 37.
475. See the concerned sections inset in the chapter.
476. See the section 'Administrative Conditions', in Chapter III.
477. See the section 'Pattern of Land Distribution', in this chapter.
478. See the sub-section 'Tenants' in Chapter IV.

CHAPTER SIX

AGRICULTURAL PRODUCTION, PRICES AND CONTROLS

AGRICULTURAL products, besides meeting the food requirements of the local populace, formed 67.94% and 87.24% of the exports that were made from the Districts of Warangal and Adilabad respectively. These consisted besides foodgrains, oil seeds, cotton and cotton seed, tobacco and chillies.[1] In other words, agricultural production had come to be the mainstay of 60 to 70% of the people in the *Suba* Districts.[2] Consequently, non-fulfilment of crop conditions to the required level, resulted in immediate experiencing of scarcity conditions.[3] The volume of agricultural production is determined by the pattern of land utilisation and the actual acreage brought under cultivation in respect of different crops, between the years.[4] These kept on changing from year to year, due to the interplay of administrative, natural and personal factors, thereby making a differential impact on the economic condition of the people and the *Suba*. The effects of the increase or decrease in agricultural production on the population in general and the cultivators in particular, were either neutralised or heightened due to the consequential effects of the deep and significant variations in the prices of agricultural products and of commodities in general that were occasioned by the two Great Wars and the Great Depression. Besides, the introduction of Food Grains Levy and Rationing and restrictions imposed by the Government on the growing of commercial crops[5] since 1942,[6] had considerably affected the efforts for increased agricultural production and also the economic condition of the agriculturists in particular and the people in general. In fact, the ills of Levy and Controls during the last decade of the period proved so unbearable and crushing that they formed one of the strong factors that goaded the people to rise against the regime.[7] A critical analysis and appraisal of these related aspects is made in this chapter.

A. *PATTERN OF LAND UTILISATION*

It can be seen from Table XXXIV and Chart No. III, that during the 14 year period of 1913 to 1926-27 for which the area figures[8] are available in respect of majority of the items as compared to the subsequent period, total Government area recorded an increase of 10.23%, 0.23% and 34.65% in respect of the *Suba* District of Warangal, Karimnagar and Adilabad. The increase in respect of Adilabad District was the highest in the State[9] which was very much in accordance with its vast area and huge natural resources.[10] If both Government and non-Government areas were taken together, as it was done in the case of the figures given for the period 1931 to 1944-45, total areas in respect of these Districts look higher by 40 to 50% approximately, showing increase at regular periods, thereby indicating the importance of the latter in this respect.[11] On the other hand, compared to total area, the area assessed and was available for cultivation looked less except in the case of Karimnagar District. Increase in this respect in the earlier period was only 8.01%, 3.36% and 16.85% in the case of Warangal, Karimnagar and Adilabad Districts. Slight improvement regarding this aspect in the case of Karimnagar District was due to the lesser preponderance of forest lands than the other two Districts.[12]

The difference in acreage between total area and that available for cultivation which was shown as *Poramboke* or unassessed waste, was considerable in respect of all the Districts of the *Suba* and they ranked highest in this respect among all the Districts in the State.[13] *Poramboke* or unassessed waste lands which in greater proportion consisted of uncultivable forest lands, formed as much as 30.2% to 39.71% of the total Government area in respect of *Suba* Districts,[14] and in this regard, they ranked next only to Nizamabad District in the State.[15] The increase in this category of land between 1912-13 to 1926-27 was the highest in Adilabad District in the entire State followed by Warangal and Karimnagar Districts.[16] Cultivable waste formed only one-fourth or even less of the total *poramboke* or unassessed waste and further it declined sharply except in the case of Karimnagar District, between the years 1931 to 1944-45, for which the division statistics is available. It declined from 25.49% and 36.43% in 1931 to 13.25% and 10.38% in 1944-45 in the case of Warangal and Adilabad Districts respectively, whereas it rose from 23.92% in 1931 to 25.44% in 1944-45 in the case of Karimnagar District. Even in respect of the State as a whole, the percentage of culturable waste to culturable area came down from 10.39 in 1911 to 7.96 in 1927.[17] The rather unwelcome trend of slight increase in cultivable waste in respect of Karimnagar District was due to the absorption of cultivators more in wet cultivation than in bringing waste lands under dry cultivation.

(*i*) *Laoni Land*[18] *Distribution* :

Fresh and uncultivated Government lands or *poramboke* were allotted either by means of auction under ordinary *Laoni* or free distribution to members of landless agricultural and backward communities like the Gonds, Koyas, Hill Reddis, etc., under special *Laoni.* The minimum bid price fixed by the Government was five times the assessment in ease of dry garden land and twice the one crop assessment if the land was wet[19] and Tahsildars had been the immediate officers who dealt with these matters.[20] But, as against lakhs of acres of land available for distribution from time to time in the *Suba*, the distribution was so meagre that it never exceeded a few thousands. In the year 1928, the total uncultivated land in the *Suba*, stood at 33,13,332 acres and 11 *guntas* out of which only 4,458 acres of land was given on *Laoni.*[21] Similarly, in the year 1947 as against a total land of 10,55,893 acres and 50 *guntas* that was available for *Laoni* distribution in the *Suba*, only 50,967 acres and 24 *guntas* of land was allotted in the year.[22] In contrast to this insignificant allotment to needy and poor ryots, Government under Colonisation Scheme granted in 1924, 1,31,000 acres to

Sir Fazalbhoy, a Bombay capitalist enterpreneur, in the Rajura and Sirpur Taluqs of the Adilabad District and 10,500 acres in 1925 in Pakhal and Mahboobabad Taluqs of the Warangal District to Sir Amin Jung, a high dignitary in the *Sarf-i-khas* Department.[23] They were made these huge grants at the nominal payment of Rs. 4 per acre.[24] But, the most unfortunate thing that turned out to be was that the former turned over the lands back to Government after only two years of actual possession but with payment from the Government three times of what he paid with practically nil development of lands and the latter after 15 years of possession and consequently payment from the Government amounting to seven times of what he paid with of course, only marginal development of one-third of the lands received by him.[25] *Sifatul-Islam,*[26] a Muslim Organisation that was started in 1933 with service motto and manned by high Government officials both in and out of service, was allowed by means of grant of *patta*, huge land donations from war-returned soldiers and others that amounted to 11,000 acres of lands, out of which 3,000 acres was there in Banki Village of Sirpur Taluq and the rest of 8,000 acres in Pakhal Talug.[27] Apart from sufferance of agriculture on account of large-scale absenteeism, this organisation, in spite of announcing an ambitious programme of starting factories, provision of electricity, railway, etc., nothing came out in cement and concrete.[28] To add to these layers of Governmental wasteful munificence, Government after the last Great War made it a policy to allot cultivable lands, even sometimes at the risk of evicting the existing cultivators, to those soldiers who distinguished themselves in the war, at the rate of 60 acres each[29] These soldiers, most of whom still continued in service and consequently away from these lands that required development, never showed any interest towards this and either allowed the lands to remain fallow, or in most of the cases, sold them away for name-sake price to the local landlords who took full advantage of the situation to further augment their land monopolization.[30] In other words, lands were distributed not to those who were in real need and craved for it as in the case of Gonds of Jodeghat,[31] but to those who had no real interest in land development but wanted to make business out of them. Chances of increased agricultural production were thus greatly retarded.

The restriction of the powers of *Suba* Revenue officials in allotting *Laoni* lands had greatly hampered the pace of distribution. Officials even upto the rank of *Subedar* did not enjoy the power of allotting lands that remained uncultivated for less than ten years.[32] When representation was made to the Government that this restriction was much responsible for greater land remaining uncultivated, it gave modification to the effect that lands below 50 acres in size could be given on *Laoni* for one year by Revenue Officials,[33] which was none the better. But, this practice of granting lands on temporary one year tenures known as the '*Eksala*',[34] was found to have caused considerable loss and inconvenience to farmers.[35] Though *Laoni* proceedings were to be transacted for every fresh year of cultivation, this was not done in practice by the slow moving Revenue echelons, with the result that the ryots continued in occupation for more than one year. But, they were subjected to summary eviction as and when the caprice of the Revenue officials dictated, irrespective of the long stay of the cultivators on the land.[36] This embarassing system was cancelled only in November, 1949[37]. Great hardship was also experienced from the side of the Forest Department in the sense that lands that had been cultivated for such a long period of 24[38] to 44[39] years were joined in *Mahsura* and even though alternate lands were shown in some cases, these in no way satisfied the frustrated ryots for they had to work afresh for the development of these new lands, added to variation in soil types and fertility. Besides this, there was another burdensome regulation that greatly affected the preparedness of the ryots to receive Government lands on *Laoni*. This rule laid down that those cultivators who were in prior occupation of the lands which they wished to receive under *Laoni* of the ordinary type, were made to pay 16 times of the assessment,[40] irrespective of their period of stay on the land, or economic status that did not exempt even *balotadars* like *Chamar*, *Hajjam*, *Dhangar*,[41] etc. The exacting nature of these demands was such that cultivators of Amin Jung's[42] lands when they demanded grant of *pattas* after cultivating the absentee lands for a period of 20 years, were asked to pay at once 30 times of land revenue for only entering their names in *Wasul Bagi Register*[43] and continue the same for 30 years.[44] Lack of co-ordination between Forest and Settlement Departments in removing timber and carrying on *Phodi* of the lands allotted, resulted in unwanted and undue delay in bringing fresh lands under cultivation.[45] The odds were thus heavy and varied that had greatly offset the *Laoni* land distribution programme and the inevitable result was that huge blocks of culturable waste lands went abegging so much so that, in 1949-50 in 55, 32 and 80 Surveyed villages of Warangal, Karimnagar and Adilabad Districts respectively, 40,931, 7,700 and 10,183 acres of land were reported unutilised by the Agriculture Department of the Hyderabad State.[46]

(*ii*) *Area Occupied and Fallow Land* :

In respect of area occupied, as can be seen from Table XXXIV, Marathwada had higher percentage than Telangana In fact, Osmanabad District in the former region recorded 100% of occupied area to arable area both in 1913 and 1922,[47] whereas the highest percentage recorded in the latter region by Karimnagar District was 95.23% in 1926-27 which incidentally was exceeded by all the eight Marathwada Districts in that year.[48] The reason for this disparity was due to the preponderance of different types of cultivation in the two regions.[49] Wet cultivation which absorbed more capital and labour, formed 11.5% of occupied area in Telangana in 1913, whereas it was only 2.5% in Marathwada. This factor coupled with the hardness and infertility of the soils in the former region,[50] induced the cultivators to leave a large proportion of dry lands cultivated in one year as fallow during the next year, thus contributing to the increase in the percentage of unoccupied land.[51] Leaving Adilabad, every other District in Telangana had higher percentage of wet land under occupation than any District in Marathwada.[52]

Regarding *Suba* Districts, the area occupied registered a regular increase throughout the period upto 1936 for which the details are available, excepting the fact that in the latter year decline was recorded (See Table XXXIV). This decline was reflected in dry rather than wet area of the Districts and accordingly the current fallows for that year in respect of Warangal, Karimnagar and Adilabad recorded as much as 41.54%, 14.90% and 22.35% of the occupied area respectively. There was excessive rainfall[53] resulting in large dry area being left fallow. It was on account of this same factor, it can be seen from the Table that whereas the net irrigated area in that year had increased in respect of all the three Districts, the net area sown had decreased considerably both in respect of Warangal and Adilabad Districts. Between 1913 and 1926-27, Karimnagar District with 87.0% of the occupied area to assesed area in 1913, 92.4% in 1922 and 95.23% in 1926-27, stood highest in Telangana, whereas Adilabad with 67.1% in 1913, 72.6% in 1922 and 73.84% stood lowest not only in the region but in the entire State.[54] Warangal District on the other hand, with 86.7% in 1913, 91.1% in 1922 and 92 54% in 1926-27 occupied second place next to Karimnagar in Telangana.[55]

If the split up of area occupied is taken up in respect of dry lands, next to Nalgonda District in Telangana, the *Suba* Districts of Warangal, Karimnagar and Adilabad occupied respectively second, third and fourth places.[56] Regarding wet lands, if the total wet area of a District is taken into consideration, the Districts of Karimnagar and Warangal occupied respectively the first and second places in the State itself and if it was considered in relation to occupied area, then these two followed Nizamabad and Medak Districts of Telangana in third and fourth places respectively in the State.[57] Adilabad District in this respect, occupied last place in Telangana, though not in the State.[58] The increases in the occupied area during the period for which the details are given in the Table were in the main, due to excess of *Laoni*[59] applications over relinquishments, resurvey operations and transfer from *Inam* or *Poramboke* to Government area [60] Greater expansion of cultivation took place between the years 1913 and 1926-27 for which the details are available, in Telangana than in Marathwada. Whereas 2,22,646 acres had been newly brought under cultivation in Marathwada during this period, as much as 9,77,861 acres had been freshly brought under the plough in Telangana. The reason was obvious that in 1913 only 1% of assessed area remained for occupation in the former region as against 20.7

in the latter. (See the Table XXXIV). In *Suba* Districts the order of increase for the period 1913-36 in the area brought under cultivation was 3,28,174 acres in Adilabad, 2,74 203 acres in Warangal and 74,033 acres in Karimnagar. But it is all the more significant to note that Adilabad, in spite of recording highest increase in occupied area during the period in the State, yet, if the area available for cultivation was taken into consideration, the District ranked lowest in the State,[61] in respect of land utilisation. Huge forests and poor hygienic conditions, lack of communications and meagre facilities for irrigation,[62] etc., had, in the main, been responsible for this insufficient utilisation of land. The prevalence of as much as 53.8% of fallow land to occupied area in Warangal District in the year 1949-50[63] had also, in another way, pointed to the inadequate usage of available land resources. Karimnagar evidently proved the better of the three and also number one in the region, chiefly aided by its record percentage of well irrigation.[64]

B. CROP ACREAGE

Paddy, jawar, bajra, maize, gram, *sesamum*,[65] groundnut, castor, cotton, tobacco and chillies had been the important crops grown in the *Suba*. Among these, rice, maize, jawar, wheat[66] and cotton were cultivated as irrigated crops. Again, among the crops that were irrigated, rice and maize predominated. The former occupied 72.82%, 71 82% and 68.05% of the total irrigated area in the respective Districts of Karimnagar, Warangal, and Adilabad and the respective percentages in the latter's case were 11.23, 9.15 and 6.74.[67] Karimnagar led in respect of both, not only in the *Suba* but in the State itself closely followed by Warangal (See Table XXXV dealing with acreage). Paddy which formed the principal article of food next only to jawar in the Dominions, was cultivated both as *abi* or winter crop and *tabi* or summer crop[68] and the proportion between them remained as 4.5 to 1 respectively.[69] Further, rice produced from the former was considered superior in quality fetching nearly 5% more per *candy*[70] than the latter.[71] The Taluqs of Warangal, Mahboobabad, Madhira, Khammam, Pakhal, Mulug, Karimnagar, Mahadeopur, Huzurabad, Jagtiyal, Sirsilla, Parkal,

TABLE XXXIV

Land Utilisation, District-wise, 1913-1951

(In acres and guntas)

Sl. No.	Fasli / Year	District	Total Government area	Forests	Area assessed and available for cultivation	Area occupied	Percentage of area occupied to assessed area	Details of occupation Dry	Wet
1	2	3	4	5	6	7	8	9	10
	1322								
1.	1913	Warangal	24,44,234	...	16,99,020	14,73,813	86.7	12,85,690	1,88,123
2.	do	Karimnagar	22,68,262	...	15,83,192	13,83,437	87.0	11,61,908	2,21,529
3.	do	Adilabad	23,26,645	...	16,07,767	10,79,060	67.1	10,49,790	29,270
4.	do	Marathwada Total	1,45,44,364	...	1,26,04,140	1,24,85,719	99.0	1,21,67,096	3,18,623
5.	do	Telangana Total	1,39,97,802	...	1,01,17,876	80,30,303	79.3	71,09,108	9,21,195
9.	do	State Total	2,85,42,166	...	2,27,22,016	2,05,16,022	90.2	1,92,76,204	12,39,818

Sl. No.	Fasli Year	District	Percentage of wet area to area occupied	Poramboke or unassessed waste	Percentage of Pormboke to total area	Current fallows	Percentage of fallow land to occupied area	Net area sown	Irrigated area (net)
			11	12	13	14	15	16	17
1.	1322/1913	Warangal	12.7	7,45,214	30.4	...	...	...	...
2.	do	Karimnagar	16.0	6,85,070	30.2	...	...	...	...
3.	do	Adilabad	2.7	7,18,878	30.9	...	...	...	...
4.	do	Marthwada Total	2.5	19,40,224	13.3	...	...	...	...
5.	do	Telangana Total	11.5	38,79,926	27.7	...	...	...	...
6.	do	State Total	6.0	58,20,150	29.4	...	...	...	...

1.	<u>1331</u>								
	1922	Warangal	26,92,017	...	17,95,985	16,36,705	91.1	14,16,805	2,19,900
2.	do	Karimnagar	22,70,463	...	15,67,300	14,49,659	92.4	12,20,760	2,28,899
3.	do	Adilabad	30,87,566	...	18,78,423	13,63,823	72.6	13,29,266	34,557
4.	do	Marathwada Total	1,46,14,177	...	1,27,25,533	1,26,69,687	99.1	1,23,03,924	3,05,763
5.	do	Telangana Total	1,50,88,859	...	1,07,46,631	87,58,927	81.5	77,76,936	9,81,991
6.	do	State Total	2,97,02,976	...	2,34,72,164	2,13,68,614	90.9	2,00,80,860	12,87,754
1.	<u>1336</u>								
	1926-27	Warangal	26,94,489	...	18,35,234	16,98,361	92.54	14,96,047	2,02,314
2.	do	Karimnagar	22,73,479	...	15,40,532	14,67,131	95.23	12,38,545	2,28,586
3.	do	Adilabad	31,32,956	...	18,88,763	13,94,717	73.84	13,58,768	35,949
4.	do	Marathwada Total	1,47,07,069	...	1,28,20,609	1,27,08,365	99.12	1,24,11,303	2,97,062
5.	do	Telangana Total	1,52,15,791	...	1,07,74,258	90,08,164	83.60	80,28,405	9,79,759
6.	do	State Total	2,99,22,860	...	2,35,94,858	2,17,16,529	92.04	2,04,39,708	12,76,821
1.	<u>1340</u>								
	1931	Warangal	38,31,058	14,90,333	...	17,50,018	...	15,44,020	2,05,998
2.	do	Karimnagar	30,24,375	6,36,027	...	14,67,005	...	12,36,931	2,30,274
3.	do	Adilabad	39,05,628	17,41,728	...	14,49,314	...	14,47,614	1,700

1.	1345 / 1936	Warangal	43,44,160	13,88,192	...	17,48,016	...	15,17,239	2,30,777
2.	do	Karimnagar	29,14,525	6,37,049	...	14,57,470	...	12,23,092	2,34,378
3.	do	Adilabad	39,15,628	18,73,631	...	14,07,234	...	13,70,604	36,630
1.	1348 / 1939-40	Warangal	50,84,000	13,75,000	...	...	...	...	...
2.	do	Karimnagar	36,62,000	6,13,000	...	...	...	...	...
3.	do	Adilabad	46,68,000	20,79,000	...	...	...	...	...
4.	do	State Total	5,29,27,000	61,85,000	...	...	...	...	...
1.	1353-54 / 1944-45	Warangal	50,84,000	13,60,000	...	...	...	...	...
2.	do	Karimnagar	36,62,000	5,38,000	...	...	...	...	...
3.	do	Adilabad	46,68,000	20,74,000	...	...	...	...	...
4.	do	Marathwada Total	2,63,65,000	7,08,000	...	...	...	...	...
5.	do	Telangana Total	2,65,61,000	54,63,000	...	...	...	...	...
6.	do	State Total	5,29,27,000	61,70,000	...	...	...	...	...
1.	1358-61 / 1949-51	Warangal	70,139-22	...	...	32,742-05	...	26,585-32	6,156-23
2.	do	Karimnagar	21,337-26	...	...	13,228-06	...	10,951-33	2,276-13
3.	do	Adilabad	44,571-17	...	...	21,874-36	...	19,587-1	2,287-35
4.	do	State (All Districts)	4,93,356-24	...	...	3,57,785-38	...	3,27,753-19	30,032-19

1.	1331 / 1922	Warangal	13.4	8,96,032	33.3	—	—	—	—
2.	do	Karimnagar	15.8	7,03,163	31.0	—	—	—	—
3.	do	Adilabad	2.5	12,09,143	39.2	—	—	—	—
4.	do	Marathwada Total	2.4	18,88,584	12.9	—	—	—	—
5.	do	Telangana Total	11.2	43,42,228	28.8	—	—	—	—
6.	do	State Total	6.0	62,30,812	21.0	—	—	—	—
1.	1336 / 1926-27	Warangal	11.91	8,59,255	31.89	—	—	—	—
2.	do	Karimnagar	15.44	7,32,947	32.23	—	—	16,83,421	—
3.	do	Adilabad	2.58	12,44,193	39.71	—	—	13,48,130	—
4.	do	Marathwada Total	2.34	18,86,469	12.82	—	—	1,27,54,407	—
5.	do	Telangana Total	10.87	44,41,536	29.12	—	—	88,56,074	—
6.	do	State Total	5.88	63,28,002	21.16	—	—	2,16,10,481	—
1.	1340 / 1931	Warangal	11.77	1,42,323∴ 4,15,866*		1,69,428	9.68	16,13,108	1,30,039
2.	do	Karimnagar	15.68	1,49,537∴ 4,75,415*		2,65,296	18.08	14,98,100	1,50,502
3.	do	Adilabad	0.11	1,59,937∴ 2,96,364*		1,37,485	9.47	15,60,114	41,901

1.	1345/1936	Warangal	13.20	2,60,200.∴ 4.31,168*	7,26,308	41.54	15,38,292	1,75,148
2.	do	Karimnagar	16.08	89,969.∴ 3,64,396*	2,17,212	14.90	16,05,899	2,14,693
3	do	Adilabad	2.60	1,78,900.∴ 2,90,964*	3,14,591	22.35	12,58,242	80,269
1.	1348/1939-40	Warangal	—	2,00,000.∴ 11,43,000*	7,54,000	—	16,13,000	1,79,000
2.	do	Karimnagar	—	17,400.∴ 12,49,000*	1,11,000	—	15,14,000	2,08,000
3.	do	Adilabad	—	1,56,000.∴ 8,54,000*	1,80,000	—	13,99,000	72,000
4.	do	State Total	—	32,74,000.∴ 1,11,58,000*	38,77,000	—	2,84,33,000	14,27,000
1.	1353-54/1944-45	Warangal	—	2,12,000.∴ 13,88,000*	8,61,000	—	12,63,000	1,79,000
2.	do	Karimnagar	—	2,82,000.∴ 8,24,000*	6,88,000	—	13,30,000	1,66,000
3.	do	Adilabad	—	92,000.∴ 7,94,000*	3,90,000	—	13,18,000	57,000

4.	do	Marathwada Total	—	19,86,000.∴ 28,44,000*	35,12,000	—	1,73,15,000	2,88,000
5.	do	Telangana Total	—	19,94,000.∴ 58,07,000*	41,37,000	—	91,60,000	10,35,000
6.	do	State Total	—	39,80,000.∴ 86,51,000*	76,49,000	—	2,64,75,000	13,23,000
1.	1358-61**							
	1949-51	Warangal	18.80	37,397-7∵	15,505-36	47.4	—	—
2.	do	Karimnagar	17.20	8,109-20∵	1,451-3	11.0	—	—
3.	do	Adilabad	11.67	22,696-21∵	4,524-52	20.7	—	—
4.	do	State (All Districts)	8.39	1,35,570-26∵	95,065-39	26.9	—	—

*Area not available for cultivation.

**Particulars are only regarding surveyed villages of 9 in Warangal, 7 in Karimnagar and 11 in Adilabad Districts at the rate of one per each Taluq.

∴Cultivable waste other than current fallows.

∵Area other than occupied area.

TABLE XXXV

Net Sown Area and Acreage of Main Crops, 1921-50

(In acres)

Sl. No.	Net sown area/Name of the crop	CROP ACREAGE, AREA-WISE 1330 Fasli (1921)				
		Warangal District	Karimnagar District	Adilabad District	Telangana	Marathwada
1	2	3	4	5	6	7
1.	Net sown area**	8,96,297	9,76,689	9,99,892	—	—
2.	Rice	50,873	63,870	25,944	—	—
3.	Jawar	4,58,437	3,73,170	5,89,100	—	—
4.	Bajra	22,879	270	3	—	—
5.	Maize	2,01,275	1,89,051	24,280	—	—
6.	Gram	17,533	12,132	1,910	—	—
7.	Other cereals & pulses**	26,465	25,192	24,033	—	—
8.	Sesamum	32,561	2,07,406	80,587	—	—
9.	Groundnut	—	—	211	—	—

10.	Castor	40,635	19,572	13,014	—	—
11.	Cotton	27,505	59,651	1,71,906	—	—
12.	Tobacco	5,974	6,013	2,109	—	—
13.	Sugar cane	—	—	—	—	—
14.	Chillies†	—	—	—	—	—
15.	Fodder crops	4,551	35,260	23,876	—	—
16.	Fruits and Vegetables crops including root crops	884	1,188	973	—	—

CROP ACREAGE, AREA-WISE AND YEAR-WISE

1331 Fasli (1922)						
State	Warangal District	Karimnagar District	Adilabad District	Telangana	Marathwada	State
8	9	10	11	12	13	14
1,52,64,266	16,31,705	14,49,659	13,63,823	—	—	—
5,39,703	82,936	75,207	78,005	—	—	—
73,52,979	3,69,169	4,60,151	7,28,274	—	—	—
40,24,375	2,38,740	98,740	35,700	—	—	—
5,52,505	3,89,440	2,49,954	35,372	—	—	—
3,77,836	29,765	25,782	13,440	—	—	—
9,90,852	2,09,891	55,368	45,679	—	—	—
4,53,576	49,101	1,73,123	53,114	—	—	—
31,950	—	—	115	—	—	—
6,47,107	40,371	16,988	6,108	—	—	—
1,80,31,866	35,642	63,147	2,31,418	—	—	—
94,064	10,875	25,740	5,798	—	—	—

20,030	—	—	—	—	—	—
—	—	—	—	—	—	—
4,76,273	85,982	1,25,671	45,470	—	—	—
92,508	2,848	5,780	892	—	—	—

*The crop areas (net sown) for the year 1319 Fasli (1910) of the *Suba* Districts and the *Suba* were as following :
Warangal : 13,46,849-17 : Karimnagar : 12,12,421-21 ;
Adilabad : 9,34,124-17½ : Total for the *Suba* : 34,94,124-17½
W.S. *File* No. 64 of 1319 Fasli (1910) & R. No. 3754 of 1321 Fasli (1912).

**These included *Tur*, *Mung*, *Masur*, *Kulthi*, *Urad* and *Lac*—*Estimates of Area and Yield of principal crops in Hyderabad State, 1925-26 to 1944-45*, (quinquennial), (Government Central Press : Hyderabad-Dn, 1938 & 1942).

†Acreage figures except those for 1943-44 & 1944-45 are not available.

††Shown blank.

CROP ACREAGE, AREA-WISE AND YEAR-WISE

1332 Fasli (1923)					
Warangal	Karimnagar	Adilabad	Telangana	Marathwada	State
15	16	17	18	19	20
16,50,526	14,49,653	13,62,382	—	—	—
91,445	96,081	36,130	—	—	—
3,61,517	4,70,540	7,05,116	—	—	—
2,37,554	53,180	68,804	—	—	—
4,05,380	1,99,069	50,262	—	—	—
35,676	44,757	4,068	—	—	—
1,92,725	62,980	56,723	—	—	—
52,507	2,00,934	46,008	—	—	—
—	—	—	—	—	—
43,761	22,341	19,907	—	—	—
40,311	81;421	3,10,130	—	—	—
11,105	15,887	6,090	—	—	—
—	—	—	—	—	—
91,779	95,214	40,300	—	—	—
3,525	9,784	668	—	—	—

CROP ACREAGE, AREA-WISE AND YEAR-WISE

1333 Fasli (1924)					
Warangal	Karimnagar	Adilabad	Telangana	Marathwada	State
21	22	23	24	25	26
16,70,573	14,60,154	13,77,267	—	—	—
85,254	1,15,957	37,018	—	—	—
6,00,617	3,43,623	6,96,588	—	—	—
2,25,215	6,602	—	—	—	—
2,91,853	1,62,872	52,849	—	—	—
3,215	55,826	4,993	—	—	—
32,006	1,72,874	51,197	—	—	—
48,335	2,35,629	52,923	—	—	—
—	—	—	—	—	—
39,134	25,344	21,489	—	—	—
1,56,504	87,492	3,11,548	—	—	—
3,801	20,307	5,274	—	—	—
—	—	—	—	—	—
—	—	—	—	—	—
1,02,874	94,945	51,862	—	—	—
1,819	9,618	781	—	—	—

CROP ACREAGE, AREA-WISE AND YEAR-WISE

1334 Fasli (1925)					
Warangal	Karimnagar	Adilabad	Telangana	Marathwada	State
27	28	29	30	31	32
16,80,118	14,65,080	13,91,609	—	—	—
1,02,053	1,16,709	42,271	—	—	—
5,96,244	3,48,641	6,97,289	—	—	—
2,21,316	6,216	—	—	—	—
2,88,311	1,62,919	53,941	—	—	—
3,325	56,281	4,875	—	—	—
31,375	1,72,850	52,296	—	—	—
50,366	2,35,271	53,148	—	—	—
—	—	—	—	—	—
39,192	26,295	21,541	—	—	—
90,776	87,537	3,13,278	—	—	—
3,100	21,422	5,341	—	—	—
—	—	—	—	—	—
—	—	—	—	—	—
1,80,019	93,652	51,963	—	—	—
2,556	9,563	792	—	—	—

CROP ACREAGE, AREA-WISE AND YEAR-WISE

1335 Fasli (1925-26)					
Warangal	Karimnagar	Adilabad	Telangana	Marathwada	State
33	34	35	36	37	38
16,80,118	13,10,464	13,84,269	87,83,280	1,27,14,393	2,68,73,939
1,52,495	2,04,383	22,876	7,07,112	76,255	8,45,867
4,30,422	4,50,424	6,47,117	23,02,049	41,74,443	90,44,292
1,64,202	5,510	—	7,52,430	15,33,002	28,72,340
1,86,070	1,24,526	62,903	5,08,954	22,352	5,94,420
74,820	42,129	20,381	9,05,225	4,76,037	8,30,781
65,190	93,945	62,869	6,90,290	12,44,364	23,33,761
36,771	1,75,498	72,015	3,87,680	22,623	5,21,347
—	—	613	2,925	1,30,488	1,90,383
30,133	33,165	5,078	6,04,564	32,818	6,72,586
27,398	64,804	2,30,030	3,70,018	27,84,014	37,81,233
—	—	—	—	—	1,55,000
50	—	119	1,193	38,224	54,624
—	—	—	—	—	—
1,19,910	45,295	35,967	9,05,373	3,16,745	12,80,827
4,050	7,906	11,269	64,397	1,93,179	2,96,691

CROP ACREAGE, AREA-WISE AND YEAR-WISE

1336 Fasli (1926-27)					
Warangal	Karimnagar	Adilabad	Telangana	Marathwada	State
39	40	41	42	43	44
16,83,421	13,48,130	13,91,876	88,56,074	1,27,54,407	2,69,84,686
97,714	73,838	25,020	4,39,010	62,460	5,39,306
4,05,349	3,73,472	3,44,944	20,02,905	40,89,959	82,08,899
89,619	7,275	—	7,61,269	11,77,091	25,02,268
1,87,611	2,86,921	1,10,882	7,01,266	37,389	8,10,618
75,526	46,001	27,824	2,19,825	4,82,503	8,53,001
69,915	1,16,447	1,27,675	11,04,140	17,99,479	33,23,638
36,669	1,99,786	61,480	3,86,293	73,388	5,04,570
—	—	250	4,804	2,30,095	3,04,538
30,431	41,117	4,412	5,43,919	30,408	6,11,410
12,751	72,604	2,05,849	3,36,729	21,80,573	32,67,483
2,905	6,737	3,838	39,413	51,397	1,15,996
—	—	115	3,547	27,782	47,256
—	—	—	—	—	—
4,82,133	67,004	96,867	13,95,781	4,49,587	19,14,479
12,959	9,263	40,763	1,20,128	1,27,582	3,88,519

CROP ACREAGE, AREA-WISE AND YEAR-WISE

1337 Fasli (1927-28)

Warangal	Karimnagar	Adilabad	Telangana	Marathwada	State
45	47	47	48	49	50
16,40,732	13,92,651	13,22,756	87,41,972	1,24,09,578	2,64,20,537
1,31,117	1,49,757	50,920	6,78,673	77,129	9,33,263
4,79,210	3,59,869	6,40,376	21,50,903	42,48,202	87,05,574
1,99,010	5,455	—	7,38,564	7,28,576	18,65,845
2,91,007	2,24,436	41,916	6,49,761	24,058	7,52,458
10,546	51,895	11,594	1,15,483	4,85,825	6,87,044
47,582	1,43,151	69,585	10,13,475	17,07,560	30,90,933
45,855	1,94,826	66,838	4,03,651	1,07,199	5,99,313
—	—	355	12,464	3,17,260	4,85,068
45,536	34,289	10,463	6,06,551	32,377	6,81,480
18,570	84,395	2,95,283	4,37,144	25,08,096	36,30,822
6,188	5,335	3,188	24,353	48,940	98,669
—	3	14	982	10,992	21,550
—	—	—	—	—	—
3,06,278	74,249	93,217	12,83,763	4,51,342	18,13,310
13,500	10,481	38,190	1,16,802	1,33,325	3,05,833

CROP ACREAGE, AREA-WISE AND YEAR-WISE

1338 Fasli (1928-29)					
Warangal District	Karimnagar District	Adilabad District	Telangana	Marathwada	State
51	52	53	54	55	56
16,48,817	14,24,344	13,54,710	88,50,853	1,26,04,045	2,64,20,537
1,47,743	1,57,160	36,634	7,28,560	90,402	9,92,453
6,15,515	3,42,300	5,84,664	23,62,584	40,06,860	91,58,128
1,60,175	2,357	—	7,00,411	8,44,037	19,45,349
2,50,517	2,18,409	52,935	6,10,505	44,508	7,34,833
11,629	41,328	22,545	1,25,342	5,28,217	7,35,770
57,716	1,61,508	88,139	10,61,369	15,24,226	29,56,380
48,131	2,26,899	70,895	4,53,808	1,14,847	6,49,942
—	—	260	52,911	4,00,358	6,50,310
48,433	40,245	9,462	5,18,058	38,080	6,59,311
17,362	1,00,827	2,77,364	4,41,991	27,28,687	40,19,331
6,130	6,415	2,885	25,965	48,940	98,669
—	6	20	609	4,282	6,095
—	—	—	—	—	—
2,47,973	68,951	85,398	11,77,672	3,96,527	16,44,546
10,817	9,269	35,529	1,25,539	98,235	2,78,270

CROP ACREAGE, AREA-WISE AND YEAR-WISE

1339 Fasli (1929-30)					
Warangal District	Karimnagar District	Adilabad District	Telangana	Marathwada	State
57	58	59	60	61	62
18,97,372	12,90,135	15,74,386	1,00,51,751	1,90,11,317	2,90,63,068
82,557	51,529	25,019	3,46,770	62,121	5,06,621
3,92,947	3,46,929	4,21,456	19,03,023	41,89,311	89,97,179
1,95,597	1,033	322	10,87,520	10,25,822	21,13,342
1,70,664	1,55,429	1,33,860	6,96,361	2,83,922	9,80,283
99,603	33,581	60,592	3,69,249	7,36,438	11,05,687
3,17,420	1,05,980	3,39,427	12,98,976	21,23,786	34,22,762
38,920	2,34,174	44,400	4,14,928	88,398	5,68,553
2,052	—	325	56,520	3,83,633	6,18,737
45,930	53,628	7,761	5,02,629	35,869	6,01,939
20,374	75,674	2,62,188	3,91,957	24,15,885	35,35,728
5,695	3,378	3,290	20,871	40,637	80,680
4	8	67	1,247	21,345	36,871
—	—	—	—	—	—
—	—	1,55,422	7,94,573	13,83,496	21,78,069
2,60,962	23,124	47,290	4,62,136	3,79,868	8,42,004

CROP ACREAGE, AREA-WISE AND YEAR-WISE

5 Years average (1335 F-1939 F)

Warangal District	Karimnagar District	Adilabad District	Telangana	Marathwada	State
63	64	65	66	67	68
17,10,092	13,53,154	14,05,599	90,56,806	1,38,98,748	2,72,15,524
1,22,425	1,27,453	33,496	5,80,025	73,673	7,63,502
4,64,689	3,74,599	5,25,711	21,44,293	41,41,755	88,22,414
1,81,721	4,326	322	8,09,039	10,61,706	22,59,829
2,17,173	2,15,974	78,499	6,33,339	82,447	7,74,522
54,267	43,041	28,589	2,07,025	5,41,804	8,42,457
1,11,564	1,24,206	1,37,539	10,53,650	16,79,133	30,24,625
41,269	2,06,237	63,126	4,09,272	85,291	5,68,745
2,052	—	375	25,925	9,93,367	4,49,807
40,093	44,489	7,434	5,55,144	33,908	6,45,345
19,291	79,661	2,54,143	3,95,568	25,23,451	36,46,903
5,230	5,466	3,300	27,651	48,722	1,11,147
27	6	69	1,496	20,525	33,279
—	—	—	—	—	—
2,89,074	63,875	93,374	11,11,433	6,99,539	17,66,246
60,460	12,009	33,008	1,77,802	2,06,438	4,22,263

CROP ACREAGE, AREA-WISE AND YEAR-WISE

1340 Fasli (1930-31)					
Warangal District	Karimnagar District	Adilabad District	Telangana	Marathwada	State
69	70	71	72	73	74
16,13,108	14,98,100	15,60,114	1,06,81,649	1,87,72,879	2,94,54,528
1,10,690	95,052	58,461	5,72,508	1,12,399	6,84,907
3,76,106	3,73,497	5,58,620	23,94,028	71,93,868	95,87,896
1,36,644	2,220	—	9,75,556	11,00,115	20,75,671
2,26,385	1,08,204	34,812	4,92,598	1,39,478	6,32,076
9,045	40,394	15,121	2,39,415	8,11,423	10,50,838
1,54,694	1,83,179	1,42,005	16,10,280	19,91,825	36,02,105
38,632	2,74,806	70,062	4,83,429	1,09,696	5,93,125
2,810	—	430	91,308	6,00,067	6,91,375
48,936	46,667	12,326	7,39,001	52,788	7,91,789
35,573	1,24,015	3,57,472	5,68,497	29,58,942	35,27,439
5,831	3,102	1,268	23,386	63,225	86,611
3	3	65	1,532	32,946	34,478
—	—	—	—	—	—
1,25,959	1,79,355	1,25,959	12,82,372	7,47,616	20,29,988
34,331	28,612	39,776	2,39,242	3,84,378	6,24,320

CROP ACREAGE, AREA-WISE AND YEAR-WISE

1341 Fasli (1931-32)

Warangal District	Karimnagar District	Adilabad District	Telangana	Marathwada	State
75	76	77	78	79	80
17,50,696	13,06,609	13,38,541	1,07,44,716	8,81,11,374	2,89,76,090
1,79,694	2,17,394	61,506	9,70,792	1,29,113	10,99,905
4,42,640	3,57,494	6,07,729	25,53,832	69,10,205	94,64,037
1,58,141	4,305	30,746	11,24,845	9,76,551	21,01,396
1.47,643	1,23,816	49,590	5,28,058	2,71,032	7,99,090
27,624	57,505	45,161	4,11,850	8,24,613	12,36,463
1,61,677	1,35,900	1,45,638	14,46,444	19,98,008	34,44,452
38,070	1,98,939	73,247	3,95,882	1,11,947	5,07,829
5,525	2,729	357	1,01,458	6,72,388	7,74,796
45,045	52,082	8,597	8,00,966	54,706	8,55,672
28,175	1,02,415	2,66,589	4,43,231	32,00,712	36,43,943
6,072	4,377	2,630	24,861	53,185	78,046
3	5	64	1,377	34,016	35,393
—	—	—	—	—	—
3,28,155	1,09,946	56,790	9,46,685	4,17,559	13,64,244
38,870	26,694	13,235	1,88,789	2,32,772	4,21,561

CROP ACREAGE, AREA-WISE AND YEAR-WISE

1342 Fasli (1932-33)

Waranagal District	Karimnagar District	Adilabad District	Telangana	Marathwada	State
81	82	83	84	85	86
18,00,696	16,47,504	14,50,500	1,12,77,863	1,87,32,026	3,00,09,889
1,74,282	1,96,389	51,482	8,62,751	1,34,491	9,97,242
5,13,449	3,70,904	5,27,143	25,69,769	67,85,432	93,56,201
2,05,299	3,929	72,685	13,32,709	12,10,826	25,43,535
1,17,677	1,72,383	45,914	5,26,815	1,62,882	6,89,697
36,155	72,490	50,707	3,75,109	8,55,758	12,30,867
1,68,491	1,67,957	1,40,180	15,48,826	23,61,485	39,10,311
49,966	2,34,936	73,577	4,73,389	1,27,251	6,00,640
9,926	2,579	467	1,48,557	9,69,532	11,18,089
33,711	65,234	8,059	7,81,861	56,021	8,37,882
33,978	77,691	2,92,761	4,58,501	31,43,144	36,01,645
5,232	4,050	2,497	35,181	51,068	76,249
29	3	76	2,144	38,068	40,212
—	—	—	—	—	—
2,27,000	1,94,321	20,497	9,96,248	4,09,374	14,05,622
43,240	58,053	45,891	2,62,700	2,34,417	4,97,117

CROP ACREAGE, AREA-WISE AND YEAR-WISE

1343 Fasli (1933-34)

Warangal District	Karimnagar District	Adilabad District	Telangana	Marathwada	State
87	88	89	90	91	92
16,16,540	16,38,892	11,22,158	1,06,56,750	1,87,01,345	2,83,58,095
2,29,153	2,16,189	62,783	11,36,138	1,72,461	13,08,599
4,91,479	3,69,191	5,39,258	26,37,275	61,97,204	88,34,479
1,52,939	3,864	—	12,10,098	13,33,535	25,40,633
1,83,394	1,54,343	30,169	5,71,513	1,68-158	7,39,671
41,992	41,400	30,816	3,13,276	9,68,436	12,81,712
1,56,970	1,90,078	30,312	12,43,741	21,60,452	34,04,193
45,551	2,41,246	69,920	4,47,728	1,33,990	5,81,718
20,090	3,236	667	1,93,024	11,91,398	13,84,422
33,763	60,336	7,639	7,64,639	61,609	8,26.248
37,094	78,757	2,80,078	4,56,737	32,41,354	36,01,645
4,085	3,683	2,750	26,872	44,277	71,149
36	4	100	3,088	43,392	46,480
—	—	—	—	—	—
3,45,164	1,63,638	1,13,638	11,83,222	4,62,492	16,45,714
2,818	58,495	19,010	1,75,055	2,42,716	4,17,771

CROP ACREAGE, AREA-WISE AND YEAR-WISE

1344 Fasli (1934-35)					
Warangal District	Karimnagar District	Adilabad District	Telangana	Marathwada	State
93	94	95	96	97	98
16,07,905	15,94,670	12,08,248	1,04,69,793	1,79,00,471	2,83,70,264
2,18,964	2,06,470	76,113	10,07,066	1,76,498	11,83,564
4,31,472	3,42,948	5,17,841	24,79,871	64,12,207	88,92,078
1,63,256	3,580	25,858	9,33,096	11,79,297	21,12,393
1,68,775	1,61,603	38,303	5,31,942	1,80,123	7,12,065
28,704	52,947	35,451	4,37,529	8,13,549	12,51,078
1,58,662	1,88,777	57.025	12,84,644	21.44,262	34,28,906
37,128	2,06,954	71,150	4,07,307	1,01,823	5,09,130
40,590	3,943	1,308	2,44,265	7,17,272	9,61,537
27,871	47,373	7,514	7,39,973	45,702	7,85,675
29,877	67,904	2,72,936	4,20,479	26,80,322	31,00,801
4,308	3,561	2,753	24,887	49,614	74,501
96	4	196	7,996	42,584	50,580
—	—	—	—	—	—
2,25,600	1,90,794	33,347	10,23,995	4,89,311	15,13,406
11,480	67,814	21,450	2,51,299	2,58,862	5,10,161

CROP ACREAGE, AREA-WISE AND YEAR-WISE

5 years' average (1340 F-1344 F)					
Warangal District	Karimnagar District	Adilabad District	Telangana	Marathwada	State
99	100	101	102	103	104
16,77,789	15,77,155	13,35,912	1,08,40,378	1,84,57,558	2,92,36,850
1,82,556	1,86,298	62,069	9,09,851	1,45,390	10,55,241
4,51,029	3,62,806	5,50,118	25,26,955	66,92,933	62,26,933
1,63,245	3,579	43,096	8,60,180	11,49,464	20,39,645
1,68,774	1,44,069	39,757	5,30,065	1,93,148	7,23,213
28,704	52,947	33,451	3,31,908	8,54,755	11,86,664
1,60,096	1,74,178	1,03,032	14,31,457	21,31,246	35,62,703
41,869	2,31,376	71,591	4,41,546	1,16,941	5,58,438
15,788	3,121	645	1,56,146	8,30,120	9,86,265
37,365	54,338	8,827	7,16,468	56,025	7,72,493
32,939	90,156	2,93,967	4,69,489	30,45,014	35,14,503
5,105	3,754	2,379	25,039	52,292	77,332
33	3	100	3,237	38,201	41,438
—	—	—	—	—	—
2,50,375	1,67,648	70,046	10,57,590	5,05,299	15,91,894
87,747	47,933	27,872	2,93,294	2,70,586	4,94,186

CROP ACREAGE, AREA-WISE AND YEAR-WISE

1345 Fasli (1935-36)					
Warangal District	Karimnagar District	Adilabad District	Telangana	Marathwada	State
105	106	107	108	109	110
15,38,000	16,06,000	12,58,000	1,02,82,000	1,88,51,000	2,91,33 000
1,53,000	1,93,000	74,000	8,87,000	1,77,000	10,64,000
4,23,000	3,29,000	4 72,000	24,59,000	63,40,000	87,99,000
1,63,000	3,000	25,000	9,62,000	12,36,000	21,98,000
1,58,000	1,62,000	36,000	4,95,000	1,80,000	6,75,000
30,000	55,000	40,000	3,39,000	9,33,000	12,72,000
1,41,000	2,35,000	94,000	11,53,000	22,47,000	33,90,000
88,000	1,83,000	64,000	4,50,000	1,38,000	5,88,000
51,000	4,000	1,000	2,58,000	8,01,000	10,59,000
69,000	46,000	7,000	7,84,000	50,000	8,34,000
17,000	71,000	2,80,000	4,39,000	32,59,000	36,98,000
4,238	4,309	2,746	26,419	45,143	71,562
83	33	195	15,231	43,274	58,505
—	—	—	—	—	—
1,28,000	2,11,000	35,000	8,91,000	2,93,000	11,84,000
62,000	62,000	46,000	3,80,000	3,25,000	7,05,000

CROP ACREAGE, AREA-WISE AND YEAR-WISE

1346 Fasli (1936-37)					
Warangal District	Karimnagar District	Adilabad District	Telangana	Marathwada	State
111	112	113	114	115	116
17,91,000	15,30,000	13,86,000	1,06,06,000	1,73,35,000	2,79,41,000
1,79,000	2,26,000	74,000	10,01,000	1,34,000	11,35,000
4,52,000	3,63,000	4,47,000	24,97,000	68,83,000	93,80,000
1,60,000	4,000	23,000	10,45,000	13,09,000	23,54,000
1,61,000	1,59,000	38,000	5,10,000	1,63,000	6,73,000
30,000	56,000	39,000	3,35,000	8,95,000	12,30,000
1,90,000	1,68,000	1,53,000	11,34,000	10,36,000	22,20,000
84,000	2,03,000	70,000	4,71,000	89,000	5,60,000
1,21,000	16,000	1,000	4,22,000	6,41,000	10,63,000
70,000	34,000	9,000	7,77,000	41,000	8,18,000
22,000	61,000	2,90,000	4,78,000	28,10,000	32,88,000
4,625	4,393	3,019	32,482	39.308	71,790
205	222	308	19,326	39,275	58,601
—	—	—	—	—	—
2,28,000	1,42,000	1,44,000	10,10,000	3,24,000	13,34,000
63,000	70,000	46,000	3,90,000	2,92,000	6,82,000

CROP ACREAGE, AREA-WISE AND YEAR-WISE

1347 Fasli (1937-38)					
Warangal District	Karimnagar District	Adilabad District	Telangana	Marathwada	State
117	118	119	120	121	122
17,04,000	14,12,000	12,32,000	92,27,000	1,71,44,000	2,63,71,000
1,68,000	1,99,000	69,000	8,31,000	1,31,000	9,62,000
4,70,000	3,29,000	4,56,000	22,89,000	61,91,000	84,80,000
1,49,000	4,000	21,000	8,58,000	12,50,000	21,08,000
1,65,000	1,54,000	37,000	4,84,000	1,67,000	6,51,000
41,000	50,000	36,000	3,24,000	9,31,000	12,55,000
1,01,000	1,79,000	1,23,000	9,97000	12,33,000	22,30,000
79,000	2,03,000	66,000	4,45,000	1,03,000	5,48,000
2,03,000	34,000	2,000	6,28,000	8,10,000	14,38,000
71,000	28,000	6,000	4,81,000	39,000	5,20,000
15,000	62,000	2,76,000	3,96,000	31,67,000	35,63,000
4,663	3,520	2,636	22,275	40,585	52,860
218	314	302	8,614	21,832	30,446
—	—	—	—	—	—
5,000	41,000	5,000	3,31,000	1,37,000	4,68,000
49,000	10,000	10,000	1,90,000	3,16,000	5,06,000

CROP ACREAGE, AREA-WISE AND YEAR-WISE

1348 Fasli (1938-39)					
Warangal District	Karimnagar District	Adilabad District	Telangana	Marathwada	State
123	124	125	126	127	128
17,11,000	15,62,000	13,47,000	99,57,000	2,70,97,000	2,70,5400
2,40,000	1,60,000	75,000	9,39,000	1,55,000	10,95,000
4,66,000	6,25,000	4,99,000	29,29,000	61,86,000	91,15,000
1,45,000	5,000	22,000	7,73,000	15,51,000	19,24,000
1,60,000	1,49,000	35,000	4,75,000	1,72,000	6,47,000
39,000	52,000	33,000	3,28,000	9,24,000	12,52,000
3,50,000	1,59,000	2,36,000	17,85,000	14,19,000	32,04,000
24,000	1,63,000	58,000	3,48,000	1,13,000	4,61,000
1,68,000	41,000	6,000	2,52,000	9,70,000	16,22,000
54,000	85,000	8,000	7,21,000	79,000	8,00,000
11,000	45,000	2,79,000	3,85,000	31,21,000	34,97,000
7,732	3,127	2,478	30,977	40,289	71,266
152	174	237	9,970	21,513	31,483
—	—	—	—	—	—
7,000	14,000	9,000	1,81,000	66,000	2,47,000
24,000	24,000	17,000	2,20,000	2,70,000	4,90,000

CROP ACREAGE, AREA-WISE AND YEAR-WISE

1349 Fasli (1939-40)					
Warangal District	Karimnagar District	Adilabad District	Telangana	Marathwada	State
129	130	131	132	133	134
16,13,000	15,14,000	13,99,000	1,02,90,009	1,81,43.000	2,84,33,000
1,38,000	1,07,000	71,000	7,79,000	1,82,000	9,61,000
6,51,000	5,23,000	5,50,000	34,23,000	69,81,000	1,04,11,000
72,000	1,000	2,000	6,33,000	9,86,000	17,19,000
83,000	1,63,000	38,000	4,28,000	1,51,000	5,79,000
17,000	24,000	27.000	2,01,000	7,44,000	9,45,000
1,68,000	2,03,000	2,05,000	15,68,000	16,15,000	31,83,000
68,000	1,46,000	75,000	4,01,000	1,47,000	5,48,000
2,13,000	68,000	6,000	8,13,000	11,46,000	19,59,000
53,000	29,000	6,000	6,70,000	45,000	6,71,009
17,000	96,000	2,68,000	4,29,000	33,02,000	37,31,000
85,585	3,846	2,621	38,457	42,678	8J,135
45	252	342	19,503	25,180	44,683
—	—	—	—	—	—
66,000	58,000	38,000	3,53,000	83,000	4,46,000
47,00	45,000	52,000	3,65,000	3,29,000	6,94,000

CROP ACREAGE, AREA-WISE AND YEAR-WISE

5 years' average (1345F-1349F)

Warangal District	Karimnagar District	Adilabad District	Telangana	Marathwada	State
135	136	137	138	139	140
15,71,000	15,25,000	13,24,000	1,00,72,009	1,77,14,000	2,77,86,00
1,76,000	1,77,000	73,000	8,87,000	1,56,000	10,43,000
4,92,000	4,34,000	4,77,000	27,19,000	65,18,000	92,37,000
1,39,000	3,000	11,000	8,54,000	11,86,000	20,40,000
1,45,000	1,58,000	37,000	3,78,000	1,67,000	6,45,000
31,000	48,000	35,000	3,05,000	8,85,000	11,90,000
1,90,000	1,89,000	1,62,000	13,38,000	15,18,000	28,56,000
69,000	1,81,000	67,000	4,23,000	1,19,000	5,42,000
1,51,000	33,000	31,000	5,55,000	1,64,000	14,26,000
63,000	64,000	7,000	6,77,000	41,000	7,28,000
16,000	67,000	2,79,000	4,25,000	31,30,000	33,55,000
5,969	3,839	2,700	30,122	41,600	71,722
141	199	277	14,529	30,214	44,743
—	—	—	—	—	—
87,000	93,000	46,000	5,55,000	1,81,000	7,36,000
49,000	42,000	34,000	3,09,000	3,06,000	6,15,000

CROP ACREAGE, AREA-WISE AND YEAR-WISE

1349-50 Fasli (1940-41)					
Warangal District	Karimnagar District	Adilabad District	Telangana	Marathwada	State
141	142	143	144	145	146
17,29,000	14,31,000	15,73,000	1,06,29,000	1,75,51,000	2,81,80,000
2,29,000	2,06,000	70,000	10,85,000	2,10,000	12,95,000
5,99,000	3,87,000	6,31,000	31,89,000	63,22,000	93,11,000
98,000	6,000	2,000	5,74,000	10,22,000	13,16,000
1,02,000	2,31,000	42,000	4,17,000	1,15,000	5,32,000
23,000	40,000	21,000	1,98,000	7,17,000	9,15,000
29,000	2,59,000	2,83,000	15,68,000	16,15,000	31,83,000
41,000	1,47,000	66,000	3,49,000	1,25,000	4,74,000
2,35,000	75,000	12,000	8,30,000	11,34,000	19,64,000
66,000	36,000	7,000	7,36,000	45,000	7,81,000
15,000	63,000	4,22,000	5,80,000	33,71,000	38,51,000
6,315	3,429	2,143	31,044	43,427	74,471
124	99	544	19,807	28,344	41,151
—	—	—	—	—	—
60,000	63,000	47,000	4,59,000	2,67,000	7,26,000
57,000	52,000	38,000	3,82,000	2,93,000	6,75,000

CROP ACREAGE, AREA-WISE AND YEAR-WISE

1350-51 Fasli (1941-42)					
Warangal District	Karimnagar District	Adilabad District	Telangana	Marathwada	State
147	148	149	150	151	152
18,31,000	15,65.000	9,59,000	96,76,000	1,65,56.000	16,65,56,000
1,23,000	77,000	47,000	6,50,000	1,34,000	7,84,000
8,07,000	4,46,000	1,69,000	31,61,000	64,77,000	96,38,000
64,000	1,007	5,000	5,43,000	8,94,000	14,41,000
1,45,000	1,48,000	42000	4,70,000	1,39,000	6,00,000
9,000	19,000	13,000	1,11,000	7,02,000	8,13,000
12,000	1,81,000	1,53,000	12,02,000	12,50,000	24,52,000
1,34,000	1,87,000	69,000	4,76,000	92,000	5,68,000
1,97,000	57,000	4,000	5,90,000	0,20,000	15,10,000
22,000	36,000	18,000	7,81,000	98,000	8,86,000
13,000	80,000	3,34,000	4,74,000	30,99,000	35,73,000
9,651	4,051	2,667	32,255	34,647	66,902
32	95	312	16,091	28,851	44,942
—	—	—	—	—	—
52,000	53,000	45,000	5,21,000	2,46,000	7,67,000
36,000	56,000	31,000	2,41,000	2,11000	5,52,000

CROP ACREAGE, AREA-WISE AND YEAR-WISE

1351-52 Fasli (1942-43)					
Warangal District	Karimnagar District	Adilabad District	Telangana	Marathwada	State
153	154	155	156	157	158
16,58,000	14,[illegible]7,000	13,12,000	95,22,000	1,70,08,000	2,65,30,000
1,87,000	1,67,000	70,000	10,90,000	1,80,000	11,80,000
5,79,000	3,85,000	5,80,000	31,50,000	66,97,000	98,37,000
78,000	1,000	2,000	5,52,000	12,50,000	18,02,000
58,000	1,49,000	42,000	3,81,000	21,000	4,12,000
4,000	14,000	10,000	80,000	5,37,000	6,17,000
6,000	1,77,000	86,000	11,30,000	18,55,000	29,59,000
64,007	1,74,000	1,18,000	4,40,000	1,26,000	5,66,000
2,08,000	70,000	4,000	8,35,000	10,45,000	18,80,000
26,000	32,000	9,000	7,27,000	47,000	7,74,000
16,000	57,000	2,42,000	3,59,000	27,58,000	31,17,000
3,233	4,027	2,826	24,950	29,429	54,372
45	72	289	14,244	27,590	41,834
—	—	—	—	—	—
21,000	50,000	31000	3,62,000	2,11,007	5,73,000
37,003	46,000	26,000	2,73,000	1,73,000	4,46,000

CROP ACREAGE, AREA-WISE AND YEAR-WISE

1352-53 Fasli (1943-44)

Warangal District	Karimnagar District	Adilabad District	Telangana	Marathwada	State
159	160	161	162	163	164
13,58,000	14,10,000	13,69,000	96,34,000	1,85,58,000	2,11,91,000
1,99,000	1,81,000	73,000	11,72,007	2,31,000	92,81,000
4,84,000	3,62,000	5,36,000	27,70,000	65,11,000	92,81,000
34,000	—	10,000	4,11,000	14,10,000	18,28,000
42,000	1,39,000	42,000	4,14,000	15,000	4,29,000
5,000	12,000	10,000	90,000	4,17,000	5,07,000
7,000	1,90,000	1,33,000	10,81,000	23,15,000	33,96000
61,000	1,82,000	1,19,000	4,83,000	1,72,000	6,55,000
4,27,000	1,48,000	6,000	14,14,000	15,93,000	31,07,000
35,000	49,000	15,000	7,73,000	53,000	8,31,000
8,000	77,000	3,44,000	4,84,000	36,21,000	41,05,000
4,816	2,157	2,418	37,362	28,066	65,428
42	84	192	21,796	41,183	62,979
6,634	17,725	3,674	64,951	23,763	88,714
6,000	11,000	2,000	26,000	32,000	58,000
5,000	6,000	1,000	43,000	30,000	73,000

CROP ACREAGE, AREA-WISE AND YEAR-WISE

1353-54 (Fasli (1944-45)					
Warangal District	Karimnagar District	Adilabad District	Telangana	Marathwada	State
165	166	167	168	169	170
23,63,000	13,30,000	13,18,000	91,60,000	1,73,15,000	2,64,75,000
1,72,000	1,57,000	99,000	50,96,000	2,03,000	12,99,000
5,75,000	3 55,000	5,49,000	27,17,000	64,17,000	91,34,000
40,000	1,000	1,000	6,16,000	13,19,000	18,35,000
56,000	1,56,000	41,000	4,22,000	11,000	4,33,000
4,000	19,000	20,000	1,18,000	6,33,000	7,51,000
11,000	2,92,000	1,73,000	14,12,000	7,15,000	21,27000
48,000	1,95,000	1,31,000	4,72,000	1,51,000	6,23,000
2,00,000	1,24,000	12,000	11,03,000	15,01,000	16,04,000
24,000	48,000	24,000	6,83,000	55,000	7,47,000
6,000	37,000	1,92,000	16,94,000	16,94,000	19,57,008
5,462	1,162	1,190	16,467	13,198	29,665
88	109	239	31,331	40,917	62,248
10,793	15,771	10,835	1,04,372	1,23,397	2,29,769
18,000	2,000	5,000	35,000	10,000	45,000
1,000	—	—	3,000	21,000	24.000

CROP ACREAGE, AREA-WISE AND YEAR-WISE

5 years' average (1349-50 F-1353-54F)

Warangal District	Karimnagar District	Adilabad District	Telangana	Marathwaaa	State
171	172	173	174	175	176
15,72,000	14,51,000	15,06,000	97,24,000	1,73,98,000	2,71,22,000
1,80,000	1,57,000	77,000	10,00,000	1,92,000	11,92,000
6,30,000	4,27,000	4,93,000	29,97,000	64,85,000	17,01,000
63,000	2,000	4,000	4,21,000	11,80,000	17,01,000
81,000	1,45,000	42,000	4,23,000	50,000	4,83,000
9,000	21,000	15,000	1,20,000	6,01,000	7,21,000
13,000	2,21,000	1,66,000	12,70,000	15,49,000	28,19,000
70,000	1,77,000	1,00,000	4,44,000	1,32,000	5,76,000
2,30,000	95,000	7,000	9,55,000	13,58,000	22,13,000
35,000	40,000	7,000	7,44,000	61,000	8,04,000
11,000	69,000	3,07,000	4,32,000	29,08,000	33,40,000
5,795	2,966	2,249	28,416	29,743	58,169
67	92	315	20,654	31,377	52,031
—	—	—	—	—	—
36,000	26,000	—	2,81,000	1,53,000	4,34,000
27,000	32,000	19,000	2,08,000	1,45,000	3,53,000

CROP ACREAGE, AREA-WISE AND YEAR-WISE

1354-55 Fasli (1945-46)

Warangal District	Karimnagar District	Adilabad District	Telangans	Marathwada	State
177	178	179	180	181	182
—	—	—	—	—	—
2,10,368	2,00,985	98,482	12,63,156	1,65,654	14,18,310
4,84,978	2,42,448	4,34,557	23,14,112	51,48,558	74,62,670
25,818	353	755	4,24,172	8,38,875	12,63,047
48,188	1,43,937	149	3,47,068	10,875	3,68,943
6,381	23,225	24,982	1,56,182	7,47,654	8,93,146
—	—	—	—	—	—
43,089	1,85,535	23,809	4,10,101	2,28,011	6,38,112
2,19,365	1,09,698	7 912	9,34,731	15,—,903	24,35,634
25,183	44,193	22,836	7,40,623	66,234	8,16,857
2,563	18,247	2,34,830	2,75,190	18,79,027	21,54,917
7,127	3,759	1,717	15,843	11,091	26,934
102	64	233	21,589	37,483	4,138
—	—	—	—	—	—
—	—	—	—	—	—
—	—	—	—	—	—

CROP ACREAGE, AREA-WISE AND YEAR-WISE

1355-56 Fasli (1946-47)

Warangal District	Karimnagar District	Adilabad District	Telangana	Marathwada	State
183	184	185	186	187	188
—	—	—	—	—	—
1,98,212	1,95,622	88,700	10,80,463	1,21,330	12,01,794
3,93,319	5,60,317	3,90,317	22,11,875	46,18,117	68,29,993
19,023	296	503	3,05,255	7,06,970	10,12,244
51,339	1,12,097	36,873	3,41,629	8,352	3,49,981
8,377	24,705	17,840	1,57,500	7,27,664	8,84,164
—	—	—	—	—	—
49,592	1,63,123	95,931	3,97,009	2,77,264	6,74,826
2,12,956	37,914	19,301	6,78,800	67,300	7,46,100
2,584	20,646	1,96,608	2,39,368	19,97,109	22,36,477
2,362	644	2,023	42,737	38,137	80,874
54	76	384	24,435	54,322	3,759
—	—	—	*R*	—	—
—	—	—	—	—	—
—	—	—	—	—	—
—	—	—	—	—	—

CROP ACREAGE, AREA-WISE AND YEAR-WISE

1356-57 Fasli (1947-48)					
Warangal District	Karimnagar District	Adilabad District	Telangana	Marathwada	State
189	190	191	192	193	194
—	—	—	—	—	—
—	—	—	—	—	13,05,000
70,882	1,46,964	2,12,104	11,71,670	16,40,119	27,11,789
17,714	373	968	3,34,080	7,74,233	11,08,313
39,280	1,16,808	34,920	3,27,713	12,100	3,39,813
8,181	15,928	14,737	1,32,338	7,97,968	9,00,306
—	—	—	—	—	—
4,590	12,021	10,140	44,662	29,677	74,339
58,134	23,348	242	2,20,222	2,91,433	5,11,655
—	—	—	—	—	—
980	17,083	1,56,120	1,89,135	17,16,832	19,95,967
—	—	—	—	—	—
2	36	197	7,841	15,291	23,132
—	—	—	—	—	—
—	—	—	—	—	—
—	—	—	—	—	—

CROP ACREAGE, AREA-WISE AND YEAR-WISE

1357-58 Fasli (1948-49)

Warangal District	Karimnagar District	Adilabad District	Telangana	Marathwarda	State
195	196	197	198	199	200
—	—	—	—	—	—
—	—	—	—	—	—
69,074	1,47,490	1,99,579	10,11,136	14,12,286	24,30,422
9,957	323	1,113	2,63,390	6,41,334	9,05,225
37,483	42,045	28,665	2,90,550	8,015	2,98,565
1,369	8,752	13f844	1,01,394	6,34,555	7,35,949
—	—	—	—	—	—
—	—	—	—	—	—
—	—	—	—	—	—
—	—	—	—	—	—
1,172	12,486	1,54,637	1,87,573	19,73,161	21,60,634
—	—	—	—	—	—
—	—	—	—	—	—
—	—	—	—	—	—
—	—	—	—	—	—
—	—	—	—	—	—

CROP ACREAGE, AREA-WISE AND YEAR-WISE

1358-59 Fasli (1949-59)					
Warangal	Karimnagar	Adilabad	Telangana	Marathwada	State
201	202	203	204	205	206
15,59,716-47	6,71,135-35	4,14,385	—	—	—
1,88,598-70	1,40,937-34	89,236	—	—	—
—	—	—	—	—	—
—	—	—	—	—	—
—	—	—	—	—	—
—	—	—	—	—	—
—	—	—	—	—	—
—	—	—	—	—	—
—	—	—	—	—	—
—	—	—	—	—	—
—	—	—	—	—	—
—	—	—	—	—	—
No cultivation	8	266	—	—	—
—	—	—	—	—	—
—	—	—	—	—	—
—	—	—	—	—	—

CROP ACREAGE, AREA-WISE AND YEAR-WISE

1359-60 Fasli (1950-51)					
Warangal District	Karimnagar District	Adilabad District	Telangana	Marathwada	State
207	208	209	210	211	212
9,54,868-10	6,40,863-300	7,848,54	—	—	—
1,36,005-25	14,527-17	29,379	—	—	—
—	—	—	—	—	—
—	—	—	—	—	—
—	—	—	—	—	—
—	—	—	—	—	—
—	—	—	—	—	—
—	—	—	—	—	—
—	—	—	—	—	—
—	—	—	—	—	—
—	—	—	—	—	—
—	—	—	—	—	—
2-0	13	406	—	—	—
—	—	—	—	—	—
—	—	—	—	—	—
—	—	—	—	—	—

Sources : 1. *Statistical Abstract of H.E.H. the Nizam's Dominions from 1321 Fasli to 1330 Fasli (1912-1921).* (For the Data of the year 1921), pp. 136-143.

2. H.E.H. the Nizam's Government, *Hyderabad District Gazetteers, Warangal, Karimnagar and Adilabad,* Tables volumes, *1340* and *1345 Fasli (1931-31 & 1936).* (For the data of the period, 1925-26 to 1924-45).

3. *Estimates of Area and Yield of Principal Crops in Hyderabad State, Quinquennial 1926-26 (1335 Fasli) to 1934-34 (1344 Fasli); 1934-36 (1345 Fasli) to 1349 Fasli (1939-40)* and *1940-41 (1350 Fasli (1334-35).* (For the details of the period, 1925-26 to 1944-45).

4. Finance Department, (Resource branch) H.E.H. the Nizam's Government, S. No. 480, *File* No. 13 of 1350 Fasli (1944). (For particulars of Tobacco crop for 1945-46 & 1946-47).

5. Sercetariat Records of former Nizam's Government, Department of Agriculture, S No. 13, *Fasli* No. 8/57 Fasli (1948). (For data of rice, bajra, jawar, maize, *sesamum* groundunt, castor, sugarcane and cotton for the years 1945-46 & 1946-47).

6. Department of Agriculture, H.E.H. the Nizam's Government, Department, S.No. 16 & *File* No. 5/57 Fasli (1948). (For *sesamum* data of 1947-48) — S. No. 14, *File* No. 7/57 Fasli (1948). (For groundnut crop particulars of 1947-48).

7. Agriculture Department, H.E.H. the Nizam's Government, S.No. 6, *File* No. 110/58 Fasli (149). (For data of maize, jawar, cotton, bajra, and gram for the years 1947-48 and (1948-49).

8. Agriculture Department, S.No. 15 and *File* No. 6/57 Fasli (1948). (For sugarcane acreage of 1947-48).

---

*The net sown area figures have been arrived at by adding the area of *kharif*, *rabi*, *abi* paddy, *tabi* paddy and sugarcane cultivation. The figures of Karimnagar District did not contain those of the Taluqs of Manthani, Jagtiyal and Metpalli, as reports have not been received at the time of compilation of the data by the Department. Further, the figures of 1359-60 Fasli (1950-51) were given up to 28-12-1950 only—Rural Reconstruction Department, H.E.H. the Nizam's Government, S.No. 47, *File* No. 269/50 Misc. of 1950. (Sugarcane details of 1949-50 and 1950-51 are quoted from the same source).

See the above in respect of Karimnagar District and regarding data given for 1950-51.

Sultanabad and Nirmal had good acreage under rice production.[72] In respect of maize which was both a food and a good fodder crop, 75.04% of the acreage in the State was contributed by the *Suba* Districts, chiefly by Karimnagar and Warangal.[73] Bajra, *mung*, *sesamum* and groundnut as *Kharif* or autumn crops, wheat, gram, *tuar*,[74] castor and tobacco as *rabi* or spring crops and jawar, maize, cotton and chillies as both *kharif* and *rabi* crops,[75] were cultivated during the period. Whereas *kharif* crops were grown with the help of monsoon rainfall, the *rabi* crops, flourished not only on rain-fed water and soil moisture caused by winter due but also enjoyed the benefit of artificial irrigation, wherever the facilities existed. (For important crop acreage trends of the *Suba* See Chart IV).

(*i*) *Food Crops Acreage in Relation to Net Sown Area* :

Net sown area whose figures are given in Table XXXV showed variations, sometimes very wide as between 1921 and 1922, directly in proportion to the amount of rainfall received in a particular crop year. In 1921, the amount of rainfall received by all the *Suba* Districts and in fact the State, was extremely inadequate,[75a] resulting in famine conditions[76] and decrease of net sown area around 40%. Rainfall in the succeeding year was excellent[77] and the result was good crop and increase in sown area to the extent of covering up the huge reduction suffered in the preceding year. Leaving the occasional increases that were caused by deep fluctuations in rainfall conditions, the net sown area as could be gleaned from the quinquennial averages that were given for the period since 1929-30, showed a declining trend as the years progressed and the fall was paradoxically more marked since 1943-44 when the Grow More Food Campaign was launched by the Government. This, to some extent, was due to deliberate faulty reporting by the village officers in collusion with influential ryots, so as to escape the compulsory grain levy contribution that was in force during this period. These crop reports were accepted with least verification by *Tahsil* officers and were in turn submitted to the *Taluqdars*[78]. But, the more contributory factor towards this development was the increase in fallow land from

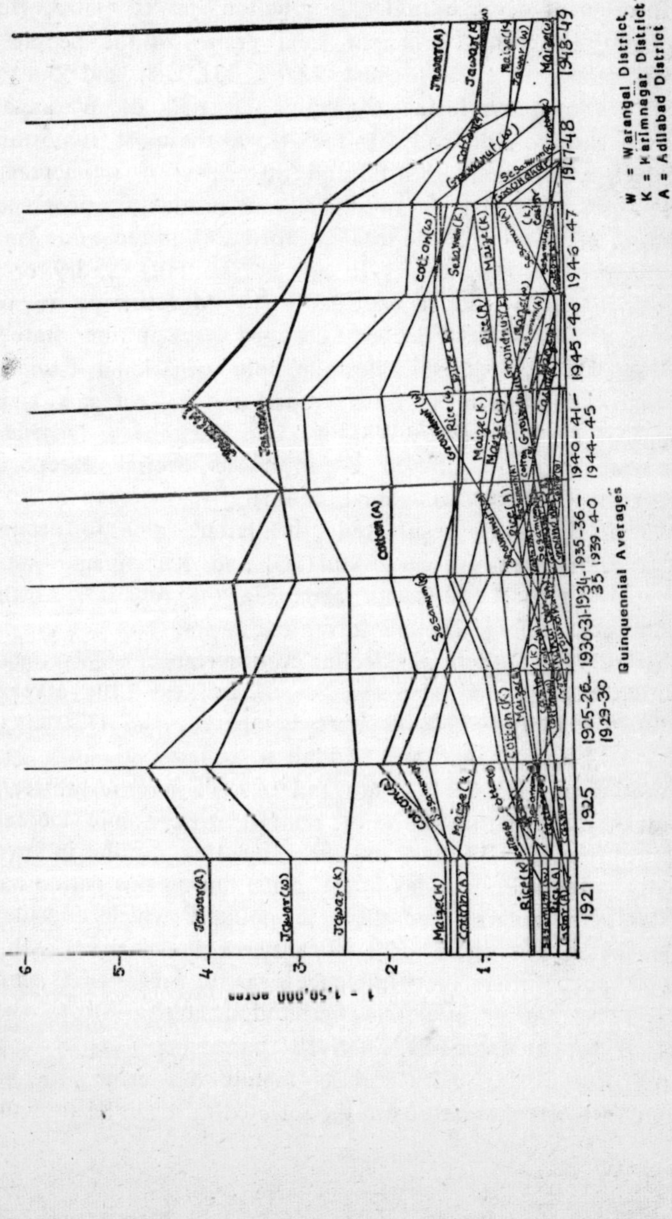

Chart No. 4 : Showing *Acreage of important crops in Warangal Suba, 1921-1948-49*

Data as per Table No. XXXV

year to year, consequent to the preponderance of wet cultivation and large scale absentee landlordism.[79]

(*a*) *Jawar*

In order of acreage under production, jawar, maize, rice and bajra, had formed principal food grains of the people[80]. Jawar in the year 1922 formed 22.0%, 31.05% and 53.40% of the net sown area in the respective Districts of Warangal, Karimnagar and Adilabad. In fact, it was the most important cereal grown in the State itself and in respect of its acreage, Hyderabad stood first among the jawar producing provinces in India. One-third of the total cropped area in the State was utilised in its production.[81] It being essentially a dry crop suitable for deep and heavier soils, the Marathwada region claimed around 45% of the total cropped area in the State.[82] Adilabad District with suitable soils, poor irrigational facilities but highest rainfall in the State,[83] stood first in Telangana right upto 1934 35, followed by Warangal and Karimnagar Districts. But, since then, it suffered a continuous decline except in 1940-41 in its acreage as against comparative increase in that of Warangal, with the result that the latter came to occupy first place in Telangana and Adilabad and Karimnagar were relegated to second and fourth places in the region,[84] as the last one also suffered decline during the period.

Since 1944-45, there was decline even in respect of Warangal, the two regions and also the State. In fact, if the acreage figures of 1933 and 1948-49 were compared, the Districts of Warangal, Karimnagar and Adilabad suffered a huge loss amounting to 3,000,95, 3,12,661 and 5,28,685 acres respectively. Besides the alternating effects of rainfall,[85] Economic Depression during 1929-33 had its effect on this decline in jawar acreage. Jawar Price index in the *Suba* during this period had suffered a fall ranging from 26 to 28 points,[87] which considerably affected the operational capacity of the farmers. But, more important than these influences was the factor that since 1922, ryots started preferring groundnut cultivation to that of jawar, for the latter was relatively unimportant as a cash crop.[88] Both being cultivated as mainly dry crops, the net income per acre assessed from the selected farms in Khammam,

Madhira, Mahaboobabad Taluqs, was higher by five times in respect of groundnut than that of jawar[89] and the natural result was tremendous and continuous increase in groundnut acreage in the period after 1929-30, in the *Suba* as well as the State.[90]

(*b*) *Maize*

This crop which was mainly concentrated in Telangana, suffered decline in acreage right from 1924-25 in respect of Warangal and Karimnagar and from 1945-46 in respect of Adilabad. There was only one bright patch between 1942-43 and 1944-45 in respect of Warangal District which was due to favourable crop conditions.[91] The late starting of decline in the case of Adilabad was due to the fact that the increase in groundnut acreage which came to be preferred to this crop along with cotton, picked up only in the forties.[92] The factors that operated regarding acreage decline in case of jawar, also applied in the case of maize also.

(*c*) *Rice*

Though the area under paddy formed only 11%, 12% and 5% of the total cultivated area in the Districts of Warangal, Karimnagar and Adilabad respectively,[93] yet, it was of prime economic importance in view of the greater yield per acre than jawar and the shortage of rice production to meet the food requirements of the State. The average outturn of rice per acre came to about 1,000 lbs. of grain as against that of 670 lbs of jawar[94] and Hyderabad on a minimum estimate, fell short of 1,00,000 tons of rice per year[95]. Rice acreage as can be seen from Table XXXV, kept on rising, with alternate years of fall depending on the amount of rainfall and supply of water for irrigation,[96] until 1925-26. There was 40 to 60% decline in acreage in 1929-30, being the acute year of Great Depression. There was good recovery in the post-Depression years of 1933-34 to 1934-35 but again, there had been a slump since 1935-36, probably due to the cultivators being drawn towards raising rich-yielding money crops. It has been observed that in spite of the launching of Grow More Food Campaign in 1942 to bring more acreage under rice and other food grains production, it was disappointing that acreage under non-food grain crops increased by leaps and bounds.[97]

(*d*) *Bajra*

It was grown as a dry crop in *kharif* season in shallow soils and even required less amount of rainfall and time for maturing than jawar. But, its consumption as a food grain was very much limited compared to other cereals. Consequently, its acreage, excepting Warangal District, was negligible in the other *Suba* Districts. Even this started diminishing right from 1924 onwards and Adilabad which had 68,804 acres under cultivation in 1923, recorded nil from 1924 to 1928-29. Similarly, Karimnagar District which had 98,740 acres under bajra acreage in 1922, suffered such a heavy and permanent decline that Warangal, whose acreage between the years put her in first to third position in Telangana, also suffered continuous and sharp decline, so much so that its acreage which stood at 2,38,740 acres in 1922 came down to 9,957 in 1948-49. Besides it being a less important cereal, other factors that worked for the acreage decline in respect of other food crops had also applied in its case in nonetheless an effective manner.

(*e*) *Pulses*

These consisted of gram,[98] red gram, black gram, bengal gram, green gram (*Mung*),[99] horse gram (*Kulthi*), Pigeon Pea (*Tuar*), lentils (*Masur*), mash gram (*Mash*) and laclong.[100] In gram as well as other pulses, taking the entire period into consideration, Karimnagar and Adilabad had, respectively, higher acreages than Warangal.[101] Gram, *tuar*, bengal gram and lentils were cultivated in *rabi* season and *mung*, red gram, black gram, green gram etc., were cultivated in *kharif* season.[102] Periodical decline in acreage was noticeable in the case of pulses also, just as it was there in the case of cereals. The percentage of gram area to total cultivated area during the quinquennium of 1930-31 to 1934-35 was 1.7, 3.4 and 2.7 in the Districts of Warangal, Karimnagar and Adilabad.[103] It came down to 0.11, 0.17 and 0.12 in the next quinquennium of 1935-36 to 1939-40[104] and further down to 0.02, 0.07 and 0.07 in the succeeding quinquennium of 1940-41 to 1944-45.[105] In the case of other pulses and grains also, the respective percentages in the three quinquennia ran in the descending order of 9.5, 11.0, 7.7 ; 0.67, 0.67, 0.57 and 0.02, 0.08 and 0.15[106] in the respective *Suba* Districts. Among these *mung* surpassed others in acreage[107] and also informing a commodity of marketable surplus.[108] In spite of the decrease in crop acreage, the consumption of pulses by the local population was inadequate to the effect that red gram, green gram and black gram amounting to 70,000 tons were allowed to be exported to British India.[109] Besides crop conditions and the effect of low prices, the one strong factor that accounted for ryots turning their acreage from pulses to money crops like groundnut was exceedingly high yields in the case of the latter—the average yield per acre in the case of the former was from 300 to 400 lbs, as against 1,000 lbs in the case of the latter.[110]

(*ii*) *Non-Food Crops*

Groundnut, *sesamum*, cotton, castor, tobacco and chillies had formed, in point of acreage, the respective and important non-food crops that were cultivated in the *Suba* area.[111] The introduction of these crops in the twenties of this century brought the ryots in the State into the fold of World market which was facilitated in turn by the opening of Suez Canal that led to a great reduction in the cost of transport and provided easy access to foreign markets.[112] Settlers that came from Krishna and Rayalaseema Districts of Madras Presidency to populate the waste and uncultivated lands in Warangal District and other border areas of the State, rendered original and significant contribution to the introduction of commercial crops in the region. Whereas the Rayalaseema settlers introduced the cultivation of the most important cash crop of Telangana in the shape of groundnut,[113] those from Krishna and Guntur Districts were responsible for the starting of the cultivation of tobacco, chillies and the all-important sugar.[114] The proportion of food as against non-food crops out of the net sown area worked out as 57.14%: 32.58%, 62.69% : 23.25% and 58.86%: 35.79% in Warangal, Karimnagar and Adilabad Districts respectively.[115] The large area covered by the last named District under jawar and cotton, was chiefly responsible for giving it a proper balance between the two crop varieties, which looks rather missing in the case of Karimnagar. Compared to the State average of 31.4% regarding cash crops,[116] all the *Suba* Districts appeared to have gone beyond this minimum. Though non-food crops had formed roughly one-third of the net sown area, yet, they brought revolutionary transformation in the agricultural economy of the area, for the exportable surplus was yielded by them.

(*a*) *Groundnut*

Among the cash crops, none had undergone such a record increase in acreage as it occurred in the case of groundnut. In the case of Warangal District which commenced groundnut cultivation rather late in 1929-30 with only 2,052 acres, expansion took place so rapidly and regularly that in 1944-45, the average touched the record figure of 2,34,000 acres—an increase of 2,31,948 acres in a period of 15 years, which amounted to 11,303.50%. Because of this rapid growth, the District though started late, came to occupy second place next to Mahaboobnagar in Telangana by 1933-34 and even third place in the State in the quinquennium of 1940-41 to 1944-45 after Raichur in Marathwada and Mahboobnagar occupied the first two places.[117] The ryots of the Taluqs of Khammam, Madhira and Yellandu were found by *Subedar* of having taken up this cash crop cultivation more than any food crop as it was more paying and the soils, being red sandy loans with lime, were also more suitable for groundnut than for jawar.[118] Karimnagar and Adilabad had also witnessed increase during this period but comparatively, it was not that spectacular.[119] During the last quinquennium out of which the acreage figures are available for the first three years, there was no significant increase in 1945-46 and 1946-47 and in the succeeding year of 1947-48, there was heavy decline for the first time amounting to 75 to 80%. Whereas shift in crop conditions affected the position in former years,[120] the disturbing political, law and order situation in the latter year[121] was mainly responsible for registering a reverse trend in this direction.[122]

(*b*) *Seasamum and Castor*

Next to groundnut came *sesamum* and castor among the prominent oil-seed crops of the *Suba*. Amongst *sesamum* growing provinces, the State ranked second in India and within the State, the chief contribution was made by Telangana region.[123] In crop acreage, Karimnagar District ranked first in the State throughout the period, contributing roughly 30 to 40% of the total acreage. Regarding the other *Suba* Districts, the significant point that deserved to be noted in this connection was that whereas until 1934-35, Adilabad occupied the second place in *sesamum* acreage, its place during the succeeding period extending upto 1941-42, came to be occupied by Warangal which hitherto was in the third place. Steep decline in the acreage of Adilabad as against increase in that of Warangal led to this change. In the forties, Adilabad could again improve its acreage and position.[124] Fluctuations in crop conditions, Depression effect on prices and unsettling internal conditions,[125] had all been contributory factors for the alternating increase or decrease in *sesamum* acreage.

With 54.3% of the total castor cultivated area of India under its occupation, Hyderabad ranked first among castor growing Provinces in India.[126] As the alluvial and red soils of deep and free type that were typical of Telangana suited the cultivation of the castor seed, 92% of the total castor area in the State was met from Telangana.[127] The principal castor Districts of Telangana, in order of acreage, were Nalgonda, Mahboobnagar, Karimnagar and Warangal.[128] In the District of Karimnagar, though all Taluqs shared in the allocation of castor area, 73% of the area was concentrated in those of Jagtiyal, Karimnagar and Sirsilla.[129] Similarly, in Warangal District, Taluq of the same name accounted for nearly three-fourths of the castor area in that District,[130] besides Mahaboobabad Taluq and in Adilabad District, the Taluq of Asifabad accounted for 63% of the total castor area in that District.[131] Though Warangal District between 1921 and 1924-25 had more acreage than Karimnagar, the latter picked up so much from 1925-26 that it came to occupy number one place among *Suba* Districts which it maintained right throughout the period. In 1929-30, the acreage in respect of all except Karimnagar District, came down under the impact of the Depression. There was increase in crop acreage during the post-Depression period until 1939-40 in respect of both Warangal and Karimnagar Districts. On the other hand, Adilabad District along with the two regions and the State recorded increase between 1930-31 to 1934-35, but decrease during the next quinquennium of 1935-36 to 1939-40. Conversely enough, during the succeeding quinquennium of 1940-41 to 1944-45, whereas Adilabad remained stationary, the two regions and the State recorded increase, as against 35 to 40% decrease in the case of Warangal and Karimnagar Districts.[132] This significant decrease was due to the large-scale shifting of castor acreage to groundnut cultivation in these Districts, for the latter proved more paying economically in view of the comparatively poor yield of the former and also its failure to meet foreign competition in world markets. During the two years that followed, there was general decrease in acreage of castor seed, due to the factors that operated in respect of groundnut and *sesamum*.[133]

(*c*) *Cotton*

97% of the fibre crops area was under cotton seed cultivation in the State,[134] which by embracing 13.9% of the total cotton area of India ranked fourth in acreage and outturn among cotton-growing provinces of India.[135] With nearly 20 lakh acres or about 77% of the net cropped area of the State, cotton crop became the second largest crop in the State, next only to jawar.[136] But, it being mostly a dry crop and best suited for black soils, 88% of the total cotton area of the State was met in Marathwada Districts. The *Suba* Districts of Warangal, Karimnagar and Adilabad had only 0.02, 1.9 and 7.8% of the total cotton area of the State[137] respectively. On the other hand, in relation to net acreage sown, the area under the cotton cultivation of these Districts formed below 1%, 1 to 5% and 20 to 25% respectively.[138] The black and dry soils of Adilabad, Kinwat, Boath, Rajura and Nirmal Taluqs of Adilabad District got well suited for cotton cultivation[139] which enabled it to occupy first place in Telangana in crop acreage throughout the period followed by Karimnagar in second place.[140] In the

State as a whole, the place of the former District in cotton acreage varied from 6th during 1925-35 to 5th during 1935-45.[141]

The cotton acreage of Warangal District which was 1,56,504 acres in 1923-24 (1333 *Fasli*) and was far higher than that of Karimnagar District which stood at 87,402 acres in the same year got declined drastically to 27,398 acres in 1925-26 and fell lower than that of the latter District whose acreage also declined to 64,804 acres. The acreage of the former went on declining further from year to year in the period that followed until it reached the nominal figure of 1,172 acres in 1948-49. The acreages of Karimnagar and Adilabad Districts were also not free from fluctuations. Apart from the decrease on account of Depression in 1929-30, there was considerable increase in the acreages during the decade of 1925-26 to 1934-35. But, there was considerable decrease during the next quinquennium of 1935-36 to 1939-40, amounting to an average of 23,000 and 15,000 acres respectively This decrease was made good and even an average increase of 13,000 acres was achieved in respect of Adilabad District during the next five year period of 1941-42 to 1944-45 but, Karimnagar District with greater deficiency could cover only 2,000 acres during this period.[142] In spite of high prices prevailing for cotton during this period, the acreage failed to increase at the pace that it achieved during 1925-35, mainly because of the restrictions that were imposed by the Government on the cultivation of cash crops by promulgating the Cash Crop Restriction Regulation and by launching the Grow More Food Campaign in 1353 *Fasli* (1943-44).[143] The restriction that the area of the Cash Crops cultivated by a ryot should not exceed 1/3 of his total cropped area,[144] the breach of which was fined by collecting an amount equalling three times of land revenue in case of groundnut and two times in case of cotton for the excess area,[145] acted as a great set-back to the efforts of the enthusiastic farmers to bring more lands under cultivation of these crops The natural consequence of the continuation of these measures during the next four years of 1945-46 to 1948-49, besides, of course, the influence of rainfall and law and order conditions, was heavy decline in cotton acreage. The acreages of Karimnagar and Adilabad Districts which stood at

57,000 and 2,42,000 acres in 1942-43, came down to 12,486 and 1,54,637 acres respectively in 1948-49.

(*d*) *Tobacco and Chjllies*

The Taluqs of Khammam and Madhira in Warangal District,[146] Manthani and Huzurabad in Karimnagar District[147] and those of Adilabad, Nirmal and Sirpur in Adilabad District,[148] took up mainly tobacco cultivation. This was grown especially on black soils as a dry crop. The area of tobacco increased or decreased according to the cultivation of chillies, for the latter was also raised under the same soil and crop conditions that applied to the former but, on the other hand, it fetched better prices with better yields and were easier to be handled. The former, after being harvested required drying, stacking and curing operations which entailed considerable skill and attention.[149] Except during the quinquennium of 1935-36 to 1939-40, the tobacco acreage throughout the period was always on the decline. The acreage of Warangal, Karimnagar and Adilabad Districts which stood at 10,875, 25,740 and 5,798 acres in 1922 came drastically down to 4,362, 644 and 1,023 acres respectively in 1946-47, the decrease during this 24 year period amounting to 59.61%, 93.61% and 82.35% respectively. Further, it can be observed from Table XXXV that Karimnagar, which until 1929-30 was higher in acreage than Warangal and infact in the *Suba*, suffered heavy decrease in the next quinquennium and only moderate increase in the succeeding one, compared to less decrease and exceedingly heavy increase in respect of Warangal. The result was that the latter came to occupy in place of the former, second rank in Telangana, first being Nalgonda District, which remained the same during the rest of the period.[150] In the State, the place of Warangal District varied from 7th during 1930-31 to 1934-35 to 4th during 1940-41 to 1944-45 and the first three places were invariably claimed by Marathwada Districts, which occupied roughly 75% of the total tobacco acreage.[151]

The general and rather characteristic unwillingness of the Telangana ryot to undertake the extra labour,[152] compared for example to groundnut cultivation, that was involved in tobacco cultivation, the low yield of only about 500 lbs per acre as against 964 lbs for the whole of the Madras Presidency and 1,200 lbs for Guntur District of the same Presidency,[153] low quality of the leaf for the manufacture of quality *bidis* without importing stronger varieties from Guntur and Gujarat,[154] late introduction of the cultivation of high grade Virginia tobacco and non-development of flue-curing facilities,[155] inadequate marketing facilities[156] and meagre Research work on tobacco cultivation,[157] had all been contributary factors for the almost continuous declining acreage in respect of this cash crop. The cultivation of Virginia tobacco became so popular that from just only 100 acres in the State, the acreage shot up to 1,500 acres in 1942, of which about a thousand acres were cultivated in Madhira and Khammamet Taluqs of Warangal District alone[158]. The organisation of a local market at Madhira in March, 1941 to save the trouble to ryots to go on carts 30 to 40 miles to Bezwada or Guntur of the Madras Presidency in 1944, designed to improve the quality and the yield[159] of locally produced tobacco,[160] were certainly welcome steps in the right direction. But, inspite of these, the oppression of ryots by tobacco tax-collectors[161] and undue suffering on account of the regulation that the ryot had to get his stock inspected by Tobacco Inspector before he sold it which got inordinately delayed on account of meagreness of the staff employed—for 180 villages in Mahboobabad Taluq of Warangal District in which there was extensive tobacco growing in the villages surrounding Dornakal, there was only one Tobacco Officer—and thereby the benefit of immediate marketing of the product denied to ryot,[162] the enthusiasm of the local farmers to bring more and more acreage under the plough was blunted, with the inevitable result that the State, though not the *Suba*, was made to import about 3,500 tons of tobacco every year to meet the domestic consumption needs.[163]

Though the acreage figures in respect of chillies, another important cash crop in *Suba* and the State, are available only for the two years of 1943-44 and 1944-45, yet they are suggestive and significant. If the figures of 1943-44 of chillies and of tobacco, both of which went hand in hand are compared, they reveal that except in Marathwada, the latter's acreage fell behind that of the former to the extent of 37.74%,

721.74%, 51.94%, 73.84% and 35.58% in Warangal, Karimnagar, Adilabad, Telangana and the State respectively. Only in Marathwada, the chilli crop fell less by 13.19%. The remarkable increase in chilli acreage of Karimnagar made it number one District in Telangana and two in the State, the first place being occupied by Nanded District of Marathwada.[164] In the second year of 1944-45 also, the chilli acreage increased in respect of all, except Karimnagar, as against decrease in tobacco acreage in respect of all. Whereas the increase in respect of the former amounted to 62.96%, 194.91%, 60.69%, 419.28% and 158.98% in respect of Warangal, Adilabad, Telangana, Marathwada and the State, the decrease in the case of the latter amounted to 7.35%, 46.12%, 50.78%, 55.98%, 52.97% and 54.67% in respect of Warangal, Karimnagar, Adilabad, Telangana, Marathwada and the State.[165] The decrease in chilli acreage of Karimnagar District in this year amounted to 11.02%. Because of this decrease, the District, though still remained in first place in the region, got relegated to fourth in the State, the first three places being occupied by Marathwada Districts.[166] This comparative data indicated that the chilli cultivation, inspite of the restriction imposed on the cultivation of cash crops,[167] grew in acreage in all the areas, its higher yields and hence, better incomes being an important criterion. But, it remained an uncertain crop, for the crop was affected by heavy or less rainfall or by cloudy weather prevailing at the time of flowering. All the same, it turned out to be a commodity of exportable surplus.[168]

(iii) *Fodder Crops, Fruits and Vegetables*

Though these did not form part of the main crops that had been cultivated during the period, yet their acreage in *Suba* Districts and especially in Warangal and Karimnagar, was considerable upto 1939-40. Between these two categories, the former far out-weighed the latter in the extent of acreage. During the quinquennium of 1930-31 to 1934-35, the percentage of area under fodder crops to the total cultivated area in Warangal, Karimnagar, Adilabad, Telangana, Marathwada and the State was 14.9, 10.6, 5.2, 9.6, 2.8 and 6.2 respectively, the percentage in the case of fruits and vegetables during the same period was 5.2, 3.0, 2.0, 2.5, 1.5 and 2.0 respectively.[169] It is significant to note that the two former Districts exceeded the percentage levels of both the regions as well as the State. In fact, both during this and the previous quinquennium, Warangal District occupied second place in Telangana and the State in respect of fodder crops acreage and first place in both, in the case of fruits and vegetables.[170] Drastic decline in acreage of both the categories took place during the next decade ending in 1944-45, mainly due to the vigorous adoption of the cash crops in preference to these. The decline amounted to an average of 2,14,000, 1,42,000, 44,000, 7,77,000, 3,52,000 and 11,29,000 acres in Warangal, Karimnagar, Adilabad, Telangana, Marathwada and the State respectively in the case of fodder crops and the same was 61,000, 16,000, 9,000, 85,000, 1,26,000 and 2,11,000 acres respectively in the case of fruits and vegetables[171]. It is important to note that the acreage decline occurred in respect of all, the heaviest, of course, among all the Districts, took place in respect of Warangal. Consequently, its place in respect of fodder crops got relegated to fourth in the third quinquennium and third in the fourth, whereas in the case of fruits and vegetables, it came down to second place in both the region and the State.[172] The maximum reductions in the case of Warangal District was naturally due to the unprecedented expansion in groundnut acreage during this decade.[173] The change, though welcome from the view point of hike in the incomes of the cultivators, had definitely led to much deficiency in cattle and human dietary requirements, thereby affecting their health condition.

C AGRICULTURAL PRODUCTION AND YIELD PER ACRE

Production of food crops and pulses[174] during the 21 year period of 1925-26 to 1946-47 for which the data is available (See *Table XXXVI*) did not show much progress. As in the case of acreage,[175] the variations were wide and frequent, both in respect of outturn and yield per acre. These variations had more often been towards the declining path rather than that of ascending. In the case of 'bajra', 'maize' and 'gram' for which the figures are available only from 1935-36, the outturn

TABLE XXXVI

Agricultural Out-turn and Yield Per Acre

(In Tons) (In Lbs)

Sl. No.	Name of the crop	year	Warangal District Outturn	Warangal District yield per acre	Karimnagar District Outturn	Karimnagar District yield per acre
1	2	3	4	5	6	7
1.	RICE	1925-26	75,101	1,100	1,29,493	1,416
2.	,,	1926-27	44,314	1,016	25,946	787
3.	,,	1927-28	52,690	900	65,562	981
4.	,,	1928-29	89,010	1,349	90,442	1,289
5.	,,	1929-30	27,863	756	17,425	756
6.	,,	5 Years average	57,796	..	65,774	—
7.	,,	1930-31	33,973	687	23,343	548
8.	,,	1931-32	60,666	756	66,721	688
9.	,,	1932-33	53,501	688	60,287	688
10.	,,	1933,34	74,230	725	64,979	673

11.	,	1934-35	69,159	707	79,158	858
12.	,,	5 Years average	58,305	713	58,897	691
13.	,,	1935-36	44,000	634	75,000	870
14.	,,	1936-37	63,000	787	97,000	966
15.	,,	1937-38	54,000	720	90,000	1,014
16.	,,	1938-39	1,13,000	898	54,000	754
17.	,,	1939-40	51,000	832	32,000	662
18.	,,	5 Years average	65,000	774	69,000	853
19.	,,	1940-41	1,07,000	1,043	1,01,000	1,101
20.	,,	1941-42	38,000	745	21,000	606
21.	,,	1942-43	89,000	1,062	74,000	997
22.	,,	1943-44	37,000	417	45,000	558
23.	,,	1944-45	62,000	808	62,000	891
24.	,,	5 Years average	66,000	815	61,000	830
25.	,,	1945-46	75,084	799	62,803	599
26.	,,	1946-47	67,244	756	57,677	660

Sl. No.	Name of the crop	year	Adilabad District		Telangana Division	
			Outturn	yield per acre	Outturn	yield per acre
			8	9	10	11
1.	RICE	1925-26	10,780	808	3,94,104	—
2.	,,	1926-27	6,702	600	1,68,869	—
3.	,,	1927-28	13,639	600	2 97,874	—
4.	,,	1928-29	8,445	516	3,40,072	—
5.	,,	1929-30	4,468	400	1,08,084	—
6.	,,	5 Years average	8,807	..	2,61,801	—
7.	,,	1930-31	14,354	550	1,54,681	—
8.	,,	1931-32	17,847	650	3,53,228	—
9.	,,	1932-33	13,790	600	2,58,247	..
10.	,,	1933-34	15,378	549	3,22,903	—
11.	,,	1934-35	17,099	503	3,10,281	—
12,	,,	5 Years average	15 ,693	570	2,81,868	—

13.	,,	1935-36	19,000	577	2,90,000	—
14.	,,	1936-37	27,000	818	3,79,000	—
15.	,,	1937-38	26,000	837	3,28,000	—
16,	,,	1938-39	19,000	556	3,74,000	—
17.	,,	1939-40	22,000	595	2,90,000	—
18.	,,	5 Years average	23,000	697	3,32,000	—
19.	,,	1940-41	20,000	639	4,53,000	—
20.	,,	1941-42	15,000	454	1,90,000	—
21.	,,	1942-43	20,000	649	4,40,000	—
22.	,	1943-44	22,000	675	3,83,000	—
23.	,	1944-45	21,000	478	4,03,000	—
24.	,,	5 Years average	20,000	579	3,74,000	—
25.	,,	1945-46	25,429	578	4,35,919	779
26.	,,	1946-47	22,728	573	3,29,664	683

Sl. No.	Name of the crop	Year	Marathwada Division		State	
			Outturn	yield per acre	Outturn	yield per acre
			12	13	14	15
1.	RICE	1925-26	6,084	—	4,17,831	1,107
2.	,,	1926-27	5,942	—	1,88,324	781
3.	,,	1927-28	15,317	—	3,44,880	828
4.	,	1928-29	14,072	—	4 03,476	910
5.	,	1929-30	13,727	—	1,50,955	667
6.	,	5 Years average	11,028	—	3,01,093	..
7.	,,	1930-31	23,293	—	1,77,974	582
8.	,	1931-32	36,142	—	3,89,370	792
9.	,,	1932-33	34,303	—	2,92,550	658
10.	,,	1933-34	41,304	—	3,64,207	624
11,	,,	1934-35	44,753	—	3,55,034	672
12.	,,	5 Years average	35,958	—	3,17,826	666

13.	,,	1935-36	46,000	—	3,36,000	706
14.	,,	1936-37	39,000	—	4,18,000	825
15.	,,	1937-38	40,000	—	3,68,000	856
16.	,,	1938-39	47,000	—	4,21,000	822
17.	,,	1939-40	39,000	—	3,29,000	837
18.	,,	5 Years average	42,000	—	3,74,000	809
19.	,,	1940-41	66,000	—	5,19,000	692
20.	,,	1941-42	25,000	—	2,15,000	596
21.	,,	1942-43	59,000	—	4,99,000	946
22.	,,	1943-44	53,000	—	4,36,000	996
23.	,,	1944-45	44,000	—	4,47,000	772
24.	,,	5 Years average	49,000	—	4,23,000	785
25.	,,	1945-46	43,643	590	4,79,562	757
26.		1946-47	30,625	566	3,60,289	671

27.	JAWAR	1925-26	72,865	379	76,725	282
28.	,,	1926-27	72,763	402	66,690	400
29.	,,	1927-28	1,15,524	540	64,262	400
30.	,,	1928-29	1,50,959	549	35,883	235
31.	,,	1929-30	49,294	281	38,720	250
32.	,,	5 Years average	92,281	—	56,456	..
33.	,	1930-31	57,928	345	41,685	250
34.	,,	1931-32	37,051	187	24,977	156
35.	,,	1932-33	64,467	281	25,872	156
36.	,,	1933-34	49,893	227	46,832	281
37.	,,	1934-35	41,413	215	29,366	192
38.	,	5 Years average	50,150	251	33,648	207
39.	,,	1935-36	38,000	199	37,000	248
40.	,,	1936-37	70,000	345	60,000	368
41.	,,	1937-38	69,000	329	55,000	376
42.	,,	1938-39	73,000	350	76,000	275
43.	,,	1939-40	1,18,000	404	67,000	288
44.	,,	5 Years average	73,000	325	59,000	311
45	,,	1940-41	1,30,000	487	65,000	377
46.	,,	1941-42	1,30,000	360	1,14,000	396

47.	,,	1942-43	1,56,000	449	69,000	404
48.	,,	1943-44	47,000	257	38,000	251
49.	,	1944-45	72,000	273	47,000	285
50.	,,	5 Years average	1,09,000	378	66,000	342
51.	,,	1945-46	68,747	354	22,830	205
52.	,	1946-47	50,362	286	26,943	232
53.	BAJRA*	1935-36	11,000	..	1,000	..
54.	,,	1936-37	10,000	..	..	..
55.	,	1937-38	9,000	..	..	..
56.	,,	1939-40	5,000	..	..	..
57.	,,	5 Years average	9,000	..	..	..

Sl. No.	Name of the Crop	Year	Adilabad District		Telangana Division	
			Outturn	Yield per acre	Outturn	Yield per acre
			8	9	10	11
27.	JAWAR	1925-26	89,736	311	3,24,394	..
28.		1926-27	58,251	300	2,80,244	..
29.	,,	1927-28	96,496	400	3,94,536	..
30.	,,	1928-29	1,21,630	504	4,22,764	..
31.	,,	1929-30	70,556	375	3,18,679	..
32.	,,	5 Years average	87,334	..	3,48,123	..
33.	,,	1930-31	85.787	344	2,92,867	..
34.	,,	1931-32	59,348	219	2,21,690	..
35.	,,	1932-33	58,833	250	2,82,661	..
36.	,,	1933-34	64,034	266	3,18,909	..
37.	,	1934-35	74,360	322	2,63,880	..
38.	,,	5 Years average	68,472	280	2,76,001	..
39.	,	1935-36	72,000	343	2,78,000	..
40.	,,	1936-37	82,000	410	3,900,00	..
41.	,,	1937-38	81,000	399	3,46,000	..

42.	,,	1938-39	72,000	327	4,07,000	..
43.	,,	1939-40	98,000	400	5,61,000	..
44.	,,	5 Years average	81,000	376	3,97,000	..
45.	,,	1940-41	1,07,000	382	5,66,000	..
46.	,,	1941-42	33,000	434	5,47,000	..
47.	,,	1942-43	1,00,000	385	5,67,000	..
48.	,,	1943-44	93,000	386	3,25,000	..
49.	,,	1944-45	79,000	317	3,64,000	..
50.		5 Years average	82,000	382	4,75,000	..
51.	,,	1945-46	40,383	208	2,78,520	270
52.	,,	1946-47	55,203	317	2,56,728	260
53.	BAJRA*	1935-36	1,000	..	60,000	..
54.	,,	1936-37	1,000	..	62,000	..
55.	,,	1937-38	1,000	..	50,000	..
56.	,,	1939-40	..	..	39,000	..
57.	,,	5 Years average	1,000	..	51,000	..

Sl. No.	Name of the Crop	Year	Marathwada Division		State	
			Outturn	Yield per acre	Outturn	Yield per acre
			12	13	14	15
27.	JAWAR	1925-26	5,15,809	..	11,11,789	275
28.	,,	1926-27	5,18,042	..	10,34,449	282
29.	,,	1927-28	7,49,735	..	14,52,905	374
30.	,,	1928-29	6,88,799	..	14,10,350	344
31.	,,	1929-30	5,71,032	..	13,15 063	286
32.	,,	5 Years average	6,08,683	..	12,64,911	..
33.	,	1930-31	10,12,408	..	13,05,275	304
34.	,,	1931-32	7,95,376	..	10,17,066	240
35.	,,	1932-33	9,92,702	..	12,75,363	305
36.	,,	1933-34	8,42,421	..	11,61,330	394
37.	,,	1934-35	7,67,822	..	10,31,702	259
38.	,,	5 Years average	8,81,545	..	11,57,547	280
39.	,,	1935-36	8,22,000	..	11,00,000	280
40.	,,	1936-37	12,00,000	..	15,90,000	381
41.	,,	1937-38	9,63,000	..	13,08,000	346

42.	,,	1938-39	9,85,000	..	13,92,000	345
43.	,,	1939-40	11,44,000	..	17,05,000	364
44.	,,	5 Years average	10,22,000	..	14,19,000	343
45.	,,	1940-41	12,74,000	..	18,60,000	418
46.	,,	1941-42	11,28,000	..	16,75,000	392
47.	,,	1942-43	11,91,000	..	17,58,000	397
48.	,,	1943-44	9,13,000	..	12,38,000	299
49.	,,	1944-45	8,61,000	..	12,25,000	299
50.	,,	5 Years average	10,73,100	..	15,48,000	360
51.	,,	1945-46	6,20,197	265	8,98,717	266
52.	,,	1946-47	6,78,623	330	9,35,351	307
53.	BAJRA*	1935-36	73,000	..	1,33,000	..
54.	,,	1936-37	77,000	..	1,39,000	..
55.	,,	1937-38	73,000	..	1,23,000	..
56.	,,	1939-40	62,000	..	1,01,000	..
57.	,,	5 Years average	72,000	..	1,23,000	..

Sl. No.	Name of the crop	Year	Warangal District		Karimnagar District	
			Outturn	Yield per acre	Outturn	Yield per acre
1	2	3	4	5	6	7
58.	BAJRA	1940-41	6,000	..	1,000	..
59.	,,	1941-42	8,000	..	..	..
60.	,,	1942-43	12,000	..	..	..
61.	,,	1943-42	3,000	..	..	..
62.	,,	1944-45	4,000	..	..	..
63.	,,	5 Years average	7,000	..	..	..
64.	,,	1945-46	2,016	174	23	145
65.	,,	1946-47	1,330	157	15	113
66.	MAIZE*	1935-36	30,000	422	24,000	344
67.	,,	1936-37	29,000	400	24,000	344
68.	,,	1937-38	30,000	400	24,000	344
69.	,,	1938-39	28,000	395	23,000	340
70.	,,	1939 40	15,000	395	25,000	338
71.	,,	5 Years average	26,000	402	24,000	342
72.	,,	1940-41	18,000	400	23,000	400

73.	,,	1941-42	13,000	200	20,000	300
74.	,,	1942-43	7,000	249	17,000	250
75.	,,	1943-44	3,000	176	11,000	180
76.	,,	1944-45	5,000	197	17,000	235
77.	,,	5 Years average	9,000	244	17,000	273
78.	,,	1945-46	3,367	156	8,968	149
79.	,,	1946-47	4,082	178	8,493	169
80.	GRAM*	1935-36	3,000	..	9,000	..
81.	,,	1936-37	4,000	..	10,000	..
82.	,,	1937-38	5,000	..	9,000	..
83.	,,	1938-39	5,000	..	9,000	..
84.	,,	1938-40	2,000	..	5,000	..
85.	,,	5 Years average	40,000	..	8,000	..
86.	,,	1940-41	2,000	..	2,000	..

Sl. No.	Name of the crop	Year	Adilabad District Outturn	Adilabad District Yield per acre	Telangana Division Outturn	Telangana Division Yield per acre
			8	9	10	11
58.	BAJRA	1940-41	..	..	42,000	..
59.	,,	1941-42	1,000	..	69,000	..
60.	,,	1942-43	..	..	80,000	..
61.	,,	1943-44	1,000	..	3,2,000	..
62.	,,	1944-45	..	..	56,000	..
63.	,,	5 Years average	..	..	56,000	..
64.	,,	1945-46	59	175	32,679	172
65.	,,	1946-47	50	222	25,496	187
66.	MAIZE*	1935-36	6,000	385	83,000	376
67.	,,	1936-37	6,000	355	83,000	372
68.	,,	1937-38	6,000	355	81,000	373
69.	,,	1938-39	6,000	369	80,000	376
70.	,,	1939-40	7,000	379	72,000	377
71.	,,	5 Years average	6,000	369	79,000	375
72.	,,	1940-41	8,000	450	76,000	422

73.	,,	1941-42	5,000	250	66,000	378
74.	,,	1942-43	4,000	200	49,000	318
75.	,,	1943-44	5,000	257	50,000	272
76.	,,	1944-45	3,000	148	52,000	274
77.	,,	5 Years average	5,000	261	59,000	335
78.	,,	1945-46	2,407	149	27,327	170
79.	,,	1946-47	3,128	190	33,713	227
80.	GRAM*	1935-36	5,000	..	50,000	..
81.	,,	1936-37	5,000	..	53,000	..
82.	,,	1937-38	5,000	..	50,000	..
83.	,,	1938-39	4,000	..	52,000	..
84.	,,	1939-40	4,000	..	34,000	..
85.	,,	5 Years average	5,000	..	48,000	..
86.	,,	1940-41	2,000	..	25,000	..

Sl. No.	Name of the crop	Year	Marath wada Division		State	
			Outturn	Yield per acre	Outturn	Yield per acre
			12	13	14	15
58.	BAJRA	1940-41	73,000	..	1,15,000	..
59.	,,	1941-42	96,000	..	1,65,000	..
60.	,,	1942-43	1,43,000	..	2,23,000	..
61.	,,	1943-44	1,34,000	..	1,66,000	..
62.	,,	1944-45	1,34,000	..	1,90,000	..
63.	,,	5 Years average	1,16,000	..	1,72,000	..
64.	,,	1945-46	59,732	160	92,411	164
65.	,,	1946-47	55,211	175	80,707	178
66.	MAIZE*	1935-36	31,000	384	1,14,000	378
67.	,,	1936-37	27,000	373	1,10,000	373
68.	,,	1937-38	27,000	372	1,08,000	373
69.	,	1938-49	29,000	379	1,09,000	377
70.	,,	1939-40	24,000	376	96,000	377
71.	,,	5 Years average	28,000	377	1,07,000	376
72.	,	1940-41	23,000	455	99,000	439

73.	,,	1941-42	30,000	497	96,000	438
74.	,,	1942-43	4,000	371	53,000	344
75.	,,	1943-44	2,000	291	52,000	272
76.	,,	1944-45	1,000	274	53,000	274
77.	,,	5 Years average	22,000	374	81,000	355
78.	,,	1945-46	1,006	207	28,333	172
79.	,,	1946-47	1,224	328	35,937	230
80.	GRAM*	1935-36	1,47,000	..	1,97,000	..
81.	,,	1936-37	1,42,000	..	1,95,000	..
82.	,,	1937-38	1,46,000	..	1,96,000	..
83.	,,	1938-39	1,45,000	..	1,97,000	..
84.	,,	1939-40	1,16,000	..	1,49,000	..
85.	,,	5 Years average	1,39,000	..	1,87,000	..
86.	,,	1940-41	1,02,000	..	1.27,000	..

Sl. No.	Name of the crop	Year	Warangal District		Karimnagar District	
			Outturn	Yield per acre	Outturn	Yield per acre
1	2	3	4	5	6	7
87.	Gram	1941-42	1,000	..	1,000	..
88.	,,	1942-43	..	..	1 000	..
89.	,,	1943-44	..	..	1,000	..
90.	,,	1944-45	1,000	..	1,000	..
91.	,,	5 Years average	1,000	..	1,000	..
92.	,,	1945-46	595	..	955	..
93.	,,	1946-47	654	..	794	..
94.	SESA MUM	1925-26	3,058	186	10,967	140
95.	,	1926-27	2,869	195	8,119	91
96.	,,	1927-28	4,744	232	12,321	142
97.	,,	1928-29	5 574	259	14,079	139
98.	,,	1929-30	6,390	368	16,821	161
99.	,,	5 Years average	4,527	..	12,461	..
100.	,,	1930-31	1 690	98	17,175	139

101.	,,	1931-32	1,428	84	6,217	70
102.	,,	1932-33	2,498	112	13,215	126
103.	,,	1933-34	1,796	88	7,198	67
104.	,,	1934-35	1,329	80	6,902	75
105.	,,	5 Years average	1,648	92	10,141	191
106.	,,	1935-36	4,000	106	10,000	111
107.	,,	1936-37	7,000	182	14,000	154
108.	,,	1937-38	6,000	164	15,000	168
109.	,,	1938-39	1,000	128	7,000	92
110.	,,	1939-40	5,000	166	8,000	121
111.	,,	5 Years average	5,000	149	11,000	130
112.	,,	1940-41	2,000	129	9,000	179
113.	,,	1941-42	10,000	170	15,000	180
114.	,,	1942-43	5,000	170	14,000	176
115.	,,	1943-44	3,000	93	8,000	103
116.	,,	1944-45	3,000	146	13,000	154
117.	,,	5 Years average	5,000	142	12,000	158
118.	,,	1945-46	2,398	122	11,839	143
119.	,,	1946-47	2,606	130	8,154	112

Sl. No.	Name of the crop	year	Adilabad District		Telangana Division	
			Outturn	Yield per acre	Outturn	Yield per acre
			8	9	10	11
87.	GRAM	1941-42	1,000	..	13,000	..
88.	,	1942-43	1,000	..	9,000	..
89.	,,	1943-44	1,000	..	9,000	..
90.	,,	1944-45	2,000	..	21,000	..
91.	,	5 Years average	1,000	..	13,000	..
92.	,,	1945-46	1,646	..	12,763	..
93.	,,	1946-47	1,147	..	13,059	..
94.	SESAMUM	1925-26	5,600	174	26,336	..
95.	,,	1926-27	3,292	120	20,239	..
96.	,,	1927-28	4,826	162	26,954	..
97.	,,	1928-29	3,932	124	27,752	..
98.	,,	1929-30	2,380	120	31,443	..
99.	,,	5 Years average	4,006	..	26,545	..
100.	,,	1930-31	5,025	161	28,530	..

101.	,,	1931-32	3,269	100	14,551	..
102.	,,	1932-33	3,284	100	24,674	..
103.	,,	1933-34	2,818	91	16,111	..
104.	,,	1934-35	2,926	92	15,014	..
105.	,,	5 Years average	3,464	109	19,676	..
106.	,,	1935-36	3,000	109	23,000	..
107.	,,	1936-37	5,000	156	32,000	..
108.	,,	1937-38	4,000	125	31,000	..
109.	,,	1938-39	3,000	136	17,000	..
110.	,,	1939-40	7,000	193	26,000	..
111.	,,	5 Years average	5,000	144	26,000	132**
112.	,,	1940-41	4,000	141	21,000	149**
113.	,,	1941-42	5,000	159	35,000	157**
114.	,,	1942-43	9,000	165	34,000	169**
115.	,,	1943-44	12,000	219	29,000	131**
116.	,	1944-45	6,000	99	28,000	136**
117.	,,	5 Years average	7,000	157	30,000	148**
118.	,,	1945-46	3,663	98	22,668	124
119.	,,	1946-47	5,296	124	19,132	108

Sl. No.	Name of the crop	Year	Marathwada Division		State	
			Outturn	Yield per acre	Outturn	Yield per acre
			12	13	14	15
87.	GRAM	1941-42	94,000	..	1,07,000	..
88.	,,	1942-43	77,000	..	86,000	..
89.	,,	1943-44	51,000	..	60,000	..
90.	,,	1944-45	78,000	..	89,000	..
91.	,,	5 Years average	80,000	..	93,000	..
92.	,,	1945-46	92,254	..	1,05,017	..
93.	,,	1946-47	91,523	..	1,04,582	..
94.	SESAMUM	1925-26	4,668	..	32,769	142
95.	,,	1926-27	3,227	..	25,470	111
96.	,	1927-28	4,353	..	36,472	135
97.	,,	1928-29	4,996	..	36,792	128
98.	,,	1929-30	3,867	..	38,441	142
99.	,,	5 Years average	4,222	..	33,989	..
100.	,,	1930-31	7,220	..	35,750	136

101.	,,	1931-32	9,111	..	23,662	106
102.	,	1932-33	10,502	..	3 5,176	130
103.	,,	1933-34	10,144	..	26,255	100
104.	,,	1934-35	6,663	..	21,677	97
105.	,,	5 Years average	8,728	..	28,404	114
106.	,,	1935-36	12,000	..	35,000	133
107.	,,	1936-37	9,000	..	41,000	168
108.	,,	1937-38	9,000	..	40,000	164
109.	,	1938-39	13,000	..	30,000	146
110.	,,	1939-40	12,000	..	38,000	152
111.	,,	5 Years average	11,000	207**	37,000	153
112.	,,	1940-41	15,000	237**	36,000	193
113.	,,	1941-42	8,000	207**	43,000	182
114.	,,	1942-43	15,000**	256	49,000	212
115.	,,	1943-44	14,000	173**	43,000	152
116.	,,	1944-45	13,000	177**	41,000	146
117.	,,	5 Years average	13,000	213**	43,000	181
118.	,,	1945-46	23,023	226	45,691	160
119.	,,	1946-47	24,904	201	44,036	146

Sl No.	Name of the crop	year	Warangal District Outturn	Warangal District yield per acre	Karimnagar District Outturn	Karimnagar District yield per acre
1	2	3	4	5	6	7
120	GROUND NUT	1925-26	—	—	—	—
121	,,	1926-27	—	—	—	—
122	,,	1927-28	—	—	—	—
123	,,	1927-29	—	—	—	—
124	,,	1929-30	—	161	—	—
125	,,	5 years average	147	—	—	—
126	,,	1930-31	720	574	—	—
127	,,	1931-32	1,233	500	609	500
128	,,	1932-33	2,495	563	576	500
129	,,	1933-34	4,476	499	960	664
130	,,	1934-35	9,418	520	1,151	654
131	,,	5 years average	3,668	531	824	580
132	,,	1935-36	11,000	487	1,000	533
133	,,	1936-37	14,000	989	6,000	829

134	,,	1937-38	75,000	827	12,000	805
135	,,	1938-39	59,000	784	17,000	942
136	,,	1939-40	3,000	869	18,000	588
137	,,	5 years average	56,000	791	11,000	739
138	,,	1940-41	72,000	691	23,000	924
139	,,	1941-42	57,000	649	19,000	751
140	,,	1942-43	85,000	909	25 000	812
141	,,	1943-44	1,24,000	848	45,000	688
142	,,	1944-45	87,000	979	45,000	807
143	,,	5 years average	55,000	815	31,000	796
144	,,	1945-46	74,782	763	26,823	547
145	,,	1945-47	68,333	718	25,529	529

			Adilabad District		Telangana Division	
			Outturn	yield per acre	Outturn	yield per acre
			8	9	10	11
120	GROUND NUT	1925-26	38	125	170	—
121	,,	1926-27	21	118	415	—
122	,,	1927-28	6	38	1,253	—
123	,,	1928-29	7	60	8,561	—
124	,,	1929-30	9	62	7,689	—
125	,,	5 years average	16	—	3,618	—
126	,,	1930-31	88	458	25,210	—
127	,,	1931-32	79	496	,24,637	—
128	,,	1932-33	104	501	51,266	—
129	,,	1933-34	159	534	60,785	—
130	,,	1934-35	330	565	60,285	—
131	,,	5 years average	112	511	44,601	—
132	,,	1935-36	—	506	74,000	—
133	,,	1936-37	—	734	78,000	—

134	,,	1937-38	—	699	2,22,000	—
135	,,	1938-39	2,000	833	2,43,000	—
136	,,	1939-40	2,000	651	2,77,000	—
137	,,	5 years average	1,000	885	1,99,000	—
138	,,	1940-41	4,000	690	2,56,000	—
139	,,	1941-42	1,000	650	1,74,000	—
140	,,	1942-43	2,000	873	3,30,000	—
141	,,	1943-44	2,000	607	5,20,000	—
142	,,	1944-45	3,000	577	3,72,090	—
143	,,	5 years average	2,000	679	3,30,000	—
144	,,	1945-46	1,596	453	2,66,417	638
145	,,	1946-47	2,269	607	2,59,394	664

			Marathwada Division		State	
			Outturn	Yield per acre	Outturn	Yield per acre
			12	13	14	15
120	Ground nut	1925-26	9,240	—	16,055	248
121	,,	1926-27	12,522	—	19,152	184
122	,,	1927-28	11,844	—	32,680	194
123	,,	1928-29	16,658	—	62,812	279
124	,,	1929-30	40,054	—	64,158	525
125	,,	5 years average	22,864	—	38,972	%
126	,,	1930-31	1,39,630	—	164,840	535
127	,,	1931-32	1,88,602	—	213,239	616
128	,,	1932-33	2,68,682	—	3,19,949	641
129	,,	1933-34	3,12,818	—	3,73,603	605
130	,,	1934-35	1,64,147	—	2,24,432	522
131	,,	5 years average	2,14,012	—	2,58,613	584
132	,,	1935-36	2,13,000	—	2,87,000	607

133	,,	1936-37	1,72,000	—	3,50,000	742
134	,,	1937-38	2,54,000	—	4,76,000	741
135	,,	1938-39	3,29,000	—	5,72,000	791
136	,,	1939-40	3,26,000	—	6.03,000	659
137	,,	5 years average	2,59,000	—	4,58,000	708
138	,,	1940-48	4,52,000	—	5,88,000	884
139	,,	1941-42	2,72,000	—	4,45, 000	665
140	,,	1942-43	3, 74,000	—	7,64,000	843
141	,,	1943-43	5,55,000	—	10,75,000	775
142	,,	1944-41	3,82,000	—	7,54,000	655
143	,,	5 years average	3,89,000	—	7,19,000	730
144	,,	1945-46	4,28,799	—	7,48,216	583
145	,,	1946-47	4,75,616	—	7,35,080	677

Sl. No.	Name of the crop	year	Warangal District		Karimnagar District	
			Outturn	Yield per acre	Outturn	Yield per acre
1	2	3	4	5	6	7
146	CASTOR	1925-26	5,685	423	1,987	134
147	,,	1926-27	7,900	582	2,754	150
148	,,	1927-28	88,350	568	2,448	160
149	,,	1928-29	6,484	320	3,183	173
150	,,	1929-30	4,633	226	5,759	241
151	,,	5 years average	7,280	—	3,212	—
152	,,	1930-31	5,018	280	2,889	139
153	,,	1931-32	3,394	189	833	36
154	,,	1932-33	2,257	150	4,368	150
155	,,	1933-34	2,770	184	3,953	147
156	,,	1934-35	8,507	121	3,381	160
157	,,	5 years average	2,989	171	3,085	126
158	,,	1935-36	5,000	860	4,000	210
159	,,	1936-37	6,000	206	4,000	233
160	,,	1937-38	6,000	177	3,000	210

161	,,	1938-39	4,000	175	9,000	246
162	,,	1939-40	5,000	211	2,000	130
163	,,	5 years average	5,000	182	4,000	206
164	,,	1940-41	6,000	190	4,000	248
165	,,	1941-42	2,000	177	3,000	218
166	,,	1942-43	3,000	282	3,000	239
167	,,	1943-44	3,000	207	4,000	193
168	,,	1944-45	2,000	207	5,000	218
169	,,	5 years average	3,000	213	4,000	223
170	,,	1945-46	2,059	183	3,832	194
171	,,	1946-47	1,528	166	2,909	172

			Adilabad District		Telangana Division	
			Outturn	yield per acre	Outturn	yield per acre
			8	9	10	11
146	CASTOR	1925-26	337	148	58,560	—
147	,,	1926-27	240	122	49,493	—
148	,,	1927-28	579	124	38,345	—
149	,,	1928-29	396	94	30,684	—
150	,,	1929-30	432	125	28,601	—
151	,,	5 years average	397	—	41,137	—
152	,,	1980-31	639	116	42,417	—
153	,,	1931-32	540	148	60,787	—
154	,,	1932-33	506	141	58,130	—
155	,,	1933-34	406	119	63,361	—
156	,,	1934-35	444	132	45,033	—
157	,,	5 years average	507	130	53,345	—
158	,,	1935-36	1,000	119	54,000	—
159	,,	1936-37	1,000	196	67,000	—
160	,,	1937-38	—	171	38,000	—

161	,,	1938-39	1,000	134	63,000	—
162	,,	1939-40	—	195	48,000	—
163	,,	5 years average	1,000	163	54,000	—
164	,,	1940-41	1,000	171	70,000	—
165	,,	1941-42	1,000	148	63,000	—
166	,,	1942-43	1,000	201	84,000	—
167	,,	1943-44	1,000	197	62,000	—
168	,,	1944-45	2,000	155	10,000	—
169	,,	5 years average	1,000	174	56,000	—
170	,,	1945-46	4,280	125	52,647	—
171	,,	1946-47	1,073	125	54,788	—

			Marathwada Division		State	
			Outturn	yield per acre	Outturn	yieid per acre
			12	13	14	15
146	**CASTOR**	1925-26	4,498	—	61,800	206
147	,,	1926-27	1,178	—	52,326	191
148	,,	4927-28	1,812	—	42,586	141
149	,,	1928-29	4,508	—	37,446	126
150	,,	1929-30	1,864	—	33,446	140
151	,,	5 years average	1,571	—	45,513	—
152	,,	1930-31	2,707	—	45,124	127
153	,,	1931·32	2,621	—	63,408	165
154	,,	1932-33	2,666	—	60,796	163
155	,,	1933-34	3,252	—	66,613	182
156	,,	1934-35	2,014	—	47,047	134
157	,,	5 years average	2,650	—	55,995	154
158	,,	1935-36	3,000	—	57,000	159
159	,,	1936-37	2,000	—	69,000	189
160	,,	1937-38	2,000	—	40,000	172

161	,,	1938-39	4,000	—	67,000	183
162	,,	1939-40	2,000	—	50,000	173
163	,,	5 years average	2,000	—	56,000	174
164	,,	1940-41	2,000	—	72,000	172
165	,,	1941-42	3,000	—	66,000	147
166	,,	1942-43	3,000	—	87,000	195
167	,,	1943-44	3,000	—	65,000	146
168	,,	1944-45	3,000	—	53,000	143
169	,,	5 years average	3,000	—	69,000	155
170	,,	1945-46	4,025	136	56,672	157
171	,,	1946-47	3,936	131	55,720	167

Sl. No.	Name of the crop	year	Warangal District		Karimnagar District	
			Outturn	yield per acre	Outturn	yield per acre
1	2	3	4	5	6	7
172	COTTON	1925-26	7,034	575	6,661	230
173	,,	1926-27	3,188	560	12,973	400
174	,,	1927-28	3,345	404	40,872	335
175	,,	1928-29	2,478	281	46,791	373
176	,,	1929-30	2,036	224	9,549	280
177	,,	5 years average	3,556	—	44,352	—
178	,,	1930-31	3,557	224	42,224	224
179	,,	1931-32	3,813	303	9,464	207
180	,,	1932-33	3,396	224	6,440	185
181	,,	1933-34	3,634	219	8,258	235
182	,,	1934-35	3,080	234	5,198	171
183	,,	5 years average	3,495	42	8,310	37
184	,,	1935-36	2,000	39	10,000	57
185	,,	1936-37	3,000	52	8,000	52
186	,,	1937-38	3,000	70	9,000	58

187	,,	1938-39	40,00	40	5,000	44
188	,,	1939-40	3,000	64	10,000	39
189	,,	5 years average	3,000	52	8,000	50
190	,,	1940-41	2,000	60	15,000	66
191	,,	1941-42	2,000	60	15,000	73
192	,,	1942-43	2,000	63	10,000	71
193	,,	1943-44	1,000	42	9,000	46
194	,,	1944-45	1,000	54	3,000	48
195	,,	5 years average	1,000	55	11,000	61
196	,,	1945-46	309	48	1,977	43
197	,,	1946-47	328	51	2,070	40

			Adilabad District		Telangana Division	
			Outturn	yield per acre	Outturn	yield per acre
			8	9	10	11
172	COTTON	1925-26	80,870	787	1,07,167	—
173	,,	1926-27	72,047	784	1,03,439	—
174	,,	1927-28	1,10,473	838	1,40,287	
175	,,	1928-29	96,192	777	1,30,591	
176	,,	1929-30	45,883	392	60,471	
177	,,	5 years average	81,093	—	1,08,380	—
178	,,	1930-31	5,3621	211	73,194	—
179	,,	1931-32	36,771	309	56,658	—
180	,,	1932-33	29,276	224	45,852	—
181	,,	1933-34	46,010	368	65,449	—
182	,,	1934-35	43,837	360	58,532	—
183	,,	5 years average	41,903	57	59,937	—
184	,,	1935-36	44 000	63	64,000	—
185	,,	1936-37	51,000	70	77,000	—
186	,,	1937-38	47,000	69	64 000	—

187	,,	1938-39	40,000	57	51,000	—
188	,,	1939-40	52,000	78	71,000	—
189	,,	5 years average	47 000	67	66,000	—
190	,,	1940-41	70 000	66	93,000	—
191	,,	1941-42	46,000	67	69,000	—
192	,,	1942-43	43,080	71	61,000	—
193	,,	1943-44	61,000	71	77,000	—
194	,,	1944-45	22,000	46	28,000	—
195	,,	5 years average	48 000	64	66,000	—
196	,,	1945-46	23 667	40	28 401	41
197	,,	1946-47	23 474	48	27,129	45

			Marathwada Division		State	
			Outturn	yield per acre	Outturn	yield per acre
			12	13	14	15
172	COTTON	1925-26	8,52,613	—	10,60,406	112
173	,,	1926-27	5,52,804	—	8,07,541	99
174	,,	1927-28	6,66,392	—	9,50,910	105
175	,,	1928-29	6,73,732	—	8,95,134	89
176	,,	1929-30	2,94,342	—	4,46,709	51
177	,,	5 years average	6,05,977	—	9,23,140	—
178	,,	2930-31	3,08,616	—	3,81,810	74
179	,,	1930-32	4,52,760	—	5,09,218	56
180	,,	1932-33	4,88,039	—	5,33,891	59
181	,,	1933-34	4,98,522	—	5,63,971	61
182	,,	1934-35	3,84,048	—	4,42,582	57
183	,,	5 years average	4,26,377	—	4,86,334	61
184	,,	1835-36	5,05,000	—	5,69,000	62
185	,,	1936-37	4,45,000	—	5,22,000	65
186	,,	1937-38	5 06,000	—	5,70,000	63

187	"	1938-39	4,67,000	—	5,08 000	58
188	"	1939-40	5,11,000	—	5,82,000	63
189	"	5 years average	4,85,000	—	5,50,000	62
190	,	1940-41	5 29,000	—	6,22,000	63
191	"	1941-42	4,81,000	—	5 50,000	66
192	"	1942-43	4 47,000	—	5,08,000	66
193	"	1943-44	4,88,000	—	5,65,000	55
194		1944-45	2,20,000	—	2,48 000	52
195	"	5 years average	4,34,000	—	5,90,000	54
196	"	1945-46	2,32,156	49	2,60,557	48
197	,	1946-47	2,67,479	53	2,94,608	52

Sl. No.	Name of the crop	year	Warangal Distrtct		Karimnagar District	
			Outturn	yield per acre	Outturn	yield per acre
1	2	3	4	5	6	7
198	TOBACCO†	1926-27	415	320	898	299
199	,,	1927-28	2,664	964	1,905	800
200	,,	1928-29	2,688	982	2,320	810
201	,,	1929-30	1,047	412	1,236	820
202	,,	5 years average	1,704	—	1,590	—
203	,,	1930-31	1,788	687	762	550
204	,,	1931-32	1,863	687	1,200	614
205	,,	1932-33	1,606	688	1,492	825
206	,,	1933-34	1,208	663	933	570
207	,,	1934-35	1,436	747	1,166	733
208	,,	5 years average	1,580	694	1,110	58
209	,,	1935-36	1,426	754	1,380	717
210	,,	1936-37	1,539	755	1,606	819
211	,,	1937-38	1,690	812	1,389	884

213	,,	1939-40	3,660	955	943	550
214	,,	5 years average	2,203	810	302	766
215	,,	1940-41	2,307	818	1,265	826
216	,,	1941-42	2,683	622	933	515
217	,,	1942-43	1,143	792	1,370	761
218	,,	1943-44	1,227	750	712	740
219	,,	1944-45	1,349	677	333	642
220	,,	5 years average	1,742	732	923	697
221	,,	1945-46	2,375	—	1,170	—
222	,,	1946-47	1,249	—	158	—
223	SUGAR CANE	1929-30	3	—	6	3,640

			Adilabad District		Telangana Division	
			Outturn	yield per acre	Outturn	yield per acre
			8	9	10	11
198	**TOBACCO†**	1926-27	102	60	5,012	—
199	,,	1927-28	279	196	6,953	—
200	,,	1928-29	272	211	6,653	—
201	,,	1929-30	411	280	4,514	—
202	,,	5 years average	266	—	5,783	—
203	,,	1930-31	265	468	5,076	—
204	,,	1931-32	550	468	5,810	—
205	,,	1932-33	523	469	5,983	—
206	,,	1933-34	600	489	5,334	—
207	,,	1934-35	683	556	5,779	—
208	,,	5 years average	524	490	5,596	—
209	,,	1935-36	638	524	6,331	—
210	,,	1936-37	885	659	9,175	—
211	,,	1937-38	634	539	6,334	—
212	,,	1938-39	668	598	8,941	—

213	,,	1939-40	636	554	11,077	—
214	,,	5 years average	691	575	8,371	—
215	,,	1940-41	539	569	9,065	—
216	,,	1941-42	546	458	7,348	—
217	,,	1942-43	635	504	5,965	—
218	,,	1943-44	390	361	8,105	—
219	,,	1944-45	207	389	3,721	—
220	,,	5 years average	463	456	6,841	—
221	,,	1945-46	350	—	3,403	—
222	,,	1946-47	171	—	10,032	—
223	SUGAR CANE	1929-30	48	201	1,777	—

			Marathwada Division		State	
			Outturn	yield per acre	Outturn	yield per acre
			12	13	14	15
198	TOBACCO†	1926-27	2,878	—	10,063	199
199	,,	1927-28	3,480	—	12,491	256
200	,,	1928-29	3,535	—	11,709	272
201	,,	1929-30	5,079	—	11,990	331
202	,,	5 years average	3,743	—	11,563	—
203	,,	1930-31	12,161	—	17,237	437
204	,,	1931-32	10,466	—	16,276	459
205	,,	1932-33	11,711	—	17,694	553
206	,,	1933-34	9,534	—	14,868	460
207	,,	1934-35	10,530	—	16,309	478
208	,,	5 years average	10,880	—	16,476	473
209	,,	1935-36	3,656	—	15,987	500
210	,,	1936-37	9,630	—	18,805	584
211	,,	1937-38	10,269	—	16,603	592
212	,,	1938-39	9,569	—	18,510	571

213	,,	1939-40	11,013	—	22,090	606
214	,,	5 years average	10,028	—	18,399	571
215	,,	1940-41	11,273	—	20,338	611
216	,,	1941-42	7,342	—	14,690	444
217	,	1942-43	6,795	—	12,760	536
218	,,	1943-44	6,129	—	14,234	505
219	,,	1944-45	3,203	—	6,924	523
220	,,	5 years average	6,948	—	13,789	507
221	,,	1945-46	2,301	—	5,709	—
222	∴	1946-47	8,616	—	18,648	—
223	SUGAR CANE	1929-30	37,415	—	39,193	2,361

Sl. No.	Name of of the crop	year	Warangal District		Karimnagar District	
			Outturn	yield per acre	Outturn	yield per acre
1	2	3	4	5	6	7
224	SUGAR CANE∴	5 years average	3	—	6	—
225	,	1930-31	3	2,240	6	3,733
226	,,	1931-32	3	2,240	5	2,240
227	,,	1932-33	29	2,240	5	3,733
228	,	1933-34	36	2,240	6	3,360
229	.	1934-35	128	3,105	6	3,360
230	,	5 years average	39	2,412	6	3,285
231	,,	1935-36	78	2,105	6	3,258
232	,	1936-37	336	3,668	6	4,192
233	,,	1937-38	206	2,116	584	4,166
234	,,	1938-39	209	3,080	253	3,257
235	,,	1939-40	67	3,360	343	3,049
236	,	5 years average	179	2,866	328	3,584
237	,,	1940-41	171	3,089	196	4,435

238	,,	1941-42	57	4,000	116	2,735
239	,,	1942-43	61	3,038	95	2,747
240	,,	1943-44	58	2,824	120	3,200
241	,	1944-45	66	1,603	146	3,000
242	,,	5 years average	83	2,911	135	3,223
243	,,	1945-46	103	2,261	29	1,015
244	,,	1946-47	76	3,153	866	2,534

			Adilabad District		Telangana Division	
			Outturn	yield per acre	Outturan	yield per acre
			8	9	10	11
224	SUGAR CANE.·.	5 years average	48	—	1,777	—
225	,,	1930-31	87	2,998	2,805	—
226	,,	1931-32	52	1,820	2,510	—
227	,	1932-33	86	2,535	3,792	—
228	,,	1933-34	103	2,308	4,825	—
229		1934-35	238	2,720	13,485	—
230	,,	5 years average	113	2,476	5,485	—
231	,,	1935-36	222	2,550	23,527	—
232		1936-37	468	3,403	40,813	—
233	,,	1937-38	485	3,597	16,528	—
234	,	1938-39	421	3,970	24,593	—
235	,	1939-40	464	3,066	42,649	—
236	,,	5 years average	412	3,319	29,622	3,738**

237	,,	1940-41	860	3,531	46,768	4,024**
238	,,	1941-42	419	3,000	32,390	6,354
239	,,	1942-43	423	3,352	33,109	3,701
240	,,	1943-44	165	1,925	45,884	3,217
241	,,	1944-45	276	3,098	56,158	2,835
242	,,	5 years average	389	2,981	42,872	3,461
243	,,	1945-46	287	2,759	49,079	5,093
244	,,	1946-47	425	2,479	36,077	3,307

			Marathwada Division		State	
			Outturn	yield per acre	Outturn	yield per acre
			12	13	14	15
224	SUGAR CANE.˙.	5 years average	37,416	—	39,193	—
225	,,	1930-31	46,638	—	49,454	3,228
226	,,	1931-32	62,054	—	64,564	4,160
227	,,	1932-33	71,982	—	75,774	4,256
228	,	1933-34	66,865	—	71,690	3,506
229	,,	1934-35	79,646	—	93,129	4,085
230	,,	5 years average	65,437	—	70,932	3,847
231	,	1935-36	75,669	—	99,196	3,759
232	,,	1936-37	84,013	—	1,24,826	4,789
233	,,	1937-38	44,743	—	60,271	4,480
234	,,	1938-39	44,737	—	69,330	4,881
235	,	1939-40	48,823	—	91,472	4,655
236	,,	5 years average	59,397	4,035**	89,019	4,513
237	,,	1940-41	62,690	4,598**	1,10,458	4,311

238	..	1941-42	55,501	4,892	88,891	5,123
239	,,	1942-43	55,157	4,017	88,266	3,859
240	,	1943-44	75,312	4,052	1,21,296	3,638
241	,	1944-45	93,008	3,653	1,09,166	3,244
242		5 years average	58,934	4,042	1,01,806	3,751
243	,,	1945-46	69,241	4,138	1,18,320	4,487
244	,	1946-47	91,158	3,759	1,27,235	3,619

*The particulars of these crops were given in '*Agriculture Statistics*' only from 1935-36. Further, the yield per acre details of 'bajra' and 'maize' and region-wise information of the same in respect of all crops (excepting few later years) were also not provided in the available sources.

**These were given as average figures of the respective regions.

†Cotton outturn figures are given in bales of 400 lbs, and yield of lint in lbs.

††The data is available only from 1926-27.

∴The outturn was of *gur* (jaggery) in tons and yield per acre also of the same in lbs. particulars are available only from 1929-30.

Sources :-1. *Estimate of Area and yield of Principal Crops in Hyderabad State, Quinquennial, 1925-26 (1335 Fasli) to 1934-35 (1344 Fasli); 1935-36 to 1345 Fasli (1939-40 (1349 Fasli)* ; and *1940-41 (1350 Fasli) to 1944-45 (1354 Fasli)*. (For the outturn and yield per acre particulars of the period, 1925-26 to 1944-45);

2. Finance Department (Resource), H.E.H. the Nizam' Government S. No. 480, *File* No. 13 of 1353 Fasli (1944). (For particulars relating to 'gram' and 'tobacco' crops for the years 1945-46 & 1946-47)

3. Secretarist Records of former Nizam's Governments, Department of Agriculture, S. No. 13, *File* No. 8/57 Fasli (1948). (For details of all the crops excepting 'gram' and 'tobacco' for the years, 1945-46 & 1946-47).

was either nil[176] of stationary for one quinquennium and there was a precipitous fall since 1940-41 which was fundamentally due to the preference of cultivators for cash crops that had become marked by this time.[177] Not only there was shrinkage in the acreage of these crops, but the yields per acre in *Suba* Districts remained far lower than the State average which in itself stood far below that of Bombay or Madras Presidencies or of All-India. In respect of 'maize' crop for which the yield per acre figures are available, none of these Districts ever exceeded during 1935-47, the yield figure of 450 lbs per acre as against that of 475 lbs in respect of the State, 635 lbs in Madras Presidency and 933 lbs in All-India.[178] In fact, the State yields and invariably those of the *Suba* Districts in respect of all the Principal crops remained far lower, forming in reality only 1/3 of what had been achieved in the neighbouring provinces like Madras[179] or distant ones like United Provinces[180] of British India, or India taken as a whole. Besides the effect of frequently changing crop conditions and that of the Great Depression which was clearly reflected in the comparatively low yields in respect of all crops in the year 1929-30[181], the factor which significantly contributed for low crop yields in the State, was of course, poor utilisation of agricultural inputs.[182]

In the case of jawar and rice, the two principal grains that formed the food of the majority of rural and urban people respectively, whereas the first decade of 1925-35 was one of general decline in outturn, the second one that began from 1936-37 showed definite growth in it. The rise in the Prices of these food stuffs during the Post-Depression period of 1935-39 by 14 to 18 points in the index in *Suba* area,[183] coupled with the various incentives offered by the Government such as free allotment of culturable lands to members of backward castes and tribes, remission of 50% land revenue on dry *kharif khata*[184] and *poramboke* lands growing food crops and even concessions upto 5 years in wet assessment under irrigation projects and supply of seeds and manure at concessional *taccavi*[185] etc, had greatly helped in their increased production. But, these benefits which were extended as part of the Grow More Food Campaign could, due to corruption and slackness of the Agricultural Department and its propaganda wing, the meagre allocation of funds to this Department and lack of proper means of transport,[186] reach only a minor fraction, definitely falling below 10% of the total agricultural population.[187] Consequently, the overall picture of food grain production, especially in respect of paddy, continued to be one of deficit for the State, though not for the *Suba*. Even during the second decade of 1935-45, there were outturn variations between the two quinquennia. Whereas jawar recorded outturn increase in respect of all the *Suba* Districts in both the quinquennia, rice was not. It showed rise in respect of all during 1935-36 to 1939-40, but slight rise in respect of Warangal amounting to 1,000 tons and heavy to moderate decline amounting to 8,000 and 3,000 tons in respect of Karimnagar and Adilabad Districts during 1940-41 to 1944-45.[188] The next two years were characterised by alternate rise and fall in respect of rice but the reverse, excepting Warangal and Karimnagar, in respect of jawar. The period thus considered as a whole, presented a spectacle of decline in outturn and also the standard yield per acre in respect of both these cereals. Regarding the latter, during this 21 year period, the standard or normal yield per acre which according to the Department of Agriculture was 1,200 lbs 1,100 lbs and 800 lbs of rice (irrigated)[189] in respect of Warangal, Karimnagar and Adilabad Districts, was reached in only one year, two years and three years respectively and regarding jawar, the standard yield of 500 lbs fixed in respect of all,[190] was reached only twice by Warangal, none by Karimnagar and once by Adilabad District. Even in respect of wheat, whose acreage and outturn was insignificant in Warangal and Karimnagar Districts and did not exceed 3,000 tons in Adilabad District which stood first in Telangana, but 8th or 9th in the State after Marathwada Districts, the outturn during these two decades was on the ever declining spree.[191]

(*ii*) *Non-Food Crops—Outturn and Yield*

Among non-food crops, groundnut was the only one which had regular increase in outturn from 1930-31 to 1944-45 and that too, in an unprecedented manner. In Warangal

District which led the *Suba* and also held third place in the State from 1936-37 to 1944-45, the outturn increased from 147 tons in 1929-30 to 11,000 tons in 1935-36 ; from 54,000 tons in 1936-37 to 85,000 tons in 1944-45. This amounted to 7,382.99% in the former period and 57.40% in the latter. As a matter of fact, no other crop had assumed such a degree of importance in the agricultural economy of Hyderabad State during this period as groundnut.[192] In the year 1934-35, Warangal District had achieved a record increase of 11.054% in groundnut production compared to previous year. During the quinquennium of 1935-36 to 1939-40, outturn growth outstripped the expansion in acreage and consequently, this District which occupied 5th place in crop acreage[193] during this period in the State, came to occupy third place in respect of outturn turnover. But, all the same, the standard yield of 1,000 lbs per acre fixed in respect of the State and also *Suba* Districts,[194] had, throughout the period never been realised either by this or other *Suba* Districts or in fact by the State as a whole.[195] The use of vegetable ghee produced out of groundnut seeds as a substitute for ghee or butter by the European Countries,[196] besides its vast use in the extraction of cooking oil in India, provided wide marketing facilities for the product, making it as the prime export commodity of the State and the *Suba*. Groundnut arrivals dominated the Regulated Markets of Marathwada, Mahboobabad, Khammam, Madhira, Karimnagar, Peddapalli, Jammikunta etc.,[197] and exports in the State gallopped from 22,00,303 *Pallas* in 1347 *Fasli* (1937-38) to 59,65,432 *Pallas* in 1353 *Fasli* (1943-44),[198] an increase of 17.11% in six years. General decline in outturn in 1945-46 and 1946-47 excepting in Adilabad and Marathwada was due to adverse crop conditions caused by untimely and less rainfall respectively.[199]

The outturn and acre yield figures of the other cash crops of *sesamum*, castor, cotton, tobacco and sugarcane were a mixture of increase and decrease, varying from one quinquennium to another, or not infrequently, even from year to year. During the quinquennium of 1925-26 to 1929-30, the average was generally on the increase, for the prices of these commodities were on a gradual and slight slump.[200] But, with the sudden and drastic reduction that came about in the price levels of these money crops during the Depression Period of 1929-30 to 1933-34, considerable reduction in five-yearly outturn averages amounting to 63.59% in respect of *sesamum* of Warangal, 58.54% in the case of castor of the same District, 26.79% in respect of cotton of Adilabad District and 30.19% in respect of tobacco of Karimnagar District, took place.[201] The price decline compared to pre-Depression year, ranging from 42% in the case of *sesamum*, 40% in respect of castor to 21% in the case of cotton had resulted in considerable lowering of agricultural incomes, which, in turn, obliged the peasants to lessen the cultivation of commercial crops as they involved more expense in the shape of investment and instead, take up more and more the food crop cultivation like jawar that involved comparatively less monetary investment and further met their food and fodder requirements.[202]

As the price situation had improved with the ending of the Depression effect by 1936-37, there was again general and in the case of some, considerable increase in outturn and acreage yields during the next two quinquennia ending in 1944-55, with of course, some exceptions in the last one. The *sesamum* production in the case of Adilabad District increased from 3,464 tons as 5-yearly average in 1934-35 to 5,000 tons in 1939-40 and further to 12,000 tons in 1944-45, the percentage in the latter being as high as 140 ; the castor outturn in Karimnagar District rose from the five-yearly average of 3,085 tons in 1934-35 to 4,000 tons in 1939-40, the increase working upto 29.65%, but remained stationary in 1944-45 which, to a greater extent, was due to the closing of the foreign markets for the product due to the Second Great War ; the cotton seed production in the leading Telangana District of Adilabad rose from quinquennial average of 41,903 bales in 1934-35 to 47,000 bales in 1939-40, the percentage of increase being 16 93 and finally to 48,000 bales in 1944-45, the decrease in the rate of increase in the latter being due to less than the average rainfall and also insect attacks in the *rabi* season for the year 1944-45,[203] as a result of which, the normal outturn rate suffered by more than 50% ; in respect of tobacco and sugar-cane crops, the trend was somewhat different in the sense that whereas there was increase in the outturn average of all the *Suba* Districs[204] in the quinquennium of 1935-36 to 1939-40, there was considerable decrease in respect of all in the next five year period of 1940 41 to 1944-45.[205] The main factor that led to outturn decrease in the latter quinquennium was considerable shrinkage in acreage,[206] which in the case of sugar-cane even amounted to 50%,[207] that took place in respect of both these cash crops.

In the last two years of 1945-46 and 1946-47 for which only the data is available, there was almost general decrease in the production of all these cash crops which, in respect of some like cotton and castor, ranged from 50 to 60% roughly. Unfavourable crop conditions coupled with the intensification of the restrictions on the cultivation of non-food crops contributed towards this end. Regarding yield per acre, it is significant to note that Warangal District had the distinction of not only exceeding the standard yield limit fixed by the Agriculture Department in its case and also of the State, but even went far ahead of the yield limits achieved by the British Indian Provinces during 1925-45, in respect of *sesamum* and castor crops. The yield per acre figures of 368 lbs of *sesamum* in the year 1929-30 and 582 lbs of castor seed in the year 1926-27 that were recorded by this District remained the highest in the country.[208] But, these record yields had been achieved only once in a way and mostly in the quinquennium of 1925-26 to 1929-30. Though Karimnagar led in the volume of production of both these commodities, its highest yields per acre during the period had been 180 lbs. of *sesamum* in 1941-42 and 246 lbs. of castor in 1938-39,[209] as against the standard yields of 224 lbs and 300 lbs arrived at respectively, in the case of both these *Suba* Districts.[210] The yields of Adilabad also remained below the normal levels set by the Department.[211] It, of course, led the Telangana Districts in cotton yield.[212] In tobacco and sugarcane, none of the *Suba* Districts, nor, as a matter of fact, any one in the State, ever reached the set yield levels, although they remained much below those of the British Indian neighbouring Provinces.[213] But, all the same, Warangal in respect of tobacco with 982 lbs. in 1928-29 and Nizamabad District in sugarcane with 5,861 lbs. in 1938-39 recorded the highest acre yields in the State,[214] during the period. In sugarcane acreage as well as outturn, the *Suba* Districts, due to soil, irrigational and investment limitations[215] and most important of all, the ignorance of the cultivators, ranked insignificant during the period in the region as well as the State, which also with only 0.4 lakhs acres under sugar-cane cultivation was obliged to meet 75% of its sugar requirements from imports.[216] (For outturn trends of main food and non-food crops of the *Suba*, see Chart No. V).

D. *PRICE VARIATIONS AND THEIR EFFECTS*

The economic condition or the well-being of the people in *Suba* in general and agriculturists in particular, had been considerably influenced by fluctuations in the prices of agricultural commodities and also manufactured goods. But, the study of the price developments in the area was greatly hindered by the non-availability of retail price statistics in respect of cash crops, which in fact, provided the much needed agricultural income to the tillers and exportable surplus to the Government.[217] In order to obviate this difficulty, the data that was given in respect of the State was studies and analysed as that broadly reflected the situation that obtained in that *Suba*[218] also. The region had its main export and import transactions with the neighbouring British Indian Provinces and just as in their case, its price system had the deep impact of the two Great Wars and the Depression.

(*i*) *1910-1928*

During the four year period before the commencement of the European War in 1914, the retail prices of rice and jawar, for which only the figure are available as could be seen from Table XXXVII, were on the rise. This feature was conspicuous in the prices of the year 1913, the reason being below average rainfall and resultant crop failure in Warangal and Karimnagar Districts.[218a] Compared to them Adilabad District had better rainfall, as a result of which jawar price did not undergo any change compared to previous year and even that of the rice also had exhibited lesser change. It is a clear indication that crop conditions had heavy bearing on prices of agricultural

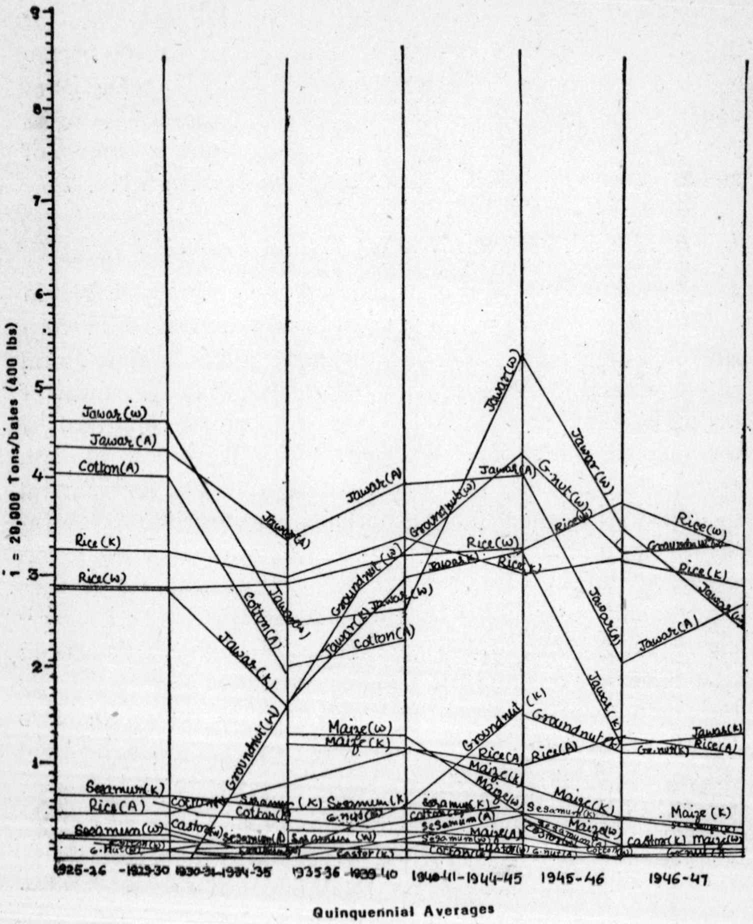

Chart 5 : Showing *Quinquennial outturn af important crops. in Warangal Suba, 1925-26—1946-47.*

W=Warangal District.
K=Karimnagar "
A=Adilabad "

TABLE XXXVII

Annual Average Retail Prices with Index Numbers of Principal Commodities

(in seers and *chataks* per Hyderabad Rupees) *in Warangal Suba, 1910-1941*).

Base for Index Numbers Average price of the quinquennium, 1902-1906 (for the period upto 1920) and January 1922 (for the period from 1921) onwards.

DISTRICT	COMMODITY	1910	1911	1912	1913	1914	1915
1	2	3	4	5	6	7	8
Warangal	RICE	7½	7¼	6½	6	6¼	8¼
,,	,,	133	129	154	167	148	121
Karimnagar	,,	6¼	7½	6½	5½	6½	8½
,,	,,	168	140	162	183	166	124
Adilabad	,,	6¾	7	6¼	6¼	6	7½
,,	,,	141	136	142	152	158	131
State	,,	6¾	7	6	5½	5½	7
,,	,,	131	125	150	163	159	127
Warangal	JAWAR	11¼	11¼	11	10	11¾	12½
,,	,,	209	200	214	235	200	188
Karimnagar	,,	10	11¾	13¾	8¾	11¼	13
,,	,,	255	217	186	291	227	196
Adilabad	,,	12	13½	13¾	13¾	13¾	17½
,,	,,	246	219	215	245	223	169
State	,,	14	14½	12¾	10¾	12	14½
,,	,,	165	155	175	207	184	153

Warangal	MAIZE*	—	—	—	—	—	—
,,	,,	—	—	—	—	—	—
Karimnagar	,,	—	—	—	—	—	—
,,	,,	—	—	—	—	—	—
Adilabad	,,	—	—	—	—	—	—
,,	,,	—	—	—	—	—	—
State**	,,	—	—	—	—	—	—
,,	,,	—	—	—	—	—	—
Warangal	GRAM	—	—	—	—	—	—
,,	,,	—	—	—	—	—	—
Karimnagar	,,	—	—	—	—	—	—
,,	,,	—	—	—	—	—	—
Adilabad	,,	—	—	—	—	—	—
,,	,,	—	—	—	—	—	—
State	,,	—	—	—	—	—	—
,,	,,	—	—	—	—	—	—

DISTRICT	COMMODITY	1916	1917	1918	1919°	1920°	1921°	1922°	1923	1924
		9	10	11	12	13	14	15	16	17
Warangal	RICE	6½	7½	6	4½	4-0	4-1	5-1	5-1	4-8
,,	,,	154	133	167	235	250	126	100	100	113
Karimnagar	,,	8½	7½	6	3½	3½	3-8	4-13	4-6	3-15
,,	,,	124	140	175	300	300	138	100	110	122
Adilabad	,,	8	7¼	5	3½	3	3-5	4-6	5-3	4-7
,,	,,	119	131	190	292	317	132	100	84	99
State	,,	7½	6¾	5	3½	3½	3-11	4-2	4-2	4-1
,,	,,	124	132	175	260	263	112	100	100	102
Warangal	JAWÂR	11¾	10¾	7½	5½	6½	5-12	7-7	8-10	9-6
,,	,,	200	229	333	427	362	129	100	86	79
Karimnagar	,,	13¾	12¼	7¾	5	6	5-3	7-6	8-2	9-11
,,	,,	186	208	329	510	425	142	100	91	76
Adilabad	,,	18	14¾	7½	6¾	8½	7-5	7-11	9-9	10-0
,,	,,	164	200	393	437	347	105	100	80	77
State	,,	15	13	6¼	5	7¼	4-15	6-11	8-11	8-14
,,	,,	151	177	357	435	314	132	100	78	77
Warangal	MAIZE*	—	—	—	—	—	6-3	10-4	8-12	9-8
,,	,,	—	—	—	—	—	166	100	117	108
Karimnagar	,,	—	—	—	—	—	5-3	8-2	7-10	10-2
,,	,,	—	—	—	—	—	156	100	107	80
Adilabad	,,	—	—	—	—	—	6-12	8-2	11-5	11-0
,,	,,	—	—	—	—	—	120	100	72	74

State**	,,	—	—	—	—	—	5-10	8-5	10-0	10-0
,,	,,	—	—	—	—	—	147	100	86	82
Warangal	GRAM	—	—	—	—	—	4-2	3-9	4-11	7-2
,,	,,	—	—	—	—	—	86	100	76	50
Karimnagar	,,	—	—	—	—	—	3-9	3-10	4-9	7-2
,,	,,	—	—	—	—	—	102	100	79	51
Adilabad	,,	—	—	—	—	—	3-5	3-10	5-1	6-15
,,	,,	—	—	—	—	—	109	100	72	52
State	,,	—	—	—	—	—	3-15	3-7	5-1	7-11
,,	,,	—	—	—	—	—	89	100	69	51

DISTRICT	COMMODITY	1925	1926	1927	1928	1929	1930	1931	1932
		18	19	20	21	22	23	24	25
Warangal	RICE	4-12	5-12	5-1	5-8	6-0	6-9	7-11	7-13
,,	,,	107	88	100	92	84	77	66	65
Karimnagar	,,	4-5	5-15	5-1	5-5	5-7	5-13	6-7	8-5
,,	,,	112	81	95	91	89	83	75	58
Adilabad	,,	4-5	5-4	4-6	4-11	4-14	5-7	6-13	8-2
,,	,,	101	83	100	93	90	80	64	54
State	,	4-1	4-10	4-2	4-6	4-15	5-2	6-3	7-6
,,	,,	102	90	100	95	85	81	67	56
Warangal	JAWAR	9-3	9-0	7-11	8-6	9-8	9-2	14-8	12-0
,,	,,	81	83	97	89	78	82	51	62
Karimnagar	,,	10-10	11-11	9-2	9-7	10-1	12-2	15-3	13-7
,,	,,	69	63	81	78	73	61	48	55
Adilabad	,,	10-14	11-14	9-6	8-14	11-12	14-12	16-9	18-7
,,	,,	71	65	82	87	65	52	46	42
State	,,	8-14	10-6	8-14	8-10	9-12	9-15	16-7	15-5
,,	,,	76	65	77	79	70	70	42	44
Warangal	MAIZE*	11-5	11-3	9-11	9-11	11-3	15-0	17-11	14-4
,,	,,	91	92	106	106	92	68	58	72

Karimnagar	,,	15-0	11-8	7-2	8-7	10-2	12-7	15-5	12-0
,,	,,	54	71	114	96	80	65	53	68
Adilabad	,,	14-0	15-0	15-2	13-6	11-5	16-0	18-11	20-9
,,	,,	58	54	52	61	72	51	44	40
State**	,,	11-3	11-9	10-9	10-2	10-10	13-4	15-12	16-2
,,	,,	77	75	81	83	80	66	55	53
Warangal	GRAM	5-11	5-11	5-13	5-4	5-14	5-0	8-5	8-11
,,	,,	63	62	61	68	73	71	43	41
Karimnagar	,,	5-11	5-2	4-5	4-3	4-14	6-10	7-8	10-4
,,	,,	64	59	84	70	62	55	48	35
Adilabad	,,	6-9	7-1	5-4	4-15	6-5	5-4	8-1	10-1
,,	,,	55	51	69	73	57	69	45	36
State	,,	6-4	5-15	5-1	5-0	5-7	5-3	7-4	10-1
,,	,,	57	60	70	69	65	70	49	34

DISTRICT	COMMODITY	1933	1934	1935	1936	1937	1938	1939	1940*	1941*
		26	27	28	29	30	31	32	33	34
Warangal	RICE	9-4	10-0	8-6	8-1	7-12	7-13	7-13	6-13	6-9
,,	,,	55	51	60	63	65	65	65	74	77
Karimnagar	,,	10-0	10-12	8-13	8-10	8-7	8-1	7-5	6-9	6-11
,,	,,	48	45	55	56	57	60	66	73	72
Adilabad	,	9-10	9-12	8-3	8-1	7-12	7-12	7-4	7-1	6-9
,,	,,	45	45	53	54	56	56	60	62	67
State	,,	8-7	8-13	7-9	7-11	7-5	7-1	7-3	6-3	6-1
,,	,,	49	47	55	54	56	51	57	67	68
Warangal	JAWAR	14-15	17-14	13-8	13-0	12-3	12-3	11-1	10-12	11-2
,,	,,	50	42	55	57	61	61	67	80	67
Karimnagar	,,	15-12	16-10	12-2	12-15	12-11	12-4	10-12	10-5	11-0
,,	,,	47	44	61	57	58	60	69	72	67
Adilabad	,,	19-15	19-11	13-10	15-5	14-10	15-2	12-10	12-13	14-9
,,	,,	39	39	56	50	53	51	61	60	53
State	,,	16-8	16-11	13-4	14-2	13-4	14-4	11-14	11-0	13-2
,,	,,	41	40	51	47	50	47	56	61	51
Warangal	MAIZE*	15-8	19-1	13-11	13-4	14-7	13-2	12-7	11-15	11-15
,,	,,	66	55	75	77	71	78	82	86	86
Karimnagar	,,	15-2	16-3	12-3	12-6	12-7	12-6	11-1	10-5	11-0
,,	,,	54	50	67	66	65	66	73	79	74
Adilabad	,,	18-9	18-5	11-9	11-7	13-1	11-6	10-15	10-15	13-15
,,	,,	44	44	70	71	62	71	74	79	61

State**	,,	17-4	17-8	12-11	12-13	13-8	12-14	12-3	11-5	12-13
,,	,,	48	48	66	65	62	65	68	73	65
Warangal	GRAM	11-5	10-11	8-14	9-5	7-13	7-8	7-4	7-2	7-8
,,	,	31	33	40	38	46	48	49	50	48
Karimnagar	,	13-7	11-14	10-7	11-2	8-7	8-1	7-11	7-12	7-10
,,	,,	27	31	35	33	43	45	47	47	48
Adilabad	,	13-7	13-2	10-13	10-3	8-12	8-2	8-1	7-10	8-8
,,	,,	27	28	34	36	41	45	45	48	43
State	,,	13-4	12-3	10-8	11-1	8-5	8-0	7-13	7-10	7-10
,,	,	26	28	33	31	41	43	44	45	45

• Famine year.

* For 'maize' & 'gram', the data is available only from 1330 *Fasli* (1921). In respect of non-food crops, no data in respect of retail prices pertaining to *Suba* Districts is available.

** Regarding the particulars given in respect of the State, the information in the case of Hyderabad City, Mahaboobnagar and all Districts of Marathwada, except Aurangabad, was not given.

Source : *Retail and Wholesale prices of Principal Commodities in H.E.H. the Nizam's Dominions, 1300-1329 Fasli (1891-1920)* pp. 31-33 (Rice) & 36-38 (Index Nos) ; 41-43 (Jawar) & 46-48 (Index Nos) ; *1330-1340 Fasli* (1921-1931), pp. 4-5 (Rice) ; 8-9 (Jawar) ; 16-17 (Grams) & 14-15 (Maize) *1341-1350 Fasli (1932-42)* pp. 6-7 (Rice) ; 10-11 (Jawar) ; 16 & 17 (Maize) & 18 & 19 (Gram).

commodities. The starting of War in the following year had its repercussions on the price situation in the Dominions. It had its adverse effect on the balance of trade of the State by the closure of the Central European markets for the cotton and oil seeds exports from it[219] and also by the shortage of freight and railway wagon facilities for their export to other countries such as Japan.[220] Huge quantities of these agricultural export products remained unsold[221], and even the prices of cereals like rice and jawar during the years 1914-17 showed decline compared to those of 1913, though the crop conditions were good. War time conditions thus, in no way proved a boon to the cultivators nor to the State. (For price trends of rice, wheat and jawar upto 1941, See Chart No. VI).

The next quinquennium of 1918-22 was attended by scarcity and unfavourable crop conditions either due to unseasonable heavy rainfall or failure of monsoons or insufficient rainfall, which obliged the Government to declare famine in the affected areas and undertake relief measures.[222] There was so much shortage of essential foodgrains that the retail price index of rice between 1917-20, shot up by 117, 160 and 186 points in Warangal, Karimnagar and Adilabad Districts respectively, as against 131 points in case of the State ; the increase was still higher in the case of jawar that the index between 1917-19 rose by 198, 302, and 237 points in respective Districts, as against 258 points in the case of the State. Price rise in an year was equally staggering. In the case of rice, the index in the year 1919 compared to that of the preceding, mounted up by 40.71%, 71.42% and 53.68% in the Districts of Warangal, Karimnagar and Adilabad respectively, as against 48.59% in respect of the State. Though increase in index was there in succeeding year, it was not comparatively significant. But, in the case of jawar, the increase was comparatively not only higher, but significant in both the years of 1918 and 1919. The index increases in the respective years had been 45.41% and 28.22%, 58.17% and 55.01% and 96.50% and 26.46% in Warangal, Karimnagar and Adilabad Districts respectively, as against 101.63% and 21.84% in the case of the State. It becomes evident that except in the last case, the Districts of Karimnagar and Adilabad exceeded the increase in State average in respect of both the cereals, whereas Warangal Districts

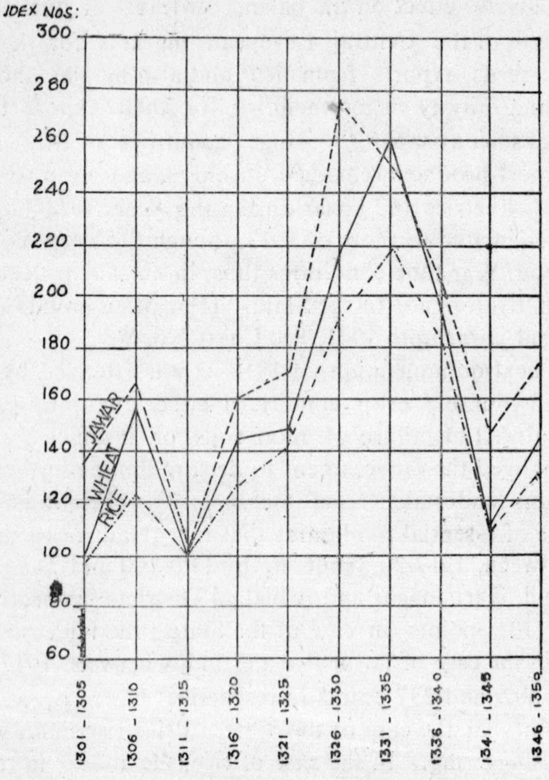

Chart 6 : *The Quinquennial Average Retail Prices of Rice, Wheat and Jawar in Hyderabad Dominions From* 1301 *to* 1350 *F.* (1891-92 to 1940-41).

Source : *Retail and wholesale prices in Hyderabad State from* 1341 (1932) to 1350 (1941) *Fasli.*

fell below it. Better sources of perennial irrigation[223] and consequently, opportunities for increased outturn enabled Warangal to claim separate status in this regard.

From 1921 to 1928, the prices of food crops,[224] pulses,[225] cotton and oil seeds,[226] were on the decrease. But, it was slow and gradual, interspersed with occasional increases. The percentage of decrease between the years ranged from 25 to 45 and it was more in the case of jawar and maize, compared to rice and gram. Among the Districts, Warangal once again[227] suffered lesser decrease. Regarding cash crops for which the price indexes are not available for this period, it can be seen from Table XXXVII that the decrease in the actual price was much less, compared to cereals and pulses. It was 23.33% in the case of *sesamum*, 13% in respect of castor and 12.60% in the case of cotton. The growing market for these products was very much responsible for this differential change. It could also be noticed that 1927, being an year of far below average rainfall,[228] resulted in outturn decrease[229] and fall in prices of almost all the commodities. Further, the huge imports of gold and silver, on account of abnormal fall in their prices to the extent of the value of O.S. Rs. 13,09,95,469 and 4,39,72.799 respectively during the period 1919-20 to 1928-29,[230] had also their effect on the slump in prices during this period. In spite of this general fall in prices during the twenties, it would be interesting to notice from the retail prices of rice and jawar that, compared to the pre-war level, the prices during 1921-28 were still much higher.[231]

(*ii*) *Depression and Recovery 1929-38* :

Except during the famine period towards the end of the second decade of the present century[232], the prices in the Dominions did not exhibit any abnormal trend so far. The onset of the Great Depression in 1929 and its continuance for a six year period ending in 1934 wrought unprecedented havoc in the economic fortunes of the cultivating masses in particular and others in general. The prices of all agricultural products went crashing down from year to year throughout the period, at an amazingly faster pace. The decline ranged from 68.47%[233] in respect of groundnut, 50% in respect of rice[234] to 20.48%

in the case of cotton. The fall in the prices of coconut, the keen competitor of groundnut in the post-war European market, the imposition of controls on groundnut imports by Germany and France and strong competition from South African groundnut which had all the advantages of better organisation, production and marketing, had cumulatively led to huge loss of overseas markets for Hyderabad groundnut[235] as against tremendous increase in production during this period[236] and the net outcome was alarming decline in price. The loss in agricultural income suffered on this count was so much that whereas groundnut production in 1933-34 registered about 500% increase compared to Pre-Depression Period, the value realised additionally was only 120%.[237] Compared to rice and gram, the price index decline in respect of jawar and maize was less, particularly in Karimnagar and Adilabad Districts. This was due to the fact that the latter cereals were in greater use and production by the small and medium farmers who, because of low agricultural incomes consequent to price depression, were not in a position to invest on inputs that were essential in extracting better yield in the cultivation of former crops, especially rice, which could be dispensed with for average yield in case of jawar and maize.[238] Less percentage of decline in cotton price index, compared to other cash as well as food crops and pulses, was due to the fact that its markets, both internal and external, did not suffer much during the period.

During this six year Depression period, peaks of decline in prices were experienced in 1931 and 1934. Between these two years, if stray cases are ignored, the increase in decline of price index was far heavier in the former and was roughly three to eleven times higher than in the latter. Depression effect was at the maximum in these years because of the unfavourable crop conditions and poor crop outturns.[239] Compared to other sections of the population, the agriculturists were subjected to special pressure under the Depressionary impact in the sense that, while they received far less for their products, they were made to pay correspondingly more for the manufactured goods like kerosene oil, salt, etc., which were required in domestic use. In other words, the slump had been pronounced in the

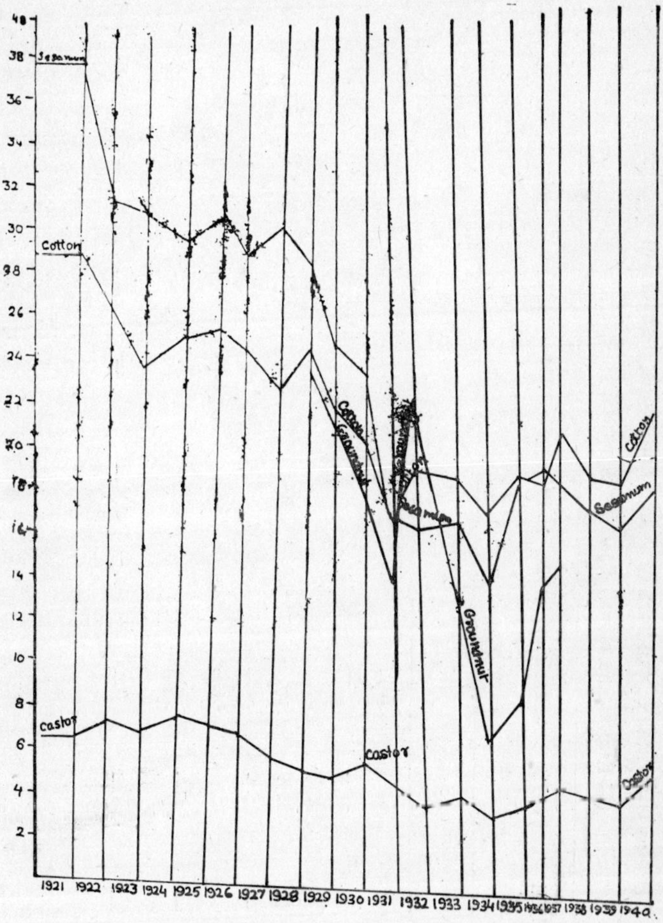

Chart 7 : Showing *Price levels of impo rtant ron-food crap*, 1921-1940.

*The prices of castor and cotton were *per maund* and those of *sesamun* and groundnut were per *palla*.

Data as per *Table No XXXVIII.*

TABLE XXXVIII

Prices with Index Numbers of Non-Food crops, 1921-1940

(In Rupees and annas) Base for Index, 1921=100

Crop	Price per	1921	1922	1923	1924	1925	1926	1927	1928	1929	1930
1	2	3	4	5	6	7	8	9	10	11	12
Castor	Maund	6-5	6-15	6-11	7-4	6-14	6-11	5-12	5-8	5-7	5-9
,,	—	—	—	—	—	—	—	—	—	78	80
Til (Sesamum)	Palla	37-11	31-9	30-13	29-13	30-15	29-7	30-8	28-15	24-13	24-0
,,	—	—	—	—	—	—	—	—	—	79	76
Cotton	Maund	28-12	26-10	23-15	25-1	25-11	24-13	23-0	25-2	22-1	20-13
,,	—	—	—	—	—	—	—	—	—	83	78
Ground-nut	Palla	—	—	—	—	—	—	—	—	23-0	18-3

Crop	Price per	1931	1932	1933	1934	1935	1936	1937	1938	1939	1940
		13	14	15	16	17	18	19	20	21	22
Castor	Maund	4-8	3-14	4-0	3-5	3-8	3-12	4-7	4-3	4-1	5-3
,,	—	65	56	58	47	50	54	64	60	—	—
Til (Sesamum)	Palla	17-2	16-5	16-8	14-5	19-9	19-14	19-9	17-14	16-11	19-7
,,	—	54	52	52	46	62	63	62	57	—	—
Cotton	Maund	17-3	19-15	19-3	17-12	19-14	19-12	21-2	19-5	18-11	22-5
,,	—	65	75	72	66	75	74	79	73	—	—
Groundnut	Palla	14-5	23-0	14-0	7-4	8-11	14-2	15-7	—	—	—

**Data not available.

Compiled from :—A.I. Qureshi, *The Economic Development of Hyderabad* pp. 248 (for data of 1921-29) ; 249 (Particulars of the period 1930-39), p. 251 (for 1940 data) ; p. 255 (Index Numbers for prices of the period 1928-29 to 1933-34) ; p. 263 (Groundnut prices 1928-29 to 1933-34) ; p. 268 (Index Numbers of the period 1935-36 to 1937-38) and p. 269 (Groundnut prices of 1934-35 to 1936-37).

case of agricultural products, whereas its influence had been less felt in the case of non-agricultural commodities.[240] Agriculture as a whole, had been rendered unprofitable and by materially increasing the real burden of the agriculturists, monetary liabilities, such as land taxes, loans etc., the position of the mass of the cultivators was rendered absolutely helpless. The result that followed in the domain of agriculture was a wave of land transfers by small and middle farmers in favour of rich peasants and landlords who began to put their extra resources in the shape of land, bullocks, grain and cash for increased food grain production so as to offset the price decline and indulge in grain and money lending that came in handy for land grabbing. The process went on so rapidly and rather alarmingly during the period that the Government thought fit to appoint an Enquiry Committee headed by S.M. Bharucha, Additional Revenue Secretary in 1937 to find out the gravity of the situation and suggest remedies for containing it.[241] Grant of remissions of land revenue[242] and *taccavi* loans[243] by the Government proved only as mere palliatives in alleviating the long drawn distress.

Price recovery, at last, started in 1935, bringing welcome relief to the much afflicted populace. Increase in the index number of all the commodities compared to that of 1934 was noticeable, ranging from 4 points in respect of gram to 26 in the case of maize.[244] But, in the next year, as there was inadequate rainfall, slight decline in prices of jawar, maize, gram and cotton ranging from 1 to 6 points, had occurred. Even the increase in respect of the price index of rice and castor was only marginal extending from 1 to 4 points, but it was significant in the case of groundnut, which, compared to the actual price of the proceding year, amounted to 62.58%, The reason for this heavy hike in groundnut price was that the production in the State fell short by 1,16,268 tons of the targeted figure[245] and consequently, the demand, which got revived after the end of the Depression Period, far outstripped the supply. 1937 and 1938, the last two years of recovery period did not also record uniform change in prices of different crops. In the former year, whereas there was increase in price index in respect of rice, jawar, gram, castor, cotton and groundnut, decrease took place in the case of maize and *sesamum*; in the latter year, as against increase or stillness in respect of rice, jawar, maize and gram, decline was there in the case of castor, *sesamum* and cotton.[246] But, these fluctuations which had been more in the direction of rise than fall, were not of a violent nature for the index either way, never changed by more than ten points. It is, of course, significant that in 1938, all the cash crops for which the figures are available, suffered decline in prices. Post-Depression boom in productivity outstripping the demand, and differential effects of crop conditions, were important factors that contributed for these price variations.

(*iii*) *Period of Inflation, 1939-50*

The outbreak of the Second World War for which the State made significant contribution in the shape of men and material on behalf of the Imperial British,[247] started the period of rising prices in 1939. Excepting slight fall in 1941 and rather heavy in 1944-45, the rest of the period, both during and after the War, was marked by a scene of ever-rising prices.[248] Sluggishness in the markets, transport bottlenecks on account of war time priorities and bumper yields in the former year in the case of crops like jawar, groundnut, cotton[249] and castor overreaching the demand, were the main factors that accounted for this exceptional decline. On the other hand, *til*,[250] in spite of decreasing outturn in both the years, had, because of the conventional and local demand for its seeds and oil, maintained rising trend in its price. The highest increase in prices and their indexes occurred in 1942-43, 1945-46, 1946-47 and 1950. During the eleven year period of 1941-42 to 1950 out of which full data[251] is available only upto 1947-48, the price increase amounted to 226.08, 346.25, 186.03, 228.92, 225.07, 523.15, 500, 398.05, 319.28 and 94.87 %, in respect of rice, jawar, bajra, gram, cotton, groundnut, *sesamum*, castor, chillies and sugarcane,[252] respectively. The rise in the case of non-food crop prices was, on the average, two to two and half times more than that was experienced in the case of food crops. The rate of increase in a single year in respect of a crop during this period was so pronounced—

chillies in 1946-47 recorded a stupendous increase of 236 points in price index compared to preceding year—that it exceeded the previous highest increase of 181 points reached in respect of jawar price[253] of Karimnagar District in the severest famine year of 1919, by 56 points. (See Chart No. VIII for price curves of this period).

But, it is all the more important for the study to realise that this spiral of rising prices could only benefit the minority section of big landlords in the rural parts and trading community in the urban areas. Paradoxically, the majority section consisting of small peasants, tenants and landless labourers or workers who were really in need of lift in their financial condition from this price inflation after having suffered heavily from the Depression effect, had got their condition really worsened.[254] Rising commodity prices led to rising costs of production. Agricultural cattle,[255] green and chemical manures, iron and timber for agricultural implements, and hides and skins for leather buckets that were used in lifting water out of wells for irrigation etc., became dearer compared to pre-War period. But, more important than these agricultural requisites, became the supply of agricultural labour and the rate of their wages. Due to manpower mobilisation for War and Wartime auxiliary industries, there came general scarcity of labour and daily wages of agricultural labourers increased between 1938-39 to 1949-50 by 166.66% in the case of men and 300% in the case of women.[256] Because of the operation of these factors, the cost of cultivation, as found out in the Economic Survey held in Madras in 1946, compared to which the conditions in the State were not better, had risen by about 100% above the level in 1939.[257] Besides this, the rise in the cost of living on account of War time scarcity and hike in prices of essential commodities such as salt, kerosene, *gur*,[257a] mill and handloom cloth[258] etc., had acted as an additional soar to the economically weaker sections of the population that included the smaller peasantry and labourers. The outcome was that the little rise that the latter had in their agricultural and wage incomes because of inflationary economy, was more than offset by the increased cultivation and living costs. Hence, their capacity to save over their

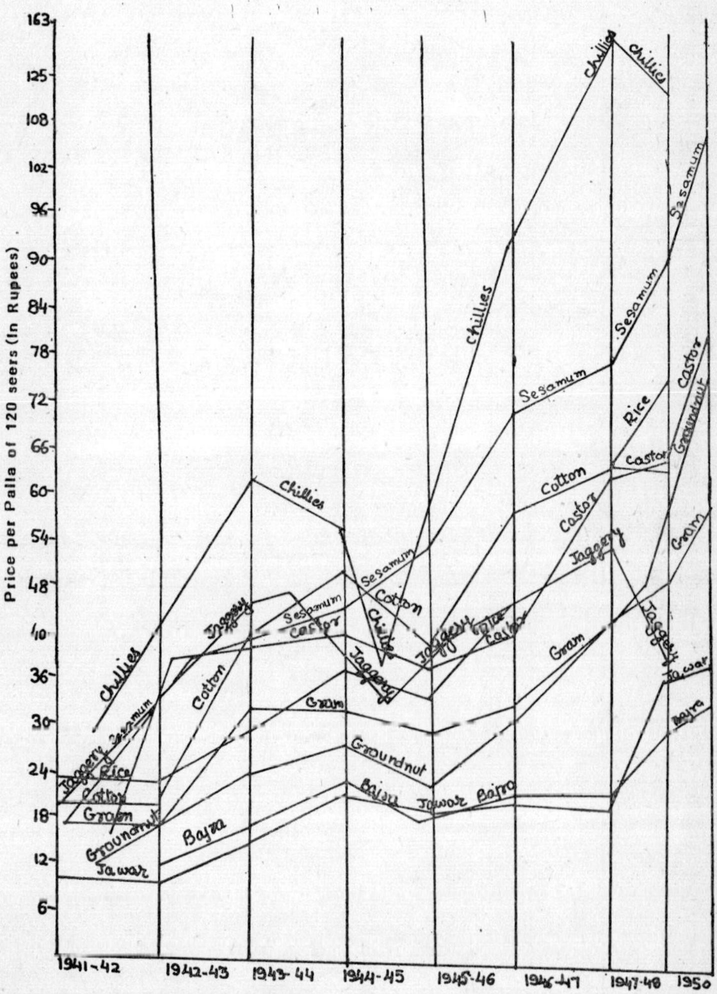

Chart 8 : Showing *Prices of all important commodities from* 1941-42 *to* 1947-48 *and* 1950.

Data as per *Table XXXIX*.

TABLE XXXIX

Annual Average Prices of Important Agricultural Commodities in Regulated Markets From 1941-42 to 1950

Prices per Palla of 120 seers)

Sl. No.	Commodity	1941-42	1942-43	1943-44	1944-44	1945-46
1	2	3	4	5	6	7
1.	Rice	23-0 (83)	28-0 (100)	37-0 (133)	33-0 (118)	47-0 (168)
2.	Jawar	9-3 (100)	14-0 (155)	22-0 (244)	19-0 (211)	21-0 (233)
3.	Bajra	11-3 (100)	17-0 (155)	23-0 (209)	18-0 (164)	21-0 (191)
4.	Gram	17-15 (129)	32-0 (229)	32-0 (229)	28-0 (200)	33-0 (236)
5.	Kapas	19-11 (155)	42-0 (323)	50-0 (385)	40-0 (338)	27-0 (438)
6.	Groundnut	11-14 (83)	24-0 (184)	27-0 (208)	23-0 (177)	30-0 (230)
7.	Til	18-0 (106)	38-0 (237)	45-0 (265)	52-0 (305)	68-0 (400)
8.	Castor	16-1 (133)	37-0 (308)	41-0 (341)	35-0 (291)	41-0 (341)
9.	Chillies	29-13 (000)	61-0 (200)	55-0 (183)	38-0 (127)	92-0 (307)
10.	Gur	19-8 (111)	45-0 (250)	47-0 (261)	34-0 (189)	41-0 (228)

		1946-47	1947-48	1948-49	1949-50	Week ending 23-12-1950	Markets from where quoted
		8	9	10	11	12	13
1.	Rice	— —	75-0 (254)	— —	— —	— —	
2.	Jawar	19-0 (211)	36-0 (400)	— —	— —	41-0** 39-0	
3.	Bajra	21-0 (191)	29-0 (263)	— —	— —	92-0	
4.	Gram	44-0 (314)	50-0 (357)	— —	— —	59-0	
5.	Kapas	64-0 (492)	66-0 (508)	— —	— —	—	
6.	Groundnut	43-0 (330)	38-0 (154)	— —	— —	74-0	
7.	Til	78-0 (459)	88-0 (518)	— —	— —	108-0	Warangal Market
8.	Castor	62-0 (517)	63-0 (525)	— —	— —	80-0	Warangal and Badapally (Mahaboobnagar District) Markets
9.	Chillies	163-0 (543)	125-0 (417)	— —	— —	— —	
10.	Gur	52-0 (305)	38-0 (211)	— —	— —	— —	

Figures in brackets indicate Index Numbers. The Year 1938-39 has been taken as the basic year with 100.
*These were given as prevailing in Warangal District by its Civil Administrator.
**The first one was for white jawar and the latter for yellow jawar, both being two varieties of the crop.
Source : *The Report of the Agrarian Reforms Committee, 1949*, Appendix 'E' (for data up to 1948-48), Secretariat Records of former Hyderabad Government, Agriculture Department, S. No. 18, *File* No. 270 50 Misc. of 1950 (for 1950 Prices).

expenditure and clear off their debt obligations, became a dim prospect. Quite in contrast, the big landholders and urban traders had enough resources at their disposal in the shape of land, cattle and capital which helped in achieving greater production and business turnover that enabled them to amass huge profits on account of rising prices, for the largeness of the operations had very much neutralised the effect of rising costs. This situation helped them in going for acquisition of further landed and business assets.

E. PRICE CONTROLS, PROCUREMENT AND RATIONING

Measures for controlling the prices of food grains were for the first time initiated by the Government, when in the middle of 1918, the Law Regulating Civil Supplies was passed[259] so as to arrest the upward tendency in prices that had set in.[260] It prohibited the export of food grains outside the Dominions except under license, restricted the profit from 2 to 3°/ₒ on cost price for wholesale transactions and 4 to 6% for retail sale and also provided for the running of cheap grains shops in some of the Districts and on a smaller scale.[261] But, these measures failed in their purpose, for a succession of bad crop years[262] coupled with the restriction or the stoppage of food imports from British Indian Provinces[263] put the entire machinery out of gear and the consequence being, the wound up of the Department of Control of Civil Supplies in 1922.[264] During the period of the latter's functioning, grain prices were more on an unprecedented rise rather than any appreciable decline even in 1921 and 1922.[265]

Price Control Committee had again come to be appointed on the 9th September, 1939[266] when a period of rising prices had started with the commencement of the Second Great War.[267] This was set up to check profiteering in grain trade and notifications were issued that persons selling food articles at a price 5°/ₒ and non-food commodities at 10°/ₒ more than that prevailing in August, 1939 would be prosecuted under Section 81 of the Defence of Hyderabad Ordinance.[268] The immediate result that followed the fixing of prices of wheat, rice, jawar, matches, kerosene, etc., was the complete disappearance of these essential commodities from retail dealers' shops.[269] This, in turn, was due to a concerted and sinister move on the part of big traders and cultivators to go for huge profiteering by indulging in large scale blackmarketing and hoarding.[270] As much as 93°/₀ of food grain production in the State was under the control of big landholders who were not prepared to part with their huge accumulated stocks except for higher prices than those fixed by the Government.[271] The prevalence of the Anti-hoarding and Profiteering Ordinance and the Food Grains Control Order that came into operation on 25th August, 1942,[272] had little effect in containing the dreaded evils.[273] Not only laxity was there in official supervision and implementation of these regulations, but the imposition of mere and meagre fines on offenders in food grain cases compared to imprisonment in British Indian Provinces, had made them little scared of Governmental action for violating food grain laws.[274] The inevitable outcome of this situation was that the general population in the area was made to suffer for essentials that ranged from rice and jawar to matches and kerosene, which could only be had on exorbitant blackmarket prices, whose increase compared to open market prices ranged from 32.72°/₀[275] in the case of rice to 275°/₀ in the case of matches.[276]

(i) *Rationing and Public Distribution System*

Local people were so much exasperated by the rising food grain prices that they raided grain shops at Khammam,[277] Hanamkonda, Matwada[278] and Yellandu[279] during 1941-43 and indulged in looting. The rise in prices was experienced not only because of blackmarketing and concealment of stocks, but also equally due to exports to Hyderabad and more to neighbouring provinces. These smuggling activities flourished on account of far higher prices prevailing in British Indian Provinces. The Statutory ceilings were fixed in *Azur*, 1353 *Fasli* (October, 1944) and these compared as below with the prices prevailing in the neighbouring provinces :

Table XL

Commodity :	Hyderabad	Bombay	Madras	C.P.
		(In B.G. Rupees per maund)		
R ..	..	..	..	..
Rice	8-11-5	11-8-0	7-13-5	10-6-9
Jawar	5-6-10	7-0-3	8-3-8	8-4-0
Bajra	5-10-9	7-9-6	6-10-8	—

Source : Office of the Financial Secretary and Financial Adviser, Supply Finance, S. No. 429, *File* No. 3/G1 of 1354 Fasli (1945), p. 97.

Excepting in the case of rice relating to Madras, the ceiling prices in British India, as could be seen from Table XL, were much higher than those of Hyderabad which naturally tempted and encouraged the traders to smuggle the grain across the borders[280] and at the same time disappointed the local farmers that they got less price for their produce compared to their brother cultivators in British India. The factors which abetted the smuggling activities had been the connivance of the local Customs Officials,[281] the unwillingness of Police and Revenue Staff to take prompt action on offenders[282] and the paltry fines inflicted for violation of Scheduled Articles Movement Control Orders.[283]

High prices coupled with scarcity, mostly artificial, impelled the Government to introduce Statutory Rationing[284] during 1944 and 1945 in the urban areas of Warangal, Khammam, Kothagudem Collieries, Bellampalli Collieries and Sasti Collieries and open cheap grain shops in the non-rationed areas that comprised Taluq headquarter towns and some villages here and there. The number of consumers served by a ration shop in respect of the latter areas was far beyond the operational optimum. Whereas it was 1,583[285] and 2,316[286] in the case of Khammam town and Warangal City respectively, it remained as high as 6,000 in the case of Chinnoor, Taluq headquarters in Adilabad District which was not covered by Statutory Rationing, for its population stood at 12,000 only.[287] The quantity of ration that was distributed had also come down by 25°/₀ between 1945-50. It fell from 8 *Chattaks* or 16 ounces per day and per head to 12 ounces or 6 *Chattaks* and it is significant to note that this entire fall was in respect of rice ration only which formed the most important staple food of the people, next to jawar only.[288] Besides the limitation of imports from India on which the State heavily depended, the loopholes in the system of distribution and the illegal transfer of godown stocks into blackmarket and across the borders, had contributed not a little to this situation of scarcity.[289] Bogus ration cards numbered as many as 47,000 in Warangal City,[290] 37,000 in Kothagudem,[291] and 15,000 in Khammam towns. In fact, the population in the Colliery town of Kothagudem was not more than 40,000, but the ration cards that had been issued there numbered 70,000.[292] The amount of grain deficiency suffered by needy non-agricultural sections on account of this malpractice was so huge that it amounted to 1,356 *Pallas* per week in the case of Warangal and Khammam[293] and 39 bags per day in the case of Colliery town.[294]

The work of Public Distribution of essential commodities in the State was supervised by the Supply Department that came into being in September, 1943[295] which, in turn, took the assistance of co-operative bodies, such as Hyderabad Co-operative Commercial Corporation,[296] Taluqa Co-operative Development Unions and Village Co-operative Grain Banks, in grain collection, purchase, sale as well as distribution. Whereas H.C.C C., started in February, 1943,[297] served as the chief agent of the Supply Department in the collection of grain levy and its purchase in the open market which was mainly aimed at counteracting the activities of hoarders and blackmarketeers, Development Unions at the Taluq level and Grain Banks[298] at the village level took part in grain lending on co-operative basis, besides acting as the agents of the

H.C.C.C. in grain collection and purchase and further as ration shops for public distribution. But these bodies, though they had been very much popular,[99] especially the latter, in view of cheaper grain-lending compared to individual and professional lenders,[300] suffered from the evils of mismanagement, red-tapism and domination by vested interesrs.[301] As many as 50°/₀ of the Grain Banks remained mere paper societies[302] Grain that was deposited came to be utilised by the village elders for their own purposes.[303] The fact that half of the Taluqa unions were located at places which were not marketing centres proved unsound[304] and their too much preoccupation with grain collection and purchase as agents of the H.C.C.C., obscured the other important functions of lending and distribution.[305] The spread of these organisations in Non-*Diwani* areas, compared to *Diwani* Villages, was very much less, thereby restricting the opportunities for food supply and grain lending in those parts. The respective percentages of Grain Banks to total number of villages in *Diwani, Jagir, Paigah* and *Sarf-i-khas* areas in the State stood at 72.6, 20.1, 10.8 and 35 7.[306] The final result that emerged out of the situation was that the *Suba* People, during the period of Rationing, experienced extreme hardship and suffering not only for food grains of rice, jawar and wheat, but also for other essential items like sugar, jaggery cloth, yarn (for weavers), iron (for agricultural implements), thread (for tailors) and even matches. The usual practice that remained in vogue regarding distribution was that out of the quota that was allotted to a dealer, only half was distributed and the remaining half was sold in blackmarket at exorbitant rates.[307] A ration of 3 seers of rice per month would hardly be enough for a rice eater for one week and thus indirectly, the non-agriculturists and the lower sections of the population were forced to fall back on blackmarketeers.[308] The non-availability of yarn, iron and thread at controlled rates had considerably affected the professional fortunes of weavers, cultivators and tailors. Majority of weavers in Khammam, Karimnagar and Sirsilla Taluqs who could not afford to purchase yarn at black market rates and find it remunerative to weave it into cloth, gave up their traditional occupation and took to unskilled labour for living.[309] The failure of the crops, which was rather not uncommon under local conditions,[310] further added to the misery of these poorer sections of the rural population. At times, these were reduced to such straits that *ballar*,[311] tree roots and tamarind seed formed their staple food.[312] The Taluqs of Mahboobabad, Khammam, Madhira and Yellandu in Warangal District, Karimnagar, Sirsilla, Mahadeopur, Sultanabad and Jagtiyal in Karimnagar District and those of Luxettipet, Chinnoor and Sirpur in Adilabad District, felt the worst impact, compared to rest of the Taluqs, of the distressing conditions that prevailed between 1944-50. It would be interesting to note that these became the very pockets of economic discontent that characterised the post 1946 scene and was exploited by the Communists to suit their power strategy.[313]

(*ii*) *Procurement Policy and its Wide-Ranging Effects*

As part of its food policy to build adequate stocks of foodgrains so as to supply them at controlled rates to non-producing sections of the population in both rural and urban areas, Government thought it best to introduce the collective levy order on 27th October, 1943.[314] Both middle and small farmers came under its severe and crushing impact. The rate of levy in respect of Paddy had been fixed at 3 maunds per acre for *abi* crop and 4 maunds per acre of *tabi* crop and in the case of all other food crops that included jawar, wheat, bajra, ragi,[315] maize, etc., the scale in Telangana Districts excepting Adilabad had been fixed at ¾th maund per acre from a cultivator of an area of less than 10 acreas and 1½ maunds per acre from cultivator of an area of 10 acreas or more. In respect of Adilabad District which has been clubbed with Marathwada and Karnatak regarding the latter variety of food crops,[316] the rate was put at one maund per acre from every cultivator holding an area of less than 10 acres and two maunds per acre from a cultivator holding 10 acres or more.[317] It is significant to note that in respect of fixation of paddy levy, no distinction was made, unlike other food crops, between small and big farmers which made lot of difference to the former in view of their meagre holdings and also the fact that paddy levy rates compared to those of other food crops proved far higher ranging from 266.66 to 400%.[318] If these paddy levy rates per crop are considered in terms of standard yields of 15, 14, and 10 maunds per acre[319] in the respective Districts of Warangal, Karimnagar and Adilabad which were rarely reached in practice,[320] they amounted to 20 to 40%.[321] Small and medium farmers whose crop surpluses over their family needs were not much, were made to suffer considerable economic loss when they were forced to sell such percentage of each of their paddy crops at a price which, when compared to open market price of rice, was drastically less by as much as 55.84%, 59.15% and 56.92% in Warangal, Karimnagar and Adilabad Districts respectively.[322] The provision in the levy order that the *Taluqdar*, if he thought that the crop was good, could in consultation with the Local Food Advisory Committee[323] and with the approval of Director-General of Supplies, increase the rate of levy on non-paddy food crops from 3/4th to 1 maund in respect of cultivating holders of less than 10 acres and from $1\frac{1}{2}$ maunds to 2 maunds per acre in respect of cultivators holding 10 acres or more[324], had further added to the discomfiture of these ryots. In other words, they were denied of the little advantage that could be enjoyed at times when crop was good.

The one thing which fell like an axe on the toiling shoulders of the cultivating masses was the draconian regulation that, besides levy grain, they were made to compulsorily sell, under what was known as '*Khushkharidi*'[325] a portion of their remaining grain to H.C.C.C. at nominal price.[326] Its rate varied from 2 maunds per acre in Karimnagar Taluq, to 3 maunds in Huzurabad Taluq and 4 maunds in Manthani Taluq.[327] Supply Department claimed in 1947 that it was doing service to the ryots when it combined both the contributions and fixed the new rate of levy at 5 maunds per acre instead of the former 3 maunds in respect of paddy ![328] The most ironical and at the same time painful part of this new arrangement was the regulation that, if at all any ryot wanted to sell any grain after paying the enlarged levy demand, he had to sell it only to H.C.C.C.[329] For a loss in price ranging from Rs. 14 to Rs 17 per *palla,*[330] the poor and helpless peasant was offered a bonus of Re. 1 per maund of paddy (But for three months only ! [331] But, more than this loss in price was the inability of many a small farmer to meet the new levy demand which now amounted to 33 to 50 % of the normal yields of paddy per acre in the *Suba.*[332] As the ryots were prevented from carrying on their agricultural transactions of daily nature until the levy grain was handed over irrespective of the fact that there was inadequacy or failure of the crop, they had no other alternative except going to big landlords and merchants who had sufficient grain reserves and further took advantage of the situation to trade in grain and thereby further strengthen their grip over the peasant community, and purchase grain from them at Rs. 30 to Rs. 40 per *palla* as against the levy price of Rs. 18 which they got from H.C.C.C. and thereby get themselves freed from the marauding clutches.[333] Those ryots who did not quickly respond to the demands of the Levy Inspectors were even subjected to Physical beating.[334] Even as per Collective Levy Order, non-payment of levy was made punishable with imprisonment or fine or both and without prejudice to such punishment, the food grains in respect of which the levy order had been contravened were made liable for forfeiture ; in case of fine imposition, an amount equal to three to ten times the value of the levy grain due from a cultivator was collected by Tahsildar as arrears of land revenue.[335]

But, the crux of the problem lay in the fact that the grain purchase was not made from those who had enough stocks to spare. Rich landlords and big merchants bribed the Levy *Girdavars* and also used their influence as village officials and consequently members of the Local Food Advisory Committee, to remain untouched and unaffected by Government's grain purchase[336]. On the other hand, they could further enrich themselves by indulging in profitable grain lending and sale to small and middle farmers.[337] As these elements who were really in a position to contribute heavily and rather in full towards grain procurement escaped, the burden fell all too crushingly on the poor peasantry, for the officials all the same strived for reaching the targets set in this respect.[338] First *Taluqdar* of Warangal in his *Confidential Report to Subedar submitted for the first fortnight for the month of Farwardi, 1355 Fasli (February, 1946)* observed that :

> "Sudden checks were made of the paddy in the possession of big *Pattedars* under Ghanpur and Ramappa tanks from Ghanpur, Ramanjapur and Jangalapalli (Villages) where the chief *pattedars* live, four thousand *pallas* of paddy over and above the target will be purchased. The *pattedars* agreed to part with this stock after great persuasion. Atmakur, a village in Warangal Taluq was also visited and 250 *pallas* of paddy were secured from the *Deshmukh.*[339]"

It could thus be seen that whereas big *pattedars*, after great persuasion by the District head, agreed to sell a portion of their huge grain reserves to the H.C.C.C., in contrast, the ryots were subjected to all types of torture until the grain was handed over at any cost.[340] It very *Deshmukh* in the *Suba* or the State had acted like that of Atmakur (see above), the region would not have experienced the shortage of food grains from year to year as it did.[341]

The levy system was associated with several other loopholes—deduction of '*seers* per *palla* from ryots towards '*Taruqu*' at the time of weighing levy grain,[342] delay extending to even four days in weighing the grain due to non-availability of more than one balance at a godown[343] ; delay in announcing the price after weighing it[344] and ryots being made to wait, sometimes for 2 years[345] to receive the payment for the levy grain that they handed over, mainly because of embezzlement of ryots' levy amounts by *patwaris,* both *asaldars* and *gumasthas,*[346] deduction of old arrears of land revenue, *tuccavi* etc , from the levy grain amount that was due to the ryots[347] etc., that made the ryots further dislike and hate it. On occasions, especially during 1946-48, they were so much exasperated at the official attempts to forcibly collect the grain, in such economically backward Taluqs like Sirpur, Boath and Minwat in Adilabad District, Huzurabad, in Karimnagar District and Borgampahad Taluq in Warangal District, that they entered into physical clash with levy officials assisted by the police, in which one Second *Taluqdar* and Six Revenue Inspectors were injured or manhandled and Six Revenue Inspectors were killed[348]. The ryots, in presenting this attitude of resistance, were immensely encouraged by the preaching of local Andhra *Maha Sabha* leaders otherwise renowned as Communists and only some passive appeals here and there by the *Arya Samajists* and the State Congress leaders[349]. The influence of the former had spread in all the *Suba* Districts which was confessed by *Subedar* himself[350]. In otherwords, it would be useful to realise that the rise of the Communists onto the scene in Telangana in 1944 had strongly coincided with commencing of the worst period of the Rationing and Levy in the State and the worker and peasant disaffection that grew out of it due to grave lapses on the part of the Administration[351], had only come strengthen and consolidate their popular image. The times and the events had ably served their purpose and the official machinery due to its joining hands with the landlordly, business and feudal interests[352], never came out boldly to remove the causes of popular discontent on the food front, although it was well aware and goaded to that effect by the State Congress[353] and Maharashtra *Parishad* leaders[354] that the removal of hunger and exploitation of the lower sections of the population regarding levy and procurement would remove the winds out of the sails of Communist propaganda.

Lesser utilization of the available land resources, general decrease in crop acreages, outturn and acre yields, unsettling and debilitating effect of agricultural prices on the economic condition of small and middle farmers, scarcity of food grains and other essential commodities due to the ineffective price controls and Rationing and lastly, the crushing impact of the levy system on the living conditions of small and middle peasants, these, infact, became the dominant features of the agrarian scene during the period under study. These different factors had only contributed for the general retardation of agricultural development in the *Suba* area. The increase in fallow land unoccupied land for exceeded that in occupied land, for the main reason that as against lakhs of acres of land available for *Laoni* distribution, only few thousands of acres were usually distributed. Further, huge blocks of land, in some cases running over several thousands of acres, were granted to absentee colonisers and war-returned soldiers, whereas the really needy and interested peasants and tenants found it hard to receive fresh and unoccupied lands for cultivation[355]. The land distribution system of the Government had thus led to not only lesser utilisation of the cultivable land, but the benefits being received more by absentees and non-agriculturists, resulted only in the neglect of agriculture. The decrease in crop acreages, outturns and acre yields was as much due to fluctuating crop conditions and price levels of agricultural commodities[356] as to excessive land monopolization absenteeism, small and fragmented holdings, lesser utilisation of irrigation potential and agricultural inputs and inadequate availability of cheap agricultural credit.[357] It was of course a welcome development that in both acreage and outturn, non-food crops like groundnut castor, *sesamum*, cotton, tobacco and chillies went far ahead of food crops which led to commercialisation of agricultural crops and also the fact that Hyderabad agricultural exports began to find world markets.[358] But, this growth of rapid and excessive preference for cash crops, coupled with artificial scarcity created by blackmarketeers and hoarders and the cuts that were effected by the Indian Government in food exports to the State, led to acute shortage of food grains, especially to non-agriculturist employees, landless labourers, small and middle farmers and tenants.[359] The collection of grain levy in a rigorous and enhanced manner from the small peasanty, had added fuel to the fire. As bigger landlords escaped from this obligation by whetting the pockets of levy inspectors and Revenue Officials, the burden fell so crushingly on these weaker agrarian elements that they, encouraged by the non-levy preachings of the local Communist leaders, dared even to physically resist the official attempts at grain collection that resulted in the killing of as many as seven Revenue Inspectors in different Taluqs of the *Suda*.[360] The wilful closing of the eyes of the Government to the dangers inherent in the situation had only thrown the real base of the rural peasantry into the waiting hands of the Reds.[361]

REFERENCES

1. Hyderabad District Gazetteers, Part II-Tables, *op. cit.*, Warangal, (p. 36) & Adilabad, (p. 39). This information is not provided by the source in respect of Karimnagar District.
2. Out of every 1,000 in the local population, agriculture livelihood persons numbered 709 in Adilabad, 683 in Warangal and 584 in Karimnagar Districts in 1951—Census, 1951, Part I, *op. cit.*, p. 124.
3. See the section 'M. Crop Conditions', in Chapter V.
4. This is of course, besides the influence of various factors outlined in Chapter V.
5. Groundnut, cotton, tobacco, chillies and oilseeds formed this category.
6. W.S. *File* No. 14 of 1351 Fasli (1942) & R. No. 974 of 1356 Fasli (1947).
7. W.S. *File* No. 4 of 1351 Fasli (1942) & R. No. 3 of 1352 Fasli (1943) ; W.S. *File* No. 25 of 1355 Fasli (1946) & R. No. 71 of 1356 Fasli (1947).
8. Government area, otherwise known as *Diwani.*
9. Decennial Report on Administration, *op. cit.*, p. 83 ; Report on the working of the Departments under the Secretary & Director-General of Revenue, *op. cit.*, p. 7.
10. See the Sections dealing with 'Area' & 'Natural Resources', in Chapter II.
11. See Table IX in Chapter IV.
12. See Table II in Chapter II.
13. Decennial Report on Administration, *op. cit.*, p. 83 ; Report on the working of the Departments under the Secretary & Director-General of Revenue, *op. cit.*, p. 7.
14. See Table XXXIV for the period 1913 to 1926-27.
15. Nizamabad District (40.5 to 40.79%) stood first in the State, Adilabad second, Warangal third and Karimnagar fourth upto 1922. In 1926-27, the places of the latter two were interchanged and the rest the same as before—Decennial Report on Administration, *op cit.*, p. 83; Report on the working of the Departments under the Secretary & Director-General of Revenue, *op. cit.*, p. 7.
16. *Ibid.*
17. Report on the working of the Departments under the Secretary & Director-General of Revenue, *op. cit.*, p. 11.
18. See the Section '*Tahud/Sarbasta/Watandars*', in Chapter IV.
19. For rates of assessment, see the section, 'Land Revenue Assessments and their incidence', in Chapter IV.
20. Office of the First Taluqdar, Warangal *File* No. 39 of 1350 Fasli (1941) & R. No. 8565 of 1356 Fasli (1947).
21. W.S. *File* No. 103 of 1338 Fasli (1929) & R. No. 3100 of 1339 Fasli (1930).

22. W.S. *File* No. 36 of 1356 Fasli (1947) & R. No. 2469 of 1357 Fasli (1948).
23. W.S. *File* No. 48 of 1351 Fasli (1942) & R. No. 1827 of 1354 Fasli (1945).
24. *Ibid.*
25. *Ibid.*
26. Means in Urdu 'Grace of Islam'.
27. W.S. *File* No. 4 of 1353 Fasli (1944) & R. No. 1946 of 1355 Fasli (1946).
28. *Ibid.*
29. W.S. *File* No. 3 of 1350 Fasli (1941) & R. No. 1365 of 1351 Fasli (1942).
30. There had been good number of such sales. They averaged roughly 1/3 of the total number of land sale transactions effected in an year in the later forties and the price for 60 acres ranged from Rs. 1,000 to 2,000 Only-W.S. *Files* No. 87 of 1353 Fasli (1944) & R. No. 1441 of 1353 Fasli; 123 of 1354 Fasli (1945) & R. No. 619 of 1355 Fasli (1946) & 49 of 1355 Fasli (1946) & R. No. 654 of 1355 Fasli.
31. It is in Asifabad Taluq of Adilabad District. Their attachment to land was so strong that they braved firing in 1940 in which 13 tribesmen were killed after which *pattas* were given to them—W.S. *File* No. 49 of 1351 Fasli (1942) & R. No. 1437 of 1352 Fasli (1943)—See the Section 'Administrative Conditions,' in Chapter III.
32. W.S. *File* No. 103 of 1338 Fasli (1929) & R. No. 3100 of 1329 Fasli (1930).
33. *Ibid.*
34. Means one year in Urdu.
35. *Hyderabad Government Bulletin on Economic Affairs*, Vol. III, No. 9, (September, 1950), p. 748.
36. *Ibid.*
37. *The Deccan Chronicle*, 10-11--1949.
38. W.S. *File* No. 15 of 1343 Fasli (1934) & R. No. 1593 of 1352 Fasli (1943).
39. W.S. *File* No. 8 of 1350 Fasli (1941) & R. No. 1477 of 1350 Fasli.
40. W.S. *File* No. 9 of 1352 Fasli (1943) & R. No. 1435 of 1352 Fasli.
41. *Chamar* stands for cobbler, *Hajjam* for barber and *Dhangar* for shepherd in Urdu—W.S. *File* No. 2 of 1352 Fasli (1943) & R. No. 2520 of 1352 Fasli.
42. See the above para.
43 Register kept at *Tahsil* Office which showed details of tax due, collected and balance remaining in respect of each *pattedar*, year-wise and village-wise.
44. W. S. *File* No. 23 of 1354 Fasli (1945) & R. No. 1769 of 1354 Fasli.
45. W. S. *File* No. 15 of 1356 Fasli (1947) & R. No. 14 of 1356 Fasli.
46. Agriculture Department of Hyderabad Government, quoted in REE., *op. cit.*, p. 111.

47. Decennial Report on Administration, *op. cit.*, p. 85.
48. Aurangabad, Bir, Parbhani, Nanded, Gulbarga, Raichur, Osmanabad and Bidar, had been the eight Districts that formed Marathwada —Report on the working of the Departments under the Secretary & Director-General of Revenue, *op. cit.*, p. 9.
49. See the Section 'Location and Natural Divisions', in Chapter II.
50. See the Section 'Soils' in Chapter II.
51. Report on the working of the Departments under the Secretary & Director-General of Revenue, *op. cit.*, p. 8.
52. Decennial Report on Administration, *op cit.*, p. 85. Report on the working of the Departments under the Secretary & Director-General of Revenue *op. cit.*, p. 9.
53. See Table XXXIII-(c).
54. Decennial Report on Administration, *op. cit.*, p. 85 ; Report on the working of the Departments under the Secretary & Director-General of Revenue, *op. cit.*, p. 9.
55. *Ibid.*
56. *Ibid.*
57. *Ibid.*
58. *Ibid.*
59. See the earlier sub-section *Laoni* land distribution', in this Chapter.
60. Revenue Administration Report, *op. cit.*, p. 84 ; Decennial Report on Administration, *op. cit.*, p. 88 ; Report on the working of the Departments under the Secretary & Director-General of Revenue, *op. cit.*, p. 9.
61. See the above para.
62. See the sections 'Forests' in Chapter II ; 'Administrative Conditions' in chapter III and 'Irrigational Facilities', in chapter V.
63. District Authorities, quoted in REE., *op. cit.*, p. 107.
64. See the sub-section 'Irrigational sources, their construction and maintenance', in chapter V.
65. Other wise known as 'gingelly' or '*Nuvvulu*' (in Telugu) from which seeds, oil is extracted that is used deliciously in cooking.
66. It has formed only 1.2% of the total cultivated area in Adilabad District and 0.003% & 0.04% in Warangal and Karimnagar Districts respectively—*Estimates of Area and yield of principal crops in Hyderabad State, 1925-26 to 1943-35* (Hyderabad, 1938), pp. 104 105.
67. Hyderabad District Gazetteers, *op. cit.*, Warangal, pp. 304-305, Karimnagar, pp. 302-303 & Adilabad, pp. 300-301.
68. *Abi* sowing is made in June-July and harvesting in November-December. *Tabi* sowing is made in January-February and harvesting in April-May—*Supply Statistics, H.E.H. the Nizam's Government, 1354 Fasli (1945)*, p. 92.

69. Agricultural Statistics, 1935-36 to 1940 & 1940-41 to 1944-45, *op. cit.*, pp. 44 & 117.
70. Measure of 20 maunds of grain.
71. Settlement Report of Warangal Taluka, *op. cit.*, p. 33.
72. Hyderabad District Gazetteers, *op. cit.*, Warangal, pp. 304-305, Karimnagar, pp. 304-305 and Adilabad, pp. 300-301.
73. See the acreage given in Table XXXV for the year 1921.
74. *Mung* and *Tuar* are two kinds of pulses ordals, used in the diet of the people.
75. *Kharif* sowings were made in June and harvesting in October-January, the latter varying according to the type of the crop grown. *Rabi* sowings were made in June-October, month varying according to the nature of the crop grown and harvesting in January-March. Crop is termed *kharif* or *rabi*, according to the time of its harvest—Supply Statistics, 1354 Fasli (1945), *op. cit.*, p. 92.

75(a) See Table XXXIII-(c) in Chapter V.

76. See the Section 'Crop Conditions', in Chapter V.
77. See the Table XXXIII-(c) in chapter V.
78. W.S. *File* No. 103 of 1338 Fasli (1929) & R. No. 3100 of 1339 Fasli (1930).
79. See Table XXXIV and sub-section 'Occupied and fallow land', in this chapter.
80. See the data for the years since 1922 given in Table XXXV of this chapter. 1921 is not taken for this purpose for the reason that it was characterised by famine conditions.
81. Agricultural Statistics (Herein after referred to as A.S.) 1935-36 to 1939-40, *op. cit.*, p. 64.
82. See the figures given for the year 1935-36 (1335 Fasli), in Table XXXV.
83. See Table V in Chapter II.
84. Third place in the region during the period was claimed by Mahaboobnagar District—Agricultural Statistics. *op. cit.*, 1935-36 to 1939-40 and 1940-41 to 1944-45, p. 68 and pp. 156-157.
85. See the sub-section 'Food Crops acreage in relation to net sown area' in this Chapter.
86. It can be seen in Table XXXV that during this period of Depression, jawar acreage declined considerably.
87. *Index Numbers of annual average retail prices in H.E.H. the Nizam's Dominions, 1319-1350 Fasli (1910-1940-41)*, (*n.y*), pp. 26-28.
88. A.S., 1935-36 to 1939-40. *op. cit.*, p. 210
89. Immediate Agrarian Problems, *op. cit.*, p. 80.
90. See Table XXXV.
91. See Table XXXIII-(c) in Chapter V and the section 'Crop Conditions', in the same chapter.
92. See Table XXXV.
93. A.S., 1930-31 to 1934-35, *op. cit.*, pp. 104-105.

94. A.S., 1935-36 to 1940, *op. cit.*, pp. 49 and 65.
95. *Hyderabad Government Bulletin on Economic Affairs*, Vol. I, No. 9, (December, 1948), p. 1071.
96. Rice crop required half an inch of rainfall for 90 days or 45 inches of water altogether—A.S., 1940-41 to 1944-45, *op. cit.*, p. 118.
97. *Hyderabad Information*, Vol. IV, No. 10, (Shahrewar, 1353 Fasli) (July, 1944), p. 10.
98. In Telugu known as '*Ulavalu*' used mainly for cattle and horse feeding.
99. In Telangana, red gram, black gram, bengal gram, green gram are popularly known as '*Kandulu*', '*Minimulu*', '*Sanagalu*' and '*Pesalu*' respectively, all used in the preparation of dishes and soups. The husk (*Pottu*) of these pulses served as a strong cattle feed.
100. A.S., 1940-41 to 1944-45, *op. cit.*, pp. 102-103.
101. See Table XXXV.
102. Supply Statistics, 1354 Fasli (1945), *op. cit.*, p. 92.
103. A.S., 1930-31 to 1934-35, *op. cit.* p. 104-105.
104. A.S., 1935-36 to 1939-40, *op. cit.*, p. 40.
105. A.S., 1940-41 to 1944-45, *op. cit.*, pp. 102-103.
106. A.S., 1930-31 to 1934-35, *op. cit.*, pp. 104-105 ; A.S., 1935-36 to 1939-40, *op. cit.*, pp. 40-41 and A.S., 1940 41 to 1944-45, *op. cit.*, pp. 102-103.
107. A S., 1940-41 to 1944-45, *op. cit.*, pp. 102-103.
108. H.E.H. the Nizam's Government, *Trade Statistics, 1352 Fasli* (*1942-43*), pp. 18-19.
109. *Meezan*, 10-3-1945.
110. A.S., 1940-41 to 1944-45, *op. cit.*, pp. 4-5.
111. See Table XXXV.
112. A. Sarada Raju, *Economic Condition in the Madras Presidency, 1800-1850*, Published Ph. D. thesis (Madras University : 1942), p. 75.
113. B.N. Chaturvedi & K. Surender Reddy, 'Irrigation in Telangana—sources and Problems', in *The Deccan Geographer* (Hyderabad : January, 1964), p. 161.
114. *Hyderabad Information*, Vol. II, No. 9, (Amardad, 1351 Fasli, (June, 1942); Also see N.G. Ranga, *Economic Organisation of Indian Villages*, Vol. II, (Bombay : 1929).
115. As these proportions are not available in a calculated shape for the Districts, it has been done for the year 1943-44, (1352-53 Fasli) based on the figures given in Table XXXV leaving last two items, as they do not belong to any of the two categories.
116. A.I. Qureshi, *op. cit.* p. 51
117. A.S., *op. cit.*, 1925-26 to 1929-30, p. 54 ; 1930-31 to 1934-35, p. 55 ; 1935-36 to 1939-40, p. 101 and 1940-41 to 1944-45, p. 216.
118. W.S. *File* No. 31 of 1352 Fasli (1943) & R.N. 5 of 1357 Fasli (1948).
119. See Table XXXV.

120. See Section 'Crop Conditions', in chapter V and also Table XXXIII-(c).
121. See the Sections 'Administrative Conditions' & 'Political Conditions' in chapter III.
122. A.S., 1930-31 to 1934-35, *op. cit.*, p. 125.
123. Its rank among *Sesamum*—growing provinces in India got changed to fifth in India during the second quinquennium of 1930-31 to 1934-35- *Ibid.*
124. See Table XXXV.
125. These applied for the heavy decrease in crop acreage in 1947-48 See the sub-section on 'Groundnut,' in the previous para.
126. A.S., 1925-26 to 1929-30, *op. cit.*, p. 105.
127. H.E.H. the Nizam's Government, *Agricultural, Industrial & Trade Statistics for the year* 1341 *Fasli* (*6th October*, 1933 *to 5th October*, 1934), (Hyderabad : 1936), p. 39.
128. *Ibid.*
129. A.P.D.G., Karimnagar, *op. cit.*, p. 86.
130. Agricultural, Industrial & Trade Statistics for the year 1343 Fasli (1934), *op. cit.*, p. 40.
131. A.S., 1925-26 to 1929-30, *op. cit.*, pp. 107-108.
132. See Table XXXV.
133. See the sub-sections, 'Groundnut' & '*Sesamum.*' in this chapter.
134. Decennial Report on Administration, *op. cit.*, p. 19.
135. A.S., 1940-41 to 1944-45, *op. cit.*, p. 291.
136. *Ibid.*
137. Department of Agriculture, H.E.H. the Nizam's Government, *File* No. 32-8, S. No. 97 of 1357 Fasli (1948), p. 9. The pereentage of Warangal District was not given in the source cited as it was below 1%. But, from A.S., 1940-41 to 1944-45, *op. cit.*, p. 108, the figure cited was given.
138. Department of Agriculture, H.E.H. the Nizam's Government, *File* No. 32-8, S. No. 97 of 1357 Fasli (1948), p. 9.
139. See the Section 'Soils,' in chapter II ; Hyderabad District Gazetteers, Adilabad, *op. cit.*, p. 10.
140. A.S., *op. cit.*, 1925-26 to 1929-30, p 72 ; 1930-31 to 1934-35, p. 73; 1935-36 to 1939-40, p. 157 & 1940-41 to 1944-45, p. 298.
141. *Ibid.*
142. See Table XXXV.
143. Department of Agriculture, H.E.H. the Nizam's Government, *File* No. 32/8, S. No. 97 of 1357 Fasli (1948), p. 9.
144. *The Deccan Chronicle*, 8-5-1947.
145. Office of the Financial Adviser and Financial Secretary (Supply Finance), H E.H. the Nizam's Government, *File* No. 528, S.No. 279 of 1353 Fasli (1944), pp. 2 & 6.
146. *Hyderabad Information* Vol. II, No. 9, (Amardad, 1351 Fasli) (June, 1942), p. 9.

147. A.P.D.G., Karimnagar, *op. cit.*, p. 86.
148. Hyderabad District Gazetteers, Adilabad, *op. cit.* p. 10.
149. A.S., 1935-36 to 1939-40, *op. cit.*, pp. 304 & 306.
150. A.S., *op. cit.*, 1930-31 to 1934-35, p. 79; 1935-36 to 1939-40, p. 164 & 1940-41 to 1944-45 pp. 308-309.
151. *Ibid.*
152. Maulvi Nazir Ahmed, *Sadr Taluqdar* (This office was later converted into that of *Subedar*) Observed regarding Telangana cultivators : 'The cultivators of Telangana are, as a class, idle, shiftless and improvident...' quoted in Syed Hussain Bilgrami, *op. cit.*, p. 299.
153. *Hyderabad Information*, Vol. IV, No. 10, (Shehrewar, 1353 Fasli) (July, 1944), p. 20.
154. *Ibid.*
155. It was introduced only in 1937 *Hyderabad Information*, Vol. II, No. 9, (Amardad, 1351 Fasli) (June, 1942), p. 9.
156. *Ibid.*
157. *Hyderabad Information*, Vol. IV, No. 10, (Shahrewar, 1353 Fasli) (July, 1944), p. 21.
158. *Hyderabad Information*, Vol. II, No. 9. (Amardar, 1351 Fasli) (June, 1942), p. 9.
159. *Ibid.*
160. *Hyderabad Information*, Vol. IV, No. 10, (Shahrewar, 1353 Fasli) (July, 1944), p. 20.
161. *Meezan*, 13-9-1947 (Editorial).
162. *Meezan*, 28-6-1944.
163. *Hyderabad Information*, Vol. IV, No. 10, (Shahrewar, 1353 Fasli) (July, 1944), p. 20.
164. A.S., 1940-41 to 1944-45, *op. cit.*, p. 276.
165. See Table XXXV.
166. A.S., 1940-41 to 1944-45, *op. cit.*, p. 276.
167. See the sub-section 'Cotton,' in this Chapter.
168. A.S., *op. cit.*, 1935-36 to 1939-40, p. 143, 1940-41 to 1944-45, p. 275.
169. A.S., *op. cit.*, 1930-31 to 1934-35, pp. 106-107.
170. A.S., *op. cit.*, 1925-26 to 1929-30, pp. 82 & 84 ; 1930-31 to 1934-35, pp. 83 & 85.
171. A.S., *op. cit.*, 1935-36 to 1939-40, pp. 168 & 170; 1940-41 to 1944-45; pp. 316-17 & 322.
172. *Ibid.*
173. See the sub-section 'Groundnuts' in this chapter.
174. Production figures of pulses other than 'gram' like *tuar*, *mung*, *masur* and *kulthi* were given only for the two years of 1943-44 & 1944-45 which, except in the case of *mung* showed a decline A.S., 1940-41 to 1944-45, *op. cit.*, pp. 199-202.
175. See Table XXXV in this chapter.
176. See the 'bajra' figures in Table XXXVI.

177. See the sub-section 'ii. Non-food crops,' in 'Acreage' Section of this chapter.
178. A.S., 1940-41 to 1944-45, *op. cit.*, p. 4.
179. *The Golkonda Patrika* (Bi-weekly), Editorial, 10-4-1939.
180. *The Hyderabad Information*, Vol. IV, No. 3, (Bahman, 1353 Fasli) (December, 1944) ; A.S., 1940-41 to 1944-45, *op. cit.*, pp. 2-11.
181. See The Table XXXVI.
182. See Chapter V.
183. H.E.H. the Nizam's Government, Index Numbers of Annual Average Retail Prices, *op. cit.*, pp. 5 & 9.
184. Unallotted Government land, but cultivable.
185. *Hyderabad Information*, Vol. IV, No. 10, (Shahrawar, 1353 Fasli) (July, 1944), p. 10.
186. *Meezan*, 25-9-1945.
187. Rural Reconstruction Secretariat, former Hyderabad Government, *File* No. 9/1, S. No. 48 of 1358 Fasli (1949).
188. See Table XXXVI.
189. A.S., 1940-41 to 1944-45, *op. cit.*, pp. 2-3.
190. *Ibid.*
191. A.S., *op. cit.*, 1925-26 to 1934-35 pp. 22-25 ; 1935-36 to 1939-40, pp. 60-61 & 1940-41 to 1944-45, pp. 142-145.
192. A.S., *op. cit.*, 1940-41 to 1944-45, p. 210.
193. See sub-section 'Groundnuts' in Section 'Crop Acreage' this chapter.
194. A.S., *op. cit.*, 1940-41 to 1944-45, pp. 4-5.
195. See the Table XXXVI.
196. A.S., *op. cit.*, 1935-36 to 1939-40, p. 96.
197. *Trade Statistics, 1352 Fasli (1942-43) H.E.H. the Nizam's Government*, p 18 Mathwada was a suburb of Warangal Town.
198. *Supply Statistics, 1354 Fasli (1945)*, (H.E.H. the Nizam's Government, Hyderabad : 1945), p. 60.
199. See the Section 'Crop Conditions' in chapter V.
200. A.I. Qureshi, *op. cit.*, p. 250.
201. Compare the 5-yearly averages of 1925-26 to 1929-30 & 1930-31 to 1934-35 in Table XXXVI.
202. A.I. Qureshi, *op. cit.*, pp. 257, 264-66.
203. See the Section 'Crop Conditions' and Table XXXIII-(c) in chapter V.
204. Excepting Karimnagar District in the case of tobacco.
205. See the Table XXXVI.
206. For reasons of decrease in tobacco average, see sub-section 'Tobacco & Chillies' in 'Non-Food Crops' item of section 'Crop Acreage' in this Chapter. In the case of sugarcane also, the unwillingness and weak financial position of the cultivators to undertake the labour and expense involved in its cultivation, besides Governmental restrictions on cash crop cultivation, were responsible for decrease in acreage. Also see Table XXXV in this chapter.

207. In the case of Adilabad District, though there was no decrease in quinquennial average of acreage, there was 40% decrease compared to this, in the acreage of 1943-44 which resulted in lower outturn average for the 5 year period—See Tables XXXV and XXXVI.
208. A.S., *op. cit.*, 1925-26 to 1934-35, pp. 94 and 97 ; 1935-36 to 1939-40, pp. 116 & 129 & 1940-41 to 1944-45, pp. 236 & 253.
209. *Ibid.*
210. A.S., 1940-41 to 1944-45, *op. cit.*, pp. 5 & 6.
211. *Ibid* ; also see Table XXXVI.
212. A.S., *op. cit.*, 1925-26 to 1934-35, p. 9 ; 1935-36 to 1939-40, p. 159 & 1940 41 to 1944-45, p. 302.
213. A.S., 1940-41 to 1944-45, *op. cit.*, pp. 10 & 11.
214. A.S., *op. cit.*, 1925-26 to 1934-35, p. 98 ; 1935-36 to 1939-40, p. 149 & 1940-41 to 1944-45, pp. 288-289.
215. See f.n. No. 206 of this Chapter.
216. A.S., 1940-41 to 1944-45, *op. cit.*, pp. 144-146.
217. See the sub-section 'ii. Non-Food Crops—Outturn and yield' in Section 'Agricultural Production and yield per acre' in this chapter.
218. See Table XXXVIII attached to this section.
218. (a) See Table XXXIII & Section 'Crop Conditions' in this Chapter.
219. *A.R. for 1324 Fasli (1914-15)*, (Hyderabad-Dn : 1916), p. iii.
220. *A.R. for 1326 Fasli (6-10-1916 to 5-10-1917)*, p. 24.
221. A.R. for 1324 Fasli (1914-15), *op. cit.*, p. iii.
222. See Table XXXIII-(c) & Section 'Crop Conditions' in Chapter V.
223. See the sub-section 'Sources of Irrigation' in Section 'Irrigational Facilities' in Chapter V.
224. Includes 'maize' also. See Table XXXVII in this chapter.
225. Only retail prices of 'gram' are available.
226. See Table XXXVIII attached to this section and also chart No. VII.
227. See the above para.
228. See Table XXXIII-(c) and Section 'Crop Conditions' in Chapter V.
229. See Table XXXI in this chapter.
230. Hyderabad Banking Enquiry Report, *op. cit.*, p. 103.
231. See Table XXXVII-Price Indexes of the two periods can't be compared as the base is different in each case. Hence, the actual prices are examined.
232. See the above sub-section, 'i. 1911-28' in this Section.
233. It is calculated on the actual price difference between 1929 and 1934.
234. It is in respect of Adilabad, arrived at by calculating the percentage of the price index difference between 1929 and 1934.
235. A.I. Qureshi, *op. cit.*, p. 264.
236. See Table XXXVI in this Chapter.
237. A.I. Qureshi, *op. cit.*, p. 264.
238. See the Section 'Agricultural Production and yield per acre' in this chapter.

239. *A.R. for 1941 Fasli* (*6-10-1931 to 5-10-1932*), (Hyderabad-Dn : 1933), p. 47 : W.S. *File* No.'125 of 1343 Fasli (1934) & R. No. 54 of 1343 Fasli ; W.S. *File* No. 49 of 1343 Fasli & R. No. (n.g) & W.S. *File* No. 48 of 1343 Fasli & R. No. (n.g)—Also see Table XXXVI in this chapter.
240. D.R. Gadgil, *The Industrial Evolution of India in recent times*, (Oxford University Press, 1942), p. 198; The whole sale price index of kerosene, oil for the State for 1929-34 ran as following : 84.82.80 74, 75, 75 & 67—Retail and wholesale prices, *op. cit.*, 1921-1931, p. 76; 1932-1941, p. 96 ; the retail price index in respect of salt ran as following : 89, pp. 90, 86, 93, 96 & 93—Retail and wholesale prices, *op. cit.*, 1921-1931, 20-21 ; 1932-1941, pp. 22-23. (Though District figures are available, for totality of picture, State figures are given). The contrast becomes clear, if these are examined with reference to prices of agricultural products given in Tables XXXVI & XXXVII.
241. The findings of this Committee and the follow-up measures taken are discussed in the Section 'L. Agricultural Indebtedness' in Chapter V.
242. See the Section 'Remissions' in chapter IV.
243. See the Section 'Agricultural loans & *taccavi*' in Chapter V.
244. See the Table XXXVII relating to this Section.
245. A.S., 1935-36 to 1939-40, *op. cit.*, p. 214.
246. Groundnut price details are not available, as could be seen from Table XXXVIII for period 1938-40.
247. The Nizam's Government made very large contributions towards the War, the most noteworthy of which were perhaps, the investment of over 44 crores in Defence Bonds and War and victory loans, the provision of two Fighter squadrons for the R.A.F. or a Corvette for the Royal Navy, bore the cost of two Infantry Battalions, two cavalry regiments and one Artillery Battery that were kept on war service outside the State, and a monthly contribution of Rs. 1,50,000. The public of the State, besides the above efforts of the Government, had contributed approximately Rs. 50 lakhs to various war purposes.—Hyderabad Residency Records, *File* No. 80—p. 1946. (Available at National Archives, Delhi).
248. See Table XXXIX attached to this section. This is mainly utilised for explaining the price trends of this period. The data of Tables XXXVII & XXXVIII can't be clubbed with this, as the index base and price units were different in this case.
249. See Table XXXVI of this Chapter. In 1944-45, increase in production occurred in this case of gram.
250. Local and Urdu name for '*sesamum*'.
251. Excepting in respect of rice in 1946-47.
252. These percentage calculations are made upto 1950 in respect of crops for which the 1950 prices are available and in respect of others, 1947-48 figures are taken as the end figures.

253. Prices of cash crops for this early period are not available.
254. REE, *op. cit.*, pp. 457 & 459.
255. The cost of a pair of plough bullocks which in 1938 stood at Rs. 109-13-0, 79-9-0 and 91-12-0 in the Districts of Warangal, Karimnagar and Adilabad respectively, shot up to Rs. 422-8-0. 268-0-0 and 265-4-0 in 1945, an increase that amounted to 3 to 4 times—Retail & Wholesale prices, 1931-1941, *op. cit.*, p. 98 (1938 prices).
256. A.P.D.G., Khammam, *op. cit.*, p. 182.
257. Rao Bahadur Dr. B.V. Narayanaswami Naidu, *Report of the Economist for Enquiry into Rural Indebtedness, 1946*, (Government of Madras : Madras, 1946), p. 3.
257. (a) Local name for jaggery manufactured out of sugarcane.
258. For verification of price levels of Kerosene, salt, *gur*, etc., see Retail and Wholesale prices, 1931-41, *op. cit.*, p 92 (*gur*) ; p. 96, (Kerosene) & p. 22 (salt) ; Statistical year Book, 1351-1354 Fasli (1942-45), *op. cit.*, pp. 790-791. (for all the three).
259. Wholesale & Retail Prices, 1889-90 to 1918-19, A.D. *op. cit.*, p. 5.
260. See Table XXXVII.
261. Decennial Report on the Administration, *op. cit.*, p. 23.
262. See Table XXXIII-(c) & Section 'Crop Conditions' in Chapter V.
263. Wholesale & Retail Prices, 1889-90 to 1918-19 A.D. *op. cit.*, p. 5.
264. Decennial Report on the Administration, *op. cit.*, p. 23.
265. See Table XXXVII & sub-section 'i. 1910-28' in the Section 'Price Variations and their effects' of this Chapter.
266. *Trade Statistics, 1349 Fasli (1939-40), H.E.H. the Nizam's Government*, p. 4.
267. See the sub-section 'iii. Period of Inflation, 1939—50' in Section 'Price Variations and their effects' in this Chapter.
268. Trade Statistics, 1349 Fasli (1939-40), *op. cit.*, p. 4.
269. Political Branch, *File* No. 6 (7)-P(S)/45, in Hyderabad, New Delhi & Simla Lists (Micro Film), *Reel 2, Acc. No. 45*, p. 1.
270 *Hyderabad Information*, Vol. V, No. 2, (November, 1944), p. 10.
271. *The Deccan Chronicle*, (Editorial), 19-8-1949.
272. Hyderabad Residency Records, *File* No. 9 (12) P (S) 42, of 1942, p. 3. It introduced obtaining of license for purchase, sale or storage of grain of 10 maunds or above.
273. *Meezan* (English), (Editorial), 26-8-1948 & 13-9-1944 (Telugu).
274. *Ibid.*
275. *Golkonda Patrika* (Daily), 26-1-1949.
276. *Meezan*, (Letter to the Editor), 22-1-1947.
277. Political Branch, Hyderabad Residency Records, *File* No. 5 (2) P (Secret), 1941.
278. W.S. *File* No. 62 of 1352 Fasli (1943) & R. No. 102 of 1352 Fasli.
279. W.S. *File* No. 77 of 1352 Fasli (1943) & R. No. 112 of 1352 Fasli.
280. Between 1943 and 1947, good number of instances of large-scale food grain smuggling across the border had been reported from the

Customs Check Posts of Rajura, Khammam, Nelakondapalli (Khammam Tq), Madhira and Karimnagar—Subedari *Files* No. 158 of 1352 Fasli (1943) & R. No. 160 of 1352 Fasli ; 15 of 1356 Fasli (1947) & R. No. 14 of 1356 Fasli ; *Meezan*, 21-6-1944 & 24-10-1946.

281. W.S. *File* No. 158 of 1352 Fasli (1943) & R. No. 160 of 1352 Fasli ; *Meezan*, 24-10-1946.

282. *Meezan*, 21-6-1944.

283. W.S. *File* No. 112 of 1356 Fasli (1947) & R. No. 21 of 1357 Fasli (1948)—According to this order, the import or export of food grains, pulses, oil and oilseeds, fibres etc., was prohibited without obtaining the permission of the Director-General and Secretary, Supply Department in the case of food grains and pulses and of *First Taluqdars* in the case of other articles.

284. As per Government's decision, this was introduced in all towns with a population of 20,000 or more—*Hyderabad Government Bulletin on Economic Affairs*, Vol. II, No. 2 (February, 1949), p. 220.

285. Finance Department, Supply Branch, H.E.H. the Nizam's Government, S.No. 74, *File* No. 8/D4 of 1354 Fasli (1945), p. 10.

286 Finance Department, Supply Branch, H.E.H. the Nizam's Government, S. No. 530, *File* No. 153/1353 Fasli (1944), p. 38.

287. *Golkonda Patrika* (Daily), 17-10-1950 (See the f.n. 284 above).

288. Finance Department, Supply Branch, H.E.H. the Nizam's Government, S. No. 74, *File* No. 8/D4 of 1354 Fasli (1945), p. 10 ; *Golkonda Patrika* (Daily), 21-12-1950.

289. *Meezan*, 29-4-1947 (Editorial).

290. *Golkonda Patrika* (Daily), 1-1-1950.

291. W.S. *File* No. 169 of 1356 Fasli (1947) & R. No. 73 of 1357 Fasli-(1948).

292. *Ibid.*

293. *Golkonda Patrika* (Daily), 1-1-1950.

294. *The Deccan Chronicle*, 16-2-1949.

295. *A Summary of Hyderabad's War Effort, 1939-44* (Government Central Press ; Hyderabad-Dn, 1944), p. 19.

296. Herein after referred to as H.C.C.C.

297. A Summary of Hyderabad's War Effort, 1939-44, *op cit.*, p. 18.

298. These Banks which covered 61% of the total number of villages in the State, could be formed in every village where 75% of cultivators were willing to join it. The noticeable feature was that 1/8th of the levy grain collected from ryots was kept as deposit to be lent to landless labourers and petty cultivators—*Hyderabad Government Bulletin on Economic Affairs*, Vol. II, No. 2, (February, 1949), p. 162 ; *The Deccan Chronicle*, 15-7-1949.

299. Grain Banks increased in number from 17 in 1938-39 to 13,828 in 1949—*A.R. for 1349 Fasli* (*6-10-39 to 6-10-40*), (Hyderabad-Deccan, 1942), p. 84 ; *Hyderabad Government Bulletin on Economic Affairs*, Vol. II, No. 2, (February, 1949), p. 162.

300. Whereas the local money lenders squeezed out 25% interest per quarter, the Grain Banks charged the same rate of interest per annum—R.V. Rao, *op. cit.*, p. 310.
301. Rural Reconstruction Secretariat, H.E.H. the Nizam's Government, *File* No. 41/58 & S. No. 35 of 1358 Fasli (1949), pp. 9-10 ; Immediate Agrarian Problems, *op. cit.*, p. 61.
302. Secretariat Records of H.E.H. the Nizam's Government, Agriculture Department, *File* No. 45/59 of 1359 Fasli (1950) & S. No. 92, p. 37.
303. *Golkonda Patrika* (Daily), 14-7-1950.
304. Agriculture Department, H.E.H. the Nizam's Government, S. No. 92 & *File* No. 45/59 of 1359 Fasli (1950), p. 39.
305. RARC, *op. cit.*, p. 171.
306. Rural Reconstruction Secretariat, H.E.H, the Nizam's Government, *File*, No. 36/58 & S. No. 36 of 1358 Fasli (1949), p. 7.
307. *Meezan*, 15-8-1944, p. 3 ; *Golkonda Patrika* (Daily), 17-10-1950.
308. *Golkonda Patrika* (Letter to the editor), 17-10-1950 ; 29-10-1950 (Correspondent's report).
309. *Meezan*, 1-9-1944 ; 5-4-1945 ; *Golkonda Patrika* (Daily), 5-12-1950.
310. See the Section 'Crop Conditions' in Chapter V.
311. A kind of pulse that is infrequently used in *dai* preparation in the area, but mostly consumed by the poor people directly, either raw or boiled.
312. W.S. *File* No. 15 of 1356 Fasli (1947) & R. No. 14 of 1356 Fasli; The *Deccan Chronicle* (Editorial), 1-10-1947.
313. This aspect was discussed in detail in Chapter VIII.
314. A.I. Qureshi, *op. cit.*, p. 314.
315. Small and red-coloured grain used by some of the poorer sections in rural parts.
316. Among Telangana Districts, only Adilabad (its northern and Western Taluqs) shared features of Marathwada and Karnataka region in respect of cropping pattern, especially, wheat and cotton growing and less of paddy cultivation. Hence Clubbing See the Section 'Rivers' in Chapter II.
317. *Hyderabad Information*, Vol. V, No. 3, Dai, 1354 Fasli (November, 1944), p. 9.
318. These percentages are calculated by comparing the two paddy rates and two in respect of other food crops stated above.
319. The yield figures given in lbs. (see the Section 'Agricultural Production and Yield per acre' in this Chapter) are converted into Mds @ 80 lbs per maund (though Oxford Concise Dictionary has given 82 2/7 lbs per Indian maund, for easy calculation, it is rounded off to 80 lbs).
320. See the Section 'Agricultural Production and Yield per acre' in this chapter.
321. Both the *abi* & *tabi* paddy levy rates cited in the para are taken into consideration for percentage calculation.

322. Finance Department (Resource Branch), H.E.H. the Nizam's Government, S. No. 522, *File* No. 4240 of 1353 Fasli (1944), p. 22. (Percentages are calculated and not given).
323. It consisted of 2 village officials and 5 residents of the village, invariably from the landlords section to give advice on all foodgrain matters and help in the collection of levy *The Deccan Chronicle*, 28-6-1949.
324. *Hyderabad Information*, Vol. V, No. 2. Dai, 1354 Fasli (November, 1944), p 9.
325. Means in Urdu 'Voluntary Purchase'. But, in this respect, it turned out to be a compulsory sale.
326. See the above para.
327. *Meezan*, 9-2-1947 (Announcement of Sri Baddam Yella Reddy, General Secretary, Andhra *Maha Sabha*).
328. *Meezan*, 4-1-1947.
329. *Ibid*.
330. Finance Department, (Resource Branch), H.E.H. the Nizam's Government, S. No. 522, *File* No. 424/53 of 1353 Fasli (1944) p. 22.
331. *Meezan*, 4-1-1947 (3 maunds made one *palla* of 120 *seers*).
332. See the above para for standard yields of paddy in the *Suba* Districts.
333. *Meezan*, 7-2-1946 : (Announcement of Sri Baddam Yella Reddy, General Secretary of Andhra *Maha Sabha*). It was reported that some times, the small and middle farmers, in order to meet the enlarged levy demand by taking the grain from big landlords and merchants on 1½ '*Nagu*' or in other words, return the grain on harvest at 1½ times the grain taken. These exigencies of the ryots were reported from Sirsilla and Jagtiyal Taluqs of Karimnagar District. Other *Suba* Taluqs, though not reported in writing, did not remain an exception to these practices—*Meezan*, 9-9-1944. (For information on Jagtial Taluq).
334. *Meezan*, 7-2-1946 (Announcement...as above).
335. *The Deccan Chronicle*, 14-7-1949.
336. *Meezan*, 7-2-1946 (Announcement...as above); A.I.S.P.C. *File* No. 67/46-47, Part I, p. 303 ; W.S. *File* No. 142 of 1355 Fasli (1946) & R. No. 30 of 1356 Fasli (1947).
337. See the above para for remarks on this aspect.
338. *Meezan*, 7-2-1946 (Announcement...as above); A.I.S P.C. *Files* No. 67 & 68/46-47, Part I, pp. 303 & 112 respectively.
339. W.S. *File* No. 16 of 1355 Fasli (1946) & R. No. 69 of 1356 Fasli (1947).
340. See the second para in this sub-section.
341. See the last two paras in sub-section 'i. Rationing & Public Distribution system' in this Chapter.
342. '*Tarugu*' means less in weightage that is likely to occur later due to individual difference in weighing and also the grain getting drier, but 6 *seers* per *palla* deduction on this count was very much heavier—S.W. *File* No. 45 of 1357 Fasli (1948) & R. No. 462 of 1357 Fasli-3 maunds made one *palla* of 120 *seers*.

343. At Parkal, Taluq headquarters in Karimnagar District, *First Taluqdar* in his tour in January, 1948 found that 800 carts with levy grain were lying there since four days as there was only one balance—W.S. *File* No. 23 of 1357 Fasli (1948) & R. No. 465 of 1357 Fasli.
344. W.S. *File* No. 105 of 1355 Fasli (1946) & R. No. 98 of 1356 Fasli (1947).
345. *Meezan*, 10-10-1945, (A.M.S. Khammam Taluq resolutions).
346. For definition of '*Asaldars*' & '*Gumasthas*' see Section 'Villages' in Chapter III. Good number of embezzlement cases are recorded. Among them a few : W.S. *File* No. 30 of 1354 Fasli (1945) & R. No. 6 of 1357 Fasli (1948) ; W.S. *File* No. 38 of 1355 Fasli (1946) & R. No. 2803 of 1355 Fasli & W.S. *File* No. 43 of 1357 Fasli (1948) & R. No. 2272 of 1357 Fasli.
347. W.S. *File* No. 105 of 1355 Fasli (1946) & R No. 98 of 1356 Fasli (1947) ; *Meezan*, 22-2-1946 ; 5-4-1945 (Announcement of K. Rajalingam, Congress leader of Warangal District).
348. W.S. *File* No. 25 of 1355 Fasli (1946) & R. No. 71 of 1356 Fasli (Manhandling of Second *Taluqdar* of Huzurabad division by villagers of Kesavapur in Huzurabad Taluq) ; A.I.S.P.C. *File* No. 70 (Part I) of 1947-48 (Killing of one Revenue Inspector by the villagers of Chowtapalli and Mallavaram in Huzurabad Taluq : injuring of five Revenue Officials in Sirpur Taluq of Adilabad District) ; *Golkonda Patrika* (Daily), 17-1-1948 (Killing of six Revenue Inspectors in Boath Taluq of Adilabad District) & W.S. *File* No. 15 of 1356 Fasli (1947) & R. No. 14 of 1356 Fasli (Beating of Special *Girdavar* by villagers of Mangapet in Borgampahad Taluq of Warangal District).
349. There are good number of records that testify to the impact of the Communists in *Suba* area ; out of them some specimens ; Financial Secretary & Financial Adviser, Supply Finance, H.E.H. the Nizam's Government, S. No. 28 & *File* No. 6/A6/1359 Fasli (1950), Regarding Warangal District) ; W.S. *File* No. 23 of 1355 Fasli (1946) & R. No. 70 of 1356 Fasli (1947), (Relating to Karimnagar District. Also of *Arya Samaj* influence there) ; W.S. *Files* No. 43 of 1355 Fasli (1946) & R.No 68 of 1356 Fasli (1947), (Rajpura, Adilabad, Kinwat, Luxettipet and Chinnoor Taluqs of Adilabad District) ; 15 of 1356 Fasli (1947) & R. No. 14 of, 1356 Fasli (Nirmal Taluq of Adilabad District) ; *The Deccan Chronicle*, 18-11-1948 (Regarding Congress appeal).
350. W.S. *File* No. 25 of 1355 Fasli (1946) & R. No. 71 of 1356 Fasli (1947).
351. For an account of these lapses, see the sub-sections 'i. Rationing and public Distribution System' & 'ii. Procurement Policy and its wide-ranging effects' of this chapter.
352. See the sub-section 'ii. Procurement Policy and its wide-ranging effects' in this chapter.
353. *The Deccan Chronicle*, 18-11-1948.
354. W.S. *File* No. 43 of 1355 Fasli (1946) and R. No. 68 of 1356 Fasli

(1947). For all accounts of the political background of Communists, Congress and Maharashtra *Parishad*, see the Section 'Political Conditions' in Chapter III.

355. See the Section 'Pattern of Land utilisation' in this chapter.
356. See the Sections 'Crop acreage' and 'Agricultural Production and yield per acre' in this chapter.
357. See chapter V for these aspects.
358. See the sub-section 'Non-food Crops' regardirg acreage and cutturn in this chapter.
359. Refer to the sub-sections, 'Price Controls,' 'Rationing and Public Distribution System' in this chapter.
360. Refer to the sub-section 'ii. Procurement Policy and its wide-ranging effects' in this chapter.
361. Communists are also known by this term, since their flag is in this colour.

CHAPTER SEVEN

INDUSTRIAL PRODUCTION, LABOUR, TRADE AND TRANSPORT

COMPARED to total population of the *Suba* Districts in 1911,[1] the number of those who earned their livelihood by industries including mines,[2] formed 17.80, 23.93 and 11.18% in the respective Districts of Warangal, Karimnagar and Adilabad.[3] Karimnagar District, in fact, with 239 out of every 1,000 persons of the total population pursuing industrial occupation, ranked high over all other Districts in the State,[4] mainly because of its predominance in the cottage industries of spinning and weaving of cotton and woollen fabrics, carpentry, brick and tiles, pottery and poultry.[5] It is important to realise that though the population supported by industry formed only 33.29, 51.38 and 16.61% of that dependent on agriculture in Warangal, Karimnagar and Adilabad Districts respectively;[6] yet, next to agriculture, industry became the major occupation of the people.[7] Industrial Production, and to a lesser extent, that of the agriculture,[8] was influenced by the working conditions, amenities and wages that were made available to labour who, next to peasantry, formed a sizeable section of the *Suba* population in the sense that they averaged from 0.3 to 0.4 per every cultivator in the field of agriculture[9] and factory workers employed per day in 1935 came of the order of 5,509, 1,028 and 1,059 in Warangal, Karimnagar and Adilabad Districts respectively.[10] In fact, Warangal with its leading textile mill of Azamjahi,[11] employing daily labour of 2,305[12] and Singareni Collieries engaging 7,560 in 1937-38,[13] the highest for any enterprise in the State, besides good number of rice, oil and flour mills, came to be the biggest labour-employed District in the State. Import and export trade that the region had mainly with neighbouring British Indian Provinces and to some extent with Western countries, had considerable bearing on the economic fortunes of the people for, whereas coal, paper, cotton and cottonseed, castor-seed, groundnut, *sesamum*, cattle, hides and skins, cotton textiles, handloom products of cotton, silk and wool, formed the chief items of export, it depended on imports from outside for piece-goods, yarn, salt, sugar, jaggery, kerosene oil, iron, tobacco, silk, fruits and also cattle.[11] Fluctuations in prices of agricultural, as well as manufactured articles that characterised the period since the commencement of the First Great War had, besides variations in crop outturns, had considerable influence on the balance of trade position, especially in view of the fact that the exports being primarily raw and unmanufactured fetched lesser prices in Indian and foreign markets compared to imports which remained mostly manufactured products.[15] Development of transport and communications formed, in fact, the nucleus for the all round economic development of the area. Agricultural marketing exports and imports of industrial goods and raw materials, mobility of labour and in fact, the supply of essential articles of non-local nature such as yarn to weavers, iron to ryots, kerosene, salt, tobacco etc., to the general population, had all been linked to the availability of good means of transport and communication. This development necessity became all the more significant in the Eastern Division in view of its vast forest and mineral resources and the backwardness of the people in tribal and forest areas.[16] But, the vital limb of road and rail transport did not receive the growth to the required level, so much so that, the P.W.D. estimate of the Post-War Period of the forties, found that the shortage worked out to 27.80% in Warangal, 64.03% in Karimnagar and 56.84% in Adilabad Districts.[17] Postal and telephone facilities proved further deficient.[18] A critical study of these factors of economic development would help in having a proper and fuller assessment of the forces at work in the economic history of the *Suba*.

A. *INDUSTRIAL ORGANISATION, MANAGEMENT AND FINANCE*

It could be seen from Tables XLI and XLII, that in *Suba* Districts, cottage or village industries far outnumbered large industrial establishments which were usually located at urban centres. Further, the bigger units among the latter such as the Singareni Collieries, the Azamjahi Mills, the Sirpur Paper Mills and the Carpet Factory at Warangal, had very much functioned as Government enterprises, for it looked after their financial and managerial wings, through Industrial Trust Fund, an agency created for this purpose in 1929[19]. On the other hand, the home-based industries such as spinning, weaving, printing, dyeing, tailoring, smithy, brick and tiles-making and basket manufacturing, involved only marginal investment and little additional labour over and above the members of the family. Besides, these trades continued as hereditary callings since countless generations in most of the families. Again, among these several cottage industries that formed part of village activity, hand-ginning of cotton, *Charkha* spinning of yarn and handloom weaving were so prominent that more than 75% of the total units in the *Suba* Districts and also of the State, had been covered by them (See Table XLII). Handloom weaving, next to agriculture, became such an important occupation of the people in the State that 3 to 4% of the total population or 4.77 lakhs of workers daily earned their livelihood by this means and the cloth woven by them met the clothing requirements of half of the total population.[20] Warangal, Hanamkonda, Warangal Fort, Karimabad, Urus, Sainpet, Waddepalli, Kazipet, Hasanparthi (all in Warangal Taluq of Warangal District), Narsapur (Mulug Taluq of Warangal District), Sirsilla (Sirsilla Taluq of Karimnagar District), Karimnagar (Karimnagar Taluq of the same District), Mahadeopuram (Mahadeopuram Taluq of the same District), Nirmal, Chinnoor and Adilabad (Respective Taluqs of Adilabad District), served as notable centres of this most important cottage industry in Warangal *Suba*.[21] *Shalis*, *Telingas*[22] among Hindus, *Julahas*[23] and *Momins* among Muslims had

TABLE XLI

Number of Cottage Industries* in Warangal Suba and State in 1941

Sl. No.	Districts	No. of handlooms			No. of spindles or *Charkas* at work of spinning yarn out of cotton	No. of houses or establishments containing two or more persons not being weavers who were engaged in dyeing yarn or cloth
		Cotton	Silk	Wool		
1	2	3	4	5	6	7
1.	Warangal	6,848	229	521	9,715	101
2.	Karimnagar	13,344	35	1,807	57,277	136
3.	Adilabad	3,246	29	47	19,827	351
	State Total	79,584	4,547	11,312	1,72,821	1,905

	No. of houses or establishments containing two or more persons not being weavers who were engaged in printing cloth	No. of hand cotton ginning machines at work	No. of tailoring establishments composed of two or more tailors using sewing establishments	Total No. of sewing machines used at tailoring establishments	No. of oil *ghanies*** at work driven by hand or bullock power	No. of sugar-cane pressing mills at work driven by hand or bullock power	No. of printing presses and Litho (hand)
	8	9	10	11	12	13	14
1. Warangal	50	1,256	586	778	394	11	17
2. Karimnagar	27	6,391	584	694	949	64	6
3. Adilabad	154	2,464	340	494	1,442	112	2
State Total	898	25,020	8,487	12,531	10,372	6,125	135

	No. of smithy workshops composed of two black-smiths	No. of gold and silver smiths	No. of Metal workshops	No. of carpenters' workshops composed of two or more carpenters including cabinet workers, wheel smiths and book builders	No. of painters' workshops where toys are painted, boxes, plates, stationery boxes, playing cards, etc. were made	No. of potters' establishments composed of two or more potters	No. of brick and tile works
	15	16	17	18	19	20	21
1. Warangal	695	752	346	891	25	1,035	96
2. Karimnagar	1,003	1,389	378	1,298	15	1,440	255
3. Adilabad	685	603	235	892	16	573	96
State Total	8,466	9,267	3,283	11,047	242	10,337	1,685

	No. of dairy establishments where butter and ghee was manufactured	Modern cream-separating machines at work	Poultry farms	No. of tanneries	No. of cane and bamboo workshops	No. of basket manufactories	No. of soap factories
	22··	23··	24	25	26	27	28
1. Warangal	11	12	25	58	117	325	5
2. Karimnagar	5	9	1,267	95	30	462	2
3. Adilabad	—	—	21	114	17	244	—
State Total	977	53	1,834	3,042	502	3,922	60

*Those industries which required a capital of Rs. 500 to 1,000 and employed only unskilled labour. I.S., *op. cit.*, p. 4.

··In *Industrial Statistics, H.E.H. the Nizam's Government, 1935-45*, p. 261, the dairy establishments in 1940 of Warangal, Karimnagar and Adilabad Districts were given as 110,6 and 7 respectively and cream separators as 19 for Warangal and blank for other Districts.

**Country type of oil mills in which a roller, operated by human or bullock-power was used in crushing the oil seed.

∴In *Industrial Statistics, 1935-45, H.E.H. the Nizam's Government*, p. 287, this number was given as 791 which looks more probable.

Source : *Census of India, 1941*, vol. XXI, *H.E.H. the Nizam's Dominions* (Hyderabad State), *Part I—Report*, pp. 764-65.

TABLE XLII

Taluqa-wise Enumeration of Large Industrial Establishments* and Average Number of Persons Employed in 1931 & 1936 (1340 & 1345 Fasli) in Warangal Suba

S. No.	Industry	Warangal	Khammam	Mahabubabad	Madhira	Pakhal	Paloncha
1	2	3	4	5	6	7	8
1.	Government Local fund Factories	3	1	2	—	—	—
	I. *Textiles*						
2.	Cotton spinning and weaving Mills	1	—	—	—	—	—
3.	Ginning Factories	10	5	—	6	—	—
4.	Pressing Factories	2	1	—	2	—	—
	II. *Engineering*	—	—	—	—	—	—
	III. *Minerals and Metals*	—	—	—	—	—	—
	IV. *Food, Drink and Tobacco*						
5.	Rice and Pulse Mills	6	6	8	9	—	—
6.	Oil Mills	3	2	1	1	—	—
7.	Decorticators	2	4	2	4	—	—
	V. *Chemicals & Drugs*						
8.	Bones and Manures	2	—	—	—	—	—
9.	Matches	—	—	—	—	—	—
	VI. *Wood, Stone, Cement, Lime & Glass*	—	—	—	—	—	—
	VI. All other Factories	—	—	—	—	—	—
10.	Total for 1345 Fasli (1936)	29	19	14	22	—	—
11.	Total for 1340 Fasli (1931)	22	6	2	1	—	—
	Average number of persons employed						
12.	In 1345 Fasli (1936)	4,322	853	1,364	540	—	—
13.	In 1340 Fasli (1931)	719	161	234	263	—	—

		Mulug	Yellandu	District Total	Karimnagar	Jagtiyal	Huzurabad	Mahadeopur	Parkal
		9	10	11	12	13	14	15	16
1.	Government Local fund Factories	—	1	7	2	2	1	—	1
	I. Textiles								
2.	Cotton spinning and weaving Mills		—	1	—	—	—	—	—
3.	Ginning Factories	—	—	21	3	—	2	—	—
4.	Pressing Factories	—	—	5	3	—	—	—	—
	II. *Engineering*	—	—	—	—	—	—	—	—
	III. *Minerals and Metals*	—	—	—	—	—	—	—	—
	IV. *Food, Drink and Tobacco*								
5.	Rice and Pulse Mills	—	4	33	2	—	1	—	—
6.	Oil Mills	—	—	7	1	—	—	—	—
7.	Decorticators	—	1	13	—	—	1	—	—
	V. *Chemicals & Drugs*								
8.	Bones and Manures	—	—	2	—	—	—	—	—
9.	Matches	—	—	1	—	—	—	—	—
	VI. *Wood, Stone, Cement, Lime & Glass*	—	1	1	—	—	—	—	—
	VII. All other factories	—	—	—	—	—	—	—	—
10.	Total for 1345 Fasli (1936)	—	7	91	11	2	5	—	1
11.	Total for 1340 Fasli (1931)	—	2	33	—	—	1	—	—
	Average number of persons employed								
12.	In 1345 Fasli (1936)	—	386	7,465	440	318	204	—	24
13.	In 1340 Fasli (1931)	—	37	1,414	—	—	156	—	—

		Sirsilla	Sultanabad	District Total	Adilabad	Chinnoor	Asifabad	Luxettipet
		17	18	19	20	21	22	23
1.	Government Local fund Factories	1	—	7	1	1	1	—
	I. *Textiles*							
2.	Cotton spinning and weaving Mills	—	—	—	—	—	—	—
3.	Ginning Factories	—	—	5	3	—	—	—
4.	Pressing Factories	—	—	3	—	—	—	—
	II. *Engineering*	—	—	—	—	—	—	—
	III. *Minerals & Metals*	—	—	—	—	—	—	—
	IV. *Food, Drink and Tobacco*							
5.	Rice and Pulse Mills	—	—	3	—	—	—	—
6.	Oil Mills	—	—	1	—	—	—	—
7.	Decorticators	—	—	1	—	—	—	—
	V. *Chemicals & Drugs*							
8.	Bones and Manures	—	—	—	—	—	—	—
9.	Matches	—	—	—	—	—	—	—
	VI. *Wood, Stone, Cement, Lime & Glass*	—	—	—	—	—	—	—
	VII. All other factories	—	—	—	—	—	—	—
10.	Total for 1345 Fasli (1936)	1	4	20	4	1	1	1
11.	Total for 1340 Fasli (1931)	—	—	5	4	4	—	1
	Average number of persons employed							
12.	In 1345 Fasli (1936)	252	—	1,238	269	174	251	—
13	In 1340 Fasli (1931)	—	195	351	205	—	—	40

		Kinwat	Nirmal	Rajura	Sirpur	Boath	Utnoor	District Total
		24	25	26	27	28	29	30
1.	Government Local fund Factories	—	—	—	*** —	—	—	3
	I. *Textiles*							
2.	Cotton spinning and weaving Mills	—	—	—	—	—	—	—
3.	Ginning Factories	2	4	3	—	—	—	12
4.	Pressing Factories	—	—	2	—	—	—	2
	II. *Engineering*	—	—	—	—	—	—	—
	III. *Minerals & Metals*	—	—	—	—	—	—	—
	IV. *Food, Drink and Tobacco*							
5.	Rice and Pulse Mills	—	—	—	—	—	—	—
6.	Oil Mills	—	2	1	—	—	—	3
7.	Decorticators	—	1	—	—	—	—	1
	V. *Chemicals & Drugs*							
8.	Bones and Manures	—	—	—	—	—	—	—
9.	Matches	—	—	—	—	—	—	—
	VI. *Wood, Stone, Cement, Lime & Glass*	—	—	—	—	—	—	—
	VII. All other factories							
10.	Total for 1345 Fasli (1936)	2	7	6	—	—	—	21
11.	Total for 1340 Fasli (1936)	—	2	1	1	—	2	11
	Average number of persons employed							

		24	25	26	27	28	29	30
12.	In 1345 Fasli (1936)	72	305	338	—	—	—	1,409
13.	In 1340 Fasli (1931)	—	265	—**	255	—	—	765

*Those industries which required Rs. 50,000 & above as capital and employed persons above 20 that included considerable skilled labour. I.S. *op. cit.*, pp. 3 & 4.

**Though one Mill was shown in the column of Rajura, persons employed was indicated as blank. As the District total in the latter case has tallied, it must be understood that the said Factory remained shut at the time of enumeration.

***Paper Factory was started in 1942.

Source : *Hyderabad District Gazetteers*, Tables Vols. *1340 & 1345 Fasli* (*1931 & 1936*).
Warangal, pp. 404-407 & 412-413 ;
Karimnagar, pp. 400-403 & 406-407
&
Adilabad, pp. 400-405 & 408-409.

been the communities that mainly took to weaving in the region.[24]

Even large establishments, though they were not very much rural-based, they, on the other hand, as could be seen from Table XLI, remained predominantly agro-based. The industries based on cotton, food products and oilseeds, even leaving out Government or Local Fund Factories among which also some did belong to this category[25], formed 92.30, 81.81 and 85.71% in Warangal, Karimnagar and Adilabad Districts respectively.[26] Among the Districts, there was however, difference regarding the proportion of industries based on cotton on one hand and those based on food products and oilseeds. The relevant proportion in Warangal, Karimnagar and Adilabad Districts had been 27 : 53, 8 : 5 and 14 : 4 respectively.[27] These numbers speak out three things ; first, in both the categories and in fact, in the total number of large industrial establishments, Warangal Districts far outweighed the other two Districts, which in turn, was chiefly due to the better transport facilities and availability of investment capital in the hands of big landlords and businessmen[28], and also power facilities[29] which, some of its Taluqs like Warangal, Khammam, Madhira and Mahaboobabad had possessed in far higher degree compared to other *Suba* Taluqs ; the number of cotton gins, and presses compared to rice and oil mills was higher in Karimnagar and Adilabad Districts than in the case of Warangal District, because of higher production of cotton in the former compared to the latter[30] and also because of lesser, capital investment and labour potential that was involved in the case of former type of industries than in the case of the latter ; third, though Karimnagar District had higher outturn of rice, gram and *sesamum*, though not groundnut and castor, than Warangal District[31], yet, the number of industries based on these agricultural products in the former District formed only one-tenth of those that were run in the latter District,[32] which again, was due to the prevalence of poor transport facilities, especially by rail, lack of power facilities and more so, sufficient capital for industrial investment not coming from landlordly element and poor attraction of outside capital[33] by the former as against better conditions in these respects in the latter.

Another important factor deserving to be noted in respect of the organisation of these agro-based industries was that almost all the cotton ginning and pressing factories remained seasonal in character, the work usually extending from December to March in a year and in order to get engaged during the off-season, took to rice milling, groundnut decorticating and also oil extraction.[34] The extent of combining depended on the capital resources of the mill owners and in a way was responsible for the total number of units seeming less, especially in Karimnagar and Adilabad Districts. Further, there was unequal distribution and rather heavy concentration of these units at particular urban centres. The Census of large industrial establishments that was taken for the year ending in March, 1941, showed that out of 33 factories of this mixed type in Warangal District, 17 were from Warangal Taluq, out of which again, 14 were located in Warangal town, similarly, out of 8 factories in Khammam Taluq of the same District, as many as 7 were located in Khammam town ; out of 7 factories in the entire District of Karimnagar, 4 were there in Peddapalli, a Taluq headquarters town and the remaining 3 at Jammikunta in Huzurabad Taluq ; and out of 13 of this type in Adilabad District, as many as 5 had been there in Adilabad Taluq and all of which were located in Adilabad town, the Taluq as well as District headquarters.[35] It was a clear indication of the flight of rural capital into urban areas, for these concerns had been mostly owned by big landlords and excise contractors of rural eminence.[36] This, together with 75 to 100% concentration at headquarters towns, had immensely affected the chances of employment for rural agriculturists and labour and the better exploitation of agricultural produce of several villages that were distant from these urban centres had been severely impaired due to lack of easy and cheap means of transport.[37] Further, due to heavy concentration at one place, the units ran in an uneconomical manner in the sense that they failed to get enough raw produce for exploitation,[38] but however, kept on their existence by the socialist way of dividing the returns at a place among all the concerns, whosoever turned out the work to any extent.[39]

ii. *Management* : The management of those industrial concerns in which Government held major shares or advanced huge loans was kept by itself and the Industrial Trust Fund discharged this duty on its behalf.[40] The Trust, in turn, instead of exercising direct supervision over these establishments appointed its Representatives or agents like Mr. C.S. Tyabjee, a noted industrialist to look after the affairs of Azamjahi Mills,[41] and these Representatives, for carrying on the work on behalf of the Trust, received 80 to 50% of the Commission which the latter claimed from the Concern.[42] It thus proved to be a combination of Government's financial backing put to use by Private managerial talent. But yet, there was too much dependence of these industries on the financial support and guidance of the Trust Fund and there was very less of private initiative and enterprise, the consequence of which was that, barring Singareni Collieries and Azamjahi Mills, the rest of the Trust-managed concerns failed to register co-ordinated growth[43] and, in fact, the Government was put to such sore straits that it felt itself unable to finance the expansion plan of Sirpur Paper Mills[44] and the installation of Sirsilk Factory at the same place[45] and both were, in 1953, turned over to the managing agency of Messrs Birla Brothers Ltd., a well-known Capitalist agency of the North and the Government Carpet Factory at Warangal was even closed down before 1949-50.[46] There was no proper check on the use of the loans provided by the Trust, as a result of which, the industries spent disproportionately large amounts on initial capital items such as huge buildings and imported machinery which over-burdened the cost structure and led to a shortage afterwards.[47]

The management of cottage industries and also of others whose capital investment was not much and in which Government had no shares, was left to the individual proprietors or Joint-Stock Companies. As far as village or home-based industries were concerned, the number of work force being confined from 2 to 5 persons, the owner also, invariably took part in the process of production, besides supervising over the work of others. It could be gathered from the census of those industrial establishments that were not under Governmental management, taken from the year ending in March, 1941 that joint proprietorship was in greater vogue in Cotton ginning, pressing and factories of the mixed type, whereas in the case of exclusive rice or oil mills, individual or single ownership was noticeable.[48] Taken as a whole, the former type was in wider prevalence, which very much suited the average economic soundness of many of the smaller industrialists of the region. Single proprietorship, on the other hand, represented bigger feudal and business interests and tended towards greater concentration of wealth.

iii. *Finance* : As majority of cottage, small-scale[49] and even larger industrial owners were not financially independent or self-sufficient, industrial growth in the area basically depended on the extent of the availability of short and long term credit. Industrial Trust Fund, Banks and indigeneous bankers formed the industrial credit agencies. But, the credit extended by these agencies proved very much inadequate to the requirement[50] and more so, in the case of smaller units. Advances from the Fund were usually extended to large-scale industries for fixed items of capital expenditure whose repayment was spread over long period of yearly instalments.[51] Though it was provided that loans and grants would be made for the development of small and cottage industries from out of the annual profits, ranging upto 4 lakhs of rupees, that accrued to the Trust by its investments in large-scale industries, yet, it being a Governmental affair, the usual delay and red tape that was involved in undergoing the procedure for the sanction of the loan and mortgaging of property and further, ignorance in rural and remoter parts about this credit facility, had led to poor utilisation.[52] The loan of Rs. 2,17,950 sanctioned free of interest by the Government to help cottage Industries during the first ten year period of Trust Fund commencing from 1929, was not fully utilised in the entire Dominions.[53] Even in respect of small-scale industries also, an amount of O.S. Rs. 5½ lakhs had been advanced in the State as a whole during the long period of 1929 to 1941 in the shape of 84 loans to 75 different parties.[54] Only heavy industries like Singareni Collieries, Azamjahi Mills, Sirpur Paper Mills, etc., in which Government held huge shares, received substantial financial assistance from the Trust Fund.[55]

b. Banks : The policy adopted by the Imperial and Joint-Stock Banks in the State was not encouraging for the industrial development of the area.[56] They came to regard Hyderabad as a deposit-receiving centre rather than a centre for investments.[57] The percentage of loans on all accounts to the deposits of all kinds received locally by the Imperial Bank and the Central Bank, the two leading Banks in Hyderabad, was surprisingly small and ranged from 5 in 1925 to 19 in 1929 in the case of the former and 35 to 24 in the case of the latter.[58] Further, the delay, formalities and strict securities that were demanded for the issue of bank loans discouraged needy industrialists and handicraftsmen so much that they became very much prepared to take the help from the local bankers and *sahukars*, even at higher rates of interest, for the latter comparatively were found much freer, informal and sympathetic in loan advancement, though of course, quite prompt and strict in collection.[59] Right until the end of the period of present study, banks, including the State Bank of Hyderabad started in April, 1942, played only a minor role as a source of industrial finance. They remained as yet commercial banks financing trade and commerce[60] and indulging in profitable exchange business.[61]

c. Indigenous Bankers and Sahukars : When Government and Joint-stock Banks, thus provided industrial credit only in a limited sphere and manner, the field for credit operations of bankers and money-lenders became wide open. Most of the bankers were *Marwaris*.[62] They had their head-offices or branches in the cities in British India. Whereas these carried on their business in Urban centres, the *Sahukars*[63] transacted in Districts. They operated largely on their own funds accrued from lending activity and subsidiary occupations such as agriculture, industry, trade, business, etc., and did not indulge in deposit-receiving from the public unlike banks.[64] Though their methods had been swift and secret and did involve much of documentation and delay, the rate of interest remained high.[65] 12 to 15% was charged in case of carpet weavers of

Warangal who took short loans from master-weavers,[66] but the most troublesome stipulation was that the finished products were to be sold only to their creditors.[67] The one factor which dealt a crushing blow to the prosperity of handloom weaving and other handicraft or cottage works like Nirmal toy making, Warangal carpet weaving, etc., and also the economic condition of weavers and craftsmen was that due to the ignorance, financial poverty and lack of credit either from the Government or the Banks to the latter, the local *sahukars* took into their hands both the supply of yarn, dyes or other raw material and the sale of finished goods and those who toiled and worked at them were paid piece-wages which, when analysed, proved to be less than what the unskilled labourers received.[68] As a result, many of the weavers in the villages took up to agricultural labour during crop season, as they failed to get sufficient work or wages in their traditional occupation.[69] It would be significant to note that this miserable condition of the industry and the craftsmen was due to the failure of the Government, Co-operative Societies and the Banks, in coming to their rescue by providing easy credit to purchase the raw material or themselves supply it in view of the blackmarketing and consequent high prices that prevailed during the forties,[70] which would, in turn, have enabled the weavers and the craftsmen to sell their products in open market and enjoy whatever benefit that would accrue over the cost price.

d. Foreign and Public Investment : No outside invest ment was noticeable in any major industrial concern of the *Suba*, during the period. Its richness in coal, iron-ore, lime-stone and forest resources, opened up vast possibilities for the starting of large-scale industries of steel, cement, thermal power, etc.[71] In fact, efforts were made in 1940 by the Hyderabad Construction Company[72] to start an iron and steel industry in Hyderabad with the co-operation of a French Company. But, the London Political Department fearing that the proposed industry would be endangering the extension of the British Indian industry suggested to the *Nizam* through Resident that it must be ensured that more than 50%

of the capital was subscribed by State-cum-British interests. There ended the matter.[73] This was how sometimes the *Nizam* and at other times he, acting under the strong suggestions of his English mentors,[74] slammed the door against entry of foreign capital into Hyderabad and also vice versa.[75] The lack of industrial power except at Warangal apart from its cheapness was also an important factor that discouraged and dissuaded the foreign capitalists from industrial investment in the area, even though they had been free from income and professional taxes.[76] A rich source of investment had thus been lost, rather by a deliberate and unwise policy at a time when the indigenous agencies could not meet a large part of industrial credit needs.

Public investment in industries by means of purchasing shares or indirectly by contributing to deposits in Post Office Savings Banks and Joint-Stock Banks was meagre and insignificant. Besides the incomes of majority of the populace being low, fluctuating and precarious, the institutional efforts for deposit mobilisation at least from the higher income groups, were not upto the mark. The per capita savings in the Post Office Savings Banks for the *Suba* in 1931 and 1945 for which the figures are available, stood at such a dismally low point as Rs. 0.21 and Rs. 1.26 respectively.[77] The number of depositors formed a very low proportion of the total population which could be seen from the fact that the amount of saving per depositor in these years in the *Suba* stood at Rs. 152.35 and Rs. 166.68 respectively.[78] Little awareness was brought among the people in rural areas about the existence of Savings Banks and the utility of investment in Savings.[79] On the other hand, the number of Savings Banks in the Districts of Warangal, Karimnagar and Adilabad got reduced from 95, 62 and 58 in 1940 to 31, 18 and 27 in 1945 respectively.[80] Even in respect of deposit-making in Imperial and Joint-Stock Banks, the same attitude of apathy was noticeable on the part of the public, which was due to the rate of interest being regarded as low by the mercantile community and the location of market centres at places where the well-to-do middle class population was absent.[81] Instead of making special efforts by advertisement,

TABLE XLIII

Coal Production in Warangal Suba, 1910-1950

(In Tons & CWT)

Sl. No.	Year	MINES AT Singareni	Sasti-Paoni	Tandur*	Kothagudem	Kanaja	Total Production
1	2	3	4	5	6	7	8
1.	1910	5,06,173	—	—	—	—	5,06,173
2.	1911	5,05,380	—	—	—	—	5,05,380
3.	1912	4,81,652	—	—	—	—	4,81,652
4.	1913	5,52,132	—	—	—	—	5,52,132
5.	1914	5,55,991	—	—	—	—	5,55,991
6.	1915	5,86,823	—	—	—	—	5,86,823
7.	1916	6,14,520	770	—	—	—	6,15,290
8.	1917	6,74,556	6,073	—	—	—	6,80,629
9.	1918	6,47,486	11,634	—	-	—	6,59,121
10.	1919	6,41,473	20,722	—	—	—	6,62,195
11.	1920	6,66,334	27,745	—	—	—	6,94,079
12.	1921	6,46,047-55	42,673-75	—	—	—	6,88,722
13.	1922	6,04,357-7	38,522-25	—	—	—	6,42,880

14.	1923	6,29,224-6	29,204-25	—	—	—	6,58,428-31
15.	1924	6,19,725	25,049-50	—	—	—	6,44,774-50
16.	1925	6,29,724-70	38,152-75	—	—	—	6,67,877-45
17.	1926	6,09,700	28,000	—	—	—	6,37,700
18.	1926-27	...	...	—	—	—	7,07,213
19.	1927-28	...	...	...	—	—	7,34,766
20.	1928-29	...	...	...	—	—	8,15,876
21.	1929-30	...	...	...	—	—	8,12,300
22.	1930-31	...	...	...	—	—	7,57,575
23.	1931-32	...	...	...	—	...**	7,68,611
24.	1932-33	...	...	...	—	...	7,47,387

MINES AT

S. No.	Year	Singareni	Sasti-Paoni	Tandur*	Kothagudem	Kanda	Total Production
1	2	3	4	5	6	7	8
25.	1934	5,27,939-2	42,940-16	1,35,838-3	—	1,08,503-14	8,15,271-15
26.	1935	5,13,259-6	50,585-19	1,63,658-1	—	12,688-0	7,40,191-6
27.	1936	6,99,117-7	63,510-17	2,29,398-0	—	—	9,92,025.·.
28.	1937	7,40,759-17	68,670-14	2,65,624 0	1,175-19. .	—	10,76,240-10
29.	1938	6,90,850-6	90,782-4	3,34,283-0	95,247-15	—	12,11,163-5
30.	1939	6,76,513-7	74,994-16	3,13,155-0	1,49,904-17	—	12,14,568-0
31.	1940	5,39,943-9	71,176,18	3,21,299-0	3,17,702-15	—	12,50,122-2
32.	1941	1,54,164-5	88,793-15	3,47,201-0	7,11,218-12	—	13,01,377-12
33.	1942	::	63,171-11	3,69,421-5	8,44,597-18	—	12,77-190-14
34.	1943-44	—	53,000	3,11,000	5,68,000	—	9,32,000†
35.	1944-45	—	65,000	3,10,000	6,48,000	—	10,23,000††
36.	1945-46	—	...	...	...	...	10,50,692
37.	1946-47	—	...	...	...	...	10,95,000
38.	1947-48	—	...	...	...	...	10,69,536
39.	1948-49	—	...	...	...	...	10,92,436
40.	1949-50	—	...	...	...	...	11,01,000

*These mines were situated at Bellamapalli near Tandur in Adilabad District and were opened in 1927-28.

*=Its output (how much not given) was included in this year's total production.

:The mines were closed in September, 1941, as the mineral was exhausted.

·· Production Commenced in 1937.

∴As against this combined total of the three mines the total production for the year of all these mines was given as 8,52,739 tons in *A.R. 1345 Fasli* (*1935-36*).

+As against this total of three mines put together given in I.S. *op. cit.*, p. 307, the total was given as 9,05,361 tons in *A.R. of C & I. Department, H.E.H. the Nizam's Government for 1353 & 1354 Fasli* (*1944 & 45*), p. 42.

++As against this total of 3 mines put together, given in I.S. *op. cit.*, p. 307, the total was given as 8,78,967 tons in A.R. of C & I. Department, H.E.H. the Nizam's Government for 1353 & 1354 Fasli (1944 & 1945), *op cit.*, p. 42.

—Production not started or stopped.

—Particulars of individual Mines in these years are not available in the sources consulted.

Sources :—*Administrative Reports, H.E.H. the Nizam's Government, 1910 & 1911* (p. 50); 1912 & 1913 (p. 52) ; *1914 & 1915* (p. 32) ; *1916 & 1917* (p. 28); *1918-19* (p. 27): *1920-21* (p. 28) *1922-23* (p. 40) ; *1924-25* (p. 43) *1926* (p. 37) ; *1926-27* (p. 45) ; *1927-28* (p. 57) ; *1928-29* (p. 61); *1929-30* (p. 59) ; *1930-31* (p. 66) ; *1931-32* (p. 67) ; *1932-33* (p. 88) ; *1933-34* (p. 79) : *1934-35* (p. 72) ; *1935-36* (p. 92) ; *1936-37* (p. 100) ; *1937-38* (p. 106) ; *1939* (p. 117) ; *1940* (p. 108) ; *1941*(p. 114) & *1942* (p. 101) ; I.S. *op. cit.*, p. 307., (for 1943-44 to 1944-45)

&

Administrative Report of Commerce and Industries Department, H.E.H the Nizam's Government for 1353 & 1354 Fasli (*1944-45*), p. 42 & *for 1355 Fasli* (*1645-46*), p. 41 ; *Trade Statistics, H.E.H. the Nizam's Government for 1356 Fasli* (*1946-47*), p. 18 ; *Report on the Administration of Hyderabad State, September, 1948 to March, 1950*, p. 204.

propaganda etc., to attract more depositors, these Banks remained content with their existing resources and hence, men of average means failed to become their customers.[82] The ultimate result that followed was that the purchase of shares in large industries was done mainly by the Government or by Managing Agents of capitalistic background. But, this was only in respect of selected few.[83] Rest of them, including small, cottage or home industries were made to get their capital requirements fulfilled from any of the other sources open to them, which, as the foregoing discussion proved,[84] looked bleak and in certain cases, fraught with sad effects.

B. LARGE-SCALE INDUSTRIAL PRODUCTION AND ITS IMPACT ON THE ECONOMY

Coal mining became the earliest large-scale industry in the *Suba* and also the Dominions.[85] Production was always on the rise, except during the 1945-49 quinquennium.[86] The increase was, however, significant in the quinquennia of 1915-19 (6.2 lakh tons compared to previous quinquennium), 1935-39 (13.33 lakh tons) and 1940-44 (5.49 lakh tons), whereas it was less, significant in those of 1920-24 (1.24 lakh tons) and 1925-29 (2.34 lakh tons).[87] 66 to 100% of the total coal output during the period upto 1937 had been contributed by Singareni Coal Mines only and from 1941 when the former were closed due to exhaustion, the Kothagudem Collieries started contributing the major share amounting to 50 to 60%.[88] Among the other mines, those at Sasti-Paoni never, during the period, turned out production touching at least one lakh tons, but on the other hand, the Tandur Mines gradually gained in production to the effect that from 1938 they came to contribute 25 to 30% of the total coal output and occupy second place, next to Kothagudem Mines, since 1941.[89] The decrease in coal production during the last quinquennium was due to 8% decrease suffered in the year 1948 which again, was caused by the disturbed conditions that prevailed before September[90] on account of which, the coal mines had to be closed for several days due to lack of essential supplies.[91]

Though there was increase in coal production for most of

the time, yet the value realised for coal changed appreciably as per variations in price levels. Thus, whereas the increase in production during the quinquennium of 1920-24 over that of 1915-19 was only 1.24 lakh tons, the value realised amounted to an increase of Rs. 55.61 lakhs ; on the other hand, even though coal production rose by 3.37 lakhs during the quinquennium of 1930-34 over that of 1925-29, the value realised fell by as much as 28.58 lakhs of rupees ; and similarly, as against a rise of 5.49 lakh tons coal production of 1940-44 quinquennium over that of 1935-39, the increase in value, true to the prevalence of inflationary conditions, amounted to as much as 112.27 lakhs of rupees.[92] Though production which stood at 5,06,173 tons in 1910 got doubled by 1937,[93] yet the rate of production vis-a-vis the resources and the capacity of the mines, remained very much inadequate. During 45 years of coal extraction by the Singareni Collieries Company that ended in 1944, only about 33 million tons of coal was extracted as against the estimated resources of 1,000 million tons in the Dominions.[94] The two large coal mines at Kothagudem and Tandur had an annual capacity of 20 lakh tons, but only 10 lakhs had been extracted[95] on an average during the period.

Low prices, rising costs of production, old, and uneconomical machinery, transport bottle-necks for export, shortage of labour and its discontent, had all contributed, each in its own way, for low production.[96] The cost of production in Hyderabad Collieries was found to be Rs. 5 to 6 per ton more than that in the collieries of Madhya Pradesh, a British Indian province, as a result of which profits got lessened.[97] One factor which accounted for this was that they lacked power supply and consequently, huge amounts had to be spent on importing generators in order that more electric drills could be used.[98] Mechanical disorders were of such magnitude sometimes that in May, 1949, when three out of four boilers got spoilt at Kothagudem Mines, 16,000 workers were forced to remain without work for more than a week.[99] Less outturn was also due to much time being spent for bringing out coal from underground to surface, due to defective application of

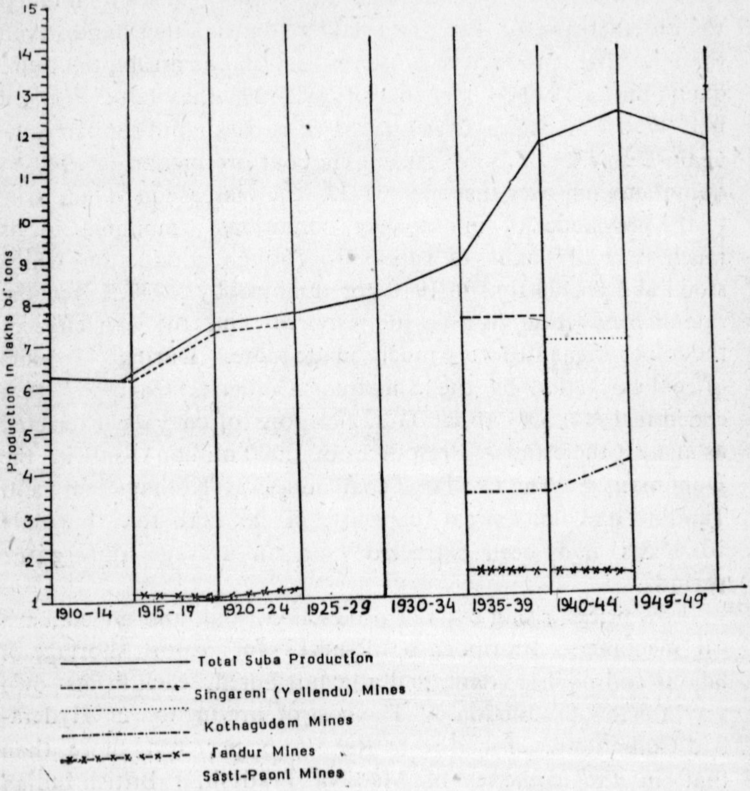

Chart 9 : Showing *quinquennial Production of Coal in Warangal* Suba, 1910-49.

Source : Data in Table No. XLIII.

TABLE XLIV

Cloth & Yarn Sales of Azam Jahi Textile Mills, Warangal, 1934-1950

(in O.S. Rs.)

Sl. No.	Balance sheet as on	Cloth sales	Cloth sold & on hand	Yarn sold
1	2	3	4	5
1.	1st July, 1934 to 5th October, 1934	—	3,76,430-10-10	—
2.	6th October, 1935	—	19,76,778-5-2	—
3.	5th ,, 1936	—	16,88,990-3-1	—
4.	5th ,, 1937	—	19,13,924-11-4	—
5.	,, ,, 1938	23,66,721-14-9	26,09,931-10-7	9,45,578-3-1
6.	6th ,, 1939	24,53,498-11-2	26,21,165-13-4	8,53,831-3-4
7.	5th ,, 1940	39,92,604-0-11	28,65,961-5-7	9,93,065-14-0
8.	,, ,, 1941	39,13,228-0-0	36,93,040-0-0	11,25,522-0-0
9.	,, ,, 1942	61,70,564-0-0	64,72,285-0-0	22,73,559-0-0
10.	6th ,, 1943	93,71,590-0-0	1,04,74,606-0-0	35,57,878-0-0
11.	5th ,, 1944	1,04,64,670-0-0	98,76,226-0-0	22,98,001-0-0
12.	,, ,, 1945	85,96,622-0-0	90,99,280-0-0	14,43,388-0-0
13.	30th September 1946	78,89,006-0-0	70,57,404-0-0	15,65,558-0-0
14.	,, ,, 1947	70,81,108-0-0	66,66,777-0-0	12,89,718-0-0
15.	,, ,, 1948	1,27,20,347-0-0	1,33,33,697-0-0	14,38,657-0-0
16.	,, ,, 1949	1,10,96,806-0-0	1,23,44,297-0-0	11,29,775-0-0
17.	,, ,, 1950	1,27,95,193-0-0	1,26,79,030-0-0	13,39,704-0-0

(*Contd.*)

Sl. No.		Yarn sold & on hand	Trading profit (*) or loss (—)	Dividend per share	Bonus
		6	7	8	9
1.	1st July, 1934 to 5th October, 1934	19,926-8-4	—7,940-7-6	—	—
2.	6th October, 1935	7,75,900-8-3	+2,10,751-1-3	—	—
3.	5th ,, 1936	19,28,530-2-10	+1,56,923-4-0	—	—
4.	5th ,, 1937	10,94,706 5-2	+4,44,144-8-5	5%	4,000-0-0
5.	,, ,, 1938	9,17,256-6-1	+4,33,524-11-5	6%	—
6.	6th ,, 1939	9,54,461-6-10	+4,39,103-2-7	7%	—
7.	5th ,, 1940	9,89,569-13-5	+3,11,361-3-11	7%	—
8.	,, ,, 1941	11,27,968-0-0	+4,03,543-0-0	12%	—
9.	,, ,, 1942	22,84,257-0-0	+19,70,833-0-0	—	—
10.	6th ,, 1943	35,49,651-0-0	+52,13,817-0-0	20%	10%
11.	5th ,, 1944	21,93,638-0-0	+41,49,778-0-0	20%	10%
12.	,, ,, 1945	14,14,398-0-0	+37,36,729-0-0	20%	10%
13.	30th September 1946	15,72,988-0-0	+22,67,389-0-0	Rs. 10/-per share	Rs. 5/-per share
14.	,, ,, 1947	12,75,767-0-0	+10,14,341-0-0	Rs. 10/-P.S*	Rs. 2/-P.S
15.	,, ,, 1948	14,28,730-0-0	+40,65,083-0-0	Rs. 10/-P.S	Rs. 5/-P.S.
16.	,, ,, 1949	13,33,276-0-0	+9,67,295-0-0	do	do
17.	,, ,, 1450	12,37,629-0-0	+4,12,083-0-0	Rs. 5/8/-P.S.	—

*Per share.

Source : *Yearly Balance Sheets*
(Available at the Mills, Warangal, Filing Section).

TABLE XLV

Input & Output Analysis of the Sirpur Paper Mills Ltd.

Sl. No.	Year	Manufacturing Expenses	Miscellaneous	Total Input	Sales	Other Revenue	Total Output	Ratio
1	2	3	4	5	6	7	8	9
1.	1443-44	37,20,101	12,59,266	49,79,367	85,50,169	19,191	85,69,350	1:1.72
2.	1944-45	45,17,467	11,45,502	56,62,969	82,57,659	36,582	82,94,241	1:1.46
3.	2945-46	42,81,969	10,59,637	53,41,606	68,41,414	47,450	68,88,864	1:1.29
4.	2946-47	37,59,475	11,48,973	59,08,448	57,80,898	47,455	58,28,353	1:0.97
5.	1947-48	43,97,142	11,76,626	15,73,768	64,01,377	59,058	64,60,435	1:1.15
6.	1948-49	47,41,386	11,28,129	58,69,515	41,83,084	78,823	42,61,907	1:1.73
7.	1949-50	52,57,860	9,42,591	62,00,451	55,37,354	10,468	55,47,822	1:0.89
8.	1950-51	50,63,132	8,85,369	59,48,501	74,47,388	13,414	74,60,802	1:1.25

Source : L.S. Habib Ahmed, *An Economic Survey of the Sirpur Paper Mills Ltd.*, M.A. (Econ) Dissertation, (Osmania University, 1960), p. 48.

'long wall work'.[100] But, the one factor which led to labour shortage and dissatisfaction that affected production growth in turn, was the hated contract system of labour recruitment and payment that was resorted by the coal mining authorities in the *Suba* area. These were not in the habit of directly recruiting most of their labour, but got them provided through middlemen-contractors who received payment on the basis of work turned over and paid the workers in turn on daily basis.[101] The system worked in such a disconcerting manner that on an average, the contractor got about 5 annas per head which was really too much when the labourer himself received only about 7 annas per day.[102] Besides, the same contractor very often happened to be the moneylender of the labourer who naturally hated to work under the latter, for his wages tended to get further reduced.[103] Due to this unhappy situation and also the fact that the wage received for hard underground work of coal mining had only little margin over that for comparatively easy, near home and less strenuous work of agricultural fields during the season, majority of the coalmine workers preferred often to quit the work and seek elsewhere.[104] The disparity and the discrimination shown by the Managing Authorities in wages and amenities between foreign labour consisting of Gorakhpur people[105] and Burma evacuees and the local labour, the better deal being given to the former, had further added to the latter's discontentment.[106] The crux of the situation lay in the fact that even though the workers raised united voice for the abolition of the contract system, the colliery managements found it convenient to carry it on, for it enabled them not only to avoid direct dealing with workers but also keep their demands for higher wages at bay.[107]

But, in spite of inadequate production and low utilisation of the potential, it is significant to note that 90% of the coal that was produced in the *Suba* was exported[108] and in this respect the State stood fourth in the country.[109] Besides the State Railway, others of Southern, Eastern and Western India depended on Hyderabad coal.[110] Power generation came next, though of course, no large scale plant had been installed during the period.[111] Further, though the coal of this region, due to its less coking nature could not be utilized for metallurgical purposes, yet it was capable of yielding liquid gas, tar, the vaporization of which under different temperatures, could result in bye-products that were highly useful in the manufacture of aniline dyes and drugs.[112] Coal industry thus formed a basic industry of the *Suba* people during the period.

i. *Other Large-Scale Mining Industries* : Marble and Mica mining and Iron-ore workings formed these in the area. The latter, though before the present century won much renown abroad for its making of steel swords, daggers and knives,[113] suffered severe decline during the period under study and consequently, it only persisted as a dying cottage industry for the manufacture of agricultural implements by using indigenous method of iron-smelting[114] in some villages of Sirpur Taluq of Adilabad District, where rich iron-ore deposits existed.[115] Even though magnetic iron-ore deposits were found existing on both banks of Godavari for over 200 miles including the Southern boundary of Singareni coal fields with an estimated reserve of more than 600 million tons and a scheme was investigated to establish steel works at Antargaon on the right bank of the river in Karimnagar District as late as 1940, nothing was practically taken up, due to Governmental inactivity and indifference.[116] The result was that the total annual import or pig-iron, wrought iron, steel and other iron manufactures into the State came of the order of 33,500 tons.

The extraction of marble and mica, as against the potential resources, was, just as in the case of coal, meagre and inadequate.[117] As against the anticipated deposits of marble ranged between 25,000 and 30,000 tons near Yellandu, Taluq headquarters in Warangal District, the output for the eleven years during which mining had taken place, i.e., 1931-1942, was only 2,597 tons and production stopped between the latter year and 1950.[118] Regarding mica, though prospecting and *Purwana*[119] licenses were issued to firms since 1941-42 and especially to Messrs. Vazir Sultan & Sons, Hyderabad, who worked the mines at Kallur and Gokavaram in Madhira Taluq of Warangal District, between 1944 and 1950[120], the quantity mined was rather so insignificant that its particulars were not to be found in the Departmental Reports or Statistics. Though mica of commercial sizes had been reported from village of both Khammam and Madhira Taluqs which had vast potentialities for export and internal use in dry lubrication, electric insulation and miconite-making,[121] the resources were allowed to remain very much unexploited by Departmental indifference and disinterestedness.

ii. *Azam Jahi Textile Mills, Ltd*: This Mill at Warangal which started production from July, 1934 became one of the two leading textile mills in the State, the other being Osmanshahi Mills at Nanded in Marathwada, both of which remained under Government control.[122] It could be seen from Chart No. X depicting production curve of the Mills[123] that the turnover of cloth as well as yarn was on a mild rise upto 1940 and then registered remarkable growth during the triennium of 1941-43. Lack of adequate machinery and labour force, introduction of novel techniques from only 1937,[124] market depression and price slump in 1939 and 1940,[125] had in a measure, led to the slow production growth upto 1940. Increase in the value of cloth sold and on hand, compared to the preceding year amounted to 8.27 lakhs of rupees in 1941, 27.79 lakhs in 1942 and 40.02 lakhs in 1943 and the corresponding increases in respect of yarn sold and on hand, were of the order of 1.38 lakhs, 11.56 lakhs and 12.65 lakhs respectively.[126] This steady and upward push was due not merely to rise in production, but more due to world shortage in the supply of cloth due to War and the restriction of supplies from Japan and England, as a result of which, scarcity and high prices came to prevail in the country.[127] But, during the succeeding four years of 1944-47, the curve came down regularly, the decline being more pronounced in 1946. This downward trend in the value of sales was more due to low controlled prices of cloth and yarn fixed by the Government rather than decline in production.[128] In 1945, the reduction in prices of cloth and yarn amounted to 30% at the end of the year, compared to their level at the year beginning.[129] The situation

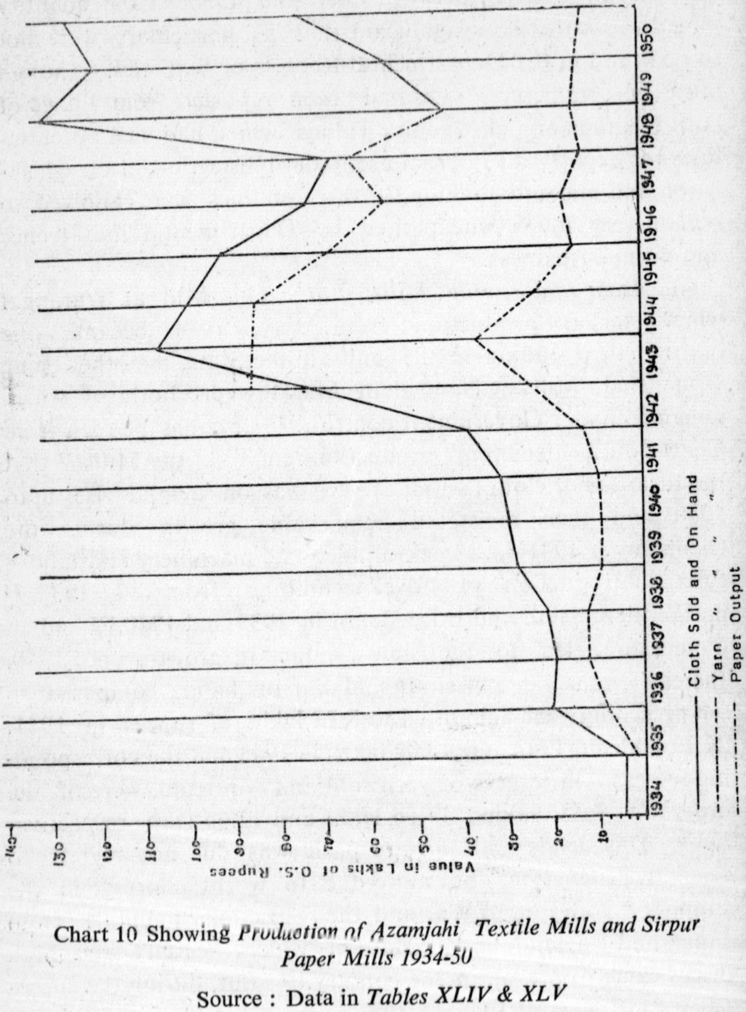

Chart 10 Showing *Production of Azamjahi Textile Mills and Sirpur Paper Mills 1934-50*

Source : Data in *Tables XLIV & XLV*

was particularly bad in 1946, for there was steady increase in the price of raw cotton as against 6½% to 11½% reduction in the controlled prices of cloth and yarn.[130] The position was slightly better in 1947 in the sense that the controlled prices remained stationary, though cotton price increased considerably.[131] It is interesting to note that 1948, though an year of disturbed condition in the area, was characterised by more than 100% increase in the value of cloth sold and on hand, and, of course about 12% in that of yarn.[132] This was because of the fact that the Mill worked in three shifts throughout the year without any loss of time due to labour strike and further, it could purchase a large quantity of cotton required at well below market price.[133] Compared to this heavy increase, there took place slight decrease in 1949 which was due to less margin that existed between the prices of cotton on one hand and cloth and yarn on the other.[134] In the year that followed, the position slightly improved as the Mill received good export orders even though raw cotton prices remained uncontrolled.[135]

The available production figures of the Mill for the period 1353 *Fasli* (1943-44) to 1355 *Fasli* (1945-46)[136] show that yarn production was more than that of piece-goods, though of course, as seen above,[137] the value realised was far larger in the case of the latter than the former. The respective production figures in the triennium were 65.04, 63.79 and 53.99 lakh lbs. in the case of yarn spun and 52.35, 53.95 and 44.24 lakh lbs. in the case of piece-goods.[138] Difference in relative prices led to the contrary trend in the value realised. As the cotton used by the Azamjahi Mill was mostly of short staple variety, it only produced in abundance coarse cloth of low quality and very little of finer variety.[139] The production of the latter which was essential for widening the markets and improve the competitive position of the Mill in the country, required the import of long staple cotton from U.S.A., which was not resorted, conditioned probably by its limited financial resources.[140] But, the coarse cloth produced by the Mill, though inferior in quality even to that of Sholapur or Ahmedabad Mills,[141] its price being cheap, was within the capacity of the poorer sections of the local population and hence found an assured market.[142] Further, the rough texture suited the requirements of the rural peasants and working classes. Besides quality, the quantum of production was also low,[143] especially in view of the fact that imports of piece-goods and yarn formed important items next to none[144] and at the same time, raw cotton of the order of 40,918 bales of 400 lbs was exported from centres like Warangal, Madhira and Rajura in the *Suba*.[145] Inadequate capital and machinery, low quality of the raw materials, lack of enough skilled labour[146] and occasional labour trouble and discontent,[147] had all been factors that contributed for the low productivity of this Mill. Yet, inspite of these shortcomings, the Azamjahi Mills, being the only large scale industry in the textile sector in Warangal *Suba*, supplying on one hand coarse and medium cloth to the low and middle income groups of the local population besides earning exports, and on the other, providing yarn to the handloom industry of the region, certainly ranked as a core industry in the Eastern Division.

iii. *The Sirpur Paper Mills Ltd.* : This was the only important large scale industry that came to be established in Adilabad District. Located at Sirpur on the Delhi-Madras Grand Trunk rail route with an annual capacity of 6,000 tons of paper or 18 tons per day,[148] the Factory went into production from April, 1942,[149] with bamboo that was available in plenty in the nearby and surrounding forests, as the principal raw material.[150] During the first three months period of 1st April, 1942 to 30th June, 1942, the Factory produced 709 tons of paper[151] whose monthly rate was less than 50% of the estimated production capacity. As a matter of fact, the actual production figures that are available for the period upto 1947-48,[152] go to show that the proposed output level had never been reached and the highest turnover achieved in 1945-46—5,102 tons[153]—fell short by 898 tons of this figure. Yearly outturns and the value realised therefore, also alternated between rise and fall but, for most part, they were on the downward path.[154] But, on the other hand, Wartime scarcity for paper and the consequent high prices, had very much boosted up the output value and thus compensated for shortfalls in production.[155] This could be seen from the fact that during the period 1942-43 to 1947-48, as against increase in production (compared to preceding year) of 457 tons in 1943-44 and 208 tons in 1945-46 decrease amounting to 189 tons in 1944-45, 735 tons in 1946-47 and 741 tons in 1947-48 had which taken place,[156] but, on the other hand, the profit of the Mill swelled upto Rs. 35.91 lakhs only came down, in spite of considerable production shortfalls in the post-war period, to 8.87 lakhs in 1947-48.[157]

The year 1948-49 had been the worst in the annals of the factory for it suffered heavy loss in production as it remained closed for about two months just before and after the Police Action and further, the cost of the raw materials had increased considerably.[158] The result was reflected in the low input-output ration for the year being 1:0.73[159] and the regular profit that the Mills had been receiving got converted into not too small a loss of Rs. 16.07 lakhs.[160] During 1949-50, though production went up by 23% the costs, due to wage rise and payment of compensation to paper merchants for non-fulfilment of previous supply commitments, had also increased by 5.80% and the result was a loss of Rs. 6.5 lakhs for the year.[161] Increase in production amounting to 27% and only 2½% increase in Factory expenses during the year 1950-51, on the other hand, led to a net profit of Rs. 5.22 lakhs.[162]

These Mills in which the Government held 75% of the shares and managerial rights[163] discharged on its behalf by the Hyderabad Construction Company[164] until September, 1949 and later by the Industrial Trust Fund[165] and which manufactured all kinds of writing and printing paper[166] and was also designed for the production of newsprint from early in 1950 with the operation of second paper-making machine,[167] came to serve as a prominent large scale industries, not only from the point of view of industrial development of the *Suba*, but also from the State and Indian requirements. During the War, the Mills, out of their average yearly production of 5,000 tons, 65% was sent to the Government of India whose requirement had enormously increased due to War.[168] It only met the State's annual consumption of 1,500 tons which earlier used to be imported at considerable expense, but also exported sizeable quantity adding in not a small measure, to the revenues of the State.[169] In 1941-42, the Mill supplied Rs. 7.39 lakhs worth of paper within the State and on the other hand exported Rs. 9.66 lakhs worth of paper.[170] Only in years of much lesser production, such as those of 1946-47 to 1948-49,[171] had the imports been resorted to.[172] Besides augmenting the revenues of the State, the paper Mills served the *Suba* and the District interests by providing employment to a strong force of about 2,000 technicians and 1,500 labourers per day. (Figure of 1941-42).[173] But, the fact that with excellent facilities to obtain raw materials of bamboo, coal, lime, water,[174] (excepting supply of some chemicals from British India),[175] and rail transport[176] along with enough capital, the Mills, throughout the period upto the end of 1950, were always nearly short of 1,000 tons by the estimated capacity of production,[177] probably pointed to managerial inefficiency and lack of co-ordinated and concerted development. The Company Directors came to consist in majority Government Officials, *Jagirdars*, rich local and Bombay merchants rather than men known for their managerial efficiency or telents.[178]

iv. *Mahbubia Match-Making Industry, Mahboobabad* : Mr. Syed Ismail had the honour of starting the first match-making industry in Hyderabad State in 1928 in the shape of the Mahbubia Match Factory at Mahboobabad in Warangal District.[179] It was a venture of private enterprise that grew rapidly into a large power-driven unit producing the highest number of match boxes in the State and providing employment to a sizeable number of persons.

The factory which was proposed with 20 men and 200 match boxes per day,[180] registered such a remarkable growth within a decade that, as could be seen from Table XLVI, the former went up on an average to 300 and the latter to 1,000 grosses, thus amounting to a percentage[181] of 1,400 and 400 respectively. The fluctuations in the number of persons employed[182] seem to have been very much influenced by the supply condition of essential chemicals such as sulphur and blue match

TABLE XLVI

Output and Employment Particulars of Mahbubia Match Factory

Sl. No.	Fasli/Year	OUT PUT Various splints (40-60-80) In Grosses		Average number of persons employed per day
		Per Year	Per Day	
1	2	3	4	5
1.	1341 Fasli (1931-32)	...	808	72
2.	1342 " (1931-33)	...	1,000	...
3.	1343 " (1933-34)	...	...	419
4.	1344 " (1934-35)	3,93,053	...	295
5.	1345 " (1935-36)	3,01,460	...	450
6.	1346 " (1936-37)	3,75,808	...	350
7.	1347 " (1937-38)	4,00,000	...	295

Compiled from : · *Administrative Reports of the Commerce and Industries Department of H.E.H. the Nizam's Government, for the years 1341 Fasli* (*1931-32*), p. 19; *1342 Fasli* (1932-33), p. 16; *1344 Fasli* (*1934-35*), p. 13; *1345 Fasli* (*1935-36*), p. 12 ; *1346 Fasli* (*1936-37*) p. 10 *Agricultural, Industrial & Trade Statistics for the year 1343 Fasli* (*1933-34*), *H.E.H. the Nizam's Government*, p.160; and *Industrial Statistics, H.E.H. the Nizam's Government, 1345-1349 Fasli* (*1935-36 to 1339-40*), p. 459.

paper from British India rather than the level of wages which generally remained low both before and after the War.[182a] The former item which was but indispensable, used to be imported from such a far off place as Calcutta.[183] In other words, the extent of production, both daily and yearly, was determined by this important factor besides others, such as shortage of transport facilities due to War requirements, levy of excise duty and strong competition from a Swedish Company based at Madras, known as the Eastern India Manufacturing Company (WIMCO).[184] Before the War, the imposition of 5% duty on foreign imports enabled the local match factories to carry on their production and sales rather unaffected.[185] But, the imposition of excise duty since 1934 @ Rs. 2-4-0 per gross which, compared to price of gross of match sticks that stood at Rs. 1-6-0, amounted to 190%,[186] and the War time delays that occurred in the grant of licenses for receiving essential chemicals and in their transhipment as well as those of other raw materials such as splints or wood, had been greatly responsible for undermining the production, especially since 1943 when scarcity of one raw material or the other became the order of the day.[187] On the other hand, WIMCO had their own chemicals-manufacturing plant and hence, were placed in a very strong competitive position.[188] The result of these cumulative factors on match manufacture in the State could be seen from its continuous and steep decrease from 8,07,784 gross in 1939 to 6,01,651 in 1940; 5,07,511 in 1941 and 3,38,236 gross in 1942.[189]

As against these disadvantages, the yearly output figures that are available for a limited period of the thirties[190] go to show that the Mahbubia Factory was striving forward in its manufacturing efforts. In fact, during this period, it always remained very much ahead of the other two or three large scale power-driven units in the State, at times its lead amounting to more than one lakh gross of match boxes.[191] But, the adverse effect of the War time situation, stated as above, seem to have continued in the post-War period as it was reported in September, 1946 that the Factory was employing only 100 workers who turned out 100 gross of boxes per day.[192] It had a further set-back in 1948-49 when the founder-owners left to Pakistan[193] as a sequel to the strained communal relations that attended the situation.[194] Though it was handed over to a refugee from Sind,[195] yet it failed to regain its former importance in the field of match manufacturing. But, however, during the period of study, it flourished as one of the prominent large scale industries of the *Suba* and the State.

v. Government Carpet Factory, Warangal : Manufacture of cotton and woollen carpets and rugs of a very superior kind had been the celebrated industry, from the time of the Kakatiyas of Warangal Taluq in which Warangal, the headquarters town, held the dominant place.[196] These carpets which included those of silk also, had been so popular in local and foreign markets right until the turn of the present century, that every year carpets aggregating in value of Rs. 25,000 were sent to Hyderabad and in 1289 *Fasli* (1879-80) carpets costing Rs. 57,000 had been sent to English markets.[197] Even as late as 1925-26, there were in Warangal 350 carpet looms that provided employment to 1,500 persons spread over 225 families, who manufactured articles to the value of Rs. 2.72 lakhs.[198] But, it was very much baffling that during the next four years only, such a vast deterioration beset this industry that in 1929-30, the number of looms came down to 90 with only 22 families manufacturing carpets of the annual value of Rs. 30,000.[199] Besides lack of former royal patronage, the immediate factors that must have accounted for this sudden and severe decline were, strong competition from the imported mill goods, raw materials such as yarn and dyes becoming costly, weak financial condition of majority of the weavers to manage these by themselves, lack of Government aid in this regard and a change in the tastes of the people, especially the middle class, in favour of the mill goods which came cheaper, though lacked the beauty and lustre of the hand-made goods.[200]

In order to restore this decayed industry by arranging for the training of local carpet weavers in the preparation of superior quality of carpets, manufacture, stock and export of carpets and rugs, and assistance to the local weavers in the manufacture and sale of cheap quality rugs, light and heavy cotton durries or *shatranjis*, the Government with a cost of Rs. 52,328 which was provided by the Industrial Trust Fund, established the Experimental Carpet Factory at Warangal in 1929.[201] But, the carpet weavers of the locality stood away from the Factory, inspite of the efforts made by the Local Advisory Board consisting of the First *Taluqdar*, Assistant Registrar of Co-operative Credit Societies, Superintendent, Central Jail and two members from the Carpet Weavers' Community, to explain the objects for which the Factory had been established.[202] As a result, it was obliged to admit some non-professional boys and train them in the Factory.[203] It was only in the fourth year that the unit was started, some change was reported in the attitude of the local weavers.[204] They probably required this time gap, to gain confidence in the efforts of the Government which earlier rather left them to their fate. The Factory had 15 looms of different sizes, more than half being of 11½' width and more than 100 boys had been trained in the art of manufacturing superior quality carpets in it.[205]

The functioning of this factory was mainly aided by the order which it secured in 1935-36 for the supply of superior carpets worth Rs. 30,000 for H.E.H. the Nizam's palace at Delhi,[206] supply of cheap quality rugs made by cottage weavers in their own houses, worth Rs. 1,36,937 to Oriental Carpet Manufacturers Ltd., London and Rs. 14,135 worth to Cottage Industries Sales Depot, Hyderabad.[207] Excluding the Delhi order, it could be seen from Table XLVII that of the three varieties of carpets, the general demand seemed to be more for cheaper, then medium and the last for superior type, which in a way reflected the general level of standard of living of the local population. The curve depicting the value realised in respect of all varieties of carpets produced and sold during 1930-31 to 1945-46 shows that upto 1938-39, there had been alternate rise or fall, but it was of a mild nature and from 1939-40 till the end, excepting in 1941-42, there has been continuous rise of a striking nature.[208] Until 1937-38, there was the sale of only superior variety of carpets, whereas from this year until the end, medium and cheaper varieties, rather in greater amounts, came to be sold along with the former type[209] and this factor, besides war-time hike in demand and price, had accounted for the variations in production and sale of the carpets, as explained above. Though the sale of the carpets very much thrived on foreign exports and the War-time restriction of luxury imports into Britain and the closure of the Mediterranean route had very much affected the sales of carpets abroad,[210] yet, the War-time demand in the country rose appreciably, thereby, leading to considerable rise in prices. This accounted for the phenomenal rise of the production

TABLE XLVII

Production of Carpets, Rugs and Durries (Shatranjis) at Government Carpet Factory, Warangal, 1930-31 to 1945-46

Sl. No.	Fasli	Year	Superior variety No.	Superior variety Value	Medium variety No.	Medium variety Value	Cheap variety No.	Cheap variety Value	Total No.	Total Value
			Carpets manufactured or sold							
1	2		3	4	5	6	7	8	9	10
1.	1340	Fasli (1930-31)	7*	1,926-9-7	—	—	—	—	7	1,926-8-7
2.	1342	,, (1932-33)	28**	4,408-0-0	—	—	—	—	28	4,408-0-0
3.	1343	,, (1933-34)	19. .	7,409-3-0	—	—	—	—	19	7,409-3-0
4.	1344	,, (1934-35)	16. .	5,591-1-7	—	—	—	—	16	5,591-1-7
5.	1345	,, (1935-36)	—	10,163-0-3	—	—	—	—	—	10,163-0-3
6.	1346	,, (1936-37)	28. .	6,283-0-0	—	—	—	—	28	6,283-0-0
7.	1347	,, (1937-38)	27	4,535-0-0	—	—	—	5,071-0-7·*	27	9,606-3-7
8.	1348	,, (1938-39)	—	4,000-0-0	—	—	—	4,536-6-1	—	8,536-6-1
9.	1349	,, (1939-40)	—	3,241-10-3	—	4,824-14-10	—	7,207-9-10	—	15,274-2-10
10.	1350	,, (1940-41)	—	8,412-13-7	—	—	—	17,140-7-0··*	—	25,553-4-7
11.	1351+++	,, (1941-42)	—	2,457-4-11	—	4,465-11-9	—	6,616-14-0	—	15,539-14-8
12.	1353	,, (1943-44)	—	20,000-0-0*	—	—	—	—	—	20,000-0-0
13.	1354	,, (1944-45)	—	7,891-1-0	—	10,390-10-10	—	36,142-11-3	—	54,424-7-1
14.	1355	,, (1945-46)	—	12,464-2-8**	—	23,731-11-6	—	33,338-15-8	—	69,540-13-10

*In some cases, the rugs were woven by individual weavers which the Factory purchased and supplied to outside firms and gained 5% commission for doing so.

++As against this purchase, the total rugs despatched during this year remained the same as last year at 8, 450-*A.R. of C.&.I. Dept. of H.E.H the Nizam's Government for 1344 Fasli* (*1934*-35), (Hyderabad-Dn, 1936)

+++The entire business conducted by the Factory during the year amounted to Rs. 24,677-2-2, fetching a commission of Rs. 2,044-4-5—*A.R. for 1351 Fasli* (*1941-42*), (Hyderabad-Dn, 1945), p. 94.

*Out of 20 carpets to be supplied to the East India Company, Amritsar (Punjab), 7 carpets have been sent during the year and 4 were ready to be despatched—*A.R. of the C.&.I. Dept., of H.E.H. the Nizam's Dominions for 1340 Fasli* (*1930-31*), pp. 27-28.

**It has already completed six finest quality carpets and 3 more were there on the looms for Delhi Palace of the *Nizam.—A.R. of the C.&.I. Dept. of H.E.H. the Nizam's Government for 1342 Fasli* (*1932-33*), p. 28.

· *These carpets were of various sizes which were supplied to the Government Cottage Industries Sales *Depot—*A.R. for 1347 Fasli* (*1937-38*), (Hyderabad-Dn, 1940), p. 104.

· · *These included both medium and cheap quality carpets—*A.R. for 1350 Fasli* (*1940-41,*) (Hyderabad-Dn, 1943), p. 110.

· They worked on piece-work system as against 20 boys last year. They gained capability of working by themselves from designs given to them—*A.R. of the C.&.I. Dept. of H.E.H. the Nizam's Government for 1343 Fasli* (*1932-33*), p. 28.

· · These were supplied to *Nizam's* Delhi Palace for which the Commerce and Industries Department received an order of the value of B.G. Rs, 60,000—*A.R. for 1344 Fasli* (*1934-35*), (Hyderabad-Dn, 1938), p. 69.

Sl. No.		Fasli	Year	RUGS Purchased, manufactured or sold					
				Supplied to Oriental Manufacturing Company, London.		Supplied to Messrs. Jessani Carpet Company, Bombay		Supplied to Cottage Industries Sales Depot, Hyderabad	
				No.	Value	No.	Value	No.	Value
				11	12	13	14	15	16
1.	1340	Fasli	(1930-31)	—	—	—	—	—	—
2.	1342	,,	(1932-33)	3,248	13,852-0-0	—	—	—	—
3.	1343	,,	(1933-34)	6,564	—	—	—	—	—
4.	1344	,,	(1934-35)	6,745	—	—	—	—	—
5.	1345	,,	(1935-36)	—	—	—	—	—	—
6.	1346	,,	(1936-37)	2,400	12,000-0-0	—	3,500/	—	4,405/
7.	1347	,,	(1937-38)	3,705	20-000-0-0	—	—	—	—
8.	1348	,,	(1938-39)	1,123	—	—	—	—	—
9.	1349	,,	(1939-40)	—	—	—	—	—	—
10.	1350	,,	(1940-41)	—	—	—	—	—	—
11.	1351†††	,,	(1941-42)	—	—	—	—	—	—
12.	1353	,,	(1943-44)	—	—	—	—	—	—
13.	1354	,,	(1944-45)	—	—	—	—	—	—
14.	1355	,,	(1945-46)	—	—	—	—	—	—

RUGS Purchased, manufactured or sold

			Total		Cotton Durries (Shatranjis) Manufactured under the supervision of the Factory		No. of looms worked in the Factory	No. of workmen employed in the Carpet Factory	No. of boys trained in Carpet weaving in the Factory
			No.	Value	No.	Value			
			17	18	19	20	21	22	23
1. 1340	Fasli	(1930-31)	—	—	—	—	—	—	30
2. 1342	,,	(1932-33)	3,248	13,852-0-0	—	—	—	—	26
3. 1343	,,	(1933-34)	6,564	—	—	—	—	—	—
4. 1344	,,	(1934-35)	6,745	—	—	—	—	—	—
5. 1345	,,	(1935-36)	—	—	—	—	—	—	40
6. 1346	,,	(1936-37)	2,400	19,905-0-0	—	—	—	35	—
7. 1347	,,	(1937-38)	3,705	20,000-0-0	—	—	—	30	8
8. 1348	,,	(1938-39)	1,123	—	—	—	—	—	—
9. 1349	,,	(1939-40)	—	—	—	—	—	—	—
10. 1350	,,	(1940-41)	—	—	62	131-9-0	—	—	—
11. 1351†††	,,	(1941-42)	—	—	—	1,025-6-6	15	40	—
12. 1353	,,	(1943-44)	—	—	—	30,000-0-0	15	—	—
13. 1354	,,	(1944-45)	—	—	—	3,270-13-0	—	—	—
14. 1355	,,	(1945-46)	—	—	—	3,490-10-3	—	—	—

*This amount was of superior and medium quality carpets and floor durries—*A.R. of C & I Dept. for 1353 & 1354 Fasli* (*1944 & 1945*), (Hyderabad-Dn, 1946), p. 9.

**This amount was of local superior quality carpets and also those made for export—*A.R. of C&I. Dept. for 1355 Fasli* (*1945-46*), (Hyderabad-Dn, 1947), p. 47.

Compiled from : *A.R. of C&I. Dept. H.E.H. the Nizam's Government for 1340 Fasli* (*1930-31*), (Hyderabad-Dn, 1938), pp. 27-28 ;

A.R. of C&I. Dept. H.E.H. the Nizam's Government for 1342 Fasli (*1932-33*), (Hyderabad-Dn, 1935), pp. 28 & 32 ;

A.R. of C&I. Dept. H.E.H. the Nizam's Government for 1343 Fasli (*1933-34*), (Hyderabad-Dn, 1935), p. 14 ;

A.R. of H.E.H. the Nizam's Dominions for 1342 Fasli (*1932-33*), (Hyderabad-Dn, 1935) p. 71 ;

A.R. of C&I. Dept. H.E.H. the Nizam's Government for 1344 Fasli (*1934-35*), (Hyderabad-Dn, 1936), pp. 12 & 39 ;

A.R. of H.E H. the Nizam's Dominions for 1345 Fasli (*1935-36*), (Hyderabad-Dn, 1938), p. 87 ;

A.R. of H.E.H. the Nizam's Dominions for 1346 Fasli (*1936-37*), (Hyderabad-Dn, 1919), p. 97 ;

A.R. for 1347 Fasli (*1937-38*), (Hyderabad-Dn, 1940), p. 104 ;

A.R. for 1348 Fasli (*1938-39*) (Hyderabad-Dn, 1941), p. 112 ;

A.R. for 1349 Fasli (*1939-40*), (Hyderabad-Dn, 1942), p. 104 :

A.R. for 1350 Fasli (*1940-41*) (Hyderabad-Dn, 1943), p. 110 ;

A.R. for 1351 Fasli (*1941-42*), (Hyderabad-Dn, 1945), p. 94 ;

A.R. of C&I. Dept. H.E.H. the Nizam's Government for 1353 & 1354 Fasli (*1944 & 1945*), (Hyderabad-Dn, 1946), p. 9 ;

A.R. of C&I. Dept. H.E.H. the Nizam's Government for 1355 Fasli (*1945-46*), (Hyderabad-Dn, 1947), p. 7.

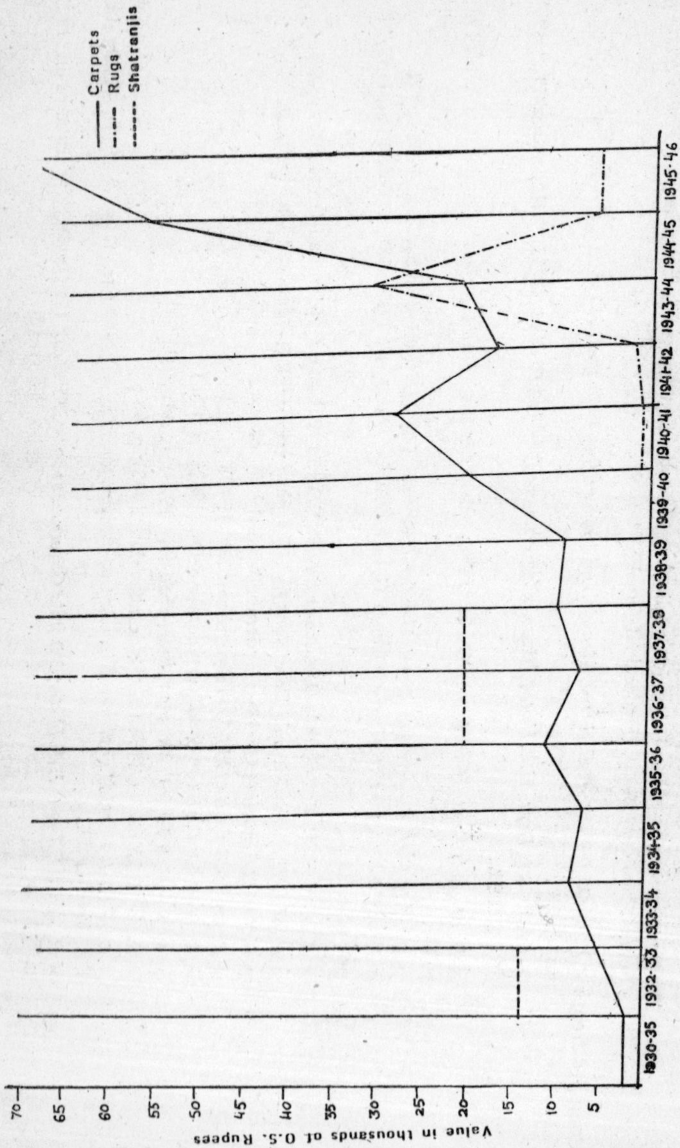

Chart 11 : Showing *Production of Carpets, Rugs Shatranjis* (Durries) *in Warangal Suba, 1930-31-1945, 46*
Source : *Table XLVII*

value in the Forties. The fall in 1941-42 was due to lesser sales in respect of both superior and cheaper carpets compared to preceding year[211], which might have been occasioned either by transport-bottleneck or by short supply of raw materials.

Regarding rugs and durries, the Factory acted as an intermediary agency by getting them produced at the houses of individual weavers by supplying them raw materials and also designs and then arranging for their sale for which they received commission.[212] More than 90 % of the former were sent to the Oriental Manufacturing Co., London.[213] But, these which in April, 1932, had been agreed to be imported at the rate of 300 rugs per month and were in September, 1932 increased to 499 per month,[214] suffered 50% decrease during the year 1935-36[215] and finally came down to 1,123 rugs for the whole year of 1938-39, after which the entire transaction got stopped.[216] Accumulation of stocks in London market[217] due to failure of the Company to create enough demand for the products and the War-time restrictions on imports into Britain led to this sufferance in exports to England. To add to this, the Jessani Carpet Company, Bombay and the Cottage Industry Sales Depot at Hyderabad, though in a position to compensate for the decline in foreign exports, failed to fill this breach and their purchase, extended to only the lone year of 1936-37.[218] The production of durries or *Shatranjis* both of floor or bed, which was started by the Factory in 1941-42 as a means of encouragement to the weavers who suffered due to failure of the market for carpets and rugs,[219] also ran well only for a very brief period.[220] During the War, this industry was in a prosperous condition as there was a good demand for the goods.[221] But, towards the close of the War and afterwards, the market had suffered considerably which could be seen from the huge ascent of the curve in 1943-44 and its steep fall in the following year.[222]

Thus, the efforts of the Government to revive and rehabilitate the decayed carpet industry, did not appear to be met with much success. In fact, the Carpet Factory ran on loss amounting to Rs. 8,262 for the period 1930-32 and Rs. 9,829 for the period 1933-36[223] and after the War-time demand and price rise was over, it was closed for good.[224] The amount of profit that was received by an artisan in this industry came to be meagre—the average daily income earned by a weaver and his wife together ranged from Re. 1-15-0 to Rs. 2-9-0[224a] and on the other, the artisans being financially incapable of buying the raw materials independently, came under the unrelenting control of either the moneylenders or master weavers who engaged them as paid workers.[225] The encouragement and assistance of the Government Factory could extend only to a limited section of local carpet and durrie weavers who initially rather felt suspicious of its efforts. They, in general, felt secure neither in obtaining raw materials nor in finding outlets for their products. The result was that the industry failed to regain its former prosperity and excellence and continued in a very much decayed form.[226]

vi. *Other Large-Scale Industries* : The Hyderabad Chemicals and Fertilizers Factory which was started in 1942 at Bellampally in Adilabad District with an authorised share capital of Rs. 1 crore and an issued capital of Rs. 20 lakhs[227] was also an important large-scale industry in the *Suba* region. It was engaged in the manufacture of sulphuric acit, nitric acid, hydrochloric acid, alum, superphosphate, mixed fertilizers, ammoniasulphate, epsom salts, etc., and employed about 300 persons per day.[228] Only the value of the production achieved in 1944-45 and 1945-46 standing at Rs. 2,16,000 and Rs. 2,17,464-5-2 respectively,[229] is available which indicates that the output was of moderate extent, though it had the impact of War-time conditions. On the other hand, the location of the Factory at Bellampally had the advantages of coal from the mines at the same place,[230] rail line, labour availability etc.

The Sirsilk Factory which was also proposed to be started in the same District at Sirpur-Kagaznagar,[231] failed, due to the financial difficulties of the Government,[232] to start production until June, 1954, even though it was registered as early as June, 1946 with Hyderabad Construction Company as the Managing Agents.[233] The construction of the building and erection of plant and machinery dragged on for such a long period that it could ultimately be completed by the new Managing Agents, being the Birla Brothers.[234] It really was a set-back to the industrial development of the *Suba* and the State that this large-scale unit with an authorised capital of Rs. 5 crores[235] and with capacity to manufacture 5 tons of acetate yarn which was to be converted into 50,000 yards of fabrics per day,[236] was allowed to remain unfinished beyond 1950.

(*a*) *Rice and Pulse Mills* :[237] Almost all the paddy grown in the *Suba* was milled there itself.[238] But, very little rice was polished as the demand in the Districts was for unpolished rice.[239] As a matter of fact, the hand-pounding of rice became so common, due probably to its taste and strength, in the villages that it was estimated to be about 36.2 % of the total production.[240] A rice mill had the capacity of pounding 200 to 300 maunds of paddy per day and according to pre-War prices did cost, Rs. 5,600 to Rs. 37,000 depending on the turnover required.[241] Most of the mills contained machinery of Bezwada type which occupied more room and the breakage of rice was also more.[241a]. But, as rice milling depended on the paddy outturn which fluctuated on the favourability or otherwise of crop conditions,[242] the mill owners employed their machinery for seasonal activities such as cotton ginning, pressing, groundnut decorticating, oil extraction and even flour grinding.[243] In majority of mills, ginning and rice-milling were carried on.[244] This combining of mill work based on agricultural produce became so predominant, that in 1933-34 out of 20 Factories in Warangal Taluq which carried on rice milling, only 4 got restricted to rice milling and as many as 16 were of a combined nature.[245] The very fact that capitalists like Pingali Venkatrama Reddy[246] and Bhicaji Dadabhai & Co.,[247] established factories of this type at more than one centre showed that rice milling proved a profitable industrial activity. As the capital involved was very much within the reach of the rural rich and urban businessmen, majority of the units came to be established by men representing these elements, especially in Warangal District which had lion's share in rice milling not only in the *Suba* but in the State itself.[248] They had taken full advantage of the shortage of rice that came to prevail during forties and enriched themselves by indulging in large-scale hoarding, black-marketeering and smuggling.[249]

(b) *Oil Mills* : Compared to the significant production of oil seeds such as groundnut, castor, *sesamum* , cotton and linseed in the *Suba* Districts,[250] the extraction of oils out of them or putting their by-products to internal use, left much to be desired. The average export of raw produce from the State in respect of these ranged as high as 59 %, 62 %, 70 %, 22.8 % and 92 % of the annual output.[251] The enormity of these exports could very well be realised from the corresponding figures of British India which stood at 28.1 %, 42 %, 31 % and 58.3 % respectively.[252] This had proved a considerable loss both economically and industrially in the sense that raw exports brought lesser return than manufactured ones, agriculturists were deprived of oil cakes and seeds which came of profitable use as cattle food and also manure to irrigated crops ; and opportunities of providing employment to local landless labourers and development of several ancillary industries based on the running of oil industries such as margarine-manufacture, soap-making paint and varnish industries, preparation of compound lubricants, printing-ink, candles, oil cloth or linoleum, hair oils and glycerine, had been lost.[253] The high tariffs on oil exports that were levied before 1931 proved a great source of discouragement to oil-seed crushing industry in the area. The effect could be understood from the fact that for crushing 6,000 tons of *mahua* seed, gingilly seed, castor seed and linseed, the miller in the State got respectively Rs. 48,000, 4,500, 18,000 and Rs. 30,000 less than his counterpart in British India, due to difference in tariff rates.[254] As a result of the *Oil Industry Survey held in the State in 1929-30* and its recommendations, the Hyderabad Government in May, 1931, removed the export duty on vegetable oils which gave such an impetus to the oil-seed crushing industry that the export of oil increased by 300%. But, this proved temporary and the reimposition of a duty of O.S. Re. 1 per *palla* of 120 *seers* from April, 1935, led to decrease in export of oil since then.[255] Quite conversely to this policy, other countries protected the interest of their oil industry by imposing import duties of at least 5 shillings per cwt. on oil, while oil seeds were admitted more or less free of duty.[256]

50% of the oil-seeds crushing in Hyderabad State was done by means of bullock-driven *ghanis* which numbered 113, 779 and 494 in Warangal, Karimnagar and Adilabad Districts respectively. These small-scale units that were locally made at very low cost were found quite suitable for crushing of *til* and *kardi* seeds.[257] On the other hand, 30 to 40% of the castor seeds were crushed in screw presses operated by hand which numbered 105, 7 and......in the three Districts respectively. Warangal, being one of the important castor extraction centres in the State, stood highest in the number of these screw presses, which, though moderately priced at Rs. 600 each (pre-War rate) could give only 42% of the oil from the seed.[258] Regarding *sesamum*, though Karimnagar District had the highest number of bullock-driven *ghanis* in view of its highest production of the seed[259], yet, if the total extraction of oil by both large and small-scale units was taken into consideration, Warangal ranked as the most important centre, from where 80 wagon loads of *til* seed oil were despatched per annum.[360] The latter had four Factories equipped with 22 power-driven rotary *ghanis*[261] employed in pressing oil from this seed at the rate of 5 tons of seed per day, besides good number of bullock-driven *ghanis*.[262] In the case of groundnut, which loomed large in oil exports, while 14 lakhs of maunds of kernel was crushed in the State by power expellers or rotary mills, only one lakh maunds of kernel was crushed by means of bullock *ghanis*.[263] Kernal was separated from pods by decorticating machines and Warangal District with 46 of them—39 run by power and 6 by hand – ranked highest among Telangana District. The husk of the pods was used as fuel and hence, the cotton ginning and pressing factories usually put up a decorticating machine and undertook decortication at a nominal charge of Re. 0-1-4 per maund of kernel.[264] Regarding the types of mills, it is significant to note that out of 503, 1,017 and 1,140 total units both small-scale and large-scale in Warangal, Karimnager and Adilabad Districts respectively,[265] the large establishments numbered only 7, 1 and 3 respectively.[266]

The heavy export of oil seeds was equally matched by considerable export of the oils that were extracted in the Dominions. Out of an estimated groundnut oil production in the State of the order 5.96 lakhs of maunds, the export and internal consumption amounted respectively to 4.21 lakhs of maunds and 1.75 lakhs of maunds.[267] The export from Warangal to Cuttack, Gondia[268] and Vizianagaram,[269] ranged from 79,409 *pallas* in 1938 to 1,52,783 *pallas* in 1941.[270] Tandur and Madhira also served as exporting stations in the *Suba.* But, oil exports formed only 1/12th of the value of seed exports. Whereas the total value of oil seeds exported was nearly Rs. 6 crores, vegetable oils exported from the State averaged only to Rs. 80.61 lakhs.[271] More than oil, the exports of 50% of oil cakes from the State as against 12½% in the case of British India, averaging 19.08 lakhs maunds annually and valued at Rs. 39.75 lakhs,[272] affected the development of agricultural manuring, cattle growth and especially milch cattle. These exports were made from *Suba* Districts to British Indian territories of Bombay, Kakinada, Masulipatam, Bezwada, Dwarapudi and Vetapalem,[273] mainly for the purpose of being used as manures for irrigated crops such as sugarcane.[274] The local ryots, out of ignorance in realising the proper value and application of this oil seed by-product and also being attracted by the higher prices amounting to even Rs. 100 more per ton prevailing in Indian provinces, made these supplies,[275] which proved detrimental to their own immediate and long term interests.

(*c*) *Cotton Ginning and Pressing Factories* :[276] Cotton ginning and pressing was undertaken in the *Suba* both on cottage-scale by means of *charkha* on hand and large-scale by means of machines.[277] The former, though slow in separating the lint from the seed,[278] yet, far outnumbered the latter, mainly because of its low cost, home-based and subsidiary nature of work for rural unemployed and agricultural labour,

As against 22, 7 and 14 large-scale factories in 1939-40 in Warangal, Karimnagar and Adilabad Districts respectively,[279] the distribution of hand-gins in the respective Districts, as per 1941 Census, was of the order of 1,256 ; 6,391 and 2,464.[280] Among the former, Warangal and Adilabad Districts occupied the first two places among Telangana Districts, whereas regarding the latter, Karimnagar District stood first in the entire State. Though the industry was seasonal and only involved preliminary process for the transhipment of the material for manufacturing units, yet, it was economically significant for the employment opportunities that it provided both in urban and rural areas.[281] The average number of persons employed daily in large-scale units were of the order of 1,015, 428 and 747 in Warangal, Karimnagar and Adilabad Districts[282] and those engaged in house hold units could easily be counted as many as the number of hand-gins, though not more, and more important, house-hold women during their leisure hours took up this work in the countryside.[283]

Regarding the set up of these factories, it is interesting to note that out of 13 factories in Adilabad District, as per the Census of 1941, as many as 9 were gins and presses; and in Warangal District, on the other hand, out of 23 factories, 11 belonged to the category of ginning, decorticating, rice and oil milling and 8 to that of ginning, decorticating and rice.[284] The fact that groundnut and rice predominated in the latter District as against their insignificance in the former District, compared to that of cotton,[285] characterised the type of alternative work undertaken by these ginning factories to get themselves engaged during slack season or unseason. But, as capitalists, both local and from British Indian Provinces, like Pingali Venkatrama Reddy,[286] The Empress Mills Co., Bhicaji Dadabhoi & Co., etc., found it convenient to establish more than one factory of this nature under their control,[287] the number of units at different places were reported to be more than what was required. The result was lack of work for many of the units.[288]

(*d*) *Bone Mills*: With Warangal and Karimnagar Districts occupying the first and second places respectively in the State of possessing the highest number of livestock and the incidence of cattle mortality being high due to inadequate veterinary facilities,[289] the scope for raw-bone output was considerable in the area. Bones of the value of Rs. 19,411 were exported as an yearly average during the five year period ending in 1921 from Warangal District[290] and if the figures of other Districts are taken together, the exports from the State of bone-meal and raw-bone during the decade ending in 1945, was worth nearly Rs. 1½ lakhs annually. 84% of this export went to foreign countries through the Madras port and 12% through the Bombay port.[291] Bone-meal which was the major product of the factories was used as a manure to more valuable crops such as sugarcane, coffee and tea, because of its high cost which ranged from Rs. 67 to 100 per ton, in making handles for knives and buttons, and also as an specifying agent in enamel industry.[292]

The industrial importance of Warangal town, the *Suba*, District and Taluq headquarters, was enhanced by the fact that both the large-scale and power-driven bone crushing factories that existed in the State, had been located there. Both were in the private sector, one owned by Ahmed Alladin and Sons, Known as 'The Warangal Bone Mill' and the other by Messrs Viccaji & Co., known as 'The Deccan Manure Works'[293]. The crushing capacity of each factory was 10 tons of bones per day of 10 hours.[294] The average number of persons employed daily numbered 21 in the case of the former and 43 in the case of latter.[295] Bones were crushed into various sizes of 1/8″, 1/2″, 3/4″, 5/16″, 3/16″, 3/22″ and below that came to be known as bone-meal.[296] A factory could crush 2,400 tons in a year as normally they worked for 8 to 8½ months during the year, probably due to limitations in raw material supply and the value at Rs. 100 per ton came to Rs. 2.5 lakhs.[297] There remained fair margin of profit as the cost of production was only Rs. 12 to 14 per ton.[298]

The production figures of only Alladin Bone Mill were available for 1945 and 1946. They stood at 769 and 1,911 tons respectively, the value being Rs. 96,125 and Rs. 1,19,100[299]. The output fell below the normal estimated annual capacity by 1,631 and 489 tons in the respective years. In spite of its varied uses and especially as a very valuable manure, no special care was taken either in the rural side or urban area, to prepare the commodity for marketing on a commercial basis. The collectors of bones threw them in heaps in open yards until a purchaser happened to visit the places[300]. The slackness in production efforts might also be due to the fact that the bone factories, besides bone crushing, were also allowed to carry on groundnut decorticating and rice milling.[301]

C. MEDIUM, SMALL AND COTTAGE INDUSTRIES AND THEIR DEVELOPMENTAL ASPECTS

The poor and the average financial condition of majority of the craftsmen in the area permitted only the establishment of industries of this type in considerable number, whose capital investment ranged from Rs. 5 to Rs. 50,000 and involved less of specialised labour and more of semi-skilled or unskilled labour.[302] Depending on the capacity of the worker-owners of cottage industries to employ labourers other than members of his family, these grew into small or medium scale units and that was how units of these three types were found occuring at the same or different places in industries such as tanning & leather works, brass-ware industry, brick and tiles manufacturing, weaving, dyeing, printing etc. In obtaining the raw materials at ready and cheaper rates and in marketing of their products, they very much needed Departmental assistance which came rather sparingly and inadequately. As a matter of fact, it was not financially in a position to fulfil this obligation, for its budget allotment remained the lowest among all the nation-building Departments of the State which, between 1912-13 and 1945-46 never exceeded Rs. 4 laks[303] and between 1934-35 to 1950-51, the expenditure on Industries Department formed only 0.40 to 0.56 of the total expenditure.[304] This neglect of the Department was reflected in the absence of any permanent District organisation for a systematic development of small-scale and cottage industries.[305] The Secretary, Commerce and Industries Department, himself confessed in his review on the *Administration Report for 1945-46* that until then, the activities of the Department were confined mainly to Hyderabad city only.[306] The failure of the State machinery naturally drove the craftsmen into the hands of rich traders or *sahukars* and master-craftsmen who reduced them to the status of piece-wage or paid workers.[307]

i. Tanneries & Leather Works : As in bone industry, Warangal District dominated in tanning also.[308] Out of 1,152 people who were engaged in tanning industry during 1918-20, as many as 670 or 58.15% were from Warangal District[309]. There was vast scope and need for the development of these industries in view of the fact that during the decade ending in 1944-45, the import of tanned leather, leather goods and belts averaged Rs. 10.52 lakhs per year as against the export of raw hides and skins from the State to the value of Rs. 12.72 lakhs per year and of leather to the value of Rs.35 lakhs.[310] The export of raw hides and skins from Warangal District during the earlier period was of far higher proportions, which was of the value of Rs. 18,58,623 being the average of the five years ending in 1920-21.[311] Even '*tarward* bark' (*Cassia auriculata*), the main raw material that was used in tanning was so much available in abundance in the District that its export during the said period amounted to as high as Rs. 79,525.[312]

As many as 30 Leather Factories were reported existing in Warangal District, but none was perennial.[313] In the month of August, 1945 (*Meher*, 1354 *Fasli*), 15 of them were closed down without ever giving notice to workers, due to shortage of leathers.[314] It is significant to find leather shortage as against huge exports of raw hides and skins. The reasons for this curious situation are to be found in the crude and primitive methods that were adopted in the process of tanning, and the local tanneries finding it profitable to export leather rather than supplying it to local Leather Factories. The tanning was so defective that out of every 16.5 lakhs of skins and hides that were tanned, only 30 thousand were selected for the export and the rest were rejected.[315] The situation was really so discouraging that with 58, 95 and 114 village tanneries, each worked by 2 or more persons in Warangal, Karimnagar and Adilabad Districts respectively and 84 large and small tanneries in the State of which 30 were of medium size giving employment to 2,000 persons,[316] the shoe-makers of Karimnagar and Warangal Districts, numbering about 300, were obliged to import leather for their requirement from outside the State.[317] The Government could think of arranging for the training of the tanners or *chamars* in modern methods of tanning only after 1944-45, but no perceptible change seem to have taken place during the remaining six years, in view of the tradition-bound mentality of the *chamars* and Government's preoccupation with problems on the food and political front.[318]

The problem was mutual. Tanned leather got exported and leather goods of the annual value of Rs. 2.73 lakhs were imported, mainly because of non-development of local leather industry to any significant stage other then shoe and *chappal* manufacture, besides agricultural requisites, by village *mochis* or cobblers[319]. The production particulars of the Leather Factories of Warangal District which used neither mechanical nor electrical power[320] are not available. The condition of village *mochis* was also none the happier. Not only they found work for only 8 months in a year, but more affecting was that they got their work financed by local money lenders and business men for a period of 4 to 6 months in a year @ of 12 to 24 %.[321] After clearing off the loan, immediately after disposing of their products, not much surplus remained for the artisans either to carry their trade independently or to develop the scale of their operations.

ii. Medium and Small-Scale Extraction of Graphite, Limestone Garnets, Talc & Soapstone, Steatite, Ochre and Clays : The extraction of these minerals, though of proven industrial utility and existence in *Suba* Taluqs,[322] was on a low key during the period. No industries based on these were established[323] and hence, the mining was done in a half-hearted manner. Whatever was extracted got exported and the Government was satisfied with the royalty that it obtained from the mining companies or agencies.[324] The extraction of graphite from Paloncha mines by Mr. R.S. Chenoy, the lease assignee, was so poor that it yielded 26 tons in 1937-38, 9-1/4 tons in 1938-39 and 27 tons, 18 cwts and 84 lbs. in 1942[325]. It definitely reflects on the type of extraction or the quality of the mineral that was kept, or its marketing, for these little quantities that were produced could not find demand and consequently, no mining was undertaken during the years 1939-40 and 1940-41.[326] Foreign export might have suffered due to advent of the War, but otherwise, the mineral was so much valuable in metal, pencil, stone polishing and electrical industries[327] that it should have found its way to British Indian provinces. The very lease expired in July, 1949.[308] Extraction particulars of the Paloncha Graphite Mines are not to be seen in the records after 1942. The graphite deposits at Hasanabad in Karimnagar District, though reported small,[329] remained completely unexploited.

Vast limestone deposits estimated at more than 900 million tons that could be used in lithography, building construction and flooring, were reported occurring in the forests of the *Suba* Districts.[330] Whereas graphite mining was carried on as a small-scale industry, limestone quarrying was undertaken as a medium-scale industry.[331] Excepting the Sirpur Paper Mills putting to use 50 million tons of fine grade limestone available in the Asifabad area of Adilabad District[332] and quarrying of Tandur Mines in the same District for flooring stones including that of polish,[333] no other industrial or economic application of this abundant and valuable mineral was undertaken during the period. Output figures of only the flooring stone that was quarried from all the mines in the State are available quinquennially from 1915-19 to 1940-44 which show that excepting the Depression period of 1930-34 and the War period of 1940-44 which were marked by considerable fall in production compared to preceding quinquennium, due to low prices, slackness of trade and transport difficulties, others were signified by growth in production. The maximum output reached during this period was 195.25 sq. feet (in lakhs) during 1925-29 valued at Rs. 5.86 lakhs.[334] But, other varieties such as the highly crystalline limestone nearing marble in Rajura Taluq of Adilabad District and black limestones occurring extensively in the hills north of Luxettipet, Taluq headquarters in the same District,[335] were allowed to go unutilised.

The collection of garnets,—small iron crystals of deep red variety that were found in Khammam, Paloncha, Yellandu and

Madhira Taluqs of Warangal District and were used in ear ornaments, watch bearings and asabrasives and had been estimated to exist in a reserve of about 35 million tons—was carried out as a small-scale industry between 1910-1929.[336] The quantity that was mined rose from 13,680 lbs. during 1910-14 to 2,32,612 lbs. during 1915-19, but since then, it slided down to 62,517 lbs. during 1920-24 and further, to 28,443 lbs. during the last quinquennium of 1925-29. Large quantities of these garnets had been sent to Madras by the Hyderabad Deccan Mining Co. Ltd., being the leaseholders, in order to be cut into semi-precious stones for use in ornamentation. The garnet collection work has since 1929 been given up on the ground that adequate market was not there and the lease of the Hyderabad Deccan Mining Co. had been surrendered by them in 1935-36.[337] The quantity that was mined formed only a negligible proportion of the estimated resources, and in view of abrasive garnets being used upto 90% in the manufacture for polishing papers and clothes and red garnets being sold as substitute for emery[338], efforts would have been made to capture distant or foreign markets rather than confining to neighbouring Indian Provinces, but that seemed not to have taken place.

Soapstone & Talc, Ochre, Kyanite, Corundum, Pyrite and Antimony were some other minerals whose occurrence was reported from different Taluqs of the *Suba* and were useful in stoneware, manufacture of toilet powders, paints, distempers, oil refining, ceramic industries, as refractory material etc.,[339] had not been, rather unfortunately for industrial development, taken up for exploitation. Only the Sirpur Paper Mills extracted 1,008 cft. of Steatite from Nittur quarry in Peddapalli area, a Taluq headquarters in Karimnagar District[340] and six quarries of clay in Asifabad Taluq in Adilabad District were mined, which, along with the one in Bidar Taluq of Bidar District of Gulbarga *Suba*, produced 2,439 tons of clay in 1948 and 1,873 tons in 1949.[341] Rest of the resources remained hidden under the strong bowels of the earth, most uncared for and unthought of.

iii. Handloom Spinning, Weaving, Printing and Dyeing : Hand-spinning by means of *charkhas* or spinning wheels, though met only partially the yarn required for handloom weaving,[342] yet formed an important home industry, especially in Karimnagar District which as in hand-ginning of cotton,[343] not only came to occupy first place in the State, but stood far above all other Districts in the number of spinning wheels that it possessed. It rose from 49,314 in 1921 to 52,255 in 1931 and 57,277 in 1941, which accounted for 1/3 of the total number in both Telangana as well as the State. Compared to this supreme importance of *charkha* spinning in Karimnagar District, the other *Suba* Districts of Warangal and Adilabad with 9,715 and 19,827 spinning wheels in 1941 respectively, came to occupy 5th and 4th places in the Region as well as the State.[344] As spinning, by way of process, followed ginning in textile manufacture, the number of cottage units in the former case, very much exhibited the same order as was experienced in the case of the latter. A woman could spin half an lb. of cotton in three days and earn 1½ annas a day.[345] *Khadi* propoganda which was carried on inthe *Suba* Districts as part of Congress activity, had given much impetus to hand-spinning.[346] Metpalli, a *Jagir* Taluq in Karimnagar District functioned as the largest *Khadi* manufacturing Centre in the entire Dominions, with the activity being spread over nearly 120 villages surrounding Metpalli, the Taluq headquarters which produced *Khadi* or *Khaddar* worth Rs. 7 lakhs every year.[347]

But, the hand-spun yarn, though provided useful employment, especially to women of the lower classes, was hardly enough to meet the needs of local handloom weavers. Even mills also failed to remove this deficiency, and the result was huge foreign imports of yarn, whose value was of the order of Rs. 6,92,242 and Rs. 92,432 as against exports of the value of Rs. 54,313 and Rs. 14, in the case of Warangal and Adilabad Districts respectively, being the average of the five years ending in 1920-21.[348] In the State as a whole also, the situation was not much different even after six large-scale Spinning and Weaving Power Mills, including that of Azam Jahi at Warangal[349], came into operation by mid-thirties. In 1942, yarn worth about Rs. 64 lakhs was imported by the handloom weavers in the State as against Rs. 20 lakhs worth yarn supplied by the local mills and less than Rs. 2 lakhs worth yarn that was hand-spun.[350] Yarn supply for silk and woollen handloom weaving was characterised by total dependence on foreign and Indian imports, except in the case of Tussore silk in respect of the former and crude or inferior stuff, though not imports, in the case of the latter. Superior silk yarn was imported from Italy costing about Rs. 38-4-0 per 1b and in its absence, inferior variety from Bangalore was purchased at Rs. 33-5-4 per 1b.[351] Though Tusser cocoons, the chief raw material for Tusser silk, were gathered primarily from the forests of Parkal and Mahadeopur Taluqs in Karimnagar District, yet, due to the insufficiency of the local output, imports were made from Chanda, Nagpur and several places in Bengal.[352] Yarn for the manufacture of woollen blankets, the well-known local cottage-industry product, was spun by means of hand *charkhas* out of the raw wool received from the local tanneries, but very much in a crude and undeveloped manner, for the spinning was done by local shepherds who, being illiterate, carried on their primitive way of spinning as well as weaving.[353] In fact, the main difficulty faced by Warangal Carpet Factory in the manufacture of superior quality of carpets was the non-availability of superior mill-spun yarn, which could have been overcome only by the establishment of a large-sized woollen mill in the area, in view of its vast raw material potential, but that never came about, as part of poor industrial exploitation of the *Suba* resources.[354]

(*b*) *Weaving : Cotton, Silk & Woollen* : Handloom weaving was of great significance in the economic history of the *Suba*, not only as the most ancient and important of the cottage industries in the Dominions, but also as a significant subsidiary occupation to agriculturists who failed to get sufficient income from their profession or found enough leisure to pursue part-time vocation. The number of such ryots formed the highest in Warangal District during the triennium of 1918-20 and it accounted for 27% of the total number of weavers in the District.[355] This, in a way, pointed to the intensity of agricultural insufficiency or poverty in this premier District of the

Suba. Out of the three types of weaving, that of cotton very much predominated, the number of cotton looms formed as much as 89.78% of the total number of looms in the *Suba*[356]. Those of silk and wool formed only 1.12% and 9.09% of total looms in the *Suba.* Even in the value of fabrics manufactured in a year also, the same striking difference was noticeable that, whereas the said value in the case of cotton was Rs. 36.5 lakhs, it remained only Rs. 1.45 lakhs in the case of silk and Rs. 1.78 lakhs in the case of wool.[357] Among the *Suba* Districts, Karimnagar District, very much in accordance with its leading position in respect of hand-ginning and spinning[358], accounted for 56.50% and 76.08% in respect of cotton and woollen looms of the *Suba.* As a matter of fact, even in the State also, Karimnagar District occupied the first place in respect of both these kinds of hand-weaving. On the other hand, Warangal District, though accounted for 78.15% of total silk looms of the *Suba*, its annual value of fabrics manufactured fell short that of Karimnagar District by more than 100%, thereby signifying to the greater volume of production in the latter District, though the number of its looms formed only 1/6th of that of the former. In the State as a whole, on the basis of number of silk looms, Warangal, Karimnagar and Adilabad Districts came to occupy 6th, 10th and 11th places, the first three places being occupied by Raichur, Nizamabad, Medak and Baghat Districts. It is important to note that in cotton and woollen handlooms, the two *Suba* Districts of Warangal and Adilabad not only stood far behind Karimnagar District, their percentages of the *Suba* total being 29.92% and 13.84% in the case of cotton and 21.93% and 1.97% in the case of wool respectively, but their ranking in respect of these in the State was also considerably lower, amounting to 6th and 8th places in respect of cotton and 7th and 16th or last place in respect of wool accordingly. The wide prevalence of this cottage industry in the *Suba* area could be understood from the fact that the number of handlooms in it formed as much as 27.35% of the total number in the State.[359]

But, it is alarming to note that the number of cotton and woollen looms, though not of silk, were on continuous decrease except in one or two stray cases during the period 1921-41, for which only the figures are available. The decrease occurred without any break in respect of Adilabad District, Telangana and Marathwada Regions and also the State as a whole. The fall in cotton looms in 1931 compared to 1921 in Adilabad District by 9,051 which amounted to 64.41% was the highest during this period ; in the case of woollen looms also, the fall experienced in this District between 1931-41 was so high that it amounted to 60.50%. The unfavourable crop conditions that prevailed for most of the time during the decade, coupled with the onset of the Great Economic Depression, the heavy competition from mill-made cloth, and lack of help from the Government to meet these conditions had been greatly responsible for this steep and unprecedented fall in cotton and woollen handloom weaving of Adilabad District.[360] Karimnagar District also, excepting an increase of 24.45% in 1931 in respect of cotton looms, suffered decline in 1941 amounting to 26.46% in respect of cotton weaving and 6.03% in respect of woollen looms. The percentage of decrease was less because majority of the weavers in this District compared to those in the former were economically of more than average soundness, so that they could weather the troublous conditions to a limited extent, though not fully.[361] Conversely to what transpired in respect of Karimnagar District, Warangal District experienced a fall of 33.63% in 1931 in cotton looms, but had a rise of 46.01% in cotton weaving and 20.60% in woollen looms in 1941. Unfavourable agricultural and business conditions that accounted for the decrease of 1931 was followed by boom conditions in the following decade after mid-thirties which, together with the better marketing, trade and transport facilities that Warangal District had comparatively, contributed for the rise in cotton and woollen looms of the District in 1941.[362] In the case of silk looms, quite contrastingly to those of cotton and woollen, increase was registered in respect of all, except Karimnagar District, during the decade of 1931-41. The affluence of the upper classes who took advantage of the high prices that came to prevail with the commencement of the War and sizeable exports to British Indian centres like Bombay, Poona and Sholapur, have led to this development.[363] The fall in respect of Karimnagar District that amounted to as heavy as 76.51% was due to the overshadowing of silk weaving by cotton and woollen weaving and also the sufferance of raw material imports due to War-time restrictions.[364]

The final position that emerged by the close of the period, in the field of handloom weaving, and even in its allied branches of dyeing and printing, was highly depressing. Majority of the weavers either migrated to border provinces of British India to work under better conditions, or resorted to factory labour or even unskilled labour such as carpentry, masonry or even *coolie* work, for whereas a weaver on his loom in a town earned not more than 5 annas per day, a worker in carpentry earned Rs. 1-4-0, in masonry work 12 annas and a *coolie* 6 annas per day. Only those weavers who were not in a position physically to bear exertion, continued in their age-old craft.[365] The most important factor that contributed for this sad plight of the handloom weavers was their complete dependence on *sahukars* or master-weavers for the purchase of yarn, dyes and also the sale of their finished products. They had, in fact, been reduced to the condition of mere piece-wage earners, being thereby deprived of the opportunity of taking benefit of rising prices for their products that were experienced during the forties. The increasing poverty of these craftsmen and the failure of either the Government or the Co-operative institutions in providing easy, though not cheap credit to them, led to this sorry state of affairs in which the whole handloom weaving industry was under the thumb of a few greedy merchants and rapacious master-weavers.[366] The Department of Industries and Commerce, rather strangely, instead of trying to remove the presence of this intermodiary class, began to depend on them for the distribution of scarce raw materials, thinking that it would be convenient to deal through them rather than directly with labour. The result was that the artisans were made not only to hover around these middlemen for the issue of their supply cards, but the cotton yarn supplied to country weavers was issued at an unduly high price compared with the price charged by the mills.[367]

Heavy competition from the cheap imported mill cloth and also to a considerable extent from the hand-woven products of British India,[368] meagre adoption of modern looms and methods of weaving and dyeing, especially in silk and blanket weaving,[369] scarcity and high prices of yarn and dyes due to black-marketing,[370] lack of support and encouragement from the Government which the industry formerly enjoyed in full,[371] change in the taste of the middle and upper classes very much in imitation of that of the Ruler and his officials and nobles from hand-woven local cloth products to imported mill-made items[372], feudal domination in the area very much stifling the free functioning of handloom weavers[373] and the crushing effect of the debt burden of these artisans,[374] had all been significant factors that contributed, each in its own way, for the decline of the handloom weaving and dyeing industries. Though cottage industry products like *Pitambars*, *Cholkhans*, *tailia rumals*, *dhoties*,[375] shirtings, blankets, etc., had been characterised by artistic excellence and variety, people began to prefer mill products, though they lacked variety and design, mainly because of cheaper prices. No protection, either by way of tariffs or by subsidies, was given to the local weavers to face this strong outside competition. Especially, the non-patronage of these products by the ruling and well-to-do sections who were very much in a position to do so with a long tradition behind them, deprived the industries the main core of their support. The mass illiteracy of the weavers, their poor housing accommodation, the inadequacy of the Demonstration staff to teach them new techniques and above all, the declining demand for their products, made the Departmental efforts to introduce new appliances and methods of production meet with only meagre effect.[376] Yarn and dyes were blackmarketed to such an extent that weavers in Warangal District were unable to get the yarn supplied by Azamjahi Mills of the same District, except at high prices that acted as a source of great discouragement to their production efforts.[377] The pleas for action against blackmarketeers remained very much unheeded.[378] Feudal domination in the area was so complete that only those weavers who obeyed their commands could carry on the trade and production was geared to suit their interests.[379] Imposition of tax on handlooms in *Jagirs* right until 1944, though it was abolished in *Khalsa* area as early as 1872, created considerable hardship to weavers in these areas.[380] With scarce supply of raw material and insecure demand, the debt contracted by handloom weavers for yarn purchase, though meant for a short period, proved a recurring burden so much so that, it became extremely difficult for them to get extricated from the unrelenting thumb of the greedy *sahukars* and master weavers. The cumulative result of these factors was that, this widely based cottage industry in the *Suba* went on declining from decade to decade since 1921.

(*c*) *Dyeing and Printing* : This was an auxiliary industry to weaving, coming down from the ancient times as the latter did. Hence, its progress or decline became very much dependent on the condition of that of the weaving industry.[381] Dyeing was practised almost at each weaving centre, either by professional dyers or by the weavers themselves. Warangal with 60 families, Hasanparti, with 45 families, both in Warangal Taluq of Warangal District, Koratla with 6 families in Jagtiyal Taluq and Sirsilla with 8 families in the Taluq of the same name, both in Karimnagar District, had flourished as important centres of cloth dyeing industry in the *Suba* area.[382] The number of cottage establishments that were engaged in cloth and yarn-dyeing rose tremendously between 1931-41 amounting to 320.83%, 58.13% and 588.23% in Warangal, Karimnagar and Adilabad Districts respectively,[383] very much prompted by increased demand and better regulation of yarn supplies. But, during the decade that followed, the industry was very much on the decline, being confronted by raw material scarcity and external competition. The system of controls that was in operation since 1944 resulted in blackmarketing and high prices of the dyeing colours,[384] which, coupled with the exhausting of natural dyes except cochineal and indigo[385] and competition from the power-driven dyeing mills from outside the Nizam's Dominions, brought the industry to sore straits.[386]

Cloth printing which was also an important ancient industry co-existing with weaving flourished in the centres of Warangal, Karimnagar, Jagtiyal and Adilabad, all head-quarter towns in the *Suba* Districts.[387] It could be seen that the first town where 40 families were engaged in printing of coarse and other types of cloth was also known for significant cultivation of dycing industry.[388] Handblock printing using red, chacolate and black shades of alizarine, included variety of cloth material such as saris, floor cloth (*Jajum*), bed cover (*Palang posh*), quilt (*Razaee*), table cloth, dinner cloth (*dastar Khan*), prayer cloth (*janimaz*), screen and curtain (*Purdah*), neckties, kerchiefs and *lambadi* clothing such as *dupattas* (covering cloth), *langas* (lady wear in place of sari), breast clothes, etc.[389] But this industry, though like that of dyeing witnessed rise in the number of units between 1931-41,[390] started declining subsequently, due to factors like competition from British Indian centres like Pamidi, Masulipatam, Chirala, Nellore, all in Madras Presidency, Bombay and Farukabad (U.P.), the printers due to their poverty, illiteracy and lack of training organised by the Government, failing to adopt modern design and new colours that led to their products not being very much in demand, which also was caused by change in fashion and rise in the standard of living.[391] The industry got confined only to a few families and the post-War Governmental efforts to rehabilitate this, were not effective.[392]

(*iv*) *Other important coitage and home industries* :

Tailoring, dairying, poultry-farming, carpentry & smithy, brass and copper-ware, silver & gold filigree work, pottery, brick and tiles manufacture, toy-making, *beedi* manufacture, basket and cane works, formed important industries in this category, next to textiles, providing employment to good number of men, women and children in the countryside of the *Suba* Districts. Excepting the manufacturing of brick and tiles, all other undertakings, remained home-based. The instruments and the methods of production employed in these concerns, remained essentially traditional, with practically no complicated machinery in operation that required skilled training on the part of the craftsmen and not more than two or three persons engaged in each unit. Apart from sewing machines, 19 cream separators that had been used in dairying in Warangal District during 1935-40, in respect of which, it stood next to Hyderabad City and Atraf-i-Balda District,[393] consisted of the only pieces of machinery used in these home industries.[394] The rate and volume of production, though naturally slow and small, could, of course, more than meet the local requirements. The products of gold and silver, filigree works of Karimnagar and Jagtiyal in Karimnagar District and Nirmal toy industry of Adilabad District, won renown, due to their artistic excellence, in markets outside the State.[395]

The number of these cottage establishments excepting those relating to toy-making and poultry-farming, had shown considerable rise during 1931-41.[396] In other words, more and more number of people in the area came to depend on these industries for their living, very much being influenced by unfavourable agricultural and trade conditions for most of the time during the decade, due to Depression and the Second War.[397] Excepting in tailoring, dairying and cane works in which Warangal District had the upper hand, in the rest of these industries, Karimnagar District came to occupy the dominant place in the State itself.[398] On the other hand, during this period, the toy-making and wood-painting works in Warangal, Karimnagar and Adilabad Districts showed a decrease of 61.53% and 59.45% in their number respectively.[399] This industry, though ancient in conception and practice, lost State encouragement during the present century[400] and hence, due to failure of demand, majority of the craftsmen turned to other available occupations for living.[401] As a result of this decline, these *Suba* Districts which occupied I, II and III places in the State in 1931, slid down to II, VI and V places respectively in 1941.[402] The number of poultry birds in Warangal, Karimnagar and Adilabad Districts, in respect of which they occupied the first two and sixth places respectively in the State in 1940, suffered also heavy fall during the next quinquennium amounting to as many as 9,41,003, 5,24,106 and 1,44,002 or a percentage of 51.81, 50.41 and 28.10 in the respective Districts.[403] Even though this industry had considerable scope for development in view of increasing demand for chicken and eggs the unprecedented loss in birds during the quinquennium was due to lack of arrangements by the Veterinary Department to provide vaccine treatment to the birds that had been attacked by *ranikhet*, a common disease in their case. Only in the year 1949-50, arrangements had been made to import this vaccine from Madras.[404] In spite of this severe loss in birds, this home-industry as such by 1945 came to be of such wide application, especially in Karimnagar District, that with 1,267 poultry farms, it covered nearly 80% and 66% of the total farms that were there in Telangana and Hyderabad State respectively.[405]

A study of these industries reveals the significant fact that as against plentiful raw material resources such as *tendu* leaves,[406] milch-cattle, bamboo & cane, soft and light wood,[407] clay,[408] poultry birds, etc., and skilled artisans that had been practising the respective trades since several generations, the product out-turn was very small when compared to huge raw material exports and imports of manufactured goods. This development was not far different from what was observed earlier in respect of large, medium and small-scale industries.[409] In the case of bamboo and baskets works to take an instance, in which Warangal and Karimnagar Districts held respectively first and second places in the State regarding the distribution of cottage units,[410] bamboo worth Rs. 3 lakhs was exported from the State, import being insignificant of the value of 0.46 lakhs and baskets worth Rs. 80,000 had been imported on an average per year during 1941-45. As a matter of fact, this was one industry where the articles were manufactured by manual labour alone with little or no capital investment and a very large number of articles of household and agricultural utility had been turned out as a means of livelihood by hundreds of poor families, otherwise called *Burods*[411] Dairy industry in the *Suba* Districts exhibited the same tendency. With 3,62,567, 2,85,604 and 2,44,099 total milch cattle in 1935, Warangal, Karimnagar and Adilabad Districts occupied respectively I, II and IV places in the State.[412] As against this resource, the number of dairy establishments where butter and ghee, etc., were manufactured, ranged from 23 in 1935 to 9 in 1945 (with, of course, 110 in 1940) in respect of Warangal District, 3 in 1935 to 6 in 1940 (nil in 1945) in respect of Karimnagar District and 7 in 1940 (nil in 1935) to 6 in 1945 in the case of Adilabad District.[413] Even in the State as a whole also, the situation was not different. Whereas import of dairy produce (ghee and butter) rose in value from O.S. Rs. 5,65,678 in 1930-31 to 12,99,473 in 1934-35, the export of the samefell down from O.S.Rs. 2,89,355 in the former year to 86,829 in the latter.[414] On the other hand, Karimnagar filigree industry and Nirmal toy industry and lacquer works, whose varied products displayed the artistic skill of the craftsmen, declined due to lack of enough support by the Department and also a change in the tastes of the people, especially of the middle and upper classes.[415] The decline had so much set in even by 1937-38 that, only three master craftsmen were found engaged in toy industry at Nirmal.[416] These ancient industries had thus been allowed to die until they had seen the light of the day after the formation of the Popular Government in the State.

D. LABOUR :

Agricultural labour, though seasonal and comparatively less paid, formed 12.15% of the *Suba* population in 1931, as against factory labour which formed only 0 53%.[417] But, if the total number of cultivators were taken into consideration, agricultural labourers numbered per every cultivator only at the proportion of 0.4 in Warangal District to 0.3 in Karimnagar and Adilabad Districts as per 1931 population Census.[418] The smallness of land holdings, the meagreness of irrigation, the primary character of agricultural occupation, the seasonal and the less remunerative nature of agricultural labour, had all been the factors that contributed for narrowing down the scope for the latter.[419] Warangal District with 1,24,319 agricultural labourers in 1931, occupied the first place in the State.[420] In the *1929-30 Economic Enquiries*, it was found that one-third of the families in the District were landless and tenancyless and about a fifth had been unskilled or dependent families.[421] Even in 1949-50, the percentage of landless tenants to the total number of tenants, proved the most conspicuous in this District, amounting to 71.19.[422] The large-scale concentration of land in the central and northern part of the District and its cultivation almost exclusively either by tenants or by *bhagelas*,[423] had been very much responsible for this particular situation in it. Further, it could be seen from Table XLVIII[424] that, in between male and female labourers in the field of agriculture, the former outnumbered the latter in Warangal District and vice versa in the other *Suba* Districts. The fact that women with lesser wages ranging upto 50% to that of men[425] could suitably be engaged in wet crop works such as sowing or transplantation, weeding and reaping,[426] was very much responsible for the latter's situation. In Warangal District, on the other hand, male labourers were employed in larger number on yearly or monthly basis as hired labourers of *Jeetagadus*[427] or as '*bhagelas*'. The number of agricultural labourers in Karimnagar and Adilabad Districts stood less by 23.79% and 48.46% respectively than that of Warangal District.[428] In fact, Adilabad District with 60,248 labourers, ranked the last but one in the State, the last being Nizamabad District with 57,563 labourers.[429] The lesser degree of rich landlord composition in Karimnagar District and poor irrigational crops in Adilabad District contributed for this lesser in take of agricultural labour.[430]

Wage Condition of Agricultural Labour: The wages of agricultural labourers, as could be seen from Table XLIX, were on the decline during the period 1927-28 in which the last wage enumeration in the State was done,[431] to 1934-35,

TABLE XLVIII

Total Number of Labourers Employed in Agriculture and Factories in Suba Districts, 1911-1945

Number Employed
in Agriculture

Sl. No.	Year	Warangal District			Karimnagar District			Adilabad District		
		Men	Women	Total	Men	Women	Total	Men	Women	Total
1	2	3	4	5	6	7	8	9	10	11
1.	1911	—	—	—	—	—	—	—	—	—
2.	1921	—	—	—	—	—	—	—	—	—
8.	1931	64,894	59,515	1,24,319	39.668	55,972	94,749	29,999	31,158	59,249
4.	1932	—	—	—	—	—	—	—	—	—
5.	1933	—	—	—	—	—	—	—	—	—
6.	1934	—	—	—	—	—	—	—	—	—
7.	1935	—	—	—	—	—	—	—	—	—
8.	1940	—	—	—	—	—	—	—	—	—
9.	1941	—	—	—	—	—	—	—	—	—
10.	1942	—	—	—	—	—	—	—	—	—
11.	1943	—	—	—	—	—	—	—	—	—
12.	1944	—	—	—	—	—	—	—	—	—
13.	1945	—	—	—	—	—	—	—	—	—

Number employed

In Factories (Daily Average)

		Warangal District			Karimnagar District			Adilabad District		
		Men	Women	Total	Men	Women	Total	Men	Women	Total
		12	13	14	15	16	17	18	19	20
1.	1911	6.872	2,192	9,962	—	—	—	33	27	62
2.	1921	19,449	3,415	13,864	—	—	—	57	2	49
3.	1931	—	—	4,142*	—	—	351	—	—	765
4.	1932	—	—	1,723	—	—	351	—	—	656
5.	1933	—	—	1,829	—	—	482	—	—	1,956
6.	1934	—	—	1,942	—	—	1,383	—	—	1,259
7.	1935	—	—	5,329	—	—	1,982	—	—	1,959
8.	1949	—	—	7,2[illegible]	—	—	1,125	—	—	743
9.	1941	—	—	8,208	—	—	1,208	—	—	855
10.	1942	—	—	5,935	—	—	514	—	—	1,063
11.	1943	—	—	9,568	—	—	143	—	—	1,304
12.	1944	—	—	9,291	—	—	590	—	—	307
13.	1945	—	—	5,534	—	—	330	—	—	2,425

*Excluding Singareni Colliaries Labour of 11,338 in 1931 Census.

Source : *Compiled from* : 1. *Census of India, 1911*, Part II, P. 295 :

2. *Census of India, Hyderabad State, 1921*, Part II. pp. 237-38 :
3. *Report on Labour Census, 1935*, p. 25.
4. *Statistical Year Book, 1349 Fasli (1939-40)*, pp. 1098-99.

&

5. *Statistical Year Book, 1351-1354 Fasli (1941-42 to 1944-45)*, pp. 1210-11.

TABLE XLIX

Wage Rates of Rural and Urban Labourers in Suba Districts, Telangana, Marathwara and the State 1927-28—1949-50

(In Rupees, annas and paise)

			Rate per day in cash			
			Blacksmiths URBAN			
Sl. No.	Year	Administrative unit	Rural	Superior	Ordinary	Rural
1	2	3	4	5	6	7
1.	1927-28*	Telangana	0-12-11	1-2-5	0-12-10	0-12-10
2.	,,	Marathwada	1-1-6	1-6-7	0-15-3	1-2-2
3.	,,	Hydcrabad State	0-15-2	1-4-6	0-14-0	0-14-6
4.	1934-35	Telangana	1-7-7	1-1-8	0-11-3	1-9-5
5.	,,	Marathwada	1-15-7	1-2-2	0-11-7	1-14-6
6.	,,	Hyderabad State	1-11-7	1-1-11	0-11-5	1-11-11
7.	,, **	Warangal District	1-3-7	1-0-0	9-11-0	1-5-0
8.	,,	Karimnagar District	2-8-5	0-12-0	0-8-0	1-11-10
9.	,,	Adilabad District	1-4-4	0-15-0	0-10-0	1-7-9
10.	1939-40	Telangana	1-8-0	0-15-0	0-11-0	1-9-0
11.	,,	Marathwada	1-10-0	1-4-0	0-12-0	1-10-0
12.	,,	Hyderabad State	1-9-6	1-2-6	0-11-6	1-9-6
13	,,	Warangal State	1-8-0	1-0-0	0-9-0	1-8-0
14	,,	Karimnagar District	2-4-0	0-10-6	0-7-5	1-8-0
15.	,,	Adilabad District	1-14-0	0-10-6	0-8-0	2-4-0
16.	1949-50	Warangal District	—	—	—	—
17.	,,	Karimnagar District	—	—	—	—
18.	,,	Adilabad District	—	—	—	—

			Rate per day in cash						
			Carpenters URBAN		Sowers & Weeders			Transplanters	
			Superior	Ordinary	Plough men	Men	Women	Men	Women
			8	9	10	11	12	13	14
1.	1927-28*	Telangana	1-3-7	0-12-11	0-4-2	0-4-0	0-2-5	0-2-4	0-2-1
2.	,,	Marathwada	1-10-1	1-0-9	0-7-2	0-7-5	0-4-0	0-5-9	0-3-5
3.	,,	Hyderabad State	1-6-10	0-14-10	0-5-8	0-5-9	0-3-3	0-4-3	0-2-9
4.	,,	Telangana	1-2-6	0-12-2	0-3-2	0-3-9	9-2-4	0-2-11	0-2-2
5.	,,	Marathwada	1-15-3	0-13-9	0-4-8	0-4-10	0-2-11	0-3.11	0-2-2
6.	,,	Hyderabad State	1-3-10	0-12-11	0-3-21	0-4-4	0-2-8	0-3-5	0-2-2
7.	,,	Warangal District	1-1-0	0-12-0	0-3-10	0-4-0	0-2-7	0-3-0	0-2-6
8.	,,	Karimnagar District	1-1-0	1-10-0	0-2-5	0-3-0	0-1-9	0-2-2	0-1-5
9.	,,	Adilabad District	1.1-0	0-11-0	0-3-1	0-2-10	0-2-2	0-2-3	0-1-10
10.	1939-40	Telangana	1-0.0	0-11-0	0-3·6	0-2-2	0-3-8	0-3-0	0-2-6
11.	,,	Marathwada	1-5-0	3-10-0	0-4-0	0-4-2	0-2-8	0-3-0	0-2-6
12-	,,	Hyderabad State	1-2-6	0-12-0	0-3-9	0-4-1	0-2-5	0-3-3	0-2-6
13.	,,	Warangal State	1-0-0	0-10-0	0-3-6	0-4-6	0-2-6	0-3-0	0-2-3
14.	,,	Karimnagar District	0-12-2	0-8-6	0-2-6	0-3-0	0-2-0	0-2-8	0-1-8
15.	,,	Adilabad District	1-2-0	0-11-0	0-3-0	0-3-0	0-1-8	0-2-6	0-1-8
16.	1949-50	Warangal District	—	—	—	—	—	—	—
17.	,,	Karimnagar District	—	—	—	—	—	—	—
18.	,,	Adilabad District	—	—	—	—	—	—	—

*Data of Districts separately is not available for this year.

**District figures are averages, arrived at by adding the rates of Taluqs in a District and then dividing it by this number of Taluqs in it.

			Rates per Day in cash				
			Reapers			Agricultural Labourers	
			Men	Women	Herdsmen	men	Women
			15	16	17	18	19
1.	1927-28	Telangana	0-4-4	0-0·1	0-2-10	0-3-9	0-2-10
2.	,,	Marathwada	0-8-6	0-4-10	0-3-10	0-6-8	0-3-8
3.	,,	Hyderabad State	0-6-7	0-4-9	0-3-4	0-5-3	0-3-3
4.	1934-35	Telangana	0-4-9	0-2-8	0-2-9	0-3-4	0-2-10
5.	,,	Marathwada	0-4-9	0-3-1	0-2-8	0-4-9	0-2-6
6.	,,	Hyderabad State	0-4-3	0-2·11	0-2-9	0-4-6	0-2-8
7.	,,	Warangal District	0-3-6	0-2-10	0-2-6	0-3-6	0-2-8
8,	,,	Karimnagar District	0-3-0	0-2-0	0-2-3	0-2-7	0-1-7
9.	,,	Adilabad Dtstrict	0-3-1	0-2-5	0-2-10	0-3-5	0--2-2
10,	1939-40	Telangana	0-4-0	0-2-6	0-3-0	0-3-6	0-2-2
11.	,,	Marathwada	0-4-6	0-3-0	0-3-2	0-4-0	0-2-4
12.	,,	Hyderabad State	0-4-3	0-2-9	0-3-1	0-3-9	0-2-3
13.	,,	Warangal District	0 3-8	0-2-6	0-2-6	0-2-6	0-3-8
14.	,,	Karimnagar District	0-3-0	0-2-0	0-3-0	0-3-0	0-2-0
15.	,,	Adilabad District	0-3-0	0-2-0	0-3-0	0-3-4	0-2-0
16.	1949-50	Warangal District	—	—	—	1-0-0	0-8-0
17.	,,	Karimnagar District	—	—	—	1-0-0	0-8-0
18.	,,	Adilabad District	—	—	—	0-8-0	0-4-0

			Rates per Day in cash					Rate per Month	
			Masons		Collies				
			Superior	Ordinary	Men	Women	Boys	Sweepers	Malis
			20	21	22	23	24	25	25
1.	1927-28	Telangana	2-5-1	0-31-5	0-6-4	0-3-10	0-2-11	4-7-3	8-10-9
2.	,,	Marathwada	8-8-6	1-0-5	2-8-9	0-4-10	0-3-9	9-13-9	11-0-6
3.	,,	Hyderabad State	1-6-9	1-14-11	0-7-6	0--4-4	0-3-4	5-00-6	9-10-9
4.	1934-35	Telangana	1-2-11	0-12-6	0-5-0	0-3-0	0-2-9	0-3-2	7-2-0
5,	,,	Marathwada	1-3-2	0-11-10	0-5-5	0-3-3	0-2-9	4-0-9	9-10-3
6.	,,	Hyderabad State	1-3-0	0-12-2	0-5-2	0-3-1	0-2-9	3-12-11	8-6-1
7.	,,	Warangal District	1-2-0	0-13-0	0-5-0	0-3-0	0-2-0	0-15-0	7-3-0
8.	,,	Karimnagar District	1-3-0	0-11-0	0-4-0	0-2-0	0-2-0	2-14-0	5-0-0
9.	,,	Adilabad District	1-2-0	0-12-0	0-4-0	0-4-0	0-2-0	2-5-0	9-1-0
10.	1939-40	Telangana	1-0-0	0-11-0	0-5-0	3-3-0	0-2-0	5-0-0	6-0-0
11.	,,	Marathwada	1-5-0	0-12-0	0-5-6	0-3-6	0-2-6	5-8-0	9-12-0
12.	,,	Hyderaaad State	1-2-6	0-11-6	0-5-3	0-3-3	0-2-3	4-12-0	7-14-0
13.	,,	Warangal District	1-2-0	0-12-0	0-6-0	0-3-0	0-2-0	4-0-0	6-0-0
14.	,,	Karimnagar District	0-14-0	0-3-0	0-3-6	0-2-4	0-1-6	3-0-0	5-0-0
15.	,,	Adilabad District	1-0-0	0-11-0	0-3-8	0-2-6	0-1-2	3-0-0	6-0-0
16.	1949-50	Warangal District	—	—	—	—	—	—	—
17.	,,	Karimnagar District	—	—	—	—	—	—	—
18.	,,	Adilabad District	—	—	—	—	—	—	—

Complied from :—1. *Report on Labour Census, 1935*, (Hyderabad-Dn, 1937), p. 41 ;

2. *Hyderabad District Gazetteers*, Tables Volumes, *1931* & *1936*, *Warangal*, pp. 398-401 : *Karimnagar*, pp. 394-397 ; *Adilabad*, pp, 394-397 :

3. *Statisical Year Book*, *H,E.H. the Nizam's Dominions*, *1349 Fasli* (*1939-40*). pp. 1029-31.

4. S. Ketava Iyengar : *Rural Economic Enquiries in the Hyderabad State, 1949-51*, (Hyderabad Dn, 1951), pp-216-17.

These had diminished between 33 to 50% mainly due to the steep decline in the prices of food grains on account of the Great Depression.[432] But, among the Districts in the State and also the *Suba*, wages of agricultural workers were particularly low in the Gondwana region or the northern Taluqs of Adilabad District such as Boath, Utnoor, Kinwat and Rajura, and also in some of the forest-bound and backward Taluqs of Karimnagar District, such as Parkal, Mahadeopur, Sultanabad and Huzurabad.[433] If comparison was made among the four *Subas* in the State, the annual average wage of a *bhagela* in Warangal *Suba* in 1936-37, which stood at 34.7 remained the lowest, falling less by 100% to the highest average obtained in Aurangabad *Suba* standing at 68.05 and by nearly 50% to the State average remaining at 50.5.[434] Even the rate of daily wages of men and women of the *Suba* of Warangal which stood at 3.5 and 1.7 respectively in the same year, ranked the lowest in the State, the highest being 4.3 for men in Gulbarga *Suba* and 2.2 for women in Aurangabad *Suba*, both being in Marathwada Region and even the State averages remaining at 4.0 and 1.9 respectively, stood above those of Warangal *Suba*.[435] The inability of the *bhagelas* to get freed from the hereditary debt burden that they owed invariably to their masters and the weak bargaining power of the rural proletariat due to their poverty and ignorance, to fight against the unilateral fixing of wage rates by landlords,[436] had accounted very much for the low agricultural wage rates in the *Suba*. On the other hand, the wage rates of blacksmiths and carpenters, both during this as well as succeeding period were generally on the rise and further far above those of agricultural labourers,[437] for the reason that they being the chief and skilled artisans in the village, had enjoyed better bargaining power in claiming payments for the work done.[438] Karimnagar District with its vast number of blacksmithy and carpentry establishments, had its artisans 40 to 50% better paid than in other Districts of the *Suba* and also the State.[439] Between rural and urban artisans of these categories, the former excepting in 1927-28, received 40 to 50% higher wages than the latter, for the reason that these trades remained essentially rural-based during the période. The exception in former year might probably be due to lapse in Census classification of rural and urban units, for the other urban workers and artisans such as masons, *coolies*, sweepers and *mails*, showed a fall in their wage rates relating to the said year.[440]

Wage rates during the next quinquennium of 1934-35 to 1939-40 showed further decline over that of the preceding seven years.[441] As agricultural production and prices did not yet make full recovery from the Depression effect,[442] the trend of low wage rates continued. With the phenomenal rise in commodity prices and demand during the next decade of War and post-War period,[443] remarkable rise in wages of agricultural labour, was experienced. From round about an annas wage in 1939-40, a male labourer received enhancement in 1949-50 ranging from 8 annas in Adilabad District to one rupee in the other *Suba* Districts, the rise amounting to 100 to 400% ; and the wage rate of female labour rose from 2½ annas in the former year to 4 annas in the Adilabad District and 8 annas in the other *Suba* Districts, the increase amounting to 60 and 100% respectively.[444] The lesser increase in respect of the former District was due to the slow and rather mild spread of the War and the post-War period effects, on account of the backwardness of the people and the difficulty of communication. But, the higher cost of living deprived the labourers of enjoying any real benefit out of this huge rise in their wages.[445] Working class cost of living indices prepared for Warangal town, for the months of August, 1947, December, 1948, April and May, 1950, along with five other industrial centres in the State showed that as much as 68.43% of the working class budget was spent on food alone, which ranked the highest of all.[446] Thus, whether it was Depression or inflation, the agricultural labourers who were principally drawn from the depressed classes such as *Dhers*, *Mahars*, *Chamars*, *Mochis* and *Mangs*, experienced a life of misery, besides the social ignominy of living in the outskirts of the villages away from the higher sections of the community.[447]

(*i*) *Industrial Labour* : As in agriculture, Warangal District, with even excluding the highest labour-consuming coal-mining industry, came to occupy the first place not only in the *Suba* but in the State itself, in respect of the employment of industrial labour by accounting for as much as 10.57% of the total employed in the State in 1935.[448] On the other hand, the number of industrial labourers employed in Karimnagar and Adilabad Districts formed only less than one-tenth of the number engaged in the former District.[449] The preponderance of large-scale industries such as the Azam Jahi Mills, cotton ginning and pressing factories, rice and oil mills in Warangal District, accounted for its sizeable absorption of factory labour.[450] Though there was not much variation in the number of industrial units during the period, there had been considerable fluctuations, now and then, in the number of persons employed.[451] The Depression and the Inflationary periods had their effects on the fall and the rise in the number of labourers engaged, for the demand for the manufactured goods varied with fluctuations in the price situation and also War-time constraints. Apart from these, the scarcity that was experienced for industrial raw materials and food grains for workers' daily consumption during the War and the post-War period had its severe bouts in 1942 and 1945 that got reflected in the considerable fall that took place in the respective years in the number of persons employed.[452] Because of the fact that the Sirpur Paper Mills started newly its production in the former year having more than enough demand for its product internally, Adilabad District registered an opposite trend during these years.[453] The fact that more number of workers emigrated from the Telangana Districts to C.P. Madras and Bombay Presidency parts externally and Marathwada Districts internally, because of the higher wages prevailing there, right from 1921 onwards, had also contributed not a little for labour shortage and the consequent decline in the number engaged by the industrial units.[454]

(*a*) *Wages and Trade Unionism* : Wage rates of industrial workers in the Hyderabad State varied very widely not only between centre to centre, and unit to unit in the same centre, but also between different individuals in the same occupation in one unit.[455] But yet, taken as a whole, it transpired that 80% of the two lakh industrial workers in the Capital and the Districts received such low wages which fell less than Rs. 18 per month or amounted to ten annas per day for male labourers. Female and child labourers, the latter being out of poverty compelled to work even before they reached the age of ten, received further low and miserable wages that amounted to Rs. 5 per month and two to four annas per day respectively.[456] The request of the labour unions such as the *Mazdoor Sangh*[457] and Singareni Collieries workers' union for the fixation of a basic wage ranging from Rs. 40 to unskilled labourer, Rs. 52 for semi-skilled labourer and Rs. 70 for skilled worker and dearness allowance to be paid on the basis of the rise or fall in the cost of living, was turned down many as time by the Government which held controlling shares in all heavy industries.[458] Only in 1949 did the new Government appoint the Rege Committee to look into these vital matters, as a result of which the basic wage for male, female and child labourers was fixed at O.S. Rs. 26, 20, and 17 respectively with a common dearness allowance of Rs. 21 per month, but these new rates were made effective only from January, 1951.[459] Before this date, only in Azam Jahi Mills of Warangal, was the basic wage which was made Rs. 26 in 1946, got further raised to Rs. 30 (both in O.S.) in 1949.[460]

But, it is significant to realise that when workers received such meagre and insufficient wages that they got starved often in view of the rising prices of food grains, the managing agents of the industries and to a lesser extent, the labour contractors rolled in wealth. In the Azam Jahi Mills, to cite an instance, while the wage bill of 4000 workers in 1943 went up to Rs. 13.63 lakhs, the managing agents' commission amounted to as much as Rs. 7.44 lakhs or 54.58% of the former.[461] The war-time abnormal profits that the Mills earned, which climaxed in the year 1946 to double the paid-up capital of Rs. 18 lakhs, very much boosted up the earnings of the latter, whereas marginal hike in the wages of the former was very much neutralised by the rise in the cost of living.[462] The contractors on whom the managements, especially of larger industries including that of coal-mining, depended for the supply of unskilled labourers who were required in greater number, earned without any manual labour more than 70% of what the labourer earned by hard physical work.[463] But for this middle man, this huge accretion of income would definitely have bettered the lot of the real worker. In the distribution of workers' wages which was done through these contractors, much corruption and harassment was indulged in by them, thereby causing further loss and suffering to the helpless and ignorant workers.[464] The managements, on the other hand, in spite of strong union representations for the removal of this much hated system of recruitment, the former found it profitable and confident to carry it on, for by this they could successfully keep the constant labour demands for higher wages, D.A., bonus and other amenities, very much at bay.

Trade Union Act came in the State only in 1945, whereas in British India, it came into operation as early as 1926.[465] Excepting N.S. Railway Employees Union which had an All-India character, the 3,000 workers of the Azam Jahi Mills of Warangal had the distinction of forming before this Act, the first Workers' Union in the State on 8th, August, 1943.[466] It was however mysterious that the two important Organisations of the locality—the *Ittehad-Ul-Muslimin*[467] and the Andhra Conference[468] combined their efforts in forming this labour union. Whereas Mr. Samad Razvi, the General Secretary of the Union held also the District Secretaryship of the former Organisation, Mr. S. Ramanadham, the Joint Secretary of the Union, had been a member of the latter Organisation.[469] Though strikes had been organised from as early as 1921 by the workers of the Singareni Collieries[470] and 1943 by those of the Azam Jahi Textile Mill,[471] either for 12½ % increase in pay, declaration of public holidays, payment of bonus and night allowance or 50% War time allowance on par with Bombay instead of 33%, these attempts and demands of the labourers had all been successfully suppressed by the respective managements with the help of the strong police support of the State. Trade Union activity gained in intensity, though the end result remained the same, during the post-War quinquennium. Singareni Collieries Workers Union, Mahbubia Match Factory Workers Union, the Sirpur Paper Mills Union and the Warangal Tanneries Workers Union, etc., had all been formed during this period. The movement grew so rapidly that the number of registered Unions in the State rose from 7 at the end of 1948 to 123 by September, 1950[472]. Activities of Central labour organisations such as the Hyderabad State *Mazdoor Sevak Sangh* and All-Hyderabad Trade Union Congress[473],the latter being a Communist-directed Organisation and an affiliate of the All-India Trade Union Congress, came to the scene since 1946-47. Their intensified representations to the Government to control greedy profiteering in the sale of essential commodities, reduce working hours, introduce a minimum living wage, grant dearness allowance on the basis of cost of living, subscribe to provident fund @ $8\frac{1}{3}\%$ of workers' wages, grant one month's wages as bonus, etc. had only roused the anger of the latter, leading to the promulgation of section 145 (Section 144 in British India) and arrest of trade union leaders.[474] When a call was given by All-Hyderabad Trade Union Congress to celebrate 17th October, 1946 as Anti-Repression Day to mark the protest of the working class against Government's policy, the latter in a pre-emptive and severe manner got the police raid and search, on 30th September, 150 houses or offices that belonged to the agitating unions, parties and their leaders that were located in Talangana Districts and the twin cities of Secunderabad and Hyderabad, in which much union correspondence was seized. Heavy police patrolling was done in industrial areas to prevent the meeting of workers.[475]

The Unions could have a sigh of relief only after the Police Action and the consequent change of the old regime. The period that followed was characterised by much labour unrest.[476] Its severity could be evidenced from the fact that during the first half of 1949, seventeen major strikes were organised in the State, out of which as many as ten related to the textile industry. The total number of workers involved in these was

29,873 and 4,34,000 man-hours had been lost.[477] As a climax, occurred the General Strike from January 11th to 30th,1950, in which 23,452 workers pertaining to textiles, engineering, mines, sugar, printing and even twin cities municipalities took part, as a result of which, 97 working days and 3,11,692 man-days were lost.[478] The grievances on account of which these disputes took place, mainly related to remuneration terms, conditions of employment, the question of amenities and recognition of trade unions.[479] The period of political and administrative transition that followed the Police Action, the considerable amount of influence that the Reds exercised over important labour unions and organisations and most important of all, the dissensions that prevailed among Central Organisations such as those that existed between Hyderabad State *Mazdoor Sevak Sangh* and All-Hyderabad Trade Union Congress,[480] had all led to a situation in which the striking lobourers, being denied any immediate benefits, were made to wait until the Rege Committee's recommendations came to be implemented[481].

(*ii*) *Bhagelas and Begaris*. These two institutions which had been in vogue in the region since a long time, involved a kind of labour that remained different and distinct from the usual rural or urban labour. Fundamentally, freedom of service that characterised the latter was woefully lacking in the former. *Bhagelas*, whose services as agricultural farm labourers were chiefly utilised in the northern and Central parts of Warangal District by rich non-cultivating landlords, functioned very much like bonded labourers. They got tied down by the debt which a *bhagela* or his family predecessors had contracted mostly for marriage celebration and which, for decades together failed to get fully cleared off because of the meagre and insufficient wages received either in kind or cash or both that hardly enabled them to maintain themselves and their families.[482] Further, because of running family needs, fresh loans were contracted from the same master, adding to the accumulated debt, thus making the latter very much a permanent thing.[483] Though the *Bhagela* Agreement Regulation limiting the period of contract for one year, setting reasonable rate of wages, interest to be recovered on the loan amount being fixed at 6% per annum and the agreement becoming null and void in case of the death of either party, was brought about in 1936, these terms were rarely observed.[484] The poverty and illiteracy of these semi-serfs, coupled with lack of alternative sources of credit and means of livelihood, lack of legal sanction behind this measure, the implementation responsibility being put on the shoulders of Tahsildars and Second *Taluqdars* who had been more amenable to the influence of the landlords than to the appeals of the affected *bhagelas*, had all been the significant factors which contributed to this unhappy outcome.[485] The lot of these farm labourers which had undergone little alteration during the period, proved worse than that of a serf, for the master under-took the responsibility of maintaining the latter but not the former, though both had unlimited service obligation.[486]

Begari labour, on the other hand, remained not only forced but also mostly unpaid or very nominally paid. This, which went by the popular name of *Vetti*,[487] was extracted essentially in two ways. First, the village officials and Government officers on tour, received this type of service from all those craftsmen who enjoyed *balota Inams*.[488] But, these grants had originally been made not for this purpose, but to serve the general or common interests of the cultivating folk.[489] Even the non-*Inam* holders such as the merchants, the weavers, the washermen, etc., were also made to render this *begari*, whenever it suited the official interests.[490] Though "*Sarbarahi*"[491] rules were made in 1926-27 enjoining the Government officials that went on tour to pay for the extra or additional services that they received over and above the help that was required in carrying out of official business, these were least observed and it became a no man's business.[492]

But, more dangerous and troublesome proved to be the second type of *Vetti* that was extracted by the feudal elements from almost all sections of the community, ranging from small and middle peasants down to craftsmen and depressed class people that comprised *Dheds*, *Chamars*, *Madigas*, *Malas*, etc. Mere ancestral practice was quoted as the rightful sanction in this regard and Government's deliberate complacency even when rightful complaints were made, had only encouraged the *watandars* to further unleash a reign of terror.[493] There was no limit on the type, extent and time of demanding this labour.[494] Failure to oblige or faltering in service, met with brutal punishments which sometimes resulted even in loss of life.[495] In spite of the avowed expressions of the Government about its removal, this much hated institution came to be practised right until 1949-50, irrespective of the change in the set-up.[496] This, together with *bhagela* system, had greatly undermined the economic prosperity of the lower and middle strata of the population in the *Suba* area as well as the Telangana Region.[497]

E. *MARKETING AND TRADE*

(*i*) *Regulated and unregulated markets* : Specialization in agriculture involving the production of cotton, oil seeds, spices and tobacco in increasing measure compared to cereals and pulses, which were retained upto 50% of the production for local and domestic consumption as against only 10% in the case of the former by the producers, created the need for markets, or outlets to receive surplus agricultural production. On average, one half proportion of the total agricultural produce, valued at seventy crores of rupees was marketed in the State either in village trade centres or market towns.[498] But, as is evident from *Table L*,[499] the marketing facilities, especially of a regulated and regular character, remained right until 1947-48, very much deficient and inadequate, compared to the unregulated and periodical ones. Karimnagar District, though a leading agricultural District, was not served by any big agricultural market excepting the one at Peddapalli.[500] The result was that the products of the District found their way to other District markets located at Warangal, Nizamabad, Kamareddi and Siddipet.[501] Not only the District was thus deprived of the benefits of export trade but it was made to depend on other markets for the import of essential commodities like kerosene, petrol, foodgrains, etc., thereby causing at times, unwanted misery to the District population.[502] Adilabad District, with two Regulated Markets[503] to serve ten

TABLE L

Number of Trading Centres in the Suba and the State, 1940-52

Sl. No.	District/ Region/ State	Regulated Markets In 1940 & 1947	Regulated Markets In 1952	Unregulated Markets (In 1952)	Total Number of Assembling centres (Cols. 4 85)	Mandis* (in 1940 & 1947)	Ganja** (In 1940 & 1947)	Total (of cols. 7 & 8)
1	2	3	4	5	6	7	8	9
1.	Warangal	2	5	1	6	2	2	4
2.	Karimnagar	..	6	1	7	2	..	2
3.	Adilabad	1	2	5	7	3	..	3
4.	Telangana	5	27	19	46	25	18	43
5.	Marathwada	10	42	51	93	31	29	60
6.	State	15	69	70	139	56	47	103

Sl. No.	District/ Region/ State	Weekly Bazaars In 1940	Weekly Bazaars In 1947	Weekly Bazaars In 1952	Periodical Bazaars (In 1940)	Number of villages where Urus, Mela or Jatra are held (In 1940)	Cattle Bazaars Weekly In 1940	Cattle Bazaars Weekly In 1947	Cattle Bazaars Periodical In 1940	Cattle Bazaars Periodical In 1947	Godowns of the Hyderabad Co-operative Commercial Corporation Ltd.
		10	11	12	13	14	15	16	17	18	19
1.	Warangal	10	10	2	3	83	. .	2	3	2	12
2.	Karimnagar	18	18	23	2	73	. .	3	2	. .	7
3.	Adilabad	60	63	80	. .	83	3	10	. .	2	11
4.	Telangana	249	280	270	11	844	21	52	11	19	—
5.	Marathwada	613	737	749	24	1,593	117	136	4	25	—
6.	State	862	1,017	1,019	35	2,437	138	188	15	44	—

*Wholesale business centres usually located in urban areas where commodities of daily use excepting food grains were dealt by auction. They had the status of secondary markets.

**Well built grain or wholesale markets where all grains, pulses and oil seeds were dealt either by auction or by sale. In marketing, they held the place next only to Regulated Markets.

. . NIL.

—Information not available.

Compiled from :
1. *Trade Statistics for 1352 Fasli (1942-43), H.E.H. the Nizam's Government*, p. 20.
2. *Statistics about Trade centres (Markets & Bazars) in Hyderabad State, 1948*, (Hyderabad State-Dn, 1950), pp. 16-17, 54-55, 57 & 87.
3. Marketing Department, Government of Hyderabad : *A note on Agricultural Marketing in Hyderabad State*, Hyderabad-Dn (1952), pp. 9, ; 6 & 5.
&
4. H.E.H. the Nizam's Government, *List of Uruses, Melas, Jatras, etc., In H.E.H. the Nizam's Dominions*, 1349 Fasli (1940 A.D.), (Hyderabad-Dn, 1940), pp. 12-43.

TABLE LI

Regulated Markets —Functionaries & Business Turn-over, 1940-41 & 1947-48—1949-50

Sl. No.	District	Taluq	Market	Traders					
				Buyers	Adatyas	Dallals	Weighmen	Petty Dealers	Total
1	2	3	4	5	6	7	8	9	10
1.	Warangal	Warangal	Warangal (Mathwada)	196	83	30	69	. . .	378
2.	,,	Khammam	Khammam	154	119	. . .	73	91	437
3.	,,	Madhira	Madhira.	—	—	—	—	—	—
4.	,,	Mahboobabad	Mahaboobad	—	—	—	—	—	—
5.	,,	Warangal	Ghanpur.	—	—	—	—	—	—
6.	Karimnagar	Sultanabad	Peddapalli	42	23	5	10	29	109
7.	,,	Karimnagar	Karimnagar	22	23	. . .	6	. . .	51
8.	,,	Jagtiyal	Jagtiyal	. . .	. . .	. . .	. . .	. . .	. . .
9.	,,	Huzurabad	Jammikunta	. . .	. . .	. . .	. . .	. . .	. . .
10.	,,	Metpalli	Metpalli.	—	—	—	—	—	—
11.	,,	Jagtiyal	Koratla.	—	—	—	—	—	—
12.	Adilabad	Adilabad	Adilabad	7	26	. . .	13	22	68
13.	,,	Lexettipet	Mancherial	—	—	—	—	—	—

Annual Arrivals in hundreds of *pallas* in 1353-54 Fasli (1944-45)

Sl. No.	District	Taluq	*Kapas*	Paddy	Jawar	*Tuar*	Gram	*Mung*	Ground-nut	*Til*	Castor	Chillies	Onions
			11	12	13	14	15	16	17	18	19	20	21
1.	Warangal	Warangal	102	26	17	17	16	30	4,077	145	185	210	36
2.	,,	Khamman	2	107	...	71	1	251	3,177	4	39	16	31
3.	,,	Madhira	—	—	—	—	—	—	40**	—	—	—	—
4.	,,	Mahboobabad	—	—	—	—	—	—	—	—	—	—	—
5.	,,	Warangal	—	—	—	—	—	—	—	—	—	—	—
6.	Karimnagar	Sultanabad	615	580	54	39	9	43	371	62	139	93	7
7.	,,	Karimnagar	...	4	6	6	14	16	88	80	59	18	2
8.	,,	Jagtiyal	2**	...	...	1	...	6	16	...	9	21	9
9.	,,	Huzurabad	13**	...	...	...	2	...	843	...	6	8	7
10.	,,	Metpalli	—	—	—	—	—	—	—	—	—	—	—
11.	,,	Jagtiyal	—	—	—	—	—	—	—	—	—	—	—
12.	Adilabad	Adilabad	631	5	118	27	15	1	29	41	1	1	1
13.	,,	Lexettipet	—	—	—	—	—	—	—	40*	—	—	—

Sl. No.	District	Taluq	1940-41(1350 Fasli) Total annual arrivals in thousands of carts	Value of commodities in lakhs of Rs.	1947-48 (May to June) Quantity	Value	1948-49 (May to June) Quantity	Value	1949-50 (April to March) Quantity	Value
			Business turn over in hundreds of *pallas* and thousands of rupees							
			22	23	24	25	26	27	28	29
1.	Warangal	Warangal	140	70,17	2,202	11,671	2,880	16,792	3,369	23,552
2.	,,	Khammam	67	41,00	1,486	7,304	1,078	6,952	2,143	13,493
3.	,,	Madhira	—	—	...	...	167	1,035	137	1,564
4.	,,	Mahboobabad	—	—	...	...	...	...	54	329
5.	,,	Warangal	—	—	—	—	—	—	—	—
6.	Karimnagar	Sultanabad	25	10.00	743	4,920	947	5,478	1,131	7,197
7.	,,	Karimnagar	...	...	277	1,519	377	2,006	521	3,393
8.	,,	Jagtiyal	...	...	242	1,367	230	1,401	285	2,629
9.	,,	Huzurabad	...	...	458	1,763	584	3,293	779	5,016
10.	,,	Metpalli	—	—	114	811	183	1,275	230	2,037
11.	,,	Jagtiyal	—	—	19	174	50	303	100	546
12.	Adilabad	Adilabad	46	8.95	925	7,118	606	3,641	636	5,722
13.	,,	Lexettipet	—	—	542	3,985	597	3,741	538	3,115

*It was 40,000 maunds as in 1938.

—*Trade Statistics, 1352 Fasli (1942-43) H.E.H. the Nizam's Government*, p. 17.

**These 'Arival' figures in respect of Madhira, Jagtiyal and Jamikunta are as in 1948. Data in respect of 1944-45 is not available.

—*Statistics about Trade Centres (Markets & Bazaars) in Hyderabad States, 1948*, p. 19.

∴The Regulated Markets of Madhira, Mahaboobabad, Ghanpur Metpalli, Koratla and Mancherial were established, respectively in 1947, 1949, 1951, 1947, 1948 and 1947. Hence, data in their respect is not available for the period before 1947-48, as it was in respect of others.

Compiled from :—*Statistical Year Book, 1351-54 Fasli (1942-45), H.E.H. the Nizam's Government*, pp. 1314-15 ; 1306-13 ; Chief Marketing Officer, Hyderabad Government, quoted in S. Kesava Iyengar, *Rural Economic Enquiries 1949-51*, Marketing Department, Government of Hyderabad, p. 346 : *A Note on Agricultural Marketing in Hyderabad State*, (Hyderabad-Dn, 1952), p. 26.

Taluqs, was none the better. The entire eastern, central and southern belt of the District remained woe fully deficient and deprived in this respect. The fact that these Regulated and big Markets were invariably established at those urban centres that were connected by railway, had mainly contributed for this poor development of big markets in both these *Suba* Districts, for they had been very meagrely served by rail transport.

In contrast, the markets at Warangal and Khamam, the two headquarter towns in Warangal District well connected by railway with the State capital as well as Madras Presidency, played a significant role in the economic development of the area. The former with an annual arrival of 1,40,000 carts loaded with produce, occupied third place in the State and first in Telangana in 1940-41.[504] Groundnut, *til*, castor and chillies were heavily traded in here, as against paddy, groundnut and *mung*[505] being indulged in large number at the latter.[506] Besides rail link, the fact that these towns were characterised by the location of a number of large-scale industries such as those of rice and oil mills, textiles and coal-mining, had in not a little measure, aided in the brisk functioning of these markets. Further, the regulation of the markets under the Hyderabad Agricultural Markets Act of 1929-30, proceeded very much unevenly during the period. Where five markets were brought under the Act in the *Suba* area during the 16 year period ending in 1946, an equal number was recorded during only the next 3 year period ending in 1949.[507] This comparatively fast increase in regulation in the latter period was because of the introduction of *ad valorem* or value-based collection of market fees since 1947, replacing the earlier system based on vehicles or carts. Because of the continuation of the inflated prices of commodities, there was considerable increase in the income of both old and new markets under the new system.[508] In spite of this increase in market fees rates, the Regulated Market, when compared to the unregulated ones, proved of considerable benefit to the cultivators and industrial manufacturers, for the dues were fixed and there was a 20 to 30% price rise.[509] Diversity in dry measures, absence of certified weights and scales, malpractices in handling the produce, free gratification given in kind from the seller's produce to the agents of the merchants and above all, the adjustments of the old debts from the sellers in the latter's sale proceeds, had been some of the many evil practices that characterised the dealings in unregulated trade centres.[510]

(*ii*) *Factors affecting market growth* : But, the most important factor that affected the free market dealings of the cultivators in general was their indebtendness to village merchants or wholesale dealers, or *adatyas*[511] of nearby assembling markets. The understanding was that the former as an obligation towards receiving loan, had to dispose of his produce to their creditors or through them, which in other words, amounted to the peasants being deprived of the benefit of marketing their products by themselves.[512] The difference between the price offered by *Sahukars* for buying and the price at which they sold ranged from Rs. 15 to Rs. 20[513] Besides this loss in price, the cultivators who usually contracted grain loan for seed purposes before the commencement of the agricultural operations[514] and repaid it after harvesting, were made to pay interest preferably in kind, ranging from 25 to 50%.[515] Further, the warehousing facilities available at market centres were poorly utilized by the cultivators, nor were they freely thrown open to small cultivators as it had been in the case of big merchants.[516] The former, out of ignorance and lack of proper awareness of market conditions, always hurried to dispose off their produce on the same day and get back to their villages, whatever be the price that prevailed. On the other hand, the latter made use of the available godown facilities to wait for a profitable rise in prices and for short periods extending upto one week, no charges were made for storage.[517] The introduction of the Foodgrains Control Levy Order, the Restriction of Non-food crops Regulation Order and the Cotton Control Order, all War-time measures, but continued during post-War period also,[518] aimed at the restrictions of the movement of foodgrains and the cultivation of commercial crops such as cotton, groundnut, *til*, castor chillies and tobacco, had greatly affected produce arrivals into the markets. The evil practices of blackmarketing, hoarding and smuggling that were associated with the system of Rationing and Levy,[519] had further curtailed the volume of open market trading. The closure of European markets during War time and the shipping difficulties had considerably affected the export trade that was carried on by the Regulated Markets.[520]

(*iii*) *Periodical Markets* : The contribution of periodical markets such as weekly *bazars*, *Melas*, *Jatras* and *Uruses*[520a], to the development of internal trade, though not of external, was very much insignificant, even though, they numbered considerably in the *Suba* Districts as well as the State.[521] Weekly *bazars* were held on particular week days differing from one place to another in which sundry articles of local use were offered for sale, but the sales in some cases did hardly exceed Rs. 100. This was for the reason that the ryots took little interest in them as grain and cattle were very rarely offered for sale in them.[522] The Markets Act had been extended to cover the sale of livestock only in the year 1950.[523] *Uruses*, *Melas* and *Jatras* which were held annually and more in the nature of social and religious gatherings of the people of the surrounding villages, had also served the purpose of exhibiting and putting for sale the field produces and industrial wares of the village community. Mahaboobabad Taluq in Warangal District with as many as 40 villages where such fairs were held and which formed nearly 50% of the District total, led in the entire *Suba* in this respect. Some of these, such as those held at Bhadrachalam in Polancha Taluq of Warangal District and Vemulwada in Sirsilla Taluq of Karimnagar District had drawn good number of participants amounting to 20,000 and 15,000 respectively and the value of the property brought in for transaction ranged in maximum up to Rs. 20,000 and Rs. 10,000 respectively.[524] But, they being annual and not being entirely trade fairs as such, they had only little effect on local trade. It could be seen from *Table L* [525] that in both weekly and annual fairs and *bazars*, the number in Telangana formed only two to three times less than that in Marathwada. This was due to the fact that producers in the former, becuase of easy and long distance movement on *chalka* soils, found it profitable to go 30 or even 50 miles to sell their products, whereas those in the latter, because of difficult long distance movement on account of blacksoils, regarded it suitable to cover smaller distances for marketing their wares.[526] Establishment of permanent merchant shops in Telangana villages which met most of the shopping requirements of the villages, had also contributed for the same result.[527]

(*iv*) *Monopolistic Tendencies in Marketing* : Compared to this minor role played by periodical markets, the business turnover of the Regulated Markets was substantial and was very much on the rise. Excepting those of Adilabad and Mancherial, all the other Markets registered tremendous increase in turnover amounting to 229.09% and 221.30% in the case of Khammam and Warangal respectively, during the decade 1940-41 to 1949-50 for which the data is available, though in an incomplete manner.[528] The decline in respect of the two former was because of the fact excepting jawar, cotton and *til*, the arrivals of other produce was very much insignificant in them[529] and further, the crop out turn of even these three commodities also suffered during the period for the reasons discussed elsewhere.[530] But, the dividends of this flourishing business had come to be enjoyed only by men of a particular community and of landed interests. Besides the *Komati*[531] merchants who dominated the trading interests from village to State level in Telangana, some of the rich landlords in their variegated role, functioned as wholesale merchants, *adatyas*, brokers and also as godown owners.[532] In the Warangal Regulated Market, to cite an instance, the list of prominent cotton dealers included besides Siddamsetty Lingayya who was a *Komti*, Pingali Venkat Janardhan Reddy and Pingali Pratap Reddy,[533] who represented landed section, out of whom the last one was known as a powerful *Deshmukh* in Warangal Taluq.[534] The concentration of market trade was so much in the hands of these urban-based capitalists that in the total produce that got gathered at assembling centres in Hyderabad and Secunderabad, the share of the actual producers and the village merchants amounted to only 1/3 and the remaining 2/3 was contributed by the traders of the District markets.[535] The growth or the emergence of new markets thus, came to further strengthen the hands of the big landlords who already had started investing in industries.[536]

(*b*) *Trade* : The prosperity or the importance of trade from the *Suba* Districts could be judged from the fact that the Customs income of Warangal Railway, Madhira and Rajura frontier posts rose respectively from O.S.Rs. 13,32,022, 1,17,697 and 2,41,488 in 1931-32 to 44,81, 615, 4,91,452 and 8,11,170 in 1946-47, the respective increases amounting to 236.45, 317.55 and 235.90% during this fifteen year period.[537] These had been the three Customs centres that operated in the *Suba* area, the former two in Warangal District and the latter in Adilabad. Out of the two latter which dealt with goods traffic by road, Rajura received nearly double the income the Madhira had earned, which was mainly due to the huge exports of cotton lint made from the former centre and in this respect, it occupied the highest places among all the thirteen frontier posts that operated in the State.[538] The levy of Customs duty that was charged on 46 import and 63 export items on the basis of weight and towards the end of the period on the cost value of commodities,[539] yielded a sizeable revenue to the State that it formed third largest source of income, after land revenue and excise.[540] But, the system of collecting these duties at the British India seaports and again on the entry of goods into the State, proved burdensome to the consumers as well as industrial importers and exporters, for the costs and prices had an additional rise compared to those in British India.[541] Though the Treaty of 1802 had conferred upon the State the right of importing foreign goods free of British Indian duties,[542] it was never regarded so by the British nor the *Nizams* had the audacity to take up cudgels in this regard. Besides, widespread corruption among Customs Officials that led to nefarious smuggling, especially of food-grains, across the border had resulted in huge loss of revenue to the Government and much misery to the local population on account of scarcity conditions that were created.[543]

(i) *Nature of Trade* : Inter-District or internal trade loomed larger than external trade in the *Suba* as well as the State,[544] Matwada, a suburb of Warangal Proper and a renowned trade centre since the time of the Kakatiyas, attracted merchandise and met in turn, the import requirements of not only Warangal and other Taluqs of Warangal Districts, but also of neighbouring Districts, especially Karimnagar.[545]

Whereas Karimnagar exported rice, jawar, maize, *sesamum* castorseed, tobacco, silk cloth, cotton, chillies, sheep, hides & leather, bones & horns and brass vessels to Warangal and Hyderabad, it received in turn from the former, carpets, cotton and woollen cloth of European manufacture, glassware, refined sugar, jaggery, gold, silver, salt, opium, kerosene oil, brass and copper sheets.[546] Next in importance in *Suba* trading came the Taluq headquarters town of Khammamet, also in Warangal District, which not only met the trading requirements of the surrounding Taluqs of Madhira, Yellandu and Paloncha of the same District, but had also very much served as the export and import centre for Nalgonda District of the Medak *Suba*. Its close proximity with Bezwada, an important trade centre in Madras Presidency, both being connected by road as well as railway, placed it in an advantageous position to carry on export as well as import trade. Similarly, by way of exchange, cotton from Warangal District was sent, besides Hyderabad, to Aurangabad and Gulbarga, both in Marathwada Region, for the latter led in cotton export trade.[547] Adilabad District, in view of its geographical location, had developed trade contacts more with Central Provinces on the east and north and Marathwada Districts on the West than with other *Suba* Districts that lay to the South. Except Sirpur and Mancherial on the Kazipet-Balharshah line, this vast District was untouched by rail transport and hence, the trade was mainly carried on by road. State Capital drew its essential requirements of grain, pulses, oil-seeds and oil from the surplus Districts. Paddy, jawar, maize, groundnut and groundnut oil, castor seeds and castor oil, *til*, chillies and tobacco from Warangal and Karimnagar Districts and jawar, linseed, timber, toys and cotton from Adilabad District, found their way into the capital. In fact, 50% of rice, 94% of wheat and 30% of jawar, the three staple food grains of the people in the twin cities, had been import from the Districts of respectively, Telangana, Marathwada and both combined.[548] In return, foreign and mill-manufactured goods, machinery, iron, salt, kerosene, diesel, sugar, gold and silver, glassware, etc. flowed from the Capital into the Districts, to be distributed in turn by the local exporting agencies and the village merchants, among the populace.

External trade from the *Suba* and in fact from the Dominions, was mainly carried on with important trading centres from the neighbouring presidencies of Bombay and Madras. Vizagpatam, Rajahmundry, Masulipatam, Guntoor, Jaggayyapeta, Bezwada, Kurnool and Adoni, all from the latter, and Barsi, Sholapur. Ahmadnagar, Bellary and Bijapur from the former, ranked as prominent centres.[549] For exports, the produce of the interior was carried to the nearest railway station by means of carts or pack-bullocks for consignment either to Madras or Bombay or even Hyderabad, for that matter. The same agencies that were employed for collecting the produce for export also performed the function of distributing imported articles to distant parts by means of the country type of transport.[550] Whereas oil seeds and cotton were exported in greater measure to Bombay than Madras, hides and skins were sent to the latter in greater number than the former. On the other hand. imports of cotton twist and yarn, cotton piece-goods, kerosene oil and salt were received largely from Bombay, rice, jawar, sugar and tea being contributed heavily by Madras.[551] In fact, 50 per cent of rice, 30 per cent of jawar, 81 per cent of tea and 46 per cent of sugar, imported into Hyderabad and Secunderabad, had been sent from parts of Madras Presidency.[552] Import of rice from Bengal and Burma, gram from the Punjab and the Central Provinces and wheat from the Punjab and the United Provinces, all also forming British Indian Provinces, was resorted to when the supplies from Madras and Bombay became inadequate to meet the demand.[553] The exports of raw cotton and oil seeds to Great Britain and countries of Central Europe, though in ordinary years went on well, suffered considerably at the time when hostilities broke out during the period of the two World Wars.[554]

(*ii*) *Exports, Imports and Trade Balance* : The chief exports from the *Suba* consisted of agricultural produce, live-stock and its by-products and forest yields. Cotton and cotton seed, castor seed, *sesamum*, linseed, groundnut seed and oil, foodgrains consisting of rice, jawar, maize and pulses, hides and skins, animals including agricultural and dairy cattle, timber, chillies and cotton, silk and wollen

TABLE LII

Chief Exports and Imports of Warangal and Adilabad Districts

(Average of the five years ending in 1330 Fasli (1920-21 A.D.)

Sl. No.	Articles	Warangal District Value of Imports (In Rupees)	Warangal District Value of Exports (In Rupees)	Adilabad District Value of Imports (In Rupees)	Adilabad District Value of Exports (In Rupees)
1	2	3	4	5	6
1.	Piece goods	6,00 279	2,39 846	4 35,418	31
2.	Yarn	6,92,242	54,313	92 432	14
3.	Silk	2 03,368	5	—	—
4.	Salt	11,75,508	—	72,729	—
5.	Sugar	5,40,097	6	46,548	29
6.	Jaggery	5,53,241	668	96,508	6 410
7.	Fruits	1,87,047	1,241	51,339	506
8.	Animals (livestock)	1,54,887	8 79,923	2,07,077	3,29,866
9.	Iron	2,14,296	796	—	—
10.	Timber	32,222	5,36,108	—	—
11.	Food grains	—	9 96,419	—	—
12.	Cotton	—	41,63,433	—	38,74,939

13.	*Sesamm*	20 902	25 04,277	616	1 89,774
14.	Castor seed	32,511	41,15 061	—	1,01,198
15.	Oils and paints	82,401	4,13,561	—	—
16.	Hides and skins	6,873	18,58,623	—	—
17.	Miscellaneous goods	2,41,276	—	41,954	—
18.	Gold	1,69,454	—	1,40,481	—
19.	Tobacco snuff, etc.,	1 18,191	59,573	5,030	33,379
20.	Cotton seed	7,189	5 21,025	62,192	10 88,300
21.	Oil cakes	11,558	1,58 023	—	—
22.	Kerosene oil	1,64,346	—	38,416	—
23.	*Tarward Bark*	802	79,525	—	—
24.	Chillies	41,442	4,53,258	2,730	19,614
25.	Bones	105	19,411	—	—
26.	Fowls	9	15 114	—	—
27.	Wool	101	24,496	—	—
28.	Bamboo	315	21,513	—	—
29.	Mills	27,623	2,401	—	—
30.	Matches	42,644	—	10 961	—
31.	Gunny bags	50,852	530	—	—
32.	Silk (foreign)	24,897	—	—	—
33.	Others	20,95,313	6,66,300	1,64 937	2,93,573
	TOTAL	80,34,409	1,92 46,616	16 77,034	60,84 117

*The same data about Karimnagar District was not given in the source, it being the only one regarding Districts in this respect.

Source : *Hyderabad District Gazetteers 1931* & *1936* (*1340-1345*) *Fasli* part II, Tables Volumes, *Warangal*, p. 37 ; *Adilabad* p. 39

piece-goods formed the principal items of export.[555] Export of oil seeds formed the major share of the total exports. which during the quinquennium ending in 1920-21, amounted to 58.76 per cent in Warangal District and 86.37 per cent in that of Adilabad.[556] It is significant to note that these percentages were obtained without groundnut seed and oil which, from thirties accounted for sizable exports, especially from Warangal and Karimnagar Districts.[557] The latter, though its import and export data is not available, it could be well ascertained from production data that in oil seeds export, it just came behind the former and far above Adilabad.[558] If the total volume or value of oil seeds exported is taken into consideration, the last-named District accounted for less than 50 per cent of that of Warangal,[559] Next to oil seeds came livestock, hides and skins, in the order of export importance, their annual average standing at Rs. 27,38, 546 in respect of Warangal District and Rs. 3,29,866 in the case of Adilabad.[560] Foodgrains, timber, chillies, oils and paints, oil cakes and piecegoods, figured in the next order of export items.[561] Regarding the total value of exports made from the *Suba* Districts during the quinquennium ending in 1920-21, it was three times more in the case of Warangal, when compared to that of Adilabad and Karimnagar's ranking stood between the two.[562]

Manufactured or semi-manufactured articles comprised the imports essentially. Salt, yarn, mill-made piecegoods, jaggery. sugar, silk cloth, iron, fruits, gold, kerosene oil, tobacco and snuff formed the main articles in order of their import value.[563] It is significant to note that whereas Warangal and Karimnagar Districts chiefly exported rice and paddy, Adilabad District, on the other hand, mainly got them imported, for it was highly deficient in rice production.[564] Even the import of livestock was also higher in the latter's case when compared to the former, for the number of working cattle per cultivator was the lowest in it, falling below even the State average[565] Next to salt whose import was rather inevitable in view of the lack of sea coast for its manufacture in the State, came the huge imports of yarn and piecegoods of mill-make. Together with silk, they accounted for more than 25% and 30% of the total imports that were received by Warangal and Adilabad Districts respectively, during the five years ending in 1921-21.[566] Handloom weaving and spinning being the most prominent industry in the *Suba* providing employment to the largest number of people than any other industry, got very much throttled because of the stiff competition from imported piecegoods on one hand and excessive dependence on outside yarn supply on the other. This situation and the consequent decay of this industry in the *Suba* Districts, had contributed not in a little measure for the spread of poverty among the masses.[567] Just as in exports, so also regarding the average of the total value of imports made during the quenquennium ending in 1920-21, for which only this data is available District-wise, Warangal District stood far above that of Adilabad, its imports proving nearly five times higher than those of the latter.[568] The greater industrial character of Warangal District necessitating considerable raw material imports, its compartively hugeness of population and especially of urban areas and preponderance of rich land lord community who very much became the patronisers of luxurious imported goods, had all been singnificant and contributory factors that helped towards this situation. If these features are taken as an index, Karimnagar District could well be assumed to have taken its place next to that of Warangal in this respect.[569]

Exports exceeded imports during this period in the *Suba* Districts. They were in the ratio of approximately 12:5 and 15:4 in the case of Warangal and Adilabad Districts respectively. The proportion of imports to that of exports was higher in the case of the former than that of the latter, amounting to one-half and one-fourth respectively.[570] Reasons were as analysed above. The condition of crops which fluctuated rather frequently, the effect of price situations such as the Depression and the Inflation and that of the two World Wars on the availability of markets, especially foreign, for produce export, restrictions on imports and transport bottlenecks had considerable bearing on this ratio. Any one of these factors was capable of bringing change in the situation and combination of them which did take place at times[571], had more telling or disastrous effects. This aspect could better be examined if the entire State was taken as one unit, not only because the data is available on it, but also because of the fact that the overall

TABLE LIII

Trade Particulars of Hyderabad State*, 1911—1949-50

Sl. No.	Year	Trade Turn-over Value in Rupees IMPORTS	EXPORTS	Value of Total Trade (In Rupees)	Balance Trade of Surplus(+) Deficit(—) (In Rupees)
1	2	3	4	5	6
1.	Average for 5 years ending in 1320 Fasli (1910-11)	7,05 26 000	8 27,80,000	15 33 06,000	+1,22,54,000
2.	1321 Fasli (1911-12)	10,18,08,000	9 85,80,000	20,03,88,000	— 32,28,000
3.	1322 ,, (1912-13)	10,77,05,000	9,21,33,000	19,98,38 000	—1,55,72,000
4.	1323 ,, (1913-14)	12,69,05,000	13,46,29,000	26,15,34,000	+ 77,24,000
5.	1324 ,, (1914-15)	8,49,87,000	8,77,65,000	17,27,52 000	+ 27,78,000
6,	Average of the decade 1322-31 Fasli (1912-22)	13,46,51 000	11,88,09,000	25,34,60,000	—1,58,42,000
7.	1923	19,12,35,000	17,10,12,000	36,22,47,000	—2,02 23,000
8.	1924	19,87,81,000	19,54,25,000	39,42,06,000	— 33,56,000
9.	1925	21,65,62,000	15,78,31,000	37,43,93,000	—5,87,31,000
10.	1926	14,60,16,000	15 85,76,000	30,45,92,000	+1,25,60,000

11.	1927			13,88,95,000	12,48,12,000	26,37,07,000	—1,40,83,000
12.	1928			18,53,44,000	20,56,34,000	39,09,78,000	+2,02,90,000
13.	1929			19,05,53,000	20,82,13,000	39,87,66,000	+1,76,60,000
14.	1930			19,02,47,000	19,90,28,000	38,92,75,000	+ 87,81,000
15.	1340	Fasli	(1931)	13,01,00,000	13,49,00,000	26,50,00,000	+ 48,00,000
16.	1341	,,	(1932)	13,35,00,000	10,13,00,000	23,48,00,000	—3,22,00 000
17.	1342	,,	(1933)	13,07,00,000	13,06 00,000	26,43,00,000	— 1,00,000
18.	1343	,,	(1934)	14,15,00,000	13,37,00,000	27,52,00,000	— 78,00,000
19.	1344	,,	(1935)	14,42,00,000	11,72,00,000	26,14,00,000	—2,70,00,000
20.	1345	,	(1936)	13,75,00,000	14,40,00,000	28,15,00 000	+ 65,00,000
21.	1346	,	(1937)	15,05,45,855	16,75,17,173	31,80,63,028	+1,69,71,318

Sl. No.	Year			Trade Turn-over Value in Rupees: Import	Export	Value of Total Trade (In Rupees)	Balance of Trade Surplus(+) Deficit(—) (In Rupees)
1	2			3	4	5	6
22.	1347	Fasli	(1938)	1497,08,829	14,64,80,989	29,61,89,818	— 32,27 840
23.	1348	,,	(1939)	14,68,66,973	13,58,06,853	28,26,73,826	—1,10,60,120
24.	1349	,	(1940)	16,60,53,020	16,86,34,524	33,46,87,544	+ 25,81,504
25.	1350	,,	(1941)	16,62,23,221	17,70,79,256	34,33,02,477	+1,08,56,035
26.	1351	,,	(1942)	17 37,68 570	14,59,50,330	31,97,18,900	—2,78,18,240
27.	1352	,,	(1943)	23,73,35,047	18,50,16,656	42,23,51 703	—5,23,18,391
28.	1353	,,	(1944)	26,74,89,000	33,15 40,000	59,90,29,000	+6,40,51,000
29.	1354	,,	(1945)	30,94,78,130	35,12,61,190	66,07,39,320	+4,17,83,060
30.	1355	,,	(1946)	36,95,89,485	36,10,36,522	73,06,26,007	— 85,52,963
31.	1356	,,	(1947)	47,64,13,356	31,47,76,647	79,11,95,003	16,16,41,709
32.	1357	,,	(1948)	—	—	60,00,00,000	—
33.	1358	,,	(1949)	57,00,00,000	29,00,00,000	86,00,00,000	— 28,00,00,000
34.	1359	,,	(First half- Year ending on 31st March, 1950)	29,00,00,000	20,00,00,000	49,00,00,000	— 9,00,00,000

*Since these particulars are not available in respect of Districts or of *Subas*, the State details are given, of which the *Suba* figures formed part and parcel, indicating the general trade trend during the period.

Compiled from :-

1. *H.E.H. the Nizam's Government Revenue Administration : Report, 1324 Fasli (1914-15 A.D.)* pp. 244 & 247 ;
2. *Decennial Report on the Administration of H.E.H. the Nizam's Dominions, 1322 to 1331 Fasli (1912-22A.D.)* p. 148;
3. *Census of India, 1931*, Vol. XYIII, *H.E.H. the Nizam's Dominions*, (*Hyderabad State*), Part I, Report, p. 27;
4. *The Economic Life of Hyderabad*, (Government Central Press : Hyderabad-Dn, 1937), P. 94 ;
5. *Trade Statistics, H.E.H. the Nizam's Government, 1346 Fasli (1936-37)* p. 67 ; *1349 Fasli (1939-40)* pp. 84-85 ; *1351 Fasli (1941-42)*, p. 65 ; *1352 Fasli (1942-43)* p. 81 ; *1356 Fasli (1946-47)*, pp. 90-91 ;
6. Agriculture Department, H.E.H. the Nizam's Government, S. No. 18, *File* No. 55 of 1354 Fasli (1944-45), pp 14-15 ;
7. *Hyderabad Government Bulletin on Economic Affairs*, Vol. II, No. 3 March, 1949, p. 362 ;
8. *Golkonda Patrika* (Daily), 22-11-1950

&

9. *Report on the Administration of Hyderabad State, September, 1948 to March, 1950*, p. 20.

trade decisions, including those affecting that of the *Suba*, were formulated by the former.

iii. Trade Development, 1911-1950 : The balance of trade during the quinquennium ending in 1910-11 was very much favourable, showing a surplus of Rs. 1.22 crores.[572] It was rather an unfortunate coincidence that trade decline in the State commenced with the start of the reign in 1911-12. The considerable quinquennial surplus was followed by a deficit of 32.28 lakhs and in the next year, it got further enhanced to 1.55 crores, thus even going beyond the opening surplus. This successive unfavourable trade balance was because of fall in grain exports and increase in imports, which again was mainly occasioned by poor crop outturn due to 8″ to 9″ less than minimum rainfall.[573] 1913-14 witnessed a return to normal crop conditions and hence, there was not only a favourable trade balance of 77.24 lakhs, but that the total trade reached the level of 26.15 crores, the highest that was ever recorded until then.[574] There had been increase in the export of grain and cotton and also in the import of piecegoods.[575]

(*a*) *First War Period* : The commencement of the War caused much dislocation in the trade of the State.[576] Both imports and exports fell considerably to the effect that the total trade of the State suffered a net decrease of 34% compared to the previous year.[577] Cotton and oil seeds being the two main exports of the Dominions, failed to find the usual markets in Central Europe on account of War hostilities and consequently, a considerable part of these crops remained unsold for a long time. Lack of freight further complicated the situation and the prices realised for the produce sold remained extremely low.[578] Imports in the shape of piece goods, yarn, silver and gold etc., also decreased considerably by 4.20 crores as against 4.69 crores in the case of exports, for the reasons that the stock of these commodities due to War reasons got restricted and consequently, prices went high and further, due to the disposal of the Hyderabad staple crops at low prices, people had less money at their disposal for the purchase of imports.

Though the situation had improved towards the end of the year when Japanese markets replaced the hostile markets and a rise in export prices was experienced, yet, due to initial set-back, the loss in the trade balance to the extent of 49.46 lakhs could not be avoided.[579]

The second year showed a rise in the aggregate trade to the extent of 4.12 crores and again, export also registered considerable increase as good and favourable crop conditions prevailed.[580] The third year of 1916-17 was again marked by an adverse trade balance of 2.01 crores, mainly caused by War time restrictions on exports and also because of heavy and unseasonal rainfall that affected rice, *kharif* and *rabi* crops.[581] The following year also experienced the same kind of crop and trade conditions, The next quadrennium ending in 1921-22 was the most disastrous and dreadful period in the reign of the last *Nizam*. Devastated by famine and epidemic conditions, those four years in the trade annals of Hyderabad State had been marked by a continuous excess of imports over exports and hence, an adverse balance of trade. The effects of the rise in prices that were experienced towards the later years of the War and the trade boom that followed the close of the War, had been very much neutralised by the adverse crop and health conditions.[582] The impact of this unhappy period was to be seen in the trade average of the decade 1912-22, which showed a deficit of 1.58 crores as against a surplus of 1.22 crores for the quinquennium ending in 1910-11.

(*b*) *Pre-Depression Period* : The six-year period of 1923-28 was also marked by adverse trade balances in as many as four years. The decline in the prices of foodgrains, pulses, cotton and oil seeds ranging from 25 to 45%[583] and unfavourable crop conditions, had been the causative factors. Only 1926 and 1928 registered trade surplus of the order of 1.25 and 2.02 crores. The former was marked by a huge decrease in imports of the order of 7.05 crores and the latter by an equally big increase in exports amounting to 8.08 crores. Good crop outturn very much contributed for these, especially in the case of the latter. In the remaining four years, imports exceeded exports and the deficit ranged from 2.02 crores in 1923 to 5.87 crores in 1925. The greater proportion of imports was caused by grain imports on account of insufficiency or failure of crops on one hand and also by considerable imports of gold and silver because of their cheapness, on the other. Bullion imports were mainly purchased by the rich cotton and oil seeds merchants and also wealthy landlords who earned enough profits or incomes at the time when high prices prevailed during War period.[584] 1927 was the only year in which both imports and exports, the latter in a considerable measure amounting to 3.37 crores, had suffered decline, the reason being extremely below average rainfall that led to severe crop failure and diminishing purchasing capacity of the people.

(*c*) *Depression and Post-Depression Period* : Trade in Hyderabad State, as part and parcel of Indian as well as world economic order had come under the strong impact of the great Economic Depression that commenced towards the end of 1929. There was steady decline in the prices of agricultural products as well as industrial manufactures. But, it proved far steeper and heavier in the case of the former than the latter. In the same terms, whereas the exports in the State during the worst Depression period of 1929-34 dwindled by more than half, the imports decreased by only one-third.[585] Agricultural price decline was as heavy as 68.47% in respect of groundnut and 50% in respect of rice.[586] Between 1929 and 1934, the value of imports, exports and total trade suffered to the extent of 23, 35 and 30% respectively. But, the maximum fall was experienced in 1932 when, compared to 1929, the import, export and total trade value declined by as much as 30, 51 and 41 % respectively.[586a] In consequence, the trade deficit in this year touched the highest level that was reached during this period, viz., 3.22 crores. The severe effect in this year was due to the fact that besides the price decline, unfavourable crop conditions prevailed which in turn, resulted in poor outturn.[587] The trade balance during the decade ending in 1938 turned a full circle. It started in 1929 with a surplus of 1.76 crores, began declining at a faster rate until it got converted into a deficit of 3.22 crores in 1932; from 1933 onwards, the huge deficit began receding, though with exceptions in 1934 and 1935[588], until it again got turned into a surplus of 1.69 crores in 1937. In the next two years, once again, both imports and exports suffered, resulting in an adverse balance of 32.27 lakhs in 1937-38 and 1.10 crores in 1938-39. In other words, trade developments indicated that the recovery which commenced from 1932-33, was slow, gradual and halting or hesitating. This, in turn, was related to the fact that the recovery in agricultural prices was slower than that in the case of the manufacturing ones.[589] Consequently, in spite of the recovery in trade that went on, the value of exports, imports, and total trade as it stood in 1938-39, fell short by 32, 20 and 27% of what remained in the pre-Depression year of 1928.

(*d*) *Second War and Post-War Period* : The eleven year period ending in 1949-50 was marked by a continuous rise in the value of imports. The increases that were obtained between 1943 and 1949 proved very much heavy. These amounted to 5.35, 3.01, 4.19, 6.01, 10.68 and 9.35 crores in 1943, 1944, 1945, 1946, 1947 and 1949 respectively.[590] These were due to the phenomenal rise in commodity prices on one hand and heavy imports of foodgrains and piece goods on the other. Between 1941-42 and 1947-48, price increase in respect of important food and non-food crops ranged from 186.03% to 523.15%.[591] As a result, the spurt in import values was more due to this astounding price rise rather than increase in quantity of goods.[592] During the nine years from 1939-40 to 1947-48, deteriorating or unfavourable rainfall and seasonal conditions that considerably affected crop yields, prevailed in as many as six years.[593] These frequent crop failures coupled with the evils of hoarding, black-marketing and smuggling that got associated with the system of Public Distribution that was in operation during this period, necessitated huge imports of food grains.[594] The magnitude of the rise in the import value of some of the basic items could be known from the fact that jawar and jawar flour imports shot up in value from Rs. 91,000 in 1941-42 to Rs. 27,74,000 in 1946-47 ; rice without husk rose from Rs. 43,89,000 to Rs. 1,19,16,000 ; and cotton piecegoods from Rs. 2,54,83,000 to Rs. 6,46,30,000 during the same period.[595]

As against imports, increase in exports was witnessed in only six out of the ten years for which the figures are available. Significant among these related to 1939-40, 1942-43, and 1943-44 and 1944-45, the amount of increase standing at 3.28, 3.90, 14.65 and 1.97 crores respectively. Textiles, oil seeds, grains and pulses, oils and livestock formed the principal commodities that showed increase in their exports in the respective order.[596] But, it is all the more important to realise that the excess of exports over imports, or in other words, favourable trade balance was obtained only in four years out of ten during this period. Efforts of the Government to grow more food and manufacture goods for local consumption in order to attain self-sufficiency[597] in this regard, coupled with rising prices of commodities, aided in achieving surplus export values. Military requirements during War time, requirements of neighbouring provinces in essential items such as oil seeds and pulses, and the new method of collecting duties *advalorem* instead of by weight, also worked towards the same end.[598] But, the closure of European and Far Eastern Markets in consequence of War, transport bottlenecks and scarcity of tonnage,[599] levy of sales tax on exports by the neighbouring provinces,[600] the restrictions imposed by the Government on the cultivation and export of important exportable items such as cotton and oil seeds,[601] and the failure of crop conditions in as many as six years during this period,[602] had all led to diminishing export trade and consequent unfavourable balance in seven out of eleven years.[603]

Total trade of the Dominions, on the other hand, showed regular increase, though of varying proportions, except in 1941-42 and 1947-48. Highest among them, amounting to 10.26,17.66 and 26 crores were recorded in 1942-43, 1943-44 and 1948-49 respectively. In all these years, there had been significant increase in both imports as well as exports. On the other hand, trade decreases coincided with export decreases.[604] If the exports, imports and total trade curves as shown in *Chart No. XII*,[605] are observed, the picture for the entire reign period would be clear. The imports curve, except during the three quinquennia of 1911-15, 1928-32 and 1933-37, was always running above that of exports. The latter, especially since 1947-48, showed considerable shrinkage compared to the

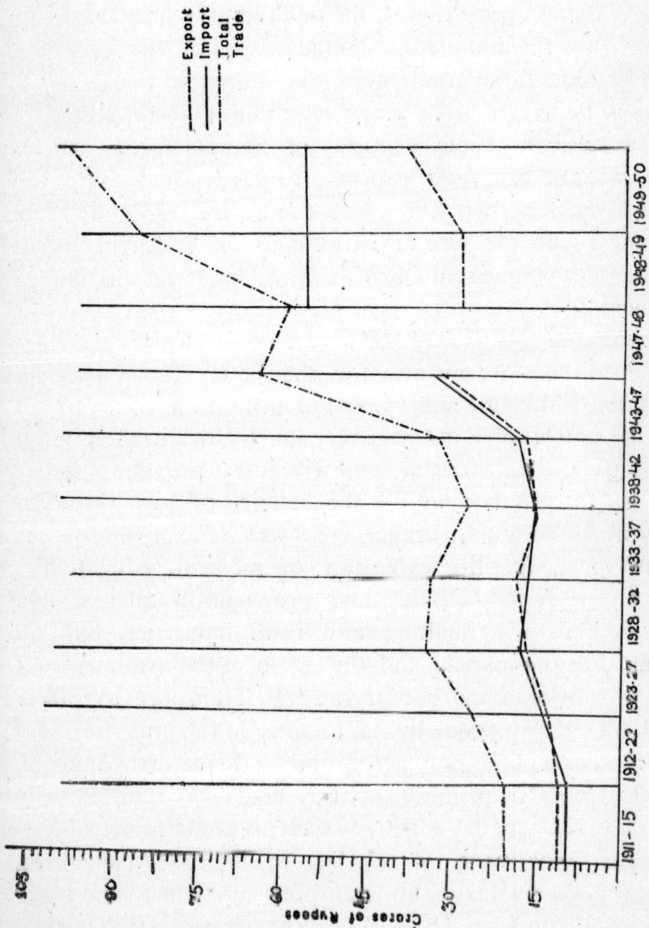

Data From : Table LIII

Chart No. 12 Showing *Trade Turn-Over in Hyderabad State, 1911-15 to 1949-50.*

Data from : *Table VIII*

former. Total trade curve, on the other hand, except during the Depression and post-Depression quinquennia and 1947-48, was also on the rise throughout and more significantly, since the Second War commencement. Nearly three-fifths of the total period was marked by more imports, less exports and hence, adverse trade balances. Besides frequent crop failures, effects of the two Wars and price trends, the one factor which basically contributed for this import-dominated nature of the economy was that manufactured goods were more imported than exported and raw materials were more exported than imported.[606] Whilst in British India exports of manufactured articles formed 26% of the total exports, in Hyderabad State the percentage was less than 4.[607] As a result, the economy more wilted under the pressure of extraneous of emergent forces rather than deriving maximum benefit or material advantage out of them.

F. TRANSPORT DEVELOPMENT :

It formed the basis not only for the better functioning of *Suba* administrative machinery,[608] and utilisation of available irrigational potential,[609] but also very much aided in the promotion of agriculture, industry and trade by providing better markets for the produce and for the import of raw materials and manufactured goods. In fact, rural welfare as a whole came to depend on it, for the extension of medical, educational, post and telegraph facilities and propagation of new and modern methods in agriculture and rural industries, had all been linked to the manner and the extent of the availability of transport facilities in the countryside.[610] Transport by water and air was conspicuous by its absence in the area, for there was neither coast line nor aerodromes. River irrigation by means of '*tokras*' or primitive country boats was resorted only occasionally for sundry purposes such as going to neighbouring villages, movement of pilgrims to Bhadrachalam[611] on Sri Rama Navami Day and transport of timber and other kinds of forest produce, which of course, due to the uneven sandy and shallow river beds, was possible only during rainy season.[612] Using of steam boats or *launches* either for export or import trade on any considerable scale was a rare or unknown phenomena during the period. Consequently, the carrying trade

TABLE LIV

Length of the Road & Rail Mileage and Requirement, in Warangal Suba, 1921-1950

WARANGAL DISTRICT						
Sl. No.	Year	Area in Sq. miles	Agricultural Area in Sq. miles	Non-Agricultural Area in Sq. miles	Net mileage required	Existing mileage of Railways
1	2	3	4	5	6	7
1.	1330 Fasli (1921)	—	—	—	—	—
2.	1344 ,, (1935)	—	—	—	—	—
3.	1349 ,, (1940)	—	—	—	—	—
4.	1351 ,, (1942)	—	—	—	—	—
5.	1352 ,, (1943)	—	—	—	—	—
6.	1353 ,, (1944)	—	—	—	—	—
7.	1354 ,, (1945)	—	—	—	—	—
8.	1358 ,, (1949)	7,944	2,520	5,424	910	182
9.	1359 ,, (1950)	—	—	—	—	—

WARANGAL DISTRICT

Sl. No.	Year			Existing Road Mileage: Metalled (Miles) P.W.D	Munici-pality	District Board or Local Board	Total	Un-Metalled (Miles) P.W.D	Munici-pality	District Board or Local Board	Total	Total Road Length (Miles) Metal-led	Un-Metall-ed	Total
				8	9	10	11	12	13	14	15	16	17	18
1.	1330	Fasli	(1921)	—	—	—	54¾	—	—	—	107½	54¾	107½	162¼
2.	1344	,,	(1935)	291¼	7⅝	2⅛	301	129⅛	—	7¾	136⅞	301	136½	437⅞
3.	1349	,,	(1940)	344	3	1	348	97	4	4	105	348	105	453
4.	1351	,,	(1942)	333	9	12	354	93	3	27	123	354	123	477
5.	1352	,,	(1943)	396	9	26	431	93	14	38	145	431	145	576
6.	1353	,,	(1944)	396	9	26	431	93	14	38	145	431	145	576
7.	1354	,,	(1945)	354	—	26	380	72	—	38	110	380	110	490
8.	1358	,,	(1949)	—	—	—	—	—	—	—	—	—	—	475
9.	1359	,,	(1950)	—	—	—	437	—	—	—	28¾	437	28¾	465¾

KARIMNAGAR DISTRICT

Sl. No.	Year	Area in Sq. miles	Agricultural Area in Sq. miles	Non-Agricultural Area in Sq. miles	Net mileage required	Existing mileage of Railways
		19	20	21	22	23
1.	1330 Fasli (1921)	—	—	—	—	—
2.	1344 „ (1935)	—	—	—	—	—
3.	1349 „ (1940)	—	—	—	—	—
4.	1351 „ (1942)	—	—	—	—	—
5.	1352 „ (1943)	—	—	—	—	—
6.	1353 „ (1944)	—	—	—	—	—
7.	1354 „ (1945)	—	—	—	—	—
8.	1358 „ (1949)	5,722	2,366	3,356	922	56
9.	1359 „ (1950)	—	—	—	—	—

Sl. No.	Year			Existing Road Mileage — KARIMNAGAR DISTRICT: Metalled (Miles) P.W.D	Metalled (Miles) Municipality	Metalled (Miles) District Board or Local Board	Metalled (Miles) Total	Un-Metalled (Miles) P.W.D.	Un-Metalled (Miles) Municipality	Un-Metalled (Miles) District Board or Local Board	Un-Metalled (Miles) Total	Total Road Length (Miles) Metalled	Total Road Length (Miles) Un-Metalled	Total Road Length (Miles) Total
				24	25	26	27	28	29	30	31	32	33	34
1.	1330	Fasli	(1921)	—	—	—	74⅝	—	—	—	55⅛	74⅝	55⅛	129¾
2.	1344	,,	(1935)	134	—	—	134	78⅝	—	21	99⅝	134	99⅝	233⅝
3.	1349	,,	(1940)	213	—	4	217	61	—	63	124	217	124	841
4.	1351	,,	(1942)	264	2	3	269	10	16	59	85	269	85	354
5.	1352	,,	(1943)	396	9	26	431	93	14	38	145	431	145	576
6.	1353	,,	(1944)	264	2	3	269	10	16	59	85	269	85	354
7.	1354	,,	(1945)	285	—	3	288	—	—	59	59	288	59	347
8.	1358	,,	(1949)	—	—	—	—	—	—	—	—	—	—	269
9.	1359	,,	(1950)	—	—	=	291¾	—	—	—	16⅝	291¾	16⅝	308⅜

Sl. No.	Year	ADILABAD DISTRICT Area in Sq. miles	Agricultural Area in Sq. miles	Non-Agricultural Area in Sq. miles	Net mileage required	Existing mileage 8 Railways
		35	36	37	38	39
1.	1330 Fasli (1921)	—	—	—	—	—
2.	1344 ,, (1935)	—	—	—	—	—
3.	1349 ,, (1940)	—	—	—	—	—
4.	1351 ,, (1942)	—	—	—	—	—
5.	1352 ,, (1943)	—	—	—	—	—
6.	1353 ,, (1944)	—	—	—	—	—
7.	1354 ,, (1945)	—	—	—	—	—
8,	1358 ,, (1949)	7,294	2,187	5,108	876	78
9.	1359 , (1950)	—	—	—	—	—

ADILABAD DISTRICT

Sl. No.	Year			Existing Road Mileage: Metalled (Miles) P.W.D.	Metalled (Miles) Munici-pality	Metalled (Miles) District Board or Local Board	Metalled (Miles) Total	Un-Metalled (Miles) P.W.D.	Un-Metalled (Miles) Munici-pality	Un-Metalled (Miles) District Board or Local Board	Un-Metalled (Miles) Total	Total Road Length (Miles) Metal-led	Total Road Length (Miles) Un-Metalled	Total Road Length (Miles) Total
				40	41	42	43	44	45	46	47	48	49	50
1.	1330	Fasli	(1921)	—	—	—	Nil	—	—	—	$36\frac{1}{4}$	Nil	$36\frac{1}{4}$	$36\frac{1}{4}$
2.	1344	,,	(1935)	$224\frac{1}{8}$	—	—	$224\frac{1}{8}$	$46\frac{5}{8}$	—	$1\frac{1}{8}$	$47\frac{3}{4}$	$224\frac{1}{8}$	$47\frac{3}{4}$	$271\frac{7}{8}$
3.	1349	,,	(1940)	294	1	—	295	—	2	3	5	295	5	300
4.	1351	,,	(1942)	301	—	5	306	—	—	36	36	306	36	342
5.	1352	,,	(1943)	301	3	5	309	—	16	20	36	309	36	345
6.	1353	,,	(1944)	301	3	5	309	—	16	20	36	309	36	345
7.	1354	,,	(1945)	301	6	5	312	—	39	20	59	312	59	371
8.	1358	,,	(1949)	—	—	—	—	—	—	—	—	—	—	300
9.	1359	,,	(1950)	—	—	—	$303\frac{1}{2}$	—	—	—	—	$303\frac{1}{2}$	—	$303\frac{1}{2}$

Compiled from :- *Hyderabad District Gazetteers*, Part II, Tables volumes, *1925*, *Warangal*, (p. 3), *Karimnagar* (p. 3) and *Adilabad* (p. 3).

Statistical Year Book, 1344 Fasli (1935), H.E.H. the Nizam's Government, pp, 462-63 ;

Statistical Year Book, 1349 Fasli (1940), H.E.H. the Nizam's Government, p. 764 ;

Statistical Year Book, 1351-1354 Fasli (1942-45), H.E.H. the Nizam's Government, p. 242 ;

'Post-War Development Scheme' prepared by P.W.D., H.E.H. the Nizam's Government, quoted in a special article 'Some Economic Aspects of Road Planning and Development with special reference to Hyderabad' by A. Gopalan in *the Hyderabad Government Bulletin on Economic Affairs*, Vol. II, No. 8-9, August-September, 1949, p. 333.

&

Public Works Department, H.E.H. the Nizam's Government quoted by S. Kesava Iyengar in *Rural Economic Enquiries in the Hyderabad State, 1949-51*, p. 333.

of the *Suba* was primarily carried by road and secondarily by rail. The mileage of the latter in 1949 formed only 38.31, 26 and 20.82% of that of the former in Warangal, Adilabad and Karimnagar Districts respectively.[613] Even if the road needs of the area were worked out at the minimum of one mile for every five miles of territory, the existing mileage fell short by 38.66, 35.24 and 55.70% in the case of Warangal, Karimnagar and Adilabad Districts respectively.[614] But, for an efficient road system, it was felt by the Chief Engineer, *Nizam's* State Railway, that one mile of road was essential for every 3.3 sq. miles,[615] which, if strived for, world further increase the deficiency.

i. Road Transpost : No cement or tar roads existed in the *Suba* Districts.[616] Metal and unmetalled or *murum*[617] had been the two types that were maintained out of which, the former accounted for 80 to 9 0% of the total road mileage.[618] It is a welcome trend to note that between 1921 and 1950, the mileage of metal roads showed an increase ranging from 300 to 700% as against decrease in respect of *murum* roads amounting to 66 to 80%.[619] In total road mileage as it stood in 1949, Warangal District was ahead of Karimnagar and Adilabad Districts by as much as 206 and 175 miles respectively.[620] This difference was reflected in their ranking in the State as a whole in the sense that, whereas Warangal claimed third place next to Nalgonda and Aurangabad, the Districts of Adilabad and Karimnagar on the other hand, came to occupy ninth and tenth places respectively.[621] 98% of the metal roads and 65% of the non-metal ones were maintained by the Public Works Department (P.W.D.) and among the Municipalities and District or Local Boards which only accounted for the remaining meagre portion, the latter's contribution was roughly three to four times more than that of the former.[622] Only in respect of Adilabad District, P.W.D's maintenance role was conspicuous by its absence regarding non-metal roads after 1935, which was probably due to the meagreness of the mileage involved or the official disinclination to spread their arm to the remoter parts. The mileage figures, however, reveal an interesting fact that whereas during the 15 years period of 1921-35, length of the road mileage showed an increase of 276, 104 and 235 miles in the respective Districts of Warangal, Karimnagar and Adilabad, the corresponding rise during the succeeding 15 year period was only of the order of 28, 65 and 32 miles respectively. This decrease in the growth rate amounting to 89.85, 37.5 and 86.38%[623] respectively, did very much reflect on the slackness of the Government during the latter period, even though there was abundant need for expansion in this regard.[624] Another trend that becomes clear is that, whereas the road mileage was regularly on the rise, though varying in intensity between the periods, upto 1943 which year particularly due to War time boom in production and trade showed the maximum rise in a single year that amounted to 54.01% in the case of Karimnagar and 20.75% in respect of Warangal,[625] it showed a general decline since then for the remaining period, with only some exceptions here and there, in Districts other than Warangal.[626]

Though some important inter-District and inter-Taluq roads like those of Hanamkonda-Karimnagar road, Karimnagar Luxettipet road, Khammam-Suryapet[627] road, Adilabad-Ichoda[628] road, Paloncha-Yellandu road, Karimnagar road links with Jagtiyal, Sirsilla and Manthani, Asifabad-Rajura road, Asifabad-Sirpur road, and Mancherial road links with Tandur and Luxettipet,[629] etc., had been executed and some of them metalled during the reign period of the VII *Nizam*,[630] yet, hundreds of villages including some Taluq headquarters in the *Suba*,[631] had no proper roads or connection with either a road or railway system at all.[632] Kinwat, Boorgampahad and Mahaboobabad Taluqs suffered considerable disadvantage in this respect.[633] Villages even 60 miles away from a *Kutcha* or unmetalled road were there.[634] Inordinate delay took place in the construction as well as repair of the roads. The laying of the road from Mahaboobabad to Abbayapalem in the same Taluq of Warangal District could not be completed even six years after the commencement.[635] Failure to take up the repair of the roads in Yellandu, Taluq headquarters of the same District, even after a six year period, made them difficult of usage for carts and other traffic.[636] The condition of the road from Nirmal to Mannore, a distance of 36 miles on the Nirmal

Adilabad road was so miserable that most of the culverts became much higher than the road level and the number of ditches and ruts was very large. And this was a part of one of the most important national highways in the country, connecting Coimbatore, Bangalore, Hyderabad and Nagpur[636]. This inadequacy of road facilities had not only affected the movement of foodgrains for distribution by the Supply Department[637] and the movement of mail between District and Taluq headquarters,[638] but essentially deprived the ryots of taking advantage of the demand and higher prices of the agricultural produce that prevailed in Regulated Markets and more so in neighbouring provincial markets. The result was its disposal at far too low prices to middlemen or village merchants who took the trouble of transporting it to wholesale markets and got richly rewarded.[639] Several lakhs of rupees income was lost annually by Adilabad farmers for not having easy access to Pandarkota and Chanda markets in Madhya Pradesh where the prices of cotton per *khandi*[640] proved higher by Rs. 50 compared to those at Adilabad or Peddapalli, a business centre in Karimnagar District.[641] The growing of fruits or vegetables or the sale of milk that gave quick and constant returns to cultivators and even the going of local people to Taluq headquarters for representation and redressal of their grievances, were greatly affected by this vital deficiency to the considerable detriment of the local population.[642]. On account of the latter handicap, the *Pairavkars* or those who acted as middlemen in transacting official business for the illiterate and ignorant rural masses, flourished by exploiting the latter to the maximum.[643]

Besides the Departmental delay and indifference, the poor and inadequate apportionment of the budget for the construction and repair of roads, contributed not a little for road deficiency. For a State with an area of 82,698 sq. miles and a road mileage ranging from 5,000 miles in 1937[644] to 5,358 miles in 1949[645], the amount spent on road and rail transport ranged from 1.02 lakhs in 1934-35 to 5.71 lakhs in 1948-49 which formed respectively as low as 0.14 to 0.22 percentage of the total expenditure.[646] The neglect inherent in the situation could better be appreciated from the fact that as against this low expenditure, the State which held the monopoly of road and rail transport since June, 1932, got revenue from this wing which ranged from 93.87 lakhs in the former year to 51.41 lakhs in the latter, touching the highest mark of 164.87 lakhs in 1945-46 and formed respectively 12.83, 1.99 and 9.22% of the total State Revenue.[647] To add to this, considerable imbalances prevailed in the division of the allotted budget between the *Subas* and again between District headquarters and Taluqs. Warangal *Suba*, which was only slightly lesser in area than Gulbarga *Suba*, but very much more than those of Aurangabad and Medak and also contained greater percentage of tribal and backward population compared to the rest, got the least amount spent on road construction and repairs.[648] On the other hand, out of the moderate resources that the Local Bodies could muster for spending on developmental works, greater proportion was spent on District headquarters and items such as water works than on Taluqs and road works.[649] The proportion between them stood respectively at 54.17& 45.83, 70.65 & 29.35 and 12.75 & 87.25 in Warangal, Karimnagar and Adilabad Districts respectively.[650] The contrary trend was noticeable in respect of last named District, mainly because of the fact that the headquarter and costly items such as water works, had not been taken up in its case.[651] Some of the neglected areas in road communication such as Mahaboobabad, Palvancha, Manthani and Sirsilla Taluqs received attention through laying of new roads in 1949-50, when the Government adopted it as one of the means to clear these areas of Communist insurgence.[652]

(*a*) *Motor Bus Service* : Motor vehicles came to be used in the area since the twenties of the present century.[653] Initially, the bus services which were operated on all P.W.D. roads and also on country tracks during fair-weather[654], had been run either by individuals such as Gulam Rasool in Boorgampahad[655] or by agencies such as the Hyderabad Motor and Oil Company in Karimnagar District.[656] These private services had been characterised by irregularity, substandardness and high rates.[657] Yet, they grew in strength,[658] for the convenience and the facility of travel and movement offered by the new means of transport was not discouraging. But, more important was the fact that they started competing with the State Railway in sharing the earnings of passenger and goods traffic.[659] Hence, the Government in order to divert this huge private income to the State and also to bring improvement in the service and more important, coordination of road and rail transport for fuller exploitation of the State's transport potential, brought into being on 15th June, 1932, the historic Road Transport Department under the control of the *Nizam* State Railways.[660] This coordination of road and rail transport and also Air Transport Service from 1936,[661] all under the direction of the State Railway Board, was a pioneering measure in the country, that was carried on with considerable vigour and success in the ensuing period upto April, 1950 when the changed political set-up in the State brought separation among these services, the Railways falling under the Indian control and Road Transport coming under the State Government's control.[662]

The introduction of nationalised road transport system was not uniform in the *Suba* Districts. Whereas it was started in Warangal at the very commencement of the service in June, 1932, the same was delayed in Adilabad upto October, 1936[663] and in Karimnagar still very much farther, upto June, 1946.[664] This delay had only benefited the private operators and the people got deprived of the benefits that were expected under the new measure. Even where the State transport service was introduced, private bus service was also allowed to be run on unmetalled or non-PWD roads mostly during fair-weather. But, the size of these buses was so small that the average number of passengers carried in a trip ranged from only 9 in Warangal and Adilabad Districts to 12 in Karimnagar District.[665] Even in the RTD service also, though the capacity of a bus was between 50-60 passengers, there used to be heavy overcrowding as the number of buses operated on a route were very much limited, mostly being confined to two only and the public request for the increase in the number of trips or buses went rather unheeded.[666] Though other grievances of the people such as two or three hours late arrival of buses daily, bus halts being kept two or three furlongs away from a village[667] and production of heavy sound by the running buses, the most important popular representation regarding the service was that the charges were high and hence, should be reduced. Even before the Second War, these were regarded as high which had been further enhanced, although there was heavy increase in passenger and goods traffic during War period compared to lesser rise in maintenance and running costs of the Department during the same period.[668] Further, in order to boost up railway receipts which was an entire State preserve, bus fares were made higher so that the traffic would get diverted to the former and controlling agency for both being the same, it was regarded that the loss if any, in road traffic would be compensated by the increase in the former.[669] In fact, the main object kept in mind while framing the Hyderabad Motor Vehicle Rules which became law in 1936 was that ultimately the railways in the State should have monopoly over all public transport services.[670] But, in spite of passenger grievances which were least met, the Road Transport Service in the State kept on growing in the sense that the number of buses rose for 27 in 1932 to 368 in 1938-39 with an operative route mileage of 4,069 miles and further increased in 1944-45 to 549 buses with 4,291 miles of route mileage.[671] All the same, for 138 *Tahsils*, comprising as many as 22,360 villages with a population of 1,63,38,534,[672] the number of buses run by the State was far too inadequate. In Adilabad District with 7,294 sq. miles of area, 2,138 villages with a total population of 8,23,622[673] comprised in as many as ten Taluqs, the RTD by the end of 1950-51 was able to put only a paltry number of 18 buses on the road, operated from the Depots of Asifabad and Nirmal, covering a route mileage of about 334 miles.[674] The inevitable result was that with all the known ills inherent in private transport service, the total mileage operated by private operators in the State during 1948-49 was 4,153.5 miles as against 4,944.9 miles operated by RTD during the same year[675] and out of 6,203 Motor vehicles registered in 1944-45, private motor cars numbered as many as 3,880.[676]

(*b*) *Carts* : In the countryside, these formed by far the most common means for general conveyance and chiefly for transporting produce to the nearby markets. As bullocks and carts, the two accessories, were invariably owned by ryots, they found it economical and rather suited to their general economic capacity, to use this means of transport than go for motor vehicles or lorries except when long distances had to be travelled or heavy quantity of produce was to be taken for sale. One bullock cart had the capacity of 12 to 21 maunds and the two bullock one, which was mostly employed, had the capacity of 27 to 33 maunds.[677] Its make had undergone considerable alteration from the primitive type of low stone wheels to the modern type of consisting of either wooden wheels topped with iron or rubber tyres.[678] In parts which were not touched by railway, the carrying of exportable goods to the rail-head and the transhipment of imports from the rail-head to the interior, was mainly performed by this country means of transport.[679] Its importance in the *Suba* and also the State could be known from the fact that not only its number in the Census[680] of 1919 and 1935 recorded increase, but that between 1940-45 when the neighbouring provinces of Bombay, Madras and Central Provinces experienced decrease in their total number of carts, the former on the other hand, registered increase.[681] But, however, Karimnagar District which until then occupied second place in the State, suffered considerable decline from 71,162 carts in 1935[682] to 64,820 in 1950,[683] which in turn, was not a little due to the scarcity and the imposition of control in respect of the supply of iron and rubber or rubber tyres that had been basically employed in the manufacture of cart wheels, during the War and the post-War period.[684] At the same time, Adilabad District which occupied third place in the State where comparatively, these components were less employed in view of the greater prevalence of stone wheels, registered increase in the number of carts from 63,842 in 1935[685] to 66,882 in 1951.[686] In Warangal District, on the other hand, due to better rail and road facilities, less number of carts-only 46,428 in 1935[687] were used when compared to the other *Suba* Districts and consequently, it came to hold fourth place in the State in this respect. All the same, transport requirements in the rural parts of the *Suba*, especially of the produce and merchandise, had been mainly fulfilled by this means than any other, throughout the period.

ii. Rail Transport : In rail mileage, Warangal District with 182 miles[688], ranked first not only in the *Suba* but in the State itself.[689] It had the distinction of being traversed by two important broad gauge lines—the Secunderabad—Bezwada line and the Secunderabad-Delhi line via Kazipet and Balharshah—,the former connecting it with Nalgonda District of Medak *Suba* and Krishna District of Madras Presidency and the latter with the *Suba* Districts of Karimnagar and Adilabad and the British Indian Central Provinces and further North upto Delhi.[690] North-South and West of the District, had thus witnessed rail line. It is significant to realise that this District had accounted for 79.24% of the mileage of the former line, for it had occupied 162 miles[691] out of 215 miles of the line.[692] Leaving out the branch lines that were laid for Singareni and Kothagudem Collieries[693], there had been as many as 17 Stations[694] that covered the Taluqs of Warangal, Mahaboobabad, Khammam and Madhira, and the principal industrial and trade centres of the District, viz., Warangal, Ghanpur, Mahaboobabad, Khammam, and Madhira had all been Stations on this broad guage line. Mulug and Parkal remained as the only Taluqs of this District that had been completely untouched by the rail line either branch or main.[695]

On the other hand, Karimnagar and Adilabad Districts were served essentially by only the Kazipet-Balharshah broad-gauge line which in turn, covered only limited territory. 56 miles of line in Huzurabad and Sultanabad Taluqs of the former District and 78 miles of line in the Luxettipet, Asifabad and Sirpur Taluqs of the latter District, formed part of this North-South Railway.[696] Jammikunta, Peddapalli and Ramagundam in the former, Mancherial, Bellampalli, Tandur, Asifabad Road, Rechini Road and Sirpur-Kagaznagar in the latter, had been the stations that mainly carried the export-import trade of these Eastern Districts. It could be noticed that these again were the same in which the key industries of these Districts such as coal paper, stone, timber, chemicals and fertilisers, oil and cotton, had been located.[697] Besides this broad-gauge line, a metergauge line of about 23 km. traversed through Kinwat and Adilabad Taluqs of the District of the latter name, the starting point of which was Mudkhed in the Marathwada region and the terminus was of course, Adilabad Station itself.[698] The completion of this line which contributed for the promotion of trade links between these two northern Taluqs and the cotton rich Marathwada regions, got dragged on, due to War, consequent scarcity of materials and to some extent the slackness of the Department, from 1939 to 1950, even though the total length of the line was only 101 miles.[699] However, compared to Warangal District, those of Karimnagar and Adilabad fell short in rail mileage, by 69.23 and 57.14% respectively.[700] Karimnagar, Jagtiyal, Sirsilla, Parkal and Manthani Taluqs in the former, Boath, Rajura, Chinnur, Nirmal and Utnoor Taluqs in the latter, remained completely untouched by rail line.

Though the railway mileage in the *Suba* Districts was less by nearly three to five times of that of the road mileage,[701] yet on the other hand, the value of rail-borne goods accounted for as much as 80% of the total trade.[702] Raw materials like coal, grain, timber, oil-seeds and cotton formed the principal items of outward traffic ; petroleum goods and petrol-manufactured cloth, sugar, oils, general goods and industrial raw materials consisted the main items of inward traffic that was carried on by the railways.[703] Coal exports from the Singareni, Kothagudem, Bellampalli and Balharshah mines that were all situated on the Kazipet—Balharshah line amounted to nearly 40% of the goods traffic turned out by the State Railways.[704] The earnings rose abnormally during the periods of War, as for instance, there was an increase of Rs. 138 lakhs in 1943-44 over that of 1938-39.[705] During this year, the railways carried out nearly double the passengers traffic and over 50% more goods traffic than what was handled in the latter year.[706] At the same time, working expenses formed only 42.8% of gross earnings,[707] thereby very much boosting up the profit margin. Compared to the value of goods traffic, that of passenger traffic showed less by more than 68% which was evident from the fact that during 1941-42 to 1944-45, the total earnings from the latter in the State amounted to Rs. 1,62,45,000 while the former's earnings ranged upto Rs. 2,69,06,000.[708] Again, during the same period, out of 1,77,39,000 passengers carried by the State Railways, as many as 1,07,32,800 were accounted for by the metre gauge, which amounted to more than 61%.[709] It otherwise, indicated that people in the area, due to their poverty and also local necessities, preferred rail travel more by branch and smaller lines than by main and bigger lines. However, the collection of a number of taxes such as the Income Tax, Excess Profits Duty and Corporation Tax on State Railways earnings by the British during the year before April, 1930, when the *Nizam* Guaranteed State Railway Company functioned under the direction of a Board in London had, to a considerable extent, reduced the Government's share of surplus earnings in the railway[710] which would otherwise have been available for the development of rail transport. The rate of British Income Tax was raised from IS,2d in the pound before the First War to 6S. in the pound in 1918-19 and then, since 1922 was kept at 4½ S. in the pound.[711] Even after State Assumption of railway control in April, 1930, the attempts of the British Indian Government to carry on extra-territorial rail jurisdiction and the ineffective resentment of the former at such activities, had also come to restrict the plans of railway expansion in the State.[712]

iii. Postal and Tele-communication Facilities · These were very much inadequate to the requirements of the population in the *Suba* Districts. The number of Post Offices, as could be seen from *Table LV*, rose during 1926-36, by only 5, 13 and 16 in the respective Districts of Karimnagar, Adilabad and Warangal. Their ratio in proportion to District area and population left much to be desired. The former, excepting the case of Karimnagar District in 1950-51,[713] never came down throughout the period, below the proportion of one Post Office for 100 sq. miles of territory and the maximum being 235 sq. miles for one Post Office and the latter, never came down below the population ratio of 10,000 per one Post Office, the maximum in this regard, touching at high as 31,035 persons per one Post Office.[714] Letter boxes and Post men had

TABLE LV

Distribution of Postal and Telephone Services in Warangal Suba, 1926-1950

KARIMNAGAR DISTRICT

Sl. No.	Year	Number of Post Offices	Number of Sq. miles per Office	Number of inhabitants per Office	Letter Boxes	Village Post men	Percentage of Postal income to expenditure	Number of telephone subscribers	Number of telecommunication stations
1	2	3	4	5	6	7	8	9	10
1.	1335 Fasli (1926)	39	147	28,088	22	27	—	Nil	Nil
2.	1336 ,, (1927)	—	—	—	—	—	—	,,	,,
3.	1340 ,, (1931)	40	143	31,035	41	23	—	,,	,,
4.	1341 ,, (1932)	—	—	—	—	—	140.3	,,	,,
5.	1342 ,, (1933)	—	—	—	—	—	136.1	,,	,,
6.	1343 ,, (1934)	—	—	—	—	—	155.4	,,	,
7.	1344 ,, (1935)	42	136	29,557	47	23	135.9	,,	,,
8.	1345 ,, (1936)	44	130	28,214	48	23	161.7	,,	,,
9.	1346 ,, (1937)							,,	,,
10.	1351-1354 Fasli (1941-42 to 1944-45)							,,	,,
11.	1358 Fasli (1949)							,,	,,
12.	1360 ,, (1950-51)	146	—	—	—	—	—	,,	,,

ADILABAD DISTRICT

	Number of Post Offices	Number of Sq. miles per Office	Number of inhabitants per Office	Letter Boxes	Village Post men	Percentage of Postal income to expenditure	Number of telephone subscribers	Number of tele-communication stations
	11	12	13	14	15	16	17	18
1. 1335 Fasli (1926)	31	235	21,146	23	26	—	Nil	Nil
2. 1336 ,, (1927)	—	—	—	—	—	—	,,	,,
3. 1340 ,, (1931)	41	—	—	40	21	—	,,	,,
4. 1341 ,, (1932)	-	—	—	—	—	90.1	,,	,,
5. 1342 ,, (1933)	—	—	—	—	—	871.8	,,	,,
6. 1343 ,, (1934)	—	—	—	—	—	106.4		,,
7. 1344 ,, (1935)	43	170	17,722	47	31	112.4		,
8. 1345 ,, (1936)	44	166	17,319	41	31	117.2	,,	,,
9. 1346 ,, (1937)	--	—	—	—	—	—	,,	,
10. 1351-1354 Fasli (1941-42 to 1944-45).	—	—	—	—	—	—	,,	,,
11. 1358 Fasli (1949)	—	—	—	—	—	—	,,	,,
12. 1360 ,, (1950-51)	67	—	—	—	—	—	,,	,,

WARANGAL DISTRICT

	Number of Post Offices	Number of Sq. miles per Office	Number of inhabitants per Office	Letter Boxes	Village Post men	Percentage of Postal income to expenditure	Number of telephone Subscribers	Number of telecommunication stations
	19	20	21	22	23	24	25	26
1. 1335 Fasli (1926)	47	169	—	—	—	—	Nil	Nil
2. 1336 ,, (1927)	—	—	—	—	—	—	70	2
3. 1340 ,, (1931)	58	137	—	—	—	—	—	,,
4. 1341 ,, (1932)	—	—	—	—	—	104.3	—	,,
5. 1342 ,, (1933)	—	—	—	—	—	146.8	—	,,
6. 1343 ,, (1934)	—	—	—	—	—	127.6	—	,,
7. 1344 ,, (1935)	—	—	—	—	—	137.9	—	,,
8. 1345 ,, (1936)	63	—	—	—	—	167.0	49*	,,
9. 1346 ,, (1937)	—	126	—	—	—	—	55	,,
10. 1351-1354 Fasli (1941-42 to 1944-45)	—	—	—	—	—	—	109*	,,
11. 1358 Fasli (1949)	—	—	—	—	—	—	—	4
12. 1360 , (1950-51)	—	—	—	—	—	—	—	,,

*Telephone connections.

Compiled from :
1. *Hyderabad District Gazetteers*, Tables Vols, *1931 & 1936 Warangal*, (pp. 114-15 & 122-23), *Karimnagar*, (pp. 114-15 & 122-23) ; *Adilabad* (pp. 114-15 & 122-23) ;
2. *Administrative Report*, *1346 Fasli* (*1936-37*), (Hyderabad-Dn, 1939), p. 128 ;
3. H.E.H. the Nizam's Government, Financial Secretariat, English Branch, *File* No. 155 of 1346 Fasli (1937) and S. No. 202 ;
4. *Statistical Year Book*, *1941-42 to 1944-45*, *H.E.H. the Nizam's Government*, p. 420 ;
5. S. Kesava Iyengar, *Rural Economic Enquiries*, *1949-51*, p. 344 ;

&

6. *Andhra Pradesh District Gazetteers*, *Karimnagar*, 1974, p. 144 ; *Adilabad* 1976, p. 110.

also been highly deficient in supply. In most of the years, their number was far less than that of the Post Offices in a District, thereby signifiying the fact that the latter existed in some cases without the former and vice-versa.[715] On the other hand, in contrast to this poor supply of the basic amenities in the field of postal communication, the percentage of postal income in relation to expenditure ranged from 90.1 to 871.8.[716]

Besides the inadequate spread of Postal Services in the *Suba* area, much delay and inconvenience was experienced by the people in receiving letters and parcels. Because of the lack of transport facilities to the interior villages, letters failed to reach them for not less than two weeks time.[717] Hence, all urgent and important messages in these parts were conveyed in person only.[718] But, it spoke of the inefficiency of the Service that even in towns where good transport facilities existed, letters were not received in time and sometimes, even the issues disappeared before being handed over to the addresses.[719] Lot of difficulty was experienced, especially by the merchants, in getting articles or goods from distant places by train. These articles were sent to the nearest railway stations which sometimes were located at a distance ranging from 60 to 100 miles, but the railway receipt was sent to the Imperial Post Office[720] at Hyderabad which, on intimation, was to be collected either by the addresses or some one on his behalf, incurring the to and fro expenditure to Hyderabad and again, similar expenditure in going over to the concerned railway station for collecting in goods.[721] It was complained that excess amounts over and above the bill amounts were charged by customs and railway authorities that added fuel to the fire.[722] Further, for sending money orders to British Indian territories, the local people were subjected to the burden of paying local commission and also the Imperial Commission.[723] Above all, the fact that nearly 50 British Post Offices existed in the Dominions very much competing with local offices and the free delivery amounting to Rs. 85 to 95 lakhs worth a year, of all articles transferred from the former by the latter, hand considerably affected the strength and the sound functioning of the local Post Offices.[724] The loss incurred on account of this unfavourable situation amounted to Rs. 2 to 3 lakhs every year by the Hyderabad Postal Department.[725] This very Department was finally merged with the Indian Postal Department from 15th April, 1950, as part of the integration of the State with the Indian Union.[726]

Telephone or tele-communication Services in the *Suba* during the period of study had been confined to only Warangal District and the remaining drew completely blank in this respect.[727] Though the need of this quick service arm both for the purposes of administration as well as business was realised as early as 1920s and representations were made by First *Taluqdars*, such as that of Adilabad to Government for the installation of trunk lines as early as 1928, nothing had emerged in concrete from the Capital right until the end of the period, in respect of the latter.[728] Only Warangal, the headquarters town, had, besides the local telephone service, the facility of trunk connection with Hyderabad since 1927.[729] Besides this premier town, only Ghanapur, a market place in Warangal Taluq had only local phone service the same year, but, no trunk service[730] and Khammam and Kothagudem, the two Taluq headquarters-cum-trading or industrial towns in the same District of Warangal, had been made the tele-communication station only since 1949.[731] Other six Taluqs of Warangal District also remained untouched by this communication facility Taluq headquarters town of Mahaboobabad in Warangal District, had not even a Telegraph Office in 1950 and the local people represented to Assistant Civil Administrator in this regard.[731a] It is important to note that even where this Service was introduced also, it was neither popular nor run on profitable lines. As could be seen from *Table LV*, the number of telephone subscribers in Warangal Exchange, came down from 70 in 1927 to 55 in 1937, amounting to a decrease of 21% over a decade, instead of increase.[732] This unpopularity of the Service was reflected in the fact that this Exchange which also served the centres of Bhongir, Alir, and Jangaon in Nalgonda District of Medak *Suba*, suffered a loss of Rs. 18,262 in 1936 and Rs. 19,723 in 1937 successively.[733] The main reason for this poor performance of the local Telephone Service was the fact that, as the important trading or business centres in the *Suba* as well as the State were not linked each other by trunk service, the merchants and other public felt no use for local Telephone

Service wherever it was provided.[734] Even, it failed to come of much use to the administration also, for there had been no inter-Taluq or District links. Finally, this Service, like the Postal Service, got merged, since April, 1950, with the All-India Service, marking the integration of the State with the Indian Union.[735]

To sum up, industrial production in the *Suba* during the period, was marked by low productivity and under-utilisation of the resources or the materials. To cite the instance of coal-mining which served as the leading large-scale industry in the *Suba* as well as the State, the Singareni Collieries Company during 45 years ending in 1944 could extract only about 33 million tons of coal as against the estimated resources of 1,000 million tons of coal in the Dominions. In the same way, as against an annual capacity of 20 lakhs tons of the two large coal mines at Kothagudem and Tandur, only 10 lakhs had been extracted on an average, during the period.[736] Medium, small and cottage industries, on the other hand, languished more due to dearth of finances, and shortage of raw materials rather than the supply of labour or the managerial element. External competition and effects of World Wars, trade cycles and price fluctuations, had only aggravated their decaying conditions. The decline of the handloom weaving industry, especially of cotton, led to considerable rural unemployment and the consequent diversion of these elements for employment in factories. Labour discontent that grew out of poor wages and rising prices led to spoilation of industrial relations and production. 80% of the male labourers received a wage of Rs. 18 per month or ten annas per day and female labourers and child workers received only Rs. 5 per month and two to four annas per day respectively.[737] These wages were hardly enough for two meal a day. Though Trade Union activity in the State was started very late in the forties, it was suppressed in the bud with an autocratic hand.[738] Regarding trade that considerably affected the fortunes of the people, nearly three-fifths of the total period was marked by more imports, less exports and hence, adverse trade balances.[739] Besides other causative factors such as crop failures, Great Wars and price variations, the principle factor that governed the trade relations was the fact that, whereas more than 90% of the exports consisted of raw produce, imports included, on the other hand, manufactured goods, almost to the same proportion.[740] Markets and trade had developed at places like Warangal, Khammam, Peddapalli, Jammikunta, Adilabad and Mancherial, where the railway line ran. But, of course, for the movement of goods and passengers between the rail-heads and the interior, bus and lorry transport and equally of carts, proved essential. Though coordination of road, rail and air service was put into operation very much as a pioneering measure, only limited parts of the *Suba* Districts had been covered, as for example, in Adilabad District with ten Taluqs and 2,138 villages, a paltry number of 18 buses operated on the road from the Depots of Asifabad and Nirmal, covering a route mileage of 334 miles in 1950-51.[741] The slackness of the Government regarding the development of road mileage was reflected in the fact that during the 15 year period of 1935-50, the rise in the length of road mileage of the Districts of Warangal, Karimnagar and Adilabad, was of the order of 28, 65 and 32 miles respectively.[742] Postal and Telephone Services were few and far between. One Post Office for more than 100 sq. miles of territory and 10,000 of population was hardly the minimum.[743] Telephone Services being extended to just 3 or 4 places of only one District in the *Suba* and even these places also not connected with other business or administrative centres by trunk line, spoke of its utter inadequacy and uselessness.[744] Hence, low production and under utilisation of the resources in industries, poor wages and labour discontent, adverse trade balances for most of the time, development of markets very much at rail towns only, extension of bus transport only to limited parts, Governmental slackness towards the extension of road mileage, meagre Postal Service and utter inadequacy and uselessness of the Telephone Service, these, in fact, characterised the economic scene of Warangal *Suba*, during the period, in the domains of industry, labour, trade, transport and communications. They certainly tended to keep the economy of the *Suba* on a low keel.

REFERENCES

1. See Table I in Chapter II.
2. Here, it refers to coalmines.
3. Census of India, 1911, Vol. XIX, Hyderabad State, Part II, *op. cit.*, p. 157. (The percentages are worked out by taking into consideration the figures of industrial and total population).
4. *Ibid.*
5. I. S., *op. cit.*, pp. 142, 155, 215, 287, 384 and 254; *Triennial Report on the Administration of the Department of Industries and Commerce for the years 1918, 1919 & 1920 A.D.* (Hereinafter referred to as *TRAIC*), (Hyderabad-Dn ; Government Central Press, 1922), pp. 19 & 22.
6. 1911 Census, Part II, *op. cit.*, p. 157. (The percentages are worked out by taking into consideration agricultural and industrial population).
7. 1941 Census, Part I, *op. cit.*, p. 173.
8. Because of greater prevalence of smaller holdings, less labour was employed in agriculture compared to industries.
9. *Report on Labour Census, 1935 (1344 Fasli)*. (H.E.H. the Nizam's Government : Hyderabad-Dn, 1937), p. 24.
10. *Ibid.*, p. 25. (Warangal's figure seem to have not included the labourers engaged by Singareni Collieries).
11. Named after Crown Prince, Azam Jah.
12. I.S., *op. cit.*, p. 168.
13. *Administrative Report of Commerce and Industries Department for the year 1346 Fasli (1937)*, (Hyderabad-1939), p. 11.
14. Hyderabad District Gazetteers, *op. cit.*, Warangal, p. 37 ; Adilabad, p. 39 (This information was not given in Karimnagar District Gazetteer, but the trend, as known from other sources, remained the same).
15. See the Section 'Price Variations and their effects' in Chapter VI.
16. See the Sections 'Forest Resources' & 'Natural & Mineral Resources' in Chapter II.
17 A. Gopalan, 'Some economic aspects of road planning and development with special reference to Hyderabad' in *Hyderabad Government Bulletin on Economic Affairs*, Vol. II, No. 8-9, August-September, 1949, p. 833. (The Percentages are worked by comparing the existing mileage with that required).
18. See the last para in the Section 'Administrative Conditions' in Chapter III.
19. Besides acting as managerial agents, the Industrial Trust Fund rendered financial assistance, either by purchasing shares or advancing loans, or both to the extent of Rs. 20 lakhs. B.G. (British Government Currency) to Singareni Collieries (*Administrative Report of*

Commerce and Industries Department, H.E.H. the Nizam's Government, for 1340 Fasli (*1931*), (1938), p. 1) ; Rs. 6. 55, 600 to Azam Jahi Mills (*Administrative Report for 1343 Fasli* (*6-10-1933 to 5-10-1934*), 1937, p. 68) ; Rs. 31 lakhs to Sirpur Paper Mills (I.S., *op. cit.*, p. 267) and Rs. 52,328, to Carpet Factory, Warangal (*Administrative Report of Commerce and Industries Department, H.E.H. the Nizam's Government for the year 1345 Fasli* (*1935-36*), 1937, p. 3.

20. I.S., *op. cit.*, pp. 153-54.
21. *Ibid.*, pp. 162-165 ; A.P.D.G., *op. cit.*, Warangal, (p. 94) ; Karimnagar, (p. 110) & Adilabad, (p. 77).
22. Otherwise known as '*Telugus*' or '*Telagas*' in Telangana region.
23. In Urdu it means 'Weaver'.
24. I.S., *op. cit.*, p. 158.
25. The division of Government and Local Fund Factories is not available from the source. But, the fact that some of them belonged to these categories just like Warangal Carpet Factory need be noted.
26. See Table XLII in this Chapter.
27. See the Section 'Transport Development' in this Chapter.
28. Excessive land monopolization and excise contracts in Warangal District helped for this in the case of landlords like Pingali Venkatrama Reddy of Waddepalli (See Section '*Tahud/Sarbasta, Watandari*' in Chapter IV) of Warangal Taluq. Besides being a big landlord, he owned one factory in Warangal Taluq and two in Madhira Taluq, engaged in ginning, pressing, decorticating, rice and oil manufacture, A member of the same family and also a rich landlord, viz., Pingali Kodandarama Reddy owned a ginning, decorticating, rice and oil factory at Warangal proper—1941 Census, *op. cit.*, pp. 776-77.
29. Whereas Warangal, the headquarters town had power facility right from 1935-36, no other place had this facility right until 1950—–A.P.D.G., *op. cit.*, Karimnagar, Warangal and Adilabad Districts.
30. See Table XXXVI in Chapter IV.
31. *Ibid.*
32. See Table XLII in this Chapter.
33. For example, Bhikaji Dadabhai & Co., an outside capitalistic firm, sought in 1935, permission for establishing 4 factories for rice, oil and cotton pressing in Warangal proper but not for a single one in Karimnagar. Better facilities, especially of transport, at Warangal might have induced him—*Administrative Report of Commerce and Industries Department of H.E.H. the Nizam's Government for the year 1344 Fasli* (*6-10-1934 to 6-10-1935*), (Hyderabad, 1936), p. 25.
34. Census, (Hyderabad State), *op. cit.*, 1931, (p. 153) ; 1941, (p. 176).

35. 1941 Census, *op. cit.*, pp. 772-73 to 778-79.
36. See f. n. No. 29 in this chapter.
37. See the Section 'Transport Development' in this chapter.
38. *Administrative Report of Commerce and Industries Department of H.E.H. the Nizam's Dominions for the year 1345 Fasli* (*7th October, 1935 to 5th October, 1936*), (Hyderabad, 1937), p. 12.
39. A.S.I.T., *op. cit.*, p. 16; *Cotton Manual, H.E.H. the Nizam's Government*, (Government Central Press : Hyderabad-Dn, 1942), p. 174.
40. See the first para in this Section and f. n. No. 19 of this chapter.
41. Azamjahi Mills, *Director's Report* for the period ending 5-10-1938.
42. A.S.I.T., *op. cit.*, p. 91.
43. M.F. Jussawalla, *Industrial Finance in the Former Hyderabad State*, (*1941-56*), Unpublished Ph. D. Thesis, (Osmania University, 1961), p. 200.
44. The expansion scheme was taken up in the middle of 1949 for which the Government gave a loan of Rs. 100 lakhs, but still it could not be completed—L.S. Habib Ahmed, *An Economic Survey of the Sirpur Paper Mills Ltd.*, M.A. dissertation, (Osmania University, 1960), p. 23.
45. It was the only Factory of its kind in India to take up Production of artificial silk by acetate process. It was registered in June, 1946 and it was expected that the production would commence in 1950. Loan advanced by Government with interest amounted to O.S. Rs. 388 lakhs, but another 150 lakhs could not be provided to complete the installation—Sharada Sitaraman, *Economic Survey of Sirsilk Ltd., Sirpur Kagaznagar*, M.A. Dissertation, (Osmania University, 1961), pp. 28-31.
46. REE, *op. cit.*, p. 545.
47. M F. Jussawalla, *op. cit.*, p. 199.
48. 1941 Census, *op. cit.*, pp. 768-69 to 780-81.
49. Those industries which required a capital of Rs. 1 to 5 thousand and employed only semi-specialised labour to a limited extent of below 20 persons—I.S., *op. cit.*, p. 4.
50. The Hyderabad Banking Enquiry Committee Report, *op. cit.*, p. 72.
51. *Ibid.*
52. I.S., *op. cit.*, p. 32 ; Banking Enquiry Committee Report *op. cit.*, p. 72.
53. *Suba*-wise figures are not available—I.S., *op. cit.*, p. 35.
54. Once again something with *Suba*-wise figures—*Ibid.*, p. 34.
55. See the first para in this Section and f. n. No. 19 in this chapter.
56. Banking Enquiry Committee Report, *op. cit.*, p. 72.
57. *Ibid.*, p. 23.
58. *Ibid.*, p. 22. Loan Statistics for other and later periods are not available.

59. *Ibid.*, pp. 26-27.
60. ASIT, *op. cit.*, p. 105.
61. See the Section 'Credit Agencies and extent of credit supplied' in Chapter V.
62. See the sub-section, 'iii. The money lenders and their contribution to agricultural credit' in Chapter V.
63. A landlord or businessman rich enough to carry on money-lending was popularly referred so.
64. Banking Enquiry Committee Report, *op. cit.*, p. 26.
65. *Ibid.*, pp. 26 & 72.
66. Weavers who were financially sound enough, most probably due to subsidiary occupation such as agriculture, not only to carry on their weaving operations independently, but also to lend money to other weavers or employ them on piece-wages just like *Sahukars.*
67. REE. *op. cit.*, p. 546.
68. I.S. *op. cit.*, pp. 158 & 160 ; REE. *op. cit.*, p. 549 ; ASIT. *op. cit.*, p. 59 ; *Triennial Report on the Administration of the Department of Industries & Commerce, H.E.H. the Nizam's Government for the years, 1918, 1919 & 1920* (Hyderabad Deccan, 1922), p. 9.
69. I.S. *op. cit.*, p. 158.
70. See the sub-section 'Rationing & Public Distribution System' in Chapter VI.
71. See the sections 'Forest Resources' & 'Natural & Mineral Resources' in Chapter II.
72. This was floated with Mir Laik Ali as Chairman, who later in 1947-48 became the Prime Minister of the State. Most of the Government construction work was carried out by this Company and the managing agencies of several industrial concerns controlled by the State (Including that of Sirpur Paper Mills) were also transferred to it—K. Munshi, *op. cit.*, p. 24.
73. Crown Representative Reports, File No. 23—1. B/40 in *Micro Film Reel No. 4 & Acc. No. 47* (The Year 1940 as the proposal year was not given as such, but was deduced from the File number).
74. See the Section 'Central system' & f. n. No. 39 in Chapter III.
75. ASIT, *op. cit.*, p. 96 ; *Meezan* (Telugu, edition), 31-3-1944, p. 4.
76. M.F. Jussawalla, *op. cit.*, pp. 22-23 ; See the second para in this Section and f. n. No. 28.
77. Statistical Abstract, 1922-31, *op. cit.*, p. 440 ; Statistical Year Book, 1351-54 Fasli (1942-45), *op. cit.*, pp. 402-3 (Per Capita figures were calculated by dividing the deposits made in the years by the total population in the respective years as given in the 1941 Census Report, Part I., *op. cit.*, p. 41).
78. *Ibid* (The amount of saving per depositor has been arrived at by dividing the amounts deposited in the respective years by the total depositors in those years).
79. Banking Enquiry Committee Report, *op. cit.*, p. 84.

80. *Statistical Year Book*, *1349 Fasli* (*1940*), p. 270 ; & 1351-54 Fasli (1942-45), *op. cit.*, pp. 402-03.
81. Banking Enquiry Committee Report, *op. cit.*, p. 86.
82. *Ibid.*
83. See the first para in this Section & f. n. No. 19 in this Chapter.
84. See the sub-section 'iii. Finance' & its items in this Section.
85. ASIT, *op. cit.*, p. 20.
86. See Chart No. IX of this Section.
87. The quinquennial output figures and the increase levels, are calculated on the basis of the 'Total production' figures given in Table XLIII of this Section.
88. See Table XLIII attached to this Section. For the background history of the individual coal mines, see the sub-section 'Coal' in Chapter II.
89. See Table XLIII included in this Section.
90. See the last two paras in Section 'Political Condition' in Chapter III.
91. *Report on the Administration of Hyderabad State, September 1948 to March, 1950*, (Government Press, Hyderabad) (n. d), pp. 203 & 204.
92. The figures of value realised are taken from : I.S., *op. cit.*, p. 310.
93. See the 'Total Production' figures in Table XLIII attached to this Section.
94. Statistical Year Book, 1941-42 to 1944-45, *op. cit.*, p. 1125.
95. I.S. *op. cit.*, p. 310. (Also see 'The Production figures' in Table XLIII included in this Section).
96. *Trade Statistics, H.E.H. the Nizam's Government for 1352 Fasli* (*1942-43*), (Government Central Press : Hyderabad-Dn 1944), p. 10.
97. M.F. Jussawalla, *op. cit.*, p. 333.
98. *Ibid.*, p. 334.
99. *Golkonda Patrika* (Daily), 10-5-1949 & 12-5-1949.
100. The work referred to the quicker process that was adopted to bring underground coal to surface—A.I.S.P.C., *File* No. 68, Part I/1946-47 (Memorandum of the Singareni Collieries Workers' Union, Kothagudem, p. 3).
101. Christoph Von Furer Haimendorf, *op. cit.*, p. 39 ; W.S. *File* No. 31 of 1352 Fasli (1943) & R. No. 5 of 1357 Fasli (1948).
102. 'Confidential Report of the *Subedar*, Warangal to the Director-General & Secretary to Government, Revenue Department, for the second Fortnight of Sherewar, 1352 Fasli (July, 1943)' in W.S. *File* No. 31 of 1352 Fasli (1943) & R. No. 5 of 1357 Fasli (1948).
103. Christoph Von Furer Haimendorf, *op. cit.*, p. 39.
104. *Meezan*, 25-11-1944 ; W.S. *File* No. 31 of 1352 Fasli (1943) & R.No. 5 of 1357 Fasli (1948).

105. From U.P. State, a British Indian territory. Labour also was brought from Madras Presidency of British India—*Meezan*, 25-11-1944.
106. 'Confidential Report of the *First Taluqdar*, Warangal to *Subedar* Warangal for, the Second Fortnight of Mehr, 1354 Fasli (November 1945)' in W.S. *File* No. 30 of 1354 Fasli (1945) & R.No. 6 of 1357 Fasli (1948).
107. W.S. *File* No. 31 of 1352 Fasli (1943)& R.No. 5 of 1357 Fasli (1948) Memorandum of the Singareni Collieries Workers' Union, Kothagudem, in A.I.S.P.C. *File* No. 68, Part I, 1946-47.
108. I.S., *op. cit.*, p. 313.
109. E.L.O.H., *op. cit.*, p. 96.
110. A Claude Campbell, *Glimpses of the Nizam's Dominions*, (Bombay & London, 1898), p. 499.
111. ASIT., *op. cit.*, p. 39.
112. A. Claude Campbell, *op. cit.*, p. 141 ; ASIT, *op. cit.*, p. 39 ; I.S. *op. cit.*, p. 313.
113. For an account of the Development of steel industry in the *Suba* area before the present century, see the Section 'Iron-Ore' in Chapter II.
114. It consisted of iron-smelting by using wood char-coal instead of the modern coke ovens.
115. I.S., *op. cit.*, p. 324.
116. Nawab Ahsan Yar Jung Bahadur, *Manufacture of Steel in H.E.H. the Nizam's Dominions*, (Hyderabad, 1940), p. 10 ; *Conservation of Coal & Manufacturing of Gasoline*, (Hyderabad, 1940), pp. 3 & 4.
117. For the extent of marble and mica minerals in the area, their prospecting and exploitation, see the Section 'Marble' and 'Mica' in Chapter II.
118. ELOH, *op. cit.*, p. 69 ; ASIT, *op. cit.*, p. 40.
119. License granted for exploitation of a mine during a particular period.
120. I.S. *op. cit.*, pp. 325 & 327 ; ASIT, *op. cit.*, p. 40.
121. I.S., *op. cit.*, pp. 325 & 327.
122. See the sub-section 'ii. Management' in this chapter.
123. Since production figures for the period as a whole are not available, the value of yearly cloth and yarn sales and stock on hand was represented in the chart.
124. Venugopal Rao, S : *Economic Survey of the Azam Jahi Mills, Ltd., Warangal*, M.A., Dissertation, (Osmania University, 1961), p. 35.
125. *Reports of the Directors, Azam Jahi Mills, for the period ending 6th October, 1939 and 1940*.
126. The increases were calculated on the basis of the data given in Table XLIV attached to this Section.
127. *Report of the Directors, Azam Jahi Mills, for the period ending 6th October, 1941*.
128. *Ibid.*, for the period ending 6th October, 1944.
129. *Ibid.*, for the period ending 6th October, 1945.
130. *Ibid.*, for the period ending 6th October, 1946.
131. *Ibid.*, for the period ending 6th October, 1947.

132. The percentages are calculated roughly on the basis of the figures given in Table XLIV attached to this Section.
133. *Hyderabad Government Bulletin on Economic Affairs*, Vol. II, No. 3, March, 1949, p. 285.
134. *Report of Directors, Azam Jahi Mills, for the period ending 6th October, 1949.*
135. *Ibid.*, for the period ending 6th October, 1950.
136. *Administrative Report of Commerce and Industries Department, H.E.H. the Nizam's Government for the years 1353 and 1354 Fasli (1943-44 & 1944-45)*, (Hyderabad, 1946), p. 41 ; *for the year 1355 Fasli (1945-46)*, (Hyderabad, 1947), p. 40.
137. Also see Table XLIV included in this Section.
138. Administrative Report of Commerce and Industries Department, H.E.H. the Nizam's Government for the years 1353 and 1354 Fasli (1943-44 & 1944-45), *op. cit.*, pp. 41
139. Venugopal Rao, S. *op. cit.*, p. 79.
140. *Ibid.*, pp. 37 & 79. (From 1960 onwards, the Mill authorities had been importing long staple cotton from U.S.A. inorder to produce fine cloth p. 23).
141. Located in Western India to the North-West of Nizam's Dominations.
142. Venugopal Rao, S. *op. cit.* p. 79.
143. *Ibid.*, p. 29.
144. *Trade Statistics, H.E.H. the Nizam's Government 1346 Fasli (1936-37)*, (Hyderabad, 1938), p. 143 ; *1351 Fasli (1941-42)*, (Hyderabad, 1944), p. 15 ; *1356 Fasli (1946-47)*, (Hyderabad, 1949), p. 117.
145. *Cotton Manual 1940* (H.E.H. the Nizam's Government, Hyderabad, 1942), pp. 130-131.
146. Venugopal Rao, S. *op. cit.*, pp. 29-30.
147. *Meezan*, 10-11-1944 & 29-12-1946.
148. I.S., *op. cit.*, p. 286.
149. *A.R. for 1351 Fasli (6-10-1941 to 5-10-1942)*, (H.E.H. the Nizam's Government : Hyderabad-Dn, 1945), p. 95.
150. *Golkonda Patrika* (Bi-weekly), 23-2-1939.
151. Agriculture Department, H.E.H. the Nizam's Government, S. No. 18, *File* No. 55 of 1354 Fasli (1945), p. 12.
152. 1942-43 ; 4,626 tons ; 1943-44 ; 5,083 tons ; (*Ibid.*) ; 1944-45 : 4,894 tons ; 1945-46 : 5,102 tons (A.R. of Commerce and Industries Department H.E.H the Nizam's Government, for 1353 & 1354 Fasli (1944 & 45) & 1355 Fasli (1946) *op. cit.*, p. 42) ; 1946-47 : 4,367 tons & 1947-48 : 3,626 tons (L.S. Habib Ahmed : *An Economic Survey of Sirpur Paper Mills Ltd.*, M.A. (Economics) dissertation, (Osmania University, 1960), p. 53.
153. See the above f.n.
154. See Table XLV and Chart No. X that are included in this Section.

155. L.S. Habib Ahmed, *op. cit.*, p. 49.
156. The increases and decreases are arrived at. See f.n. No. 152.
157. L.S. Habib Ahmed, *op. cit.*, p. 53.
158. *Ibid.*
159. See Table XLV attached to this Section.
160. L.S. Habib Ahmed, *op. cit.*, p. 53.
161. L.S. Habib Ahmed, *op. cit.*, pp. 53-54.
162. *Ibid.*, p. 54.
163. See the Section 'Industrial Organisation, Finance and Management' (Para I) and f.n. No. 19 in this Chapter.
164. See the Section 'Foreign and Public Investment' in this Chapter.
165. L.S. Habib Ahmed, *op. cit.*, p. 36.
166. *Ibid.*, p. 20.
167. *Hyderabad Government Bulletin on Economic Affairs*, Vol. III, Nos. 1-3. January-March, 1950, p. 211.
168. L.S. Habib Ahmed, *op. cit.*, p. 20.
169. I.S., *op. cit.*, p. 269.
170. *Ibid.*
171. See the earlier two paras in this sub-section.
172. *Trade Statistics, H.E.H. the Nizam's Government for 1356 Fasli (1946-47)*, pp. 18 & 63.
173. A.R. for 1351 Fasli (6-10-1941 to 5-10-1942), *op. cit.*, p. 95.
174. *Golkonda Patrika* (Bi-weekly), 23-2-1939.
175. *Meezan* (English edition), 15-8-1948.
176. *Golkonda Patrika* (Bi-weekly), 23-2-1939.
177. See the earlier two paras in this sub-section.
178. *Golkonda Patrika* (Bi-weekly), 23-2-1939.
179. I.S., *op. cit.*, p. 459.
180. Office of the *First Taluqdar*, Warangal, *File* No. 2 of 1327 Fasli (1928) & R. No. 3406 of 1339 Fasli (1930) ; *Report on the working of the Commerce and Industries Department of H.E.H. the Nizam's Government, for the year 1337 Fasli (1927-28)*, (n.p), (n.d.) p. 3.
181. It is calculated.
182. See Table XLVI contained in this sub-section.
182. (a) *Meezan*, 5-9-1946.
183. Office of the First *Taluqdar*, Warangal, *File* No. 2 of 1327 Fasli (1918) & R. No. 3406 of 1339 Fasli (1930).
184. Finance Department, Resource Branch, H.E.H. the Nizam's Government, S. No. 66 *File* No. 58 of 1355 Fasli (1945-46), pp. 21-23.
185. *Ibid.*, p. 21.
186. *Golkonda Patrika* (Bi-weekly), 5-4-1934.
187. Finance Department, Resource Branch H.E.H. the Nizam's Government, S. No. 66, *File* No. 58 of 1355 Fasli (1945-46), pp. 10 & 21-24.
188. *Ibid.*, p. 21.
189. *Ibid.*, p. 10.
190. See Table XLVI included in this sub-section.

191. *Administrative Report of Commerce and Industries Department, H.E.H. the Nizam's Government for the years 1344 Fasli* (*1934-35*), p. 13& *1346 Fasli 1936-37*), p. 10.
192. *Meezan*, 5-9-1946.
193. *Golkonda Patrika* (Daily), 14-3-1950.
194. See the last two paras in Section 'Political Conditions' of Chapter III.
195. *Golkonda Patrika* (Daily), 14-3-1950.
196. For the renown of carpets during Kakatiya days and later, see the second and third paras in Chapter I ; Settlement Report of Warangal Taluka, *op. cit.*, p. 17.
197. Settlement Report of Warangal Taluka, *op. cit.* p. 17.
198. I.S., *op. cit.*, pp. 220 & 222.
199. *Ibid.*, p. 222.
200. Gadgil, The Industrial Evolution of India, *op. cit.*, pp. 36-42 ; I.S., *op. cit.*, pp. 14-15.
201. I.S., *op. cit.*, p. 220.
202. *Administrative Report of the Commerce and Industries Department, H.E.H., the Nizam's Government, for 1340 Fasli* (*1930-31*), p. 28.
203. *Ibid.*
204. *Administrative Report of the Commerce and Industries Department, H.E.H. the Nizam's Government for* (*1342 Fasli 1932-33*), p. 28.
205. See Table XLVII attached to this section ; I.S. *op. cit.*, p. 221.
206. I.S. *op. cit.*, p. 221.
207. *Ibid.*
208. See Chart No. XI included in this Section. The data for 1942-43 is not available and hence, could not be represented in the Chart.
209. See Table XLVII included in this Section.
210. *Administrative Report, H.E.H. the Nizam's Dominions for 1349 Fasli* (*1939-40*), p. 104.
211. See Table XLVII included in this Chapter.
212. *Administrative Report of the Commerce and Industries Department of H.E.H. the Nizam's Government for 1341 Fasli* (*1931-32*), p. 13 ; *Administrative Report of H.E.H. the Nizam's Dominions for 1350 Fasli* (*1940-41*), p 110.
213. See the Table XLVII in this Section.
214. *Administrative Report of the Commerce and Industries Department of H.E.H. the Nizam's Government for the year 1342 Fasli* (*1932-33*), p. 28.
215. *Administrative Report of H.E.H. the Nizam's Dominions for 1345 Fasli* (*1935-36*), p. 87.
216. *Administrative Report of H.E.H. the Nizam's Dominions for 1348 Fasli* (*1938-39*), p. 112.
217. Administrative Report for 1345 Fasli (1935-36), *op. cit.*, p. 87.
218. See Table XLVII in this Section ; *Administrative Report of H.E.H. the Nizam's Dominions for 1346 Fasli* (*1936-37*), p. 97.

219. *Administrative Report of H.E.H. the Nizam's Dominions for 1350 Fasli (1940-41)*, p. 110.
220. See Table XLVII in this Section.
221. REE, *op. cit.*, p. 547.
222. *Ibid.*, See Chart No. XI in this Section.
223. *Administrative Report of Commerce and Industries Department of H.E.H. the Nizam's Dominions for the year 1345 Fasli (1935-36)*, p. 37.
224. REE, *op. cit.*, p. 545.
224(a). REE, *op. cit.*, p. 546.
225. ASIT, *op. cit.*, p. 70 ; *Administrative Report of the Commerce and Industries Department of H.E.H. the Nizam's Dominions for the year 1342 Fasli (1932-33)*, p. 30 ; See the sub-section 'iii. Finance' in this Chapter.
226. Only 20 families as against former 350, were engaged in this industry REE, *op. cit.*, 545.
227. ASIT, *op. cit.*, p. 36.
228. *Ibid.*
229. *Administrative Report of the Commerce and Industries Department, H.E.H. the Nizam's Government for the year 1355 Fasli (1945-46)*, (Hyderabad-Dn, 1947), p. 41.
230. See the f.n. in Table XLIII included in this Section ; Also see the sub-section 'Coal' in Chapter II.
231. The same place where Sirpur Paper Mills are located—see sub-section iii. in this Section.
232. See the sub-section 'ii. Management' in this Chapter and f.n. No. 45.
233. Sharada Sitaraman ; *Economic Survey of Sirsilk Ltd.*, M.A. (Econ) dissertation, (Osmania University, 1961), pp. 28 & 32.
234. The Managing Agency was transferred to them from the Industrial Trust Fund. (This took from the Hyderabad Construction Company in 1949) in 1953 *Ibid.*, pp. 31-32.
235. *The Deccan Chronicle*, 14-12-1949.
236. Sharada Sitaraman, *op. cit.*, p. 29.
237. For the number, character and organisation of these Mills, see the 2nd and 3rd paras in Section 'A.Industrial Organisation, Management and Finance' of this Chapter.
238. ELOH, *op cit.*, p. 78.
239. I.S., *op. cit.*, p. 590.
240. *Ibid.*, p. 591.
241. *Ibid.*, p. 590.
241(a). ELOH, *op. cit.*, p. 78.
242. See the Section 'Crop Conditions' in Chapter V.
243. See the paras 2 & 3 in the Section 'A. Industrial Organisation, Finance and Management' of this Chapter.
244. H.E.H. the Nizam's Government : *Agricultural, Industrial & Trade Statistics for the year 1343 Fasli (1933-34)*, (Hyderabad-Dn, 1936), pp. 168-169.

245. *Ibid.*, pp. 159-160 & 168-169.
246. See the 2nd para in the Section 'A. Industrial Organisation, Finance and Management' of this Chapter and f.n. No. 29.
247. See the same para as the above and f.n. No. 33 ; This Company had established such mills at Warangal and Khammam in Warangal District and even one at Nizamabad in Medak *Suba*—1941 Census Report, Part I, *op. cit.*, pp. 303, 326 & 343.
248. 1931 Census Report, Part I—Report, *op. cit.*, p. 154.
249. See the sub-section 'ii. Procurement Policy and its wide-ranging effects' in Chapter VI.
250. See the crop outturn Tables in Chapter VI.
251. I.S., *op. cit.*, pp. 521, 529. 534, 537 & 541.
252. *Ibid.*
253. *Ibid.*, pp. 507 & 513.
254. *Annual Report on the Administration of the Department of Industries and Commerce, H.E.H. the Nizam's Government for the year 1921*, (Hyderabad-Dn, 1923), p. 9.
255. I.S., *op. cit.*, p. 508.
256. *Ibid.*, p. 530.
257. *Ibid.*, p. 510—*ghanis* refer to country-made mills of pestle and mortar.
258. *Ibid.*, pp. 510 & 529 ; ELOH, *op. cit.*, p. 73.
259. See Table XXXVI in Chapter VI.
260. I.S., *op. cit.*, p. 542
261. Output small compared to power consumed. But, it was cheap in initial cost—*Ibid.*, p. 510.
262. *Ibid.*, p. 542.
263. *Ibid.*, p. 524.
264. *Ibid.*, pp. 523-524.
265. *Ibid.*, p. 509. The number of different types are clubbed together to arrive at the total figure of units in respect of each District.
266. See Table XLI included in the first Section of this Chapter.
267. I.S., *op. cit.*, p. 525.
268. In Central Provinces where Warangal oil was very popular—*Annual Report on the working of the Commerce and Industries Department, H.E.H. the Nizam's Government for the year 1346 Fasli (1937)*, (Hyderabad-Dn, 1939), p. 9.
269. In Madras Presidency.
270. *Supply Statistics, H.E.H. the Nizam's Government for 1354 Fasli (1945)*, (Hyderabad-Dn, 1945), p. 64.
271. I.S., *op. cit.*, p. 507.
272. *Ibid.*, pp. 518-519.
273. Other than Bombay, all other places were located in Madras Presidency.
274. I.S., *op. cit.* p. 526.
275. See the Section 'Manures and their application' in Chapter V.

276. For this organisation, see paras 2 & 3 in Section 'Industrial Organisation, Finance and Management' in this Chapter.
277. I.S., *op. cit.*, p. 137.
278. With a hand-ginning *charkha*, a women could separate lint from cotton seed at the rate of 1½ *seers* of cotton lint per day—*Ibid.*, p. 138.
279. *Ibid.*, p. 163.
280. *Ibid.*, p. 138.
281. Gadgil, the Industrial Evolution of the India, *op. cit.*, p. 54.
282. I.S., *op. cit.*, p. 163.
283. *Ibid.*, p. 138.
284. 1941 Census Report, Part I—Report, *op. cit.*, pp. 772-73 to 780-81.
285. See Table XXXVI in Chapter VI.
286. See para II in Section 'Industrial Organisation, Finance and Management' and f.n. No. 29 in this Chapter.
287. Out of these two British Indian capitalist firms. The Empress Mills & Co., established two Ginning and Pressing Factories at Limha in Nirmal Taluq of Adilabad District and Bhicaji Dadabhai & Co., established Ginning, Decorticating and Rice Factory at Warangal town of the same Taluq and District, Ginning, Decorticating, Rice and Oil Factory at Khammam, Taluq headquarters in Warangal District and Ginning, Pressing and Oil Factory at Peddapalli, Taluq headquarters in Karimnagar District—1941 Census Report, Part I. *op. cit.*, pp. 772-73 to 778-79.
288. *Administrative Report of Commerce and Industries Department of H.E.H. the Nizam's Government for the year 1345 Fasli (1935-36)*, (Hyderabad-Dn, 1937), p. 12.
289. See the Section 'Animal husbandry as an adjunct of agriculture' (last but one para) in Chapter V.
290. Hyderabad District Gazetteers, Warangal, Part II, Tables, *op. cit.*, p. 37 ; The export value of bones & bone-meal from Warangal kept on increasing from Rs. 16,850 in 1331 Fasli (1922) to Rs. 74,139 in 1344 Fasli (1935), touching the maximum of Rs. 1,04,340 in 1336 Fasli (1927). It was the highest in the State and from 1332 Fasli (1923) came to from more than 60 to 80% of the total State export—H.E.H. the Nizam's Government, *Labour Census*, 1935, p. 70.
291. I.S., *op. cit.*, p. 241.
292. *Ibid.*, p. 244.
293. *Ibid.*, 1941 Census Report, Part-I, *op. cit.*, pp. 770-771.
294. I.S., *op. cit.*, p. 244.
295. 1941 Census Report, Part-I, pp. 770-771.
296. I.S., *op. cit.*, p. 244.
297. *Ibid.*
298. *Ibid.*, p. 244.
299. *Administrative Report of the Commerce and Industries Department, H.E.H. the Nizam's Government for the year 1355 Fasli (1946)*, (Hyderabad-Dn, 1947), p. 40.

300. I.S., *op. cit.*, p. 243.
301. Office of the First *Taluqdar*, Warangal, *File* No. 21 of 1353 Fasli (1944) & R. No. 738 of 1355 Fasli (1946).
302. The monetary or investment scale prescribed in the State was : medium-scale : Rs. 5 to 50,000, small-scale : Rs. 1 to 5,000, cottage-scale : Rs. 500 to 1,000 and home-industries : Rs. 500. I.S., *op. cit.*, p. 4.
303. R.V. Rao, *op. cit.*, pp. 249-251.
304. Memoranda submitted to the Taxation Enquiry Committee, 1953, *op. cit.*, p. 189.
305. *Administration Report of the Commerce and Industries Department for the years 1353 and 1354 Fasli* (*1944 & 1945*), (Government Central Press : Hyderabad-Dn, 1946), p. 2.
306. *Administration Report of the Commerce and Industries Department, H.E.H. the Nizam's Government for the year 1355 Fasli* (*1945-46*), (Hyderabad-Dn, 1947). p. i.
307. See the sub-section 'C. Indigenous Bankers & *Sahukars*' covered under 'Finance' in this chapter.
308. See the sub-section '(d) Bone Mills' in this Chapter.
309. *Triennial Report on the Administration of the Department of Industry and Commerce, H.E.H. the Nizam's Government for the years 1918, 1919 and 1920*, (Hyderabad-Dn, 1922), p. 5.
310. I.S., *op. cit.*, p. 228.
311. Hyderabad District Gazetteers, Warangal, Part-II, Tables Volume, *op. cit.*, p. 36.
312. *Ibid.*
313. W.S. *File* No. 30 of 1354 Fasli (1945) & R. No. of 6 of 1357 Fasli (1948).
314. *Ibid.*
315. I.S., *op. cit.*, p. 229.
316. *Ibid.*, pp. 229 & 233.
317. REE, *op. cit.*, p. 538 ; ASIT, *op. cit.*, p. 62.
318. I.S., *op. cit.*, pp. 229 & 230 ; *The Deccan Chronicle*, 10-7-1947.
319. I.S. *op. cit.*, p. 233
320. W.S. *File* No. 30 of 1354 Fasli (1945) & R. No. 68 of 1357 Fasli (1948).
321. REE, *op. cit.*, p. 538 ; ASIT, *op. cit.*, p. 62.
322. For an account of their utility and places of location, see the Sections dealing with them in Chapter II.
323. ASIT, *op. cit.*, p. 40.
324. For example, Messrs Gouthami Mining Works of Kovvur (Madras Presidency) who worked graphite for Mr. R.S. Chinoy of Hyderabad, the assignee of the Paloncha Graphite lease, paid a Royalty amounting to B.G. Rs. 479-10-4 on 142 tons 53 lbs. of refined graphite sold by the Company during 1941 & 42—*Administrative Report for 1350 Fasli* (*1940-41*), (Hyderabad-Dn, 1943), p. 102.

325. *Administrative Reports for 1347 Fasli* (*1937-38*), p. 108 ; *1348 Fasli* (*1938*), p. 118 ; & *1351 Fasli* (*1941-42*), p. 102.
326. *Administrative Reports for 1349 Fasli* (*1939-40*), (Hyderabad-Dn, 1942), p. 109 ; *1350 Fasli* (*1940-41*), (Hyderabad-Dn, 1943), p. 115.
327. See the concerned Section in Chapter II.
328. *Report on the Administration of Hyderabad State, September, 1948 to March, 1950*, p. 205.
329. I.S. *op. cit.*, p. 336.
330. See the relevant Section in Chapter II.
331. I.S., *op. cit.*, pp. 336 & 343.
332. See the Section 'Limestone' in Chapter II.
333. I.S., *op. cit.*, p. 344.
334. *Ibid.*, p. 344-45.
335. *Ibid.*, p. 346.
336. *Ibid.*, pp. 332-34 ; See the relevant Section in Chapter II.
337. *Ibid.*, p. 333.
338. *Ibid.*, p. 334.
339. *Ibid.*, pp. 337, 338, 429 & 430. See the concerned Sections in Chapter II.
340. *Report on the Administration of Hyderabad State, September, 1948 to March 1950*, p. 205.
341. *Ibid.*
342. See the para down below on this point.
343. See the sub-section 'C. Cotton ginning and Pressing Factories' in this Chapter.
344. I.S., *op. cit.*, p. 142
345. *Ibid.*
346. *Ibid.*
347. W.S. *File* No. 30 of 1352 Fasli (1943) & R. No. 4 of 1357 Fasli (1948).
348. Hyderabad District Gazetteers, Part-II—Tables., *op. cit.*, Warangal, (p. 37) & Adilabad, (p. 39).
349. See the sub-section 'Azam Jahi Mills' in this Chapter.
350. A.S. I.T. p. 44.
351. REE, *op. cit.*, p. 494.
352. All these places were there in British India-*Ibid.*,
353. I.S., *op. cit.*, p. 211 ; REE, *op. cit.*, p. 537.
354. *Administrative Report of Commerce and Industries Department, H.E.H. the Nizam's Government for 1355 Fasli* (*1945-46*), (Hyderabad-Dn, 1947), p. 8.
355 Triennial Report on the Administration of the Department of Industries and Commerce for the years 1918, 1919 and 1920, *op. cit.*, p. 19.
356. This percentage was for the year 1941. It was calculated by taking the totals of the three types of looms in the *Suba*- I.S., *op. cit.*, p. 155.

357. *Ibid.*, pp. 155, 192 & 215.
358. See the relevant sub-sections in this Chapter.
359. *All* the percentages referred to in the para are calculated I.S., *op. cit.*, pp. 155, 192 & 215.
360. See the Section 'Crop Conditions' in Chapter V—Also see REE, *op. cit.*, p. 558.
361. The wide distribution of the weaving establishments in the District enable the weavers to improve their fortunes during the periods of rising prices and easy or cheap supply of yarn that were experienced before 1941.
362. See the Section 'Crop Conditions' in Chapter V and also those on 'Marketing, Trade' & 'Transport' in this Chapter.
363. ASIT, *op. cit.*, p. 48.
364. REE, *op. cit.*, p. 494. (All the percentages referred to in the para are calculated).
365. Labour Census, 1935, H.E.H. the Nizam's Dominions, quoted in *Golkonda Patrika* (Bi-weekly), 11-8-1938 ; REE, *op. cit.*, p. 556.
366. See the last para in sub-section 'Finance' in this Chapter ; Also refer I.S., *op. cit.*, p. 160.
367. REE, *op. cit.*, p. 558 ; RARC, *op. cit.*, p. 193.
368. REE, *op. cit.*, p. 496 ; *Report on the working of the Commerce and Industries Department, H E.H. the Nizam's Government, for the year 1339 Fasli (1929-30)*, (Hyderabad-Dn, 1931), p. 1.
369. REE, *op. cit.*, pp. 494 & 558 ; I.S , *op. cit.*, p. 216.
370. See the sub-sections 'System of Rationing and Black-Marketeering' in Chapter VI and 'Handloom-Spinning, Weaving, Printing & Dyeing' (Para II) in this Chapter ; Refer also REE, *op. cit.*, pp. 494 & 556.
371. *The Hyderabad Government Bulletin on Economic Affaris*, Vol. III, Nos. 1-3, January-March, 1950, p. 100 ; R.V. Rao, *op. cit.*, p. 363.
372. The Industrial Evolution of India, *op. cit.*, pp. 40-41 ; *Golkonda Patrika* (Bi-weekly), 11-8-1938.
373. M.F. Jussawalla, *op. cit.*, pp. 21-22.
374. REE, *op. cit.*, pp. 546 & 559.
375. *Pitambars* referred to solid bordered silk saris ; *cholkhans* referred to bodice cloth (for ladies' upper garment); *taulia rumals* stood for kerchiefs or towels and *dhotis* for men's upper wear—I.S., *op. cit.*, p. 193.
376. *Administration Report of Commerce and Industries Department, H.E.H. the Nizam's Government, for the years 1353 and 1354 Fasli (1943-44 & 1944-45)*, (Hyderabad-Dn, 1946), p. 5. Also see I para of Section 'C. Medium, small and cottage industries and their developmental aspects' in this Chapter.
377. *Meezan*, 28-6-1944 (Telugu edition).
378. *Ibid.*
379. M.F. Jussawalla, *op. cit.*, pp. 21-22.

380. *Meezan*, 3-6-1944—For definition of *Jagir* see f.n. No. 8 in Chapter I and for *Khalsa*, see para II of Chapter IV.
381. 1931 Census Report, Part I, *op. cit.*, p. 190.
382. I.S., *op. cit.*, pp. 147 & 149.
383. *Ibid.*, p. 148 (The percentages are calculated).
384. *Meezan*, 28-6-1944 (Telugu edition).
385. 1931 Census Report, Part I, *op. cit.*, p. 190.
386. *Ibid.*
387. I.S., *op. cit.*, pp. 640-41.
388. *Ibid.*, p. 641, See the above para for information on dyeing.
389. A.P. D.G., *op. cit.*, Warangal, (p. 96) & Karimnagar, (p. 112) ; I.S., *op. cit.*, p. 640.
390. Between 1931-41, the number of dyeing and printing establishments arrived at by population censuses, rose by 400% and 285% in the case of Warangal and Adilabad Districts, but a decline of 30.76% in respect of Karimnagar District was witnessed. It being an allied industry, the reasons for rise and fall in the number of units as noted in the case of weaving and dyeing applied here also—See the above para on 'dyeing' and sub-section on 'weaving' in this Chapter; I.S., *op. cit.*, p. 642.
391. 1931 Census Report, Part I, *op. cit.*, pp. 190-91,
392. A.P. D.G., Warangal, *op. cit.*, p. 96.
393. *Sarf-i-khas* or crown lands surrounding the capital of the State, were formed into this District which was free from *Diwani* jurisdiction.
394. I.S., *op. cit.*, p. 261.
395. A.P. D.G., *op. cit.*, Karimnagar, p. 105 ; Adilabad, p. 72.
396. I.S., *op. cit.*, pp. 636. (Sewing and tailoring) ; 287. (carpentry workshops); 384. (Pottery); 293. (Bomboo and basket works) ; and 261. (dairying).
397. See the Sections 'Agricultural Production' & 'Prices' in Chapter VI.
398. See the source mentioned in f.n. No. 396 in this Chapter.
399. The percentages are calculated—I.S., *op. cit.*, p. 644.
400. ASIT, *op. cit.*, p 59.
401. *Administrative Report of H.E.H. the Nizam's Dominions for 1345 Fasli (1935-36)*, (Hyderabad Dn, 1938), p. 86.
402. I.S., *op. cit.*, p. 644.
403. *Ibid.*, p. 254. (The percentages are worked out).
404. *Hyderabad Government Bulletin on Economic Affairs*, Vol. II, No. 2, February, 1949, p. 172.
405. The other two *Suba* Districts of Warangal and Adilabad had only 25 and 21 farms respectively and Telangana and the State had 1,571 and 1,814 units respectively—I.S., *op. cit.*, p. 254.
406. Used for wrapping of *beedis* (country cigars).
407. For making of toys.
408. Raw material for pottery, brick and tiles manufacture.
409. See the relevant Sections in the earlier pages of this Chapter.

410. Warangal District with 117 bamboo works in 1941 as against 302 in Telangana and 502 in the State occupied first place, and Karimnagar District with 462 basket works as against 2,774 in Telangana and 3,912 in the State , occupied 2nd place, first being Nalgonda District with 562 units. Karimnagar and Adilabad Districts had 30 and 17 bamboo works and Warangal and Adilabad Districts had 325 and 244 basket works—I.S., *op. cit.*, p. 293.
411. *Ibid.*, p. 292. In telangana Districts, the communities of basket makers are popularly known as *Erukalas* and *Yenadis*.
412. *Livestock Census, 1935*, H.E.H. the Nizam's Dominions, p. 24.
413. I.S., *op. cit.*, p. 261.
414. Livestock Census, 1935, *op. cit.*, p. 62.
415. See the earlier observations in this sub-section.
416. ELOH, *op. cit.*, p. 87.
417. H.E.H. the Nizam's Government, *Report on Labour Census, 1935* (*1344 Fasli*), (Hyderabad-Dn, 1937, Percentages are calculated), pp. 24-25.
418. *Ibid.*, p. 24.
419. For information on land holdings, irrigation and character of agriculture, see the relevant Sections in Chapter V.
420. Report on Labour Census, 1935, *op. cit.*, p. 24.
421. S. Kesava Iyengar, *Economic Investigations in the Hyderabad State, 1929-30, Vol. I* (Hyderabad-Dn, 1931), p. 22.
422. REE, *op. cit.*, pp. 55-56.
423. Agricultural labourers of bonded type. For more information, see the relevant Section that followed in this Chapter.
424. Attached in this Section.
425. See Table XLIX attached in this Section and also refer to Report on Labour Census, 1935, *op. cit.*, p. 30.
426. A.I. Qureshi, *op. cit.*, p. 68.
427. Telugu name for annual farm labourer used in the region.
428. Report on Labour Census, 1935, *op. cit.*, p. 24. (Percentages are calculated).
429. *Ibid.*
430. For 'Landlord Composition' and 'Irrigational Facilities', see the relevant Sections in Chapter V.
431. Report on Labour Census, 1935, *op. cit.*, p. 48.
432. For food grain prices decline during the Depression, see the Section on 'Prices' in Chapter VI.
433. Report on Labour Census, 1935. *op. cit.*, p. 30.
434. S.M. Bharucha, *op. cit.*, pp. 50 & 51.
435. *Ibid.*
436. Report on Labour Census, 1935, *op. cit.*, p. 29.
437. See Table XLIX included in this Section.
438. Report on Labour Census, 1935, *op. cit.*, p. 29.
439. See Table XLII included in the 'Industries' Section of this Chapter

and Table XLIX attached in this Section. Percentages are calculated.

440. See Table XLIX included in this Section.
441. *Ibid.*
442. See the relevant Sections in Chapter VI.
443. *Ibid.*
444. See Table XLIX incorporated in this Section.
445. *The Deccan Chronicle*, 9-2-1950.
446. *The Hyderabad Government Bulletin on Economic Affairs*, *Vol. I*, No. 12, December 1947, p. 232 ; *Vol. II*, No. 2, February 1949, p. 33 & *Vol. III*, Nos. 10-11, October-November 1950, p. 980.
447. H.E.H. the Nizam's Government, *Report on Labour Census, 1940*, (*1349 Fasli*), (Hyderabad-Dn, 1943), p. 5.
448. Report on Labour Census, 1935, *op. cit.*, p. 25. (percentage is calculated).
449. *Ibid.*
450. See Table XLI included in this Chapter.
451. See Table XLVIII attached in this Section.
452. See the Section on 'Prices and Controls' in Chapter VI. Besides these factors, the tales of War horrors brought by refugees from Rangoon and Vizagpatam and the stationing of the army at the Collieries in 1942 and the feeling of the workers in 1945 that they were paid lower wages compared to outside labourers and lack of good relations between the Management and the coal mine workers, had also been responsible for major exodus of workers from Kothagudem amounting to 80%—W.S. *File* No. 78 of 1351 Fasli (1942) & R. No. 19 of 1352 Fasli (1943) ; *Meezan*, No 25-11-1944 ; W.S. *File* No. 30 of 1354 Fasli (1945) & R.No. 6 of 1357 Fasli (1948).
453. See the sub-section 'Sirpur Paper Mills' in this Chapter.
454. Report on Labour Census, 1935, *op. cit.*, pp. 73 & 74.
455. *Ibid.*, p. 47.
456. Romesh Thapar, *Storm over Hyderabad*, (Kutb publishers : Bombay, 1947), p. 11.
457. Hyderabad State *Mazdoor Sangh*, a Central labour organisation and a non Communist led body, was started on 12-6-1946, Mr. B.S. Mahadev Singh, its Secretary, claimed in August, 1946, that its following was nearly 12,000 strong—All India Trade Union Congress, *File* No. 110, p. 93. (Available in NMML, New Delhi).
458. *The Deccan Chronicle*, 4-6-1949.
459. *Golkonda Patrika* (Daily), 23-12-1950.
460. Venugopal Rao, S., *op. cit.*, p. 23—Though this rise was effected, the Mill workers were made to fight for other grievances regarding payment of bonus, War allowance on par with Bombay, night duty allowance, supply of cheap grains, etc.—W.S. *File* No. 26 of 1352 Fasli (1943) & R.No. 78 of 1352 Fasli ; *File* No. 4 of 1351 Fasli (1942) & R.No. 3 of 1352 Fasli (1943) & *Meezan*, 10-11-1944.

461. P. Sundarayya, *Telangana People's Struggle and its lessons*, (Calcutta, 1972), p. 17 ; AISPC *File* No. 243/1946-47, p. 393.
462. Venugopal Rao, S., *op. cit.*, p. 21.
463. W.S. *File* No. 31 of 1352 Fasli (1943) & R. No. 5 of 1357 Fasli (1948).
464. Memorandum of the Singareni Collieries Workers Union, Kothagudem, in *File* No. 68, Part I (A.I.S.P.C.), 1946-47, p. 4, (NMML, New Delhi).
465. *The Deccan Chronicle*, 10-12-1948 ; Report on Labour Census, 1935 *op. cit.*, p. 67.
466. Comrade S.A. Dange, *All India Trade Union Congress Papers* (Available in NMML, Delhi).
467. See the last but one para in the Section 'Political Conditions' in Chapter III.
468. An Organisation in Telangana representing the interests of agriculturists.
469. S.A. Dange, AITUC papers, *op. cit.*
470. Report on the internal situation of Hyderabad State for the fortnight ending on 31st August, 1921, in Foreign and Political Department, *Micro Film, Reel No. 72* and *Acc. No. 65.*
471. W.S. *File* No. 26 of 1352 Fasli (1943) & R.No. 78 of 1352 Fasli.
472. *Hyderabad Government Bulletin on Economic Affairs*, Vol. III, No. 9, September, 1950, p. 805.
473. This functioned as a Communist-led Central labour organisation in the State, with late Mr. Makhdoom Mohiuddin as President and Mr. Raj Bahadur Goud, as Secretary, from 15th August, 1946. It claimed affiliation of 200 unions, big and small that comprised more than 50,000 workers—AITUC *File* No. 110, p. 15 ; AISPC, *File* No. 243/1946-47.
474. AISPC, *File* No. 243/1946-47 ; *The Deccan Chronicle*, 10-12-1948.
475. AITUC Papers, *File* No. 110, p. 15.
476. *Hyderabad Government Bulletin on Economic Affairs*, Vol. II, No. 6-7, June-July, 1949, p. 676.
477. *The Deccan Chronicle*, 16-6-1949.
478. *The Deccan Chronicle*, 23-2-1950.
479. *Hyderabad Government Bulletin on Economic Affairs*, Vol. II, 1949, p. 91.
480. AITUC, *File* No. 110, p. 93.
481. See the first para in this sub-section.
482. Economic Investigations in Hyderabad State, Vol. III, *op. cit.*, p. 12.
483. A.I. Qureshi, *op. cit.*, p. 72.
484. *Ibid.*, p. 73.
485. *Hyderabad Information*, Vol. I, No. 2, November, 1941, pp. 17 & 19.

486. A.I. Qureshi, *op. cit.*, p 73.
487. For definition see f.n. No. 31 in Chapter III and for its wider application see 'the systems of land tenure' in Chapter IV.
488. For elaboration see Section 'villages' and f.n. No. 23 in Chapter III.
489. Nawab (Mushtaq Hussain Khan) Vicar-ul-Mulk Bahadur, *Description of a Tour in the Eastern Division in 1294 Fasli* (*1885*), p. 4.
490. *Golkonda Patrika* (Bi-weekly), 7-11-1933; 8-9-1938, & *Meezan*, 18-7-1945.
491. In Urdu it means supply.
492. *Golkonda Patrika* (Daily), 24-5-1949.
493. Economic Investigations in Hyderabad State, Vol. III, *op. cit.*, pp. 13-14.
494. *Ibid.*
495. *Golkonda Patrika* (weekly), 10-6-1933.
496. *Golkonda Patrika* (Daily), 18-5-1949 ; *The Deccan Chronicle*, 21-5-1949.
497. Economic Investigations in Hyderabad State, Vol. III, *op. cit.*, p. 13.
498. The Marketing Department, Government of Hyderabad : *Note on the Agricultural Marketing in Hyderabad State*, (Hyderabad-Dn, 1952), p. 3.
499. Attached to this Section.
500. See Table L incorporated in this Section.
501. Nizamabad and Kamareddy were there in Nizamabad District and Siddipet in Medak District, both in Medak *Suba*.
502. W.S. *File* No. 30 of 1352 Fasli (1943) & R.No. 4 of 1357 Fasli (1948).
503. See Table L included in this Section.
504. See Table LI in this Section.
505. See sub-section 'Pulses' in Chapter VI.
506. Statistical Year Book, H.E.H. the Nizam's Dominions, 1351-54 Fasli (1942-45), *op. cit.*, pp. 1306-15.
507. A note on Agricultural Marketing in Hyderabad State, *op. cit.*, p. 26.
508. *Ibid.*, p. 20.
509. *Ibid.*, p. 16. A.I. Qureshi, *op. cit.*, p. 214.
510. A note on Agricultural Marketing Hyderabad State, *op. cit.*, p. 7.
511. Commission agents of big or wholesale merchants.
512. A note on Agricultural Marketing in Hyderabad State, *op. cit.*, p. 7.
513. Hyderabad Banking Enquiry Report, 1930, *op. cit.*, p. 39.
514. *Ibid.*, p. 38.
515. *Statistics about Trade Centres* (Markets & Bazars) *in Hyderabad State, 1948*, (Hyderabad-Dn, 1950), p. 9.
516. REE. *op. cit.*, p. 345.

517. Hyderabad Banking Enquiry Report, 1930, *op. cit.*, p. 41.
518. See the Sections 'Crop Acreage', 'Agricultural Production' & 'Price Controls and Rationing' in Chapter VI.
519. See the Section 'E. Price Controls, Procurement & Rationing' in Chapter VI.
520. A.I. Qureshi, *op. cit.*, p. 214 ; Report on the Administration of Hyderabad State, September, 1948 to March, 1950, *op. cit.*, p. 189.

520(a). These were named after and celebrated in the name of a God, Goddess or Saint of either Hindus or Muslims.

521. For their number, see Table L included in this Section.
522. Settlement Report of Warangal Taluka of the Warangal District, *op. cit.*, p. 15.
523. A note on Agricultural Marketing in Hyderabad State, *op. cit.*, p. 11.
524. *List of Uruses, Melas, Jatras, etc. in H.E.H. the Nizam's Dominions*, 1349 Fasli (1940 A.D), (Hyderabad-Dn, 1940), pp. v, 13-43.
525. Attached in this Section.
526. A note on Agricultural Marketing in Hyderabad State, *op. cit.*, p. 4.
527. *Ibid.*
528. See Table LI in this Section. (percentages are calculated)
529. *Ibid.*
530. See the Section 'Agricultural Production and its effects on the economy' in Chapter VI.
531. See the sub-section 'Money-lenders' in Chapter V.
532. A note on Agricultural Marketing in Hyderabad State. *op. cit.*, p. 6.
533. Cotton Manual, H.E.H. the Nizam's Government, *op. cit.*, p. 259.
534. About the extent of Pingali Pratap Reddy's landlordship, see the Section on 'Irrigational Facilities' in Chapter V.
535. A note on Agricultural Marketing in Hyderabad State, *op. cit.*, p. 10.
536. Regarding landlord investment in industries, see the Section 'A. Industrial Organisation, Management and Finance' in this Chapter.
537. *Trade Statistics, H.E.H. the Nizam's Government, 1933-34* (*1343 Fasli*), p. 25 and *1946-47* (*1356 Fasli*), p. 138. (percentages are calculated).
538. *Cotton Manual, 1940, H.E.H. the Nizam's Government*, (Hyderabad-Dn, 1942), pp. 130-31.
539. *Hyderabad Government Bulletin on Economic Affairs*, Vol. II, No. 2, February, 1949, p. 221.
540. *Golkonda Patrika*, 25-8-1938 ; Statistical Year Book, 1351-54 Fasli (1942-45), *op. cit.*, p. 578.
541. *Hyderabad Government Bulletin on Economic Affairs*, Vol. I, December, 1947, No. 2, p. 210.

542. *Ibid.*
543. *Golkonda Patrika*, 25-8-1938 ; for an account of smuggling activities with the connivance of Customs Officials, see the sub-section 'i. Rationing and Public Distribution System' in Chapter VI.
544. IGI, *op. cit.*, p. 43.
545. Settlement Report of the Warangal Taluka of the Warangal District, *op. cit.*, p. 14.
546. IGI, *op. cit.*, p. 180.
547. *Ibid.*, p. 168.
548. *H.E.H. the Nizam's Government, Agricultural, Industrial and Trade Statistics for the year 1343 Fasli (1933-34)*, (Hyderabad-Dn, 1936), p. 59.
549. A.S. Raju : *Economic Conditions in the Madras Presidency, 1800-1850* published Ph. D. thesis, (University of Madras, 1941), p. 214 ; IGI, *op. cit.*, p. 44.
550. IGI, *op. cit.*, pp. 43 & 44.
551. *Ibid.*, p. 44.
552. Agricultural, Industrial and Trade Statistics for the Year 1343 Fasli (1933-34), *op.cit.*, p. 59.
553. H.E.H. the Nizam's Government, *Report on the Working of the Departments under the Revenue Secretariat, 1328 Fasli* (1918-19), (Hyderabad-Dn), (n.d.), p. 1.
554. *Administrative Report for 1324 Fasli (1914-15)*, (Hyderabad-Dn, 1916), p. iii.
555. See Table LII attached in this sub-section
556. *Ibid.* (percentages are calculated).
557. See Table XXXVI in chapter VI for an idea about the tremendous growth in groundnut production.
558. *Ibid.*
559. See Table LII included in this sub-section, Warangal's total oil seed exports amounted to Rs. 1, 13,03,976 and of Adilabad to Rs. 52,55, 211. (percentage is calculated).
560. See Table LII in this sub-section.
561. *Ibid.*
562. *Ibid.*
563. *Ibid.*
564. IGI, *op. cit.*, pp. 168, 180 & 189 ; For Adilabad's low rice production, see Table XXXVI in Chapter VI.
565. See Table LII in this Chapter and Table XXVII in Chapter V ; Livestock Census, 1935, *op. cit.*, p. 27.
566. See Table LII in this sub-section. (percentages are roughly calculated).
567. See the sub-section 'iii. Handloom-spinning, weaving, printing and dyeing' in this Chapter.
568. See Table LII in this sub-section.
569. Regarding industries, see the I section in this Chapter ; for popula-

tion, see the relevant Section in Chapter II and for rich landlord composition, see the Section 'B. Pattern of land distribution' in Chapter V.

570. See Table LII in this sub-section. Ratios and extents are calculated roughly.

571. During the period of Second World War, for instance, inflation, closure of European markets and transport bottlenecks, had all operated at the same time.

572. See Table LIII included in this sub-section. Except otherwise referred, it should be assumed that the figures of imports, exports, total trade and balance of trade are hence quoted from this Table.

573. See Table XXXIII and Section 'L. Crop Conditions' in Chapter V ; *Administrative Report for 1322 Fasli* (*1912-13*), p. 46 ; *Decennial Report on the Administration, 1322-31 Fasli* (*1912-22*), p. 147.

574. Decennial Report on the Administration, *op. cit.*, p. 147.

575. *Administrative Report for 1323 Fasli* (*1913-14*), (Hyderabad-Dn, 1915), p. v.

576. *Administrative Report for 1324 Fasli* (*1914-15*), (Hyderabad-Dn, 1916), p. vii.

577. RAR. *op. cit.*, p. i.

578. A.R., for 1324 Fasli (1914-15), *op. cit.*, p. iii.

579. *Ibid.*, p. vii.

580. Decennial Report on the Administration, *op. cit.*, p 147 ; also see the Section 'L. Crop Conditions' in Chapter V. Herein after, for any reference on crop conditions, until and unless otherwise stated, this Section may be looked into.

581. *A.R. for 1326 Fasli* (*1916-17*), (Hyderabad-Dn, 1918), p. 24 ; see also Table XXXIII-(c) in Chapter V for rain fall. Hereinafter, for references on rainfall, this may be looked into.

582. Decennial Report on the Administration, *op. cit.*, pp. 147-48 ; The Industrial Evolution of India, pp. 222-23.

583. See the Section 'D. Price variations and their effects' in Chapter VI.

584. *Administrative Report for 1329 Fasli* (*1919-20*), (Hyderabad-Dn, 1921), pp. iv & 24.

585. A.I. Qureshi, *op. cit.*, p. 275.

586. See the sub-section 'ii. Depression and Recovery, 1929-38', in the Section 'Price variations and their effects' in Chapter VI.

586(a). The percentages are calculated upto lakhs.

587. *Ibid.*

588. In these two years, there was an excess of imports over exports which resulted in the deficit going up, instead of receding.

589. A.I. Qureshi, *op. cit.*, p. 274.

590. For 1949, the increase was arrived at from that of 1947, for the figure of 1948 is not available.

591. See the sub-section 'iii. Period of Inflation, 1939-1950' in Chapter VI.
592. *Trade Statistics for 1351 Fasli (1941-42), H.E.H. the Nizam's Government*, (Hyderabad-Dn, 1944), p. 17 ; *Trade Statistics for 1352 Fasli (1942-43)*, (Hyderabad-Dn, 1946), p. 25.
593. See the Section 'L. Crop Conditions' in Chapter V.
594. For an account on these evils and their effects, see the Section 'E. Price Controls, Procurement & Rationing' in Chapter VI.
595. Trade Statistics for 1351 Fasli (1941-42), *op. cit.*, pp. 116-17 ; *Trade Statistics, 1356 Fasli (1946-47)*, (Hyderabad-Dn, 1949), pp. 116-117.
596. Trade Statistics for 1352 Fasli (1942-43), *op. cit.*, p. 60.
597. *Trade Statistics for 1349 Fasli (1939-40)*, (Hyderabad-Dn, 1941), p. 20 ; *Trade Statistics for 1350 Fasli (1940-41)*, (Hyderabad-Dn, 1942), p. 19.
598. Trade Statistics for 1352 Fasli (1942-43), *op. cit.*, p. 60 ; Report on the Administration of Hyderabad State, September 1948 to March, 1950, *op. cit.*, p. 20.
599. Trade Statistics for 1350 Fasli (1940-41), *op. cit.*, p. 1 ; A.R. for 1351 Fasli (1941-42), *op. cit.*, 14
600. Report on the Administration of Hyderabad State, September, 1948 to March, 1950, *op. cit.*, p. 14.
601. *Hyderabad Government Bulletin on Economic Affairs*, Vol. II, No. 3, March, 1949, p. 362 ; see the sub-section dealing with 'Acreage of non-food crops' in chapter VI.
602. See the para above.
603. 1948 is also taken as a deficit year, for there was a decline in total trade.
604. This could be seen from the total trade figure of 1941-42 and of earlier decreasing years, though not of 1947-48 which is not available.
605. Attached in this sub-section.
606. See the sub-section 'i. Nature of trade' in this Chapter.
607. Revenue Administration Report, *op. cit.*, p. 240.
608. See the last paragraph in the Section 'Administrative Conditions' in Chapter III.
609. See the last para in sub-section 'iv Reasons for low utilisation of irrigational resources' in Section 'C. Irrigational Facilities' of Chapter V.
610 Report of the Royal Commission on Agriculture in India, *op. cit.*, p. 498.
611. It is located in Paloncha Taluq of Warangal District, on the banks of river Godavari. As there is the celebrated Sri Rama Temple here, pilgrims from far and near collect here on the Lord's birthday festival.
612. APDG, *op. cit.*, Warangal, p. 125 ; Adilabad, p. 108.
613. See Table LIV enclosed in this Section. (percentages are calculated).

614. A. Gopalan: 'Some Economic Aspects of Road Planning and Development with special reference to Hyderabad in *The Hyderabad Government Bulletin on Economic Affairs*, Vol. II, No. 8-9, August-September, 1949, p. 836 and see Table LIV in this Section, (percentages are calculated).
615. *Hyderabad Government Bulletin on Economic Affairs*, Vol. I, No. 2, December, 1947, p. 130.
616. REE, *op. cit.*, p. 333.
617. The name is derived from *Murum* or sand gravel that was used as cover for these roads.
618. See Table LIV incorporated in this Section. Percentage was roughly calculated taking especially the figures of 1950 into consideration.
619. The figures of only Warangal and Karimnagar Districts were taken for calculation as those of Adilabad left a void.
620. All references on road and rail mileage hereinafter made, until otherwise stated, should be supposed to have been made from Table LIV attached in this Section.
621. A. Gopalan, *op. cit.*, p. 833.
622. 1941 Census Report Part I, *op. cit.*, p. 27.
623. Percentages are calculated.
624. See the end part of the Section para 'F. Transport Development' in this Chapter.
625. It was only 0.8% increase in respect of Adilabad District, which probably, was due to the reasons cited in the middle of this paragraph.
626. These exceptions were there for the year 1950 in the case of Karimnagar District and 1945 & 1950 in the case of Adilabad District, which was due to marginal differences in the trends of development.
627. It was a Taluq headquarters in Nalgonda District of Medak *Suba* lying to the West of Khammam.
628. In the neighbouring State of Madhya Pradesh or Central Provinces.
629. For the identification of the Taluqs, see Table VI in Chapter III.
630. APDG, *op. cit.*, Warangal, p. 118; Khammam, p. 159; Karimnagar, p. 134; Adilabad, p. 100; Decennial Report, *op. cit.*, p. 158.
631. See the last para in the Section, 'Administrative Conditions' in Chapter III.
632. I.S., *op. cit.*, p. 607; *Golkonda Patrika* (Daily), 21-5-1950; 25-8-1938.
633. For Kinwat and Boorgampahad, see the last para of Section, 'Administrative Conditions' in Chapter III; *Golkonda Patrika* (Daily), 28-6-1949.
634. N.G. Ranga, *op. cit.*, p. 9.
635. *Golkonda Patrika* (Daily), 28-6-1949.

636. *Meezan* (Telugu edition), 18-10-1946.
636(a). REE, *op. cit.*, p. 323.
637. W.S. *File* No. 43 of 1355 Fasli (1946) & R.No. 68 of 1356 Fasli (1947).
638. W.S. *File* No. 16 of 1355 Fasli (1946), & R.No. 69 of 1356 Fasli (1947).
639. *Golkonda Patrika* (Daily), 21-5-1950.
640. See f.n. No. 285 in Chapter V.
641. REE, *op. cit.*, p. 321.
642. *Golkonda Patrika* (Daily), 21-5-1950.
643. *Ibid.*
644. ELOH, *op. cit.*, p. 109.
645. A. Gopalan, *op. cit.*, p. 333.
646. Memoranda submitted to the Taxation Enquiry Committee, *op. cit.*, p. 189.
647. *Ibid.* p. 183.
648.

Suba	Area in Sq. miles	Expenditure O.S.Rs.
Medak	19,584	7,13,523
Aurangabad	18,858	5,96,001
Gulbarga	21,661	4,49,652
Warangal	20,294	2,82,206
Total State	80,397	20,41,382

A.R. for 1320 and 1321 Fasli (1910-1912), H.E.H. the Nizam's Government, p. 44.
649. W.S. *File* No. 38 of 1354 Fasli (1945) & R.No. 706 of 1354 Fasli.
650. RAR, *op. cit.*, p. 231.
651. W.S. *File* No. 38 of 1354 Fasli (1945) & R.No. 706 of 1354 Fasli.
652. *Golkonda Patrika* (Daily), 8-1-1950.
653. APDG, Warangal, *op. cit.*, p. 122.
654. Economic Investigations in the Hyderabad State, Vol. III, *op. cit.*, p. 20.
655. W.S. *File* No. 16 of 1355 Fasli (1946) & R.No. 69 of 1356 Fasli (1947).
656. W.S. *File* No. 23 of 1355 Fasli (1946) & R.No. 70, of 1356 Fasli (1947).
657. *Statistical Year Book, 1941-42 to 44-45, H.E.H. the Nizam's Government*, p. 380 ; Economic Investigations in the Hyderabad State, Vol. III, *op. cit.*, pp. 20 & 36.
658. APDG, Warangal, *op. cit.*, p. 122.

659. 1941 Census Report, Part I, *op. cit.*, p. 29 ; Statistics about Trade Centres, 1948, *op. cit.*, p. 8.
660. 1941 Census Report, Part I, *op. cit.*, p. 29.
661. I.S. *op. cit.*, p. 609.
662. Statistical Year Book, 1941-42 to 1944-45, *op. cit.*, p. 380 ; A Survey of Industries in Telangana, *op. cit.*, p. 9 ; *Golkonda Patrika* (Daily), 21-3-1950.
663. APDG, Adilabad, *op. cit.*, p. 105.
664. Confidential Report of *First Taluqdar*, Karimnagar to *Subedar* for the first fortnight of Amardad (June), 1355 Fasli (1946) in W.S. *File* No. 23 of 1355 Fasli (1946) & R.No. 70 of 1356 Fasli (1947).
665. H.E.H. the Nizam's Government, *Agricultural, Industrial and Trade Statistics for the year 1343 Fasli (1932-34)*, Hyderabad-Dn, 1936), p. 147.
666. *Golkonda Patrika* (Bi-weekly), 11-7-1938.
667. *Ibid.*
668. *Meezan* (Telugu edition), Editorial, 19-8-1945.
669. Census of India, 1941, Hyderabad State, Part I-Report, *op. cit.*, p. 29.
670. ELOH, *op. cit.*, p. 101.
671. ASIT, *op. cit.*, p. 9.
672. 1941 Census, *op. cit.*, Part II, Tables, p. 2.
673. *Ibid.*
674. APDG, Adilabad, *op. cit.*, p. 106.
675. Report on the Administration of Hyderabad State, September, 1948 to March, 1950, *op. cit.*, p. 79.
676. Statistical Year Book, 1941-42 to 1944-45, *op. cit.*, p. 361.
677. Statistical about Trade Centres, 1948, *op. cit.*, p. 8.
678. APDG, Warangal, *op. cit.*, p. 122.
679. ELOH, *op. cit.*, p. 104.
680. Labour Census held in the respective years.
681. I.S., *op. cit.*, p. 613.
682. Labour Census, 1935, *op. cit.*, p. 12.
683. APDG, Karimnagar, *op. cit.*, p. 138.
684. See Section 'I. Agricultural Implements' in Chapter V.
685. Labour Census, 1935, *op. cit.*, p. 12.
686. APDG, Adilabad, *op. cit.*, p. 104.
687. Labour Census, 1935, *op. cit.*, p. 12.
688. See the Table LIV attached in this Section.
689. A. Gopalan, *op. cit.*, p. 833.
690. See the 'Road Map of Hyderabad' enclosed in this Section.
691. Includes the 16 mile long mineral line laid from Dornakal Junction to Yellandu Collieries,—IGI, *op. cit.*, p. 168.
692. *Statistical Abstract, 1922-31, H.E.H. the Nizam's Government*, pp. 388-89.
693. The branch line to Yellandu Collieries was laid in 1888, whereas that to Kothagudem mines from Karepalli Junction, consisting of

25 miles was laid in 1927—Statistical Year Book, 1351-1354 Fasli (1942-45), *op. cit.*, pp. 336-337.

694. IGI, *op. cit.*, p. 168.
695. See the 'Road Map' enclosed in this Section.
696. See the Table LIV and the 'Road Map' included in this Section. The mileage of Adilabad District seem to include the 23 Km. Mudkhed-Adilabad Railway.
697. See the Sections dealing with 'Industries' and mainly large-scale, in this chapter.
698. APDG, Adilabad, *op. cit.*, p. 106 ; *The Deccan Chronicle*, 13-5-1950.
699. *The Deccan Chronicle*, 29-6-1947 ; 13-6-1948.
700. Percentages are calculated on the basis of the mileage given in Table LIV attached in this Section.
701. See Table LIV included in this Section.
702. *Hyderabad Government Bulletin on Economic Affairs*, Vol. I. No. 9, December, 1948, p. 963.
703. APDG, *op. cit.*, Warangal, p. 125 ; Karimnagar, p. 141 ; Adilabad, pp. 107 & 108; *Eleven years of progress of Hyderabad State Transport, 1930-41* (Hyderabad-Dn, 1941), p. 14
704. Eleven Years Progress of Hyderabad State Transport, *op. cit.*, p. 16.
705. *Hyderabad Information*, Vol. III, No. 11, August, 1943, p. 5.
706. A Summary of Hyderabad's War Effort, *op. cit.*, p. 11.
707. ELOH, *op. cit.*, p. 99.
708. Statistical Year Book, 1941-42 to 1944-45, *op. cit.*, p. 328.
709. *Ibid.*, Percentages are roughly calculated.
710. Decennial Report on the Administration, *op. cit.*, p. 159.
711. *Ibid.*
712. Syed Abid Ali Hassan, *op. cit.*, pp. 92-93.
713. In this particular case, the ratio worked out to one Post Office for 34 Sq. kms. of the District area. As an increase of 102 Post Offices was shown between 1936 and 1950-51, a rise not witnessed at any time before or by any other District, the figure as given in Table LV is open to doubt.
714. See the Table LV enclosed in this sub-section.
715. *Ibid.*
716. *Ibid.*
717. See the last para in the Section 'Administrative Conditions' in chapter III.
718. *Golkonda Patrika* (Daily), editorial, 5-8-1950.
719. See the last para in the Section 'Administrative Conditions' in Chapter III—also *Ibid.*
720. It refers to British Indian Post Office.
721. *Golkonda Patrika* (Bi-weekly), 7-6-1933.
722. *Ibid.*
723. Statistical Year Book, 1941-42 to 1944-45, *op. cit.*, p. 410.
724. Syed Abid Ali Hassan, *op. cit.*, pp. 93-94.

725. *Ibid.*
726. *Golkonda Patrika* (Daily) 21-3-1950.
727. See the last para in the Section, 'Administrative Conditions' in Chapter III.
728. H.E.H. the Nizam's Government, Financial Secretariat, English Branch, *File* No. 166 of 1337 Fasli (1928).
729. Statistical Year Book, 1941-42 to 1944-45, *op. cit.*, p. 419.
730. *Ibid.*
731 R.V. Rao, *op. cit.*, p. 364 ; REE, *op. cit.*, p. 344.
731(a) *Golkonda Patrika* (Daily), 15-7-1950.
732. See the Table LV attached in this sub-section.
733. *A.R. for 1346 Fasli (6-10-1936 to 5-10-1937), H.E.H. the Nizam's Government*, (Hyderabad-Dn, 1939), p. 128. The balance sheet of the Exchange as on 30th Aban, 1345 Fasli (30th December, 1936), showed a total loss of Rs. 1,22,625-7-5—H.E.H. the Nizam's Government, Financial Secretariat, English Branch, *File* No. 155 of 1346 Fasli, (1937), S. No. 202.
734. A.R. for 1346 Fasli (1936-37), *op. cit.*, p. 129.
735. APDG, Warangal, *op. cit.*, p. 127.
736. See para two in Section 'B. Large-scale Industrial Production and its impact on the Economy' of this Chapter.
737. See the first para in sub-section 'a. Wages and Trade Unionism' of this Chapter.
738. See the sub-section 'a. Wages and Trade Unionism' in this Chapter.
739. See the last para in sub-section 'iii. Trade Development, 1911-1950' of this Chapter.
740. See Table LII attached in the Section on 'Trade' in this Chapter.
741. See the last para of the sub-section 'a. Motor Bus Service' in this Chapter.
742. See the first para of the sub-section 'i. Road Transport' in this Chapter.
743. See the first para of the sub-section 'iii. Postal and Tele-Communication Facilities' in this Chapter.
744. See the last para in sub-section 'iii. Postal and Tele-communication Facilities' in this Chapter.

CHAPTER EIGHT

WELFARE ASPECTS : EDUCATION, HEALTH, URBAN & TRIBAL CONDITIONS AND TELANGANA STRUGGLE

POVERTY, ill-health, illiteracy and low productivity form a vicious circle which in turn, leads to economic underdevelopment.[1] The spread of education would enable the ryot to show interest in the land by understanding the principles guiding his Land Settlement, the records prepared, and verify the correctness of the entries made in his respect,[2] besides of course, gaining better knowledge of the application of agricultural inputs. Literacy also had the power of enabling the labourers to augment their bargaining power. But, illiteracy which presents the most formidable single obstacle to rural development in the widest sense,[3] has come to prevail in greater degree in the State and more so in the Eastern Division. In the rural area of the latter which comprised more than 90% of the total population,[4] the literacy percentage in 1951 stood at only 5.0, 4.7 and 3.8 in the respective Districts of Warangal, Karimnagar and Adilabad, the last-named ranking the lowest in the State, the highest being 8.3 in Osmanabad District.[5] In other words, the number of literates in the vast countryside of the State stood comparatively higher in the Western and Northern Districts of adjoining Bombay State and it diminished as one proceeded towards the East, touching the lowest mark in the forest tracts along the Penganga, the Wardha, the Pranhita and the Godavari in the extreme Eastern parts of the State bordering Madhya Pradesh and Madras Provinces of British India, the evident factors of influence being plains and better transport facilities in the former as against hilly and forest features with comparatively poor transport facilities in the latter.[6]

Public health and economic development act and react on each other, in the sense that a poor standard of general health is one of the chief causes of low output per head and of economic inefficiency.[7] But, the medical facilities in the State, even by the middle of 1949, had been in such a sad state that the average ran at the rate of one dispensary for 235 sq. miles and one hospital bed for 68,000 of the population.[8] Not only this distribution was highly inadequate, but even the staff and equipment position of the hospitals that had been functioning, remained highly unsatisfactory in the *Suba* area. These remained such that Second *Taluqdar* of Adilabad who was down with Malaria fever in 1947 could not get treated at the District Headquarters Hospital, Adilabad, for no Civil Surgeon was there nor equipment for the examination of blood and as a result, was obliged to go elsewhere for treatment.[9] If that was the medical facility enjoyed by an Assistant Collector of a District at the headquarters hospital, the condition of the people at large could well be imagined in a region where public health activities for the most part, were limited to towns only.[10]

Though the number of persons in towns per 1,000 of total population, stood in 1951 at only 182, 125 and 85 in the respective Districts of Warangal, Adilabad and Karimnagar, as against 186 persons in the State,[11] yet, the urban areas or towns whose population was above 5,000 and which again, numbered 14, 13 and 15 respectively in the year,[12] proved of much economic significance in the history of the *Suba*, for the reason that these became renowned centres of industry, commerce and trade. Warangal City with a population of 1,33,130[13] and maximum concentration of administrative, historical, industrial, trading and transport interests unequalled by any other centre in the State[14] and which took its place as the second largest urban centre in the State, next to the Capital City of Hyderabad[15], stood as the supreme specimen in this respect. On the other hand, very meagre existence of large-scale industries, trade and rail facilities in Karimnagar District and slightly better position in this respect in the case of Adilabad District,[16] was very much responsible for keeping them much behind Warangal District in respect of urbanisation. But, even in the all-important and an earliest established Municipality of Warangal, neither the sanitary workers were employed in enough number, nor were they paid sufficient salaries, the natural result being accumulation of dirt and dust and strikes of the workers.[17] The condition of lesser and other Municipalities in the *Suba* proved no better.[18]

The study of tribal conditions in the *Suba* is significant for the very simple reason that its tribal population accounted for as much as 9.38% of its total population in 1941 as against the corresponding percentage of only 4.15 in respect of the State. On the other hand, in respect of the *Suba* Districts of Warangal and Adilabad, the same stood still further higher at 14.07 and 15.24 respectively, though of course, Karimnagar's was only 1.24. The prominent aboriginal and hill tribes of Gonds, Koyas, Lambadas or Banjaras and Hill Reddis had been so widely prevalent in the two former Districts that their tribal populations formed respectively as much as 56.63% and 38.23% of that of the *Suba* and 27.42% and 18.51% of that of the State.[19] But, excepting the Banjaras which was an immigrant tribe that came from Rajputana at the time of Mogul conquest,[20] all other aboriginal tribesmen of the area, right until 1946-47, got subjected to severe exploitation at the hands of the varied agencies that dealt with them such as the *Watandars*, forest officials and contractors, non-aboriginal immigrant landlords and moneylenders, which resulted in the expropriation of the former, both in land and their earnings in cash and kind.[21] As a result, including the famous Raj-Gonds who during the medieval period enjoyed ruling power in the Gondwana region of Madhya Pradesh,[22] all these oppressed tribesmen got reduced to the wretched position of landless labourers.[23] The tribal welfare measures of the State had been brought into operation rather late when the dispossession was over and the tribesmen very much got resigned to their fate.[24]

Peasant Revolt, popularly known as the Telangana Struggle, figures prominently in the economic history of the *Suba* since the middle of 1946. The Taluqs of Mahaboobabad, Khammam, Madhira, Palvancha, Yellandu and Mulug in Warangal District, Sirsilla, Jagtiyal, Mahadeopur, Huzurabad and Sultanabad in Karimnagar District and Chinnoor, Luxettipet and Sirpur in Adilabad District, got mainly involved in this Struggle. Led by the Communists, it was directed first against the dominant feudal elements of *Jagirdars* and *Deshmukhs* and in the secondary stage against the rich peasants. Whereas all the peasants including the richer got united in the Struggle against the feudal lords, smaller peasants, tenants and agricultural labourers, on the other hand, ranged themselves against the rich peasants.[25] Land for landless tenants, ownership rights for cultivating tenants, better wages for agricultural labourers, grant of *Laoni* land and freedom from landlord oppression for small and middle peasants, freedom from food-grain levy, cash crop restrictions and *Razakar* atrocities for rich peasants and the united desire of these and other sections of the rural population including the non-agricultural for the removal of the much hated *Jagirdari* and *Deshmukhi* oppression, had in general, become the objectives for which the Movement was launched. As the continuation of these evils was associated with the *Nizam's* rule, the longing for the removal of the former tantamounted to the change of the latter also. Revenge and retribution for the misdeeds and the misery that were inflicted in the past by the aristocracy and the regime, was also very much noticeable during the course of the Resistance.[26] The fact that the percentage of landless to occupancy tenants had increased in the Surveyed villages of Warangal District from 24 to 71 between 1929-30 and 1949-50[27] and highest area of land amounting to one-fifth of that of the State has undergone transfer in the same District, as found in the latter year, mostly from cultivating into the hands of non-cultivating persons belonging to cultivating families,[28] proved potent factors for the fiare up of the situation in it. It was followed by Adilabad District, though in a lesser degree, in these explosive features of the agricultural situation in the *Suba*. Comparatively, these became far less significant in Karimnagar District.[29] The intensity and the extent of this Peasant Struggle was naturally in the same proportion in these *Suba* Districts.

A. EDUCATIONAL CONDITIONS : These proved highly unsatisfactory in various directions. Spending on this welfare item by the Government as well as the Local Boards was, compared to total revenue or expenditure, not in commensuration with the need.[30] Expenditure on education in the State by the Former, for instance, during the developmental period of 1938-39 to 1949-50, accounted for only 10.27% in the former year to 10.73% in the latter year, of its total revenues.[31] As a percentage of total Governmental expenditure, it ranged between 8.65 in 1945-46 to 14.27 in 1950-51, which remained as the minimum and the maximum levels during the 16 year period ending in the latter year.[32] The Local Boards, which were expected to spend on education 3 pies out of 12 pies or one anna that they received on every one rupee of land revenue that was collected in an year,[33] proved none the better. In the year 1918-19, excepting in Karimnagar District, which met the requirement, this expenditure in the other *Suba* Districts of Warangal and Adilabad had amounted to only one-eigth and one-tenth respectively of the Local Cess collections that had been received.[34] Added to this deficiency in allotment, it often occurred that the Local Boards failed to spend the allotted amounts fully and the P.W.D. made wrong preferences in its spending of the funds. Thus, in 1930-31 when the Taluq Boards and the District Boards were allotted by the Government, Rs. 15.87 and Rs. 11.47 lakhs respectively for expenditure on various developmental schemes respectively, they could spend only Rs. 11.61 and Rs. 7.90 lakhs respectively out of them.[35] Similarly, when the High School Building at Manthani, Taluq headquarters in Karimnagar District,[36] stood in the need of immediate repair work as early as 1943-44, it had not yet been taken up by the P.W.D. even after five years had elapsed and on the other hand, amounts were spent on whitewashing the roof which if utilised for the laying of temporary sheds, would have, for sometime served the purpose, the ultimate consequence being that the institution was forced to be closed for instruction.[37]

(*i*) *Medium of Instruction and Private Schools* : In the *Suba* Districts as early as 1921, the Telugu and Urdu-speaking population accounted for respectively, 87.50, 98.47, 56.06 and 5.64. 3.74 and 5.89% of the total population in Warangal, Karimnagar and Adilabad respectively. In the State as a whole, on the other hand, these respectively formed 48.23 and 10.35% of the total population,[38] the latter being preponderant only in the metropolitan City of Hyderabad.[39] Very much ignoring this language ratio, Urdu, the language of the Rulers, was made not only the State language, but also medium of instruction right from Secondary to University level.[40] Telugu, Marathi and Kannada, the mother tongues of the ruled, could only be studied as second language, except being the instructional medium at the primary level.[41] The effect of this irrational policy adopted by the Government in respect of the instructional media could be seen from *Table LVII*[42] that, as against 1,130 Primary Schools in the *Suba* in 1936, the Colleges, High Schools and Middle Schools numbered respectively only 1,6 and 15. Popular organisations such as the Hyderabad People's Educational Conference, the Hindu *Praja Mandal*[43] the Maharashtra Parishad etc., besides the Hindu Press[44] such as the *Meezan* (Telugu edition)[45] and the *Golkonda Patrika*,[46] constantly went on impressing their strong resentment and condemnation of this short-sighted policy of the Government, which rather came to be regarded as communally-tinged even by the British Resident at Hyderabad,[47] supposed to be favourably inclined towards the *Nizam* and his policies on many an occassion. Since the regime staked its power on the continuance of this policy,[48] however unsound it was, these public representations which, during the Second War period, even culminated into what was known as 'the mother-tongue agitation,[49] failed to bring any material change in this regard.

The sparsity of the general educational institutions in the *Suba* to the effect that excepting Warangal and Karimnagar Taluqs, none of the other 23 Taluqs had until 1936, at least one High School and one Middle School, the requisities to

Table LVII

Number of Educational Institutions (Government Recognised and Unrecognised) and the Number of Students Attending them 1331-1345 Fasli (1922-36)

Sl. No.	District and Taluqs		Colleges	Students	School Education General				
					High Schools		Middle Schools	Primary Schools	
					Institutions	Students	Institutions	Students	Institutions
1	2		3	4	5	6	7	8	9
1.	Warangal	Taluq	1	76	3	1,004	1	663	146
2.	Mahaboobabad	,,	—	—	—	—	1	327	88
3.	Khammam	,,	—	—	1	401	—	—	82
4.	Madhira	,,	—	—	—	—	—	—	50
5.	Yellandu	,,	—	—	—	—	1	303	18
6.	Pakhal	,,	—	—	—	—	—	—	27
7.	Mulug	,,	—	—	—	—	—	—	14
8.	Palvancha	,,	—	—	—	—	—	—	10
9.	Total of Warangal District in 1345 Fasli (1936)		1	76	4	1,405	3	1,293	435
10.	-Do- in 1340 Fasli (1931)		1	46	3	750	3	704	422
11.	-Do- in 1335 Fasli (1926)		—	—	2	768	3	899	404
12.	-Do- in 1331 Fasli (1922)		—	—	2	650	3	799	358
13.	Jagtiyal	Taluq	—	—	—	—	2	767	88
14.	Sultanabad	,,	—	—	—	—	—	—	57

15. Karimnagar	,,	—	—	1	479	2	426	98
16. Sirsilla	,,	—	—	—	—	1	383	75
17. Huzurabad	,,	—	—	—	—	1	279	90
18. Parkal	,,	—	—	—	—	1	317	57
19. Mahadeopur	,,	—	—	—	—	1	350	25
20. Total of Karimnagar District in 1345 Fasli (1936)		—	—	1	479	9*	2,718*	490
21. -Do- in 1340 Fasli (1931)		—	—	1	495	7	2,365	492
22. -Do- in 1335 Fasli (1926)		—	—	1	501	5	1,427	470
23. -Do- in 1331 Fasli (1922)		—	—	—	—	6	1,591	438
24. Adilabad	Taluq	—	—	—	—	1	..	26
25. Asifabad	,,	—	—	—	—	1	..	19
26. Rajura	,,	—	—	—	—	1	..	17
27. Chinnoor	,,	—	—	—	—	1	..	23
28. Luxettipet	,,	—	—	—	—	—	—	28
29. Sirpur	,,	—	—	—	—	—	—	21
30. Utnoor	,,	—	—	—	—	—	—	2
31. Nirmal	,,	—	—	1	403	—	—	35
32. Boath	,,	—	—	—	—	—	—	15
33. Kinwat	,,	—	—	—	—	—	—	16
34. Total of Adilabad District in 1345 Fasli (1936)		—	—	1	403	4	..	205
35. -Do- in 1340 Fasli (1931)		—	—	1	372	5	1,221	198
36. -Do- in 1335 Fasli (1926)		—	—	—	—	3	960	178
37. -Do- in 1331 Fasli (1922)		—	—	—	—	3	943	188

Sl. No.	District and Taluq	Students	Special Education: Training Schools Institutions	Training Schools Students	Technical Schools Institutions	Technical Schools Students	Special Schools Institutions	Special Schools Students
		10	11	12	13	14	15	16
1.	Warangal Taluq	9,849	1	55	—	—	2	53
2.	Mahaboobabad ,,	4,004	—	—	1	192	—	—
3.	Khammam ,,	3,689	—	—	—	—	—	—
4.	Madhira ,,	2,063	—	—	—	—	—	—
5.	Yellandu ,,	781	—	—	—	—	—	—
6.	Pakhal ,,	968	—	—	—	—	—	—
7.	Mulug ,,	595	—	—	—	—	—	—
8.	Palvancha ,,	638	—	—	—	—	—	—
9.	Total of Warangal District in 1345 Fasli (1936)	22,587	1	55	1	192	2	53
10.	-Do- in 1340 Fasli (1931)	20,054	2	220	1	177	2	46
11.	-Do- in 1335 Fasli (1926)	18,410	1	55	1	140	2	52
12.	-Do- in 1331 Fasli (1922)	15,994	1	76	1	134	1	18
13.	Jagtiyal Taluq	4,613	—	—	—	—	—	—
14.	Sultanabad ,,	2,720	—	—	—	—	—	—
15.	Karimnagar ,,	5,678	—	—	—	—	1	50
16.	Sirsilla ,,	3,942	—	—	—	—	1	38
17.	Huzurabad ,,	4,390	—	—	—	—	—	—
18.	Parkal ,,	2,541	—	—	—	—	—	—
19.	Mahadeopur ,,	1,279	—	—	—	—	—	—

20. Total of Karimnagar District in 1345 Fasli (1936)	25,163	—	—	—	—	2	88
21. -Do- in 1340 Fasli (1931)	23,953	—	—	3	202	50	1,217
22. -Do- in 1335 Fasli (1926)	20,872	—	—	—	—	157	2,596
23. -Do- in 1331 Fasli (1922)	16,898	—	—	—	—	—	—
24. Adilabad Taluq	1,449	—	—	—	—	—	—
25. Asifabad ,,	943	—	—	—	—	—	—
26. Rajura ,,	943	—	—	—	—	—	—
27. Chinnoor ,,	1,090	—	—	—	—	—	—
28. Luxettipet ,,	1,114	—	—	—	—	—	—
29. Sirpur ,,	1,064	—	—	—	—	—	—
30. Utnoor ,,	63	—	—	—	—	—	—
31. Nirmal ,,	1,874	—	—	—	—	—	—
32. Boath ,,	659	—	—	—	—	—	—
33. Kinwat ,,	878	—	—	—	—	—	—
34. Total of Adilabad District in 1345 Fasli (1936)	10,188	—	—	—	—	—	—
35. -Do- in 1340 Fasli (1931)	8,754	—	—	—	—	—	—
36. -Do- in 1335 Fasli (1926)	8,029	—	—	—	—	—	—
37. -Do- in 1331 Fasli (1922)	6,805	—	—	—	—	—	—

* These total figures of Cols. 7 and 8 should, as per the given Taluq figures, have been 8 and 2,522 respectively, but instead, the source gave inflated figures as found in the Table.

.. Figures are not given for this year but, however, for 1340 *Fasli* (1931), these respectively, stood at 312, 206, 243 and 255.

Source : H.E.H. the Nizam's Government, *Hyderabad District Gazetteers*, Tables Volumes, *1340 & 1345 Fasli* (*1931 & 1936*), *Warangal*, pp. 222-225 ; *Karimnagar*, pp. 222-225 and *Adilabad*, pp. 222-225.

complete Secondary Education, let alone that of the College which was strictly confined to Warangal Proper only,[50] was, besides Governmental neglect and wrong medium policy,[51] due in a considerable measure, to the restrictions that had been imposed from time to time, in the case of the establishment as well as the day-to-day functioning of the private schools. Private enterprise in the shape of well-to-do and philanthropic persons, especially from the business community like Sri. Chandra Kantaiah of Warangal Proper who made a liberal donation of Rs. 1,40,000 for the establishment and also functioning of Andhra *Vardhani* School at the same place in 1945,[52] readily came forward to promote the cause of education, which along with that of libraries, was pursued as an ideal by the Andhra *Maha Sabha* and its sister organisations to bring about cultural and literary renaissance among the people.[53] Permission of the Education Department was made obligatory, until 1942, for the starting of primary, middle and high schools, but subsequently it was removed in the case of the former two, which however, did not make much difference for these along with the latter had been subjected to periodical as well as instant checking by the Department.[54] Things went on in such an atmosphere of suspicion and lack of trust that permission was refused by the Department even when the sponsorors had agreed to fulfil all the conditions prescribed by it[55] and further, even when the villagers had themselves contributed for the construction of a school building[56] or the maintenance of a teacher not provided by the Government or the Local Board, but found essential for the instruction of their children,[57] the institutions were closed peremptorily and on frivolous grounds, much to the disappointment and chagrin of the innocent villagers. The effect of these restrictions imposed on private schools was so devastating and harmful to the spread of education in the State that these schools which numbered 4,053 before the introduction of these rules in 1924, came down to as low as 929 in 1936 and similarly, the number of students in these institutions which stood at 76,654 in the former year came down to as less as 25,865 in the latter year, the respective decrease, instead of increase, amounting to 77.07% and 66.25% within a period of only twelve years.[58]

(*ii*) *Conditions in Non-Diwani Areas* : The utter backwardness of educational facilities in non-*Diwani* areas was largely responsible for the meagre percentage of literacy and educational development in the *Suba* and the State as a whole. The sparseness of schools, including those of Primary level, was far worse in them when compared to *Diwani* areas. This could be clearly seen from the *Report of the Education Department for 1938* which states that in the *Jagir* areas which occupied one-third of the area of the State and covered one-fourth of its population, there were only 108 schools out of 5,131 in the State, the percentage working out to the dismal figure of 2.10 and in the same proportion, it was found that, whereas in the *Diwani* area one school existed for every 17 square miles of territory, the same existed in the *Jagir* area for every 231 sq. miles of territory, the percentage again working out to as low as 7.35.[59] This situation, when reviewed again after a decade in 1949, showed no signs of improvement at all. As against 5,000 Primary Schools spread over 14,000 Government-administered villages covered by 50,000 sq. miles of area, 9,000 villages administered by non-Governmental agencies, covering 33,000 sq. miles of territory and peopled by more than 40,00,000 had only 158 Primary Schools.[60] It is significant to note in this latest situation that, whereas in respect of the number of schools, the percentage of the latter to the former worked out to the miserable figures of 3.16, the same in the case of area and population worked out respectively to as high as 66 and 64.28.[61] The main reason for this dismal record in respect of non *Diwani* areas was due to the fact that the Government had no direct control over them in arranging for welfare activities such as education, public health, supply of drinking water, etc.[62] and the tenure-holders in general, on the other hand, indulging in extravagance and pomp over and above their means and with by-gone habits and less than reasonable amount of education, showed by themselves, little interest in spending over them. As a result, it came to be doubted whether there was atleast one *Jagir* which spent on education at least, minimum of one rupee out of every hundred rupees of its annual income.[63] The effect was that, as the 1949 figure given above indicated, as many as 98.25% of these non-*Diwani* villages remained without even Primary Schools[64] and fourteen towns with a population of more than 5,000 had no facilities for post-primary education.[65] To cite from *Suba* area, in Karimnagar District out of 20 *Sarf-e-khas* villages, only 4 had lower Primary Schools[66] out of which again, one was an aided institution[67] and only three were run by the *Sarf-i-khas* administration,[68] on which the actual expenditure incurred in 1933 was Rs. 1,097-15-0[69] as against the tax collection of Rs. 63,632-13-0 made from these villages by the Administration.[70] Further, neither the staff was adequate in these schools nor they paid reasonable salaries which, in effect, remained as meagre as Rs. 8 p.m. to a teacher and Rs. 15 p.m. to an Headmaster.[71] In view of these extreme unsatisfactory conditions prevailing, the Royal Commission on *Jagir* Administration and Reform in 1947 recommended for the take-over of education and other welfare subjects by the Government,[72] but this suggestion not only came rather late but, on the other hand, was not acted upon by the *Nizam's* Government, in view of its overwhelming preferences for the feudal noblesse than the interests of the people at large. Even the change of the regime also did not usher the development that the people hoped for in these long neglected areas.[73]

(*iii*) *Literacy and Educational Development* : It could be seen from *Table LV*[74] that except in 1931, the literacy percentages of all the *Suba* Districts remained well below those of the State. This was for the obvious reason that only 19.8% of the total number of Primary Schools of the State existed in this *Suba* as against 33.1% in Aurangabad *Suba*, 23.7% in Medak *Suba* and 21.6% in Gulbarga *Suba*.[75] The number of these basic institutions was, as could be observed from *Table LVII*,[76] particularly less in the forest-bound and consequently less exposed Taluqs of Pakhal, Yellandu, Mulug, Palvancha, Mahadeopur, and in fact, almost all the Taluqs of Adilabad District and more so, those of Utnoor, Boath, Kinwat, Rajura, Asifabad, Chinnoor and Sirpur. As a matter of fact, none of the Taluqs of the latter District had more than 35 Primary Schools as against the average number of 250 villages in each of them, the ratio working out to 1 : 7.1, but the lowest ratio

TABLE LV(a).

Literacy Percentages, 1911-51.

Sl. No.	District/ State	1911	1921	1931	1941	1951
1	2	3	4	5	6	7
1.	Warangal	2.5	2.7	4.2	5.8	8.2
2.	Karimnagar	2.0	1.9	2.1	4.8	6.1
3.	Adilabad	1.3	1.5	2.4	3.5	5.9
4.	State	2.8	2.9	4.1	6.8	9.2

Source : *Census of India, Hyderabad State, 1951*, Part I-A, Report, pp. 450 and 473.

in this District, which also was the same in the *Suba* as well as the State, amounted to 1 : 129.5 in Utnoor Taluq where, as against 259 villages, an utterly miserable number of two of these Schools were there.[77] This central Taluq being noted for its huge tribal composition of population, 96% of whom, being the highest among all the *Tahsils* in the State, had been principally dependent on agriculture,[78] it could be very well imagined as to why the people in these parts remained the most backward and also the most exploited in the State. On the other hand, the lowest ratio in Warangal and Karimnagar Districts, stood respectively at 1 : 18 in Palvancha Taluq and 1 : 9.52 in Mahadeopur Taluq.[79] Though the number of Middle and Primary Schools was more in the latter than in the former,[80] the number of literates per 10,000 of the total population[81] as well as the percentage of literacy in the District as a whole,[82] on the other hand, proved very much higher in Warangal District than in Karimnagar District. The comparatively better facilities of transport and communications that the former had,[83] its greater percentage of urban population, especially of Warangal and Khammam towns[84] and slightly better facilities of libraries and reading rooms,[85] had served as contributory factors towards this development.

Not only the ratio between the number of villages and that of Schools in the *Suba* area was highly inadequate, but even the rate of growth in the number of the latter over the years

TABLE LVI

Proportion of Persons belonging to Various Educational Standards for every 10,000 of the Total Population (as in 1951)

Sl. No.	District	Total Literates	Mere Literates	Primary School level	Middle School level	Matri-culates	Intermediate	Graduates	Post-Graduates
1	2	3	4	5	6	7	8	9	10
1.	Hyderabad State	916	706	99	58	30	5	4	1
2.	Hyderabad District	2,525	1,529	344	292	204	48	31	7
3.	Aurangabad ,,	1,082	802	172	68	25	3	2	..
4.	Warangal ,,	817	695	41	41	23	3	2	..
5.	Karimnagar ,,	614	497	70	30	9	1	1	..
6.	Adilabad ,,	591	431	98	35	15	1	2	..

Sl. No.	District	Teaching	Engineering	Commerce	Legal	Medical	Agri-cultural	Veterinary	Others
		11	12	13	14	15	16	17	18
1.	Hyderabad State	2	1	..	2	1	..	..	7
2.	Hyderabad District	5	7	4	8	7	,.	..	37
3.	Aurangabad ,,	3	1	..	1	1	..	..	3
4.	Warangal ,,	2	1	..	1	1	..	..	5
5.	Karimnagar ,,	1	..	..	1	..	..	.	3
6.	Adilabad ,,	1	1	..	1	..	..	..	6

N.B. : Figures are not indicated in cases where the actual proportion is less than 1 per 10,000 of the total population.

Source : *Census of India, Hyderabad State, 1951*, Part I-A, *Report*, p. 460.

was also exceedingly meagre or sometimes, even nil. Thus, during the period 1922-36, in respect of Colleges, only one institution was there in Warangal and others drew blank ; in the case of High Schools, they remained at only one in Karimnagar and Adilabad Districts and from two to four in the case of Warangal District ; in respect of Middle Schools, there was nil growth in respect of the latter and two and one in the case of the former respectively and in respect of Primary Schools, the increase amounted to 77, 52 and only 17 in the case of Warangal, Karimnagar and Adilabad Districts respectively.[86] This being the development spread over 14 years, progress in the remaining period could well be imagined. The functioning of institutions existing, right from University down to village Primary School, left much to be desired. In Osmania University, started in 1918 in the metropolis to carry out the first over experiment of teaching through Urdu, a regional language, at the graduate and the post-graduate level also, neither the staff was adequate in number nor were they well qualified and competent to deliver the goods.[87] These deficiencies which were also reported from the District institutions, led to student protest demonstrations. It was complained that the Department, instead of completely providing for the building accommodation, staff, etc., of the existing institutions, went for the creation of new ones, thereby affecting the growth of the former.[88] In villages, the teachers very often with the connivance of the Inspecting Officers of the Department, never attended to their school duties but, instead looked after their agriculture or other private errands in the same or nearby villages where they stayed and villagers' complaints against them either to the Inspecting Officers or through the Press, went unheeded.[89]

Special Education Schools, except in the case of Karimnagar District for the year 1926 and 1931 appear exceptionally few in number in the *Suba* Districts.[90] About the functioning of these schools which were established in or around the District headquarters such as those of Warangal and Karimnagar for the purpose of mainly providing training in teaching, industrial or cottage crafts, information is lacking. These being professional or vocational, their contribution for the advancement of literacy in the area was negligible. Their mite on the industrial side was discussed elsewhere. It could also be seen from *Table LVII* that Adilabad District, being not that much significant as the other *Suba* Districts in respect of small or cottage industries, drew blank in the matter of these special schools. In view of the related factors analysed as above, Adilabad and Karimnagar Districts of the *Suba*, remained as the most backward among all the Districts in the State, in respect of literacy percentage that obtained in the Districts as a whole.[91]

It is, however, important to note that both in respect of the total number of literates and also in the proportion of persons that have attained different educational standards, Hyderabad District, of all, had maintained throughout, its dominant position, followed next by that of Aurangabad.[92] The former, which of course, included the all-important metropolitan City of Hyderabad, had with just comprising 8% of the State's population, came to monopolise 80% of the latter's post-graduates as well as persons qualified in commerce, 72% of its Intermediates, 67% of its graduates, 56% of its matriculates as well as persons qualified in Veterinary, 54% in engineering, 53% in Medicine, 41% of those who passed in Middle School examination as well as those qualified in judicial and law examinations, 30% in agriculture, 23% in teaching and even 18% of its literate men.[93] In fact, it exceeded the State average in the proportion relating to all educational standards and also the total literates ranging from 3 to 7 times of the latter.[94] On the other hand, mofussil Districts excepting Aurangabad in some standards and also total number of literates, had fallen much behind the State averages, let alone those of Hyderabad District.[95] The essential thing that transpired out of this unequal situation was that, to the exclusion of the Districts and the countryside, Hyderabad City which formed the essential component of Hyderabad District, shone as the single and unified centre representing literary, professional, commercial, educational, and legal interests. This predominance of urban area in the field of education was also reflected in the comparatively better proportions of Aurangabad and Warangal Districts for, they contained respectively the important cities of the same name. Adilabad and Karimnagar Districts, which remained deficient in this respect, naturally accounted for lower averages in the educational standards and also the total number of literates.[96]

Besides the causative factors that had been analysed as contributing for low percentage of literacy, the very atmosphere in the contemporary rural society did not prove conducive to the spread of education in the countryside. The Hindu parents who formed around 85% of the local population[97] and were tradition-minded with deep devotion to their religion and its tenets, felt discouraged at the neglect of study based on these aspects in Government schools and consequently, they preferred to send their wards to what came to be known as "*bazaar* schools"[98] which met with their requirement on the payment of a few *dubs*[99] and where no regular hours were insisted nor examinations held unlike the former.[100] This type of functioning suited majority of the parents in the rural parts, for due to their meagre incomes and comparatively large family units, they expected their children when the latter came of earning capacity, to add to the family income or to help in field work or cattle tending. Further, employers in the countryside and *Sahukars* who functioned as the key controlling agency of the rural production and distribution system, desired to keep the children of their clients in uneducated slavish ignorance to the maximum possible extent, so as to perpetuate their hegemony. A *Sahukar* was reported saying "If a Hindu speaks English, I have no use for him."[101] The *Jagirdars* or the semi-independent feudal lords too, were in no way behind, in sharing and striving for keeping the peasant community under their charge, in the same unprogressive condition of illiteracy so as to cement their authoritarian rule, which was amply reflected in the poor establishment and functioning of schools in non-*Diwani* areas of the *Suba* as well as the State.[102] The inadequate means of transport and communications in most of the areas excepting selected Taluqs of the *Suba* Districts,[103] had only further aggravated the situation by allowing a free hand for those reactionary and conservative forces and at the same time closing the channels of enlightenment from the outside to the much suppressed masses.

(*iv*) *Press and Freedom* : Freedom of the press and freedom of speech, writing and assembly that are capable of quickening the literary and intellectual faculties of the people, had, especially from 1929, been restricted considerably in the State. The slow but rising consciousness of the people in cultural, economic, social and political fields, which sprouted from the activities of Andhra *Jana Sangham* since 1921, made the Government apprehensive of the developing situation and led to the clamping of the draconian '*Ghasti* No. 53,' otherwise known as '*Kali Ghasti*',[104] in November, 1929.[105] Either for starting a printing press or a newspaper, prior permission of the Government had to be obtained which in majority of the cases, was rejected without assigning any reasons for doing so.[106] Persons of much respect and popular standing like Messrs. Hanumantha Rao, Vinayak Rao and Digambar Rao, all practising lawyers at the State High Court, were refused permission. The consequence of these stringent laws was that five weeklies were printed from outside the State by Hyderabad on totally Hyderabad affairs.[107] Once again, Urdu claimed its predominance both among dailies as well as periodicals that remained in circulation. During the quarter of 1941-42 to 1944-45, out of 29 total dailies, as many as 16 belonged to Urdu, all of which were printed in Hyderabad City, 4 to English and the remaining to other languages and out of 64 periodicals published in different languages of the State, Urdu claimed as many as 39 and English 14.[108] But, the more intriguing factor was that Government's financial aid was received in a large measure by some of the newspapers which consequently, came to serve as the mouth-pieces for official policies.[109] On the other hand, those papers that were not in the receipt of Governmental financial assistance and as a result, adopted an independent and even critical attitude on the actions and policies of the Government and more so, the excesses of the feudal and aristocratic elements, such as '*Prajasakti*',[110] and *Wagt*'[111] the former of Telugu and the latter of Urdu, had been prescribed.[112] Besides popular agitations being carried on for the removal of such clampings, the harmful effect that ensued out of this policy of discrimination and suppression adopted by the regime was that a fair and non-distorted picture of the affairs in the State could not be had from the newspapers and further non-official opinion or actions were given least prominence in their columns.[113]

Other media of public information such as the libraries, meetings and publications, had also received unequal treatment and restricted growth during the period. In State Library at Hyderabad, considered to be the biggest of its kind in the State, the collection of books in languages other than Urdu, was very much neglected.[114] Books in Telugu, Marathi and Kannada to the value of Rs. 20,000 had been sought for purchase to this Centre.[115] Condition of District Libraries was still worse. Whereas the Urdu Library at Karimnagar, known as the *Osmania Public Library* had been well provided with newspapers, staff and also Local Fund aid, the Telugu library at the same place known as Sri Osmania Andhra *Bhasha Nilayam*, on the other hand, was in such a poor condition that neither there was Local Fund aid nor the supply of newspapers which, ultimately, a private citizen of the town by gathering subscriptions, could arrange in respect of two papers. But, these efforts by one gentleman could hardly suffice the needs of this unit.[116] The former type which proved the better of the two, were hardly existent in Adilabad District and numbered mere one in Karimnagar District and three in Warangal District.[117] Even in the books printed and published also, those of Urdu figured so prominently out of proportion to those of other languages that, during 1941-42 to 1944-45, the former accounted for as many as 278, as against only 36 in Telugu, 30 in Marathi, 24 in English, 10 in Hindi and one in Gujarati.[118] It would be interesting to note in this connection that those who spoke the former language formed only 10.35% of the total population in the State as against 89.65% in the case of the latter put together.[119]

Circular No. 53 which forbade the holding of meetings without prior permission of the higher authorities who were required even to approve the meeting agenda, was aimed at severely restricting this type of activity on the part of students and party leaders.[120] The mass educative value inherent in the free exercise of this right, has been lost to a considerable measure, on account of this restriction imposed. Further, the full import of the reformatory steps that the Government undertook in administrative, economic and social fields since the clamping of the order, could not be brought home well to the people, due to the operation of the same difficulty. The implementation of the *Tenancy Act, the Bhagela Agreements Regulation Act, the Money Lenders' Act, the Debt Conciliation Act*, etc. had all testified to this.[121] But, the fear of the assertion of democratic values and forces loomed large in the minds of the authorities than those weighty considerations, in consequence of which, representations and demonstrations by all the parties in the State excepting one,[122] for the restoration of the freedoms of people in this regard, went unheeded, though not ineffective.

B. PUBLIC HEALTH ORGANISATION : Organisation of Public Health which remained essentially curative than preventive, remained during the period primarily confined to District and Taluq headquarter towns. Even among these, as could be seen from *Table LVIII*,[123] the former, with the exception of Warangal, were provided with two bigger establishments or hospitals and the latter, with the lone exception of Pakhal, had been, as in 1936, equipped with only one smaller unit or a dispensary. The latter with a meagre staff, medicines and with beds not exceeding ten in number for both men and women, was hardly expected to meet even a semblance of the health and medical requirements of a population spread over, on an average, as many as 206 villages in the *Suba*.[124] Even if the State as a whole was taken into consideration, the situation for the vast rural population was not at all encouraging in the sense that, as late as 1951, one hospital or dispensary existed for every 338 sq. miles, meant to serve as many as 76,770 persons.[125] The backwardness of this position could be judged from the fact that in Mysore State, another princely territory to the South, even in 1935, there was one such institution for every 94 sq. miles of area and 20,653 persons.[126] The little interest that the Government showed towards this welfare

TABLE LVIII

Number of Hospitals and Dispensaries, Beds and Patients Treated and Died, 1331-1345 Fasli (1922-36)

Sl. No.	Taluqs and District		Number of hospitals and dispensaries	Number of beds available		Total Number of Patients treated	
				Men	Women	Indoor	Outdoor
1		2	3	4	5	6	7
1.	Warangal	Taluq	3	46	16	957	59,906
2.	Mahaboobabad	,,	1	1	1	45	13,600
3.	Khammam	,,	1	4	2	103	22,349
4.	Madhira	,,	1	1	1	35	8,758
5.	Yellandu	,,	—	—	—	—	—
6.	Pakhal	,,	2	5	5	53	34,884
7.	Mulug	,,	1	1	1	44	8,039
8.	Palvancha	,,	1	4	4	86	10,124
9.	Palvancha (*Samasthan*)	,,	—	—	—	—	—
10.	Total of Warangal District for 1345 Fasli (1936)		10	62	30	1,323	1,57,660
11.	-Do- for 1340 Fasli (1931)		11	30	18	773	1,17,528
12.	-Do- for 1335 Fasli (1926)		11	23	2	288	90,380
13.	-Do- for 1331 Fasli (1922)		8	15	3	199	76,962
14.	Karimnagar	Taluq	2	8	4	—	—
15.	Jagtiyal	,,	1	5	1	—	—
16.	Sultanabad	,,	1	2	—	—	—

17.	Sirsilla	,	1	4	4	—	—
18.	Huzurabad	,,	1	3	3	—	—
19.	Parkal	,,	1	4	4	—	—
20.	Mahadecpur	,,	1	1	1	—	—
21.	Total of Karimnagar District for 1345 Fasli (1936)		8	27	17	—	—
22.	-Do- for 1340 Fasli (1931)		8	11	7	—	—
23.	-Do- for 1335 Fasli (1926)		8	15	6	—	—
24.	-Do- for 1331 Fasli (1922)		5	10	3	—	—
25.	Adilabad	Taluq	2	2	2	47	15,307
26.	Asifabad	,	1	4	4	118	12,642
27.	Rajura	,,	1	2	1	17	10,784
28.	Chinnoor	,,	1	—	—	—	11,291
29.	Luxettipet	,,	1	4	4	11	6,760
30.	Sirpur	,,	1	2	1	11	5,866
31.	Utnoor	,,	1	1	1	6	4,245
32.	Nirmal	,,	1	4	4	74	20,367
33.	Boath	,,	1	2	2	24	6,284
34.	Kinwat	,,	1	1	1	5	9,675
35.	Yelgadap *Paigah*		—	—	—	—	—
36.	Total of Adilabad District for 1345 Fasli (1936)		11	22	20	316	1,03,221
37.	-Do- for 1340 Fasli (1931)		12	13	8	186	68,691
38.	-Do- for 1335 Fasli (1926)		12	12	7	104	38,858
39.	-Do- for 1331 Fasli (1922)		8	11	5	116	43,253

Sl. No.	Taluqs and District		Daily average of in-patients treated	Daily average of out-patients treated	Number of outdoor patients died during the year
			8	9	10
1.	Warangal	Taluq	—	—	51
2.	Mahaboobabad	,,	—	—	3
3.	Khammam	,,	—	—	2
4.	Madhira	,,	—	—	2
5.	Yellandu	,,	—	—	—
6.	Pakhal	,,	—	—	5
7.	Mulug	,,	—	—	4
8.	Palvancha	,,	—	—	6
9.	Palvancha (*Samasthan*)	,.	—	—	—
10.	Total of Warangal District for 1345 Fasli (1936)		—	—	73
11.	-Do- for 1340 Fasli (1931)		—	—	48
12.	-Do- for 1335 Fasli (1926)		—	—	17
13.	-Do- for 1331 Fasli (1922)		—	—	25
14.	Karimnagar	Taluq	9.76*	192.75*	
15.	Jagtiyal	,,	3.50	155.62	—
16.	Sultanabad	,,	1.07	48.81	—
17.	Sirsilla	,,	1.18	48.53	—
18.	Huzurabad	,,	1.00	59.05	—
19.	Parkal	,,	1.38	41.61	—
20.	Mahadeopur		0.65	56.45	—

21.	Total of Karimnagar District for 1345 Fasli (1936)		18.54	602.82	
22.	-Do- for 1340 Fasli (1931)		8.42	427.26	—
23.	-Do- for 1335 Fasli (1926)		5.54	288.22	—
24.	-Do- for 1331 Fasli (1922)		7.80	245.03	—
25.	Adilabad	Taluq	—	—	5
26.	Asifabad	,,	—	—	8
27.	Rajura	,,	—	—	4
28.	Chinnoor	,,	—	—	—
29.	Luxettipet	,,	—	—	—
30.	Sirpur	,,	—	—	1
31.	Utnoor	,,	—	—	—
32.	Nirmal	,,	—	—	7
33.	Boath	,,	—	—	3
34.	Kinwat	,,	—	—	2
35.	Yelgadap *Paigah*		—	—	—
36.	Total of Adilabad District for 1345 Fasli (1936)		—	—	30
37	-Do- for 1340 Fasli (1931)		—	—	16
38.	-Do- for 1335 Fasli (1926)		—	—	5
39.	-Do- for 1331 Fasli (1922)		—	—	6

* This data was given only in respect of Karimnagar District in whose case, on the other hand, information pertaining to Cols. 6, 7 & 10, was not given, unlike the other *Suba* Districts.

Source : H.E.H. the Nizam's Government, *Hyderabad District Gazetteers*, Tables Volumes, *1340 & 1345 Fasli (1931 & 1936) Warangal*, pp. 256-257 ; *Karimnagar*, pp. 256-257 & *Adilabad*, pp. 254-255.

activity was evident from the fact that its spending on this item as a percentage of total expenditure progressed from 3.46 in 1934-35 to only 3.55 in 1948-49, in other words, an increase of 0.9 over a period of 14 years.[127] Even the expenditure met from Local Fund Receipts formed only around 7%, 8% and 5% of the total expenditure made from this source in the case of Warangal, Karimnagar and Adilabad Districts respectively.[128]

The Administration of Public Health had also suffered from dual control. Whereas the Health Department exercised general supervision and control of the sanitary services, the actual administration was left in the hands of Revenue Officials consisting of First *Taluqdar* at the District level and Tahsildar at the Taluq level, who in turn, were assisted by District and Taluq Boards respectively, consisting of nominated non-official members, the District Health Officer of the rank of a Civil Surgeon, the Executive Engineer and also the Superintendent of Police.[129] A qualified Health Inspector was employed by each District Board who reported to it through the District Health Officer about the condition in the area.[130] This division of control that characterised the functioning of these bodies failed to ensure co-ordination in between, which resulted in the non-spending of a greater percentage of funds at their disposal, thereby marring the chances of rural development in its welfare aspects. Thus, in 1942 the various District Boards in the State had spent only Rs. 30,18,374/- against the funds available totalling Rs. 1,15,96,692/- and consequently, the unspent balance stood at as high as Rs. 85,78,588/-, the expenditure thereby forming only around 28% of the amount available.[131] Another organisational aspect that hindered the development in the health arena was that both Medical and Public Health Services, right from 1911, continued under the control of the Medical Department and only in February, 1947, the latter were given a separate status.[132] This affected in the sense that, as comparatively heavy expenditure was incurred on Public Health schemes which included well-sinking also, little remained in the medical cess budget of the Local Funds to be spent on the equally important wing of Medical Service.[133]

(*i*) *Condition in Non-Diwani Areas* : The independence that the non-*Diwani* areas enjoyed in the organisation of Health Services had, as in respect of education,[134] an impairing effect. *The Hyderabad Administration Report for 1950-51* reveals that out of 243 hospitals and dispensaries in the State, those in *Jagir* areas numbered only 45, the percentage of the latter to the former amounting to only 18.5.[135] The sparsity and under-development in respect of these institutions in non-*Diwani* areas could be well realised from the fact that as against this meagre percentage in respect of health institutions, their area and population accounted for as much as 66% and 64.28% respectively of the total area and population in the State.[136] Not only the health institutions remained scarce in these areas, but the administration there neither took any control over relief measures at the time of the outbreak of epidemics, nor atleast made arrangements for the supply of drinking water which is very much vital for public health.[137] Due to their inaction, there always stood the danger of infectious diseases spreading to *Diwani* areas which were interspersed with *Jagir* villages. The most unfortunate of it was that these feudal masters did not even relish the visiting of *Diwani* officers to arrange for relief in the distressed alienated villages.[138] It was right in consequence that the Royal Commission on *Jagir* Administration and Reform recommended though late in 1947, for the take over of the administration of these Services by the Government,[139] which of course, due to its known preference for aristocracy and the prevailing complexity of political and administrative conditions,[140] did not immediately act on it. The change, however, came with the inauguration of the new regime.[141]

(*ii*) *Incidence of Diseases and the Extent of Preventive and Relief Measures* : Plague, cholera, Small-pox, malaria, influenza fever, leprosy, tuberculosis, filaria and guinea-worm, formed the chief epidemic and endemic diseases that stalked the land. Poor and ill-ventilated houses, unswept streets, lack of proper drinking water facilities, water-logging in irrigated areas, heavy consumption of intoxicants and the custom of marrying among near and blood relations, had figured as some of the important factors that helped the prevalence of these afflictions. Among the non-epidemic diseases, the incidence of malaria had been the greatest among the *Suba* people. Though it did not often lead to the immediate death of the affected, it, on the other hand, resulted in sapping their vitality. The forest tracts of Mulug, Pakhal, Palvancha, Yellandu, Sultanabad, Mahadeopur, Boath, Kinwat, Utnoor and Adilabad[142] had been so full of thick and most uncleared woods that they became vast breeding grounds for mosquitoes, so much so that the *ayacut* areas of Ramappa, Pakhal, Laknavaram and Bhimghanpur remained largely unexploited for, neither the ryots nor the agricultural labourers ever willingly came forward to settle in these areas for fear of the dreaded scourage.[143] It was observed in *1929-30 Economic Enquiry* that not even a single family was free from this endemic disease in the Central and Northern parts of Warangal District.[144] Even in 1946-47, Reports indicated that these *Suba* areas did not remain free from this trouble[145] On the other hand, the preventive measures of removing cess pools of cleaning the drains in urban areas and providing for drainage system in irrigated areas, were poorly undertaken to the effect that even in such a big town and *Suba* headquarters like Warangal, no anti-malarial squads had been organised.[146] In fact, no town in the area had an efficient drainage system to provide against malarial breeding.[147] As against this all-pervading character of the menace, the medical arrangements provided by the Government had been so utterly inadequate that even at District headquarters hospital like that of Adilabad or Taluq headquarters like that of Utnoor, for months together Civil Surgeon or Medical Officer was not posted and there was no equipment to test parasites in the blood.[148] Consequently, Officers at these places, moved out, mostly to Hyderabad City, informing none, for treatment.[149] The dumb and innocent masses had no other go but to succumb to this demon disease.

Mosquito prevalence had also resulted in the attack of filariasis or swelled legs which incapacitated the people from actively carrying on their customary operations. This was widely prevalent in Karimnagar District,[150] for it enjoyed the highest amount of irrigation in the State and hence, the scope for water-logging and drainage accumulation was considerable. No curative measures on any considerable scale ever seem to have been undertaken by the Department and prevention also remained out of the question, as no serious and sincere efforts have been made either by the Irrigation Department or by the Local Boards for the organisation of a proper drainage system either in irrigated or urban areas.[151]

(*a*) *Leprosy, Tuberculosis and Gninea-Worm* : As many as 60,000 lepers were estimated to be existing in the State in 1931 and the alarming fact was that this number was more than ten times to what was recorded in the 1921 Census.[152] Once again, Karimnagar District which, during this period registered a record 96% increase from 50 lepers per every 100,000 of its population in 1921 to 96 per 100,000 of its population in 1931, ranked the highest in the State.[153] As a matter of fact, even in respect of other physical infirmities such as insanity, deafmuteness and blindness, this *Suba* District with 2,68,476 and 1,067 afflicted persons respectively—lepers standing at 612 and the total number of male and female persons afflicted being 2,423 in 1931 Census—stood first among all Districts in the State.[154] Warangal and Adilabad Districts, on the other hand, with a total number of 1,105 and 575 persons respectively—168 and 63 insane persons, 255 and 156 deaf-mutes, 525 and 268 blind persons and 157 and 88 lepers respectively—had accounted for only 45.64% and 23.73% respectively of the total number of infirm persons in Karimnagar District.[155] Greater amount of rice eating,[156] mal-nutrition, skin diseases like syphillis, joint family system[157] and marrying in the same branch for generations together, smoky housing and polluted water, had all become significant contributory factors in this regard. Leprosy was more prevalent among Muslims of poorer sort than among cultivators[158] and blindness occurred more in the case of women than men,[159] the former due to non-manual labour and shabby living conditions and the latter due to constant exposure to smoke in ill-ventilated dingy houses or huts. Though leprosy hospital established in 1916 by the Wesleyen Mission at Dichalli in Nizamabad District had grown into bigger dimensions with the support of the *Nizam* and the nobles[160], yet, besides distance involved, the facilities were not adequate for as many as 3,738 lepers in the State as per 1931 Census,[161] so much so that the Hyderabad State Minister for Public Health, expressed as late as October, 1950, his anxiety that news had been reaching him that the ugly-looking and dreaded disease had been increasing in different parts of the State.[162] The prevention of these infirmities proved not only a medical but also a social and economic problem in the sense that improvement in the standard of living, education and undertaking of public health measures on an independent and greater footing, became the essential pre-requisites for the removal of these maladies.[163] The *Suba* or State administrative machinery never rose to the occasion to tackle the problem on these basic fronts.

Tuberculosis or consumption prevailed both amongst the rich and the poor.[164] There was regular increase in the number of cases treated in Government hospitals and dispensaries to the effect that the cases of indoor patients treated rose from 866 in 1935 to 1,547 in 1939 and those of out-door patients treated increased from 6,890 in 1935 to 10,042 in the State, the respective increases working out to 98.52% and 45.31%.[165] The evils of smoking and drinking which were widely prevalent among all classes of people, the former even among boys of twelve years of age besides tobacco chewing by women and the latter among all peasant families including women,[166] contributed rather heavily for the onset of this disease. In possessing maximum number of liquor shops in the State, Warangal District occupied first place, whereas in toddy *Sendhi* shops, the second and third places in the State had come to be occupied by the former and Karimnagar District respectively.[167] No restraining influences worked on these corroding practices and it was but natural that the Hyderabad State Minister for Public Health, while expressing the inadequacy of medicines and equipment for treatment, stated in 1950 that this life-taking disease was increasing rapidly in different parts of the State and especially in Telangana.[168]

Guinea-worm, a parasitic disease was widely prevalent in Warangal among the *Suba* Districts. The former in 1931 had as many as 3,071 afflicted persons, as against 326 in Karimnagar and 308 in Adilabad Districts.[169] It is significant to note that 53.1% of the total affected persons represented agriculturist classes and 40.2% by beggars and vagrants.

In this latter class, there was a slight excess of females over males.[170] Lack of proteinous food and potable water unpolluted, must have aided in the occurrence of this endemic disease. As in the case of malaria, though there was no immediate danger to human life, this worm-sickness had resulted in crushing the vigour and vitality of the affected. No noticeable curative or preventive measures seem to have been taken in this regard.

(*b*) *Yaws* : This fever type disease known as 'Koya *rogam* or disease' was widely prevalent among the nomadic and aboriginal tribes such as Koyas, Gonds and Hill Reddis residing in the Taluqs of Palvancha and *Samasthan* Palvancha, jungle tracts known as *Kurvapatti* comprised in Madhira, Pakhal and Mulug Taluqs of Warangal District; Manthani, Jagtiyal and Parkal Taluqs of Karimnagar District and Utnoor and Luxettipet Taluqs of Adilabad District.[171] This special type of disease was stated to be existing among those tribesmen since 200 years, but it came to the official notice only in 1930.[172] As late as 1945, it was observed that in every four of five Reddi houses in Palvancha *Samasthan*[173], one adult was suffering from *yaws* and the number of children passing through the early stages of this disease was considerable.[174] This sickness had the effect of emaciating its victims in the initial stages and then, if not treated properly and timely, resulting in slow but sure death. Though this life-sucking disease yielded to arsenical preparation and Thiosarmine injections[175], the existence of hospitals in the affected areas was scarce such as those at Palvancha and Boorgampahad in Warangal District and further, even the medical service available to the tribal population at these few and far-away centres was found to be very much inadequate.[176] The functioning of touring dispensaries such as the latter one, had suffered whenever river Godavari was in floods, for good number of tribal villages lay on its left bank.[177] Above all, the illiteracy and the ignorance of the tribals made them most often to seek their country and quack remedies rather than utilize the distant and the inadequate medical aid that was extended to them. The great prevalance of this disease and the meagre facilities available for its treatment in the *Suba* Districts and especially in the tribal belt, had considerable bearing on the economic fortunes of the tribal population which formed as much as 14.07% and 15.24% of the total population in Warangal and Adilabad Districts respectively.[178]

(*c*) *Epidemic Diseases* : In no decade during the period, were the *Suba* Districts free from the attack of the known eipidemic diseases of plague, cholera and small-pox, the former occasioned by an acute infection of the blood by a bacillus which was usually introduced by the rat-flea and the two latter by contaminated water and food-stuffs, done largely through the agency of flies.[179] The huge breeding of rats in grain godowns owned by big landlords and businessmen[180] and the fact that in majrity of the villages people drank tank water which got dirty and polluted, for they also washed their clothes, cleaned the utensils and also their domesticated animals in the same source, and people with guinea-worm and other skin diseases freely used tanks as well as wells, for the latter had mostly steps rather than walled circular structures, had served as significant sources for contamination and pollution.[181] The usual unswept streets in villages and the lack of a good drainage system even in a major Municipality like Warangal,[182] had led to accumulation of dirt and filth which in turn, bred flies and mosquitoes.[183] The periodical famines caused by either less or heavy rains, coupled with the out-break of epidemics, had resulted in utter devastation of the health condition of the people, as was witnessed during the decade of 1911-21.[184] The arrival of increasing number of immigrants from British Indian Provinces since 1946, due to the reasons other than economic, but neither vaccinated nor inoculated, into the *Suba* towns such as Warangal, had also contributed for the spread of cholera and other epidemics in the area.[185] As it is also the fact that only one vaccinator for a Taluq as against 13 in Hyderabad City and that too only since 1922, had been appointed to carry on the preventive work in an average of 206 villages,[186] and further, the fact that cholera inoculation medicine tubes were not there at District Headquarters hospital of Adilabad, at a time when in 1945 the epidemic had already claimed the lives of more than 250 people and the rest of the population eagerly clamoured for preventive inoculation, but dejectedly turned back on the score of no medicine[187], very well go to show the poor attention paid by the Department to this most vital and preventive health measure.

These epidemics, together with influenza and malarial fevers and also coinciding with unfavourable crop conditions and the out-break of the First Great War, had extracted the most unprecedented and heavy toll of human life during the first decade of the period. It was an unfortunate and strange coincidence that the plague epidemic entered the State Capital in August, 1911, which witnessed the inauguration of the reign of the last *Nizam.*[188] During the year as many as 27,367 persons fell victims to this disease, out of whom 183, 131 and 67 were from Karimnagar, Warangal and Adilabad Districts respectively.[189] It was still more in virulent form in 1916-17 when it had claimed 50,000 lives in the Dominions and still more deadly had been the influenza and malaria in the successive and respective years of 1918-19 and 1919-20, when they had claimed the record number of 3,50,000 and 80,000 lives in the State.[190] The effect of these disasters was so telling that the natural population [191] of Karimnagar District between 1911-21 showed a decrease of 5.7%, though of course, Warangal and Adilabad Districts showed increases of 5.0% and 8.2% respectively,[192] but these appear slight when compared to the growth percentages of the respective Districts that obtained during the next decade 1921-31 which was fairly free from such severe epidemics, standing at 20.8 and 16.2.[193] The incidence of these diseases during the decade 1921-31 was not insignificant in the sense that cholera alone claimed 42, 048 deaths in the State.[194] During the next decennium of 1931-41, small pox, plague and cholera, along with malaria had not only been regular visitants, but had also hit the population severely in particular years. Thus, small pox in 1935 proved so widespread that it caused 18,549 deaths ; [195] Similarly, plague in 1933 and 1934, claimed 11,038 and 14,529 lives respectively in the State [196] and the mortality due to cholera out-break in the State rose from 4,291 persons in 1938 to 16,335 in 1940.[197] The significance of the particulars as furnished by the Public Health Department for the period 6-10-1940 to 31-3-1951, could be realised from *Table LIX.*

TABLE LIX

Epidemic Diseases and Mortality, 1940-51

Sl. No.	District/State	Cholera		Plague		Small-Pox		TOTAL	
		Attacks	Deaths	Attacks	Deaths	Attacks	Deaths	Attacks	Deaths
1	2	3	4	5	6	7	8	9	10
1.	Hyderabad State	1,28,001	66,653	59,050	31,999	70,758	18,613	2,57,809	1,17,265
2.	Warangal District	—	—	—	—	—	—	17,116	6,384
3.	Karimnagar ,,	—	—	—	—	—	—	12,541	4,108
4.	Adilabad ,,	—	—	—	—	—	—	14,011	5,918

Source : *1951 Census, Hyderabad State*, Part I-A, *Report*, p. 39.

Though the incidence figures of the last decade looked in toto, somewhat lesser than the previous one, yet the number of deaths inflicted by each disease and the ratio of the former to the number of attacks were not insignificant. In the case of individual diseases, the latter worked out to around more than 50% in respect of cholera and plague and less than 25% in the case of smallpox.[198] On the other hand, if the three diseases were considered together, the ratios naturally stood less, working out to 45.48% in respect of the State and 37.29, 32.75 and 42.23% in case of Warangal, Karimnagar and Adilabad Districts respectively.[199] It could be observed that whereas the incidence was at a lower rate in the *Suba* Districts when compared to that of the State, on the other hand, within the *Suba*, Adilabad and Warangal Districts, because of the greater exposure of their predominantly tribal population to the epidemic ravages, had experienced higher rates when compared to that of Karimnagar District.[200]

Epidemics had thus been regular visitants during the period, but the efforts made to meet or prevent them had neither been prompt nor effective. Shortage in technical personnel, equipment and medicines had considerably affected the functioning of the health units.[201] The deficiency was such that even the District and Taluq headquarters hospitals remained for months together without their Chief Medical Officers[202] and the inoculation or the vaccination tubes could not be had even when the epidemics had been taking a heavy toll.[203] The arrangements in *Jagir* areas suffered still further in these respects.[204] More than these shortcomings the lack of improvement in the sanitary condition of the people, either the drinking water facilities or the street cleanliness and the drainage system[205] formed the essential reasons for the persistence of these ravages. Even the Municipalities of bigger towns such as Warangal,[206] Khammam,[207] and Mahboobabad[208] failed to ensure satisfactory conditions in this regard. Besides the conservatism of the rural population in hesitating to utilize the meagre preventive facilities that were made available, the lack of proper means of transport connecting the interior villages with the District of Taluq headquarters had, to a great extent, impaired the quick and fair enforcement of the preventive as well as the curative measures of the Department in the needy and the affected areas.[209]

(*iii*) *Mal-nutrition and its Effect on the Health Condition of the People* : The health condition of the people and also their working capacity, depended basically on the type of the food that was consumed by them in their daily life. It mainly consisted of jawar and bajra whose flour was essentially used in the preparation of cakes and then rice, in a smaller measure. The latter was, of course, used as essential food and also wheat, by the upper and well-to-do sections. But, as it could be seen from *Table IX*,[210] the consumption of these cereals by the people in the State was 71.42% more than what is required in a balanced diet as recommended by experts.[211] As against this, the proportion in all other items of diet was dismally low in the State as compared to the requirements of a proper diet. Pulses and vegetables were used by the peasants only to the extent and if they were grown in their fields, which received only least attention in preference to the cultivation of foodgrains.[212] In respect of milk and its products which, next to cereals formed the most important item in balanced diet, the consumption in the State was very much negligible,[213] thereby causing greatest deficiency in the proteinous character of the food. This position was very much unfortunate, if the fact was taken into consideration that Warangal, Karimnagar and Adilabad Districts occupied first, second and fourth places respectively in the possession of milch cattle in the State.[214] Not only the milk yield was less due to poor feeding and inferior breeding,[215] but even almost the entire quantity that was obtained was converted into curds to extract ghee out of it, whose sale acted as one of the subsidiary sources of income to the rural population. Majority of the lower sections of the population got contented with consuming butter milk only.[216]

The consumption of fruits, being considered very much a luxurious item for the means of an average villager, almost totally was non-existent in the daily diet of the people at large.[217] Eating of meat and fish was also, in the rural area, resorted mostly on festival and ceremonious occasions rather

TABLE LX

Balanced Diet and its Composition in Hyderabad State

(In ounces)

Sl. No.	Food items	Composition of a balanced diet	Diet composition in Hyderabad State
1	2	3	4
1.	Cereals	14	24
2.	Pulses	3	0.5 to 1
3.	Green leafy vegetables	4	Small quality
4.	Non-leafy vegetables	6	0.5 to 1
5.	Fruits	3	Almost Nil
6.	Sugar and jaggery	2	Small quantity
7.	Vegetable oil or ghee	2	0.5
8.	Milk and milk products	10	Negligible
9.	Fish and meat	2	0.5
10.	Egg	1	

Source : A.I. Qureshi : *The Economic Development of Hyderabad*, Vol. I, (Madras, 1947), pp. 342-343.

than as a daily or even a monthly item of food. Compared to pulses and vegetables, this was considered as a dearer item and moreover, it could be had only when some one had cut a goat in the village for some purpose or the other. Though the *Suba* Districts, especially Karimnagar and Warangal predominated in the State in respect of keeping of poultry birds,[218] yet, the local people mostly resorted to the sale of eggs and chicks rather than use them for family consumption. Sugar, jaggery and vegetable oil also, though locally manufactured to some extent, did figure very little in the food consumption of the people, for their cost proved prohibitive for the common man's purse and hence, their purchase was dispensed with, except on festive or special occasions.[219]

The daily diet of the people thus, in the *Suba* as well as the State, was highly mal-nutritious and defective in the sense that it lacked animal proteins, fats, calcium and A & C vitamins. It came to be too much dominated by cereals and the lack of variety was compensated by the consumption of a high quality of condiments like chillies and also salt.[220] The non-consumption of protective foods like milk, fruits, eggs, fish and meat, even to a reasonable extent, made the people physically deficient and less resistant to the diseases that infected. The fact that both the different epidemic and endemic diseases haunted the land throughout the period, at times in a demon-like form, to which the hapless people succumbed everytime in their thousands, was due in not an inconsiderable measure, to the unsatisfactory physical and the consequent health condition of the people.

C. *URBAN DEVELOPMENT*

Urban population in 1911 formed only 8.10, and 4.80 and 3.89% of the total population in Warangal, Karimnagar and Adilabad Districts respectively. Also in the *Suba* taken as a whole, it accounted for only 5.71% as against 19.05% in the State as a whole.[221] The number of towns in the same year whose population stood above the minimum limit of 5,000, remained respectively at 5, 7 and 3 in Warangal, Karimnagar and Adilabad Districts as against 85 in the State.[222] Even these few urban areas were concentrated in particular headquarter spots like Warangal Proper which, within a radius of 3 or 4 km. had encompassed the three towns of Hanamkonda, Urus-Karimabad and Warangal Fort, out of the total five in the District.[223] Besides being the *Suba*, District and Taluq headquarters, the agglomeration contained two railway stations, one being an important junction on the North-South line,[224] the large Azam Jahi Textile Mill, Carpet Industry, Wool, Skin and Hides Factories, a big and Regulated Grain Market, number of oil and rice mills and above all, the urban amenities of electricity, protected water supply and drainage. This was an indication that urbanisation or urban development proceeded in the area, as in other parts of the country, along the lines of administrative, transport, industrial and trade development.[226] These developmental factors, as traced before,[227] had been less marked in Adilabad District and further less in the other *Suba* District of Karimnagar, which got amply reflected in the fact that, the number of urban residents per mile of the total population as late as in 1951, accounted in them respectively, only to 68.68 and 46.70% of what had obtained in the case of the premier District of Warangal.[228]

On the other hand, it could be observed from *Table LXI* that the number of towns, except in 1921, had always figured more in Karimnagar District than either in Warangal or Adilabad Districts. This was due to the fact that the former, though deficient in respect of prevalence of large-scale industries or rail facilities, came out more than compensated by the predominant adoption of cottage and home industries such as handloom spinning and weaving, carpentry, brick and tiles making, pottery and poultry in consequence of which it recorded the highest percentage in the State, of people who earned their livelihood by means of industrial occupation.[229] It is equally significant to note in this connection that except in 1931, the average population per town was approximately 40 to 50 per cent less in this District than that of Warangal and even that of Adilabad in 1921 and 1941, though not in other Census years.[230] Out of 13 towns in Karimnagar District, none excepting Karimnagar, Jagtiyal and Peddapalli had ever until 1941, crossed or even reached the 10,000 margin of persons. Even among these three towns also, the first one obtained this level only in the third decade and the latter in the fourth.[231] In contrast, this mark was far exceeded by the Warangal combine and the coal town of Yellandu right from the first decade and by Khammam town from the second decade.[232] Adilabad District in this respect, stood none the better than Karimnagar District in the sense that, only Nirmal town from 1931 and Adilabad town from only 1941 could reach this population mark.

TABLE LXI

Growth of Towns and Urban Population, 1911-1951

Sl. No.	District/Region	Number of towns					Urban Population			
		191_	1921	1931	1941	1951	1911	1921	1931	1941
1	2	3	4	5	6	7	8	9	10	11
1	Warangal District	5	6	7	11	14	73,373	81,261	1,17,579	1,78,018
2.	Karimnagar ,,	7	6	11	13	15	54,418	43,142	82,818	1,09,495
3.	Adilabad ,,	3	3	9	4	13	24,137	22,433	48,084	40,290
4.	Warangal Suba*	15	15	27	28	42	1,51,928	1,46,836	2,48,481	27,803
5.	Telangana Region	—	—	—	—	—	—	—	9,96,262	13,84,251
6.	Hyderabad State	85	89	133	138	240	12,95,305	11,87,297	16,16,981	21,94,294

Sl. No.	District/Region	Average Population per town in					Number of persons Per mile residing in towns			
		1951	1921	1931	1941	1951	1921	1931	1941	1951
		12	13	14	15	16	17	18	19	20
1.	Warangal District	2,88,395	13,549	6,797	16,183	20,600	88	105	134	182
2.	Karimnagar ,,	1,34,323	7,190	7,529	9,115	8,955	39	67	81	85
3.	Adilabad ,,	1,13,105	7,477	5,343	10,072	8,700	35	63	49	125
4.	Warangal Suba*	5,35,823	9,789	9,203	11,350	12,751	55	78	88	130
5.	Telangana Region	21,28,490	20,226	—	—	15,790	104	—	—	—
6.	Hyderabad State	34,76,159	13,340	12,158	15,900	14,484	95	112	135	186

*The Figures given in Col. Nos. 5, 6 & 7 and those from Cols. 10 to 14 and from 18 to 20 are not given in the source material. Hence the average of the District figures was calculated and put.

...Information lacking.

Source : *Census of India, Hyderabad State*, Part II, *1911*, pp. 2 & 3 ; *1921*, pp. 2 & 49 ; *1931*, pp. 2 & 58 ; *1941*, pp. 2 & 16 and *1951*, p. 4, Part I-A, p. 229 and Part I-B, pp. 66 & 68.

In spite of serving as District and also Taluq headquarters, the latter, due to the backward conditions that prevailed, could thus show only poor and delayed population growth.

(*i*) *Growth of Towns* : Among all the 42 towns that came to exist in the *Suba* by 1951, the historic city of Warangal right throughout the period,[234] registered record growth. The percentage increase in its population which, excepting 3,524 of its inhabitants belonged to municipal area, stood successively at 33%, 49% and 43% during 1921-31, 1931-41 and 1941-51 respectively.[235] In spite of the slight decrease during 1911-21,[236] its population the 40 year period progressed so tremendously from 35,627 persons in 1911[237] to 1,33,130 persons in 1951[238] that, the overall increase amounted to 301.74%.[239] The varied factors that contributed for this appreciable regular rise had already been narrated.[240] Khammam, which besides being Taluq headquarters, gained prominence as an important trading and industrial centre in the District as well as the State, also accounted for sizable growth which during the 50 years ending in 1951 amounted to 224 per cent.[241] The coal town of Yellandu, on the other hand, though showed considerable increase in its poulation level in the first and second decades, suffered decline at an increasing pace during the succeeding dscades.[242] The changes in this case, had been very much influenced by the differing trends of coal production that obtained at this centre,[243] which got amply reflected in the fact that with the closure of the Mines in 1941 due to exhaustion,[244] this town which had been enjoying the status of a Municipality,[245] was brought down to that of a non-Municipality.[246] Karimnagar, Jagtiyal, Nirmal, Adilabad, Paddapalli and Kothagudem figured as other prominent urban areas in the *Suba* Districts.[247] the contributary factors being administrative and industrial, though mostly of cottage and textile character in the case of the first four towns, business and rail transport in respect of the fifth and increasing coal production since 1938 in respect of the last one.[248] The lack of any large-scale industries excepting in the last-named town, rail transport facilities excepting in the latter three and big trading activity except in the case of the fifth, acted as big retarding forces in the growth of these towns as prominent and flourishing urban centres.[249]

On the other extreme, the conditions had been so poor and backward that even by 1931, Asifabad, Rajura, Luxettipet Sirpur, Boath and Kinwat. in spite of being Taluq head-quarters. failed to reach even the minimum population limit of 5,000 persons.[250] But, yet, all of them, located in Adilabad District, had been given not only the status and recognition as towns, but were also endowed with municipal organisation.[251] These forest-ridden and malaria-infested areas had been so sparsely populated that their densities per square mile even in 1951, ranged from less than 100 in the case of Rajura to less than 150 in the case of the remaining, in consequence of which the District, throughout the period had the distinction of recording the lowest density in the State.[252] Besides these disadvantageous factors, the poor means of road and rail transport in these areas, which was far short of the minimum that was required for the overall economic development,[253] has put a great snag in the growth of these towns, for except Sirpur[254] which was on the main North-South rail line, others in spite of vast natural and mineral resources,[255] failed to attract during the period, either the establishment of any large-scale industries other than coal mining or the development of trade centres in any of them.

The condition of *Jagir* ahd *Samasthan* towns remained far worse in respect of this growth aspect. During the successive decades of 1921-31 and 1931-41 for which only the figures are available. the *Samasthan* town of Palvancha in Warangal District and Dharmapuri, the *Jagir* town in Karimnagar District registered such meagre population growths that amounted respectively to 30.32%, 4.93% and 8.95% and 0.72%.[256] Vemalwada, an independent *Jagir* and pilgrim town in the latter District,[257] it is distressing to note, experi-enced during the 30 year period of 1911-41, a 17.77% decrease in its population,[258] Even Paddapalli, also an exempted *Jagir* and a leading business and rail centre in the same District,[259] could only obtain 47.80% increase during this tri-cennium which appears trifle when compared to 160.49% and 108.20% obtained respectively during the same period, by the *Khalsa* towns of Warangal (City) and Khammam in the neighbouring *Suba* District of Warangal.[260] The utter neglect of the associate factors of development, such as those of industries, transport and trade, besides poor agricultural conditions, was primarily responsible for this highly inadequate growth of the urban areas in Non-*Diwani* lands.[261] Further, these got so scarcely distributed in the *Suba* area and in fact, in the State that in 1941, Warangal District contained 2 *Samasthan*, 1 *Sarf-i-khas*, 1 *Jagir* town, Karimnagar District 4 *Jagir* towns and Adilabad District none.[262] The *Suba* Districts taken as a whole, these towns formed only 28.57 per cent of the number contained in *Diwani* areas as against however, 25.84 per cent obtained in respect of the State in 1921.[263] Out of these few again, the town status was obtained by 2 in 1911, 1 in 1921, 2 in 1931,3 in 1941, which unmistakably points to the torrid urbanisation in the area.[264]. Its value was least realised by the feudal overlords who took no pains to promote the requisite conditions.[265]

(*ii*) *Municipalities and Town Life* : Until 1929, there remained in the State only one budget for the rural and urban areas of the districts, the result of which was that greater spending was made by the District headquarters at the expense of the former.[266] *The Revenue Administration Report of 1914-15* states that in as many as 8 out 15 Districts in the State including Warangal and Karimnagar, more than 50 per cent of the Local Fund expenditure was incurred at the respective District headquarters towns. The respective percentages of the *Suba* Districts cited were 54.17 and 70.65, the latter standing second highest among all Districts, first being Medak District with 91.34 per cent.[267] It was observed that, even after 1921, finding the taxes collected from the Warangal town citizens inadequate, the hard-collected tax amount from the ryots in the villages to the extent of Rs. 24,000/- per year had been utilized for spending at the headquarters.[268] This unequal and unjust utilisation was in a way added by the filling up of almost all the non-Official members of the District and Taluq Boards by those residing invariably in headquarter towns.[269] The neglect of rural health, education and other welfare activities in the area, could well be understood under these circumstances.[270] The other *Suba* District of Adilabad, on the other hand, stood a contrast in this respect. With only 12.75 per cent expediture of the Local Funds at District headquarters and as much as 87.25 per cent in respect of the Taluqs, it occupied the second place in the State in this manner of spending, first being of course, Nalgonda District with 12.49 per cent and 87.51 per cent[271] respectively. The lack of any special grounds of preference for Adilabad, the headquarters town, either on trade industrial or even administrative factors, has to a considerable extent influenced this differential trend in expenditure. Due to the prevalence of unsatisfactory conditions or amenities here, the Officials that were obliged to serve treated it, even in the late forties, very much as a sort of punishment and hence bade their time.[272]

It was only in 1935 that separate Municipal Committees apart from Local Boards, had been brought into being for the administration of bigger and smaller towns.[273] Warangal was one of the 8 major Municipalities created in this year, each Committee consisting of 5 Official members and from 9 to 15 non-official members, depending on the population of the town.[274] The process of extending such bodies to other towns in the *Suba* Districts went on considerably slow to the effect that by 1941-42, only Khammamet and Karimnagar had been further equipped so.[275] These major Municipalities had generally been set up only in towns whose population exceeded the limit of 15,000 persons.[276] In towns of lesser size that had inhabitants exceeding 5,000 such as Mahaboobabad in Warangal District, Manthani and Koratla in Karimnagar District, Nirmal, Adilabad and Chinnoor in Adilabad District,[277] the town Committee functions had come to be discharged by the District Board in case of a District headquarter town and Taluq boards in respect of Taluq headquarter and also other towns.[278] Taluq headquarter towns of Asifabad, Rajura, Luxettipet, Sirpur, Boath and Kinwat, all in Adilabad District, had been provided with such Committees, during the third decade, even though their population stood below the 5,000 mark,[279] but however, this arrangement appeared temporary for it was discontinued in 1941.[280] Giving the margin for the periodical inclusions and exclusions that were effected, the number of both major and minor Municipalities put together in the *Suba* during the 30 year period of 1911-1941 for which only the Census data is available, proceeded inexorably tardily from 7 to 10, the towns being Warangal (City), Khammamet and Mahaboobabad in Warangal District, Karimnagar, Jagtiyal Manthani and Koratla in Karimnagar District, Nirmal, Adilabad and Chinnoor in Adilabad District.[281]

Municipalities in the *Suba* area were not only scarcely distributed, but the services provided by them to the urban population during the period, proved equally inadequate and wanting. Water supply arrangements were completed only in Warangal City towards the end of the thirties,[282] and the same in other towns lagged far behind. In Khammam, which ranked in importance next only to the former, and where drinking water problem was experienced by the residents, especially during summer and due to greater prevalence of saltish water,[283] water supply system was put into commission as late as 25th October, 1949.[284] In Adilabad, the District headquarters town, this work was taken up in 1940-41,[285] but had not yet reached its completion by the end of December, 1943,[286] Regarding the other civic amenities of drainage, lighting and internal roads, the condition was far more disappointing in almost all the Municipal towns, including Hanamkonda, the *Suba* headquarters. The surface drainage laid in the latter was not subjected to cleaning even once in a month, resulting in stagnation and mosquito breeding.[287] In lesser towns like Mahaboobabad, there was not even this system and the rubbish and filth was found in heaps at each and every spot.[288] Municipal workers even in bigger Municipal towns like Warangal and Karimnagar were not only insufficient in number to take up cleaning work in its entirety, but good number of them were utilised for work at Officers' residences instead of the former.[289] Thus, in Karimnagar Municipality where 25 women and 20 men workers were engaged to look after the sanitary needs of a 20,000 population in 1945, 7 worked at First *Taluqdar's* house, 3 at *Motemad* (Superintendent), Local Fund's residence and 1 at Sanitary Inspector's and punishments ranging from salary cut to beating were effected for refusal of failure in this regard.[290] Further, the meagre wages that were paid to Municipal workers which ranged from Rs. 8 to 16 p.m. and the consequent resorting to strikes of the former, the prevalence of the grades system[291] among them on account of which young workers preferred to join in other professions and the reluctance of the private owners to hire carts for the removal of garbage on account of the poor charges that were paid, had all been the factors that further hindered the sanitary work in the towns.[292]

Maintenance of roads in Khammam town was stated to be in such a worst condition that passage on either during the rainy season or summer, turned out to be an unpleasant task.[293] Dust accumulation and its non-removal was complained regarding the roads in Hanamkonda town.[294] Failure to repair the roads in Yellandu, the coal town and Taluq headquarters in Warangal District, even after a period of six years, reduced them to such a miserable state that even carts and other traffic found it extremely difficult to pass through them.[295] Compared to District of Taluq Boards, the Municipalities spent three to four times less on road construction or repair[296] and further, compared to water works and other items of public utility, the latter, or to that matter the Local Bodies, expended approximately three to four times less on the former.[297] As power supply until 1950 was restricted only to Warangal town,[298] other towns in the *Suba* Districts were provided with street lamps whose number and functioning remained highly inadequate and unsatisfactory to the inhabitants.[299] The foregoing account of the Municipal conditions would thus go to show that, the provision of the basic amenities was least adequate and satisfactory and hence, town life did not prove that much happier as it should be or hoped for.

(*iii*) *Composition, Character and Functioning of Local Bodies* : Besides the Town Municipalities that have been dealt with in the foregoing sub-sections,[300] 3 District Boards, 24 Taluq Boards[301] and a few village Panchayats,[302] comprised the Local Government structure in the *Suba*. Whereas a District Board consisted of a president who was ex-officio the First *Taluqdar*, and 13 members, of whom 6 were Officials and 7 non-officials, a Taluq Board, on the other hand, consisted of 4 Officials and

4 non-officials and was presided by either the Tahsildar or the Second *Taluqdar*, depending on the nature of the headquarters where the Board sat.[303] These bodies very much functioned as unrepresentative and official-dominated organisations in the sense that, besides the Officer-president and members were also selected and nominated by the First *Taluqdar* from among the *Zamindars*, lawyers, big traders and merchants of the District who mostly resided in headquarter towns, for a period of every three years, subjected of course, to the approval of the Government in the Revenue Department.[304] The control of these bodies and even of District headquarter Municipalities and mofussil Town Committees, rested with District Collectors, who as ex-officio presidents and superior Officers over Second *Taluqdars* and Tahsildars, but subject however, to the supervision of the *Subedar* and the Local Fund Department of the the Government,[305] exercised dominating influence in their functioning.[306] Another factor which contributed for this situation was that the Local Bodies had few Officers of their own and in general, worked through the regular district establishment of the Government. This in turn, was not due to financial stringency as such, for the Local Fund Engineers that were latterly instituted at the District, Divisional and State levels, were paid from the funds of the Local Bodies, though appointed by the Government and were made subject to its control,[307] but more probably, due to lack of system and direction from the popular side. Even the Local Funds annual budget was prepared according to rules prescribed by the Government and was not valid until approved by the latter.[308]

The major source of income to Local Bodies, as could be seen from *Table LXIII*,[309] was the Local Fund or Cess amount, collected at the rate of one anna per rupee of land revenue.[310] Out af this, 7 pies share was enjoyed by the District Boards[311] that amounted to 58.33% and hence, a prosperous condition, especially when compared to Taluq Boards which received less than one paisa share each. The levy of house tax, lighting tax, water tax, *barbardari* toll.[312] market fees, vehicle tax,[313] profession tax, entertainment tax and tax on the transfer of immovable property, formed certain other forms of

TABLE LXII

Towns and Population Growth, 1911-1941

S. No.	Town	Description	District	Population in++ 1911	1921	1931	1941
1	2	3	4	5	6	7	8
1.	Warangal City	Municipality	Warangal*	5,542**	46,791	62.119	92,808
2.	Yellandu	,	,,	15,914	22,938	19,872	15,907**
3.	Khammam	,,	,,	9,117	11,532	13,002	18,982
4.	Hasanparthi	Non-Muncipality	,,	—	4,780	6,198	6,331
5.	Mahaboobabad	Municipality	,,	—	3,499	5,824	7,463
6.	Palvancha	*Samasthan*	,,	—	4,082	5,330	5,593
7.	Mandarpalli	,,	,,	—	4 492	5,234	55,069
8.	Kothagudem	Non-Municipality	,,	—	—	—	9,669
9.	Garla	Non-exempted *Jagir*	,,	—	—	—	5,848
10.	Zafargadh	*Sarf-i-khas*	,,	—	—	—	5,177
11.	Waimur	Non-Municipality	,,	—	—	—	5,177
12.	Jagtiyal	Municipality	Karimnagar	11,688	9,682	13,882	16,294
13.	Karimnagar	,,	,,	8,347	9,399	10,903	17,437

14.	Manthani	,,	,,	7,759	6,731	7,560	8,286
15.	Koratla	,,	,	6,068	6,004	6,996	8,161
16.	Vemalwada	Exempted *Jagir*	,,	8,075	5,986	7,645	6,640
17.	Peddapalli	,,	,,	7,260	5,340	8,945	10,731
18.	Huzurabad	Municipality	,,	—	4,534	6,251	8,161∴
19.	Sirsilla	,,	,,	—	4,360	5,752	6,836∴
20.	Dharmapuri	Non-exempted *Jagir*	,,	—	5,082	5,537	5,577
21.	Gambhiraopet	Non-Municipality	,	—	4,453	5,006	5,394
22.	Manakondur	,,	,,	—	4,302	4,341	5,500
23.	Metpalli	Exempted *Jagir*	,,	—	—	—	5,316
24.	Jammikunta	Non-municipality	,,	—	—	—	5,162
25.	Nirmal	Municipality	Adilabad	9,588	9,457	12 585	14,499
26.	Adilabad	,,	,,	7,560	7 271	8,096	11,128
27.	Chinnoor	,,	,,	6 989	5,705	7,751**	8,369
28.	Asifabad	,	,,	—	2 590	3,075	+
29.	Rajura	,	,,	—	—	2,968	+
30.	Luxettipet	,	,,	—	1,839	3,124	+
31.	Sirpur	,,	,,	—	2,965	3,877	+

32. Boath	,,	,	—	3,067	3,351	+
33. Kinwat	,,	,	—	2,970	3,257	—
34. Bellampalli	Non-Municipality	,,	—	—	—	6,294

*It comprised the four suburban and Municipal units of Mathwada (Municipal—20,998), Hanamkonda (Municipal—14,782) and Urus-Karimabad (*Jagir* and Suburban-5,589) and Warangal Fort (*Jagir* and Suburban-5,422) —1921 Census, Part II, *op. cit.*, p. 14

**Became a Non-Municipality—1941 Census, Tables Volume, *op. cit.*, pp. 50-51.

∴Classified as a Non-Municipality—1941 Census, Tables Volume, *op. cit.*, pp. 50-51 & 52-53.

+The figures were given only in those Census years when the places were made either towns or Municipalities and not otherwise.

***This figure which was given in *1931 Census*, Part II (pp. 10-13) referers to only that of Warangal Proper, for the other Municipal and suburban areas of Hanamkonda, Urus-Karimabad, and Warangal Fort which later (see f.n.*) got merged with the former into Warangal City, had not only each crossed the minimum town population limit of 5,000, but on the other hand, the increase itself recorded for the decade ending in 1911 in respect of Hanamkonda stood at 14,996 and Urus-Karimabad peopled to the extent of 7,173 in the same year. In view of these facts, the population of Warangal City of the future years would have been in 1911, around 40,000 persons—Refer to 1911 Census, Part I, *op. cit*, pp. 9-11.

. . Not referred as a Municipality—1931 Census, Part I, *op. cit.*, p. 60.

| Did not figure in enumeration either as Municipalities or towns—1941 Census, Part II, Tables volume, *op, cit.*, pp. 52-53

Source : *Census of India, Hyderabad State*, 1921, Part II, Imperial Tables, p. 14; 1931, Part I, p. 60 ; 1941 Tables volume, pp. 50-53. & Part II, pp. 10-13.

income to Local Bodies, next to Local Cess levy[314]. But, these brought only minor revenue to these units,[315] probably in view of their limited applicability in the different areas. Village Panchayats were, of course, given a grant equal to 15% of the land revenue of a particular village, from the State funds.[316] Though tax income to the Local Bodies was very much less, yet, at the same time, it was of much relief to the people that the incidence of taxation was only about 12 annas, whereas in 1929-30, excluding tolls, it was as high as Rs. 3 in a Municipal town of the Madras Presidency.[317] Non-tax revenue, which also except at District headquarters such as Warangal and Karimnagar, did not form a sizable source of income to the Local Bodies,[318] comprised mostly of fees, fines, rent and other miscellaneous items.[319] Though the running of commercial, transport and other undertakings on a commercial basis, was a source of considerable income to the Town Municipalities, no such efforts were made in the *Suba* nor in the State. Even the water works were not run on these lines and in most cases, they turned a liability rather than an asset or source of income to the Local Bodies.[320]

Great divergence had come to prevail between the levels of total income enjoyed by Local Government units comprised in the District headquarters Taluq and the forest-bound or the least populated Taluq in *Suba* District, excepting of course, Adilabad District. Thus, in 1936, whereas the Taluq of Warangal, Karimnagar and Nirmal had claimed respectively around 35 per cent, 31 per cent and 24 per cent of the total amounts pertaining to their Districts, the backward and the least populated Taluqs of Mulug, Mahadeopur and Utnoor in the same Districts could claim the pitiably low percentages of approximately 2, 5 and 2 respectively of their District total incomes.[321] It was not a surprise that, under the circumstances, the welfare services of education, health, water works, roads etc., were miserably let down in the latter by the Local Bodies.[322] Nirmal Taluq, because of its comparatively greater population and fertile lands, its timber resources[323] as well as its location on the Bangalore-Nagpur highway,[324] was able to receive nearly 2½ times more income than what Adilabad, the District headquarters Taluq could receive.[325] Further, it could also be seen from *Table LXIII*[326] that the income of the Local Bodies in the *Suba* Districts varied according to the changes in trade and price cycles, in the sense that compared to 1922 level, it showed considerable rise in 1926 and 1936 and decline, on the other hand, in the Depression and post-Depression years of 1931[327] and 1935. It is also significant to note regarding the financial position of these Bodies that in the State, no share as such, of revenue from specific taxes levied and collected by the Government was available to them, excepting the grant allowed to Village Panchayats.[328] Left to fend themselves, the Taluq Boards in the *Suba* with none excepting the one at the District headquarters or the District Board,[329] having an yearly income of Rs. 50,000 and some even having an income of less than Rs. 10,000 per year,[330] had been obviously in sound financial position at all, to execute the welfare and public utility activities among the people under their jurisdiction.

The expenditure pattern of the Local Bodies, as could be gleaned from *Table LXIII*, stood obviously very much linked with their income and balances position. The striking and rather unwholesome fact that appears is that the Boards relating to the District headquarters of Warangal, Karimnagar and Asifabad had shared such a huge proportion of the total Local Boards' expenditure in the concerned Districts that in 1936, it amounted to 74.43 per cent, 71.76 per cent and 39.67 per cent respectively.[331] The dominating influence and control of the First *Taluqdar* over these Bodies and the filling up of their non-official members from headquarters residents who very much represented vested interests,[332] could well be considered as significant factors that contributed towards this situation. Next to these District centres, spending on Welfare services and Civil works by the Local Bodies was considerable in those Taluqs where important Municipalities existed such as those of Khammam and Mahaboobabad in Warangal District, Jugtiyal in Karimnagar District and Nirmal and Chinnoor in Asifabad District.[333] The heartening effect of this unequal and disproportionately heavy expenditure in the former was that inexorably paltry amounts had been spent by other Taluq Boards on these nation-building services, to the effect that in 1936, Mulug in Warangal District spent Rs. 194 on education,

TABLE LXIII

Composition, Income and Expenditure of Taluq and District Local Boards, 1331-1345 Fasli (1922-36)

(In O.S. Rs)

S. No.	Taluqs & District		Number of Boards	Number of Members		Income	Excluding	Balance
				Officials	Non-Officials	From Local Fund	From rates and taxes	Other sources
1	2		3	4	5	6	7	8
1.	Warangal	Taluq	1	7	7	61,825	169	26,960
2.	Khammam	,,	1	4	4	43,209	20	587
3.	Mahaboobabad	,,	1	4	4	37,820	169	1,233
4.	Madhira	,,	1	4	4	33,960	280	289
5.	Yellandu	,,	1	4	4	14,917	309	535
6.	Mulug	,,	1	4	4	3,095	1,643	387
7.	Pakhal	,,	1	4	4	9,203	280	307
8.	Palvancha	,,	—	—	—	10,613	433	76
9.	Warangal District Total for 1345 Fasli (1936)		7	31	31	1,14,641	3,303	30,375

10.	-Do-for 1344 Fasli (1935)	7	31	31	2,15,699	—	5,225
11.	-Do-for 1340 Fasli (1931)	3	35	35	2,42,796	—	2,992
12.	-Do- for 1335 Fasli (1926)	8	35	35	2,02,869	—	53,027
13.	-Do- for 1331 Fasli (1922)	8	35	35	1,82,999	—	22,617
14.	Jagtiyal Taluq	1	5	3	34,434	312	2,677
15.	Sultanabad ,,	1	11	16	26,322	622	217
16.	Karimnagar	1	7	7	49,721	12	35,955
17.	Sirsilla ,,	1	10	11	42,098	37	162
18.	Huzurabad ,,	1	3	3	37,759	23	1,104
19.	Parkal ,,	1	5	4	28,511	16	161
20.	Mahadeopur ,,	1	3	4	12,077	441	86
21.	Karimnagar District Total for 1345 Fasli (1936)	7	44	48	2,30,958	1,463	40,373
22.	-Do- for 1344 Fasil (1935)	7	31	31	2,21,320	1 191	13,254
23.	-Do- for 1340 Fasli (1931)	7	31	31	2,27,770	909	42,152
24.	-Do- for 1335 Fasli (1926)	7	31	31	2,29,597	3,197	6,644
25.	-Do- for 1331 Fasli (1922)	7	31	31	1,99,913	1,928	6,908
26.	Adilabad Taluq	1	4	4	10,423	413	—
27.	Asifabad ,,	1	7	7	4,642	—	—
28.	Rajura ,,	1	4	4	12,632	1,575	285

29. Chinnoor	,,	1	4	4	11,935	1,196	—
30. Luxettipet	,,	1	4	4	11,184	889	—
31. Sirpur	,,	1	4	4	5,843	432	105
32. Utnoor	,,	1	4	4	1,935	—	278
33. Nirmal	,,	1	4	4	25,147	448	—
34. Boath	,,	1	4	4	5,295	—	36
35. Kinwat	,,	1	4	4	9,868	417	—
36. Adilabad District Total for 1345 Fasli (1936)		10	43	43	98,904	5,370	704
37. -Do- for 1344 Fasli (1935)		10	46	45	29,357	—	3,590
38. -Do- for 1340 Fasli (1931)		10	45	45	93,749	—	11,275
39. -Do- for 1335 Fasli (1926)		10	45	45	92,304	—	15,805
40. -Do- for 1331 Fasli (1922)		10	45	45	71,410	—	12,056

	Total	Expenditure Education	Civil Works	Sanitation & Hospital	Miscellaneous	Total
	9	10	11	12	13	14
1. Warangal Taluq	88,954	25,629	3,410	32,806	25	1,61,870
2. Khammam ,,	43,816	10,124	29,905	2,458	2,644	45,131
3. Mahaboobabad ,,	39,222	12,489	9,956	16	300	22,761
4. Madhira ,,	34,529	4,919	5,359	360	279	10,917
5. Yellandu ,,	15,761	2,943	8,685	240	—	11,868
6. Mulug ,,	5,125	194	653	—	—	847
7. Pakhal ,,	9,790	1,511	2,677	—	1,283	5,973
8. Palvancha ,,	11 122	5,275	4,598	1,734	993	12,660
9. Warangal District Total for 1345 Fasli (1936)	2,48 319	63,084	1,65,243	37,614	5,526	2,18,467

10. -Do- for 1344 Fasli (1935)	2,18,924	67,629	1,20,495	2,3,336	645	2,18,105
11. -Do- for 1340 Fasli (1931)	2,45,698	44,371	75,552	22,758	1,348	1,43,929
12. -Do- for 1335 Fasli (1926)	2,55,896	32,799	38,261	18.126	78,737	1,67,423
13. -Do- for 1331 Fasli (1229)	2,05,616	36,837	41,469	17,051	18,402	1,13,759
14. Jagtiyal Taluq	37,423	5,236	5,203	5,477	10,061	25.977
15. Sultanabad ,,	27,161	3,238	132	1,333	2,596	7,299
16. Karimnagar ,,	85,698	29,524	70,919	23,649	34,335	1,78,427
17. Sirsilla ,,	42,297	3'842	50	2,268	3,532	10,392
18. Huzurabad ,,	38,922	9,213	822	926	4,725	10,382
19. Parkal ,,	28,688	2,844	7	1,351	2,451	6,553
20. Mahadeopur ,,	12,605	1,735	627	1,790	5,450	9,602
21. Karimnagar District Total for 1345 Fasli (1936)	2,72,794	70,222	77,770	37,493	63,152	1,48,637
22. -Do- for 1344 Fasli (1935)	2,35,765	83,067	67,979	38,782	51,729	2,41,557
23. -Do- for 1344 Fasli (1931)	2,70,831	1,07,934	24,793	25,185	30,781	1,88,693
24. -Do- for 1335 Fasli (1926)	2,39,438	43,798	24,485	9,050	1,22,343	1,99,476
25. -Do- for 1331 Fasli (1922)	2,08,748	50,478	26,611	1,873	79,888	1,56,850
26. Adilabad Taluq	10,836	1,787	3,390	—	30	5,007
27. Asifabad ,,	4,642	978	25,101	3,586	450	00,115
28. Kajpura ,,	14,492	1,028	3,844	—	2,487	7,359
29. Chinnor ,,	13,131	3,147	2,215	1,657	280	6,399
30. Luxettipet ,,	12,074	3,243	3,079	—	24	6,346
31. Sirpur ,,	6,380	1.566	2,648	—	56	4,273
32. Utnoor ,,	2,213	84	2,723	—	—	2,807
33. Nirmal ,,	25,595	2,722	5,071	300	72	8,165

34.	Boath ,,	5,331	877	740	180	91	1,888
35.	Kinwat ,,	10,285	1,562	2,087	—	—	3,649
36.	Adilabad District Total for 1345 Fasli (1936)	1,04,978	13,794	50,898	5,723	3,490	75,905
37.	-Do- for 1344 Fasli (1935)	95,965	28,845	13,543	62,511	—	1,04,899
38.	-Do- for 1340 Fasli (1931)	1,05,024	26 185	10,424	59,613	—	96,122
39.	-Do- for 1335 Fasli (1926)	1,08,109	13,498	9,667	49,747	4,836	77,748
40.	-Do- for 1331 Fasli (1922)	84,866	14,442	9,729	51,429	—	75 600

Source : H.E.H. the Nizam's Government, *Hyderabad District Gazetteers*, Tables Volumes, *1340* & *1345* *Fasli* (1931) & 1936 *A.D.*) *Warangal*, pp. 346-47 ; *Karimnagar* pp. 344-47 ; and *Adilabad*, pp. 342-45.

Parkal in Karimnagar District spent Rs. 7/- on civil works and Boath in Asifabad District spent Rs. 180/- on sanitation and hospitals.[334] Another interesting fact that emerged in this connection was that, whereas the three District headquarters Boards spent 80 to 100% over and above their incomes, but excluding previous balances and slight excess of around 5% in the case of Khammam Taluq Board, all other Taluq Boards in 1936, were found spending fat less than their incomes, apart from balances, the deficiency ranging from 25% to 75%.[335] The same tendency was observed in their case in the State as a whole in 1931[336] as well as 1942.[337] The weak Engineering executive at the disposal of the Taluq Boards as against an efficient wing in the hands of the major Municipalities and lack of control by the Government over the Local Cess collections in *Jagir* areas of the *Suba* and its consequent non-spending by the feudal chiefs, had been among the factors that accounted for this poor spending by the former as against increased expenditure by the latter.[338] The ultimate consequence that followed was that excepting in the major Municipal towns such as Warangal, Khammamet, Karimnagar and Adilabad, the contribution of Local Boards towards the development of education, health and public works in the *Suba* area, remained very much meagre and insignificant.[339]

iv. Immigration and Urban Development : The movement of the population from rural to urban areas which became a regular phenomenon in the State from 1921 onwards,[340] has come to greatly influence the growth of the latter in the *Suba* area. The meagre increase in the cultivable area,[341] unsatisfactory crop yields either due to failure of crop conditions or due to lesser application of inputs[342] and the withering condition of village industries,[343] had all resulted in the swelling of the ranks of the rural unemployed. On the other hand, the concentration of heavily labour-oriented large-scale industries in urban areas, the growth of trade, commerce, rail and road transport, banking institutions and even the greater spread of the activities of Local Bodies to these centres only and also the location of either District or Taluq headquarters, or in the case of some, even both at the same towns, had all provided ample avenues of employment both for the skilled and unskilled persons.[344] As a matter of fact, the point that Azam Jahi Textile Mills at Warangal and Singareni Collieries at Yellandu, the two leading among the large-scale industries in the *Suba*, District of Warangal, could employ daily labour of the order of 2,305 and 7,560 respectively,[345] stood as ample indicator of the vast employment opportunities that presented themselves in the *Suba* towns. Immigrants, especially into the coal mining towns of Yellandu and Kothagudem in Warangal District, Bellampalli and Sasti in Adilabad District, the Textile Mill at Warangal and the Paper Mill at Sirpur in the latter, flocked not only from Karimnagar, Nalgonda, Nizamabad and other contiguous Districts in the State including that of Hyderabad city, but also considerably from the British Indian Provinces of Madras, Madhya Pradesh and to a lesser extent from those of Rajasthan and Uttar Pradesh.[346]

These immigrants, as could be seen from *Table LXIV*, primarily and rather obviously belonged to non-agricultural classes. As many as 85,222 persons who formed 62% of the total number of immigrants into Warangal District, and 57,439 persons that formed 60% of the total number of immigrants into Adilabad District in 1951, belonged to these classes. On the other hand, these numbered only 17,105 in Karimnagar District, which however, accounted for. 60% of the total number that came into it.[347] Both the classes put together and when compared to the total urban populations of these Districts, the percentages stood at 22.8, 27.9 and 5.5 in Warangal, Adilabad and Karimnagar respectively.[348] The seeming contradiction between these percentages of the two former as against their predominant non-agricultural immigrants cited above, was due to the huge difference that existed between their total urban populations which stood at 2.88,395 and 1,13,105 respectively.[349] In fact, in respect of the total number of immigrants that entered into a District, Warangal District stood second only to Hyderabad District which included the Capital city of Hyderabad.[350] Further, it had the distinction of attracting the largest number of non-agricultural immigrants from beyond the borders of the State, especially from the Madras Presidency areas, who accounted for as much

TABLE LXIV

Population Movement in Urban Areas

Sl. No.	District/ State	Percentage of Immigrants to total urban population	Immigrants belonging Agricultural classes		Immigrants belonging to Non-Agricultural classes	
			Percentage to urban population	Percentage of females	Percentage to urban population	Percentage of females
1	2	3	4	5	6	7
1.	Warangal	22.8	1.4	49	21.4	45
2.	Karimnagar	5.5	0.6	64	4.9	50
3.	Adilabad	27.9	1.4	56	26.5	49
4.	Hyderabad State	18.2	1.2	54	17.0	47

Source : *1951 Census Part I-A, Report* P. 241.

as 30% of the total number of immigrants that entered into this District.[351]

It could be observed from *Table LXIV* that regarding the percentage of immigrants to total urban population, whereas Warangal and Adilabad Districts stood far above that of the State, Karimnagar District, on the other hand, stood far below that of the latter. In fact, the latter District had the unequal distinction in the State, of registering the lowest number of immigrants and at the same time, sending the highest number of emigrants, the respective totals standing in 1951 at 28,467 and 1,52,826 persons.[352] Whereas the coal-miners at Yellandu and Kothagudem, the Azam Jahi Textile Mill at Warangal, rice, oil, ginning and pressing factories at Warangal, Khammam and Madhira towns, bone and leather factories at Warangal, Match Factory at Mahaboobabad, Carpet Factory at Warangal[353] and above all, the urban, administrative and even historical importance of Warangal and to some extent of Khammam town, besides the growth of trade and transport wings in these two centres,[354] all in Warangal District and the Bellampalli and Sasti Collieries, the Sirpur Paper Mills, the Chemicals and Fertilizer Factory at Bellampalli,[355] ginning, pressing, rice, pulse and oil Mills in Adilabad, Kinwat, Nirmal and Rajura Taluqs,[356] all in Adilabad District, the administrative importance of most of these towns, besides sparsity of population in almost all of them except Nirmal town,[357] had been the varied factors or sources that provided enough ground for immigrants into the urban areas of these two Districts, Karimnagar District, on the other hand, besides being the most densely populated District in the State,[358] and excepting some ginning, pressing, rice, pulse and oil Mills in Karimnagar and Huzurabad Taluqs[359] and languishing handloom and other cottage industries at Karimnagar, Jagtiyal, Koratla, Mahadeopur and Metpalli centres,[360] it lacked any large-scale industries or urban areas known for any big development of trade, transport and administrative interests,[361] as a result of which all, it could least absorb persons from outside than send its own in considerable numbers to mostly contiguous Districts of the *Suba* and the State and to a lesser extent to non-adjoining areas.[362]

Karimnagar District immigrants numbered 45,902 in Warangal District, 40,085 in Adilabad District and 23,999 in Nizamabad District, of whom, non-agricultural urban immigrants ranked 28,567, 22,510 and 9,248 respectively, with of course, 18,297 persons of the latter category in Hyderabad District, or in other words, wholly in Hyderabad City.[363] In fact, in respect of both the classes, immigrants from Karimnagar District, when compared to those from other areas or Districts, ranked highest in Adilabad District which had the overall give and take ratio of 4,000 : 40,000 with the former.[364] Even the little amount of immigration that occurred in Karimnagar District was more by way of marriage relations rather than due to economic reasons, for the percentage of female immigrants was higher here, when compared to other *Suba* Districts or the State.[365] On the other hand, the movement into Warangal and Adilabad urban areas was influenced more by economic considerations than otherwise.[366] Next to Karimnagar, the highest number of immigrants into Adilabad and Warangal Districts had been witnessed respectively from Madhya Pradesh and Nalgonda District, the urban non-agricultural immigrants amounting respectively to 3,358 and 1,808 persons, with of course, the Madrasi immigrants being excepted in the latter case.[367] The enormity of the situation in respect of the *Suba* Districts could be well understood from the fact that urban and non-agricultural emigrants vis-a-vis the immigrants of the same character carried a percentage of 612.14, 25.91 and 13.47 in Karimnagar, Warangal and Adilabad respectively.[368] The latter, as a matter of fact, formed the lowest in the State in contrast to the former being the highest.[369] These percentages, as the preceding sub-sections dealing with urban development have indicated, stood as prominent pointers towards the opportunities and the levels of urban development in the Districts of the *Suba* area.

D. TRIBAL CONDITIONS : No Taluq in the *Suba* remained entirely devoid of tribal population, though the extent differed from one to the other.[370] Mahaboobabad, Yellandu, Palvancha (*Samasthan*), Khammam and Warangal Taluqs in Warangal District and Kinwat, Boath, Rajura, Sirpur and Utnoor Taluqs in Adilabad District, contained in the order, good numbers of tribal people in the Districts of the Eastern Division.[371] In contrast, Karimnagar District had none such Taluqs.[372] Considered in terms of total population of Taluqs, the line up was altogether different, or rather somewhat, the inverse of the former. Utnoor,[373] Palvancha *Samasthan*, Yellandu, Kinwat, Boath, Rajura, Mahaboobabad, Sirpur, Khammam and Warangal Taluqs with respectively 56.34, 40.40, 33.38, 26.81, 25.58, 22.35, 15.49, 13.96, 7.31 and 4.01% of their total population as tribals,[374] stood in fact in order, as the key centres in the panorama of tribal life not only in the *Suba*, but very much in the State itself. The two Districts considered as a whole, the position in this respect showed the same trend in the sense that, whereas the actual tribal population of Warangal District in 1931 was higher by 33.10% than that of Adilabad District, it, on the other hand, formed 12.48% of the former's total population as against 13.75% of that of the latter.[375]

This difference was due not only to greater number of total population in the former than the latter, but also not in a lesser degree, due to much higher rate of growth of tribal population in the latter than in the former.[376] Between 1911-41, the increase in tribal population per 10,000 of total population was only 92 in Warangal District, 39 in Karimnagar District and 201 in the State, as against as much as 462 in Adilabad District.[377] The latter, as could be seen from *Table LXVI*, maintained continuous growth during all these three decades, though of course, little in 1921-31, whereas the former two *Suba* Districts suffered considerable decrease during the decade of 1911-21 and showed nominal rise in the next decade.[378] Further, compared to total population, tribal population had witnessed a faster growth in Adilabad District than in Warangal and Karimnagar Districts. The respective percentages of increase in these two types of populations during the decade 1921-31 in Warangal, Karimnagar and Adilabad Districts, for instance, stood at 20.8, 21.0 ; 13.3, -24.08 & 16.2 and 57.9 respectively.[379] The comparatively less accessible, sparsely populated and meagrely exploited forest and land resources in the latter District, had very much met the requirements of the secluded type of living and the *podu* type of cultivation,[380] as well as

TABLE LXV

Tribal Population, Taluq-wise, 1340 Fasli (1931 Census)

Sl. No.	Taluq	Total Population	Tribal Population
1	2	3	4
1.	Warangal	3,00,571	12,054
2.	Mahaboobabad	2,10,228	32,570
3.	Khammam	1,65,846	12,127
4.	Madhira	1,42,510	9,721
5.	Yellandu	84,591	28,237
6.	Pa*l*hal	74,633	7,547
7.	Mulug	39,329	7,410
8.	Palvancha	35,112	3,582
9.	Palvancha (*Samasthan*)	64,973	26,251
10.	Total of Warangal District in 1340 Fasli (1931)	11,17,693	1,39,499
11.	Total of Warangal District in 1330 Fasli (1921)	9,25,041	1 15,287
12.	Percentage increase (+) or decrease (—)	+20.8	21.0
13.	Jagtiyal	2,92,553	2,348
14.	Sultanabad	1,64,920	751
15.	Karimnagar	2,21,947	1,238
16.	Sirsilla	1,88,221	368
17.	Huzurabad	1,73,761	2,171
18.	Parkal	1,16,493	280
19.	Mahadeopur	83,510	3,238
20.	Total of Karimnagar District for 1340 Fasli (1931)	12,41,405	10,394
21.	Total of Karimnagar District for 1330 Fasli (1921)	10,95,444	13,961

22. Percentage of increase(+) or decreas (—)	+13.3	+31.7*
23. Adilabad	86,674	7 652
24. Asifabad	70,263	7,349
25. Rajura	61,462	13,742
26. Chinnoor	84,609	5,487
27. Luxettipet	87 379	5,604
28. Sirpur	87,032	12,155
29. Utnoor	20 639	11,628
30. Nirmal	1,02,816	2,748
31. Boath	64,756	16,565
32. Kinwat	71,919	19,284
33. Yelgadap (*Paigah*)	23,481	2.593
34. Total of Adilabad District for 1340 Fasli (1931)	7,62,030	2 593
35. Total of Adilabad District sor 1330 Fasli (1921)	6,55,536	89·785
36. Percentage increase(+) or decrease (—)	+16.2	+57.9

*As there was a decrease of 3,297 persons in tribal population figures of 1921 and 1931, the percentage should be —24.08 and not the figure given.

Source : H.E.H. the Nizam's Government, *Hyderabad District Gazetteers*, Tables volumes, *1340 & 1345 Fasli* (*1931 & 1936*), *Warangal*, pp. 10 & 11 ; *Karimnagar*, pp. 10 & 11 & *Adilabad*, pp. 10 & 11.

much dependence on forest produce that had been usually associated with tribal living in the area. Areas in the former such as *Samasthan* Palvancha, Yellandu and Mahaboobabad that presented similar conditions, also encouraged tribal concentration. Compared to these two, Karimnagar District with a meagre forest area which fell in extent even below the Telangana average,[381] did not offer congenial conditions for the tribes much to settle in. Only the forest tracts of Mahadeopur Taluq in this District on the banks or Godavari, could offer such, though of course, highly malaria-infested and hence, people felt not encouraged to settle on these lands.[382] Besides these natural or geographical factors, the condition of the tribals in the area has come to be influenced considerably by other attendant factors, administrative, economic social and personal.[383] An examination of the condition of the main tribes that prevailed in the *Suba* area during the period, will bring these factors into proper focus.

i. *Gonds* : Next to Lambadas or Banjaras who immigrated from the North,[384] Gonds or Raj-Gonds[385] ranked as the most prominent aboriginal tribe in the *Suba* as well as the State, both in numbers and historical importance. Whereas they accounted for 22.56% of the State's tribal population, the corresponding percentage in the *Suba* was 43.02. It is significant to note that almost the entire Gond tribe amounting to 99.51% inhabited in the *Suba* Districts only. Among these again, Adilabad and Warangal Districts together, had almost accounted for the entire Gond population, the respective percentages being 50.60 and 47.33 and Karimnagar's share, on the other hand, was only negligible 1.57%.[386] Even if the Gawaris, a Teluguized branch of the Gond race[387] that numbered 3,971 in the latter District, rather the highest in this branch, was considered along with the number of Gonds as such, the total number in Karimnagar District formed only around one-eleventh of that contained in the other *Suba* Districts.[388] However, the significance of the Gond element in the total tribal population of the *Suba* Districts is evident from the fact that the former amounted to 57.22, 36.14 and 13.24% of the latter in Adilabad, Warangal and Karimnagar Districts respectively.[389] The central and northern Taluqs of Adilabad District such as Utnoor, Asifabad, Boath, Kinwat, Rajura and Adilabad, the riverine and forest tracts of Warangal District such as Palvancha, Mulug, Pakhal, Yellandu and Mahaboobabad and Mahadeopur, Huzurabad and Jagtiyal Taluqs in Karimnagar District, formed their real centres of habitation.

Agriculture formed the principal occupation of these tribesmen who mostly cultivated *Kharif* crops[390] and oil seeds on light soils[391] that were found on plateaus and slightly inclined slopes. They practised shifting cultivation by changing the plots for every two or three years, on the latter getting exhausted of their fertility.[392] Depending on the rainfall, the crop yields were not meagre to the effect that a generation before, individual Gonds were found owning up to a thousand head of cattle, thereby indicating their days of prosperity.[393] That period had also been marked by smaller revenue charges both in feudal and Government villages and at the same time freedom from the exactions of the forest and subordinate Government Officials.[394] But, the development of communications such as the laying of Nirmal-Adilabad Road, Mancherial-Rajura Road, Nirmal-Mancherial Road, Asifabad-Rajura Road, Asifabad-Sirpur Road, Palvancha-Yellandu Road, Hanamkonda-Mulug Road, Mankota-Korvi Road, Narsampet-Pakhal Road, Karimnagar-Mahadeopur Road, Karimnagar-Jagtiyal Road, Kazipet-Balharshah rail line connecting the forest tracts of Huzurabad, Sultanabad, Asifabad and Sirpur Taluqs and the Adilabad-Mudkhed rail line traversing through Kinwat and Adilabad Taluqs, connecting the aboriginal areas with non-tribal areas of the *Suba* and the State and even outside the State,[395] had resulted in seriously endangering the stability of the tribal economy.[396] Immigrants belonging to both cultivating and non-cultivating communities from such areas where there was dense population and pressure on the land such as Karimnagar District in the *Suba*, Berar and Central Provinces to the north of Adilabad District and Krishna and Guntur Districts of the Madras Presidency to the south of Warangal District etc., started trekking into tribal areas right from almost the commencement of the last *Nizam's* reign,[397] in search of land and exploitation of forest produce.

Government, as a policy measure, encouraged the arrival of these non-aboriginals to bring more and more lands in these areas under the plough which, in turn, resulted in enhanced revenue to the State.[398] But, in the process, the Gonds came to be dispossessed in one village after another, except in the inaccessible hilly areas such as the Manickgarh block in Rajura Taluq, the Daboli block in Utnoor Taluq and the Dhanora and Tilani blocks in Asifabad Taluq, from the lands which they had been cultivating for several generations.[339] The tribesmen

TABLE LXVI

Growth of Tribal Population, 1911-1941

Sl. No.	District/ State	Tribal population per 10,000 of total population in 1911	1921	1931	1941
1	2	3	4	5	6
1.	Warangal	1,315	1,246	1,248	1,407
2.	Karimnagar	85	1,265*	84	124
3.	Adilabad	1,063	1,370	1,375	1,525
4.	State	214	345	377	415

* This appears to be an improbable figure, for the tribal population of this District was never during the period, known to have reached such a level that the proportion per 10,000 of total population even exceeded that of Warangal District, the latter being, next to Adilabad District, known for its large content of tribal population.

Source : *Census of India, Hyderabad State, 1941, Part II*, pp. 677-78.

in this respect, were handicapped in both the ways that, on the one hand they were not required to hold land *Pattas* under Gond *rajas* or feudal overlords, for no individual ownership right was recognised under the latter,[400] and on the other, when on resumption of the latter's estates by the State, the efforts of the former to establish and defend their claims to land ownership, were completely overcome by the guile methods employed by the newcomers who could influence the Revenue Officers in getting their claims recognized, even if it involved change of Revenue records.[401] The latter were further greatly strengthened in these designs and the tribesmen inconvenienced to the same extent by the fact that, except in fully aboriginal and hilly villages, the non-aboriginals in most of the villages that they entered, the *Watans* of *Patwari*, Police and *Mali Patels*, fell into their hands, in certain cases covering not only several villages but Taluqs, which enabled them not only to expropriate aboriginal lands, but also extract from the poor and ignorant

TABLE LXVII

Distribution of the Main Tribes, 1941

Sl. No.	Tribe	STATE		WARANGAL		
		Persons	Males	Females	Persons	Males
1	2	3	4	5	6	7
1.	Gonds(a)	1,42,026	71,890	70,136	67,229	33,958
2.	Koyas (b)	31,094	15,913	15,181	22,481	11,522
3.	Lambara (c) or Banjaras	4,04,614	2,08,867	1,95,747	85,259	43,987
4.	Erakala (d)	45,771	23,184	22,587	8,397	4,420
5.	Pardhi	4,805	2,480	2,325	128	82
6.	Gawari	4,036	1,791	2,245	—	—
7.	Hill Reddis	1,834	932	902	1,697	855
8.	Andh	19,313	9,732	9,581	—	—
9.	Pardhan	1,583	859	724	731	378

10.	Kolam (e)	746	436	310	—	—
11.	Koli (f)	237	125	112	—	—
12.	Bhil	18,021	9,085	8,936	—	—
13.	Chenchu	3,865	1,819	2,046	31	14
14.	Yenadi	169	85	84	41	20
15.	Baiga	18	10	8	4	3
16.	Desandra	17	13	4	—	—
	Total	6,78,149	3,47,221	3,30,928	1,85,998	95,239

			KARIMNAGAR			ADILABAD	
		Females	Persons	Males	Females	Persons	Males	Females
		8	9	10	11	12	13	14
1.	Gonds (a)	33,271	2,232	1,155	1,077	71,874	36,411	35,463
2.	Koyas (b)	10.959	601	298	303	7,990	4,079	3,911
3.	Lambara (c) or Banjaras	41,272	3,814	2,112	1,702	39,984	19,981	20,002
4.	Erakala (d)	3,977	6,040	2,982	3,058	208	106	102
5.	Pardhi	46	10	4	6	10	5	5
6.	Gawari	—	3,971	1,761	2,210	—	—	—
7.	Hill Reddis	842	—	—	—	—	—	—
8.	Andh	—	—	—	—	4,076	1,997	2,079
9.	Pardhan	353	72	41	31	416	225	161
10.	Kolam (e)	—	—	—	—	746	436	310
11.	Koli (f)	—	—	—	—	237	125	112
12.	Bhil	—	—	—	—	17	9	8
13.	Chenchu	17	107	54	53	—	—	—

14.	Yenadi	21	—	—	—	—	—	—
13.	Baiga	1	—	—	—	14	7	7
16.	Desandra	—	—	—	—	17	13	4
	Total	90,759	16,847	8,407	8,440	1,25,589	63,424	62,165

(a) + Rajgond 1,142 persons
+ Naikpod 777 Male
365 Female

(b) + Raj Koya 640 persons
+ Bhim Koya 325 Male
215 Female

(c) + Mathula 3,489 persons
1,852 Male
1,637 Female

(d) + Korvi 4,456 persons
+ Korwa 2,289 Male
2,167 Female

(e) + Mannervarlu

(f) + Raj Koli

Source : *Census of India, Hyderabad State, 1941*, Part II, pp. 683-685.

tribesmen, several levies in cash, kind and labour.[402] Severe epidemics, like the one of 1919 either due to cholera or influenza, had also resulted in large-scale land relinquishment by the Gonds in the area, for many villages got deserted and very few were in a position either to pay the land revenue or cultivate the lands.[403]

The worse of the situation was that the dispossessed tribesmen were not even allowed to continue as tenants on their lands, for the new absentee landlords that came to occupy their lands covering large stretches or entire villages, began to lease their lands to non-aboriginal cultivators, for the latter paid higher rents and had better knowledge of cultivating methods than the former.[404] Even if a few were allowed to continue, they could not do so for long for, the non-cultivating landlords resorted to frequent hiking up of the land rents which, the former with their primitive type of cultivation failed to cope with.[405] The inevitable result that followed was that, by 1943 majority of the tribal villages in the plains as well as near the urban areas and on road side, got converted into non-aboriginal villages and even in the few that still retained their tribal majority, the *Watan* rights and proprietorship of non-Governmental land were in the hands of the new landlords that came from outside, even as far as Uttar Pradesh.[406] Thus, out of 20 villages within a 3 mile distance from Asifabad, 12 no longer contained aboriginals, 5 in part and only 3 in full[407] and in Renganghat village in the same Taluq, located on the Asifabad-Utnoor Road, which remained a purely Gond village one generation before, only one Gond house was found in 1943.[408] Driven from the plains, the Gonds were, rather unfortunately, not allowed by the Forest Officials to cultivate the lands of their choice in the hilly areas. Thus, when a section of the tribe was cultivating for a considerable time lands at Babjhari, located 11 miles to the west of Asifabad, the Forest authorities insisted on keeping this area under Reserved Forest limits, the former in exasperation and out of their strong attachment to those particular lands, resisted the vacation orders resulting in firing and loss of precious and poor souls.[409] Even after this sacrifice, the decimated number were allowed to inhabit not at Babjhari, but at Jodeghat, a spot further down the former.[410]

Added to such offensives, the Forest Authorities exhibited much high-handedness and injustice towards the tribesmen in the implementation of the rules that many *Patta* lands held by the aboriginals have been included in the Reserved Forest without compensation being granted, the result being that the owners in may cases still paid the revenue for lands they were no longer allowed to cultivate.[411]

Economically, the tribesmen were also subjected to suffering by the *mamuls* extracted by the Revenue Subordinate staff such as *Girdawars*,[412] *Patwaris* and Tahsil *chaprasis* and constables of the Police Department. The latter made frequent visits to Gond villages and collected all types of provisions including foodstuffs, chicken, ghee, etc., which were at times carried away comfortably in carts they had with them. In villages near Police Stations, free supply of milk and ghee were demanded and those who delayed their turns were subjected to fines.[413] In return for these contributions, the Police failed to offer protection to Gond villagers from the armed raids of beggar parties who extracted provisions and cash also.[414] At the same time, the former always came forward to enforce the claims, genuine or otherwise, of non-aboriginals against the tribesmen.[415] The cumulative result of exploitation at different hands had been the development of a feeling of frustration in the minds of the Gonds that they were not allowed to lead a life of their own and came to believe that the Government Officials neither protected them against non-aboriginal competition nor remained themselves free from inflicting unjust demands on them.[416]

The Government which had an inkling of this attitude of tribesmen in the Babjhari resistance,[417] took charge of some remedial measures with the appointing of a Special Tribes Officer in 1943 to carry out the double-pronged programme of preventing the alienation of aboriginal lands into the hands of caste people on the one hand and free grant of lands to the tribesmen under *Laoni khas*.[418] Under the latter in Adilabad District, between 1944 and the beginning of 1948, a total of 1,30,000 acres land was given on *patta* to the aboriginals which amounted to nearly 50% of the total Gond population in the District holding some land or other on *patta* rights.[419] The Gond Education Scheme was also started to develop the Gondi language and train the tribesmen as school teachers and village officers. Under it, as many as 60 aboriginal schools were opened due to whose efforts, it was claimed that the percentage of literacy among them rose from 6 to 10.[420] However, the incidence of drink evil that was excessive among the Gonds,[421] the delay committed by the District Forest Officials in surveying the area marked for allotment and the Survey Department Officials in arranging for *phodi*[422] of the said lands, had been some of the factors that slowed down the pace of remedial measures.[423] Political and internal disturbances that stalked the land had their own deleterious effect on these programmes.[424] Further, the amounts allotted for spending on different aspects of tribal development did not appear to be adequate in the sense that for Warangal District with a total tribal population of 1,85,998, the sum provided was Rs. 3,28,000.[425] The Governmental measures rather came late when the non-aboriginal settlers had already become the dominating force in the so-called tribal zones.

(*ii*) *Koyas* : Among the aboriginal tribes, these formed, next to Gonds, the predominant section both in the *Suba* as well as the State. As in the case of the latter tribes, so also the former, excepting the paltry figure of 22 persons was completely inhabitant in the *Suba* Districts, and more so in Warangal and Adilabad.[426] The respective percentages of the total Koya population in these two Districts and Karimnagar are 72.30, 25.69 and 1.96.[427] The riverian tracts of Palvancha, Mulug and Pakhal and the forest region of Yellandu, Kothagudem and Boorgampahad, all in Warangal District, besides areas of such description in the other *Suba* Districts, formed during the period, significant centres of Koya habitation in the State. Whereas the Koyas in the riverian region of Godavari, covering essentially a strip of 20 to 30 miles wide, spoke the Gondi dialect, influenced to some extent by Telugu and practised tribal culture and customs, those in the inland and forest areas spoke Telugu akin to other rural population and followed customs that were some what different from those of the former.[428] These linguistic and cultural differences were also characterised by variation in economic development, in the sense that those tribesmen living in the inland tracts were found to be less backward in this respect than those residing in the river areas, such as that of Palvancha *Samasthan.*[429] In the latter and the Boorgampahad areas, these lived in symbiosis with Konda Reddis, another aboriginal tribe whose level of culture and material development were, of course, on a slightly higher plane than those of the former.[430]

At the beginning of the present century, the Koyas were found so predominantly pursuing agricultural occupation that in the country between Kothagudem and Yellandu, they formed the main population.[431] Whereas in the forest areas, they carried on *podu* or shifting cultivation even beyond the period of present study, methods of settled type of cultivation were tried to be adopted in the other areas.[432] But, just as it happened in the case of Gonds, the development of communication facilities in the area and the arrival there of affluent and shrewder landhungry new settlers that went with it, had resulted in the creation of thoroughly unfavourable conditions for the Koya tribesmen.[433] On the other hand, the reservation of forests, demarcation of boundaries and the restrictions thus came to be imposed on free felling of forests, led to the impairment of shifting cultivation too.[434] Land dispossession through the means of village Officers, merchants and money-lenders during the 10 or 15 year period preceding the Land Alienation Act of 1939-40 was so severe and extensive that, even in the predominantly aboriginal villages, the majority of Koyas had no land of their own and for the most part, continued their existence either as tenants or as daily labourers.[435] Even when in the early forties, some 6,000 acres of open forest had been allotted in Yellandu Taluq of Warangal District on *Siwai-i-Jamabandi* tenure,[436] none of it came to Koyas but, on the other hand, it was mainly big land owners who profited from this measure under the 'Grow More Food' campaign.[437] The provisions of the Land Alienation Act also could not be strictly applied in the case of Koyas, for they claimed to belong to "*Dorlasatam*" or lordly descent with different status from that of an aboriginal community.[438] On the other hand, in the Godavari river tract which remained inaccessible by cart-track, the conditions remained most backward that, the aboriginals due to the restrictions imposed by the Forest Department were not only deprived of the most ordinary chances of survival, but also subjected to unscrupulous exploitation by a group of timber merchants from the Madras Presidency who enjoyed monopoly rights over the extraction of bamboo and timber in the area.[439]

The habits of the Koya tribesmen contributed not a little for their economic backwardness. They were neither industrious nor thrifty.[440] They never cultivated more than what they thought needed for their annual maintenance. As a result, very often they were obliged to borrow cereals from non-aboriginal ryots at 50 or 75 % interest for consumption in summer and also for payment to labour in the transplantation season.[441] Further, they had a poor idea of money-economy that they paid away their debts not in money but in kind.[442] Because of their inefficiency and disinclination for hard work, the Koyas were not preferred by the immigrants for agricultural labour.[443] But, they however, proved experts in hunting, cattle breeding and wood-cutting or deforestation and were paid at the rate of a rupee for every tree that was cut.[444] The addiction of these tribesmen to excessive drinking has acted not only as a huge drain on their limited earning, but has also led to gradual health impairment.[445] Added to this, the scarcity of drinking water wells in the Koya villages made them usually drink water from the nearby rivers and tanks, in some cases situated at a distance varying from 5 to 10 miles, but dirty, stinky and highly contaminated, which proved a potent source for the attack of diseases like dysentry, typhoid and other fevers including the dreaded *yaws*.[446] Facilities for the spread of education among the Koyas, also remained very much meagre. In Palvancha *Samasthan* which had 116 villages,[447] only 12 Primary Schools and 11 aided schools were there in 1942-43 in which the Koya pupils numbered about 75 and again, two-thirds of the latter were there in the school at Ankampallam, a pure Koya village.[448] Neither free books nor school materials were provided in them. The total expenditure incurred by the *Samasthan* authorities on education in that particular year stood at paltry Rs. 500 and hence, it is not surprising that the literacy percentage came so low to 3.45.[449] Conditions were not much different in the Koya habitats of *Diwani* areas in the *Suba*.[450]

Rehabilitation measures by the Government to allay the feelings of discontentment and sense of frustration that lay deep in the minds of these aboriginals, had been instituted only in 1946, when a Teachers' Training Centre was opened at Sudimalla in Yellandu Taluq of Warangal District, in order to train Koya boys to be later appointed as independent school teachers in tribal areas. Another such centre was started in 1948 at the Koya village of Kamaram in Mulug Taluq of the same District.[451] The tribal areas along the Godavari gorge in Palvancha Taluq of the same District was covered by the Godavari valley Rural Welfare Scheme whose main feature, besides the educative, medical and agricultural aspects, was the co-operative exploitation of forest coupes, Primarily intended for the benefit of aboriginal labourers.[452] Allotment of lands on *patta* under Special *Laoni* to the landless and deserving Koyas was taken up when a Social Service Officer was posted in 1947 with powers for the purpose.[453] It was reported in this regard that, until the end of 1951, nearly 25,000 acres of land was distributed among 2,500 families in Yellandu and Mulug Taluqs,[454] which, considering the period covered and the previous record was not insignificant though, of course, the number of persons or families yet to be covered in the District was nearly seven to eight times of the one presently covered.[455] It is however important to realise that the so-called *Tribal Areas Regulation* in which rules were framed regarding the remedial programme to be executed, was brought into force only in 1949-50 and the rehabilitation of the Koyas from the interior and less accessible villages to centrally located ones which formed part of the programme under the Regulation, was commenced only in March, 1950.[456] Further, the Welfare work was brought to a standstill by the Political trouble that overtook the region during 1948-49.[457] The Koya rehabilitation work thus, which was started towards the close of the period, failed to bring much transformation in their unhappy condition.

(*iii*) *Hill Reddis* : Among the aboriginal tribes that inhabited the Godavari riverine tract, the Hill Reddis or also known as Konda Reddis,[458] figure significant during the period. They were fully concentrated in the Palvancha *Samasthan* of Warangal District to the extent of 92.53% of their total number.[459] In physical appearance, these looked decidedly more primitive than the Koyas who also inhabited the same belt of territory[460] and spoke a corrupt form of Telugu, but was ignorant of the Gondi dialect spoken by the latter.[461] For quite a long time, the Reddi tribesmen subsisted entirely by shifting cultivation, the collection of wild fruits and roots and hunting with bow and arrow. They came down to live on the river only in recent times, where they variedly occupied themselves with bamboo and timber cutting and plough cultivation of the flat alluvial pockets of land in the Godavari valley, besides of course, their usual cultivation of forest lands and hill slopes, otherwise known as *Podu*.[462] It is interesting to note that whereas advanced tribes like Gonds[463] used developed instruments like hoes in their shifting cultivation, the Konda Reddis on the contrary, employed none such, but instead, primitive tools like bamboo sticks or iron-tipped digging sticks. The crops cultivated by the latter included jawar, *ragi*, *korra*,[464] small millets and several kinds of pulses as well as large beans.[465] Besides plough land, these also came to own cattle, both of which not only helped them in securing credit from the money-lenders and merchants, but at the same time aroused the covetousness of the latter to capture them by taking advantage of the lack of shrewdness of the tribesmen in transacting business either with outsiders or people from the plains.[466]

During the period, the major change that had overtaken the economic system of these aboriginal tribesmen was that, due to the unfavourable conditions that obtained in the domain of cultivation, they began fast turning from the former occupation to forest labour.[467] In the generation before 1945, much flat and cultivable land suitable for rain-fed rice crop had changed hands in Palvancha *Samasthan*, passing from Konda Reddis and Koyas into the hands of the non-aboriginal *Patwaris*[468] and timber merchants or forest contractors that hailed from the East Godavari District of the Madras Presidency. The ironical feature of this situation was that the new masters got their lands cultivated by employing the dispossessed tribesmen as daily labourers or hiring out the lands against 50% of the crop.[469] Redrawing of the boundaries of Reserved Forests leaving only small slopes around villages for *Podu* cultivation,[470] higher revenue rates on such lands and their unjust collection amounting to six times by the *watandar patwaris*[471] and the fact that the tribesman was made to pay to the former for giving up old *Podu*, cutting new *Podu* and its measurement, all three separately, besides fees to Forest Guard,[472] had considerably restricted the scope for carrying on this type of cultivation by the Hill Reddis, for apart from area being curtailed, the vexatious and too many demands far outweighed the value of the produce[473] that was normally received from such lands. On the other hand, on the other side of the river in East Godavari District of the British territory, not only the forest boundaries were fixed far distant from villages thereby providing much opportunity for *Podu*, but also that the revenue rate was less by 50% and no illegal hiking nor sundry payments were there either to village Officers or to Forest Guards.[474] The ultimate and natural consequence of these conditions was that a considerable number of the Hill Reddis in the *Samasthan* had emigrated to this British area and the rest gave up their traditional shifting cultivation in later years and started subsisting on their only income forest labour and collection of jungle produce.[475]

Even in the case of permanently cultivated and plough land also, similar unequal and discouraging conditions existed in the Reddi area that huge excess revenue collections ranging upto five times the prescribed rate, had been made besides exacting plough fee of Rs. 3 per plough and often 10 to 20 *seers* of grain by the Forest Guards.[476] The bordering British area was again free from these unjust and illegal exactions.[477] As though these dues were not enough, grazing fees which in practice amounted to Re. 1 per buffalo was also levied in the area and it was most unfortunate that the Reddis who practically inhabited in the hilly and forest areas were made to pay a house tax of Re. 1 if they were non-cultivating and others had to offer gratifications to Forest Guards for house-building, ranging from Rs. 2 to Rs. 10. Tribals on the other side of the river were not aware of such payment.[478] It is significant to note that under the circumstances, emigrating tribesmen as well as others who continued their stay, expressed rather complainingly that their lot under the previous direct administration of Raja of Palvancha was far better and happier than the present on under the Court of Wards,[479] for during the former period, it was stated that the revenue demands were low, enough area for *Podu* cultivation and more important, much immunity from the vexatious inflictions of the *Patwaris* and the Forest Guards.[480] The Reddis and Koyas being known for their tribal innocense and had no particular attitude of hatred or vengeance against the *Diwani* administration, it could be strongly assumed that the latter was definitely more harder and severe in their case and the *Raja* appeared to have been more considerate and sympathetic in this respect.

The lot of these tribesmen as forest labourers also, did not prove beneficial.[481] The timber merchants from East Godavari who monopolised forest contracts in the *Samasthan* area and who freely indulged in methods of terrorisation,[482] came to regard them, for all practical purposes, as their personal property and an article of trade.[483] As the land revenue dues of the Reddis were not collected direct from them but from their timber employees, this arrangement was exploited not only by *Patwaris* in collecting the maximum without proper accounting or receipting, but also by the merchant contractors who made the former work for them the whole year for negligible payment in the form of millet, under the pretext of debts incurred by the payment of land revenue.[484] In that area, the latter functioned as the most influential section, not afraid of adopting any method to keep the tribesmen under their grip. Either supply of grain would be withheld during the rains when it was most needed, land revenue payment would be refused or resort would be made to even physical violence. Neither *Samasthan* nor Government Officials ever thought or attempted to check these marauding profiteers.[485] On the contrary, on the British side of the Agency tracts from which the latter domiciled, there were regulations on their activities such as the *coupe* system,[486] exclusion of undesirable merchants by expulsion from Agency tracts and demand of security amount, out of which the District Forest Officer could pay any wage arrears,[487] the net result of which would be the smallness of profits that would accrue to them. As a result, these merchants gave up business in their native lands and found instead, the exploitation of forests in the Reddi areas as highly profitable and at the same time, least risky.[488]

Until 1945-46, no definite programme aimed at the welfare of Konda Reddis had been taken up either by the Government or by the *Samasthan* authorities.[489] Schools were conspicuous by their total absence in the area.[490] Regarding medical service, though there was a dispensary at Boorgampahad, it was distantly located from Reddi habitations and no touring Medical Officers or Veterinary Surgeons had been appointed for close service in the area. As a result, no Reddis had ever been to this lone medical centre.[491] The Godavari Valley Rural Welfare scheme was the one launched in this area around 1946-47 under which, as an important feature, the tribal workers were encouraged to form into Co-operatives for which long term loans had been granted for the exploitation of the forest wealth.[492] But, even this activity received a set back with the onset of the Political turmoil in the State in 1948.[493] No other activity concerning the welfare of the Hill Reddis seems to have been undertaken during the period. It could thus be seen that, these aboriginal tribesmen received little in return for the heaviest exploitation to which they had been subjected at the hands of both official and non-official agencies.

(*iv*) *Other Aboriginal Tribes* : *Erakala*, *Andh*, *Pardhan*, *Kolam* and *Koli*, figured as other significant aboriginal tribes, especially in respect of numbers, in the *Suba*. Whereas *Erakalas* were found in considerable number in Warangal and Karimnagar Districts, *Andhs*, *Kolams* and *Kolis* on the other hand, were entirely concentrated in Adilabad District, with of course, *Pardhans* being distributed among all the three Districts, around 60% of whom were resident in Warangal District alone.[494] Telugu-speaking *Kolis*, who called themselves as *Mutrasa*, *Tenegoru* and *Bantavarlu*, were stated to be residing in good number in Karimnagar District,[495] though of course, its mention was missed in the Census enumeration of 1941.[496] Bamboo and basket works formed the chief occupation of *Erakalas* and to some extent, of *Kolams*.[497] Different articles of agricultural and domestic utility were manufactured, all by manual labour. Whereas Warangal District occupied the first place in the State in respect of bamboo works, Karimnagar District on the other hand, stood second in the State, in the case of basket production.[498] Cultivation, either *Podu* or plough type did not seem to have been carried prominently by any of these tribes, except by *Kolams* to a meagre extent during the days when forest reservation did not interfere with their shifting cultivation on the higher reaches of the hill slopes. The latter settled mainly in the higher parts of the Tilani and Dhanora Forests in Asifabad Taluq, the Manickgarh Forest in Rajura Taluq, the eastern part of Daboli block in Utnoor Taluq and the Eastern part of the Satmala Forest which belonged partly to Utnoor and partly to Adilabad Taluqs, all in Adilabad District.[499] Domestic and agricultural labour ranked the second major source of livelihood, next to basket making, for these tribes including *Kolams*, *Pardhans* and *Andhs*.[500]

Even though some among these tribesmen like *Kolams* were interested and had the knowledge of methods of permanent or plough cultivation, they were not allowed to practise them, essentially due to the squeezing methods adopted in their case by the *Patwaris* and the forest officials.[501] The latter once again created the same unsettling or unfavourable conditions as was done in the case of the leading aboriginal tribes of Gonds, Koyas and Konda Reddis.[502] The result that followed was that these tribesmen, in spite of their awareness of an efficient mode of agriculture, were tied down to the service of non-aboriginal landlords as agricultural labourers or serfs.[503] Even in respect of basket making pursued by majority of these tribesmen, the conditions were not conducive for the latter to strive for a profitable growth in production. The tribesmen who carried on this trade, were made to buy the bamboo at high and unprofitable rates from the contractors.[504] These high rates of the raw material was in turn, due to the unwise policy adopted in the State in this regard that bamboo worth Rs. 3 lakhs was exported as against an insignificant import of the value of 0.46 lakhs and its inevitable result being the import of baskets worth Rs. 80,000 on an average per year during for instance, 1941-45.[505] No concessions had been provided to the poor tribesmen in the purchase of their raw material and the conditions naturally benefited the non-aboriginal and in majority of the cases, outside contractors of the forest produce.[506] Without any agricultural base and being mainly dependent on wage earnings, the economic condition of the aboriginal tribesmen dealt in this sub-section appears to be even worse than that of the major tribes discussed earlier.[507] Little remedial measures had been undertaken by the Administration in their behalf in the *Suba* area.

(*v*) *Lambadas or Banjaras* : This non-aboriginal and immigrant tribe formed the most numerous of all the tribes in the State and also the Warangal District, accounting respectively for 59.66 and 45.83% of the total tribal population in the respective units.[508] The latter with 85,259 *Banjaras*, being largely concentrated in the area surrounding the village of Turoor in Mahaboobabad Taluq, and accounting for 20.57% of the total *Lambada* population in the State, ranked the foremost among all the Districts in the State, in this respect.[509] Compared to this significant position of Warangal District, the *Banjara* population in Adilabad and Karimnagar Districts formed respectively only 31.83% and 22.63% of their respective total tribal population. In the second-named District, this tribe mainly inhabited in those Taluqs where the Gonds had also mostly prevailed, such as Utnoor, Boath, Kinwat and Adilabad Taluqs and in the latter, the *Banjara* population numbered only 3,814, hence claiming no prominent habitations as such. If viewed in terms of the total *Lambada* population in the State, the latter two *Suba* Districts accounted for only 9.88% and 0.94% respectively.[510] The country taken as a whole, these tribesmen though they were distributed all over it, were found in greater numbers in Hyderabad State than in any other part of it.[511] The opportunities for good cattle-breeding, carrier trade and also land occupation that presented themselves in considerable measure inareas like those of Warangal and Adilabad Districts, of course in varying degrees, served as significant incentives for the greater immigration of *Banjara* tribe into these parts of the Deccan. They had their own racial characteristics, custom, language and even dress, especially of women and hence, claimed the status of a separate tribe by themselves.

The names '*Lambadi*' and '*Banjara*' to this tribe are derived from '*Lavana*' meaning salt and '*Banijar*' referring to traders.[512] They entered the Deccan during medieval times[513] as carriers of salt, grain and even soldiers' luggage from coast to inland and vice versa.[514] With the introduction of quicker means of transport, these pack-bullock traders shifted to less developed areas and adopted the agricultural profession.[515] With the money that they earned from their trading transactions, the *Lambadas* could easily purchase the lands that were put to auction and which had been until then cultivated on *Siwai-Jamabandi* tenure by aboriginal tribesmen such as Gonds.[516] The fact that in mixed Gond-*Lambada* villages *Patelgi* rights were held by the latter tribesmen had, combined with their natural shrewdness compared to the former, considerably enabled the immigrants to occupy best and vast lands.[517] This development in the agricultural domain was manifest in greater proportions in the northern and Gond-concentrated Taluqs of Adilabad District to the effect that many absentee landlords arose from the *Banjara* tribe, letting huge percentage of their lands to Gonds.[518] Thus, the *Lambada Patel* of Mahagaon in Utnoor Taluq owned more than 600 acres, but cultivated himself only a fraction.[519] The lands were let out not usually at a fixed rate, but under an agreement that the cultivator provided bullocks and seed grain and gave half of the crop in lieu of the rent.[520] It is evident that this arrangement naturally proved beneficial for the immigrant landlords than for the aboriginal tenants.

In the matter of welfare services such as education also, the *Banjaras* showed their advancement compared to their fellow aboriginal tribesmen. The *Lambadas* of Turoor[521] had been so much aware and anxious about imparting instruction to their children that they had organised a private school well before the Government initiated measures in this direction in 1947, as in the case of other important tribes in the area.[522] The latter's efforts also, through the establishment of a *Banjara* Welfare

Centre at the same village in 1947[523] and the launching of the *Banjara* Welfare Scheme in Mahaboobabad Taluq, had been primarily directed for the same cause. Altogether ten *Lambada* Schools had been set in motion in the area, besides a Training Centre to prepare young *Banjaras* as teachers for the village schools.[524] But, even these activities of a sectional nature did not seem to have been extended, on the basis of a separate tribe, either to Adilabad or Karimnagar Districts. However it could be observed from their increasing numbers as compared to the total tribal population in the State and *Sub* Districts, occupation of vast agricultural lands in aboriginal villages, especially in the northern belt of Adilabad District and their comparative advancement in the field of education, especially in Warangal District, all go to show that the economic condition of the *Banjaras* or *Lambadas* was definitely far better than that of the aboriginal tribes with whom they lived in association in many of the areas. Their natural shrewdness, temperament even to sustain hard work and the incomes which they earned from their trading activity had in the main, though not the latter Governmental measures enabled the former in registering this improvement, compared to the latter.

E. THE TELANGANA STRUGGLE :

The Communist party which spearheaded this Struggle had its origin and headquarters in the Krishna District of the Madras Presidency. It came to be officially established in this area by September, 1934,[525] the operational headquarters town being Bezwada which bordered the Khammamet and Madhira Taluqs of Warangal District and Suryapet and Huzurnagar Taluqs of Nalgonda District.[52] Besides trained instructors, '*Prajasakti*' (strength of the people) a Telugu journal run by this party from this centre with its own press that enabled the publication of party literature served as an important mouth-piece for propagating the programme and the functioning of the party units. The active and the dynamic among the youth in the Telangana Region had by 1938, been roused into action because of their participation in one or the other contemporary movements such as the Non-Co-operation Movement in Andhra area of the

Madras Presidency or the *Satyagraha* against the ban on the Hyderabad State Congress or the Osmania University Students' strike.[527] But, the more militant and extremist among them such as Baddam Yella Reddy, K.V. Muralidhar, Prabhakar Rao and P. Shankariah from Karimnagar District, Devulapalli Venkateshwar Rao, S. Ramanadham, Chirravuri Lakshminarasaiah, D. Seshagiri Rao and P. Chalapathi Rao from Warangal District and Ravi Narayana Reddy, Arutla Lakshminarasimha Reddy and Ramachandra Reddy from Nalgonda District, got disillusioned with the moderate and the non-militant policy being pursued by the Andhra *Maha Sabha*, the then most widely supported popular organisation in the Region.[528] This, coupled with the failure of the Civil Disobedience Movement of 1930 in the Andhra area and *Satyagraha* for the lifting of the ban imposed on the State Congress in 1938 and Nehru's articles on Socialism in 1933-34 and his work '*The Glimpses of World History*' had impelled these elements towards the Communism that infiltrated from the southern border, resulting towards the close of 1939 in the organisation of party units in the Region.[529] Intensive and sustained efforts had been made by the party organisers in the respective areas for enrolling members from ryots, factory workers, especially those belonging to large-scale industries such as the Azam Jahi Textile Mills and the Singareni Collieries, municipal workers including those relating to Warangal Municipality, *hammals*, cartmen and other sections of the toiling population.[530]

The remarkable success of these efforts could be seen from the fact that the 12th session of the Andhra *Maha Sabha* sponsored by its Communist Wing and held at Khammam in Warangal District from the 26th to 28th April, 1945, under the presidentship of Ravi Narayana Reddy, the young and dynamic left-wing leader in the Region,[531] was attended by a record number of 15,000 to 20,000 participants.[532] It is also significant to note that good number of Communists from the Andhra Districts of the Madras Presidency, spearheaded by P. Sundaraiah, the Secretary of the Communist Party, Bezwada[533] and R. Sathyanarayana, editor of '*Prajasakti*', took an active part in the deliberations of this Conference, thereby indicating the continuity of link between the parental organisation and the newly sprung branches in the Hyderabad State, which, of course, was not only maintained but rather strengthened, including at the All-India level during the remaining period.[534] The tours undertaken by prominent rightwing or Nationalist Section leaders of the Andhra *Maha Sabha* such as Mandumula Narasinga Rao and Konda Venkat Ranga Reddy in the villages of Warangal and Nalgonda Districts at this time in a bid to counteract the growing influence of the Communist wing, made little headway,[535] for they represented the more moderate and propertied classes and never, unlike the left wing, came forward to work for the redressal of the grievances of the poor peasants, tenants and labourers or adopt means other than resolutions and petitions.[536] The interests of the latter, in fact, ran counter to those of the former. On the other hand, the fact that those persons who volunteered their services to the Communist Party were paid Rs. 80 per month besides daily food, though subject to veracity, might have served as considerable inducement for the unemployed, the underfed and the agricultural labourers to join in it.[537] Even otherwise, the considerations that this Party through its *Sanghams*,[538] consisting of ryots as well as labourers, fought for the removal of the much-hated *Jagirdari* and *Deshmukhi* exploitation, the distribution of lands for the landless tenants and prevention of eviction of tenants and also the raising of the wages of agricultural and industrial labourers, had in the main, enabled it to command enough following in the areas of its influence.

(*i*) *War Period* : In the initial period of 1942-45 or the War period, the party directed its struggle for freeing the *Begaris*[539] and *Balotadars*[540] from customary and unremitted service to *Jagirdars*, *Deshmukhs*, village officials and Government officials, the solving of the difficulties experienced by small and middle peasants as well as tenants in respect of levy grain, land revenue and War Fund collections and the supply of essential and rationed agricultural items like iron bands for bullock-carts, plough-shares, yarn for weavers and skinned-leather for cobblers and the all-important and serious problem of preventing the eviction of tenants from vast *Jagirdari* and *Deshmukhi* lands.[541] As a measure of gaining the following of

Scheduled classes such as *Dheds, Chamars, Malas* and *Madigas,* who mostly served as *Begaris* and Balotadars, they were encouraged to desist from discharging hereditary service remained mostly unpaid or nominally remunerated.[541] Warangal *Subedar* himself confessed that the Communists had been partly successful in these endeavours in Warangal District.[542] More than this, the procurement of levy grain and the collection of '*Khush Kharidi*'[543] both of which left little grain for small and middle peasants to carry on and on most of the occasions when the crop yields were not adequate obliging them to contract grain loans at prices that ranged 2 to 2½ times more than the levy price that they received, together with the unfortunate contingency that under the rigours of the inefficient Rationing system, they were forced to purchase iron for agricultural implements at exorbitant black market rates, created the most suffocating and intolerable conditions embracing these sections of the peasantry.[544] *Ryotu Sanghams* under the Communist banner vitally exploited these conditions by encouraging the peasants to resist, even with force, the imposition of these unequal and unjust levies—unequal and unjust in the sense that big landholders who controlled 93 % of the total food production in the State, contributed little levy grain and indulged in large-scale hoarding and smuggling for the enjoyment of higher prices and profits than what the low Government levy prices could offer them[545]—and thereby emerged as their real friends and saviours. It was essentially due to their encouragement that during the years 1946-48, the physical resistance of the poor peasants to the forcible collection of levy grain in the backward Taluqus of Kinwat, Boath and Sirpur in Adilabad District, Huzurabad in Karimnagar District and Boorgampahad in Warangal District, resulted in the Killing of six Revenue Inspectors and injuring or manhandling of one Second *Taluqdar* and six Revenue Inspectors.[546]

The instigation of the Communists in respect of non-payment of land revenue was referred by *Subedar* in the case of Warangal District for the year 1945-46.[547] Even otherwise, the revenue demand in respect of both dry and wet land in the *Suba* was not only on the constant rise throughout the period proving 2½ to 3 times higher than the rates prevailing in the neighbouring areas of the Madras Presidency, but remained very much inelastic and irrational in the sense that the differing price levels of agricultural commodities had no effect in the fixation of the assessments.[548] The grant of revenue remissions also which was mainly done in respect of wet lands, benefited only the wealthy landlords who monopolised these lands and enjoyed easy access to Revenue Officials.[549] War Fund collections, though supposed to be voluntary, proved in reality very much burdensome and obligatory to the *Suba* people. The inspectors that had been appointed to make the people purchase the War Bonds subjected the ryots to severe trouble by trying to sell the maximum, for they received commission on this basis.[550] The fact that during the year 1943-44, Rs. 3,61, 417-1-8 and Rs. 50,351-12-1 had been collected from *Suba* Districts towards Victory Fund and purchase of War Bonds respectively[551] and Government's readiness, as early as 1939-40, to advance three months' salary as loan to employees to enable them to purchase War Bonds,[552] stand as indications that the collections loomed large, very much to the suffering of the already famished population. Failure to meet the demands of the Inspectors were threatened with opening of the grain stores of the concerned villagers for accounting, which amounted to their mouths being shut.[553] The Communist units were stated to have strived in this regard, for lessening the rigours of these collections on the lower strata of the population, evidently by standing behind them in effecting denials and by taking the Administration to task through the press. Much Public sympathy was gained by the party on this score for organising a mass movement in the ensuing years.[554]

It has already been seen that frequent and easy eviction of tenants, even of long-standing nature, became the common characteristic of both *Diwani* and non-*Diwani* land tenures that were in vogue in the *Suba* Districts during the period. The difference between the two in this respect remained only of a degree but not of a kind, in the sense that in the latter, unlike in the former, even *Pattedars* cultivating the lands for as long a period as 90 years, had come to be regarded as *Shikmidars*.[555] To retain the leverage for frequent hike in rents and to prevent the cultivators from gaining prescriptive rights under the terms of the Act, these methods of dispossession had been resorted.[556] It is significant to realise in this connection that in respect of the percentage of landless tenants to total number of cultivators in the Surveyed villages of 1949-50, Warangal and Adilabad Districts occupied respectively the first and fourth places among all the Districts in the State, with Karimnagar District of course, due to 79.9% of its total being occupant cultivators (third in the State), having landless tenants to the percentage level of only 8.2, being the third lowest in the State.[557] In fact, the percentage of landless to occupancy tenants had increased rather alarmingly from 24 to 71 in Warangal District between 1929-30 and 1949-50.[558] But, with the emergence of the leftist wing of the Andhra *Maha Sabha*, landlordly or *Jagirdari* attempts at land evictions had come to be physically resisted. To cite some of the instances, in Allipuram and Thimmapuram, *Jagir* villages of Anwar Pasha, Mulakalagudem village held by *Zamindar*[559] Pingali Ranga Reddy and Vasikallu village controlled by the landlord Vengal Narasimha Reddy, all in Warangal District, when large-scale evictions of the tenants had been attempted by the concerned feudal lords during 1944-46, the land involved, for example being 1,000 acres in the last-named village, the tenants gathering their strength under Communist leadership and armed with *lathis*[560] and slings were able to successfully repulse attack of *goondas* and Police employed by the former and retain their possession over the land.[561] Incidents of similar nature that occurred in landlord-dominated villages in the area and mainly in the former District, had only served to strengthen the morale of the Party to take up wider issues like land seizure and rise in agricultural wages, during the Struggle period of 1946-48.

(*ii*) *Character of the Struggle* : Telangana insurrection of 1946-51 started and ended in the villages. Even though Communists were there in sizeable numbers in the workers' Unions at urban and industrial centres such as Warangal, Kothagudem, Khammam and Hyderabad, these working classes had not been organised to demonstrate their solidarity behind the Peasant Movement.[562] As a matter of fact, the demands and interests of the agricultural labourers also had not been fought for, for they ran counter to the desires of small landlords and rich peasants, which the Party least tried to disturb in the multi-class alliance which it proposed during the Struggle.[463] The Movement consequently became a Peasant Partisan Struggle facilitating its enemies to base their counter-operations from the towns and cities and at the same time obliging the former to draw its essential supplies including medicines from the distant Indian towns and cities across the border.[564] This factor had exercised considerable difference for the success of the Conflict.

A survey of the events during the Struggle would go to indicate that the major scene of operations was confined to those *Suba* Taluqs where land monopolization was at its maximum and simultaneously where the Communist *dalams*[565] were in commanding influence. Such conditions obtained in general in Warangal District and the Taluqs of Sirsilla, Jagtiyal, Huzurabad and Sultanabad in Karimnagar District. In Adilabad District, though there had been certain pockets of heavy land concentration such as those in Luxettipet, Chinnoor and Sirpur Taluqs,[566] the Struggle was not intense even in these areas, for the Andhra *Maha Sabha* activity in this District was started only in 1942, twenty one years after the founding of the parent organisation of Andhra *Jana Kendra Sangham.*[567] Further, prominent figures of the District such as J.V. Narsing Rao, K.V. Keshavulu, Murali Manohar Rao,[568] etc., had all subscribed to Hyderabad State Congress, whose branch Offices in all the Taluq headquarters of the District had also come to be established only around 1946-47.[569] In Warangal District as early as 1929-30, it was found in the Survey that 1.7% of the occupants held more than 35% of the total dry land in the Surveyed villages and 2.5% of the occupants held more than 50% of the total wet area in them.[570] Again, during the 25 years preceding 1949-50, land transfers including inheritances and partitions, stood highest in this District among all others in the State, in respect of both dry and wet land, followed of course, by Adilabad District.[571] The extent of this evil of land concentration in this District could be gauged from the fact that the *Deshmukh* of Kallur in Madhira Taluq owned, 1,00,000 acres of land, being the second biggest holder in the State, first being Janna Reddy Pratap Reddy in Suryapet Taluq of Nalgonda District, owning 1,50,000 acres.[572] It became further manifest that in Mahaboobadad Taluq where there was highest degree of land monopolization in *Diwani* as well as non-*Diwani* feudal lords, 96 out of 147 Killings that occurred in Warangal District between the Police Action and the middle of 1949 (roughly one year), had been reported from this Taluq only, amounting to 65.30% of the District total.[573]

Besides the economic objectives of resisting the feudal exploitation and gain out of it the benefits of surplus land distribution among the landless, protection of tenancy rights and enhancement of the wages of agricultural labourers, the Party and the Struggle led by it had entertained some makeshift political stances. During the Second War period influenced by the Party policy at the All-India level of contributing for smooth relations between the British and the Soviet Union in view of the War front, it failed to make strong and clear demands, either for the real transfer of power by the former of for the abolition of the *Nizam's* regime in the State. On the other hand, placing unfounded confidence in the secular and popular claims of the Muslim League and the *Ittehad-ul-Muslimeen*,[574] it advocated the parity of representation in the proposed interim executive councils between the former and the Congress at the India level and between the latter and the State Congress, otherwise based in the Andhra *Maha Sabha*, Maharashtra and Karnataka *Parishads* at the State level. Movement leaders such as P. Sundaraiah and Ravi Narayana Reddy subsequently confessed that these attitudes proved on the wrong side.[575] During the post-War and Struggle period also, no consistency in the stand of the party was maintained. When the *Razakars* had perpetrated their destructive raids on the local population during the pre-Police Action days of 1946-48, these provided the opportunity for the *Reds* to take up the cudgels on the opposite side.[576] The entry of the Indian Army on to the scene following Police Action or even before it since the days of Indian Independence when the *Nizam's* Government had come to adopt an anti-Indian stand on the question of accession and in that mood lifted the ban that was earlier continuing on the Communists in the State, had brought the two former enemies together against their new common enemy.[577] It was further maintained by the New Administration that arms flowed from the *Razakars* and the Police to the Communist insurgents.[578] These differing and inconsistent political stances of the Party both before and during the Struggle made it incapable of fully concentrating its energies on issues relating to land and further, on this score, it got deprived of the support to its economic programme of those sections of the local population which did not subscribe to its views on the political front.[579]

(*iii*) *Stages of the Conflict* : The imminent withdrawal of the British from India and the refusal of the *Nizam* to accede to the latter, led to political emergency that came in handy for the Communist Party to start its machinations in 1946-47 in the Telangana Districts bordering the Madras Presidency.[580] The time gap that would be available before the Indian Union intervenes in the matter and the anarchical conditions that would result in the State, consequent on the forcible suppression of its Ruler, were designed to be utilised for the realisation of nothing short of an ultimate Red Raj in the region.[581] It hoped further that any military intervention by the Indian Government would lead to a Kashmir type of stalemate, or in other words, complication of the issue by the intervention of external agencies.[582] But, as would be seen, its expectations proved very much belied. The events of the Struggle and their import could better be appreciated if examined under the captions of (*a*) the pre-Police Action period, (*b*) Warfare in the plains and (*c*) forest and guerilla raids.[583] Whereas Khammam-Madhira-Palvancha area, with its rich economic and natural resources and greater social and economic links with the Krishna and Godavari Districts of the Madras Presidency, figured prominently in the events that occurred until the close of 1948, the Mulug-Mahabooba-bad-Warangal area, on the other hand, with its thick forests and heavy composition of big landlords was chiefly associated with the events of 1949-51,[584] Rich and middle peasantry rather than poor peasantry and agricultural labourers predominated in the former the Movement here was based more than in other areas, on their demands instead of those of the latter.[585] The other known centres of Sirsilla, Jagtiyal, Huzurabad, Sultanabad and Manthena in Karimnagar District and Chinnoor, Sirpur and Adilabad in Adilabad District, being marked by forest and riverine tracts, exhibited revolutionary activity much in the latter period than in the former which, in these areas as well as in Mulug-Mahaboobabad-Warangal area, was due to the fact that the Communists after losing their battle in the plains with the army units deployed by the Indian Government, retreated since the beginning of 1949 into the forest, riverine and inaccessible tracts to carry on the guerilla offensives. The latter in these areas were essentially directed against the hated feudal lords and their supporters or followers by the lower peasants and agricultural labourers.

(*a*) *I Stage* : Revolutionary feeling during the 1946-48 days originated in the troubles of the people that arose from the ills of the Procurement System.[586] As early as 8th February, 1946, restrictive orders curtailing the movement outside the native village, were imposed for one year on the persons of Baddam Yella Reddy, the General Secretary of Andhra *Maha Sabha*, Prabhakara Rao, P. Shankaraiah and K.V. Muralidhar, all being Party leaders from Karimnagar District, for the obvious reason that these were going to the ryots and explaining about the loopholes in the System.[587] But, such order only served to further intensify popular disaffection on this score.[588] Political and constitutional complications that had set in with the starting of the State Congress agitation in June, 1947 for State's accession to the Indian Union and the efforts of the Administration to supress it by employing the services of not only the Police and the army, but also the *Majlis* and the *Razakars*, had fully aggravated the situation in the *Suba* as well as the State by unleashing a reign of terror and insecurity, affecting the richer and the poorer sections alike. The whole of Warangal District was declared a 'disturbed area' in July, 1947 and all meetings and processions were banned[589]. *Razakar* camps had been set up in all towns and Key centres like Khammam, Madhira, Bonakalu, Nelakondapalli, Kallur and Wyra, all in

Warangal District and military squads were posted at every railway station, besides a regular military patrol train on the railway line from Madhira to Warangal.[590] Loot, arson, murder and rape became so much the order of the day at the hands of these agencies along with the Reserve Police[591] that the people affected were obliged to seek help from the Communist squads who established centres of resistance and could successfully free the villages under their control that were estimated to be 2,000 in the beginning of 1948,[592] from this reactionary repression.[593] Big land lords and *Deshmukhs* in Taluqs like Mahaboobabad extended their active and full co-operation to these repressive elements, for they eagerly tried to wreak vengeance on the leftist elements who began opposing servictude to feudal elements.[594] Though the number of persons that lost their lives in the *Suba* Districts during the *Razakar* days as given by Sundaraiah, appeared to be small except in Jangaon and Warangal Taluqs,[595] the actual amount of destruction caused to property and distress to inhabitants, was so colossal and horrible that an inkling of it could be had from the fact that, when some of the villages in Palvancha Taluq of Warangal District declared, befitting the prevailing political and popular sentiment, their independence from the *Nizam's* yoke,[595a] a raid by 2,000 strong *Nizam's* Armed Forces and *Ittehad Razakars* on 20th February, 1948 on them resulted in the burning of 50 villages to ashes, thereby rendering 20,000 villagers homeless and evacuating.[596]

The new alliance that developed between the *Nizam's* Government and the Communists in March or April, 1948, had proved a blessing for the latter, but not for the people[597]. The former were able to strengthen their hold over the villages that were already under their influence and started the seizure of land, cattle and the grain from wealthy *watandars* for distribution among the agricultural labourers and poor peasants.[598] But, the latter programme especially that relating to land, seemed according to the claims of the Party, mainly confined to Madhira Taluq of Warangal District, totalling around 20,500 acres, out of which again, 20,000 acres were stated to have been permanently seized from the *Deshmukh* of Kallur alone.[599] On the other hand, during this pre-

Police Action period, Mahaboobabad Taluq alone, of the same District figured in respect of foodgrain distribution to the extent of 12,000 bags for which Rs. 1,35,000 was collected. As many as twenty squads consisting of about 400 members carried on raids on *Deshmukh gadis*[600] in this Taluq for this purpose and also for the very fact that these remained as the centuries old hated fortresses of the feudal lords.[601] Confining of these agrarian and economic results to such a far limited portion of one District in the *Suba* was, it is very much significant to note, due to the all-important fact that the Struggle objective of the Party units except in Nalgonda District and in a few adjacent Taluqs of the Warangal District such as the above, remained essentially the State Congress goal of attaining union with India, instead of achieving agrarian demands.[602] Consequently, it was claimed that 70% of the total land that was redistributed pertained to Nalgonda District only.[603] The lone dedication of the Nalgonda District Committee for the carrying on of agrarian struggle[604] and the hobnobbing of units in other areas with rightist parties like the Congress that did not believe in the practical realisation of economic democracy,[605] had been the factors for these differential Struggle results, though of course, the domination of the rich peasants elements in the multi-class alliance that the party had projected, led to the general set back of the agrarian movement.[606] On the other hand, the three pronged raids by the Communists, the Police and *Ittehad* during this period had, besides the loss of valuable property, shaken the morale of both the rich and the poor people to such an extent that they began to take shelter either in forests or the border British Indian areas.[607] In view of the communal relations being affected under such conditions of lawlessness, even merchants from towns including that of Warangal, fled for safety to British Indian towns such as Guntur, Bezwada, Bangalore and Rajahmundry, thereby very much paralysing the business and the trading interests in the area.[608]

The Indian armed intervention in Hyderabad led to significant changes not only in State administration, but also in the course of the Telangana Struggle and even the general tenor of people's life. The entry of the Union forces in the

Telangana region was followed in a day or two by mob attacks on *Deshmukh gadis* and railway godowns in Mahaboobabad and Warangal Taluqs of Warangal District, where landlord oppression attained a pronounced degree. Along with the grain seizure and destruction of the landlord mansions, the masses in their outburst of fury and indignation had also indulged in the assassinations of the hated *Deshmukhs* and their male heirs. Some of the latter even took their lives by themselves, instead of falling into the hands of the insurgents.[609] Huge stocks of levy grain kept in the Railway Stations at Dornakal, Papatapalli and Garla, all in the same District, amounting to 10,000 bags of paddy at the former, 300 bags of rice and 200 bags of paddy at the second one and the entire lot at the latter were snatched by mass raids, the one at Dornakal on September 15th, comprising as many as 10,000 people and the grain got distributed mostly among the participants.[610] *Razakar*, police and military camps that had been functioning in Warangal and Karimnagar Districts during the preceeding two years and had incurred much displeasure and anger of the people, had also been made targets of attack, inflicting casualties and also seizing arms from the fleeing or the dead victims.[611] The fear that the newly arrived Indian Army contingent would stall their activities, had probably prompted the insurgent masses to indulge in such pre-emptive strikes against their sworn enemies and their vestiges.

But yet, during the four months period before the Police Action, the C.P.I. failed to made any preparations even though there was wide speculation about Indian armed intervention.[612] Further, in spite of the fact that it brought under its control a large number of villages in Nalgonda and Warangal Districts by the beginning of 1948, no large military units other than village squads, covering atleast three or four villages were developed[613] nor any military training on an elementary scale either to operate the weapons or to plan the armed operations, was imparted to the members.[614] Larger operations, in a way, were not possible for there was no Party organisation above the village level that could bring about coordination at a higher level.[615] The result was that when

Gen. Chaudhri's men started their offensive within a fortnight of their entry into Hyderabad on 18th September, 1948, neither the village *dalams* nor the tactics of the Struggle organisers proved any match to the former,[616] besides the disappointment that the Party's hopes regarding the expected stalemate in the armed intervention affair did not come true.[617] The latter had always been put on the defensive and in retreat, so much so that when by the end of December, 1948, the military attacks, reinforced by those of the Police, were intensified,[618] the fighting insurgents were obliged to move from the plain areas of Khammam, Madhira, Warangal, parts of Mahaboobabad and Yellandu Taluqs, to the nearby forest and riverine tracts of Yellandu, Palvancha, Mulug and Pakhal Taluqs of Warangal District and to Mahadeopur and Chinnoor Taluqs in Karimnagar and Adilabad Districts respectively.[619] The latter tracts being less exposed and more inaccessible and composed of good number of tribals, very much suited the guerilla type of raids that were carried on during 1949-51.

(*b*) *II Stage* : It is significant to realise that during this second stage of the Struggle, not only was there a shift in the theatres of the fighting, but also a radical transformation in the class content of the participants and their War aims. In the first place, whereas the CPI leaders and members from Suryapet[620]—Khammam—Mahaboobabad areas stood firm to continue the Struggle after the Police Action for the protection and consolidation of the economic gains that had been achieved during the preceding period, those in the other area of the *Suba* Districts on the contrary, led by the thinking of leaders like Ravi Narayana Reddy, Baddam Yella Reddy and Nallamala Giri Prasad,[621] strongly opted for the withdrawal of the Struggle after the merger of the State with the Indian Union and adoption of legal and other available struggle forms for the latter purpose.[622] This attitude of the latter regarding Struggle aims, was responsible for the slowing down of the agrarian movement as it was hitherto coming.[623] Consequently, with the take-over of the State's Administration by the Military Governor, many of the squad members surrendered or buried their arms in the latter areas and returned to their villages[624] and the few that still carried on the Struggle, being influenced by the former ideology propagated by the left CPI leaders like Devulapalli Venkateshwara Rao and P. Sundaraiah,[625] did from jungle and hilly hideouts in the area.

In the second place, the rich peasants and the smaller lords who got offended by the levy grain impositions and *Razakar* raids had joined the Struggle during the first stage, now began to withdraw their support, for they could not get reconciled to the extremist demand.[626] These latter classes who, during the first stage remained mainly preoccupied with the resistance of food grain levies and extraction of *begari* or *vetti*,[627] now began to make insistent demands for more and more land distribution and increase in agricultural wages.[628] The satisfaction of both these requirements necessitated cooperation and sacrifice from the rich peasants who, on the other hand, showed their utmost reluctance, although in fighting against the *Jagirdari* and *Deshmukhi* exploitation during the pre-Police Action days, they were fully supported by these poorer sections.[629] Even the village squads also functioned very much under the leadership of rich peasants and landlords.[630] The latter shared the conviction that the meeting of these demands would lead to undermining their all-important position among the peasantry and the unfortunate fact in the agrarian fact of the Struggle was that the Communist Party, except in Nalgonda District, had accorded so much significance to this rich peasantry in its multi-class front that it got ready to restrain the development of the Struggle so as to gain the support of this upper layer whose role, especially after 1948, remained very much passive in the history of the Movement.[631] Hence, in effect, the Party in this area lined up behind the State Congress in voting for the demands of this bourgeois group to the effect that the State's accession was fought as the main issue of the Struggle which called a halt on its realisation, just at the time when the left-oriented poor peasants and agricultural labourers were becoming more aggressive in their demands in Mahaboobabad, Mulug and Warangal areas.[632]

(*iv*) *Conclusion of the Struggle* : However, on account of the Telangana Struggle, the abolition of the *Jagirdari* system and the passing of the Tenancy and Agricultural Lands Act in

June, 1950[633] were, in not a small measure, due to the effect and the impression created by this Peasants Movement.[634] These salient measures had the effect of taking the sail out of the winds of Communism by trying to remove the two proven breeding grounds of feudal exploitation on which the former thrived. It is, of course, significant to observe in this connection that the *Jagirs* removal by August, 1949, had, in a way, resulted in a concentrated and all-pronounced attack on *Deshmukhs*, the second order of feudal lords, during the remaining period of the Struggle.

The dissensions in the CPI which grew like an insidious evil culminating in an unforgeable split, centred round the aspects of support to Nehru's Government, adoption of non-militant, legal and constitutional methods and the rich peasantry or the bourgeosie element dominating in the multi-class front proposed for Peasant or Agrarian Movement, etc. It thus started that, when P.C. Joshi as Secretary of the Party during the post-Independence period raised the slogan of support to Nehru's Government, it was not received well by other leaders in the Party who had their upper hand by getting their representative B.R. Ranadive elected as Secretary in the place of the former. A violent and terroristic method of struggle was carried on under his leadership in Telangana, Andhra and other places in the country.[635] Internal criticism became intense. Whereas P.C. Joshi's group accused the former of violent activities, the Party in its announcement stated that under his leadership, it failed to implement its programme in villages, unity of ryots was broken and they were made helpless before exploitation.[636] Things led to the replacement of Ranadive by C. Rajeshwar Rao in May, 1950.

Further, the Party was incapable of taking up the Struggle for the protection of the gains that had already been achieved, because of the fact that it involved the question of State power and the ruling class, at that particular time, both in Hyderabad and in India, was in no mood to grant any concession either to poor peasants or to agricultural labourers.[637] Even, the direction of the Struggle and a call to its halt, in areas other than Nalgonda District, symbolished the interests of the bourgeois elements rather than those of the former.[638] The differing and the make-shift political stances that the Party held both before and during the course of the Struggle was also responsible for dissipating its energies on issues other than land and wages and depriving it of the support of those sections of the population, including the industrial workers that did not subscribe to its differing political creed.[639] Added to these, the lack of any independent organisations of the peasants or agricultural labourers other than the disorganised masses or hordes that collected under the force of temporary emotion or expedient, had also served as a considerable handicap in organising an independent struggle for the consolidation of the gains that had already been secured.[640]

The conduct of the Struggle from the base of the forest region, especially that banking on the river Godavari, during the last three years of the Movement, had resulted in the separation of the plains people from its mainstream who, as a matter of fact, formed its essential segment of support.[641] Hence the Struggle could maintain only a starved and depleted existence, not in a position to strike any offensive, but always on the defensive. Further, the lack of communications, atleast by road, to the rebel habitations, though served as a protection cover from the enemy attacks, had at the same time, made it a difficult task for the former to secure essential supplies like medicines or ammunition and also information that became requisite, from beyond the hills which, in turn, led to slowing down or hampering the operations. These difficulties were further heightened by the fact that the Movement, due to non-mobilization of the working classes, did not spread to the urban areas which would have well fulfilled such Struggle requirements.[642]

Split in the Party leading to clashes among the fighting members, the non-inclination of the Struggle organisers in the *Suba* area to carry it on any longer after the Indian armed intervention was over, let alone fighting for the realisation or protection of agrarian gains, the difficulites and the ordeals that were involved in carrying on forest warfare for nearly three years and above all, the eagerness of the CPI leaders to contest in the 1952 General Elections, had brought about a feeling of war-wearism both among the fighting insurgents and their leaders.[643] Though the CPI Central Committee in its 1951, May, meeting held only around five months before the conclusion of the Struggle, decided that no eviction of ryots from occupied lands should be made, lands forcibly seized from them should be given back and tribal people should have freedom in the extraction and sale of forest produce and cultivation of lands of their choice in thier areas of habitation.[644] These never seem to have been insisted as guarantees for the ending of the Struggle. Let alone these demands, the desperate position of the Communists at this time was so well realised and exploited by the Indian Government that even after the withdrawal of the Struggle, the ban that had been earlier imposed on them by the latter had not been lifted so as to enable them to contest the elections on their Party name and symbol, in consequence of which they took part as PDF (Progressive Democratic Front) candidates, though won convincing victories.[645]

The organisation of educational and health services, vital for the economic development of the land, was at its lowest ebb in Warangal *Suba* during the study period. With 6.1 and 5.9 percentages of literacy in 1951, Karimnagar and Adilabad Districts ranked respectively the two lowest and most backward among all Districts in the State.[646] The number of even Primary Schools was not more than 35 out of an average number of 250 villages in any one of the Taluqs of the latter District. Comparatively, better facilities of transport and communications, greater percentage of urban population and slightly better library and reading-room facilities, gave Warangal District a slightly better literacy percentage of 8.2, which however, stood less than that of the State, the latter remaining at 9.2.[647] Among the manifold factors that contributed for this educational backwardness of the area, those that deserved mention are, less spending on this service by the Government, the *Jagirs* and the Local Bodies, imposition of minority language as the medium of instruction, discouragement to the establishment of private schools, poor encouragement to public libraries and restrictions that were kept on press and freedom.[648]

Public Health Service which remained essentially curative

than preventive, got confined only to District and Taluq headquarter towns.[649] The medical facilities in the State, even by the middle of 1949, had been so meagre and inadequate that on an average, one dispensary existed for 235 square miles and one hospital bed for 68,000 of the population,[650] which figures compare so poorly with those of Mysore State, another princely State in the South that in the latter, as early as in 1935, one such institution existed for every 94 square miles of area, serving 20,653 persons.[651] The little interest that the Government showed on this welfare activity was evident from the fact that its spending on this item as a percentage of total expenditure ran from 3.46 in 1934-35 to only 3.55 in 1948-49, in other words, an increase of 0.9 over a period of 14 years.[652] Lack of pure drinking water facilities for majority of the villages, utter neglect of drainage and road-cleaning even in big towns like Warangal, mal-nutritious diet and excessive consumption of liquor etc., had been the major disease-prone and causative factors in the *Suba* Districts. In no decade during the period, were the latter free from the known epidemic diseases of plague, cholera and small-pox or the endemic diseases of malaria, *yaws*, tuberculosis, leprosy and guinea-worm. No preventive or curative measures ever seem to have been undertaken either by the Government or the Local Bodies in an effective manner.[653]

Urban development during the period got confined to limited centres and in general, remained slow and tardy. Warangal, Khammam, Yellandu, Karimnagar, Jagtiyal, Nirmal, Adilabad, Peddapalli and Kothagudem figured as important urban areas in the *Suba* Districts. Among these, the former two because of the better growth of industrial, trade and transport interests, recorded remarkable development to the effect that Warangal during 1911-51 registered an increase of 301.74% in its population and Khammam during 1901-51 showed an increase of 224 % in its population. On the contrary, such conditions had been so poor and backward that even by 1931, Asifabad, Rajura, Luxettipet, Sirpur, Boath and Kinwat, all in Adilabad District, in spite of being Taluq headquarters, failed to reach even the minimum population limit of 5,000 persons in order to be recognised as towns.[654]

The development was so tardy that during 1911-41, the number of major and minor municipalities rose from 7 to 10 in the *Suba.*[655] The control, composition, income and expenditure of these and other Local Bodies was very much determined by urban and official elements to the suppression of others.[656] The maintenance of sanitary and civic functions by these Bodies left much to be desired even in major municipalities like Warangal and Khammam.[657]

Tribals such as Gonds, Koyas, Hill Reddis and *Banjaras* formed important segments of rural population in Warangal and Adilabad Districts. Their peaceful, prosperous and even tenor of life was rudely shaken by road development connecting their habitations with the plain areas during the second and third decades of the present century which, in turn, brought the rapacious and greedy cultivators, money-lenders and forest contractors from the latter, to exploit the tribal resources in land, cattle and labour to the maximum. The immigrant *watandars*, forest, police and revenue officials had further aided in the total expropriation of the aboriginals, in consequence of which, majority of the latter left their ancestral habitations and migrated to neighbouring British Indian tracts where the conditions were regarded to be far better, especially in the Agency area of East Godavari District of the Madras Presidency. The condition of *Banjaras*, an immigrant tribe, looked very much different from that of the aboriginals, for the former by their shrewdness and income from carrying trade, were able to occupy good and vast stretches of land and also *watan* rights in aboriginal villages that they settled in.[658]

Telangana Struggle of 1946-51 came as a grand finale to the suffering and distress of the millions in Telangana Region and especially of the common people of the Eastern Districts. What with feudal exploitation, *Vetti*, land evictions, high rents and grain procurement, the peasants, tenants, small landlords and agricultural labourers, had been so much vexed and exasperated that they were in a mood of conflagration. The non-agricultural classes like merchants, weavers and other craftsmen also had bitter experiences of *Jagirdari* and *Deshmukhi* oppression. Communism that infiltrated from the

Madras Presidency towards the beginning of the Second War had, by 1945, got well entrenched as the left-wing of the Andhra *Maha Sabha* in Nalgonda, Warangal and Karimnagar Districts. Starting initial resistance in 1945-46 against land evictions, procurement loopholes, *begari* and War Fund collections and after gaining initial successes, the Party launched the real Struggle towards the close of 1946, choosing the opportune time of *Nizam's* refusal to accede to the Indian Union. It met with such astounding success that at the beginning of 1948, it had not less than 2,000 villages under its control. But, having sensed that Indian armed intervention was in the near offing, it failed to make adequate preparations nor was its political organisation which never extended above village level, was capable of taking up such a task. As a result, when the inevitable came, it wilted under its pressure and retreated in 1949 from plains to forests. Though the Struggle was continued until October, 1951, by means of guerilla raids and mostly in the shape of individual terroristic raids against *Deshmukhs* and their minions, it was a divided command in the sense that compaign organisers in the *Suba* Districts called it off, for the most part, after the Police Action. Rich peasants, poor peasants, tenants and agricultural labourers who had all fought together against feudal and landlord oppression in the first stage of the Struggle, now found their interests clashing as the latter three groups began to make insistent demands for land distribution and higher wages that antagonised the former. The CPI units except in Nalgonda District, followed the line of the Congress in protecting the interests of the rich peasantry rather than continue the Struggle in support of the demands of the left-oriented poor peasants, tenants and agricultural labourers. Riven by such dissensions resulting towards the end of 1950 in mutual clashes among fighting Party members, with guerilla raids proving ineffective and purposeless[658a] and the eagerness of the Party leaders to contest in the 1952 General Elections, the Struggle was finally withdrawn.[659] Irrespective of the gains made and the extent to which they were allowed to be retained, which is impossible to assess in view of the lack of records regarding them,[660] the Struggle and its leaders deserve all credit for transforming the dumb, meek and innocent Telangana peasants into an active, defying and *lathi*-wielding determined lot ready to fight and sacrifice for defending the rights which they believed with full heart.

•

REFERENCES

1. M.L. Gujral 'Health Organization and Medical Relief' in V.B. Singh (Ed.), *Economic History of India*, (New Delhi, 1975), p. 704.
2. R.D. Choksey : *Economic History of the Bombay, Deccan and Karnatak* (1818-68), (Poona, 1945), p. 128.
3. Royal Commission Report on Agriculture in India, *op. cit.*, p. 559.
4. See Table I and Section 'Area and Population' in Chapter II.
5. 1951 Census, Part I-Report, *op. cit.*, p. 455.
6. See the Sections 'Location and Natural Divisions' in Chapter II and 'Transport Development' in Chapter VII.
7. Vera Anstey, *Economic Development of India*, (London, 1929), p. 66.
8. Remarks of Hon'ble *Nawab* Zain Yar Jung Bahadur, Member, Public Health, Government of Hyderabad, in *The Deccan Chronicle*, 3-6-1949.
9. Confidential Diary for the month of Dai, 1356 Fasli (November, 1946-47) submitted by *Taluqdar Saheb*, Adilabad to *Subedar* Warangal, in W.S. *File* No. 15 of 1356 Fasli & R. No. 14 of 1356 Fasli.
10. Romesh Thapar, *op. cit.*, p 11.
11. 1951 Census Part-I, Report, *op. cit.*, p. 229.
12. *Ibid.*, Part II, Tables, p. 4.
13. *Ibid.*, p. 243.
14. See Chapters I, III and VII in this respect.
15. 1951 Census, Part I-Report, *op. cit.*, p. 23.
16. See Chapter VII.
17. *Golkonda Patrika* (Bi-Weekly), 11-5-1939 ; *Meezan* (Telugu edition), 29-12-1944. The Warangal Municipality, being the first in Telangana was established along with six others in Marathwada in 1934-35 *Administrative Report for 1345 Fasli* (*1935-36*), (Hyderabad-Dn, 1938), p. 135.
18. *Golkonda Patrika* (Daily), 18-9-1949. (Regarding Mahaboobabad Municipality in Warangal District) ; *Golkonda Patrika* (Bi-Weekly), 5-6-1939. (Regarding Khammam Municipality in Warangal District).
19. 1941 Census, Part II - Tables, *op. cit.*, p. 680. (Percentages are calculated).
20. Syed Khaja Abdul Gafoor, *op. cit.*, p. 49.

21. Observation of W.V. Grigson, Revenue and Police Member of H.E.H. the *Nizam's* Executive Council, in 1941 Census, Part I – Report, *op. cit.*, p. XLI (Appendix-I), See the relevant Section in this Chapter for vivid account on this.
22. See the Second Paragraph in Chapter I.
23. Christoph-Von-Furer-Haimendorf, 'Tribal Populations of Hyderabad Yesterday and Today' (essay) in 1941 Census Report, Part I-Report, Appendix I, *op. cit.*, p. LI.
24. Syed Khaja Abdul Gafoor, *op. cit.*, p. 38.
25. I. Thirumali, *op. cit.*, p. 95.
26. Attacks were made in thousands on *gadis* or mansions of *Deshmukhs*, *Razakar* and Police camps, seizing grain, cattle, etc., and putting to death the sworn enemies of the people—P. Sundarayya, *op. cit.*, pp. 183-84 & 87-88.
27. See the first para in the Section 'b, Tenants' in Chapter IV.
28. See Table XIII (b) and para third in sub-section 'c. The Prevention of Agricultural Land Alienation Act' in Chapter V.
29. See Table VIII in Chapter IV, Table XIII (b) & third para in Sub-section' (a) Land Transfers' and also third para in sub-section 'C. The prevention of Agricultural Land Alienation Act' in Chapter V.
30. Note the meagre percentages of Literacy that obtained in the *Suba* Districts mentioned in the first para of this Chapter.
31. *The Hyderabad Government Bulletin on Economic Affairs*, Vol. III, Nos. 1-3, January-March, 1950, p. 104.
32. Memoranda submitted to the Taxation Enquiry Committee, *op. cit.*, p. 48.
33. See the Section 'Local Government' in Chapter III.
34. Report on the Working of the Departments under the Revenue Secretariat, *op. cit*, p. 2 (Section V).
35. Gangaraju Raghunadha Rao, 'Village Problems in *Nizam's* State' in *Golkonda Patrika*, (Bi-Weekly), 5-4-1934.
36. See para three in the Section 'Administrative Changes' in Chapter III.
37. *Golkonda Patrika* (Daily), 14-7-1949.
38. 1921 Census, Part II, *op. cit.*, p. 194—The comparatively lesser percentage of Telugu-speaking population in Adilabad District was compensated by 23.22% Marathi-speaking population, 8.44% Gondi-speaking and 4.23% Lambadi-speaking population.
39. P. Sundarayya, *op. cit.*, p. 7.
40. Swami Ramananda Tirtha, *Memoirs of Hyderabad Freedom Struggle*, (Bombay, 1967), p. 65 ; P. Sundarayya, *op. cit.*, p. 7. (Private Middle Schools in mother tongue were allowed with the special permission of the *Nizam* and his administrators. which of course, became a very rare thing to be had).
41. Madapati Hanumantha Rao Vol. I, *op. cit.*, p. 13.
42. Enclosed in this Section.

43 Fortnightly Report on the political situation in the Hyderabad State for the year 1942 in *File* No. 9, (12)-P (S) 142, Political Department, 'P' Branch, p. 2, para 4.
44. Fortnightly Report, dated 30-9-1944, in *Micro Film Reel No. 2* & *Accession No. 45*, Para 7.
45. *Meezan*, 28-5-1947 (editional).
46 *Golkonda Patrika* (Daily), 14-7-1950 (editorial).
47. Crown Representative Reports, File No. 29 (45) I.A. 1938 in *Micro Film Reel No. 4* and *Accession No. 47*.
48. *Golkonda Patrika* (Daily), 14-7-1950.
49. Fortnightly Report dated 30-9-1944 in *Micro Film Reel No. 2, Accession No. 45*, Para 7.
50. See Table LVII attached in this Section.
51. See the earlier two paras in this Section.
52. Confidential Report of the First *Taluqdar* of Warangal to *Subedar*, Warangal, for the second fortnightly of Dai, 1354 Fasli (November, 1945) in W.S. *File* No. 30 of 1354 Fasli and R. No. 6 of 1357 Fasli (1948)—Emulated by his example, the merchants of Mathwada (Suburb of Warangal Proper) contributed Rs. 30 000 for the running of Andhra *Balika Patashala* (Girls School), F. N. Report of Bahman, 1354 Fasli (December, 1945).
53. Madapati Hanumanth Rao, Vol. I, *op. cit.*, p. 30 ; see para one in the Section 'Political Conditions' in Chapter III.
54. *Hyderabad Information*, Vol. II, No. 7, April, 1942, p. 22.
55. *Golkonda Patrika* (Daily), 14-7-1950.
56. Villages of Rayannapeta in Khammam Taluq contributed Rs. 1,500 for the construction of school building, but the school was suddenly closed without reason——*Meezan* (Telugu edition), 29-6-1944.
57. As English was not taught and Telugu and Urdu were taught only upto III class, some villagers to get their children better and higher instruction, in Edulabad (taken to be Adilabad) engaged a private teacher at their own expense, the Government Headmaster objected to it saying that Private Schools were banned and hence, it was forced to be withdrawn--*Meezan* (Telugu edition), 12-8-1944.
58. Suravaram Pratap Reddy : *Pradhamika Swatvamulu*, (Hyderabad-Dn, 1-11-1938), p. 47. (Percentages are calculated).
59. Report of the Education Department for 1347 Fasli (1938), in *Golkonda Patrika* (Bi-Weekly), 23-11-1939 (editorial). (Percentages are calculated).
60. *Hyderabad Government Bulletin on Economic Affairs*, Vol. II, No. 2, February, 1949, pp. 173-174.
61. Percentages are calculated.
62. *Jagir* Administrator, '*Jagir* Administration,' Vol. I, cited in A.M. Khusro., *op. cit.*, p. 11.
63. See the last para in the Section 'Other *Jagirs*' in Chapter VI.

64. See the observation made in the earlier part of this para and percentage is calculated.
65. *Hyderabad Government Bulletin on Economic Affairs*, Vol. II, No. 2, February, 1949, p. 174.
66. Providing instruction for classes upto third only.
67. Only given some monetary aid by the Government of the *Sarf-i-khas* but not completely administered by it.
68. W.S. *File* No. 3 of 1341 Fasli (1932) & R. No. 447 of 1343 Fasli (1934).
69. *Ibid.*
70. W.S. *File No.* 1 of 1343 Fasli (1934) & R. No. 492 of 1343 Fasli & No. 2 of 1343 Fasli & R. No. 481 of 1343 Fasli.
71. W.S. *File No.* 3 of 1342 Fasli (1933) & R. No. 465 of 1343 Fasli (1934).
72. Report of the Royal Commission on *Jagir* Administration and Reform, *op. cit.*, p. 81.
73. *Golkonda Patrika* (Daily), 7-10-1950.
74. Attached in this sub-section.
75. *Administrative Report for 1320 and 1321 Fasli* (*1910-12*), H.E.H. the Nizam's Government, p. 63.
76. Incorporated in this Section.
77. For Taluqwise number of villages, See Table VI in Chapter III.
78. 1951 Census, Part I-A, Report, *op. cit.*, pp. 19-20
79. Ratios are calculated.
80. See Table LVII included in this sub-section.
81. See Table LVI attached in this sub-section.
82. See Table LV included in this sub-section.
83. See the Section 'Transport Development' in Chapter VII.
84. See the third para at the beginning of this Chapter.
85. See the last but one para in the Section 'Administrative Conditions' in Chapter III.
86 See Table LVII included in this sub-section.
87. *Meezan*, (editorial) 17-10-1946.
88. *Ibid*—Chaderghat School, established years back in Hyderabad, suffered from lack of accommodation and some classes consequently, had to be run under trees and in huts.
89. *Meezan*, 19-8-1946.
90. See Table LVII—The exact character of 'Special School' mentioned in respect of Karimnagar District for the years 1926 and 1931 is not known. Though their number in these years was comparatively huge, yet the rise proved temporary only, as can be seen by the corresponding figure for the years 1922 and 1936.
91. 1951 Census, Part I—A, Report, *op. cit.*, p. 474.
92. The literacy percentages of Hyderabad District amounted to 8.5, 10.4, 16.4, 19.2 and 25.2 in 1911, 1921, 1931, 1941 and 1951 respectively—1951 Census, Part I-A, Report, *op. cit.*, p. 474—See Table LVI for total number of literates and those belonging to different educational standards.

93. 1951 Census Report, Part I-A, *op. cit.*, p. 460. See Table LVI included in this sub-section.
94. See Table LVI in this sub-section.
95. *Ibid.*
96. *Ibid.* See the third paragraph in the beginning of this Chapter.
97. 1931 Census, Part I-A, Report, *op. cit.*, p. 244.
98. Private schools in the countryside where a single teacher, very rarely with an academic degree, taught the boys as per his own method of training.
99. These are being understood as equivalent to Paise, or lowest denominations of a rupee.
100. John Law, *Modern Hyderabad* (Deccan), (Calcutta, 1914), p. 111.
101. *Ibid.*, pp. 111-12.
102. *Ibid.*, p. 116-See the sub-section 'ii. Conditions in Non-*Diwani* areas' in this chapter.
103. See the section 'Transport Development' in Chapter VIII.
104. Black Circular.
105. See the fifth Paragraph in the Section 'Political Conditions' in Chapter III.
106. Letter from R.B. Sharma, Secretary, Hyderabad People's Conference, Poona, to Babu Subhas Chandra Bose, President, Indian National Congress, in AISPC, *File* No. 65, Part I. p. 239.
107. *Ibid.*, pp 239 & 241.
108. *Statistical Year Book, 1941-42 to 1944-45.*, H.E.H. the Nizam's Government, p. 223.
109. AISPC, *File* No. 65, Part I., p. 241 ; *Meezan* (Telugu edition), editorial, 27-7-1945.
110. Printed from Vijayawada in Madras Presidency and became noted for its Communist character—*Meezan* (Telugu edition), 11-7-1946.
111. *Golkonda Patrika* (Daily), 2-12-1947.
112. AISPC, *File* No. 65, Part I., p. 241 ; N. Ramesan, Vol. IV., *op. cit.*, p. 86.
113. *Meezan.*, 11-7-1946 (Telugu edition) ; *Meezan*, 27-7-1945 (Telugu edition, editorial).
114. 'Library Movement' (editorial) in Hyderabad Bulletin; 7-7-1936 quoted in *Golkonda Patrika* (editorial), 13-7-1936.
115. *Ibid.*
116. *Golkonda Patrika* (Bi-weekly), 30-1-1939.
117. In Warangal District, besides 3 Libraries, there existed one Reading Room and one Travelling Library—A.K. Waghmare, 'Education in Hyderabad', a printed pamphlet cited in AISPC *File* No. 70 (Part I), 1947-48, p. 217.
118. *Statistical Year Book, 1941-42 to 1944-45*, H.E.H. the Nizam's Government, p. 223.
119. See the first para in the sub-section 'ii. Medium of Instruction and Private Schools' in this Section.

120. See the fifth paragraph in the Section 'Political Conditions' in Chapter III ; *Meezan*, 2-11-1944.
121. For *Tenancy Act*, see the Section 'b. Tenants' in Chapter IV ; for *Bhagela Agreements Population Act*, see the sub-section '*Bhagelas*' in Chapter VII and for *Money Lenders' Act and Debt Conciliation Act*, see the relevant sub-sections of similar title in Chapter V.
122. This exception refers to *Ittehad-ul-Muslimeen*, which very much identified Government policies and interests.
123. Attached to this Section.
124. For the average number of villages in a Taluq, see the Section 'Districts' in Chapter III.
125. 1951 Census Report, Part I-A. *op. cit.*, p. 39.
126. *Ibid.*
127. Memoranda submitted to the Taxation Enquiry Committee *op. cit.*, p. 189.
128. Report on the working of the Departments under the Revenue Secretariat, *op. cit.*, p. 2 (The percentages are calculated).
129. The ELOH, *op. cit.*, p. 143.
130. *Ibid.*
131. *Hyderabad Information*, Vol. III. No. 12, Aban, 1352 Fasli (September, 1943), p. 12 (Percentage is calculated).
132. R.V. Rao., *op. cit.*, p. 216 : See also 'Leprosy in Hyderabad State' a note by Dr. John Lowe in 1931 Census Report, Part I., *op. cit.*, p. 144.
133. *Hyderabad Information*, Vol. III, No. 12., Aban, 1352 Fasli (September, 1943), p. 10.
134. See the sub-section 'ii. Conditions in Non-*Diwani* Areas' in the Section 'A. Educational Conditions' in this Chapter.
135. 1951 Census, Part I-A, Report., *op. cit.*, p. 39. (Percentage is calculated).
136. Regarding these percentages, see the sub-section 'ii. Conditions in Non-*Diwani* Areas' in the Section 'A. Educational conditions' in this Chapter.
137. Office of the *Jagir* Administrator, Government of Hyderabad, '*Jagir* Administration.' Vol. I cited in A.M. Khusro, *op. cit.*, p. 11.
138. *Ibid.*
139. Report of the Royal Commission on *Jagir* Administration and Reform, *op. cit.*, p. 81.
140. See the Sections 'Administrative Conditions' & 'Political Conditions' in Chapter III.
141. See the third para in the Section 'Administrative Changes' in Chapter III.
142. See the Section 'Area and Population' in Chapter II.
143. See the last but one paragraph in the sub-section 'iv. Reasons for low utilisation of irrigational resources' in Chapter V.

144. Economic Investigations in the Hyderabad State, Vol. III., *op. cit.*, p. 21.
145. Confidential Report of First *Taluqdar* of Warangal to *Subedar* for Isfandar, 1356 Fasli (January, 1946-47) and Confidential Diary of First *Taluqdar*, Adilabad to *Subedar* for *Dai* & Bahman, 1356 Fasli (November and December, 1946-47) in W.S. *File* No. 15 of 1356 Fasli (1947) & R. No. 14 of 1356 Fasli.
146. Confidential Report of First *Taluqdar* of Warangal to *Subedar* for Isfandar 1356 Fasli (January, 1946-47) in W.S. *File* No. 15 of 1356 Fasli (1947) & R.No. 14 of 1356 Fasli.
147. Note of the Director of Medical and Sanitation Department, Hyderabad State, cited in 1931 Census, Part-I-A, Report, *op. cit.*, p. 32.
148. W.S. *File* No. 15 of 1356 Fasli (1947) & R. No. 14 of 1356 Fasli.
149. *Ibid.*
150. A note on 'Public Health' by Dr. Mohammad Farooq, Deputy Director of Public Health, H.E.H. the Nizam's Government, contained in 1941 Census Report, Part I., *op cit.*, p. 123.
151. Refer to the previous paragraph in this sub-section.
152. 'Leprosy in Hyderabad State'—a note by Dr. John Lowe, former Medical Superintendent, Leprosy Hospital, Dichpalli, contained in 1931 Census, Part I-Report. *op. cit.*, p. 139.
153. 1931 Census, Part I-Report, *op. cit.*, p. 135 (Percentage is calculated).
154. *Ibid.*, Part II., p. 196.
155. *Ibid.*
156. K. Krishnaswamy Mudiraj : *Pictorial Hyderabad*, Vol. II, (Hyderabad-Dn, 1934), p. 541.
157. 'Leprosy in Hyderabad State'—a note by Dr. John Lowe, contained in 1931 Census, Part I-Report, *op. cit.*, p. 141.
158. *Ibid.*
159. Pictorial Hyderabad, Vol. II., *op. cit.*, p. 541.
160. 1941 Census Report, Part I., *op. cit.*, p. 120.
161. 1931 Census, Part II, *op. cit.*, p. 106.
162. *Golkonda Patrika* (Daily), 25-10-1950 ; The disease, during the 12 years preceding 1942-43 has so much spread even in Adilabad District that in a village about 4 miles from Adilabad town, there had been as many as 70 lepers—Confidential Diary for the Second Fortnight of Farwardi, 1932 Fasli (February, 1943) sent by First *Taluqdar* of Adilabad to Director-General of Revenue through *Subedar*, Warangal, contained in W.S. *File* No. 28 of 1352 Fasli (1943) & R.No. 2 of 1357 Fasli (1948).
163. Dr. John Lowe 'Leprosy in Hyderabad State' in 1931 Census, Part I, *op. cit.*, p. 141.
164. 1941 Census, Part I-Report, *op. cit.*, p. 121.
165. *Ibid.*, (Percentages are calculated).
166. REE, *op. cit.*, p. 588.
167. See the fourth paragraph in the sub-section 'i. Causes of Indebtedness' in Chapter V.

168. *Golkonda Patrika* (Daily), 25-10-1950.
169. 1941 Census, Part II, *op. cit.*, p. 742.
170. *Ibid.*, Part I., p. 148.
171. H.E.H. the Nizam's Government, *Administrative Report for 1348 Fasli* (*6-10-1938 to 6-10-1939*), (Hyderabad-Dn, 1941), p. 151.
172. *Ibid.*, & ELOH, *op. cit.*, p. 152.
173. See the sub-section 'i. *Samasthan* or *Peshkash*' in Chapter IV.
174. Christoph Von Furer Haimendorf., *op. cit.*, p. 15.
175. Administrative Report for 1348 Fasli (1938-39), *op. cit.*, p. 151.
176. Christoph Von Furer Haimendorf, *op. cit.*, p. 57.
177. *Ibid.*, p. 15.
178. See the introductory fourth paragraph in this Chapter.
179. Vera Anstey, *op. cit.*, pp. 73 & 75.
180. Confidential Report of Warangal District for the month of Isfandar, 1356 Fasli (January, 1947) sent by First *Taluqdar*, Warangal. to *Subedar*, Warangal, contained in W.S. *File* No. 15 of 1356 Fasli (1947) & R. No. 14 of 1356 Fasli.
181. Economic Investigations in Hyderabad State, Vol. I, *op. cit.*, p. 38.
182. *Golkonda Patrika* ((Bi-weekly), 11-5-1939.
183. See the first para in the sub-section 'ii. Incidence of diseases and the extent of Preventive and Relief Measures' in this Chapter.
184. See the first paragraph in the Section 'M. Crop Conditions' in Chapter V.
185. News Bulletin of Andhra Provincial Congress Committee, Bezwada, Publicity Office, dated 19-10-1947 in AISPC *File* No. 68/46-47, Part I., p. 25—The imigrants mostly belonged to Muslim Community who were welcomed for reinforcing their community's strength vis-a-vis the majority community of Hindus.
186. Statistical Year Book, 1941-42 to 1944-45, *op. cit.*, p. 131 ; ELOH, *op. cit.*, p. 149—For average number of villages of a Taluq, see the Section 'Districts' in Chapter III.
187. Announcement of Secretary, Andhra *Mahila Sabha*, Adilabad District, in *Meezan.*, 29-8-1945.
188. *Report on the Administration of His Highness the Nizam's Dominions for the two years 1320 and 1321 Fasli* (*6th October, 1910 to 5th October, 1912*), (Hyderabad-Dn, 1914), p. 64.
189. *Ibid.*, p. 60.
190. Census Report, Part I, *op. cit.*, pp. 5 & 6.
191. Includes emigrants and immigrants besides actual population.
192. 1921 Census, Part I-Report., *op. cit.*, p. 35.
193. 1931 Census, Part I-A., Report., *op. cit.*, p. 4.
194. *Ibid.*, p. 32.
195. 1941 Census, Part I-Report., *op. cit.*, p. 116.
196. *Ibid.*, p. 120.
197. *Ibid.*
198. See Table LIX enclosed above. Percentages are roughly calculated.

199. See Table LIX. (Percentages are calculated).
200. *Ibid.*
201. *Hyderabad Government Bulletin on Economic Affairs*, Vol. III, Nos. 4-6, April-June, 1950, p. 332 (Budget Note of the Finance Minister for the year 1950-51).
202. See the first para in the sub-section 'ii. Incidence of the diseases and Preventive and Relief Measures' in this Chapter.
203. See the first paragraph in the sub-section 'c. Epidemic Diseases' in this Chapter.
204. See the sub-section 'i. Condition in non-*Diwani* areas' (regarding health) in this Chapter.
205. Pictorial Hyderabad, Vol. II. *op. cit.*, p. 569.
206. *Golkonda Patrika* (Bi-weekly), 11-5-1939.
207. *Golkonda Patrika* (Bi-weekly), 5-6-1939.
208. *Golkonda Patrika* (Daily), 18-9-1949.
209. See the second paragraph in the sub-section 'i. Road Transport' in Chapter VII.
210. See the following page.
211. The Medical and Public Health Department in the State set up in 1939, a Special Staff under a Nutrition Officer and extensive surveys were held. Some family surveys had also been held in the Osmania University under the supervision of A.I. Qureshi—*op. cit.*, p. 341.
212. See Table XXXV in Chapter VI.
213. See Table LX included in this Section.
214. See the last para in the sub-section 'iv. Other important Cottage and Home Industries' in Chapter VII.
215. Refer to the second and third paras in the Section 'J. Animal Husbandry as an agricultural adjunct' in Chapter V.
216. REE, *op. cit.*, p. 583.
217. Note the comparatively least acreage that was utilised for the cultivation of fruits and vegetables in the *Suba* Districts-See Table XXXV and sub-section 'iii. Fodder Crops, Fruits & Vegetables' in Chapter VI.
218. See the second para in the sub-section 'iv. Other important Cottage and Home Industries' in Chapter VII.
219. Refer to the last para in the sub-section 'i-Non-food crops outturn and yield' in chapter VI and sub-section 'b. Oil Mills' in Chapter VII'
220. A.I. Qureshi, *op. cit.*, p. 341.
221. For population figures of the *Suba* and its Districts, see Table I in Chapter II and for those of the State, refer to 1911 Census, Part II, *op. cit.*, pp. 2 & 3.
222. Refer to Table LXI enclosed in this Section.
223. 1911 Census, Part II, Imperial and Provincial Tables, *op. cit.*, pp. 14-20.
224. This important railway junction is at Kazipet, a suburb of Warangal, located on the Madras-Delhi grand trunk line.

225. For an idea on the value of the location of these industries and also the existence of rail facilities, see the relevant items in Chapter VII.
226. Refer to the third paragraph in the beginning of this Chapter.
227. See Chapter VII for an idea on the comparative rate of development in these spheres relating to these *Suba* Districts.
228. Refer to Table LXI incorporated in this Section and the third paragraph in the beginning of this Chapter.
229. See page 1 in Chapter VII.
230. Refer to Table LXI attached in this Section.
231. See Table LXII included in this Section.
232. *Ibid.*
233. *Ibid.*
234. Except during the calamitous decade of 1911-21, when it suffered 3% decrease in its population (1951 Census, Part I-Report, *op. cit.*, p. 243), as against 4% in respect of the State as a whole—1921, Census, Part I, *op. cit.*, p. 6.
235. 1951 Census Part I-A., *op. cit.*, p. 243.
236. See the f.n. No. 234 in this Chapter.
237. This figure which was not directly given, was assessed from the population classification made in Table III of Part II, 1911 Census, *op. cit.*, pp. 6 & 7 (See f.n.*** in Table LXII enclosed in this Section).
238. 1951 Census, Part I-A, *op. cit.*, p. 243.
239. Percentage is calculated.
240. Refer to the first paragraph in the Section 'C. Urban Development' in this Chapter.
241. 1951 Census, Part I-A, *op. cit.*, p. 246.
242. See Table LXII attached in this Section.
243. See Table XLIII in Chapter VII.
244. Refer to the sub-section 'Coal' in Chapter II.
245. 1911 Census, Part II, *op. cit.*, pp. 14-20.
246. 1941 Census, Tables volume, *op. cit.*, pp. 50-51.
247. Refer to Table LXII.
248. For an appreciation of these factors of influence, see the relevant Sections in Chapter VII.
249. *Ibid.*
250. See Table LXII.
251. 1921 Census, Part I-Report, *op. cit.*, p. 42 ; Also refer to Table LXII.
252. 1951 Census, Part I-A, Report, *op. cit.*, p. 10 ; Also see the Section 'Area and population' in Chapter II.
253. Refer to the Section 'F. Transport Development' in Chapter VII.
254. See the sub-section 'iii. The Sirpur Paper Mills, Ltd.' in Chapter VII.
255. Refer to the Section 'Natural and Mineral Resources' in Chapter II.
256. See Table LXII. Percentages are calculated.
257. Refer to second paragraph in Chapter I and sub-section 'iii. Periodical Markets' in Chapter VII.
258. Percentage is calculated from the figures given in Table LXII.

259. Refer to Table LI and second paragraph in the sub-section 'ii. Rail Transport' in Chapter VII.
260. See Table LXII. Percentages are calculated.
261. For relevant items, refer to chapters IV, V and VII.
262. See Table LXII.
263. Percentages are calculated on the basis of the figures given in Table LXII included in this Section. For data in respect of these towns in the State as a whole, which is available latest for 1921 only, see 1921 Census, Part I-A, *op. cit.*, p. 37.
264. Refer to Table LXII.
265. For an idea on their attitude and activities, refer to the Sections relating to non-*Diwani* lands in Chapter IV.
266. See the Section 'Local Government' in Chapter III.
267. RAR, *op. cit.*, p. 231.
268. Madiraju Ramakoteswara Rao, *op. cit.*, p. 256.
269. Local Government, *op. cit.*, p. 3.
270. For an idea on this refer to the Sections 'A. Educational Conditions' and 'B. Public Health' in this Chapter.
271. RAR, *op. cit.*, p. 231.
272. Confidential Diary of Adilabad District for the month of Dai, 1356 Fasli (November, 1947) by First *Taluqdar*, Adilabad to *Subedar*, Warangal contained in W.S. *File* No. 15 of 1356 Fasli (1947) & R.No. of 1356 Fasli.
273. Local Government., *op. cit.*, p. 4.
274. *Ibid.*, p. 5 ; H.E.H. the Nizam's Government, *Administrative Report for 1344 Fasli (6-10-1934 to 6-10-1935)*, (*Hyderabad-Dn*, 1938), p. 107.
275. H.E.H. the Nizam's Government, *Administrative Report for 1351 Fasli (6-10-1941 to 5-10-1942)*, (Hyderabad-Dn, 1945), p. 151.
276. Check up the Population levels of these and of Warangal in 1941 from Table LXII included in this Section. Also refer to *the Deccan Chronicle*, 26-11-1948 ; *Report of the Reforms Committee* (1938, Hyderabad-Dn), p. 131.
277. See Table LXII.
278. Local Government, *op. cit.*, p. 3 , Report of the Reforms Committee, *op. cit.*, p. 131.
279. Refer to Table LXII and also 1931 Census, Part I, *op. cit.*, p. 60.
280. See Table LXII and also 1941 Census, Table volume, *op. cit.*, pp. 50-53.
281. 1911 Census, Part II, *op. cit.*, pp. 14-20. (In the case of Warangal, the Municipal and Suburban components are all treated as one city unit) ; 1941 Census, Tables volume., *op. cit.*, pp. 50-53 ; See also Table LXII.

282. H.E.H. the Nizam's Government, *Administrative Report for 1346 Fasli (6-10-1936 to 5-10-1937)*, (Hyderabad-Dn, 1939), p. 132.

283. *Golkonda Patrika* (Bi-weekly), 5-6-1939.

284. Report on the Administration of Hyderabad State, September, 1948 to March, 1950, *op. cit.*, p. 88.

285. H.E.H. the Nizam's Government, *Administrative Report for 1350 Fasli (6-10-1940 to 6-10-1941)*, (Hyderabad-Dn, 1943), p. 149.

286. *Hyderabad Information*, Vol. IV, No.3, Bahman, 1353 Fasli (December, 1943), p. 2—The year of its completion could not be ascertained from the sources consulted.

287. *Golkonda Patrika* (Bi-weekly), 11-5-1939.

288. *Golkonda Patrika* (Daily), 18-9-1949.

289. *Meezan* (Telugu edition), 29-12-1944.

290. *Meezan* (Telugu edition), 14-11-1945.

291. This might have resulted in the payment of lower wages for beginners, though work remained the same.

292. Towards hiring charges for carts (Probably per month), Rs. 35 was paid as against a demand for Rs. 60—*Meezan* (Telugu edition), 29-12-1944.

293. *Golkonda Patrika* (Bi-weekly), 5-6-1939.

294. *Golkonda Patrika* (Bi-weekly), 11-5-1939.

295. Refer to the second paragraph in the sub-section 'i. Road Transport' in Chapter VII.

296. See the first para in the sub-section 'i. Road Transport' in Chapter VII.

297. Administrative Report of Warangal *Suba* for 1353 Fasli (1944) in W. S. *File* No. 38 of 1354 Fasli (1945) & R.No. 706 of 1354 Fasli.

298. Refer to the second para in Section 'A. Industrial Organisation, Management and Finance' in Chapter VII.

299. *Golkonda Patrika* (Bi-weekly), 5-6-1939 ; *Golkonda Patrika* (Daily), 18-9-1949.

300. See also Table LXII.

301. Refer to Table LXIII included in this Section. The number of Taluq Boards would have been 25, but for that of Palvancha in Warangal District which appears to have been discontinued some time after 1931.

302. Their number in the *Suba* is not available, but even in the entire State only 378 Panchayats existed by March, 1950—See the sub-section 'ii. Village Panchayats' in Chapter V.

∴ For an account on village Panchayats, see the Section 'Local Government' in Chapter III and sub-section 'ii. Village Panchayats' in Chapter V.

303. M. Fathulla Khan, *op. cit.*, p. 132 ; see also the Section 'Local Government' in Chapter III.
304. RAR, *op. cit.*, p. 229.
305. Local Government, *op. cit.*, p. 7.
306. RAR, *op. cit.*, p. 230.
307. Local Government, *op. cit.*, pp. 7 & 8.
308. *Ibid.*, p. 8.
309. Attached in this sub-section.
310. Refer to the Section 'Local Government' in Chapter III.
311. M. Fathulla Khan, *op. cit.*, p. 132.
312. Toll-gate levy on the movement of goods traffic.
313 Cycle tax was levied at one rupee per year—Report on the Working of the Departments under the Secretary and Director-General of Revenue, 1926-27, *op. cit.*, p. 92.
314. *Ibid.* ; Memoranda submitted to the Taxation Enquiry Committee, *op. cit.*, p. 34.
315. See col. 7 in Table LXIII.
316. Memoranda submitted to the Taxation Enquiry Committee, *op. cit.*, p. 33.
317. *Ibid.*, p. 133.
318. Refer to col. 8 in Table LXIII.
319. Memoranda submitted to the Taxation Enquiry Committee, *op. cit.*, p. 33.
320. *Ibid.*
321. Refer to col. 9 in Table LXIII attached in this sub-section.
322. For an idea on educational and health backwardness in these Taluqs, refer to Tables LVII and LVIII in this Chapter.
323. Refer to the Section 'Area and Population' ; 'Soils' and 'Forest Resources' in Chapter II.
324. See the f. n. ∴ (after 634) in the sub-section 'i. Road Transport' in Chapter VII.
325. See Table LXIII.
326. Examine the District total income figures given in col. 9 for the years 1922-36.
327. Karimnagar District showed rise instead of decline in this Depression year, due to comparatively less rigours of Depression in its case—Refer to the first para in the sub-section 'ii. Depression and Recovery, 1929-38' in Chapter VI.
328. Memoranda submitted to the Taxation Enquiry Committee, *op. cit.*, p. 33—Regarding the grant made to Village Panchayats, see the preceding paragraph in this sub-section.

329. Adilabad District formed exception in this case.
330. Refer to Table LXIII and col. 9 in it.
331. The percentages are calculated from the figures given in col. 14 of Table LXIII.
332. See the first para in this sub-section and also in the sub-section 'ii. Municipalities and Town life' in this Chapter.
333. Refer to col. 14 of Table LXIII.
334. Sec col. 10-12 in Table LXIII.
335. Compare the figures in cols. 9 and 14 in Table LXIII.
336. Refer to Section 'A. Educational Conditions' in this Chapter.
337. See the second para in the Section 'B. Public Health Organisation' in this Chapter.
338. Local Government, *op. cit.*, pp. 3 & 7.
339. Refer to this and the preceding paras in this sub-section and first paragraph in the sub-section 'ii. Municipalities and Town Life' and Table LXIII in this Chapter.
340. 1951 Census Part I-A, *op. cit.*, p. 199.
341. See the first para in the Section 'A. Pattern of Land Utilisation' in Chapter VI.
342. Refer to the first paragraph in the Section 'C. Agricultural Production, and Yield per acre' in Chapter VI.
343. See the sub-sections 'iii. Handloom—spinning, weaving, printing and dyeing 'and' iv. Other important Cottage and Home Industries' in Chapter VII.
344. Refer to the third paragraph in the beginning of this Chapter and sub-section 'ii. Municipalities and Town Life' (first paragraph) and also the last para in the preceding sub-section of this Chapter.
345. See the first para in Chapter VII.
346. 1951 Census, Part I-A, *op. cit.*, pp. 527 & 537.
347. *Ibid.*, pp. 526, 532 & 537.
348. Refer to Table LXIV included in this sub-section.
349. See col. 12 in Table LXI enclosed in this Section.
350. 1951 Census, Part I-A, *op. cit.*, p. 537.
351. *Ibid.*
352. *Ibid.*, pp. 59 & 532.
353. Refer to Table XLII in Chapter VII.
354. See the first paragraphs in the Section 'C. Urban Development' and sub-section 'i. Growth of Towns' in this Chapter.
355. See the sub-sections relating to these in the Section 'B. Large-scale Industrial Production and its impact on the Economy' in Chapter VII.
356. Refer to Table XLII in Chapter VII.

357. See the second paragraph in the sub-section 'i. Growth of Towns' in this Chapter.

358. Refer to Table I and second para in the Section 'Area and Population' in Chapter II.

359. See Table XLII in Chapter VII.

360. Refer to the sub-sections 'iii. Handloom-spinning, weaving, printing and dyeing' and 'iv. Other important Cottage and Home Industries' in Chapter VII.

361. See the first paragraphs in the Section 'C. Urban Development' and sub-section 'i. Growth of Towns' in this Chapter.

362. 1951 Census, Part I-A, *op. cit.*, p. 532.

363. *Ibid.*, pp. 532, 535-536—Regarding the counting of non-agricultural immigrants, only the numbers relating to the leading occupations of production, domestic services, barbers, washermen etc. were taken into consideration in respect of the leading Districts.

364. *Ibid.*, pp. 526-28.

365. See Table LXIV.

366. 1951 Census, Part I-A, *op. cit.*, pp. 500 & 537.

367. *Ibid.*, pp. 527 & 540—The Madrasi immigrants into Waranagal urban areas numbered as many as 5,400 persons, p. 540.

368. *Ibid.*, pp. 526-27, 532, 535 & 537-38. (percentages are calculated).

369. *Ibid.*, pp. 527 & 532.

370. Refer to Table LXV included in this Section.

371. *Ibid.*

372. *Ibid.*

373. See the administrative importance given to this Taluq, in view of its preponderant backward tribal population f.n. ∴ after No. 8 in the Section 'Districts' in Chapter III.

374. Refer to Table LXV. Percentages are calculated.

375. See the District total figures given in Table LXV. Percentages are calculated.

376. Refer to Tables LXV and LXVI.

377. See Table LXVI attached in this Section.

378. *Ibid*; the figure of Karimnagar District in 1921 was taken as 65 (instead of 1,265—See the note* in the Table).

379. See Table LXV; In the case of Karimnagar District, 24.08 stands for decrease (the only case among the *Suba* Districts)—Refer to f.n.* in the same Table.

380. Shifting type of cultivation in which the tribesman changed their lands after every 2 or 3 years, on account of the loss in the natural fertility of the soil.

381. Refer to Table II in Chapter II.

382. Bhimghanpur Project was located in this tract and typified the conditions—see the last three paras in the sub-section 'iv. Reasons for low utilisation of Irrigational Resources' in Chapter V.
383. For a glimpse on these, see paragraph third in the beginning of this Chapter and Table LXVII.
384. Refer to third paragraph in the beginning of this Chapter and Table LXVII included in this sub-section.
385. *Ibid.*
386. Refer to Table LXVII. Percentages are calculated.
387. Christoph Von Furer Haimendorf, 'Tribal populations of Hyderabad Yesterday and Today' an essay in 1941 Census, Part I, (Appendix I), *op. cit.*, pp. XXIV—XXV.
388. The total comes to only 6,203. See Sl. Nos. 6 & 1 in Table LXVII.
389. Refer to Table LXVII. Percentages are calculated.
390. See the Section 'B. Crop Acreage' in Chapter VI.
391. Refer to second paragraph in the Section 'Soils' in Chapter II.
392. Christoph Von Fuhrer Haimendorf, *op. cit.*, pp. 66-67.
393. *Ibid.*, p. 66.
394. *Ibid.*, p. 67.
395. Refer to the first para in the sub-section 'i. Road Transport' and second para in the sub-section 'ii. Rail Transport' in Chapter VII ; Hyderabad District Gazetteers, Part II, Tables, *op. cit.*, Warangal, p. 3 ; Karimnagar, p. 3 ; Christoph Von Fuhrer Haimendorf, *op. cit.*, pp. 65-66.
396. Godfrey Barras, *op. cit.*, p. 67.
397. Large Scale land relinquishment by Gonds in Utnoor Taluq of Adilabad District in favour of outsiders was recorded in a Tahsil office File of 1324 Fasli (1914-15)—Christoph Von Fuhrer Haimendorf, *op. cit.*, p. 75.
398. *Ibid.*, p. 67.
399. *Ibid.*, p. 81.
400. Godfrey Barras, *op. cit.*, p. 67.
401. Christoph Von Fuhrer Haimendorf, *op. cit.*, pp. 67-68.
402. W.V. Grigson, Revenue and Police Member in his 'foreward' in 'Christoph Von Fuhrer Haimendorf' : *op. cit.*, pp. 85-88 & 90.
403. *Ibid.*, p. 78.
404. *Ibid.*, pp. 68-69.
405. *Ibid.*, p. 157.
406. Keremi was a village in Asifabad Taluq owned by a resident Muslim landlord from Uttar Pradesh. In 1918, there had been more than 100 Gond houses in this village, but in 1945 only 25 were there--*Ibid.*, p. 70.
407. *Ibid.*, p. 69.

408. *Ibid.*, p. 70.
409. H.E.H. the Nizam's Government, Office of the Secretary to Government, Judicial, Police and General Departments, Confidential *File* No. 15/P.A/49, F.No. 2 ; See also the fourth para in the Section 'Administrative Conditions' in Chapter III.
410. W.S. *File* No. 4 of 1351 Fasli (1942) & R. No. 1437 of 1352 Fasli (1943).
411. Christoph Von Fuhrer Haimendorf, *op. cit.*, p. 92.
412. Refer to the Section 'Districts' in Chapter III.
413. Christoph Von Fuhrer Haimendorf, *op. cit.*, p. 127.
414. *Ibid.*, pp. 128-129.
415. *Ibid.*, p. 131.
416. Syed Khaja Abdul Gafoor, *op. cit.*, p. 19 : Christoph Von Fuhrer Haimendorf, *op. cit.*, pp. 135-136.
417. See the fourth para in this sub-section.
418. Syed Khaja Abdul Gafoor, *op. cit.*, p. 19—For an idea on *Laoni khas*, refer to the sub-section 'i. *Laoni* land distribution' in Chapter VI.
419. *Ibid.*, p. 21.
420. Report submitted by the Department of Aboriginals and Backward classes to Secretary, Rural Reconstruction Department, in Agriculture Department, H.E.H. the Nizam's Government, *File* No. 148/1358 Fasli (1949) & S. No. 81 of 1358 Fasli, p. 18.
421. Syed Khaja Abdul Gafoor, *op. cit.*, p. 16.
422. It refers to the work of delimitation and demarcation of agricultural lands.
423. W.S. *File* No. 15 of 1356 Fasli (1947) & R. No. 14 of 1356 Fasli.
424. Refer to the last two paragraphs in the Section 'Political Conditions' in Chapter III.
425. *The Deccan Chronicle*, 17-12-1949.
426. See Table LXVII—Refer also to the first paragraph in the preceding sub-section 'i. Gonds' in this Chapter.
427. Percentages are calculated.
428. Syed Khaja Abdul Gafoor, *op. cit.*, p. 37.
429. Confidential Report of Warangal District for the second fortnight of the month of Isfander, 1355 Fasli (January, 1946), in W.S. *File* No. 16 of 1355 Fasli & R. No. 69 of 1356 Fasli (1947).
430. Syed Khaja Abdul Gafoor, *op. cit.*, p. 37.
431. Christoph Von Fuhrer Haimendorf, *op. cit.*, p. 41.
432. Syed Khaja Abdul Gafoor, *op. cit.* p. 38.
433. Christoph Von Fuhrer Haimendorf, *op. cit.*, p. 41 ; for Gonds, refer to the second, third and fourth paragraphs in the sub-section 'i. Gonds' in this Chapter.

434. Syed Khaja Abdul Gafoor, *op. cit.*, p. 38.
435. Christoph Von Fuhrer Haimendorf, *op. cit.*, pp. 41&43 ; Syed Khaja Abdul Gafoor, *op. cit.*, p. 38.
436. Refer to the third paragraph in the sub-section 'a. Survey and Settlement' and f.n. No. 258 in Chapter IV.
437. Christoph Von Fuhrer Haimendorf, *op. cit.*, p. 43 ; for an idea on 'Grow More Food' campaign, see the second para in the sub-section 'c. Cotton' in Chapter VI.
438. *Ibid.*
439. Syed Khaja Abdul Gafoor, *op. cit.*, p. 39.
440. N.G. Ranga, *op. cit.*, p. 28.
441. *Ibid.*
442. *Ibid.*
443. *Ibid.*, p. 27.
444. *Ibid.*, p. 29.
445. *Ibid.*, pp. 28-29.
446. Confidential Report of Warangal District for the second fortnight of the month of Isfandar, 1355 Fasli (January, 1946) in W.S. *File* No. 16 of 1355 Fasli & R. No. 69 of 1356 Fasli (1947) ; N.G. Ranga, *op. cit.*, p. 29 ; Also refer to sub-section 'b. *Yaws*' in this Chapter.
447. See Table IX in Chapter IV.
448. Christoph Von Fuhrer Haimendorf, *op. cit.*, pp. 57-58.
449. *Ibid.*, p. 57.
450. For an idea on these, see the Sections 'A. Educational Conditions' and 'B. Public Health Organisation' in this Chapter.
451. Syed Khaja Abdul Gafoor, *op. cit.*, p. 38.
452. Report submitted by the Department of Aboriginals and Backward classes to the Secretary, Rural Reconstruction Department H.E.H. the Nizam's Government, in Agriculture Department, S. No. 81 & *File* No. 148/1358 Fasli (1949) of 1358 Fasli, p. 19.
453. Syed Khaja Abdul Gafoor, *op. cit.*, p. 38.
454. *Ibid.*, p. 45.
455. Compare 2,500 families with the number of persons of Warangal District as given in Table LXVII attached in this Section.
456. Syed Khaja Abdul Gafoor, *op. cit.*, pp. 41-42.
457. Report submitted by the Department of Aboriginals and Backward classes to the Secretary, Rural Reconstruction Department, in Agriculture Department, H.E.H. the Nizam's Government, S. No. 81 & *File* No. 148/1358 Fasli (1949) of 1358 Fasli, p. 19.
458. In Telugu Language, 'Konda' stands for hill. Because of hilly habitation, the tribe might have earned this prefix.

459. Refer to Table LXVII. Percentage is calculated.

460. See the first paragraph in the sub-section 'ii. Koyas' in this Chapter.

461. Christoph Von Fuhrer Haimendorf, *op. cit.*, pp. 1-2.

462. *Ibid.*, p. 2. Regarding *Podu*, see the f.n. No. 380 in this Chapter.

463. Refer to second para in the sub-section 'i. Gonds' in this Chapter.

464. Out of these cereals, jawar was cultivated in non-tribal areas also. *Ragi* and *Korra* had been mainly grown by tribesmen only, both looking smaller grains, compared to the former, the first one looking dark brown and the second one resembling white wheat in colour. The former requires much water and the latter much less, for growing, both being short-term or less than 3 month crops.

465. Christoph Von Fuhrer Haimendorf, *op. cit.*, p. 2.

466. Christoph Von Fuhrer Haimendorf, 'Tribal Populations of Hyderabad Yesterday and Today' an essay in 1941 Census, Part I-Report, Appendix I, *op. cit.*, p. 3.

467. Christoph Von Fuhrer Haimendorf, *op. cit.*, p. 3.

468. See the Section 'Villages' in Chapter III.

469. Christoph Von Fuhrer Haimendorf, *op. cit.*, p. 8.

470. This was done around 1942-*Ibid.*, p. 4.

471. It was *Annas* 8 per acre in East Godavari District as against Re. 1 per *biga* in the *samasthan*--*Ibid.*, p. 12.

472. For all the three items, the *Patwari* was paid a Re. 1—per each and the Forest Guard, Re. 1— to Rs. 4— *Ibid.*, pp. 12-13.

473. The revenue per *biga* came to only Re. 1— per *biga*—*Ibid.*, p. 5.

474. Refer to f.n. Nos. 471 & 472 that are included in this sub-section.

475. Christoph Von Fuhrer Haimendorf, *op. cit.*, pp. 5 & 27.

476. The revenue rates for permanently cultivated land : Re. 1 for dry land and Rs. 3— for wet land per *biga*. By way of excess collections, many Reddis paid between Rs. 12 and Rs. 20 per *biga*—*Ibid.*, p. 13.

477. In this District the average per household or per acre assessment ranged from Rs. 6 to 7 with no plough fee collection—*Ibid.*

478. The usual grazing charges that had been fixed were : *Annas* 8 per buffalo and *Annas* 4 per cow—*Ibid.*

479. Right from 1935, the *Samasthan* was continuously until the end of the period under the management of the Court of Wards—Refer to f.n. No 148 and second and third paras in the sub-section 'i. *Samasthan* or *Peshkash*' in Chapter IV.

480. Christoph Von Fuhrer Haimendorf, *op. cit.*, pp. 7 & 28.

481. *Ibid.*, p. 3.

482. *Ibid.*, p. 20.

483. *Ibid.*, p. 18.
484. *Ibid.*, p. 5.
485. *Ibid.*, pp. 20 & 25.
486. Systematic exploitation of forest timber under Governmental supervision.
487. Christoph Von Fuhrer Haimendorf, *op. cit.*, p. 13.
488. *Ibid.*, p. 19.
489. *Ibid.*, p. 3.
490. *Ibid.*, p. 13—In the Agency tracts of East Godavari District on the other hand, Elementary Schools were there in some Reddi villages and scholarships were given to Higher Elementary and High School students ranging upto Rs. 13 per boy.
491. *Ibid.* In contrast, in East Godavari District, the dispensary at Kunavaram was in easy reach of most of the villages and touring Medical Officers and Veterinary Surgeon, had been there.
492. Godfrey Barras, *op. cit.*, p. 66 ; See also the last para in the subsection 'ii. Koyas' in this Chapter.
493. Refer to the last para in the sub-section 'ii. Koyas' in this Chapter.
494. See Table LXVII included in this Section. Percentage is calculated.
495. Christoph Von Fuhrer Haimendorf, *op. cit.*, p. 162.
496. Refer to S. No. 11 in Table LXVII. The great reduction of this tribe from 52,472 in 1931 to 237 in 1941 was felt to be due to wrong identification, such as Telugu-speaking *Kolis* returning as Hindu and Marathi-speaking *Kolis* as Marathas—Christoph Von Fuhrer Haimendorf. 'Tribal Populations of Hyderabad Yesterday and Today' in 1941 Census Part I, Appendix I, *op. cit.*, p. IV.
497. Christoph Von Fuhrer Haimendorf, *op. cit.*, 158.
498. See the last para in the sub-section 'iv. Other important Cottage and Home Industries' in Chapter VII.
499. Christoph Von Fuhrer Haimendorf, *op. cit.*, p. 98.
500. *Ibid.*, pp. 101-104 ; 162.
501. *Ibid.*, pp. 101-103.
502. Refer to the preceding three sub-sections in this Section.
503. Christoph Von Fuhrer Haimendorf, *op. cit.*, p. 104.
504. *Ibid.*, p. 158.
505. See the last paragraph in the sub-section 'iv. Other important Cottage and Home Industries' in Chapter VII.
506. Christoph Von Fuhrer Haimendorf, *op. cit.*, p. 158.
507. Refer to the three preceding sub-sections in this Section.
508. See S. No. 3 in Table LXVII. Percentages are calculated.

509. Syed Khaja Abdul Gafoor, *op. cit.*, p. 52 ; also refer to Table LXVII ; percentages are calculated.
510. Christoph Von Fuhrer Haimendorf, *op. cit.*, pp. 79 & 159-60 ; See also Table LXVII. Percentages are calculated.
511. Syed Khaja Abdul Gafoor, *op. cit.*, p. 49.
512. *Ibid.*
513. See the fourth para in the beginning of this Chapter.
514. Syed Khaja Abdul Gafoor, *op. cit.*, p. 49.
515. *Ibid.*
516. Christoph Von Fuhrer Haimendorf, *op. cit.*, p. 79.
517. *Ibid.*
518. *Ibid.*, pp. 79 & 159-160.
519. *Ibid.* p. 79.
520. *Ibid.*
521. See the first paragraph in this sub-section.
522. Syed Khaja Abdul Gafoor, *op. cit.*, p. 53.
523. *Ibid.*
524. Report submitted by the Department of Aboriginals and Backward classes to Secretary, Rural Reconstruction Department, contained in Agriculture Department, H.E.H. the Nizam's Government, S. No. 81 & *File* No. 148/58 of 1358 Fasli (1949) pp. 19-20.
525. P. Sundaraiah, *op. cit.*, p. 169.
526. Refer to 'Warangal *Suba* (1911) Map' and last paragraph in this Section 'Rivers' in Chapter II.
527. See the seventh and eighth paragraphs and f.n. No. 155 in the Section 'Political Conditions' in Chapter III.
528. *Ibid* ; *The Deccan Chronicle*, 19-3-1949 ; P. Sundaraiah, *op. cit.*, p.89 ; Confidential Report of Warangal District for the first fortnight of Amardad, 1356 Fasli (June, 1946-47) from First *Taluqdar* of Warangal to *Subedar*, Warangal, contained in W.S. *File* No. 15 of 1356 Fasli and R. No. 14 of 1356 Fasli, *Meezan*, 22-4-1946 (Telugu edition).
529. K. Subhas Chandra Reddy, *op. cit.*, p. 47.
530. Confidential Report of the First *Taluqdar*, Warangal to *Subedar*, Warangal, for the first fortnight of the month of Aban, 1354 Fasli (December, 1944-45) contained in W.S. *File* No. 30 of 1354 Fasli and R. No. 6 of 1357 Fasli (1948) ; Similar Report for the second fortnight of the month of Khurdad, 1355 Fasli (April, 1945-46) contained in W.S. *File* No. 16 of 1355 Fasli & R. No. 69 of 1356 Fasli (1946-47).
531. Refer to the sixth paragraph in the Section 'Political Conditions' in Chapter III.

532. Hyderabad Residency Records, Fortnightly Report for the fortnight ending on 15th April, 1945 in File No. 6 (7), P/45, contained in *Micro Film, Reel No. 1, Accession No. 44.*

533. He, as an important Leftist leader, took an active part in guiding the post-1948 Telangana Struggle.

534. Hyderabad Residency Records, Fortnightly Report for the fortnight ending on 15th April, 1945 in File No. 6 (7) P/45, contained in *Micro Film, Reel No. 1, Acc. No. 44.*

535. *Ibid.* (Fortnightly Report for the fortnight ending 31st May, 1945).

536. See the sixth paragraph in the Section 'Political Conditions' in Chapter III ; also I. Thirumali, *op. cit.*, p. 126.

537. V. Veerabhadra Rao & V. Ramachandra Rao, 'India's Police Action against Hyderabad' quoted in *The Deccan Chronicle*, 13-3-1949.

538. These referred to the associations or local units that functioned under Communist direction and control.

539. Refer to the second paragraph in the sub-section 'ii. *Begaris* and *Bhagelas*' in Chapter VII.

540. P. Sundaraiah, *op. cit.*, pp. 89, 27-28.

541. Confidential Report of the First *Taluqdar*, Warangal to *Subedar*, Warangal, for the second fortnight of Aban, 1354 Fasli (September, 1944-45), contained in W.S. *File* No. 30 of 1354 Fasli & R. No. 6 of 1357 Fasli (1947-48) ; also see the section 'villages' In Chapter III and sub-section 'ii. *Begaris* and *Bhagelas*' in Chapter VII.

542. Confidential Report for the first fortnight of Bahman, 1355 Fasli (December, 1945-46) of Warangal *Suba*, contained in W.S. *File* No. 25 of 1355 Fasli & R. No. 71 of 1356 Fasli (1946-47).

543. Refer to the second para in the sub-section 'ii. Procurement Policy and its wide-ranging effects' in Chapter VI.

544. See the first and second paras in the sub-section 'ii. Procurement Policy and its wide-ranging effects' and last para in the sub-section 'i. Rationing and Public Distribution System' in Chapter VI.

545. Refer to the second para in the Section 'E. Price controls, procurement and Rationing' and third paragraph in the sub-section 'ii. Procurement Policy and its wide-ranging effects' in Chapter VI.

546. See the third para in the sub-section 'ii. Procurement Policy and its wide-ranging effects' in Chapter VI.

547. Confidential Report for the first fortnight of Bahman, 1355 Fasli (December, 1945-46) contained in W.S. *File* No. 25 of 1355 Fasli & R. No. 71 of 1356 Fasli (1946-47).

548. Refer to the third and fourth paragraphs in the sub-section 'ii. Land Revenue Assessments and their incidence' in Chapter IV.

549. See the last para in the Section 'Remissions' in Chapter IV.

550. Letter to the Editor, *Meezan*, 3-8-1945, by Vattikonda Nageswara Rao, President, Andhra *Maha Sabha*, Madhira Taluq, Warangal District.

551. Administrative Report of Warangal *Suba* for 1353 Fasli (1943-44) in W.S. *File* No. 38 of 1354 Fasli (1944-45) & R. No. 706 of 1354 Fasli.

552. Finance Department, H.E.H. the Nizam's Government Circular No. 12 dated 29th Shaharewar, 1349 Fasli (July, 1940) in W.S. File No. 1 of 1349 Fasli (1939-40) & R. No. 512 of 1352 Fasli (1942-43).

553. *Meezan*, 3-8-1945.

554. P. Sundaraiah, *op. cit.*, p. 27.

555. Refer to the Section 'b. Tenants' in Chapter IV.

556. See the last two paras in the Section 'b. Tenants' in Chapter IV.

557. R.E.E., *op. cit.*, p. 78 ; also, refer to the second paragraph in Section 'b. Tenants' in Chapter IV.

558 See para one in the Section 'b. Tenants' in Chapter IV.

559. In popular parlance, big landlords such as *Deshmukhs* were referred to as '*Zamindars*' in the Region, though their functioning and powers differed.

560. *Lathis* referred to wooden sticks and slings to animal skin-straps used for throwing stones at a distance, the latter being used even in driving away bird attack on crops.

561. P. Sundaraiah, *op. cit.*, pp. 33-34.

562. Ian Bedford, *op cit.*, P. Sundaraiah, *op. cit.*, p. 136 ; Barry Pavier : 'The Telangana Armed Struggle' in *Economic and Political Weekly*, Special Number, vol. IX, August, 1974, p. 1419.

563. Barry Pavier, *op. cit.*, p. 118 ; also refer to 5th para in the beginning of this Chapter.

564. P. Sundaraiah, *op. cit.*, pp. 136-137.

565. Armed insurgent units that were in action.

566. In Luxettipet Taluq, Mandamarri Madhava Rao had 10,000 acres, Pusukuri family 10 to 20,000 acres, and Narsapur *Samasthan*, 50 to 100 thousand acres—P. Sundaraiah, *op. cit.*, pp. 19 (Telugu Edition) & 265.

567. Meezan, 4-1-45 ; see also the first para in the Section 'Political Conditions' in Chapter III.

568. He enjoyed the *watan* of *Sirdeshmukh* and *Mali* and Police *Patelgi* rights over 22 villages in Lixettipet Taluq. His son, Sudhakar Rao

is an active Congress leader in the present Andhra politics, having even served in the Ministry also— W.S. *File* No. 24 of 1937 & R.No. 859 of 1938. J.V. Narsing Rao and K.V. Keshavulu had also represented the District in the Andhra Pradesh Ministry in the post-1952 period.

569. *Golkonda Patrika* (Daily), 3-12-1949 ; Fortnightly Confidential Report of Adilabad District for the second half of Khurdad, 1356 Fasli (April, 1946-47) in W.S. *File* No. 15 of 1356 Fasli & R. No. 14 of 1356 Fasli.

570. Refer to the Section 'B. Pattern of land distribution' in Chapter V.

571. REE, *op. cit.*, p. 113.

572. P. Sundaraiah, *op. cit.*, p. 19 (Telugu edition) ; also see Table XXI in Chapter V.

573. *The Deccan Chronicle*, 8-7-1949 ; *The Golkonda Patrika*, 9-7-1949 ; also refer to Table IX in Chapter IV. (Percentage is calculated).

574. Refer to the last but one paragraph in the Section, 'Political Conditions' in Chapter III.

575. P. Sundaraiah, *op. cit.*, pp. 24-27 ; Ravi Narayana Reddy, *op. cit.*, pp. 20-21.

576. K.M. Munshi, *op. cit.*, pp. 91-92.

577. Extract from 'Hyderabad Reborn', cited in *the Deccan Chronicle*, 26-6-1949 ; the ban was lifted on May 4, 1948 K.M. Munshi, *op. cit.*, pp. 154-155.

578. *Meezan*, 4-12-1948 ; *The Deccan Chronicle* (Editorial), 19-6-1949 ; *Golkonda Patrika* (Daily), 30-3-1950.

579. P. Sundaraiah, *op. cit.*, p. 415.

580. Kathleen Gough, 'Indian Peasant Uprisings' contained in *Economic and Political Weekly*, Special Number, August, 1974, p. 1406 ; Ian Bedford, *op. cit.*, p. 348 ; Barry Pavier, *op. cit.*, p. 124.

581. Kathleen Gough, 'Indian Peasant Uprisings' in *the Economic and Political Weekly*, Special Number, August, 1974, p. 1406 ; the Communist literature seized from the house of Mr. Azmatullah Khan, General Secretary of the League of Democratic youth, contained a paper that revealed the advance formation of a Communist Ministry in which Mr. Makdoom Mohiuddin figured as Prime Minister, Mr. Azmatullah Khan as Deputy P.M. Mr. Ravi Narayana Reddy as Foreign Minister, Dr. Raj Bahadur Goud as Education Minister, etc.,—*The Deccan Chronicle*, 17-7-1949.

582. Barry Pavier, 'Telangana Armed Struggle' in *the Economic and Political Weekly*, Special Number, August, 1974, p. 1418 ; regarding the issue of Kashmir in 1947, the dispute between India and Pakistan remained unsolved, as UNO has intervened in it.
583. It is significant to note that earlier writers on this theme such as Ian Bedford, Barry Pavier and I. Thirumali had adopted division on the basis of class struggle which restricts the representation of various facts of the scene. Hence, a different treatment is given.
584. P. Sundaraiah, *op. cit.*, pp. 89 & 256.
585. *Ibid.*, p. 89.
586. Refer to the first paragraph in the sub-section 'i. War period' in this Section.
587. *Meezan*, 22-2-1946 ; see also para I in the Section 'E. Telangana Struggle' in this Chapter.
588. Ian Bedford, *op. cit.*, p. 178 ; also refer to sub-section 'ii. Procurement Policy and its wide-ranging effects' in Chapter VI.
589. See the 9th paragraph in the Section 'Political Conditions' in Chapter III.
590. P. Sundaraiah, *op. cit.*, p. 89.
591. *The Hindu*, Madras (Editorial), 21-1-1948.
592. Romesh Thapar, *op. cit.*, p. 28.
593. K. M. Munshi, *op. cit.*, pp. 91-92.
594. A.I.S.P.C. *File* No. 67-68, 46-47, part I, pp. 463-64 & 21.
595. P. Sundaraiah, *op. cit.*, pp. 471-480, 483 & 486-494.

595(a). See the 9th para in the Section 'Political Conditions' in Chapter III.

596. A.I.S.P.C. *File* No. 70 (part I), 1947-48, p. 171.
597. Refer to the last para in the sub-section 'ii. Character of the Struggle' in this Section ; see also K. M. Munshi, *op. cit.*, p. 154.
598. K.M. Munshi, *op. cit.*, p. 155.
599. P. Sundaraiah, *op. cit.*, pp. 91-92 ; refer to the second paragraph in the sub-section 'ii. Character of the Struggle' in this Section.
600. Fortress-like mansions of *Deshmukhs* were popularly known so in the region.
601. P. Sundaraiah, *op. cit.*, p. 93.
602. Barry Pavier, *op. cit.*, pp. 131 & 163.
603. Devulapalli Venkateswara Rao (Struggle organiser, especially after Police Action in Nalgonda District) interview, 1974, cited in Barry Pavier, *op. cit.*, p. 163.
604. Barry Pavier, 'The Telangana Armed Struggle' in *The Economic and Political Weekly*, Special Number, August, 1974, Vol. IX, p. 1420.

605. Barry Pavier, *op. cit.*, p. 129 ; P. Sundaraiah, *op. cit.*, p. 118.
606. Refer to the first para in the sub-section 'ii. Character of Struggle' in this Section.
607. *Golkonda Patrika* (Daily), Editorial, 28-1-1948 ; also see the preceding paragraph.
608. *The Deccan Chronicle*, 12-7-1947.
609. P. Sundaraiah, *op. cit.*, pp. 183-184; Edumaddula Sesha Reddi, *Deshmukh* of Tatikonda in Warangal Taluq, was stated to have committed suicide—p. 187.
610. *Ibid.*
611. *Ibid.*, pp. 187-188.
612. Barry Pavier, *op. cit.*, p. 149.
613. Barry Pavier, 'Telangana Armed Struggle' in *The Economic and Political Weekly*, Special Number, August, 1974, pp. 1418-19--Village squad consisted of 120 members.
614. P. Sundaraiah, *op. cit.*, p. 134.
615. Barry Pavier, 'Telangana Armed Struggle' in *The Economic and Political Weekly*, Special Number, August, 1974, p. 1419.
616. P. Sundaraiah, *op. cit.*, pp. 192.
617. Refer to the first para in the sub-section 'iii. Stages of the Conflict' in this Section.
618. P. Sundaraiah, *op. cit.*, p. 192.
619. *Ibid.*, p. 246.
620. Taluq in Nalgonda District connected by road with Khammam.
621. He was the leader of the Palvancha area in Warangal District. At present, he is the leader of the right-wing CPI in the Andhra Pradesh State Legislative Assembly.
622. P. Sundaraiah, *op. cit.*, pp. 178-79 & 181.
623. See the third paragraph in the sub-section 'iii. Stages of the Conflict' in this Section.
624. Giri Prasad and Baddam Yella Reddy interviews, 1974, in Barry Pavier, *op. cit.*, p. 169.
625. Refer to the f.n. Nos. 533 & 603 in this Chapter.
626. I. Thirumali, *op. cit.*, pp. 129-130.
627. See the first para in the sub-section 'i. War period' and second paragraph in the sub-section 'iii. Stages of the Conflict' in this Chapter.
628. Barry Pavier, 'Telangana Armed Struggle' in *The Economic and Political Weekly*, Special Number, August, 1974, p. 1418.
629. P. Sundaraiah, *op. cit.*, p. 125.
630. Barry Pavier, 'Telangana Armed Struggle' 'in *The Economic and*

Political Weekly, Special Number, August, 1974, p. 1418.

631. *Ibid.*, Barry Pavier, *op. cit.*, p. 186 ; also see the first paragraph in the sub-section 'ii. Character of the Struggle' in this Section.

632. Barry Pavier, 'Telangana Armed Struggle' in *The Economic and Political Weekly*, Special Number, August, 1974, p. 1418.

633. Refer to the 3rd and 5th paras in the Section 'Administrative changes' in Chapter III.

634. *The Deccan Chronicle*, 3-12-1948, 8-2-1949 & 12-2-1949.

635. *The Golkonda Patrika* (Daily) Editorial, 13-4-1950.

636. *The Golkonda Patrika* (Daily) Editorial, 21-7-1950.

637. Barry Pavier, 'Telangana Armed Struggle' in *The Economic and Political Weekly*, Vol. IX, Special Number, August, 1974. p. 1419.

638. Refer to the second para in the sub-section, 'b. II Stage' in this Section.

639. See the last paragraph in the sub-section 'ii. Character of the Struggle' in this section.—The majority of the industrial workers did not agree with the Party stand that *Ittehad* was a popular and non-communal organisation—Barry Pavier, 'Telangana Armed Struggle' in *The Economic and Political Weekly*, Vol. IX, Special Number, August, 1974, p. 1419.

640. Refer to the last para in the sub-section '(a). I Stage' in this Section.

641. Barry Pavier, 'Telangana Armed Struggle' in *The Economic and Political Weekly*, Vol. IX, Special Number, August, 1974, p. 1419.

642. See the first paragraph in the sub-section 'ii. Character of the Struggle' in this Section.

643. Refer to the first paragraph in the sub-section 'iv. Conclusion of the Struggle' in this Section and also sub-section '(b). II Stage' in the same.

644. Makineni Basava Punnaiah, *Telangana Sayudha Poratam—Vastavalu* (Telangana Armed Struggle—Realities), Vijayawada, 1972, p. 59.

645. P. Sundaraiah, *op. cit.*, p. 431—50 out of 100 seats for State Legislature and 7 out of 14 Lok Sabha seats meant for Telangana, were won by these candidates.

646. See Table LV and first paragraph in the sub-section 'iii. Literacy and Educational Development' in this Chapter.

647. *Ibid.*

648. Refer to the relevant items in Section 'A. Educational Conditions' in this Chapter.

649. See the first para in the Section 'B. Public Health Organisation' in this Chapter.

650. Refer to the second paragraph in the opening of this Chapter.

651. See the first para in the Section 'B. Public Health Organisation' in this Chapter.

652. *Ibid.*

653. Refer to the concerned items in the Section 'B. Public Health Organisation' in this Chapter.

654. See the first and second paragraphs in the sub-section 'i. Growth of Towns' in this Chapter.

655. Refer to second paragraph in the sub-section 'ii. Municipalities and Town Life' in this Chapter.

656. See the sub-section 'iii. Composition, character and functioning of Local Bodies' in this Chapter.

657. Refer to the third and fourth paragraphs in the sub-section 'ii. Municipalities and Town Life' in this Chapter.

658. Refer to the relevant sub-sections in the Section 'D. Tribal conditions' in this chapter.

658(a). In view of the abolition of *Jagirs* and the passing of the Tenancy Act.

659. Refer to the relevant sub-sections in the Section 'E. Telangana Struggle' in this chapter.

660. Only P. Sundaraiah made some references on these aspects which are not adequate and exhaustive. Further, he being a party leader who had taken part in organising the Struggle, his remarks could be accepted only with the necessary reservations.

CHAPTER NINE

CONCLUSION

WARANGAL *Suba* which, during the period ran from Penganga in the north to Krishna in the south,[1] had, during the two and half centuries rule of the Kakatiyas of medieval times, comprised not only the Telangana of H.E.H. the *Nizam's* Dominions but further extended upto the sea, touching Kanchi in the south-east.[2] The headquarters town of Warangal lying 1,050 feet above the sea level on the watershed separating the basins of the Godavari and the Krishna in their lower reaches, shone not only as a brilliant trade centre in the region but also because of its huge granite boulders and basaltic dykes and climate being both hot and temperate, it had been chosen as an impregnable centre for the construction of a military fortress by the former rulers. In fact, the names '*Orugallu*', 'Warangal' and '*Ekasilanagaram*' to this town adopted by Muslim and Hindu writers during the medieval times respectively, were believed to have been derived from the big and solitary cliff that stood in the centre of this fort.[3] From the economic point of view, it is important to realise that the Warangal Kakatiyas more than any other in the pre-modern period, strived to bring more land under cultivation by encouraging the cutting down of forests and further to bring the red and sandy soils of Telangana that were considered until then infertile, under wet cultivation and thereby contribute immensely for the augmenting of food production for the first time, by the construction of dams across the flow of rivers or streams by suitable bunding between hill gorges.[4] The Gond kings of Chanda who covered a large part of the Adilabad District of the last *Nizam's* period and whose rule extended for five centuries preceding the middle of the eighteenth, also evinced similar zeal for the promotion of tank irrigation by making excellent provision, that any ryot who constructed a tank by his means was given a revenue-free grant of land lying beneath it, as a result of which inducement, a large number of small irrigation tanks were constructed in the Penganga Valley that continued to serve during the period of present study also.

During the Muslim period[5] that intervened between the Kakatiya and Qutb Shahi reigns, there was little encouragement for the development of industrial and agricultural production[6] as the rulers got themselves preoccupied with the suppression of internal disturbances and waging of foreign wars.[7] The loss was twofold ; on one hand, raids by conquerors on towns like Warangal as they had taken place in 1323 and 1424 A.D., led to the plunder of wealth that had been accumulated during the hundred years preceding them, thereby fully impoverishing the local administration and the people ; and on the other, the neglect of former irrigational works led to large cultivated rice fields getting converted into huge forest blocks, just as it was believed to be the case in respect of Pakhal *Shikargah*. Feudal system in its most dangerous form, unlike that of the Asafjahi times, was in operation under the Qutub Shahis that held the reins of power in the area for nearly 150 years preceding 1687. On the theory that the king was the owner of all the land in his kingdom, agricultural land was "farmed" or auctioned to the highest bidder and there was a whole ladder of infeudations right up to the actual tiller.[8] The latter with his poor means was not in a position to compete in the bid and hence was obliged to pay the rent demanded by the "farmers" who were definitely prone to charge higher and higher in view of the large number of intervening gradations. Even during the succeeding Mughal and Asafjahi rule[9] also, though not land-farming, tax-farming was very much in vogue until it was abolished in 1854 by Sir Salar Jung. The latter system, though unlike the former did not affect the ownership rights of the ryots, proved equally torturous for the latter. The nobles who usually obtained these tax-collection rights by offering large *nazars*[10] to the sovereign, never went to the countryside for the purpose, but staying in the capital city of Hyderabad and leading a pompous life, appointed their deputies from the rich landlord section, otherwise known as *Tahuddars* or *Sarbastadars* who indulged in the extraction of amounts far above and over what they had to remit to their normal masters at the capital. Further, the latter kept for themselves as much as they could out of the revenues to the extent of not incurring the displeasure or the wrath of His Majesty and even the meagre remainder poured into Hyderabad, with the distressing result that scarcely anything was spent on the economic requirements of the countryside, such as roads, communications and sources of irrigation. The demands made on the cultivating community proved so much extravagant that landholding became a burden than a valuable right and hence many peasants, as a last resort, gave up their lands which in turn, had its adverse effect on agricultural production and also the revenues of the State.

Though this evil system was replaced by direct collection of the State at the very commencement of Salar Jung I's Premiership, frequent failures of rain and the recurrent famines that occurred during the second half of the 19th century, had a debilitating effect on the condition of the lower and poor peasantry. Many of the latter got dispossessed of their lands, besides a good number giving up their lives. On the contrary, the well-to-do agricultural classes made huge profits on account of these calamities, as their plentiful stocks of foodgrains fetched fabulous incomes in view of the high prices of foodgrains prevailing at the time.[11] The condition of the tenants during this period, was not much different from that of the peasantry, for they were not in a position to grain enough produce that could sustain them after meeting huge rents. The periodical rise in assessments either by Settlement or by Revision, especially in the case of wet lands, not being influenced by the changing prices of agricultural and other commodities, proved a drag on the cultivating masses.[12] Even the grant of remissions which generally referred to wet lands, was also taken advantage only by big landlords as the poor peasants found it beyond their means and intelligence to go through an elaborate system of red-tape and bribery before hoping to receive the required concessions. Instead, the latter preferred to remit the full assessment, however difficult it was in view of the failure of adequate water supply to the crops or the visitation of famine conditions. The administration during this period in 1878, had, however, under the wise direction of Salar Jung I, initiated the salient measure of granting vast number of villages in the *Suba* Districts that lay deserted on account of the mal-administration of the previous regimes, the major lapse being land and tax-farming, on *Ijara* leases with nominal and progressive rates of taxation and *watan* benefits, for the purpose of land development and gradual enhancement of State revenue. As many as 317 villages that formed 89% of the total, were brought under this tenure in the *Suba*, in spite of the fact that fresh grants under this system were abolished since 1909, as by then enough demand and value had arisen for land. But, it is significant to notice that even under this *Diwani* tenure, the *Ijaradars* who were usually absentee landlords, enjoyed such liberal and extensive concessions in land allotment, revenue payment and the grant of *watan* rights that they functioned no less than *Jagirdars* in infringing and encroaching on the land rights of ryots and tenants in their villages which could be remedied only when the Hyderabad Land Revenue Act was suitably amended in 1952.

The economic development of the *Suba* was primarily influenced by the fact that 81.8, 91.5 and 87.5% of the population in the respective Districts of Warangal, Karimnagar and Adilabad resided in rural areas and again, out of them 76.1, 61.5 and 78.3% respectively, belonged to agricultural classes. The interests of this preponderant agricultural population and in a large perspective the agricultural development of the area, in turn, were essentially and manifestly guided by the land tenurial relations that existed between the different classes that had been engaged in agricultural production. Even though 83% of the total number of villages in the *Suba* were of *Diwani* and again 75% of the total *Suba* villages belonged to *Ryotwari* tenure, these only differed from non-

Diwani and non-*Ryotwari* tenures in degree but not in kind, in respect of peasant and tenant exploitation. Whereas *Jagirdars* here and there, like those of Teldarpalli in Khammam Taluq,[13] Garla in Mahaboobabad Taluq[14] and Allipuram in Warangal Taluq,[15] all in Warangal District, became notorious for the atrocities that they perpetrated on the cultivators and tenants in particular and sections of non-agricultural population in general, the *Deshmukhi* oppression on the other hand, such as those of Kallur in Madhira Taluq, Naspur (Narsapur) in Luxettipet Taluq, Kamarkunta,[16] Madugulapalli[17] and Kesavapuram[18] in Mahaboobabad Taluq, Waddepalli and Kanthamakur in Warangal Taluq and Kanthatimmapur in Parkal Taluq, all being in Warangal District, except the second being in Adilabad District, was far more widespread and severe in the *Suba* area during the period of study. This was sufficiently reflected in the terroristic and mob attacks that had been made in these areas on the person and property of the latter rather than the former during the days of the Telangana Struggle. Further, some of the *Jagirdars* like those of Peddapalli in Sultanabad Taluq and Potharam in Karimnagar Taluq, both of Karimnagar District, due to their unproductive and vainglorious spending had been reduced to such financial straits that the former contracted loans from as many as 15 persons, the lowest in value amounting to as low as Rs. 21 and the latter having failed, in spite of repeated notices, to clear off tax arrears amounting to Rs. 4,951-11-7, suffered the ignominy of his *Jagir's* confiscation by the State. On the contrary, *Deshmukhs* like Kalluri Rajeshwar Rao (Kallur), Venkat Murali Manohar Rao (Nasapur), Pingali Venkatrama Reddy (Waddepalli), Pingali Kodanda Rama Reddy (Kanthamakur), Pingali Pratap Reddy (Kanthatimmapur) and Chenna Reddi Lakshminarasimha Reddy (Kamarkunta), had wielded such huge landed power, supplemented by excise contracts[19] and industrial investment that *Subedar* could not take any measure against them and their influence in higher Governmental circles was such that the third-named was made the Deputy Prime Minister in the Cabinet of 1947-48. It is further significant to observe that 75 to 80% of these *Diwani* feudal lords hailed from the Reddi cultivating class, good number of whom again as in the case of 'Pingali' belonged to the same family branch, while only the remaining 15 to 20% belonged to the non-agricultural but cultivating class of 'Brahmins' or '*Karnams*'.[20]

Concentration of landed power extending to one or several villages became the keynote feature in all the different land tenurial systems that had been in vogue in the area during the last *Nizam's* reign. But, more than this, the power of revenue collection enjoyed by tenure-holders either as immediate overlords such as *Jagirdars*, *Maqtedars*, *Ijaradars* and *Agraharikś* or as *watandars* such as *Mali Patel* and *patwari*, had entailed major suffering to the cultivators and tenants, for the former on account of this authority came to regard themselves as the owners of the entire land under their charge and as a result, hereditary *pattedars* came to be regarded as tenants-at will and the tenants as such, were neither allowed security of tenure nor fixity of rent. The latter, on the other hand, though not like the former were entitled for the sharing of the revenue either in part or in full, had considerable opportunities for self-enrichment in discharging their duties of revenue collection and preparation of land records at the village level. The *Deshmukhs* or the *Deshpandyas* had not only claimed the hereditary status of headmanship and *rusum* that went with it but often, besides their incredible land power, had combined in themselves the offices of either *patel* or *patwari* or in some cases, even both. Their grain and money-lending, excise contracts and also industrial investment, had provided them with additional levers of economic wealth and exploitation that were not so much manifest in respect of any other tenure-holders in the area. Hence, *Deshmukhi* oppression at its peak during the period in Taluqs where they had been predominant, such as Mahaboobabad, Madhira, Warangal, Jagtiyal, Sirsilla, Luxettipet, Chinnoor and Kinwat. In contrast, it could be observed that in *Sarf-i-khas* villages where the presence of the immediate overlord was not there and in *Inam* villages where the tenure-holder was not vested with any powers of revenue collection or sharing, nor with any additional accretions of power, no peasant or tenant oppression was complained of unlike in other tenure areas, though of course, economic backwardness due to poor attention being paid by the managers, was there.

The character and the conditions of agriculture during the period, had once again, operated to the benefit of the bigger landlords and to the detriment of the smaller peasants and tenants, with the ultimate consequence of slow and a very little agricultural development in the area. The pattern of land distribution that was characterised by a large number of small, uneconomic and fragmented holdings on one hand and a few heavily concentrated and absentee holdings on the other, produced conditions that retarded agricultural production growth in the sense that, whereas the former incapacitated the cultivators from attempting any investment on agricultural inputs such as improved seeds, fertilisers, implements and wells construction, the latter resulting in huge and unwieldy holdings being mostly cultivated by tenants and *bhagelas*, the former of whom again being subjected to insecurity of *kowls* and high rents, led to diminishing returns in productivity. As against small *pattedars* in 1945 holding land from 5 acres to 10 acres who formed 60.21 %, 58.02% and 46.49% of the total number of *pattedars* in the respective Districts of Warangal, Karimnagar and Adilabad, big *pattedars* owning from 100 acres to above 5,000 acres accounted for only 4.15%, 4.45 % and 4.81 % of the total number of *pattedars*. The amount of land monopolization enjoyed by the latter could be well seen from the fact that in the 12 Surveyed villages of Warangal District in 1929-30, 1.7% of the occupants came to hold 35 % of the total dry land area and only 2.5 % of them held more than 50 % of the total wet area. The fact that the situation in this respect did not change in the latter period could be verified from the fact that in 1945 as against 444 holdings of the size of 1,000—2.500 acres, 49 holdings of the size of 2,500—5,000 acres and 11 holdings of the size of over 5,000 acres in the State, Warangal *Suba* accounted for respectively 257 (57.88%), 30 (61.22%) and 5 (45.45 %) holdings and Warangal District for 77 (17.34 %), 10 (20.40 %) and 1 holding (9.09%) ; Karimnagar District for 53 (11.93 %), 6 (12.24%) and nil (0 %) holding and Adilabad District for 127 (29.60 %), 14 (28.57 %) and 4 (36.36%) holdings respectively[21]. The reason that the latter District was first in this line-up followed by Warangal and Karimnagar Districts was due to the fact that whereas during the period 1913-36, 3,28,174 acres of land had been newly brought under cultivation in Adilabad District, the corresponding figures for the two latter Districts had been 2,74,203 acres and 74,033 acres respectively. It is important to notice that the size of both dry and wet land holdings in the area which remained far below the minimum recommended for reasonable living by *Keshava Iyengar in his 1929-30 Enquiry* and by *the Agrarian Reforms Committee in 1949*, suffered reduction during the period 1913-50 amounting to 4.8 and 3.4 acres in respect of dry lands and 1.30 and 0.36 acres in respect of wet lands relating to Karimnagar and Warangal Districts respectively, as against slight increase of 0.6 and 0.82 acres that obtained in the case of dry and wet land holdings of Adilabad District, which in turn, was due to lesser percentage of occupied area as compared to area assessed and available for cultivation in the latter when compared to the former. The fragmentation of holdings which was on the rise throughout due to family divisions of property, rise in value of land, lack of subsidiary occupations and conservatism of the rural peasantry had, besides hindering the growth of agriculture, proved a potent source for agricultural indebtedness.

The importance of irrigation for the raising of paddy, maize and other food crops on the predominantly sandy lands of the *Suba* area that had been well recognised and attended to by the Kakatiya and Gond rulers, but neglected during the succeeding regimes, had once again been, during Mir Osman Ali Khan's reign, accorded considerable attention, though, of course, the development that was obtained remained far below the potential. As many as 18,726, 31,919 and 1,779 sources of irrigation were found existing in 1926 in Warangal, Karimnagar and Adilabad Districts respectively. But when in that year, 2,798, 4,109 and 724 sources were found unserviceable in the three respective Districts, the restoration work either by private or Departmental agencies was so poor and meagre that only 11, 154 and 55 sources had been repaired in the respective Districts, the percentages of the latter to the former standing at 3.96, 3.74 and 7.59 respectively. Further, it really proved suicidal to the interests of wet cultivation in the area that even in the case of projects such as Pakhal, Ramappa and Laknavaram where enough water was there for *'Do-Fasla'* cultivation, full *ayacuts* under them as set by the P.W.D. or the Settlement Department had never been brought under cultivation, the prominent among manifold factors being the big absentee landlords acting as stumbling block for the carrying on of full-scale cultivation under some of these Projects, inordinate delay in the construction of field channels, *phodi* and Settlement of the *ayacuts*, no effective measures either for the removal of the malarial incidence that was widely prevalent in many of the forestbased projects or for the laying of roads connecting the canal villages even after 28 to 30 years had elapsed after the commissioning of some of these projects, etc. Even the spending by the State on this nation-building service during the period was not worth emulating. It rose from 23.27 lakhs in 1911-12 to 30.17 lakhs in 1948-49, an increase of 6.90 lakhs over a period of 37 years, with of course, wide falls in between amounting to 9.36 lakhs in 1934-35 and 8.01 lakhs in 1935-36. This policy had its repercussions in the way that the Manair River Project, the only one of its kind in Karimnagar District proposed to irrigate 23.000 acres in 18 villages of Sirsilla Taluq and also produce 1,076 K.W. of electricity at an estimated expenditure of Rs. 35,80,000, though earnestly submitted by the First *Taluqdar* for sanction of the Government as early as 1928, it was approved by the P.W.D. only in 1939 and the actual work was commenced only in 1945 to be completed towards the end of 1949. The ultimate result that transpired as a result of these cumulative factors was that, in spite of vast irrigational potential that ranked Karimnagar and Warangal Districts in the forefront of wet cultivation in the State, the percentage of cultivated area that was irrigated in them fell, except for small rise during 1911-21, abysmally from 12.9 in 1911 to 5.1 in 1931 and 4.2 in 1941 in the case of the latter District and from 16.5 in 1911 to 12.4 in 1931 and 6.6 in 1941 in the case of the former District and Adilabad District which on the contrary, ranked as the most backward one in respect of irrigational sources, had also witnessed the same trend that its respective percentage fell from 2.7 in 1911 to 2.1 in 1931 and 0.8 in 1941.

The methods of cultivation that had been adopted by 90% of the farmers in the area had remained essentially primitive and conservative with little application of improved seeds, manures, pesticides and implements. As more than 80% of the lands were under dry cultivation being dependent on fluctuating monsoons and *chalka* lands being poor in fertility and yield without irrigation, the cultivators of these lands, who felt, at times of unfavourable crop or trade conditions, even the payment of land revenue assessment as a burden on their heads, either regarded it as unprofitable to use improved seeds or even the cattle manure on these lands or majority of the lower peasantry and tenants were financially not in a position to afford their use. Even among wet cultivators also, only a few big farmers had taken to the use of these improved inputs with the result that only 5% of the total cultivated area in the State had come under the use of the improved seed developed by the Agriculture Department. It could thus be seen that for *abi* 1356 *Fasli* (1946-47), the supply of paddy seeds by the latter covered only one cultivator in one village under Palair Project in the shape of 30 bags for 90 acres and similarly under Wyra Project with an *ayacut* area of 17,390 acres and an actually irrigated area of 870 acres in 1942, only 337 cultivators spread over 60 villages in Khammam and Madhira Taluqs of Warangal District were supplied for *abi* crop with *taccavi* seed of 2,543 bags, the average working roughly at 6 cultivators per village and 8 bags of seed per ryot. The propagating personnel and the demonstration farms had been highly inadequate to the task, to the effect that they did not extend their activities to Karimnagar District until 1936 and to Adilabad District even beyond that excepting Sirpur Taluq and further, these had been mostly confined to Taluq headquarters only. This sparseness of the Departmental activities in the area was in a large measure due to the poor spending by the Government on this vital arm which as a percentage to total State expenditure ranged from 0.94 in 1934-35 to only 1.57 in 1950-51. The wrong use of cowdung for fuel purposes by some of the ryots in the area, the large export of castor and groundnut cakes to British Indian parts due to higher prices prevailing there, amounting to even a difference of Rs. 100 per ton, and the high cost of fertilisers such as Ammonium Sulphate and Nicifos, especially for the middle and lower peasantry, had all resulted in the poor use of both cattle and chemical manures by the ryots. Thus, for *abi* 1356 *Fasli* (1946-47), among the manures of groundnut cake, bonemeal and super phosphate, only 194 ryots spread over 15 villages under Palair Project and 313 cultivators of 17 villages under Wyra Project had been supplied with only 4,137 bags of groundnut cake (Area 1,400 acres) and 7,901 bags of the same (Area 2,935 acres) respectively, both being in Warangal District. Though insect pests and crop diseases had taken a heavy toll every year due to especially irrigation and double cropping in the area, it was a great set-back to agricultural production that until the end of 1949, the Agriculture Department had neither studies nor evolved any systematic or scientific crop control measures and the conventional methods such as setting up of light traps, rat poison-baits and 15″ deep tractor ploughing that had been advocated for the removal of weeds and insects, proved neither feasible nor effective. Above all, agricultural implements especially ploughs and carts and working cattle in the shape of oxen and buffaloes, being the prime requisties in the traditional methods of agriculture adopted in the *Suba* had, apart from the former lacking in modernity and the latter in strength, fallen short of even the required minimum number. Thus, when the cultivating population of the *Suba* Districts was well above 50% of their total population, the number of ploughs mostly of wooden per 100 of the population in 1935 in Warangal, Karimnagar and Adilabad Districts averaged respectively only 15.7, and 12.4 in respect of carts, being invariably of wooden, the averages were still far lower, standing at 4.1, 5.7 and 8.3 respectively. On the other hand, regarding the number of working animals per *pattedar* of both *Diwani* and non-*Diwani* areas in 1930, as against 2 pairs in Karimnagar District and one in Warangal District, there was not even one animal in the case of Adilabad District. Heavy incidence of cattle mortality, more so of working animals, poor and highly inadequate veterinary facilities, no preventive measures being undertaken by the Department, no attention and arrangements for proper breeding, ever diminishing grazing facilities and above all, livestock exports during 1921-35 outstripping the imports three to four times, had all led to this shortage and weakness of working cattle and also in consequence, to insufficient cattle manurial supply in the *Suba*.

The manner and the extent to which the credit requirements of the farmers had been met and the amount of their debt burden and the way in which it had been scored off in the *Suba* area had exercised overwhelming influence on its agricultural development. Uneconomical and fragmented holdings that loomed large in the area, coupled with frequent failure of crops and expenditure incurred on ceremonies like marriage and funerals and revenue and rent payments, besides several other factors, had put majority of the peasants and *kowldars* into the pangs of debt. The real factor of importance to be noted in this connection was that, out of the total debts among the Surveyed villages of 1949-51, more than 95 % of them were due to money-lenders and only less than 5 % to Co-operative Societies and the Government. Credit from the latter sources being not easily available and involved much hankering around officialdom tainted with red-tape and mal-practice, the cultivators opted for the easy-flowing credit from the former, which provided even for their unproductive expenditure but at a heavy price. Not only heavy rates of interest ranging from 12 to 18 % in cash and 25 to 125% in kind had been charged but these were compounded for every two to three years and the debtors were invariably made to repay in kind only at 20 % less than the prevailing market price, failing which, this expected gain in the transaction had to be compensated in cash besides the usual rate of interest. These transactions usually went on in such a manner that the ordinary cultivator, with his poor repaying capacity and occasional failure of crops and decline in price levels, when once he entered into the stranglehold, rarely got himself extricated from it without of course, alienating his only piece of land which, as a matter of fact, was chiefly coveted by his creditors and more so from those of the cultivating families who had the added advantage of being leading *watandars* such as *Deshmukhs*, *Deshpandyas*, *Patels* and *Patwaris*. The latter, more than in any other District of the State, had been responsible for financing 50.43% of the total debts in Warangal District and the corresponding percentages in Adilabad and Karimnagar Districts had been 40.89 and 30.03 respectively. On the other hand, professional money-lenders figured more in the latter than in the former, though of course, again non-cultivating and non-professional money-lenders operated more in Warangal District than in the other two *Suba* Districts. But all the same, the debt burden as per the limited data available, rose between 1931-39 by 22.09, 27.16 and 196.30% in Warangal, Karimnagar and Adilabad Districts respectively which, during the succeeding period ending in 1949-50 rose, excepting in the latter District, further up recording 100.40, 35.97 and 62.19% respectively. Big increase in respect of Warangal District, smaller one in Karimnagar District and considerable decrease in respect of Adilabad District in the latter year compared to 1939, was due to wide variations in the percentage of families requiring additional capital out of the total number of resident families in the surveyed villages, which stood at 55.2, 31.1 and only 24.2 in the respective Districts as against 36.3 for the State. It is significant to note in this regard that as much as 57.18 % of this additional capital was sought for land purchase in Warangal District as against only 33.5 % in the case of the latter. Intensification of lending transactions by big landlords, strengthened besides their vast agricultural incomes, by rich and copious dividends from their investments in toddy and liquor contracts and running of agrobased industries, had also been a contributary factor towards this increasing debt burden, especially in the former District. It would be very much appreciative of the situation that between 1931 and 1949-50, debt burden in Warangal, Karimnagar and Adilabad Districts rose by 144.67, 27.95 and 380.59 % respectively as against 199 % in the State as a whole. Land transfers that resulted in consequence, took place in the same proportion in the *Suba* Districts. Even in the 11 and 9 Surveyed Villages of Adilabad and Warangal Districts, 787-32 acres and 670-16 acres of dry land and 53-16 acres and 65-9 acres of wet lan respectively, had changed hands towards settlement of de claims, compared to which only 108-8 acres of dry, wet ar garden land put together had undergone transfer in Karir nagar District, which former one of the least in the State ar only $\frac{1}{8}$th of the former District and $\frac{1}{7}$th of the latter Distri which in this respect, ranked respectively first and second respect of dry land and second and first in respect of wet lan among all the Surveyed Districts in the State. In fact, Warar gal *Suba* by accounting for 50% of dry land transfer 81.25 % of wet land transfers and 20 % of garde land transfers that had been effected towards adjustment prior debt among all the Surveyed Districts in the State 1949-50, proved the highest among all the *Subas* in the Stat These large-scale land transfers, as a result of which the forme cultivating owners but now the dispossessed, had not beer especially in Warangal District, allowed to continue on thei lands as tenants, for the fear that these would gain occupanc rights by virtue of the *Asami-shikmi Act*, generated much heart burning and discontent of the dispossessed elements that go sufficiently demonstrated in the Peasant Outburst of 1946-48 Debt legislation and control measures that were in operatio since 1940, proved to a large extent ineffective, first due to th opposition of the vested interests that enjoyed wider influenc among official circles to circumvent and take advantage of th loopholes in the Acts, and second, the lack of alternative an adequate sources of credit other than money-lenders, th absence of Land Mortgage Banks and the consequen reluctance of the ryots to forsake their next door financers however tormenting their transactions had been. Besides lan dispossession, indebtedness, especially the one of accumulate nature, among average cultivators and tenants in the area, had the effect of incapaciating them from making any investment on improved inputs which in turn, resulted in low productivity. The heavy and compound interest burden, together with the fact that they were obliged to sell their grain at a lesser than market price to their greedy creditors, left little surplus in their hands after striving hard to make both ends meet.

Crop acreage, production and yield per acre in the *Suba* area, during the period 1925-26 to 1946-47 for which only adequate data is available, was, with the lone exception of groundnut in the case of Warangal District, on the downward path in the main, though occasional rises were there. Their extent and volume had come to be determined, besides rainfall and irrigational facilities, by the pattern of land utilization, price levels, the impact of the two European Wars and the degree of the application of improved inputs. Fresh and cultivable land distribution was made not only on a meagre scale as against lakhs of acres of land being available, but further, it was done in favour of absentee magnates like Sir Fazalbhoy Karim Bhoy, Sir Amin Jung, or organisations like *Sifatul-Islam*, and soldiers in service who showed more interest in trying to reap profits out of the allotments rather than put the lands to fuller and proper utilisation. In contrast, Revenue, Settlement and Forest Laws came in the way of land occupation by the needy and self-cultivating ryots. The process went on in such a slow and indifferent manner that in 1947, as against a total land of 10,55,893 acres and 50 *quntas* that was available for *Laoni* distribution in the *Suba*, only 50.967 acres and 24 *quntas* of land was allotted. Further, in view of the preponderant wet cultivation in the *Suba* Districts, especially in Warangal and Karimnagar areas that demanded more capital and labour, the dry land areas that were known for their hardness and infertility were, after being cultivated for one year allowed to remain fallow during the following year, thus contributing to the rise in unoccupied land. Its impact on the retardation of agricultural production in the *Suba* could be imagined from the fact that in 1949-50 in Warangal District, fallow land accounted for as much as 53.8 % of occupied area. The period of the First War proved the initial set back to agricultural development in the area. The closure of the Central European markets for the cotton and oilseeds exports from the State, the shortage of freight and railway wagon facilities for their export to other countries such as Japan, the fall in the prices during 1914-17 including of rice and jawar, being the two main food crops in the area and scarcity and famine conditions during 1918-22 characterised by abnormal rise in prices, had all led to low productivity and extreme suffering to the agricultural population, especially during the latter quarter. Better sources of perennial irrigation, transport and industrial development in the case of Warangal District enabled it to experience these rigours in a lesser degree compared to other *Suba* Districts and also the State. When agricultural production seemed to have recovered by 1927-28 from the effects of the War period, a bigger catastrophe had overtaken it with the onset of the Great Depression in 1929-30. Prices of all agricultural products went crashing down from year to year during the six year period ending in 1934-35, amounting to 68.47 % in respect of groundnut, 50 % in respect of rice, 26 to 28 points in respect of jawar and 20.48 % in the case of cotton which coupled with unfavourable crop conditions as in 1931 and 1934, had the disastrous effect of leading to precipitous fall in crop acreages amounting to 40 to 60% and outturn decreases ranging far higher, from 100 to 500 % especially during 1929-30 and 1931-32. Commodities that depended on exports to foreign countries like groundnut suffered greater loss than those that depended on internal demand only, like cotton. The loss in agricultural income during this period could be realised from the fact that, whereas groundnut production in 1933-34 registered as high as 500 % increase compared to pre-Depression period, the additional value realised on this count amounted to only 120 %. Further, the fact that the cultivators were made to pay correspondingly more for the non-agricultural goods like kerosene, salt etc., in view of lesser price decline in their case and substantial rise in the real burden of ryots' monetary liabilities such as land taxes, loans, etc., had brought them into such financial distress that in the sequel, a wave of land transfers by small and middle peasants in favour of rich peasants and big landlords had taken place. Grant of land revenue remissions and *taccavi* by the Government acted only as mere palliatives in this regard. It is however, significant to note that compared to the pre-Depression and Depression period, the post-Depression period turned out to be one of greater and increasing agricultural production, what with the rising prices of agricultural commodities, especially since 1939 characterised by the Second War period excepting 1941 and 1944-45, the average price hike during the period ending in

1950 ranging from 226.08% in the case of rice to 523.15% in respect of groundnut, incentives offered by the Government since 1943-44 for the growing of food crops and more than the latter which were extended, due to the poor and ineffective efforts of the Agriculture Department, to only below 10% of the total agricultural population in the State, the increasing realisation among the ryots in the *Suba* about the greater productivity per acre and hence, income that would be derived from the growing of cash crops for which, during this period considerable demand arose in foreign markets also. In spite of Governmental efforts and even the imposition of restrictions, the growing of food crops including those of rice and jawar, had been subordinated to the cultivation of the profitable commercial crops such as groundnut, chillies, *sesamum*, castor and cotton, with the result that groundnut production in Warangal District between 1936-37 to 1944-45 rose by 57.40%, *sesamum* production in Adilabad District during 1939-40 to 1944-45 rose by 140%, castor production in Karimnagar District between 1934-35 to 1939-40 increased by 29.65% and cotton seed production in Adilabad District during 1934-35 to 1939-40 rose by 16.93%. This development, though contributed for the rise of agricultural incomes, had at the same time, led to the acceleration of the food deficit in the State, though not in the *Suba*, for the *Suba* Districts ranked in the forefront of food grain product on in the State. But, it is all the more important to observe in this regard that the simultaneous rise in cost of agricultural production and cost of living had very much neutralised the gain that the smaller peasants and tenants had derived by way of rise in prices of crops that was experienced during this period and on the contrary, big landlords in rural parts by their large-scale production and business men in urban areas by indulging in blackmarketing of the essential foodgrains and other goods of daily and industrial use, reaped such immense profits by means of these inflationary prices that they turned them for the acquisition of further landed and business assets. The under utilisation of irrigational potential in the *Suba* and the meagre 5% adoption of improved inputs that had considerable influence on the low agricultural output that usually obtained there has already been recounted. The cumulative facts that presented themselves in the agricultural arena had been that not only there was, excepting groundnut crop in the case of Warangal District, general shrinkage in the crop acreage of all the principal commodities during the period of study, but the yields per acre that had been achieved in the *Suba* Districts proved far below the standard levels set by the State Agriculture Department and in reality amounted to only 1/3 of what had been achieved in the neighbouring provinces like Madras or distant ones like United Provinces of British India or India taken as a whole. Thus, during the 21 year period of 1925-26 to 1946-47, the standard yield per acre in respect of rice set at 1,200 lbs, 1,100 and 800 lbs for Warangal, Karimnagar and Adilabad Districts respectively, had been reached in only 1, 2 and 3 years respectively and in the case of jawar, the standard yield of 500 lbs fixed in respect of all these three Districts, was obtained only twice, none and once by the respective Districts. The vital sector of development was thus allowed to languish in the area with consequences highly detrimental to the majority interests of the people.

The system of rationing and grain levy that had been put into operation in the wake of War time scarcity during 1943-44, resulted in great amount of suffering to the middle and lower peasantry in particular and the artisans and labourers in general. In fact, these sections had been so much hampered and hindered in the free conduct of their professional activities and even general sustenance by the new exactions and arrangements that, the popular disaffection that grew on these scores became one of the potent grounds for exploitation by the Communist-led uprising of 1946-51. The levy collection, somewhat reminiscent of the taxation system of pre-Revolutionary France, proved unequal and oppressive ; unequal in the sense that big landholders in the State who controlled 93% of total food grain production gave, by bribing the levy *Girdavars* and by using their influence as village officials and consequently members of the Local Food Advisory Committee, only nominal or nil grain towards levy and as a result, the collection targets were reached by throwing the full burden on small and marginal farmers who were made to surrender as much as 33 to 50% or normal paddy yield per acre, with their small and fragmented holdings that gave little grain surplus over and above their subsistence needs; oppressive in the sense that, when the latter, either due to inadequacy or failure of crops were not in a position to readily attend to the levy demand, the levy officials exerted so much pressure and intimidation on them either by preventing them from carrying on their daily agricultural transactions or even physical beating or fines that the former were obliged to approach big landlords and merchants for grain purchasing @ Rs. 30 to Rs. 40 per *palla* as against the levy price of Rs. 18 that they received from H.C.C.C. It is important to recognise that it was to enjoy this huge differential price income that ranged from 66 to 122% that the latter evaded levy payment and indulged in large-scale hoarding that enabled them to do profitable grain lending and also exports to neighbouring provinces of Madras, Bombay and Central Provinces of British India, where the food grain ceiling prices proved considerably higher than those of the Hyderabad State. But at the same time, it was ironical and paradoxical that a regulation was applied in the case of the poor and hapless peasantry, that their excess grain over and above the levy demand, if at all to be sold, was to be given only to H.C.C.C. and thereby get deprived of even a rare possibility of gaining a little margin of income by selling in the open market. Popular wrath proved so vehement against this inequitous arrangement that during 1946-48 heightened by the Telangana Struggle, official attempts to forcibly collect levy in some of the Taluqs of the *Suba* were resisted, resulting in the killing of as many as six Revenue Inspectors, besides manhandling another six of them and also a Second *Taluqdar*. The system of rationing, on the other hand, which was extended not only to foodgrains, but also to articles such as yarn, iron and thread that formed the basic material in the crafts of weaving, agriculture and tailoring, failed to ensure either adequate or prompt distribution, in consequence of which, the masses were made to fall back on blackmarket purchases at very high prices or else get starved. The quantity of ration in the shape of rice distribution which formed the most important staple food of the people next to jawar, had been, between 1945-50, reduced by 25% and 3 *seers* quantity allotted per month for a person would hardly be enough for a week if he happened to he a real rice eater. Bogus ration cards that numbered as many as 47,000 in Warangal City, 37,000 in Kothagudem Coal town and 15,000 in Khammam town, all in Warangal District, formed a potent source for causing scarcity to real and genuine card holders. But, more significant factor in this direction was the usual practice in the area that out of the distribution quota allotted to a dealer, only half was distributed and the remaining half was sold in blackmarket at exorbitant rates. The meagre fines that had been imposed on them for the violation of the regulations compared to imprisonment in British Indian Provinces, made them little scared of Governmental action in this regard. Besides these defects in the Distribution System, the illegal transfer of godown stocks into blackmarket and across the border, definitely with the connivance of Revenue and Customs Officials and the restriction of the imports from British India on which the State heavily depended, being influenced by political and expedient considerations, had been other significant factors that contributed for the scarcity of the essential commodities that was keenly and bitterly experienced during this period. The final result that emerged in the economic situation was that not only the weavers, agriculturists and tailors, unable to buy yarn, iron and thread at high blackmarket rates suffered much curtailment in their trade activities and majority of the former in Khammam Taluq of Warangal District and Karimnagar and Sirsilla Taluqs of Karimnagar District had taken to unskilled labour for living, but also that the masses had been so much exasperated by the rising high prices and scarcity of foodgrains that they raided grain shops at Khammam, Hanamkonda, Matwada and Yellandu, all in Warangal District during 1941-43 and indulged in looting and at times, accentuated by crop failures, the rural poor had been reduced to such straits that *ballar*, tree roots and tamarind seed formed their staple food. The conditions looked highly ominous and portentous to be well utilized for the emergence of the peasant conflagration of the later forties in the region.

Industries in the *Suba* Districts had been more of cottage and small-scale type rather than of large-scale nature and hence, mostly rural-based rather than being located in urban areas. It is because of the predominance of industries of the former nature such as cotton and woollen spinning and weaving, carpentry, brick and tiles making, pottery and poultry farming in Karimnagar District that the percentage of its total population who earned their livelihood by means of industrial occupation formed 23.93, being the highest among all the Districts in the State, as against 17.80 and 11.18 in Warangal and Adilabad Districts respectively, in which was home and village-based industries remained comparatively less in number. Even the *Suba* and the State taken as a whole, more than 75% of the total industrial units comprised of only hand-ginning of cotton, *charkha* spinning of yarn and handloom-weaving, the latter especially looming so large that 3 to 4% of the total population or 4.77 lakhs of workers earned their livelihood daily by means of this single calling. On the other hand, large-scale industries such as the collieries, the textile industries, rice and oil mills that had been fully confined to urban areas numbered as many as 91 in Warangal District in 1936, being the highest in the State, as against only 21 and 20 in Adilabad and Karimnagar Districts respectively. Even these also remained chiefly agro-based, in the sense that 92.30, 81.81 and 85.71% of them in Warangal, Karimnagar and Adilabad Districts respectively related to cotton, food-products and oil-seeds. Further, there was heavy concentration of these industries in particular towns like Warangal and Khammam in Warangal District, Peddapalli and Jammikunta in Karimnagar District and Adilabad in Adilabad District which, besides being Taluq or District headquarters or both, had especially been characterised by the promotion of good business and transport interests, chiefly of the railway, all of which had served as industrial catalysts. The concentration which amounted to 75 to 100% had not only immensely affected the chances of employment for rural peasantry and labourers and the better exploitation of the agricultural produce of several villages that were far distant from these urban areas and at the same time locked road or transport facilities, but also resulted in low and below the capacity turnover of these units for the reason that, they failed to get enough raw produce for exploitation. Further, the latter condition was also very much influenced by the fluctuating and seasonal arrivals of agricultural produce for milling and other industrial purposes. The output levels that had been reached during the period in the case of non-agro-based industries such as the coal-mining, paper mills, carpet industry, match factories, bone and leather factories, also stood far below the expected standards or production capacities, although unlike in the case of the former, the raw material supply was abundant and unrestricted. Thus, during 45 years of coal extraction by the Singareni Collieries Company ending in 1944, only about 33 million tons of coal had been extracted as against the estimated resources of 1,000 million tons and further, as against an annual capacity of 20 lakh tons, only 10 lakh tons of coal had been extracted on an average during the period by the two large coal mines at Kothagudem in Warangal District and Tandur in Adilabad District. Similarly, with excellent facilities to obtain raw materials of bamboo, coal, lime and water excepting supply of some chemicals from British India and also rail transport, the Sirpur Paper Mills in Adilabad District had, throughout the period upto the end of 1950, fell always nearly short of 1,000 tons by the estimated capacity of production that was fixed at 6,000 tons of paper. Managerial inefficiency, inadequate and less up-to-date machinery, labour discontent and shortage, introduction of novel methods of production only towards the end of the thirties, transport bottlenecks and changes in market trends occasioned by the two Wars and variations in raw material and commodity prices and costs of production, had all been significant factors that contributed in one way or the other, towards low production in the case of these large-scale industries. The Company Directors, for instance, of Sirpur Paper Mills, came to consist in majority Government officials, *Jagirdars*, rich local and Bombay merchants rather than men known or equipped for managerial efficiency. Mechanical disorders sometimes, proved of such magnitude that in May, 1949, when three out of four boilers got spoilt at Kothagudem coal mines, as many as

16,000 workers were forced to remain without work for more than a week. Under the hated system of contract labour which the managements always upheld against strong and continuous labour opposition so as to keep their demands for higher wages at bay, the wages of industrial labour, as in coal mines proved so meagre for the hard labour that was involved that they preferred to quit it and seek seasonal agricultural field work that was comparatively less strenuous, but not less paid. The fact that labour form other provinces was given a better deal in the case of wages and work conditions than the local labour, had further added to the discontent of the latter. On the contrary, small, medium and cottage industries in which, in most of the cases, the owner had not only supervised the work of others but himself had taken part in the process of manufacture, languished to a far greater extent, not because of managerial, labour or mechanical deficiencies like the former ones, but due to severe dearth of investment capital, scarce supply of raw materials, competition from outside and mill goods, lack of patronage by the State, non-adoption by the upper and middle classes due to a change in their preferences or fashions towards the mill products and most important of all being, the lack of independence in marketing their products due to their bonds of indebtedness to *sahukars* or master craftsmen. As little amount of credit tinged with too many formalities and red-tape was provided by the Industrial Trust Fund and Banks, the artisan-entrepreneurs were forced to fall back on the nearby money-lenders who by taking over the supply of industrial raw material and also the sale of the finished products, reduced the former to the mere status of piece-wage earners, whose real wages proved even less than those of the unskilled labourers in consequence of which, many of them took to agricultural labour during the crop season leaving their traditional occupations. Blackmarketing in the supply of raw materials such as yarn, thread and iron, had considerably affected the outturn levels of the related industries such as weaving, tailoring, blacksmithy and carpentry in the sense that even the few debt-free artisans found it with their limited demand and range of profits extremely prohibitive to purchase the raw materials at exorbitantly high black prices. The decline that has set in respect of some of the traditional and renowned callings like the toy industry at Nirmal in Adilabad District, was so severe and drastic that by 1937-38, in this once flourishing industry only three master-craftsmen were found engaged. Industrial production in the area being on a low key was also due to the fact that hand or bullock-drawn instruments of production far outnumbered those that were power-driven, whereas the output turnover was several times higher in the case of the latter than the former. Thus, as against 1, 72, 821 hand *charkhas* that had been employed in the State for spinning yarn out of cotton, the number of power-driven spindles numbered 1, 38, 594,[22] the production result being that whereas Rs. 2 lakhs worth of yarn was turned out by the former, the latter produced as much as Rs. 20 lakhs worth of yarn in 1942, the ultimate consequence being huge imports of foreign yarn worth about Rs. 64 lakhs by the handloom weavers in the State. Similarly regarding oil extraction, whereas bullock-driven *ghanis* in the State numbered 8,650 as against 1, 320 power-driven *ghanis* in 1945, the result of course, being that as against the crushing of only one lakh maunds of groundnut kernel by the former, the latter could crush as much as 14 lakh maunds of kernel. The reasons for this situation being that, apart from the larger interest of providing employment, in some cases subsidiary, to a larger number of the populace through the employment of hand or bullock-powered instruments of production, the lack of power facilities except in Warangal town of the *Suba* until the close of the period left no other alternative excepting the former, with its attendant consequences of low and insufficient production. It is, however, essential to realise that a lop-sided export-import policy pursued by the Government throughout the period and poor spending as well as neglect of industries located in areas other than Hyderabad city until 1945-46 by the Industries Department, had served as significant factors that contributed for low and inadequate industrial development in the *Suba* as well as the State. The fact that exports consisted mostly of raw produce and imports mostly of manufactured or semi-manufactured goods made all the difference, not only in the balance of trade but essentially, in respect of industrial development or resource exploitation. Whilst in British India exports of manufactured articles which fetched more value formed 26% of the total exports, in Hyderabad State they formed only 4%. On the contrary, whereas exports of the raw oil seeds that fetched lesser value, such as groundnut, castor, *sesamum*, cotton and linseed formed 28%, 42%, 31% . . . and 53% respectively of the total annual output in the former territory, the same respectively accounted for as high as 59%, 62%, 70%, 22.8% and 92% of the annual output in the latter. Oil exports on which injudicious and highly discouraging tariffs were imposed throughout the period excepting the quarter ending in April, 1935, formed in the State only 1/12th of the value of seed exports. The same disadvantageous principle from the view point of industrial and economic growth was there in operation in the *Suba* area in respect of coal, bamboo, hides and skins, timber, cotton-seed, oil-cakes, etc. Further, even the existing medium, small and cottage industries which very much required timely and adequate financial assistance from the Department either in obtaining the raw materials at ready and cheaper rates or in marketing of their products, failed to receive it, for the latter was not financially in a position to extend the help in the sense that among all the nation-building Departments of the State, it received the lowest budget allotment that never exceeded Rs. 4 lakhs between the whole period of 1912-13 to 1945-46 and further, between 1934-35 to 1950-51, the expenditure on it formed only 0.40 to 0.56% of the total State expenditure. The neglect was further visible in the fact that there was no permanent organisation in the Districts to work for a systematic development of small and cottage industries which naturally, was due to the situation that until 1945-46, the activities of the Industries Department had been chiefly confined to the State capital only.

The condition of agricultural and industrial labour who, next to peasantry formed a sizeable segment of the *Suba* population was in such a miserable state that it contributed neither for agricultural nor for industrial advancement. The wages of both the categories during the period remained one of the lowest which obliged the workers to move to the neighbouring provinces of Madras, Bombay and C.P. externally and to Marathwada Districts internally, where comparatively higher wages prevailed. The wages of agricultural labourers who formed as much as 12.15% of the *Suba* population and the largest number of whom were in Warangal District in the entire State, were on the continuous decline during the period amounting to 33 to 50% during 1927-28 to 1934-35, except during the War and the post-War period when there was a considerable rise ranging from 60 to 400% which, of course, was very much neutralised by the huge rise in cost of living that forced them to spend as heavy as 68.43% of their monthly budget on food alone. The factory workers also, though formed only 0.53% of the *Suba* population but numbered as many as 15,490 in Warangal District alone which, once again ranked highest in the State accounting for more than 10% of the total industrial labour employed in the State, received throughout the period excepting in the case of Azamjahi Textile Mill workers of Warangal since 1946, such meagre and low wages that amounted to less than Rs. 18 p.m. for male workers, Rs. 5 p.m. for female workers and 2 to 4 *annas* per day to children. Whereas the debt burden of the *bhagelas* and the poverty, ignorance and landlessness of the agricultural labourers had put them in a helpless and weak bargaining position against the unilateral fixing of low wages by landlords and rich peasants, the late starting of trade union activity only after 1945, the dissensions that prevailed among central labour organisations such as the Hyderabad State *Mazdoor Sevak Sangh* and All-Hyderabad Trade Union Congress and most important of all, majority shares of the Government in all the leading and heavy industries such as the Singareni Collieries, the Azamjahi Textile Mills, the Sirpur Paper Mills, etc., on the other hand, had resulted in complete suppression of all attempts that had been made by the workers unions since 1921 sporadically, but most intensively since 1946-47 for the fixation of a basic wage ranging from Rs. 40 to an unskilled worker to Rs. 70 for skilled worker, payment of dearness allowance on the basis of the rise or fall in the cost of living, subscription to Provident Fund @ 8$\frac{1}{3}$% of wages, grant of one month's wages as bonus, reduction of working hours, etc. Only in Azamjahi Mills of Warangal where the first workers union consisting of 3,000 workers had been formed in the State in August, 1943 before the enactment of the Trade Union Act in 1945, the basic wage was made Rs. 26 in 1946 which was further raised to Rs. 30 in 1949 and in all the rest of the concerns, no change was effected in workers' wages or amenities until January, 1951, when the Rege Committee recommendations in this regard were brought into enforcement. But, it is significant to note that as against this unhappy and half-starved existence of the labourers, the managing agents by their huge commission which in the case of Azamjahi Mills in 1943, amounted to as much as 54.58% of the wage bill of as many as 4,000 workers for the year, and the labour contractors by enjoying more than 70% of what the workers earned by hard manual labour, rolled in wealth and luxury. Besides, the latter indulged in much corruption and harassment in distributing workers' wages that further made the latter suffer and feel unhappy. Repeated representations of the labour unions to end this hated system proved unavailing for the managements found it as a convenient instrument for keeping the workers' demands for higher wages constantly at bay. This situation of inequity and oppression could not but become a fertile ground for Communist exploitation in the post-War period to who the labouring classes, mainly of agriculture, and to a certain extent, those of industry especially in towns like Warangal, Khammam, Kothagudem, Madhira and Sirpur, all in Warangal District, except the last one being in Adilabad District, for joining in the Peasant Struggle that broke at this time in the Region. The subjection of *bhagelas* in large parts of northern and Central Warangal District to virtual serfdom with, of course, no protection rights of a serf, by the big and non-cultivating landlord community and the extraction of *begari* from the *balotadars*, merchants, weavers and other non-agricultural sections and *vetti*, in a more severe and oppressive manner from all the sections of lower and middle strata of rural populace by *Deshmukhs* and *Deshpandyas* in particular and village officials and touring Revenue officials in general, has only added fuel to the fire. The *Bhagela* Agreement Regulation of 1936 and the *Sarbarahi* Rules of

1926-27 that had been aimed at lessening, though not abolishing, the evil effects of *bhagela* and *begari* systems, proved mere scraps on paper, for the feudal and official elements combined to defeat these efforts to which were added the poverty, ignorance and lack of alternative sources of credit for the members of the victimised sections. Expressions of the Government about the removal of *vetti* remained only pious and avowed, with the result that this most obnoxious practice continued in the area right until 1949-50. These systems of social and economic tyranny reduced the lives of the labouring and other lower sections of the rural population to such misery and deprivation that the launching of a direct struggle for their removal under communist leadership in 1944 and 1945, was heartily welcomed and joined by these long-oppressed elements.

Marketing and trade in the area had only limited and restricted development during the period. Since the establishment of Regulated Markets was invariably confined to only those urban centres that had been served by rail transport which in turn, extended to very few tracts in Karimnagar and Adilabad Districts, the result was that right until the end of the year 1947-48, the former was served by only one Established Market and the latter by two. Even, wholesale grain markets otherwise known as '*Ganjs*' were also conspicuous by their total absence in these two Districts until the year cited. On the other hand, though periodical markets and fairs figured comparatively more, neither their transactions had been extended to grain and livestock in which the ryots were primarily interested nor the dealings had been of any significant quantum. As a result, in spite of possessing significant channels of agricultural and industrial production, these were made to depend for their export and import purposes on continuous and other District markets such as the former depending on the markets at Warangal, Nizamabad, Kamareddi and Siddipet and the latter on those located in the border Districts of Marathwada and Central Provinces. Not only the cultivators and the artisans in these *Suba* areas were deprived of the full marketable worth of their hard-earned products, the real surplus value in these cases being devoured by the middle and wholesale tradesmen and their agents, they, along with other sections of agricultural and non-agricultural population had been at times such as the War, scarcity and inflationary periods, put to much misery and suffering on account of scarce supply and high prices of essential imports such as kerosene, foodgrains, jaggery, sugar, iron, yarn, leather, mill-made piece-goods, petrol, etc. Warangal District, in contrast, presented a different picture. Rail and Road transport facilities in conjunction with industrial and trade promotion had enabled the Warangal and Khammam markets to rank among the leading ones in the State, followed by Madhira and Mahaboobabad markets in a secondary role. Not only the District requirements were comparatively well met, but these even served as outlets for the trading needs of neighbouring Districts of Karimnagar and Nalgonda, though not Adilabad. Market establishment in the *Suba* area proceeded at a very slow pace until 1946 in the sense that during the 16 year period ending in this year, only five markets had been brought into being, whereas the same number had been achieved during only the next three years ending in 1949, the factors of influence towards the latter development being, among others, greater expansion in the volume of trade and the introduction of *advalorem* collection of market fees instead of the earlier one based on vehicles or carts, which due to high commodity prices, yielded greater market incomes. In spite of this enhancement in market fees rates, the Regulated Markets proved of considerable benefit to the ryots than the unregulated ones which numbered twice to those of the former in Adilabad District, for in the former, unlike in the latter, not only the dues were fixed and there was a price rise of 20 to 30% but also the malpractices such as less weighing, diversity in dry measures, absence of certified weights and scales and most important of all, adjustment of old debts from the sale proceeds of the sellers, etc., that had been indulged in by the latter, had not been resorted to. But, more than the latter evils, the marketing benefits and opportunities of the peasantry had come to be greatly curtailed by the manifold factors such as their indebtedness to *sahukars*, contracting of grain loans, poor utilization of warehousing facilities available at market centres, Governmental restrictions imposed in the later forties on the movement of food crops and the growing of commercial crops, blackmarketing, hoarding and smuggling that had been associated with the system of Rationing and Levy put into vogue during the same period and the closure of European markets and freight difficulties during the War period. It is however necessary to realize that whereas the debt burden of the ryots incapacitated them from even marketing their produce, grain loans and levy payments, on the other hand, had the effect of enhancing the former liability. As against this grievous development, the *komti* and the big landlord sections who respectively dominated and shared the growing business interests of the Regulated as well as the grain markets in the area in general and Warangal District in particular, whose profit range could be gauged from the fact that the Regulated Markets of Khammam and Warangal during the nine year period of 1940-41 to 1949-50 registered such a tremendous increase in business turnover that it amounted to 229.09 and 221.30 respectively. This had further heightened wealth concentration in the hands of the latter section who had already been associated with industrial investment besides their vast landed estates.

District-wise trade particulars were available only for the quinquennium ending in 1920-21 and again, only in respect of Warangal and Adilabad Districts, whereas for the rest of the period and in the case of all the administrative units, only State particulars are available. As against the former period showing excess of exports over imports, the latter one exhibited more of adverse trade balances rather than favourable ones. This contrast was for the reason that whereas in the case of the *Suba* Districts, the export value of raw produce such as coal, groundnut, cotton, til, castor-seed, cotton-seed, rice, jawar, hides and skins, livestock, etc., had far outweighed the import value of manufactured and semi-manufactured articles such as salt, yarn, piece-goods, sugar, jaggery, etc., the reverse development became more true in the case of the State as a whole during the period. Except during the quinquennia of 1911-15, 1928-32 and 1933-37, the imports curve of the latter during the period 1911-1949-50, ran always above that of its exports, the rise being the highest in the last two years which, in turn, was due to the huge rise in the prices of the heavily imported food grains and piece-goods, the former again, being occasioned by frequent crop failures and also the evils of hoarding, blackmarketing and smuggling that had been associated with the Public Distribution System that was then in vogue. On the other hand, the exports, what with crop failures, effects of the Wars on marketing and tonnage, price depression, famines and restrictions on foodgrain movement and the growing of non-food crops, etc., became so scarcely excessive over imports in the State that during the Second War and post-War period ending in 1949-50, favourable trade balance was obtained in only four out of ten years. It is, however, useful to realise that the vital principle that stood behind this import-dominated nature of the economy was the fact that manufactured articles that were comparatively high-priced, were imported more than exported and on the other hand, raw materials or raw produce that was comparatively less priced, had been more exported than imported. The respective ratios when compared to those of British India were highly contrasting, with points of heavy disadvantage being on the former side than on the latter. This condition of imbalance, as has already been seen, was essentially due to low degree of industrialisation that had been adopted in the State as well as the *Suba*. Further, the system of collecting the customs duties at the British Indian sea-ports and again on the entry of goods into the State and vice versa had proved of considerable burden not only to the consumers but to the industrial importers and exporters as well, for the commodity costs had, on account of this, an additional rise compared to those in British India. Though the treaty of 1802 conferred duty-free trade through British Indian lands, neither the British ever recognized it nor the *Nizam's* Government ever tried for assertion of its rights in this regard. Besides, large-scale smuggling of foodgrains across the border that became possible because of wide spread corruption among Customs Officials, had resulted not only in loss of huge trading revenue to the Government, but also much misery to the local population on account of grain scarcity conditions that had been created.

Transport and communication facilitics that lay at the cornerstone of the all-round economic development and general progress of the *Suba* people, remained at a very low ebb during the period. Road and rail mileage had so much fallen below the level of requirement that good number of villages and Taluqs suffered total deprivation. Even in 1949, if the road needs are worked out at the minimum of one mile for every five miles of territory as against the expert recommendation of one mile for every 3.3 square miles of area, the mileage that existed fell short by 38.66, 35.24 and 55.70% in the respective Districts of Warangal, Karimnagar and Adilabad. It is to be noted that forest and tribal-infested Taluqs like Boorgampahad, Mahaboobabad and Mulug in Warangal District, Mahadeopur and Parkal in Karimnagar District and Boath, Kinwat, Utnoor and Rajura in Adilabad District, had been the worst sufferers in this regard. Villages that were even 60 miles away from a *kutcha* or unmetalled road were to be found. In respect of rail line, the deficiency was far higher in the sense that the entire Taluqs of Mulug and Pakhal in Warangal Districts, Karimnagar, Jagtiyal, Sirsilla, Parkal and Mantheni in Karimnagar District, and Boath, Rajura, Chinnoor, Nirmal and Utnoor in Adilabad District, remained untouched by it. Thus, 48% of *Suba* Taluqs went without this chief transport wing that acted as a great setback to the industrial and trade development of these areas. The loss on this count could be understood from the fact that though the railway mileage in the *Suba* was less by nearly three to five times of that of the roads, yet, the value of the carrying trade of the railways accounted for as much as 80% of the total trade. Further, compared to the value of the goods traffic, that of passenger traffic proved less by more than 68%. The utter slackness of the Government in extending this facility to new areas in the *Suba* could by ascertained from the fact that it had taken more than a decade between 1939-50, to lay the Mudkhed-Adilabad line running for a distance of only 101 miles, even though it was capable of promoting the trade links in this cotton belt and a margin could be given for the delay on account of War constraints in the first half. Similar lack of concerted effort and negligence of the Government was also witnessed in the case of adding to road mileage to the effect that during the 15 year period ending in 1950, the decrease in the mileage growth rate compared to the preceding 15 year period of 1921-35, amounted to as huge as 89.85, 37.5 and 86.38% in Warangal, Karimnagar and Adilabad Districts respectively. There was a general decline in road mileage since 1943, with some exceptions here and there in Districts other than Warangal. Not only inordinate delay extending to even a period of six years took place in the construction as well as repair of roads that also included highways and those relating to Taluq headquarters, but also poor spending was made on this all-important nation-building branch of road and rail transport which amounted to only 0.14 to 0.22% of the total State expenditure between 1934-35 to 1948-49, which stood in contra-distinction to the considerable revenue that the State received from this service which formed in the respective years 12.83 and 1.99% of the former's total revenue. Added to this, imbalances in inter-*Suba* allotment of the apportioned budget on this wing and apportioning of the Local Bodies' resources between the District headquarters and Taluqs, had further worsened the s tuation. Besides the deficiency of road and rail mileage, motor transport that had been nationalised since June, 1932, not only proved highly inadequate thereby giving room for the simultaneous operation of the sub-standard private service, but the charges which were already regarded as high before the Second War, were further enhanced during it, in spite of heavy increase in passenger and goods traffic and lesser rise in maintenance and running costs of the Department during the period and popular representations for their reduction went unheeded. Even the introduction of this new service was delayed by more than 4 years in Adilabad District and even 10 years in the case of Karimnagar District. Further, cart manufacture and railway expansion, being the two other means of transport, had come to be considerably curtailed due to the controlled supply of iron, rubber or rubber tyres that had been used in the former case during the forties and the extra-territorial rail jurisdiction and control of the British Indian Government in the latter's case. This inadequacy of the means of transport in the area had the immediate and the important consequences of not only affecting the movement of foodgrains for distribution by the Supply Department and the exchange of mail between District and Taluq headquarters but essentially in depriving the ryots of taking advantage of the demand and higher prices of the agricultural produce that prevailed in Regulated Markets and more so, in neighbouring provincial markets, the growing of fruits or vegetables or the sale of milk and their going to Taluq headquarters for representation and redressal of their grievances. The handicaps of the cultivating and other local population in this regard, were exploited to the maximum possible self-aggrandisement by the village merchants on one hand and *pairavkars* on the other.

Postal and tele-communication facilities in the area had been still worst. The number of Post Offices, Post Boxes and Post Men had been highly inadequate in relation to area and population, the former ranging at the rate of one Office per 100 to 235 sq. miles of territory and 10,000 to 31,035 persons. Letter Boxes and Post Men numbered less than Post Offices in a District for most of the years, thereby testifying to the name-sake existence of the latter. The poor spending and the utter Governmental neglect of this basic communication arm in the *Suba* area during the period could be realised from the fact that between 1932-36 for which only the figures are available, the percentage of Postal income in relation to expenditure ranged from 90.1 to 871.8. Besides being meagre in number, the Postal Service had been characterised by inefficient functioning in the sense that, considerable delay, even amounting in certain cases to two weeks' time, expense and inconvenience was experienced by the business and other sections of the local population in receiving letters and parcels even in towns with good transport facilities, what with lack of transport for the interior villages, cumbersome procedure in respect of railway parcel receiving and the functioning of 50 British Post Offices in the Dominions, very much affecting the interests and revenue of the local Post Offices and more important than this, subjecting the local customers to extra payments, such as in the case of money order commission. Telephone or tele-communication Service, on the other hand, had been confined to only Warangal District and further, in fullness of the Service and the period, only to Warangal town, rest of the *Suba* remaining in complete oblivion regarding this modern wing, in spite of the fact that representation by First *Taluqdars* such as that of Adilabad had been made as early as 1928 for the installation of trunk lines. It further speaks on the poor attention of the Government in this regard that even the lone Warangal Exchange ran into considerable loss, for the Service was poorly put to use in view of the fact that, neither it was connected with other trading centres of the *Suba* and the State, nor with other District and Taluq headquarters excepting Hyderabad city. Only the merger of this Service along with that of the Postal in April, 1950, with the All-India Service, had brought this saga of inadequacy and inefficiency to a close.

Literacy as a factor of economic development played a negligible role in the *Suba* area, for its percentage during the 40 year period ending in 1951 progressed from 2.5 to 8.2 in Warangal District, from 2.0 to 6.1 in Karimnagar District and from 1.3 to 5.9 in Adilabad District, all these throughout the period except that of Warangal in 1931 being lower than that of the State which recorded progress during the period from 2.8 to 9.2 and, as in fact, the latter two *Suba* Districts recorded respectively, as in 1951, the two lowest levels of literacy among all the Districts in the State. The poor establishment of educational institutions, the discouragement and the suppression of the private establishment of schools and their free functioning, the imposition of minority language of Urdu as the medium of instruction from Secondary to University level, complete neglect of educational activity in non-*Diwani* areas, poverty and the conservative attitude of the masses as against the reactionary and vested interests of the upper classes and the suppression of press and freedom, had all been contributary factors, each in its own way, towards this poor achievement of the *Suba* in the field of education during the period. Not only inadequate amounts that did not exceed 10.73% of the total State Revenue as in 1949-50 had been spent on education, but the Local Boards failed to spend even the allotted funds as in 1930-31. To be still worse, it was doubted whether there was any *Jagir* in the State which spent on education at least one rupee out of every hundred rupees of its annual income. The result was that during the 14 year period of 1922-36 for which the data is available, the growth in the number of Colleges, High Schools, Middle Schools and Primary Schools was respectively of the order of 1, 2, nil and 77 in Warangal District; nil, 1, 2 and 52 in Karimnagar District and nil, 1, 1 and only 17 in the case of Adilabad District. Let alone College education which was exclusively confined to Warangal town only, even the Middle and High Schools that are required for the completion of the Secondary education had been so sparse that out of 25 Taluqs in the *Suba*, only Warangal and Karimnagar Taluqs had, until 1936, at least one High School and one Middle School. Its Primary Schools which formed only 19.8% of their total in the State, numbered the lowest among all the *Subas* in the State, with forest and tribal-infested Taluqs proving poorer and poorer in this respect, the ratio of these Schools to the total number of villages in a Taluq touching during this period, as low as 1 : 129.5 in Utnoor Taluq of Adilabad District being the lowest in the *Suba* as well as the State, 1 : 18 in Palvancha Taluq of Warangal District and 1 : 9.52 in Mahadeopur Taluq of Karimnagar District, which situation was directly and mainly responsible for the poor literacy standards in the *Suba* Districts. It would be useful to note that though the number of Middle and Primary Schools was more in Karimnagar District than in Warangal District, the number of literates per 10,000 of the total population as well as the literacy percentage of the District as a whole, on the other hand, proved very much higher in the latter than in the former, which in turn, was due to the better transport and communication facilities, library and reading room arrangements and greater percentage of urban population that Warangal District had, especially in Warangal Khammam towns. It is significant to note that Hyderabad city in Hyderabad District, Aurangabad town in Aurangabad District and Warangal town in Warangal District, because of their huge accretions of urban population, were able to put the concerned Districts in the respective order as the foremost centres in the State in respect of literacy as well as different educational standards. Among these again, especially the former District because of the metropolis, with just only 8% of the State's population, had very much become the single and monopolistic centre for professional, legal, commercial, post-graduate, agriculture and veterinary degree holders as well as lower branches of collegiate and school certificate holders and even mere literates, in all of which it exceeded the State average by three to seven times. Comparison of this position with that of the rural areas such as that of Utnoor, Palvancha and Mahadeopur Taluqs of the *Suba*, would clearly indicate that the regime strived for the all-round educational advancement of the capital city and to a lesser extent of the leading *Suba* headquarter towns, only to the almost total neglect and exclusion of the vast countryside. Not only the educational institutions in the area had been few and highly inadequate in number, but they remained ill-staffed and ill-equipped besides the former being incompetent, right from University to Primary School level which often led to student protest demonstrations in Districts. The Education Department resorted to the erroneous policy of going for the creation of new units instead of providing for the deficiencies of the existing ones, resulting in the sufferance of the latter. In villages most commonly, with the connivance of the Inspecting Officers, the teachers who stayed in the nearby or the same villages, attended to their private errands instead of school duties. Further, even the salaries paid to them, especially in *Jagir* and *Sarf-i-khas* schools had been so low that, in Karimnagar District of the latter affiliation, a teacher was paid Rs. 8 p.m. and a Headmaster Rs. 15 p.m. and hence, the incentive on this count was nil. Thus, all the various possible avenues for the progress of the education of the people in the area, both private and public, got choked down by a self-willed, distorted and undemocratic policy of the regime, tinged with an excessive amount of repression and suspicion. The inevitable result was wide illiteracy that stood as a stumbling block to rural development in its widest sense.

Arrangements for the health condition of the *Suba* people during the period, remained far more inadequate and poor. Public health measures turned out to be essentially curative and not preventive, as a result of which, the incidence of diseases both epidemic and endemic, had been severe and even deadly. No serious or sustained efforts had been made by the Public Health Department, including in the major municipal town of Warangal for the maintenance of proper drainage system in residential and irrigated areas, street cleanliness, supply of potable water and especially steps for keeping such sources uncontaminated and unpolluted and elimination of rat menace in storage godowns, all of which happened to be sources for the spread of diseases like malaria, filariasis, cholera, influenza, fever and plague. The thick and mostly uncleared forests in such tracts as Mulug, Pakhal, Palvancha, Yellandu, Sultanabad, Mahadeopur, Boath, Kinwat, Utnoor and Adilabad of the *Suba*, became, with little anti-malarial measures undertaken by the Department, such intense mosquito breeding grounds that however it may be the need, both the ryots and the agricultural labourers never willingly came forward to work or cultivate the rich lands with plentiful water sources under Ramappa, Pakhal, Lakhnavaram and Bhimghanpur Projects and hence, large areas of their *ayacuts* remained unexploited. Smoking, drinking, rice eating, joint family system and the practice of marrying in the same family branch for generations together, were widely prevalent among the *Suba* people, leading to diseases like tuberculosis, leprosy and guinea-worm that had considerable sway in the area. On the other hand, tribal people such as Koyas, Gonds and Hill Reddis that inhabited in the forest and riverine tracts, became largely susceptible to *yaws* or a fever-like disease which, if not cured in time, proved deadly. But, the one factor that chiefly made majority of the lower and middle sections of the population disease-prone and non-resistant, was the highly malnutritious and imbalanced diet which they had as their daily intake, influenced mainly by their poor economic means and to a lesser extent, ignorance of the principles of sound health. It consisted chiefly of cereals, chillies and salt, but nothing or negligible quantities of pulses, vegetables and proteneious foods like fruits, milk, meat and eggs. On the other hand, it is very much important to notice that apart from not undertaking any preventive steps for disease eradication, even in the case of those that proved of longer origin and of contagious character, the Department miserably failed to make at least reasonable curative arrangements or facilities for the affected victims. One smaller unit or a dispensary located at a Taluq headquarters town, with a meagre staff, medicines and with only 10 beds for both men and women, indoor-patients could hardly be expected to meet at least even a semblance of the health and medical requirements of a population spread over, on an average, as many as 206 villages in the *Suba*. In the same terms, the ratio for the State stood in 1951 at one hospital for every 338 sq. miles and as many as 76,770 persons, the utter backwardness of which, could be seen from the comparative position that obtained in another princely territory of Mysore as early as 1935, which gave one hospital for every 94 sq. miles of area and 20,653 persons only. Staff, medicines and equipment supply, even at these limited number of units was extremely deficient so as to doubt the utility of their very existence. Things went on in such a manner that for months together and in spite of repeated representations in 1947, Medical Officer was not posted to the dispensary at Utnoor and in the same year and in the same District of Adilabad, Second *Taluqdar* of the latter place, when he was down with malaria fever, could not get himself treated at the District Headquarters Hospital of Adilabad neither Civil Surgeon was there nor equipment to test parasites in the blood and hence, obliged to go out. When such was the facility enjoyed by a Deputy Collector, the fate of common people proved to be the most horrible and worse. This was reflected in the fact that when in 1945, 250 people had already been devoured by the cholera demon and the rest of the people eagerly clamoured and approached the District Headquarters Hospital of, once again Adilabad, for preventive inoculation, they had been most shamefully and dejectedly turned back on the score that no medicine tubes were there, thereby throwing the hapless lot into the pangs of death. In the case of other widely prevalent diseases like filariasis, guinea-worm, tuberculosis, leprosy and *yaws*, either no systematic curative measures had been ever undertaken as in the case of the former two, or the measures were ineffective and inadequate as in the case of the latter three, the result being the proliferation of the victims of these endemic diseases in the *Suba* area, right until 1950. The health condition of the people in non-*Diwani* lands, as in respect of education, was further deplorable, for the assignees with the independence that they enjoyed in these matters and their lack of interest in them, not only neglected the establishment of hospitals and their maintenance but did not even provide for relief measures when epidemics broke out, or at least not allowed the *Diwani* officials to take up them nor at least strived for the supply of drinking water, an essential pre-requisite governing the health condition of their people. The poor interest that the Government showed towards this welfare activity was evident from the fact that its spending on this item as a percentage of total State expenditure progressed from 3.46 in 1934-35 to only 3.55 in 1948-49, in other words, indicating an increase of 0.9 over a 14 year period. Further, the administration of public health under dual control and the non-separation of the Medical and Public Health Services until February, 1947, had considerably impaired the free and efficient delivering of goods to the people under this nation-building arm. Cumulatively, public health in the *Suba* during the period, was allowed to suffer in such a way that it affected efforts for augmenting economic production and efficiency. Frequent failure of crops and impact of the two Wars and trade cycles had only further worsened the situation in this regard.

Though urban population of Warangal *Suba* formed, as in 1911, only 5.71% of its total population as against 19.05% in the State as a whole, yet, the towns being centres of industry, trade, administration, education and culture, with better transport and communication facilities, had not only attracted huge number of internal as well as external immigrants, but, in fact, exercised such a tremendous influence on the economic development at District, *Suba* and State levels that, they very much functioned as torch-bearers. Warangal, Khammam, Yellandu, Kothagudem, Madhira and Mahaboobabad in Warangal District, Karimnagar, Jagtiyal, Peddapalli, Sirsilla, Manthani, Jammikunta and Metpalli in Karimnagar District and Nirmal, Adilabad, Chinnoor, Sirpur, Mancherial, Bellampalli and Rajura in Adilabad District—if these prominent urban areas of the *Suba* are set aside for a moment, its economic history would appear very much deformed and rather meaningless. But, among these again, the intensity and the degree of development directly varied with the extent to which the contributary factors analysed as above, presented themselves in a particular town. Thus, Warangal and Khammam which combined all these elements, the former in a greater proportion and the latter in a lesser degree, registered during the tricennium of 1911-41, population growth amounting to 160.49% and 108.20% respectively, as against Peddapalli which, though a trading and rail centre, lacked in large-scale industries and administrative importance, achieving only 47.80% growth in its population during the same period. It is also a point to note that the latter remaining during the period as an exempted *Jagir* with little bent of mind from its holder to take stops for the promotion of the lacked elements, acted as not a little setback to its further accelerated growth. This could be confirmed from the fact that the *samasthan* town of Palvancha in Warangal District and *Jagir* towns of Dharmapuri and Vemalwada in Karimnagar District, registered, during 1921-31, and 1931-41, such meagre population growths that they respectively amounted to 30.32% and 4.93%; 8.95% and 0.72% and the latter one, in a highly distressing manner, recorded during 1911-41, a 17.77% decrease in its population. Similarly, whereas coal-mining and rail line shot Yellandu, Kothagudem, Tandur, Bellampalli, Mancherial and Ramagundam into prominence, Paper Factory at Sirpur, agro-industries and trading interests at Madhira, Mahaboobabad and Nirmal, all except the last one being served by rail transport, served as significant growth factors in the respective cases. On the other hand Karimnagar, Jagtiyal, Sirsilla, Manthani, Metpalli and Koratla which lacked large-scale industries, trade or rail line though abounded in declining cottage and home industries, and Asifabad, Luxettipet, Boath and Kinwat, all in Adilabad District, which not only remained without any of the growth elements, but on the other hand, got surrounded by forest-ridden and malaria-infested tracts, failed to make any significant progress in urban development during the period. Town administration, whether it was under Municipalities which tardily progressed from 7 to 11 during 1911-41 in the *Suba*, or under Town Committees, has, during the period, come to be controlled by Revenue Officials, headed by First *Taluqdar* and influential non-official members representing legal, business and feudal sections that invariably resided in District headquarters. Among District and Taluq Boards that attended to wider interests also, these same district headquarter and urban forces prevailed in the income and expenditure allotment of the Local Bodies, much to the exclusion of the Taluq Boards and the rural interests. This was reflected in the fact that in 1936, out of the total Local Boards' expenditure of each district, the Boards relating to the District headquarters of Warangal, Karimnagar and Adilabad accounted respectively for as much as 74.43%, 71.76% and 39.67% in consequence of which, Taluq Boards had been left with such meagre amounts that in the same year, Mulug in Warangal District spent Rs. 194 on education, Parkal in Karimnagar District spent Rs. 7 on civil works and Boath in Adilabad District spent Rs. 180 on sanitation and hospitals. Even more depressing was the situation that, whereas the latter, due to their weak and slow-moving engineering personnel, were not able to spend 25 to 75% of their incomes in the above cited year, the former, with their efficient engineering men, were able to spend 80 to 100% over and above their incomes in the year. Thus, in the vast countryside of the *Suba*, other than major Municipalities such as Khammam and Mahaboobabad in Warangal District, Jagtiyal in Karimnagar District and Nirmal and Chinnoor in Adilabad District which had substantial and varied sources of income, the contribution of Local Bodies proved to be meagre and insignificant towards the development of nation-building services like education, health and public works. The provision of civic amenities even by the latter, including those administering the important towns of Warangal, Khammam and Karimnagar, remained much unsatisfactory and imperfect. By 1949, out of ten Municipalities, only those of the former two and Adilabad had been provided with water supply, but again respectively, only towards the end of the thirties, October, 1949 and in the mid or later forties. The condition of roads in Khammam and Yellandu towns was complained to be such that it proved difficult not only for people but even for carts to move on them both during summer and rainy season. Only surface drainage was introduced in the key town of Hanamkonda and in others not even that. Its cleaning was not done even once in a month, resulting in stagnation and mosquito breeding. Not a little part of this negligence was due to the fact that a good number of Municipal workers meant for this work had been engaged for private errands at officers' residences such as those of First *Taluqdar*, Local Fund Superintendent and Sanitary Inspector, besides payment of meagre wages that ranged from Rs. 8 to Rs 16 p.m. and reluctance of private owners to hire carts for garbage removal on account of poor charges. Lighting arrangements that consisted of only street lamps except at Warangal, were equally found to be inadequate and unsatisfactory by the inhabitants. Thus, the fully nominated and official-dominated Municipal bodies had very poorly met the civic requirements of the town dwellers, for whom, in consequence, life did not appear to be that much happier and comfortable as it was hoped for or was to be.

Tribals such as Gonds, Koyas, Hill Reddis and *Banjaras*, who accounted for as much as 14.07% and 15.24% of the total population of Warangal and Adilabad Districts respectively and in fact, got distributed in each and every Taluq of the *Suba* but in differing intensities, gained prominence in the *Suba* economic history during the period, as the most oppressed and exploited elements at the hands of the immigrant and non-aboriginal landlords and forest contractors as well as forest, revenue and police officials. Until the former's hilly and riverine habitations had been, during the second and third decades of the present century, connected by road and rail links with the plain and non-tribal areas of both internal and external jurisdiction, they were enjoying a happy, peaceful and even a reasonably prosperous life, both by means of shifting and plough cultivation, cattle-breeding and also exploitation of the forest produce. With this opening up of the tribal areas and at the same time, Government as a policy measure to bring more lands under cultivation for enhanced revenue and also agricultural production, encouraging the arrival of new settlers into them, a flood of land-hungry ryots from densely populated districts of the State such as Karimnagar, and from areas of the neighbouring provinces such as Berar and Central Provinces to the north and Krishna, Guntur and East Godavari Districts of the Madras Presidency to the south of the *Suba*, along with rapacious forest contractors from the last-named District and also *Banjaras*, a shrewd non-aboriginal tribe that originally hailed from Rajasthan, had all rushed into different tribal zones that were found suitable for their exploitation. The capturing of *patwari* and *patel watans* by the immigrants in the settled villages which, in some cases embraced even whole Taluqs, and their consequent and easy influencing of higher Revenue, Forest and Police Officials, even with huge bribing, enabled the former to easily evict the innocent tribesmen from the lands that they had been already cultivating since a pretty long time, even by the change of entries in Revenue records and also acquire monopolistic rights in timber cutting and its export. The aboriginals on the other hand, such as the Gonds, were not issued under the former regimes, land *pattas* irrespective of the periods of ownership as the concept of State or kingly ownership prevailed and as a result, with their meekness and ignorance, they were found to be at a loss to prove their land claims in the present regime, when they got ranged against the wily and resourceful immigrant non-aboriginals. The situation became so worse for the former that not only had they been dispossessed from their lands, but they were not even allowed to continue as tenants on their former lands, nor the Forest Department permitted them to take up the cultivation of new lands at sites of their choice. The new absentee landlords preferred to let their lands to non-aboriginal cultivators in expectation of higher rents and also better cultivation on one hand, and the Forest officials, on the other hand, resorted to reservation of forests in such a way and so close to cultivated lands that little fresh land was available for the *podu* or the plough cultivation of the dispossessed tribals. The inevitable consequence that followed was that the latter were forced to fall back on forest labour to eke out their livelihood. But, even in this calling also, they had been subjected to severe exploitation at the hands of the immigrants forest contractors who, either under the cover of supply of grain or the payment of land revenue on behalf of the former, handed over only paltry amounts for labouring all throughout the year. The poor tribesmen had no other alternative but to receive them, failing which they were either put to starvation or even physical violence was used by the exacting merchants contractors. On the other hand, it is worth noting that considerable number of Hill Reddis from Palvancha *samasthan* in Warangal District, imigrated to the other side of the river Godavari in the Agency tract of East Godavari District of the Madras Presidency, when they found that the conditions there in respect of cultivation and forest labour was very much better. But, those who continued to remain in the *Suba* areas, nursed by 1940s, deep feelings of sullen resentment and frustration that they were neither allowed to lead unfettered a life of their own nor were they cared for. This attitude got reflected in the Babijhari incident of the same year led by Gonds, which prompted the Government towards ameliorative measures. Prevention of tribal land alienation into non-tribal hands, grant of land to tribesmen under *Laonikhas*, establishment of schools and hospitals in tribal areas and co-operative exploitation of forest *coupes*, etc., had been undertaken since 1944-45, but rather it became too late and further, the magnitude of those measures was not at all in commensuration with the need. By the time Government commenced its remedial action, the non aboriginal settlers had already become the dominating force in the once tribal zones and the tribals very much got resigned to their fate. Allotment of funds was so inadequate that for Warangal District with a total tribal population of 1,85,998, the sum provided was only Rs. 3,28,000 the per capita not even working out for Rs. 2. Similarly, land distribution among Gonds and Koyas touched only 50% and less than 10% of their number respectively. Among Hill Reddis, it was completely nil. 1948-49 convulsions put a stop to even these meagre operations. Tribal life thus during the period, excepting that of the non-aboriginal *Banjaras* who proved equal to the situation, never, since 1920s and 30s, remained free from non-aboriginal and official exploitation and became one of want and destitution. Their discontent in turn, formed a source of Communist exploitation during the latter stages of the Telangana Struggle.

Peasants' Struggle of 1946-49, came as the violent expression of deep discontent and frustration that had been brewing in their minds as well as those of agricultural labourers, occasioned by *Deshmukhi* and *Jagirdari* excesses in general and Procurement System in particular. The fact that as many as six Revenue Inspectors had been killed and same number along with one Second *Taluqdar* also had been manhandled during 1946-48, when they tried to forcibly extract levy grain from poor peasants in the forest-infested and backward Taluqs of Kinwat, Boath and Sirpur in Adilabad District, Huzurabad in Karimnagar District and Boorgamphad in Warangal District, stood as an indicator of the unbearable misery and suffering that the latter had inflicted on the small and middle peasantry. Even the rich peasants also showed their resentment against this collection along with *Razakar* excesses by joining in the pre-Police Action stage of the Struggle, of course, not for the reason that they, unlike the former, found it difficult to pay the levy, but that they had been deprived of the opportunity of selling grain in the open market and thereby earn higher prices than what the H.C.C.C. offered them. Hunger for land among the small peasants and landless tenants became the most compelling demand of vital significance. It is interesting to notice that in Warangal District where, on one hand intense land monopolization and on the other, vast number of landless tenants, small and uneconomic landholders were there, the struggle had taken a severe and intense form and further, it had been directed essentially against those big landlords like the Kalluri *Deshmukh* in Madhira Taluq, who commanded huge landed estates that gave enough room for distribution. But, of more immediate significance became the security of tenants against frequent evictions indulged in by the absentee and non-cultivating landlords, in order to bring about periodical hiking in rents and more important, to deny the former, opportunity to gain prescriptive rights or even *shikmidari* status under the *Asamishikmi* Act. These issues provided sufficient ground for the Communists who established their party units in the Region by the close of 1939, to spearhead the Peasant Resistance that gained momentum by 1944-45. The prospect of imminent declaration of Indian Independence and the anti-accession stand of the *Nizam* in 1946-47, was chosen as the right opportunity to commence the Struggle. Whereas Khammam-Madhira and Palvancha belt dominated by rich and middle peasantry interests figured essentially in the 1946-48 period of the Struggle, the Mulug-Mahaboobabad-Warangal zone, both of Warangal District on the other hand, with its thick forests constituted the scene of action in 1949.

In panorama, economic history of Warangal *Suba* during 1911-50 presents a spectacle of low and imbalanced growth in different economic spheres, characteristic of a backward economy even though it, of all the *Subas* in the State, had been endowed with rich natural, mineral and industrial resources. In fact, in the fields of irrigation, coal-mining, handloom and cottage industries, agro-based industries and rail transport, it enjoyed pre-eminent position. Leaving a margin for the influence of extraneous factors such as the failure of monsoons, visitation of epidemics, trade cycles and the two Wars etc., the case remained essentially one of poor and under-utilisation of the economic potential and a lop-sided and unbalanced regulation of the agricultural, industrial and trade forces. Absentee landlordism, rack-renting and evictions that became the dominant characteristics of land tenurial systems, served as retarding forces for augmenting agricultural production. Excessive land monopolization matched by none the lesser degree of meagre holdings and landlessness, which found their supreme expression in Warangal District for the State as a whole, had further, in an intense way, led to the same result. Considerable water resources of Projects like Ramappa, Pakhal, Lakhnavaram and Bhimghanpur went unutilised either due to non-eradication of malarial menace or the disinclination of absentee landlords to take up '*do-fasla*' cultivation under them, or due to the inordinated delay that was caused in the grant of wet land *pattas*, with the unfortunate consequence that the percentage of the cultivated area that was irrigated came down crashing in all the *Suba* District during 1911-41, with its inevitable impact on the trend and tempo of agricultural production. Repair of unserviceable sources including those of the Government, was neglected in a most harmful manner. The poor capital means of an average peasant, little availability of cheap credit other than the tormenting one from Reddi or *Komati sahukars*, the burden of accumulated debt and that precariousness of rainfall conditions, had all made the former reluctant to apply for improved seeds, manures and implements which in consequence, had come to be utilised only by the rich for wet cultivation, such land forming only 5% of the total cultivated land in the State. This poor utilisation of improved inputs was also not in a little measure due to the negligible spending by the Government on the vital Department of Agriculture that ranged from only 0.94% in 1934-35 to 1.57% in 1950-51 of the total State expenditure. These varied factors analysed as above, coupled with differing effects of the two Wars and price changes had the depressing effect of registering falling crop acreages and outturns in general, except during the inflationary period of the forties whose production and price increases had, of course, been neutralised to a considerable extent, as far as the smaller peasantry was concerned, by the rising costs of production as well as the scarcity and high prices of essential manufactured goods. Production was carried on in such an inefficient and unprogressive manner in the *Suba* Districts that the standard yields per acre set by the Agriculture Department in respect of even such staple crops like rice and jawar which, in reality amounted to only 1/3 of what had been achieved in the neighbouring or distant provinces of British India like Madras or United Provinces, had not been attained by any of the former for more than three years during the 21 years period of 1925-26 to 1946-47, for which only the figures are available. It is significant to realise in this connection that the industrial, trade and transport promotion also suffered from inadequacy, imbalance and stunted growth, all these economic wings being primarily confined to selected urban areas, with the result that the vast rural masses, especially those that failed to earn their livelihood from the predominant agricultural occupation, could not also get succour from the former. Whereas heavy industries like the Singareni Collieries, the

Azamjahi Textile Mill and Sirpur Paper Mills suffered from low utilisation of the plentiful raw material sources, the cottage and small-scale industries, on the other hand, languished from dearth of capital, scarce raw material supply and lack of proper demand and marketing facilities. The agro-industries that consisted mainly of rice, oil and cotton mills, had come to serve as outlets for the industrial investment of big landlords that flourished in the *Suba* Districts, which only became further accretions to their concentrated land power. The contract system of labour that was adopted in the labour-intensive heavy industries against strong and constant worker criticism, resulted in the payment of poor and highly inadequate wages to labour and all trade union efforts to get them bettered, though commenced rather late, were still suppressed with heavy hand, right until the close of 1950. Due to the poor industrial development and a mis-directed trade policy, raw produce such as groundnut, castor, *sesamum*, linseed, cotton, hides and skins, bamboo and by-products such as groundnut cake, castor-cake and cotton-seeds, had been heavily exported ranging from 59 % in the case of groundnut to 92 % in the case of linseed of the annual output in the State at a lesser value and large-scale imports of manufactured goods of these and others such as oils, yarn, piece-goods, baskets, leather, iron, sugar, etc., had been obtained at comparatively higher value, thereby leading to an adverse trade balance which, in fact, characterised 3/5th of the total period under study. As Regulated Markets had invariably developed only at those towns that had been served by big industries and rail transport, Karimnagar and Adilabad Districts had been poorly served by the former, for these remained very much deficient in the latter requisites, with the result that they were made to depend for their export and import requirements on contiguous or outside markets. The utter inadequacy and neglect of the road and rail transport as well as postal and tele-communication facilities in the *Suba* areas stood at the bottom of backwardness in marketing, educational, health and also general administration fields. Lowest rates of literacy, poor health standards and highest disease-incidence, limited urban development and ineffective and undemocratic functioning of Local Boards and subjection of the aboriginal tribes to the maximum possible exploitation and oppression at the hands of the non-aboriginal immigrants as well as the Revenue, Forest and Police Officials, had been the unhappy results, in essence, in the related sectors during the period. Climaxing these manifold failures of the Government and sufferings of the people at large, came the Telangana Struggle. The huge amount of trouble and suffering inflicted on the masses in general and ryots in particular by the hated grain levy and Rationing System, *Jagirdari* and *Deshmukhi* excesses in the shape of *begari*, *vetti* and land evictions, coupled with the fervent hunger for land and the desire of the Communists to take advantage of the complex political situation that had arisen in the State, had all been the chief motivating factors for the former's onset. The Struggle had gathered such a momentum that by the beginning of 1948, as many as 2,000 villages were stated to have been brought under the controlling influence of the Communists. Land and foodgrains distribution had also been undertaken, though on a paltry basis. But, the Struggle objective, except in areas bordering Nalgonda District, being limited in aiming only at accession with India, it petered out after the latter being achieved. The left elements that strongly urged for land distribution and increase in wages, though carried on guerilla warfare for more than two years and a half from forest bases and riverine tracts of Godavari, failed to make headway for, the odds were heavy against them. Further, the raids turning revengeful and destructive had alienated popular sympathies for the cause. Desperation set in the end and due to war-weariness and an overwhelming desire of the Party activists and leaders to contest in the 1952 General Elections, the Politbureau in October, 1951, called it off without any pre-conditions or even the ban on the Party being lifted. However, heroism and the sacrifices displayed by the Telangana peasantry during the Struggle, deserves commendation. The old, uneven and undemocratic regime had already given place to a popular and responsive Government encompassing the former Warangal *Suba* area, and a new chapter has begun in its economic, social and political history.

REFERENCES

1. Dr. Hirananda Sastry : *Shitab Khan of Warangal* (published by H.E.H. the Nizam's Government : Calcutta, 1932), p. 1.
2. *Proceedings of the Hyderabad Archaeological & Historical Society, January to August, 1941*, (Hyderabad-Dn, 1942), pp. 12-13.
3. Maremanda Rama Rao (Editor) : *Kakatiya Sanchika*, (published by Andhra Historical Research Council, Rajahmundry, 1935), p. 203.
4. Dr. Venkata Ramanayya and Sri M. Somasekhara Sarma : 'The Kakatiyas of Warangal' in G. Yazdani (editor), *The Early History of the Deccan*, Vol. II, Part IX, pp. 678, 680 & 682.
5. This refers to the period between 1323 and 1543 A.D. when the Tughlaqs and then the Bahamanis from 1347 reigned in the Deccan.
6. J.D.B. Gribble : *A History of the Deccan*, Vol. I, (London, 1896), p. 26.
7. Wars of succession and differences between Deccan and foreign Amirs on the internal side and wars with Vijayanagar rulers and Hindu feudatories such as those of Warangal on the external side, are significant.
8. Moreland, 'Relations of Golconda', pp. 77, 79 & 81, cited in Prof. H.K. Sherwani, *the Qutub Shahis of Golkonda*, (Hyderabad, n.p., n.d.), p. 476.
9. Moghal rule in the area dated from 1687 to 1724 and Asafjahi from 1725 to 1948.
10. Gifts or tributes of a compulsory nature.
11. K. Subramaniam, 'Famines in Hyderabad State during the second half of the 19th century' (Mimeographed article) in I. Thirumali, *op. cit.*, p. 4.
12. H.E.H. the Nizam's Government : *Administration Report for 1320 & 1321 Fasli* (*1910-1912*), pp. 2 & 5.
13. Amjad Ali was the *Jagirdar*. The atrocities complained against him proved so strong that his *Jagir* was taken over by the Government in 1945-46—*Meezan* (Telugu edition), 10/11-10-1945 ; W.S. *File* No. 31 of 1355 Fasli (1945-46) & R. No. 53 of 1356 Fasli (1946-47).
14. *Meezan*, 13-4-1946 (Telugu edition). It had a railway station which was raided for the sake of seizure of foodgrains during October, 1948).
15. Statement of Secretary, Andhra *Maha Sabha*, Khammam Taluq and Warangal workers in *Meezan* (Telugu edition), 4-12-1945.
16. In 1929-30, he held 1,900 acres of land in 4 villages of the Taluq, besides enjoying 920 acres of pasture land from 1907-08 to 1929-30 in Antaram village of the same Taluq, which was later cancelled due to Forest Department's objection.
17. E. Raghava Reddi was the *Deshmukh* who was complained of forcibly evicting *Shikmidars* from their lands and selling them to others and subjecting the complainants to beating with police help—*The Deccan Chronicle*, 5-11-1949.

18. Nookala Jagannadha Reddy was the *Deshmukh*, one of the leading in the Taluq, also served as Police and *Mali Patel* in which capacity, it was complained that by giving 3 *kundas* (72 *seers*) of jawar as loan to some ryots, he captured 18 acres of *chalka* land—*Meezan* (Telugu edition), 26-3-1946.
19. These had come to be enjoyed by the Pingali family since the time of Venkatrama Reddi's father, the former, of course, monopolizing for the entire Telangana during the study period—*The Deccan Chronicle*, 12-3-1947 ; P. Sundaraiah, *op. cit.*, p. 12.
20. This observation made on the basis of eight prominent ones given as above, will not be much different even if total figures are assessed in this case, which, of course, was not done by anybody on the subject so far.
21. The percentages given in brackets relate to the proportion that the respective holdings bear with those of the State.
22. *The Hyderabad Government Bulletin on Economic Affairs*, Vol. I, No. 2, December, 1947, p. 182 (Col. No. 10 in the Table and figure given for the year 1349 Fasli 1940).

APPENDIX

13. "If I intend extending the period of lease, I shall execute a new deed, three months before the expiry of the present deed. If not, I shall give you a release notice and take receipt from you. Otherwise, I shall not only pay the tenancy dues of the next year but also quit the land.

17. If ever, I go against any of the above mentioned conditions, on the same day I may be removed from my possession, cancelling the lease. In addition, I will be liable to pay whole amount of money and grain calculated to cover the remaining period of lease. I shall meet all the expenses, penalty or loss you are put to on that account."

—Form No. 39 : Tenancy Agreement in Ammapalem, Warangal District, 1929-30.

Source : S. Kesava Iyengar, *Rural Economic Enquiries, 1949-51.*, p. 355.

BIBLIOGRAPHY

Unpublished Original Sources :

Board of Revenue, Hyderabad
Warangal *Subedari Files*

Warangal Collectorate :

First *Taluqdar* Warangal *Files*
D.G.R. Telangana Range *Files*

Nehru Memorial Museum Library, New Delhi :

All India State People's Conference *Files*
Jawaharlal Nehru Subject *Files*
All India Trade Union Congress *File* (n.y.)
All India Trade Union Congress Papers (ed) by S.A. Dange.

State Archives, Hyderabad :

Rural Reconstruction Secretariat *Files*
Rural Reconstruction Department *Files*
Agriculture Department *Files*
Office of the Secretary to Government, Judicial, Police and General Departments, *File* No. 15/P.A./49, F. No. 2

Interim Repository, A.P. Secretariat, Hyderabad :

Financial Secretary and Financial Adviser (Supply Finance) Office *Files*
Revenue Department *Files*
Finance Department, Supply Branch *Files*
Finance Department (Resource Branch) *Files*

National Archives, Delhi :

Crown Representative *Reports* (Micro Films), Fortnightly
Hyderabad Residency *Files*

PUBLISHED ORIGINAL SOURCES

Official Reports and Resolutions :

General Administrative Reports
Trade Statistics
Industrial Statistics
Agricultural Statistics
Revenue Administration Report, 1324 *Fasli* (1914-15 A.D.)
Report of the Departments working under the Secretary and Director-General of Revenue, 1336 *Fasli* (1926-27)
Settlement Report of Warangal Taluka of Warangal District, 1302 *Fasli* (1893)
Selected Laws and Rules of the Revenue Department, 1950.
Report on the working of the Departments under the Revenue Secretariat, 1328 *Fasli* (1918-1919)
Annual Administration Reports of the Director of Agriculture
Annual Report of Research and Experimental Work of the Department of Agriculture for the years 1345-46 *Fasli* (1936-37) and 1341 *Fasli* (1931-32)
The Banking Enquiry Committee Report, 1930
Labour Census Reports
Proceedings of the Conference of *Subedars* held at the Revenue Secretariat on 18th *Sharewar* (July) 1342 *Fasli* (1933)
Statistical Abstracts
Statistical Year Books
Livestock Census Report, 1935
Report of the Reforms Committee, 1935
Local Government (n.y)
Report of the Agrarian Reforms Committee, 1949
Report of the Tenancy Committee, 1940
Village Lists, Warangal, Karimnagar and Adilabad Districts, 1941
Indian Famine Commission Report, 1901
Census of India, Hyderabad State Reports

Report of the Royal Commission on Agriculture in India, Bombay, 1928.

Report of the Royal Commission on *Jagir* Administration and Reforms, 1947.

Memoranda submitted to the Taxation Enquiry Commission, 1953.

Government of Madras : Report of the Economist for Enquiry into Rural Indebtedness, 1946.

White Paper on Hyderabad, 1948.

Fifth Annual, Report on the working of the Co-operative Societies of H.E.H. the Nizam's Government for the year 1328 *Fasli* (1919) and Third Annual Report for the year 1326 *Fasli* (1917).

Wholesale & Retail Prices, 1889-90 to 1918-19 A.D.

Annual Average Retail Prices of Principal Commodities in H.E.H. the Nizam's Dominions, 1319-50 *Fasli* (1920-41).

Index Numbers of Annual Average Retail Prices in H.E.H. the Nizam's Dominions, 1319-1350 *Fasli* (1910-1940-41).

Retail & Wholesale Prices, 1931-1941.

Estimates of Area and Yield of Principal Crops in Hyderabad State, 1925-26 to 1934-35.

Supply Statistics, H.E.H. the Nizam's Government, 1354 *Fasli* (1945).

Agricultural, Industrial & Trade Statistics for the year 1343 *Fasli* (1933-34).

Triennial Reports on the Administration of the Department of Industries and Commerce for the years 1918, 1919 & 1920 A.D.

Administrative Reports of Commerce and Industries Department.

Azam Jahi Mills Directors Reports.

Statistics about Trade Centres (Markets & Bazaars) in Hyderabad State, 1948.

List of Uruses, Melas, Jatras, etc. in H.E.H. the Nizam's Dominions, 1349 *Fasli* (1940 A.D.).

Gazetteers and Manuals :

Imperial Gazetteer of India, Provincial Series, Hyderabad State, 1909.

Hyderabad District Gazetteers, Warangal, Karimnagar and Adilabad, 1340 & 1345 *Fasli* (1931 & 1936).
Andhra Pradesh District Gazetteers, Warangal (1976).
Khammam (1977), Karimnagar & Adilabad (1974 & 1976).
The Hyderabad Survey and Settlement Manual, 1952.
Cotton Manual, H.E.H. the Nizam's Government, 1940.

NEWSPAPERS & JOURNALS

Golkonda Patrika (Daily, Bi-Weekly & Weekly).
The Deccan Chronicle (Daily).
Meezan (Daily).
The Hindu (Daily).
Hyderabad Information, (Monthly).
The Hyderabad Bulletin (Monthly).
The Hyderabad Government Bulletin on Economic Affairs (Monthly).
Proceedings of the Hyderabad Archaeological & Historical Society, January to August, 1941, Hyderabad-Dn, 1942.
Itihas (Bi-annual).
The Hyderabad Forest Magazine (Quarterly).
The Economic and Political Weekly, Special Number, August 1974.
The Deccan Geographer.

SECONDARY SOURCES

Unpublished Dissertations :

Bedford, Ian., *Telangana Insurrection : A Study in the cause and development of Communist Insurrection in Rural India*, Ph. D. Thesis (Microfilm in NMML, Delhi).

Bawa, V.K., *Hyderabad in Transition under Salar Jung I, 1853-1883, An Indian State under British Influence*, Ph. D. thesis, (Microfilm in NMML, Delhi), Tulane University, 1967.

Habib Ahmed, L.S., *An Economic Survey of the Sirpur Paper Mills Limited,* M.A. (Economics) dissertation , Osmania University, 1960.

Muttalib, M.A., *The Administration of Justice under the Nizams (1724-1947)* Ph. D. thesis, Osmania University, 1957.

Pavier. Barry., *Telangana Movement, 1944-51* (Available in JNU, Delhi).

Subhas Chandra Reddy, K., *Telangana, A Study in Regionalism*, Ph. D. thesis, Osmania University, 1978.

Venkataraman, V., *Land Reforms in India with special reference to Hyderabad*, Ph. D. thesis, Osmania University, 1957.

Venugopal Rao, S., *Economic Survey of the Azam Jahi Mills Limited, Warangal*, M.A. dissertation, Osmania University, 1961.

Sitaraman, Sharada, *Economic Survey of Sirsilk Ltd., Sirpur Kagaznagar*, M.A. dissertation, Osmania University, 1961.

Souvenirs :

Maremanda Rama Rao (ed), *Kakatiya Sanchika*, Andhra Historical Research Society, Rajahmundry, 1935.

Articles :

Abdul Qayyum Khan, 'Irrigation in Hyderabad State' in *Hyderabad Government Bulletin on Economic Affairs*, Vol. I, No. 9, (December, 1948).

Ali Baig, M.M., 'Cattle improvement in Hyderabad' in *the Hyderabad Forest Magazine* (Quarterly) No. II, (July, 1942), No. I.

Gopalan, M., 'Scheme for the Agricultural Development under the Irrigation Projects in Hyderabad' in *Hyderabad Government Bulletin on Economic Affairs*, Vol. I, No. 9, (December, 1948).

Ganu, L.G., 'Land Revenue and Rural Indebtedness' in (Finance Department, English Branch No. I of 1937) *The Hyderabad Bulletin*, 28-8-1937.

Kazim Syed, 'Mineral Resources of Hyderabad' in *the Deccan Chronicle*, 27-5-1950.

Madhava Rao, Anvari, 'The Co-operative Movement in Hyderabad' in *Hyderabad Government Bulletin on Economic Affairs*, Vol. I, 1947-48.

Madhava Rao, Anvari, 'Are existing Co-operative Societies being squeezed out?' in *the Deccan Chronicle*, 19-6-1949.

Pavier, Barry, 'The Telangana Armed Struggle' in *the Economic & Political Weekly*, Special Number (August, 1974), Vol. IX.

Pradhan, H. Prasad, 'Reactionary Role of Usurer's Capital in rural India' in *Economic & Political Weekly*, Special Number, August, 1974.

Ramnarsu, B.V., 'Banking Structure in Hyderabad' in *Hyderabad Government Bulletin on Economic Affairs*, Vol. I, 1947-48.

Raghunadha Rao, Gangaraju, 'Village Problems in Nizam's State' in *Golkonda Patrika* (Bi-Weekly), 5-4-1934.

Sarojini Regani, 'The Social Background for the rise of the Andhra Maha Sabha Movement in Telangana' in *Itihas*, Journal of Andhra Pradesh Archives, Vol. I, No. I, (January to July, 1973).

Sreenivasachar, P., 'Political, Social and Religious Conditions of the Deccan under the Kakatiyas' in *the Proceedings of the Hyderabad Archaeological & Historical Society*, January-August, 1941.

Venkataranga Rao, K., 'Causes of debt' in *Golkonda Patrika* (Bi-Weekly), 19-5-1938.

Veerabhadra Rao, V. & Ramachandra Rao, V., 'India's Police Action against Hyderabad' in *the Deccan Chronicle*, 13-3-1949.

Waghmare, A.K., 'Education in Hyderabad' in A.I.S.P.C. *File* No. 70 (Part I), 1947-48.

Chaturvedi, B.N. & Surender Reddy, K., 'Irrigation in Telangana—Sources and Problems' in *The Deecan Geographer*, Hyderabad, January, 1964.

Director of Agriculture, Hyderabad State, 'A Note on Agricultural Conditions in Hyderabad State in the year 1947-48' in Agriculture Department, S. No. 103 & *File* No. 40/8 of 1357 *Fasli* (1948).

Dr. Mohammad Farooq, Deputy Director of Public Health, H.E.H. the Nizam's Government, 'A Note on Public Health' in *1941 Census Report*, Part I, p. 123.

Dr. John Lowe, former Medical Superintendent, Leprosy, Hospital, Dichpalli, 'A note on Leprosy in Hyderabad State' contained in *1931*, *Census*, Part I- Report, p. 139.

Gough, Kathleen, 'Indian Peasant Uprisings' in *Economic and Political Weekly*, Special Number, August 1974.

Gopalan, A., 'Some economic aspects of Road planning and Development with special reference to Hyderabad' in *Hyderabad Government Bulletin on Economic Affairs*, Vol. II. Nos. 8-9, August-September, 1949.

Haimendorf, Christoph Von Furer, 'Tribal Populations of Hyderabad, Yesterday and Today' in *1941 Census*, Part I-Report, Appendix I. P. XV.

——'Library Movement' (editorial) in Hyderabad Bulletin, 7-7-1936, quoted in *Golkonda Patrika* (editorial), 13-7-1936.

Books:

Ahsan Yar Jung Bahadur, Nawab., *Manufacture of Steel in H.E.H. the Nizam's Dominions*, Hyderabad, 1940.

——*Conservation of Coal and Manufacture of Gasoline*, Hyderabad-Dn, 1940.

Abid Ali Hassan, Syed, *Whither Hyderabad*, the B.N. Press, Madras, 1935.

Anstey Vera, *Economic Development of India*, London, 1929.

Agriculturists' Association: *Immediate Agrarian Problems, Hyderabad State*, Hyderabad-Dn, 1949.

Bharucha, S.M., *Agricultural Indebtedness*, Hyderabad, 1937.

Bilgrami, S.H. & Willmott, C., *Historical and Descriptive Sketch of His Highness the Nizam's Dominions*, Vols. I & II, Bombay, 1883.

Basava Punnaiah, M., *Telangana Armed Struggle—Realities*, Vijayawada, 1972.

Baden Powell, B.H., *Administration of Land Revenue and Tenure in British India*, New Delhi, 1978.

Cheragh Ali, Moulvi., *Hyderabad (Dn) under Sir Salar Jung*, Vol. I, Bombay, 1884.

Claude Campbell, A., *Glimpses of the Nizam's Dominions*, Bombay & London, 1898.

Choksey, R.D., *Economic History of the Bombay, Deccan and Karnataka (1818-68)*, Poona, 1945.

Department of Statistics, H.E.H. the Nizam's Government, *Some Economic Facts and Figures of H.E.H. the Nizam's Dominions*, Hyderabad-Dn, 1937.

Department of Agriculture, Government of Hyderabad,

Towards Self-Sufficiency in Hyderabad, 1950-51 to 1951-52, 1952.

Department of Information & Public Relations : *History and Legend in Hyderabad*, Osmania University Press, Hyderabad, 1953.

Dube, S.C., *The Indian Village*, London, 1955.

——*The Economic Life of Hyderabad*, Government Central Press, Hyderabad-Dn, 1937.

Fathullah Khan, M., *A History of Administrative Reforms in Hyderabad State*, Secunderabad-Dn, 1955.

Government of Hyderabad, *A Summary of Hyderabad's War Effort, 1939-44*, Government Central Press, Hyderabad-Dn, 1944

Gribble, J.D.B., *A History of the Deccan*, Vol. I, London, 1896.

Government of Hyderabad, *Jagir Administration*, Vol. I, 1952.

Gadgil, D.R., *The Industrial Evolution of India in recent times*, Oxford University Press, 1942.

Hanumantha Rao, Madapati : *Teangana Andhrodyamam*, 2 vols, Hyderabad, 1949 & 1950.

Haimendorf, Christoph-Von-Furer, *Tribal Hyderabad*, Hyderabad, 1945.

Dr. Hirananda Sastry, *Shitab Khan of Warangal*, Published by H.E.H. the Nizam's Government, Calcutta, 1932.

Information Bureau, *Some Aspects of Hyderabad*, Hyderabad-Dn, 1941.

Khaja Abdul Gafoor, Syed, *Tribes and Tribal Welfare in Hyderabad*, Government Press, Hyderabad-Dn, 1953

Khusro, A.M., *Economic and Social effects of Jagirdari abolition and Land Reforms in Hyderabad*, Hyderabad, 1958.

Kesava Iyengar, S., *Rural Economic Enquiries in Hyderabad State, 1949-51*.

——*Economic Investigations in the Hyderabad State, 1929-30 Vol. III, Warangal District*, Government Central Press Hyderabad-Dn, 1932.

——*Economic Investigations in the Hyderabad State, 1929-30, Vol. I*, Hyderabad Dn, 1931.

Law, John., *Modern Hyderabad (Deccan)*, Calcutta, 1914.

Munshi, K.M., *The End of an Era*, Bombay, 1957.

Mudiraj, Krishnaswamy. K., *Pictorial Hyderabad*, Vol. II., Hyderabad, 1934.

Marketing Department, Government of Hyderabad, *A Note on the Agricultural Marketing in Hyderabad State*, Hyderabad-Dn, 1952.

Mahdi Ali, Syed Moulvi., *Hyderabad Affairs*, Vol. I, Bombay, 1883.

Mirza, Khurshid., *A Brief outline of the Geological History of Hyderabad with reference to its Mineral Resources*, Hyderabad-Dn, 1937.

Narayan, B.K., *Agricultural Development in Hyderabad State 1900-56*, Secunderabad, 1960.

——*A Survey of Industries in Telangana*, Secunderabad, 1962.

Narsing Rao, Mandumula, *Fifty Years Hyderabad*, Hyderabad, 1977.

Narayana Reddy, Ravi, *Heroic Telangana ; Reminiscences and Experiences*, Communist Party of India, Delhi, 1973.

——*Eleven Years Progress of Hyderabad State Transport, 1930-41*, Hyderabad-Dn, 1941.

Pratap Reddy, Suravaram., *Pradhamika Swatvamulu*, Hyderabad-Dn, 1938.

Qureshi, A.I., *The Economic Development of Hyderabad*, Vol. I, The Orient Longman's Ltd., Madras, 1941.

Rao, R.V., *A Review of Hyderabad Finance*, Hyderabad, 1951.

Ramakoteswara Rao, Madiraju, *Sweeya Charitra*, Warangal, *Sarvari* (Telugu Calender).

Ranga, N.G., *Economic Organisation of Indian Villages*, Vol. II, Bombay, 1929.

Raju, A.S., *Economic Conditions in the Madras Presidency, 1800-1850*, University of Madras, 1941.

Rao, D.V., *Manual on groundwater and well-sinking*, Hyderabad, 1947.

Ray. S.C., *Agricultural Indebtedness in India and its remedies*, Calcutta, 1917.

Ramesan, N., (ed)., *The Freedom Struggle in Hyderabad*, Vol. IV, Published by the Andhra Pradesh State Committee appointed for the compilation of a history of the Freedom Struggle in Andhra Pradesh, 1966.

Swamy Ramananda Tirtha ; *Memoris of Hyderabad Freedom Struggle*, Bombay, 1967.

Sarojini Regani, *Highlights of the Freedom Movement in Andhra Pradesh*, Hyderabad, 1972.

Sundarayya, P., *Telangana Armed Struggle and its Lessons*, Calcutta, 1972.

——*Veera Telangana Viplava Poratam-Gunapatalu*, Vijayawada, 1973.

Singh, V.B., (ed)., *Economic History of India*, New Delhi, 1975.

Sherwani, H.K., *The Qutub Shahis of Golkonda*, Hyderabad, (n.d).

Thapar, Romesh., *Storm over Hyderabad*, Kutb Publishers, Bombay, 1947.

Vicar-ul-Mulk Bahadur (Mushtaq Hussain Khan), Nawab., *Description of a Tour in the Eastern Division in 1294 Fasli* (1885).

Venkateswar Rao. D., *Telangana Armed Struggle and the Path of Indian Revolution*.

Yazdani, G., (ed)., *Early History of the Deccan*, Vols. I & II.

INDEX